BIDDING SUMMARY

SUIT

TYPE OF SUIT		UIRED
One biddable suit	One of a suit	14 or more
Any other suit or suits	One of a suit	13 or more
Five cards	Two of a suit	24 or more
Six cards.	Two of a suit	23 or more

RESPONSES TO OPENING BIDS OF ONE OF A SUIT

RESPONSE	SHOWS IN POINTS
Single Raise	6-12
Double Raise	13-16
Triple Raise	11-14
A new suit at the one level	6 or more
A new suit at the two level	10 or more
A new suit–single jump (forcing)	19 or more
One no trump	6-10
Two no trump	14-15
Three no trump	16-17

NO TRUMP BIDDING

OPENING BID	SHOWS IN POINTS
One no trump	16-18
Two no trump	22-24
Three no trump	25-27

RESPONSES TO AN OPENING ONE NO TRUMP

Respond according to your hand pattern and strength. In taking out a no trump opening into a suit, distributional points should be counted.

RESPONSES TO TWO OR MORE NO TRUMP

Respond with three or more points, according to your hand pattern.

CONTRACT

Containing: Basic and Advanced Bidding Methods, Play of the Hand, Practice Hands and Completely Diagramed Explanations, Quizzes and Answers, Rubber Bridge and Tournament Scoring, The Official Code of Laws

With Articles on Their Specialties and Inventions by:

Giorgio Belladonna	The Roman Club
Easley Blackwood	The Blackwood Convention
Harry Fishbein	The Fishbein Convention
John Gerber	The Gerber Convention
José Le Dentu	Canape
Terence Reese	Acol
Lawrence Rosler	Astro
Alvin Roth	Roth-Stone
Alfred Sheinwold	Kaplan-Sheinwold
Thomas M. Smith	The Precision System
Samuel M. Stayman	The Stayman Convention

(A revised edition of *Modern Point Count Contract Bridge*)

BRIDGE COMPLETE

Completely Revised and Updated Edition

A Comprehensive Text and Reference Book for Everyone, from Beginner to Expert

by ERNEST W. ROVERE

Introduction by Oswald Jacoby

SIMON AND SCHUSTER, NEW YORK

PUBLISHED BY SIMON AND SCHUSTER
ROCKEFELLER CENTER, 630 FIFTH AVENUE
NEW YORK, NEW YORK 10020
SBN 671-21437-3 CASEBOUND
LIBRARY OF CONGRESS CATALOG CARD NUMBER: 73-2149
MANUFACTURED IN THE UNITED STATES OF AMERICA

1 2 3 4 5 6 7 8 9 10

GRATEFUL ACKNOWLEDGMENT IS MADE TO THE AMERICAN CONTRACT BRIDGE LEAGUE FOR PERMISSION TO INCLUDE THE COPYRIGHTED 1963 INTERNATIONAL CODE OF THE LAWS OF CONTRACT BRIDGE.

AUTHOR'S FOREWORD

Any text, to be worthy of the name, should tell not only what to do but, even more important, *why it is being done.*

This book, I hope, accomplishes that purpose.

Grateful acknowledgement is made to the hundreds of thousands of television viewers who, using this text, learned to play bridge via that medium; to the many thousands who, during the years, have attended classes conducted by the author. Their experiences, reactions and suggestions have molded this book.

To my twelve co-authors who have so generously contributed their names and articles, giving the book what comprehensiveness and authoritativeness it possesses, even the most fervent of "thank yous" seem insufficient.

And to those others whose efforts in various ways made this work possible: my wife, Lucille; *The San Francisco Chronicle;* Brenda Cox-Moore; Nat Schmulowitz; R. Adm. Wyatt Craig, U.S.N. (ret.); Daisy Paletti; and countless others—again, my most fervent thanks.

—ERNEST W. ROVERE

GUIDE TO CONTRIBUTORS

Articles by the greatest collection of world-famous authors and experts of many nations ever assembled in one book on bridge are contained on the pages to follow. Each expert has written on his own specialty, convention or system, and to give the article complete authenticity has signed his contribution.

To assist the reader in finding each article, the following supplementary table, arranged by author and nationality, will be of assistance.

CONTENTS

INTRODUCTION

One of the great difficulties in writing a book on bridge is to decide for whom it should be written. If you write for the beginner, neither the fair nor good player will bother with your book; if you write for the fair player, the expert and the beginner won't be interested; while if you write for the expert, you omit everyone else.

To write a book for every bridge player is a truly Herculean task. Until this book by Ernest W. Rovere, no one has both successfully attempted it and accomplished it.

Ernie has!

He has the background for it. For many years he has written a column on the game for the San Francisco *Chronicle*. He is an expert player. As a former partner, I can testify to that. As a teacher, he is outstanding and a fine writer.

His book covers bridge — from soup to nuts. It starts from the very beginning — omitted in most books — and includes virtually every modern convention. I don't agree with every word of it — no two experts are ever in complete agreement — but I can assure all players, writers and teachers that every word is worth reading and reading carefully.

—OSWALD JACOBY

HOW TO USE THIS BOOK AS A SELF-TEACHER

The first portions of this book are for the beginner—the person who either has never played bridge or has only rudimentary knowledge. As the reader progresses from lesson to lesson, the text becomes increasingly more advanced, so that in its middle stages the intermediate player will find much that is new. In the 16th lesson, over 116 pages include the latest and most advanced techniques used by the experts.

Where one or more persons are learning to play bridge without a teacher, let me make the following suggestions:

If you are fortunate enough to have a bridge television course in your locale synchronized to this textbook, watch the show and avail yourself of its facilities.

To learn by yourself or with a few friends, read the text carefully. If some of the terms are not clear to you, use the glossary beginning on page 798.

Don't try to master bridge in one evening. Take it a little at a time. When you have learned what you have read, then go on.

Complete the quizzes before consulting the answers. Play out the practice hands and compare your methods with those diagramed.

Read the bridge column in your local newspaper.

Visit the bridge clubs in your locality! Almost every city has its bridge club and most have duplicate tournaments. They enjoy having kibitzers. After all, you're a future player. Drop in and watch. Ask the club director who are the best players, ask their permission to watch (which is always happily granted), draw up a chair and kibitz.

Don't interrupt the players by asking questions while they are bidding or playing, but after the hand is over or while the next hand is being shuffled or dealt, then ask your question.

The players will be happy to answer. Nothing flatters an expert's ego more than to be asked his opinion. And you will learn a great deal!

HOW TO USE THIS BOOK — FOR TEACHERS

The text is divided into 16 chapters or lessons intended to span a 16-week course. Lesson One on fundamentals consists entirely of a lecture, with no play period. Beginning with Lesson Two, the two-hour lesson is divided, with the first hour for instruction, the second for play and practice.

The text should be read by the student in advance of each lesson. This makes it possible for the teacher to cover more ground and for the student to follow the lesson more readily.

Before each lesson, a quiz is given on the previous week's work. The quiz will be found at the end of the corresponding lesson, with the answers immediately following the quiz. Ten minutes should suffice for fully answering the quiz, and the answers should be filled in in the classroom. While the students are filling in their papers, the teacher should circulate among the players and note the various degrees of proficiency and offer personal coaching. On completion of the allotted time period, the students should then correct their own papers by comparison with the answers.

A blackboard permitting writing large enough to be visible from the rear of the room will be of great assistance in diagraming hands and answering students' questions.

Players should be arranged four at each table. Extra players should kibitz (watch) or alternate with other players rather than be left alone at unfilled tables. Four practice hands, together with diagramed play of the cards, are included in each lesson. Bidding and play on each hand are so designed that each student at the table will play one hand during the session.

Starting with the second lesson, a deck of cards should be on every table. Before starting the play period, the deck should be assorted into suits. On completion of sorting, each player should have 13 cards of one suit. It is now a simple matter to lay out the hands illustrated for each lesson. The dealer is designated on each hand.

Beginning with the 12th lesson, duplicate boards should be used and players instructed in arranging their cards duplicate fashion. By the 16th lesson, the class should have had sufficient experience in playing and scoring duplicate so that they can enter tournaments with confidence.

It has been a happy custom of the writer to have a graduation party and tournament for each class. Groups of students, in addition, have formed their own duplicate clubs for additional practice. The competitive features of duplicate whet the students' interest and are highly recommended.

"The greatest skill at cards is to know when to discard. The smallest of current trumps is worth more than the ace of trumps of the last game. When in doubt, follow the suit of the wise and the prudent; sooner or later they will win the odd trick."

—Gracian

Lesson I

Fundamentals of the Game

How to Score

LESSON ONE

THE FUNDAMENTALS OF THE GAME

There are 52 cards in a deck. These cards are divided into four groups known as 'suits.' They are respectively known as spades, designated by the symbol ♠ ; hearts, ♡ ; diamonds, ◇ ; and clubs, ♣ .

Cards are said to possess rank, that is, some are greater in capturing power than others. The rule to remember is that the more spots on a card (the correct card term for spots is 'pips'), the greater its capturing power over cards with fewer spots. The only exception is the ace which has but one spot, very large, in the form of its suit symbol in the center of the card. The ace is the highest card of its suit.

Directly beneath the ace in rank and higher than the spot cards are three cards bearing pictures. These are sometimes called 'court cards' or 'face cards' and are individually known as the king, queen and jack. They rank in that order directly beneath the ace and are readily identifiable by their pictures and the letters, K, Q, and J in their corners. A complete suit of 13 cards would rank, from high to low :

Ace, king, queen, jack, 10, 9, 8, 7, 6, 5, 4, 3, 2.

Suits, too, have rank, one over the other. The spade suit is the highest ranking. Then comes hearts, next diamonds and lastly, clubs. This order of suit rank is extremely important in competitive bidding to determine the trump suit where a bid, let us say, of four spades, would supersede one of four diamonds since spades outrank diamonds. This order of rank will hold true until the bidding is concluded when the suit in which the highest bid was made becomes the ranking suit as trump and the remaining three suits become equal in value during the play of the cards. The rank of the cards within each suit remains the same, however.

The following 'gimmick' will be of great assistance to the new player in remembering the rank of one suit to another. Think of the four suits in terms of the alphabet - S for spades, H for hearts, D for diamonds, C for clubs. The highest ranking letter alphabetically, S, represents the highest ranking suit - H is next alphabetically, then D and finally C. And that's exactly the way the suits rank - S - H - D - C

Suit rank enters into the choice of partners at the start of a game where the four players each select a card at random from the deck. The two players selecting the highest cards become partners as do the pair selecting the lowest cards. In cases where identically sized cards are drawn, suit rank becomes the determining factor in choosing partnerships.

Thus if one player pulls out the king of clubs, another the 10 of spades, the third player the 10 of diamonds and the fourth the five of hearts, the players drawing the king of clubs and the 10 of spades would be partners since while two players drew 10's, the fact that spades outrank diamonds make the 10 of spades the higher card.

Primarily, it is the size of the card drawn which determines partnerships. Suit rank is only used for breaking ties.

THE OBJECTIVES OF THE GAME

The object of bridge is to score points. At the conclusion of play, the player or pair with the greatest number of points is the winner. The length of time you will play is usually determined by mutual consent of the players.

Bridge is a partnership game. Four players are necessary and form a "table" or "foursome." Each player sits at one side of a small, square table and each pair facing each other are called "partners." To a pair sitting one way of the table, the players sitting in the opposite direction (to the left and right) are termed "opponents" or "adversaries."

In order to simplify identification, newspaper columnists and bridge writers assign the names of the four cardinal points of the compass to the players. Thus North and South are partners as are East and West. On the printed page, South is at the bottom of the hand with North on top, West to the left and East to the right, exactly as on a compass.

Partners may be chosen by choice as John Jones inviting Alice Adams to be his partner, or by draw, as previously described. The player cutting (selecting) the highest card has the choice of seats at the table, the choice of which color deck to deal if, as in most games, two decks are on the table. Home and rubber bridge are usually played with two decks, one being used while the other is shuffled and made ready for the next deal. Thus the decks alternate. Generally they will have backs or patterns of contrasting colors to avoid mixing the two decks. One pair of players will deal throughout the hand with, let us say, the blue deck, the other pair of players with the red deck. Some highly superstitious players will insist on sitting a certain way of the table or using a particular color deck. If their luck is bad, they may cut again for a new choice of seats and cards.

Whatever fate befalls one player equally affects his partner. If North does well, South benefits to the same extent, winning or losing the identical number of points and if the partnership does badly, both partners suffer equally.

It is for this reason that accuracy and precision between the partnership, both in bidding and play of the hand, is vital. Each player must know how to match his cards as accurately as possible to those of his partner.

Should partners be chosen by personal preference, a cut or draw is still made to determine choice of seats, cards and dealer, these privileges going to the player selecting the highest card. All four players now seat themselves at the table and the game begins.

SHUFFLING AND DEALING

The deck of cards selected by the dealer is shuffled by the player sitting to the dealer's left. By shuffling is meant mixing the cards so that whatever order the cards have previously fallen into will be broken up for the next deal. In other words, the same hands will not be dealt again. For those unfamiliar with shuffling, it is a matter of manual dexterity.

The shuffle completed, the cards are passed to the player on the dealer's right who "cuts" the cards. By cutting is meant splitting the deck into two parts, face down, of course. Neither part should contain less than six cards and it is usually best to have the two sections nearly equal. The dealer then reassembles the two sections into one in the opposite order from which they were before the cut. In other words, the half that originally was at the bottom is now uppermost and vice-versa. The deck is now ready to deal. In informal games, the shuffle is often done by the dealer.

The dealer then picks up the "live" pack (the deck not in use is termed the "still" pack) and starts to deal, one card at a time, starting with the player to his left. The top card is slid off the deck, face down, close to the top of the table so that its face cannot be discerned and goes to the left hand opponent. The next card is dealt to the dealer's partner, the third to the right hand opponent and the fourth to the dealer, himself. This process is continued until the deck is exhausted, the dealer receiving the last card. Each player will now have 13 cards. Cards are dealt from left to right or to use a familiar expression, "clockwise."

Do not deal more than one card at a time to any player or peek at the bottom card when dealer. In pinochle and a few other card games, cards are dealt three or more at a time. This is not true in bridge. Dealing one card at a time further assists the shuffle in breaking up the deck into new patterns. Also, when cards are being dealt to you, do not pick up any of them until the deal is completed and you have all 13 cards before you.

Each player will then pick up his or her 13 cards and arrange them by suits, placing hearts in one group, spades in another, etc. To avoid the possibility of mistaking clubs for spades, since both are black, or hearts for diamonds, both red, best practice is to alternate suits of different colors in assembling the hand. This reduces the possibility of visual error.

The full 13 cards, separated into suits, are held in front of each player in the shape of a half-opened fan with the card faces towards the holder. It stands to reason that the cards should be held so that no other player at the table will be able to obtain a surreptitious peek. The fan should be held open only enough to permit the identifying corners (indices) of each card to be seen. The fan is held close to the player and is not extended far over the top of the table. Most players arrange the cards of each suit in the order of rank. This simplifies selecting the right card.

SCORING

The idea behind bridge is similar to football, baseball, hockey and the like. The side with the greater number of points wins. It doesn't matter if one side has 40 points if the other has 50 points and the same is tr ue in bridge.

Points are obtained in one or more of three ways. These are :

1 - Successful completion of a contract by the pair making the winning (highest) bid.

2 - Bonuses.

3 - Penalties paid by the side that failed to fulfill its contract.

Only points from the first method - successful completion of the contract, count towards "game." If a pair bids, let us say, three spades and takes the required number of tricks, they receive a certain number of points. Your logical questions should be, "What is a trick? How many points do they receive?"

A trick consists of four cards, each player at the table having contributed one card in clock-wise order. The very first play (lead) is made by the player sitting to the immediate left of the winning bidder and subsequent leads are made by the player who has won the previous trick.

The suits have different values in points. Spades and hearts, which are known as the "major" suits, yield 30 points per trick; diamonds and clubs are called the "minor" suits, producing 20 points for each trick. Only the successful bidders' side can count their tricks (in terms of points) towards game. The defenders, the pair who either were outbid or perhaps did not even enter the bidding, cannot.

Let me point out that if spades or hearts are trumps, each trick taken by the declarer (the person playing the hand) is worth 30 points, even if the trick itself consists of four clubs or as commonly happens, a combination of cards from different suits. It's the trump contract itself that gives each trick its point value, not the actual cards contained in the trick.

During the play of the hand, the declarer keeps the tricks won by his side and one defender keeps his side's tricks. Once a trick has been completed, its four cards are taken by the winning side and turned over so that their faces are no longer visible. The four cards of each completed trick are combined into one trick. Each trick is kept in a staggered arrangement from other tricks so that after completion of play on a hand, any particular trick can be inspected for irregularity such as a revoke (which is failure to follow suit when able to do so).

THE GAME

What is a game ?

A game consists of 100 points won by means of tricks bid and won. Since clubs and diamonds count 20 points for each trick, it is necessary to bid and win five tricks in either of these suits to score the 100 points for game. In a major suit, at 30 points per trick, a bid of four will produce a game since four times 30 yields 120, more than is actually needed. Three in a major or four tricks in a minor will obviously not suffice since scores of 90 and 80 points respectively will result.

There are three important things you should know in this connection.

1 - All of the 100 points for game need not be made at one time or on one hand. Any number of scores may be combined. Once these scores total 100 or more points, that side has scored a game. Trick scores of less than 100 points are known as *'part-scores'* or *'partials.'*

2 - If you make more than 100 points on any one hand or if your combined part-scores total more than 100, the surplus over 100 does not count towards the next game. It's just as though a home run, instead of merely clearing the fence, went a block further. It's still only one run.

3 - When one side makes a game (scores 100 or more points in tricks bid and won) any and all part scores by the other side are nullified so far as counting towards game is concerned. The process of accumulating 100 points for the next game, for both sides, begins from scratch.

THE BOOK

Thus far, we have discussed contracts and the number of tricks to be taken in terms of 'one spade' or 'two hearts' or 'three clubs' or whatever the case may be.

Since with a deck containing 52 cards, there are 13 tricks (of four cards each) to be won, it stands to reason that the pair winning the auction at, let us say, two spades, must do more than merely win two tricks since the opponents in that case would have won 11 !

Were this the case, the bidding side would be taking fewer tricks (and getting credit for them) than the opponents who may have been too weak to bid. Obviously, this is impossible.

The number of tricks required to fulfill any contract is the actual amount of the bid *plus six.* The latter *six* is termed the *'declarer's book'* which is always contracted to the expression, *'the book.'* Thus a pair bidding 'two spades' would need eight tricks to fulfill their contract - two plus the book of six. A bid of 'three' would correspondingly require the winning of nine tricks, four anything 10 tricks, a bid of five 11 tricks, etc.

The book, then, is the number of tricks the declarer must win before counting additional tricks towards the contract. That number is *six.*

DEFENDERS' BOOK

The defenders, too, have a book. Their book is the amount of the opponents' bid subtracted from seven. In other words, if the opponents have bid four spades, defenders' book is three; if the bid was two hearts, the defenders' book would be five tricks.

Tricks in excess of the defenders' book will be the exact number by which the declarer failed to fulfill his contract. One defender keeps all of the tricks won by his partner and himself. The defenders' book varies with the amount of the opponents' bid; the declarer's book is always the first six tricks.

NO TRUMP

So far we have dealt with tangible objects that could be seen as the four suits, spades, hearts, diamonds and clubs; the book, which is six for the declarer and can vary for the defenders.

Before going ahead with learning to score, I would like to introduce a fifth suit which is really not a suit at all but a combination of the previously mentioned four. That suit is no trump.

No trump consists of all four suits having equal value. In other words, when a spade is led, the highest spade played to that trick wins that trick. No suit has any higher value in play than any other suit compared with trump (suit) contracts where the highest bid was in a suit which became trump and outranked the other suits for trick-taking purposes.

In no trump, tricks are frequently won with low cards of a suit since when a low card of a suit is led, it must win that trick if no other player at the table plays a higher card of that particular suit to that trick. Even the deuce (two-spot) will win a trick in no trump if no player has a higher card of that suit. Exactly as the name implies, there is no trump or trump suit.

This equalizing of all four suits into a common trick taking value is done by a player bidding no trump rather than a suit. For example, when it was your turn to bid, you bid one or more no trump rather than one or more spades, hearts, diamonds or clubs.

The first thing to learn about no trump is that it is higher in rank than any of the four suits. Since spades are the highest ranking suit, the inclusion of no trump would give the following:

IN ORDER OF RANK

1 - No Trump
2 - Spades
3 - Hearts
4 - Diamonds
5 - Clubs

Thus a bid of no trump will take precedence (outbid) the same number of any suit. No trump is the highest denomination.

ADVANTAGES OF NO TRUMP

No trump's greatest advantage over suit contracts is that it scores more points per trick. Tricks bid and won in no trump are scored as follows: 40 points for the first trick and 30 points for each subsequent trick. Thus a bid of three no trump, if completed, would produce the needed 100 points for game as against three of a major yielding 90 points and three of a minor only 60. If a straight line is the shortest distance between two points, no trump is the quickest way to game. You need win fewer tricks.

The other advantage of no trump is the fact that it outranks the four suits. A bid of three no trump, for example, will outbid one of three spades; were the suit you intended to bid hearts, diamonds or clubs, you would have to bid four to outbid the three spade bid.

Why, then, aren't all hands played in no trump? Why bother with suit contracts at all ?

The answer is simple. All hands are not suited to play in no trump. Suppose you held ♠ 8 ♡ AKQ1087 ◇ AJ62 ♣ 43. Were hearts trumps, you would have a marked superiority in that suit over the opponents. No more than one spade trick need be lost since after the eight of spades had been played, you could win the next round of spades by trumping (playing a heart) were hearts trumps. Yet were you to play the same hand in no trump, the opponents could lead spades and spades, taking spade tricks ad infinitum. Unless you or your partner had a high spade capable of winning a trick when spades were led, you would not be able to win any tricks with your heart suit until you gained the lead.

If South played the accompanying hand *(figure one)* in no trump, West, having the first (opening) lead, would immediately play his three high spades. Thereafter, each low spade he played would win a trick since no other player would have a spade, much less a higher spade.

West		East
	♠ J107 ♡ J963 ◊ KQ5 ♣ AK2	
♠ AKQ943 ♡ 52 ◊ 1098 ♣ 65	N W E S	♠ 652 ♡ 4 ◊ 743 ♣ QJ10987
	♠ 8 ♡ AKQ1087 ◊ AJ62 ♣ 43	

Figure One

Thus in no trump, south would be forced to discard five times on the spade suit, throwing away cards that would have won tricks in a suit contract. If played in no trump by South, West would win six tricks, all in spades, with South winning the remaining seven tricks in the other suits.

For the slightly greater scoring advantages offered by no trump, attendant risks are proportionately greater since the opponents may take tricks with cards which in a suit contract could have been trumped.

What kind of hands should be played in no trump?

In general, they will be hands of even or almost evenly balanced distribution (the bridge term is balanced or semi-balanced) with no voids, singletons or worthless doubletons in unbid suits so that there is some protection against the debacle illustrated in *figure one* where a hand capable of winning 12 tricks in a suit contract won only seven in no trump.

If a long suit is present in the hand playing no trump, it will usually, though not always, be a minor. Hands containing long major suits are seldom played in no trump.

I do not wish to give you too much on no trump bidding at this point. These bids will be amply discussed in future chapters.

PENALTIES

A few pages ago, I stated that the principal objective of bridge is to score more points than the opponents.

The points received from penalties are those paid by the side making the highest bid and failing to win the necessary tricks.

The amount of the penalty paid per trick varies according to the number of tricks by which the contract failed, vulnerability and whether the contract was undoubled, doubled or redoubled. Let's explain what these words mean.

VULNERABILITY

A partnership of two players is said to be vulnerable after completing a game. It might be easier to understand if every time someone at the table stated that a side is vulnerable, you merely said to yourself, "Why, that side has a game." That's how simple it is.

Since either side can bid and make a game, it follows that each side or both can be vulnerable. Vulnerability does not affect the per trick score but it does greatly increase the penalty rates for non-fulfillment, as you will see, and also additional bonuses.

It is a good idea to associate vulnerability with a great big red sign saying "Be Careful."

DOUBLES AND REDOUBLES

Suppose you as a defender felt that the other side had bid too much, that you had so many high cards and taking tricks in your hand that they couldn't possibly make their contract.

When it becomes your turn to bid, you should say the word, "double." This greatly increases the penalty the opponents will pay for non-fulfillment. Before going further, let me stress the fact that a double is made only of the opponent's bid when it is the doubler's turn to bid. Any of the four players at the table has the right to double but it must be of a bid made by the other side. You cannot double your own or your partner's bid.

Similarly, a redouble can be made by either partner of the side that has been doubled. If side A has doubled side B, only a player on B can redouble. The same side cannot both double and redouble any more than you can redouble before you have been doubled.

It stands to reason that if the doubling side can increase the penalty by doubling, the doubled side should certainly receive something additional if they fulfill the doubled contract. Otherwise, it would be pretty one-sided.

They do! The trick value is doubled, too. Thus when each trick in spades and hearts normally counts 30 points towards game, they become worth 60 points each when doubled. The minors are increased to 40 points each by doubling and no trump to 80 points for the first trick and 60 points each for subsequent tricks.

Do you see what that means? Undoubled, a pair would have to bid and make four spades, for example, to complete a game. Making two spades, doubled, yields the equivalent score, 120 points.

In addition to the doubled trick value when the doubled contract is made, there is a bonus of 50 points for successful completion of the contract. The same 50 point bonus is also awarded for completion of a redoubled contract.

Tricks in excess of the doubled contract receive a 100 point bonus for each trick if not vulnerable, 200 if vulnerable. These amounts are the same for each suit and no trump and are scored above the line.

THE REDOUBLE

Every now and then, the side which has been doubled may feel confident that it can fulfill the doubled contract. Let us say that the adverse contract is four spades. You feel that you can win at least four tricks against that bid. You double. That is the equivalent of your saying, "I feel I can defeat the opponents' contract since I think they bid too much. Accordingly, by doubling, I wish to increase the penalty they will pay for non-fulfillment."

Whereas, either player on the other side (when it is his turn to bid) can multiply your double by two by saying "redouble." This is the equivalent of his saying, "Mr. Adversary, when you doubled our four spade bid, you thought you could defeat us. Well, I think you're wrong so I'll redouble."

Of course, in this imaginary dialogue, I am giving you the literal meaning and spirit of these bids. In actual play, all that is ever said is "double" or "redouble."

Since doubling doubles the trick score, redoubling quadruples it. One spade, for example, is worth 30 points undoubled, 60 points doubled and 120 points redoubled. Penalties and bonuses are both increased. Only the bonus for fulfillment of contract, 50 points, remains the same.

Over-tricks when the contract has been redoubled are worth 200 points each when not vulnerable, 400 points each vulnerable. These points (for over-tricks) are scored above the line. The actual doubled trick score goes *below the line*.

For example, let's say the contract is four hearts, redoubled. Five hearts are made. It is scored as follows: 480 points for the tricks actually bid and made, redoubled, below the line; 200 or 400 points for the over-trick above the line depending upon vulnerability and 50 points for fulfillment, also above the line.

One tremendous advantage of redoubling is that a redoubled and fulfilled contract of one in a major or one no trump or two of a minor will produce more than the 100 points needed for game. On the other hand, to balance the scale, the penalties in case of non-fulfillment are also greatly increased.

You should be careful about doubling less-than-game contracts unless fairly certain of defeating them; otherwise, you may present the opponents with a game they otherwise would not have had. Moreover, a penalty double may sometimes locate cards in the doubler's hand that declarer might have misguessed, making his task easier.

However, if you feel that you can beat the opponents' bid, then you should double. It is not necessary that all of the tricks needed to defeat the contract be in the doubler's hand. Frequently doubler's partner will have bid and the doubler has every right to assume his partner has the strength promised by his bid. This marked strength plus that held by the doubler should be sufficient to defeat the opponents. A double is in order. That is the beauty of good partnership bidding.

Later in this text, and as your knowledge of the game expands, you will learn that doubles and redoubles can be used to give information as to high card holdings. Used in this manner, they are termed "*informatory*." But for the present, we will not concern ourselves with any other type of double but the penalty variety where the use of the double expresses the belief that the other side cannot make its bid. The redouble, conversely, says they think they can.

THE SCORING TABLE

By this time, you should have a general idea of bridge scoring. You know your side will receive a certain number of points for each trick bid and made in excess of the book of six. Also you will receive points for each trick by which the opponents fail to make their bid and they similarly will receive identical amounts for each trick by which your side may fail. Points paid for failure are termed '*penalties*' and vary according to vulnerability. The suit (or no trump) in which the hand was played does not affect the amount of penalty *which is the same for all denominations.* Doubling and redoubling increases both trick scores and penalties.

When a partnership has accumulated 100 points for tricks bid and made, it is said to have a game (be vulnerable).

Now, there are several ways of obtaining points. We have already mentioned:

1 - For tricks bid and made;
2 - Bonuses for doubled or redoubled over-tricks;
3 - 50 point bonus for fulfillment of a doubled or redoubled contract;
4 - From penalties.

Points are also awarded for:

1 - Undoubled over-tricks;
2 - Rubber;
3 - Honors;
4 - Slams.

This will seem like a lot of things to remember when you first look at it but it really isn't. Scoring will dovetail into place very easily.

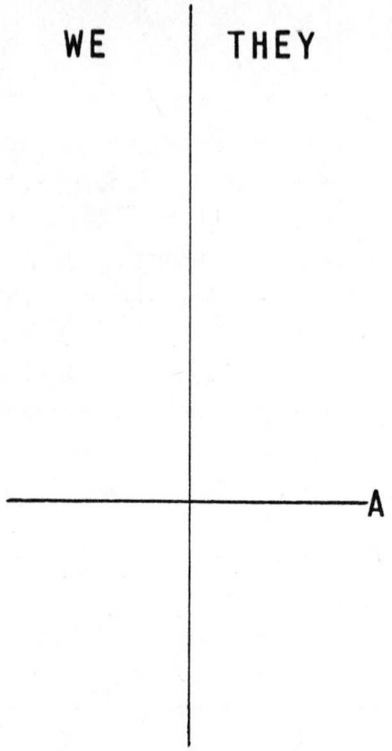

Figure Two

But what you should now learn is how to record the score. For this purpose, we use a simple cross shown as *figure two* with the upper half about twice as long as the lower section.

The long, vertical line divides "WE" from "THEY." In other words, all of the scores that your side makes will be entered on the "WE" side and all those credited to the opponents under "THEY."

The short, horizontal line which I have designated as "A" is known in bridge parlance as "the line." Beneath it go only the trick scores bid and made by both sides. Above the line, under the proper side of "WE" or "THEY" goes everything else, as over-tricks and all bonuses and penalties.

When you hear a player remark, "**We have 60 points below the line,**" he is stating that his side has 60 points towards game at that moment. When one side has won two games, that particular rubber is over and the points for each side are added from top to bottom of the columns. The lesser sum is subtracted from the greater and the difference is the margin of victory.

We are now going to discuss each form of bonus in detail. When we have done that, we will practice scoring together, entering scores on blank scoring crosses for each type of bid, penalty and bonus.

But the main thing for you to remember is this - only the points from tricks actually bid and made by the highest bidder's side are placed "below the line." Every other kind of score goes above. The upper, longer half is known as the "honors" column, the lower section as the "trick score" column. Bridge players seldom use these terms. They say "**below the line**" or "**above the line.**" So shall we.

OVER-TRICKS

Since only tricks actually bid and made count towards game, what happens to tricks won in excess of an undoubled contract? Suppose a pair bids two spades and makes four?

Tricks won in excess of the number actually contracted are termed 'over-tricks.' The actual trick value for these over-tricks is placed above the line.

In the case mentioned above where two spades were bid and four made, 60 points would go below the line, 60 above. A game would not be won since only 60 points (for the two spades bid) count towards game. The points for the extra tricks merely count in total scoring.

That, incidentally, is the main difference between contract and auction bridge. In contract, only the tricks bid and made count towards game; in auction, the entire trick score counts towards game. Bidding one spade, making four would produce a game in auction while in contract the yield would be 30 points below, 90 points above the line.

DOUBLED OR REDOUBLED OVER-TRICKS

In the foregoing paragraphs, you have learned that over-tricks, made but not contracted are scored above the line. When the contract is doubled or redoubled and extra tricks are won, they are similarly placed above the line but their values are greatly increased.

Instead of merely receiving the actual trick score for each extra (doubled or redoubled) over-trick, a bonus is given the successful side which varies according to vulnerability and also whether the contract was doubled or redoubled.

These bonuses are the same for all suits and no trump - are for each trick - and are in addition to the 50 points awarded for successful completion of the doubled or redoubled contract.

	Not Vulnerable	Vulnerable
Doubled	100	200
Redoubled	200	400

These points, of course, go above the line.

TRICKS IN EXCESS OF A CONTRACTED GAME

"Game," you say, "is bidding and making 100 points or more in tricks. Suppose I bid five spades and make it, receiving 150 points. Can I count 100 of them towards one game, the remaining 50 towards the next game?"

No! Only one game can be bid on one hand even though you may score more than the needed 100 points.

HONORS

The five highest cards of any suit are called 'honors.' These cards are the ace, the king, the queen, the jack and the 10.

When a hand is played in a suit contract, possession of any four honors *of the trump suit in any one hand* gives the holder's side a bonus of 100 points. All five honors *in one hand* yields 150 points to that partnership.

To receive either bonus, the honors cannot be divided between the partnership as three in one hand and the balance in the other. All four or five honors must be in the same hand.

I would like to emphasize a few important points. First, the bonus for holding honors is not claimed until after the hand is played. You may say, **"Why, that's strange. After the cards are all mixed up, anyone could say they held four or five honors."**

The answer to that is that players soon learn to remember the cards they have just held and played, particularly the high trumps. The principal reason for delaying announcement of honors until conclusion of the hand is that should honors be announced earlier, valuable information is given the other side as to the location of the high trumps. The opponents have no more right to know the other side's trump holding than any other cards in their hands.

Another point I would like to make is that any player, even a defender, is eligible to receive the bonus for honors. If your side plays a spade contract and an opponent holds ♠ KQJ10, the opponents receive the 100 point bonus.

In other words, 'honors' go to him that 'has,' not necessarily to the side that made the highest bid. Moreover, honors are scored *only if that particular suit is trump*. If you held ♡ AKQJ10 and spades were trumps, you wouldn't receive a single point bonus although were hearts trumps, you'd have received 150 points. With spades trumps, your heart honors are just so much Confederate money.

SLAMS

Somewhere among your bridge-playing friends, you may have heard the word 'slam.' It may have been 'big slam' or 'little slam' or 'grand slam' or 'small slam.'

Well, a grand slam and a big slam are the same thing - the bidding and taking of all 13 tricks. The small or little slam refers to the bidding and winning of 12 of the possible 13 tricks.

For the successful completion of a slam contract, a considerable bonus is awarded which varies in proportion to vulnerability and also whether the slam was a grand slam or a small slam. Obviously, bidding and making a slam when vulnerable should and does pay off better than when not vulnerable since the attendant penalties for failure to make the contract are greater when vulnerable. Similarly, it is more difficult to win 13 tricks than 12.

If you don't believe me, wait until you try it!

Bidding and making a small slam is worth 500 points not vulnerable; 750 points if vulnerable.

A completed grand slam yields a bonus of 1,000 points not vulnerable; 1,500 points if vulnerable.

These points go above the line, in the honors column, to the credit of the successful bidders.

Doubling and redoubling *do not* change the value of the slam bonus. They do, however, multiply the actual trick score below the line exactly as described under 'Doubling and Redoubling.'

SCORING UNSUCCESSFUL CONTRACTS

The reader may ask, "Suppose I bid four hearts and make three. Do I get credit for making three hearts?"

No!

In the event you or your partner fail to make your bid, you do not receive anything for the tricks you won. Instead, you pay in penalties for each trick by which you failed to make your bid.

In the preceding example, having bid four hearts and made three, you would be 'down one.' This means you would pay a one trick penalty, the amount depending on vulnerability and whether undoubled, doubled or redoubled.

HONORS IN NO TRUMP

When the hand is played in no trump, holding all four aces in one hand is termed "150 aces." That side receives a bonus of 150 points.

As in suit contracts, it is preferable to claim "150 aces" in no trump after completion of play on the hand rather than before or during play. Any player when the hand is played in no trump, whether declarer's side or defenders', receives the bonus if holding all four aces in one hand.

THE RUBBER BONUS

To the side first winning two games, an additional bonus is awarded. It is called the "rubber bonus." Sometimes one side will score two games without the other side scoring one game. Other times, each side will have made a game before one side scores its second game.

In the event that a partnership wins two games before the other side has won one, a bonus of 700 points is awarded the former pair. This is called the "rubber bonus" or as it is usually known, "the rubber." If at the end of the rubber, the score in games is two to one, the winning pair receives a 500 point bonus.

When a pair has won two games, the rubber is completed. Points are totaled in both columns, both "WE" and "THEY" and the lesser amount subtracted from the greater. The side with the greater amount has "won the rubber" and the difference in points is awarded the winners. The losers receive nothing regardless of their total.

There is a possibility that a pair that had won the rubber might still be the loser in total points. Suppose our pair, "WE," had overbid, been doubled and set 1,100 points. Later we win the rubber but since the opponents had a game, your bonus is but 500 points. You can see the vast difference between 1,100 in penalty and 500 in bonus still leaves you behind. The victory is Pyrrhic.

BONUSES FOR UNCOMPLETED RUBBERS

Every now and then, it will be found impossible to finish a rubber due to lack of time or some equally valid reason. The scores in each column are totaled. In addition, a bonus of 300 points is awarded for each game bid and made. A 50 point bonus is given for having one *or more* part scores towards an unfinished game. *A side cannot receive more than one 50 point part-score bonus.* For example, you have part scores of 20, 40 and 30 below the line. That gives you a partial of 90 points towards game. You receive one 50 point bonus, not 50 points for each. Of course, had your partials been cancelled by the opponents making a game, they would yield no bonus over and above their actual point value in the final total.

This method of scoring is quite common in bridge played for short, limited periods as commuter bridge, where the arrival of the train limits time of play.

SCORING TABLES

Scoring tables will be found on the back inside cover and enclosed with each deck of bridge playing cards. Consult them until you are familiar with the figures.

THE BIDDING PERIOD

The dealer has the privilege of the first bid. He may elect to bid or not. If he decides his hand does not have sufficient strength to bid, he says "pass" or "no bid." After he bids or passes, the next opportunity to bid or pass goes to the player at the dealer's left and this continues until all four players have had the opportunity of bidding.

A player may bid or pass only when it is his turn to bid. The fact that a player *did not bid on one round does not affect or preclude his right to bid on a future round and vice-versa.*

If no player at the table makes a bid, the hand is said to be "passed out" and taken out of play. The next hand is then dealt by the player to the left of the previous dealer. The dealer of a passed out hand does not deal twice in a row.

(a)

North, Dealer	East	South	West
pass	pass	pass	pass

In the above example, we have a passed out hand. East would deal the next hand. No score is given to either side since none was made.

The bidding on a hand will be concluded when there have been three consecutive passes following any bid.

(b)

North, Dealer	East	South	West
1 heart	pass	1 spade	2 clubs
2 hearts	pass	4 hearts	pass
pass	pass		

Since there have been three consecutive passes following the four heart bid, that is the final contract. North-South need to win 10 tricks.

A double or redouble is identical to any bid in requiring three passes to follow for the bidding to conclude. Incidentally, you cannot double a pass, only a bid by the opponents.

	North	
	♠ J862 ♡ 543 ◇ KQ2 ♣ A84	
West ♠ Q103 ♡ AJ10 ◇ J1098 ♣ J52	N W E S	**East** ♠ 97 ♡ 9876 ◇ A76 ♣ 10976
	♠ AK54 ♡ KQ2 ◇ 543 ♣ KQ3	

Figure Three

In the above hand *(figure three)*, East was the dealer and the bidding proceded:

(c)

East	South	West	North
pass	1 spade	pass	2 spades
pass	pass	pass	

While we will not go into bidding requirements at this time, there are several points to be noted.

First, the last bid was two spades and the bidding was over the moment it (the two spade bid) was followed by three passes.

Second, South is the declarer (player of the hand) in the two spade contract. To fulfill that contract, the combined cards of the North-South partnership must win eight tricks. The declarer is the person who first bid the final trump suit (or no trump), not the member of the partnership who bid the greatest number of that suit.

In *figure three,* North bid two spades, South only one spade. Yet South is the declarer because he was the first player on that side to bid spades.

The first card played to any hand is called "the opening lead." It is made by the player to the left of the declarer. Since in *figure three,* South is the declarer, the player to his left is West and that player would lead the jack of diamonds for reasons you will learn later when you study leads and defensive play.

FOLLOWING SUIT

Playing a card of the same suit led by another player is known as "following suit" or "to follow suit." You *MUST* follow suit to a trick when able to do so. In other words, when a spade is led, you must play a spade if you have one in your hand.

Let's suppose the player to your right leads the eight of spades. You hold the jack and deuce of spades. As long as you follow suit, viz., play a spade, *you may play any spade you wish.*

On the next few pages you will discover that a player who has won a trick leads (plays first) to the next trick. The fact that a spade was led to one trick *does NOT make it mandatory that a spade be led to the next trick.* Each trick is a separate unit to itself. The obligation to follow suit applies only within each trick, not from one trick to the other.

However, lacking a card of the led suit, you may play a card of any suit to that trick, including a trump, if you desire.

It is just as important to follow suit when trumps are led as any other suit. There are no exceptions to following suit, whether suit contract or no trump. When a player fails to follow suit when able to do so, it is usually from inadvertence or oversight and the rules provide severe penalties for such occurences.

Failure to follow suit when able to do so is known as a 'revoke' or 'renege.' To revoke deliberately is the equivalent of cheating.

TRUMPING

When unable to follow suit, any player may play a card of the trump suit to the current trick. This trump card outranks any card of any other suit. The only card that can outrank one trump is a still higher trump.

For example, spades are trumps and West leads the 10 of hearts. Dummy, North, follows suit with the six of hearts. East discards the queen of clubs and South trumps with the two of spades.

Who won the trick ?

North-South, of course, since South trumped the trick.

While any player can trump if void of the led suit, *it is not compulsory to trump.* A player has the right to discard from any suit he holds if unable to follow suit. Trumping is optional, not mandatory.

Trumps may be led or played by any player at any time including the opening lead. There are many hands in which a trump is a defender's opening lead.

THE DUMMY

On preceding pages, we have referred to one of the players as 'the dummy.' That individual is the declarer's partner or in other words, the partner of the successful bidder who is playing the hand.

After the bidding is over and *after the opening lead has been made*, the dummy places his cards, arranged in suits, face up on the table. The cards are placed along the edge of the table nearest the dummy. The declarer then plays not only his cards (which remain concealed in his hand) but also those of the dummy (which have been placed face upwards on the table). The entire choice of which card to play from dummy's hand and his own rests entirely with declarer.

While the dummy is actually silent after the conclusion of the bidding, he does have certain rights. He can remind his partner (the declarer) as to which hand has the lead and call attention to revokes and infractions of the laws by the opponents.

Some players, when dummy, have the habit of first placing their trumps on the table *before* the opening lead has been made. This is neither correct or desirable. There is no more reason to show the opponents the trumps held by dummy than any other cards held by that player. Moreover, there are many, many times the opponent on opening lead will not know which suit to lead and if, before making the opening lead, he can see that a trump lead is safe or advantageous to his side, can lead that suit in safety without jeopardizing a defensive trick.

THE CHANGING LEAD

The jack of diamonds in *figure three* would be covered by dummy's queen and taken by East's ace.

It is now East's turn to lead. He has won the trick.

We'll play out the hand in *figure three* from start to finish with the winning card to each trick underlined so you can see how the winner of the current trick leads to the next trick.

	North	
	♠ J862	
	♡ 543	
	♢ KQ2	
	♣ A84	
West		**East**
♠ Q103	N	♠ 97
♡ AJ10	W E	♡ 9876
♢ J1098		♢ A76
♣ J52	S	♣ 10976
	South	
	♠ AK54	
	♡ KQ2	
	♢ 543	
	♣ KQ3	

Figure Three
Reprinted for convenience

TRICK	W	N	E	S
1	♢J	♢Q	♢A	♢3
2	♢8	♢K	♢7	♢4
3	♡A	♡3	♡6	♡Q
4	♢10	♢2	♢6	♢5
5	♡J	♡4	♡7	♡K
6	♠3	♠2	♠7	♠K
7	♠10	♠6	♠9	♠A
8	♣2	♣4	♣6	♣K
9	♣5	♣8	♣7	♣Q
10	♣J	♣A	♣9	♣3
11	♠Q	♠8	♡8	♠5
12	♡10	♡5	♡9	♡2
13	♢9	♠J	♣10	♠4

It can be seen that North-South successfully completed their two spade contract, winning the needed eight tricks.

A PRACTICE EXCERCISE IN SCORING

WE	THEY
	300 (b)
(a) 60	

Figure Four

Pretend you were South, the declarer, in the preceding hand. Having bid and made two spades, your side has earned 60 points towards game, spades being worth 30 points per trick. The score is entered directly below the line in the "WE" column. We mark that score (a).

On the very next hand, we have the misfortune to overbid. Our final contract is two hearts which an opponent doubles and defeats us by two tricks. Since we are not vulnerable, we pay a penalty of 300 points according to our table and we enter that directly above the line under "THEY." This is designated as (b).

It is now the third deal. On the first, East dealt and the North-South partnership bid and made two spades. On the second deal, South was the dealer and North-South were penalized 300 points at two hearts, doubled. On the third hand, West dealt and since no player bid, the hand was passed out. On the fourth hand, North is the dealer.

What I am trying to show is that each player deals in clockwise rotation, regardless of who played the previous hand and whether the hand was played or passed out.

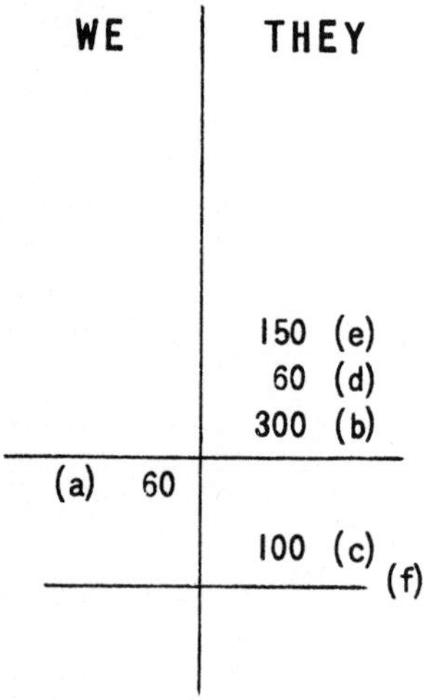

Figure Five

On the fourth hand, dealt by North, the opponents (East-West) arrive at three no trump, make five. We enter 100 below the line under "THEY" for the three no trump bid and made (c), 60 above the line for the two over-tricks (d). In addition, the declarer (East) held 150 aces. These honors are entered to their credit as (e).

Our part score of 60 has been wiped out, so far as counting towards game is concerned. To show completion of a game, a line is drawn directly beneath the game-yielding score (f).

Note that in recording scores below the line, I started directly beneath the line and wrote downwards. In entering scores above the line as (b), (d) and (e) in *figure five*, I started from immediately above the line and wrote upwards. Scores are recorded *below each other if below the line or above each other if above the line*. Everything is written from the line - down for tricks bid and made - up for everything else.

I would like to call attention to a very commonly used short-cut in scoring. Where the score for tricks bid and made exceeds 100 points, either because more than 100 were made on one hand or because the combined partials now total more than 100 points, the entire result of the hand is scored below the line in one posting rather than making two entries; tricks bid and made below the line and over-tricks above the line.

WE	THEY
	150 (e)
	300 (b)
(a) 60	
	160 (cd)
	(f)

Figure Six

Since in bidding three no trump and making five, the two extra tricks in excess of game have no value other than total scoring, they are usually posted as one score as (cd) in *figure six.*

But if a game had not been completed, then the unbid but made over-tricks must go above the line. Had "THEY" bid two no trump, made five, it would be scored as 70 below, 90 above. Had "THEY" a partial, let us say, of 30, so that 70 points would have completed their game, then the entire 160 points could go below the line. This is purely a short cut but it is one that is standard practice everywhere.

Continuing the rubber, fortune now favors us. We bid six spades which is a small slam. An opponent doubles and our partner redoubles. The defensive tricks our opponent counted on fail to materialize and we make seven. This is shown in *figure seven.*

WE	THEY
(j) 50	
(i) 500	150 (e)
(h) 200	300 (b)
(a) 60	
	160 (cd)
	(f)
(g) 720	
	(k)

Figure Seven

Below the line we receive 720 (g). Let's see how this figure was reached. Six spades ordinarily would be six times 30 or 180. Doubled would be 360 and redoubled, 720 points.

Above the line we place 200 for the redoubled, non-vulnerable overtrick, 500 (i) for small slam bonus not vulnerable and 50 (j) for fulfilling the redoubled contract. Another line (k) shows a game was made.

Both sides are now vulnerable and the rubber bonus will go to the side first to make a second game. The rubber bonus will only be 500 points since no matter which side wins, the other side has scored a game.

	WE	THEY		
(p)	500			
(m)	30			
(j)	50			
(i)	500	150	(e)	
(h)	200	300	(b)	
				The Line
(a)	60			
		160	(cd)	
			(f)	— *1st Game*
(g)	720			
			(k)	— *2nd Game*
(l)	90			
(n)	70			
			(o)	
	2,220	610		*TOTALS*

Figure Eight

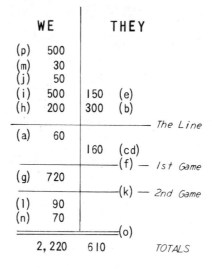

Three spades is our next bid and we make four. The 90 points for three spades bid and made is shown as (l) in *figure eight;* the 30 for the overtrick (m) above the line. We now bid one no trump, make two. The 70 points are scored below the line as (n). The 70 and 90 total 160 points, more than the 100 needed for game so the rubber is over. "WE" have won two games. To indicate this, we draw a double line (o) below the second game. We receive a 500 point bonus (p) for winning the rubber.

Total points for both sides are added. "WE" have 2,220 points. "THEY" have 610. "WE" win by 1,610 points.

If the partnerships remain the same for the next rubber, "WE" would start the next rubber with 1,610 points to our credit. Where the partnerships change after each rubber, called 'pivot' games, scores are computed in units of 100 points each, 50 or more points being considered 100. *For example, each member of a partnership winning 1750 points would be 'plus 18' in a pivot game.*

In the case of the "WE" partnership of *figure eight,* each partner in a pivot game would be 'plus 16,' each member of the losing pair 'minus 16.' I particularly want to emphasize that the losers receive no credit for the 610 points scored other than deducting it from the winners' greater total. The losers are minus 1,610 points.

QUIZ ONE

1 - Which of the four suits is the highest ranking?

2 - Which suit counts more in scoring, clubs or diamonds?

3 - How many points are needed for game?

4 - Can you combine two or more scores towards game?

5 - A bid of 'three' contracts for how many tricks?

6 - Can you refuse to follow suit, if able to do so?

7 - Must you attempt to capture a trick if you hold both higher and lower cards of a led suit?

8 - Must you trump if unable to follow suit?

9 - Can you bid at a later opportunity if you have previously passed?

10 - Your side bids three spades and wins eight tricks. Can you take credit for the eight tricks?

11 - Even though you continually pass, your partner single-handed bids four spades, is doubled and penalized 1,100 points. Can you disavow responsibility and avoid paying the penalty?

12 - Your side has made a game. Are you vulnerable or not vulnerable?

13 - The opponents play the hand with hearts trumps. You hold in hearts ♡ KQJ10. Can you, as a defender, receive a bonus for honors? If so, how much with the above?

14 - You have been doubled at four spades, not vulnerable, and make five. How many points do you receive below the line? Above?

15 - Your side, not vulnerable, bids four spades, makes six. What slam bonus do you receive?

ANSWERS TO QUIZ ONE

1 - Spades.

2 - They both count the same, 20 points per trick.

3 - 100 points.

4 - Yes.

5 - Nine.

6 - No. You must play a card of the suit being led, if you hold one at that time.

7 - No. As long as you follow suit, the size of the card you play is a matter of personal preference.

8 - No. You may play a card of any suit you wish.

9 - Yes, providing you have another chance to bid.

10 - No. You pay a one trick penalty.

11 - No. Both partners pay equally, each losing 1,100 points.

12 - Vulnerable.

13 - Yes. 100 points.

14 - 240 below the line, 150 above. The latter figure represents 100 for the over-trick, 50 for fulfillment.

15 - None. To receive a slam bonus, it is necessary to contract for the slam in addition to making it.

Lesson II

PART ONE

Opening the Bidding

PART TWO

Basic Play of the Cards

OPENING THE BIDDING

The privilege of making the first bid belongs to the dealer. The lowest bid he can make is "one" (seven tricks) which may be in any suit or no trump. If the dealer does not feel he has sufficient strength to open the bidding, he says "pass" or "no bid" and the privilege of bidding goes to the player on the dealer's left. He, too, may bid or pass, depending on the strength of his hand. Should he elect to pass, the next player to his left has the option until all four players have had a turn to bid. In the event all four players pass, the hand is then said to be 'passed out' and a new hand dealt, the deal progressing to the player who sits at the left of the previous dealer.

The initial bid at the table, regardless of whether made by the dealer, second-hand, third or fourth-hand, is the 'opening bid.' So, if the dealer and the next player passed and the third player made a bid, that would be the opening bid.

Next, the fact that a player has once passed does not bar him from entering the bidding at a later point. A bid made by a player who has previously passed is known as a 'secondary bid.'

A player may bid again and again, if he wishes, and whenever it is his turn to bid. This stands to reason since a player may have two or more suits to show or support to give partner's suits.

A bid, defined, is a contract or obligation by the bidder for his side to win a given number of tricks. The amount of the bid, as one, two or more, is always added to the book of six so that a one bid contracts for seven tricks, two for eight, three for nine, etc. Since there is a maximum of 13 tricks to be won, the highest possible bid is seven, known as a 'grand slam.'

Some of you may now be saying, **"Well, suppose someone on the other side opens the bidding. Can I bid?"**

Of course you can. Bidding is competitive and the highest bid determines the trump. That is why possession of the major suits is an advantage, since a bid of four of a major would take precedence over a bid of four of a minor. Bids made after the other side has opened the bidding are known as 'overcalls.' There are strong and weak overcalls. Their requirements will be discussed in Lesson XI under Defensive Bidding.

At present, we will be concerned only with the requirements for making an opening bid.

♠ QJ109876
♡ 43
◇ 32
♣ 32
Figure Nine

♠ AK42
♡ AK4
◇ A63
♣ 875
Figure 10

Suppose you held the hand in *figure nine*. What suit would you prefer to be trumps? Why, spades, naturally.

How many tricks could that hand win were spades trumps? *Five*, since you hold seven cards of that suit and the moment the ace and king were forced out, your remaining five spades would be winning tricks.

Here is another hand in *figure 10*, entirely different in type. Were spades trumps, it would similarly win five tricks under ordinary circumstances. The ace and king of spades would win two tricks, the ace and king of hearts two more and the ace of diamonds another.

Let's compare the two hands. Each could win five tricks were spades trumps. The former hand, by virtue of a long trump suit, was the equal in offensive trick taking ability to the second with no long suit but three aces and two kings.

So there is our first lesson - To win a given number of tricks, the longer the trump suit, the fewer high cards are needed.

But the second hand possesses one great advantage: no matter what suit is trump, it will ordinarily win five tricks, whereas the hand shown in *figure nine* cannot win any tricks unless spades were trumps. In bridge language, *figure 10* has defensive as well as offensive values.

It stands to reason that there has to be a happy meeting ground in opening bids, some kind of compromise between long suits and high cards. In order to bid, fewer high cards should be needed when holding a strong suit and conversely, with a weak suit, a greater number of high cards should be present.

This is the case !

During this discussion, you may have wondered how a player might bid one, thus contracting for seven tricks, on hands which are capable of winning but five. Where are the other two tricks coming from?

The answer is - from partner's hand. You see, he holds his share of the cards, too. If the high cards of the deck were evenly distributed between all four players at the table, each would have one ace, one king, one queen, one jack, etc. This is called 'normal expectancy.'

When a player opens the bidding with one of a suit, he is contracting or obligating his side to win more than their share of tricks - seven out of a possible 13. That's why the opening bidder must have more than his normal share of high cards and long suits. He is endeavoring to take more than his normal share of the 13 tricks.

High cards alone do not determine an opening bid any more than suit length. Each bulwarks the other.

High cards have both offensive and defensive abilities. By offensive, I mean the tricks your high cards and long suits will win if your side makes the highest bid and names the trump suit; defensively, I refer to the tricks your side will win if the opponents play the hand.

If your side were playing the hand, you would in most cases have control of the trump suit. Once trumps were led ('pulled' is the bridge player's term for trump extraction) you would be able to use your high cards in other suits to their fullest values.

Let me give you a specific example.

♠ 8
♡ AKQJ109
◊ AKQJ
♣ 32
Figure 11

In *figure 11*, were hearts trumps, how many tricks would you normally expect to win? Ten, of course, since once you gain the lead, you can pull the opponents' trumps, cash your four diamond tricks. You will lose only three black cards.

Yet how many tricks do you think the self-same hand would win if the opponents named spades trumps? In other words, how many defensive taking tricks does it contain? Let's look at the heart suit first. The suit has six cards. That leaves seven hearts to be divided between the remaining three players. If these seven cards were divided by three as evenly as possible, two players would each hold two hearts and the third, three cards of that suit. Thus two players would be able to trump the third round of hearts.

The shorter diamond suit of four cards offers a greater possibility that the suit might be played three times without being trumped. But since this is only a possibility, in the interests of accurate and conservative valuation, the maximum number of defensive taking tricks that can be counted in any suit, no matter how short, is two! Even if you held ◊ AKQ alone against an adverse contract, you could count only two defensive winners. If you take three tricks, regard it as a pleasant surprise.

Succeeding pages will contain a table of defensive winners.

HIGH CARD POINTS

CARD	VALUE IN POINTS
Ace	4
King *	3
Queen *	2
Jack *	1

* *Deduct one point from normal value if singleton.*

DISTRIBUTIONAL POINT COUNT
(For Suit Bidding)

FOR EACH	VALUE IN POINTS
Void	3
Singleton	2
Doubleton	1

High card points will always be the same for both suit and no trump bidding. Distribution is counted only for suit bidding. For conciseness, the following abbreviations will be used:

HIGH CARD POINTS	HC
DISTRIBUTIONAL POINTS	DIS

WHAT IS A DEFENSIVE TRICK?

A defensive trick is any card or combination of cards that will take a trick no matter what suit is trump. The ace of spades, for example, could be expected to win a trick whether spades, hearts, diamonds or clubs were trumps. Similarly, if you held the ace and king of spades, you could with some assurance hope to win two tricks.

TABLE OF DEFENSIVE TRICKS

AKQ	Of same suit	2 plus	A		1
AKJ	" " "	" "	KQ	Of same suit	1
			KJ10	" " "	1
AK	" " "	2			
			Kx	" " "	½
AQ	" " "	1 ½	QJx	" " "	½

DO NOT count more than two defensive tricks in any one suit!

♠432
N
♠J10 W E ♠987
S
♠AKQ65
Figure 12

Low cards, too, play their part in taking tricks. Suppose you held the South cards in *figure 12.* With spades trumps, you could lead out your three high spades. Now your six and five, little cards to be sure, are winners since the opponents no longer hold spades higher than the five and six spots.

♠ 5432
♡ void
◇ AKQJ2
♣ AKQJ
Figure 13

Here on the left in *figure 13* is another example of how low cards can win tricks, this time by trumping. Let's suppose your partner opened the bidding with one spade and the opponents have bid hearts. Do you see how useful your hand will be to your partner? Why, whenever a heart is led, your partner can trump the trick with a spade from your hand.

Your trumps, coupled with your void in hearts, are the equivalent of holding the ace, king, queen and jack of hearts in their ability to win tricks when hearts are led. In fact, if your partner's spade suit is solid and has no losers, your combined hands should be able to contract for and win all 13 tricks with spades trumps, giving you the grand slam bonus.

Sometimes, you may not have a void. You may possess one card of a suit. This lone card is known as a 'singleton.' Correspondingly, a two card holding is a 'doubleton.' The singleton permits trumping the second round of that suit (providing trumps are present) and the doubleton affords third round trumping ability.

OPENING BIDS OF ONE IN A SUIT

Ninety percent or more of all opening bids are of one in a suit. There are two things to learn.

1 - Values for high cards as aces, kings, queens and jacks.

2 - Values assigned for distribution (the ability to trump).

The advantage of point count bidding is that both types of values are expressed in the same common denominator - points!

TYPES OF SUITS FOR OPENING BIDS

THE BIDDABLE OR POOR SUIT

A biddable suit is the bridge player's name for a poor suit. Someone may ask, "Well, if it's poor, why bid it at all?" The answer is - it's the best available. It isn't always possible to hold long, solid suits. You'll hold far more four and five card suits than six, seven or eight-carders. And if your hand contains 14 points or more, you should open the bidding, even with a poor suit. If you have two or more poor suits, you should open the bidding with 13 points.

You see, the fact that you open the bidding with one suit doesn't mean that you are condemned to play the hand with that suit as trump. Unless your partner can support your suit, the probability is that the hand will be played in some other contract.

"How poor a suit can I bid?" you enquire.

ANSWER - To open the bidding with a four card suit, it should contain at least three points in high cards as queen-jack or king; any five card or longer suit may be bid, regardless of high cards. These are minimums. If the suit is stronger, so much the better.

EXAMPLES

(a)	(b)	(c)	(d)	(e)	(f)	(g)
QJ64	AJ75	K862	KJ105	AKQJ	J8432	76543

Even (e) would be classed as poor since it is only of four cards in length, even though they are the highest cards in the suit.

In order to make a satisfactory trump suit, four-carders and weak five-carders require a great deal more bolstering in supporting cards from partner than do their stronger, rebiddable brothers. That is why all four card suits and weak five card suits are classed as poor.

REASONS FOR HIGH CARDS IN THE BID SUIT

I want to show you reasons for never opening the bidding with a four card suit unless it contains at least the queen-jack or the king.

The first reason is that even though you may have opened the bidding, that is no guarantee that you will play the hand. The opponents may very well outbid you for the final contract. Accordingly, when you bid a suit, you should be prepared to have your partner lead that suit if your side becomes defenders. Therefore, your opening bid should, if possible, indicate a safe opening lead to partner.

By 'safe,' I mean a lead that will help your side win a trick so that if your partner leads a high card of your bid suit, it will not be thrown away but rather, will win a trick or help promote a future trick in your hand.

The second reason is that in the event your side has made the highest bid and your suit becomes trump, you should have high cards capable of capturing those cards held by the opponents.

GOOD OR REBIDDABLE SUITS

(h)	(i)	(j)	(k)	(l)	(m)
KQ543	AJ852	AK876	QJ432	1076432	8765432

Any five card suit headed by two or more of the top four honors (ace, king, queen or jack) is rebiddable.

Any six card or longer suit, even without any high cards, is rebiddable. While hands (l) and (m) have no defensive values, the extra trumps furnished by six card and longer suits make them 'must' opening bids with 13 or more points.

The beauty of rebiddable suits is that they may not only be opened but that they may be bid again (rebid) without previously being supported by partner.

In other words, having opened the bidding with one spade on any of the hands shown as (h) to (m) inclusive and your partner responded with, let us say, 'two hearts,' you can now bid 'two spades.'

From the very fact that you were able to bid your suit twice before your partner supported that suit, he knows it to be a good suit. Had you not rebid it, he would have every right to surmise it to be merely a biddable, poor suit.

You are beginning to see how bidding paints a picture of your hand.

EXCELLENT OR TWICE-REBIDDABLE SUITS

Sometimes you will be fortunate enough to hold a suit so strong in itself that it will require practically no supporting cards from partner to be an ideal trump suit.

Suits of this sort are termed 'solid' or 'near-solid.' They have either no losers in the suit or at most, one or two losers in a suit that possesses both great length and solidity.

Suits like these that can stand on their own two feet can naturally be rebid several times without support in that suit from partner. They are usually called 'twice-rebiddable' or 'excellent' suits. They are usually six cards or longer, contain at least five sure winners in the suit itself.

1 - QJ109876	Five winners
2 - KQJ762	Five winners
3 - AKJ1087	Five winners
4 - AKQ432	Six winners
5 - AKQJ4	Five winners. This is the only case where a five card suit can be classed as twice-rebiddable.

THE MEANING OF REBIDDING

On previous pages, we have described four card suits and weak five card suits as poor or merely biddable.

Does that mean that they can't ever be rebid?

Well, hardly!

What it does mean is that the so-called poor suit cannot be bid again by the player who first bid it until after it has been supported (raised) by partner. After the poor suit has been supported by partner, it can be rebid as much and as often as warranted by the strength of the opening bidder's hand and the strength shown by partner's raise.

Let's suppose, holding the hand shown as *figure 14,* we open the bidding with one heart.

	HIGH CARDS	DISTRIBUTION
♠ A64	4	
♡ KJ98	4	
◇ J432	1	
♣ KQ	5	1

Figure 14

Your hand totals 15 points, 14 in high cards and one in distribution for the doubleton. You open with 'one heart.' Your partner responds with a raise to 'three hearts.'

Can you rebid your poor heart suit?

Yes - since your partner not only supported your heart suit but by giving your heart suit a strong (jump) raise, showed excellent supporting cards not only in hearts but in the other suits as well.

It is only when a poor suit HAS NOT been supported that it should not be rebid voluntarily.

NOT REBIDDING A REBIDDABLE SUIT

It may seem strange to the reader that there are times when, after a player has opened the bidding holding a rebiddable suit, he does not rebid it. But a few words of explanation will help make things clear.

♠ AK432
♡ J87
◊ A65
♣ 42
Figure 15

Holding the hand shown in *figure 15,* you open the bidding with one spade. The bidding then continues as:

You, South	West	North, Partner	East
1 spade	2 hearts	PASS !!	4 hearts
?			

Should you now bid four spades merely to tell your partner that your spade suit is rebiddable?

Well, if you do, you'll get your head chopped off!

You'll be doubled and heavily penalized.

How in the world do you expect to win the 10 tricks needed to fulfill the contract with a partner so weak that he is unable to bid, both opponents showing strength and only 13 points in your hand?

So you have to put your pride in your pocket and pass. While you have a rebiddable suit, you just can't afford to show it's rebiddable. The price is too high.

Now, let's take another kind of example.

♠ AK432
♡ KJ8
◊ Q432
♣ 2
Figure 16

With the hand shown in *figure 16,* you open the bidding with one spade in the following sequence.

You, South	West	North, Partner	East
1 spade	pass	2 hearts	pass
?			

Should you rebid your spade suit by saying 'two spades?' You could because your spade suit is rebiddable.

However, you have excellent support for your partner's heart suit. Your choice, then, is between rebidding your spade suit by saying 'two spades' or showing support for partner's suit by raising him to three hearts.

In this case, the raise to three hearts is preferable.

The problem of whether to rebid one's own suit or support partner frequently arises. With a good hand and a desire to make a constructive rebid which might lead to a higher (game) contract, it is generally better with support for partner's suit to raise it rather than merely show one's own suit to be rebiddable. You will learn more about this in your lessons on 'rebidding.'

So you see, the fact that you have opened the bidding with a rebiddable suit does not make it mandatory or even sometimes desirable that you rebid it. It only means that you can rebid it - *PROVIDING* - and it's a big *'providing'* such a rebid is warranted by the course of subsequent bidding.

ASSEMBLING THE OPENING BID

Now that you have learned that suits vary in trick-taking abilities in proportion to their length and solidity, we'll put our high card points and suits together and see what we need to open the bidding with a bid of one of a suit.

TO OPEN THE BIDDING WITH ONE OF A SUIT

HOLDING	POINTS REQUIRED
One biddable (poor) suit	14 or more
Two or more biddable (poor) suits	13 or more
Any other suit or combination.	13 or more

With an aceless hand, add one point to each of the above.

There are several things I'd like to point out.

First, you'll notice the expression 'or more' repeated under the 'points required' column. That is because the more strength you have, the better. It is quite all right to open the bidding with more points than required but ordinarily, you should not open the bidding with less.

Next, you will have noticed that with any good or excellent suit or with two or more poor suits, you need only 13 points for an opening bid; with only one poor suit, you need 14 points or better. This is in accordance with what we have already demonstrated - that the weaker or shorter the suit, the more high cards are required to win a given number of tricks.

Lastly, you may ask, **"Must all of the points required to open the bidding be in high cards? Can you include points for distribution?"**

Yes. To open the bidding with a suit, both high card and distribution points are counted. Further, the necessary 13 or more points need not be in the bid suit. They can be anywhere in the hand, as long as the suit itself is biddable.

VULNERABILITY AND POSITION AT THE TABLE AS AFFECTING THE OPENING BID

You will sometimes hear some poorly informed player say, **"Why, I was vulnerable. I couldn't open the bidding on 't-h-a-t'."**

Forget it!

Vulnerability or lack of it plays no part in determining whether an opening bid is present. An ace is going to take a trick, vulnerable or not. If you have enough points to open the bidding, go ahead and bid.

From the old days of auction bridge, you may hear someone quote that **"to open the bidding fourth hand (in last position af after three passes) you must be able to make game in your own hand."** That, too, is complete bosh. No more strength is required in one seat than another.

The player sitting third hand (after two passes) *may* (and notice that I didn't say *'should'*) open the bidding with as little as 11 or 12 points providing he holds a fairly solid suit and intends to pass thereafter.

The light third hand opening bid, sparingly used and then only with a good partner, does have the strategic advantage of telling partner, as a defender, what suit to lead. The suit should resemble ♠ KQJ98 or ♠ AQJ95. It would be silly to open the bidding third hand with a spade on ♠ 87654 ♡ AQ8 ◊ Q43 ♣ K2. What could you possibly hope to gain having your partner lead a spade unless it happened to be his normal opening lead?

My recommendation to you during the early stages of your bridge development is to keep your opening bids sound and solid in all positions - first hand, second, third and fourth. Later on, as you become more experienced, you may employ light third-hand opening bids. Even experts get in trouble by opening the bidding when they 'ain't got what the bid shows.'

COUNTING THE OPENING BID

	HIGH CARDS	DISTRIBUTION	TOTAL
(a)			
♠ KJ86	4	0	4
♡ Q97	2	0	2
◇ AK84	7	0	7
♣ 75	0	1	1
			14
(b)			
♠ Q73	2	0	2
♡ AK743	7	0	7
◇ A52	4	0	4
♣ 103	0	1	1
			14
(c)			
♠ A7543	4	0	4
♡ A843	4	0	4
◇ 7	0	2	2
♣ AJ2	5	0	5
			15
(d)			
♠ A743	4	0	4
♡ A83	4	0	4
◇ A65	4	0	4
♣ J43	1	0	1
			13
(e)			
♠ J10876	1	0	1
♡ AK9	7	0	7
◇ KQ4	5	0	5
♣ 86	0	1	1
			14

BIDDING FOOTNOTES

(a) One spade. 14 points and two biddable suits. The reason for bidding one spade rather than one diamond is explained in Lesson Four.
(b) One heart. 14 points and a rebiddable suit.
(c) One spade.
(d) Pass. 14 points are needed with only one biddable (poor) suit.
(e) One spade.

(f)	HIGH CARDS	DISTRIBUTION	TOTAL
♠ 3	0	2	2
♡ KQJ10764	6	0	6
◇ AJ43	5	0	5
♣ 2	0	2	2
			15

(g)			
♠ K109	3	0	3
♡ QJ4	3	0	3
◇ AJ874	5	0	5
♣ K2	3	1	4
			15

(h)			
♠ QJ107432	3	0	3
♡ AK	7	1	8
◇ 6543	0	0	0
♣ void	0	3	3
			14

(i)			
♠ AKQJ	10	0	10
♡ K95	3	0	3
◇ 432	0	0	0
♣ 853	0	0	0
			13

(j)			
♠ AQJ732	7	0	7
♡ KQ	5	1	6
◇ J754	1	0	1
♣ Q	1	2	3
			17

(k)			
♠ KQ432	5	0	5
♡ KQ5	5	0	5
◇ QJ4	3	0	3
♣ 86	0	1	1
			14

BIDDING FOOTNOTES

(f) One heart.
(g) One diamond.
(h) One spade
(i) The hand contains 13 points but only one biddable (poor) suit.
(j) One spade. One point was subtracted from the high card value of the queen due to being a singleton.
(k) One spade.

PART TWO

PLAY OF THE HAND

The number of tricks that the declarer can win with his 13 cards and those of the dummy depend upon two sets of things. The first set includes distribution, probabilities and location; the second set is the declarer's skill and that of the defenders.

All of us have had or will have the sad experience of leading an ace only to have an opponent, void of the suit, trump it. Something nullified the value of that ace. That something is what we term *distribution.*

Distribution is the way the cards of a suit and the suits themselves are divided. The fact that the cards of this particular suit were divided into such a pattern that an opponent lacked even one card and was able to trump your ace resulted from uneven or what we call unbalanced distribution.

Probabilities deals with the percentages of the various divisions of cards; the way missing cards will be divided among the players, the number of high cards and long suits each player will hold over a period of time and all of the possibilities to be encountered at the bridge table.

Location relates to the whereabouts of certain cards. Once the deal has been completed, the cards are in fixed position to each other. They cannot be moved or exchanged between the players. Location greatly affects the trick-taking abilities of cards.

LEADING UP TO STRENGTH

It is generally true that in attempting to win a trick with a card or cards not already established as winners, their trick taking values can be increased by leading towards them (from the other partnership hand) rather than leading from the hand containing the cards with which you plan to take tricks.

In *figure 17,* South is playing a four spade contract. West opens the king of clubs, continues with the ace and South trumps the third round of clubs.

	North	
	♠ KJ98	
	♡ 432	
	♢ AQJ	
	♣ 853	
♠ 43	N	♠ 2
♡ Q109	W E	♡ AJ876
♢ 543		♢ 10987
♣ AKJ97	S	♣ Q106
	♠ AQ10765	
	♡ K5	
	♢ K62	
	♣ 42	

Figure 17

Any two rounds of trumps exhaust those of the defenders. (Had one opponent three trumps, it would have been necessary to lead three rounds of trumps to 'pull' trumps). With the numerous high diamonds and spades between the partnership, South has no difficulty getting back and forth between the dummy, North, and his own hand.

South has already lost two club tricks and certainly must lose at least one heart trick to the ace. If he loses two heart tricks, he will fail to make the bid. Correct play is to win the second round of spades in the dummy (North) and lead a heart from that hand towards the king in the South hand.

East, who plays second hand, is powerless to prevent South from taking a trick with the king of hearts. If East plays the ace, South will follow with the five. Should East play a low card, South puts up the king which wins. Thus by leading towards the king, we have enabled it to win a trick.

Contrast this treatment with a first lead (in the heart suit) of the five-spot from the South hand. He must now lose two tricks in the suit. The reader may ask, "**Suppose West held the ace of hearts?**" In that case, the king would not win a trick no matter whether led to or from. However, when the ace is 'right,' i.e., in front of the king, leading towards the king will develop a trick whereas leading away from it must lose.

This treatment of leading towards high cards in an effort to make them winners is applied to combinations of high cards as well as single high cards.

In *figure 18,* South is playing a four heart contract. West, who has bid diamonds, opens the king of that suit. The ace wins.

	♠ QJ7 ♡ Q109 ◇ A2 ♣ J8432	
♠ A109 ♡ 2 ◇ KQ109876 ♣ 65	N W E S	♠ K862 ♡ 543 ◇ 54 ♣ Q1097
	♠ 543 ♡ AKJ876 ◇ J3 ♣ AK	

Figure 18

It is apparent that South must lose one diamond and at least two spades to the missing king and ace. If he loses any more than two tricks in the spade suit, the hand will be defeated. His problem, then, is to hold the spade losers to two.

After taking the first diamond with the ace, three rounds of trumps are led, the third being won in the South hand. The trey of spades is then led. Let's say that West plays the nine. Dummy's jack loses to East's king. East will return his remaining diamond. South trumps the third lead of diamonds.

	♠ Q7	
♠ A10	N W E S	♠ 862
	♠ 54	

Figure 19

The remaining cards of the spade suit are diagrammed in *figure 19.* South now leads the four of spades and West cannot prevent North's queen from winning a trick. If West plays the 10, the queen wins. Should West win with the ace, North follows with the seven, the queen winning the third round. Either way, South holds his spade losers to two.

In *figure 20,* South is the declarer in a four spade contract. West cashes two high hearts, then switches to a diamond. The success of the hand pivots on the handling of the trump suit. Obviously, one trick must be lost to the ace. Yet South cannot afford to lose more than one trump trick or he will be defeated.

West	North / South	East
	♠ 432 ♡ 87 ♢ AQ109 ♣ KQJ6	
♠ 109 ♡ AKJ106 ♢ 432 ♣ 875	N W E S	♠ AJ8 ♡ Q542 ♢ 876 ♣ 1092
	♠ KQ765 ♡ 93 ♢ KJ5 ♣ A43	

Figure 20

South will now lead *twice* towards the king-queen of spades, hoping to find the ace 'right.' The diamond lead is won in dummy. The spade deuce is led. East will play the eight. South covers with the queen which wins. A low club is led and won in the dummy. The spade process (of leading a low card from the dummy towards South's remaining honor) is *repeated* and East cannot win more than one spade trick.

The principle of leading towards strength applies to all cards *not already winners!* If the card in question is already a winner, it is immaterial whether it is led or led towards.

West	North / South	East
	♠ K876 ♡ Q9 ♢ AQ8 ♣ 10654	
♠ A3 ♡ 65 ♢ J10762 ♣ J972	N W E S	♠ Q1052 ♡ 8743 ♢ 953 ♣ Q8
	♠ J94 ♡ AKJ102 ♢ K4 ♣ AK3	

Figure 21

In *figure 21,* the contract is four hearts by South. West opens the spade ace and after seeing dummy, switches to the jack of diamonds. Declarer wins with the king. Four rounds of high trumps pull those of East. South's losing spade is then thrown on dummy's third diamond. It is obviously immaterial whether declarer leads towards the king of spades or plays that card since once the ace has been played, the spade king is already a winner.

There is one more matter to be discussed in leading towards high cards and that is the matter of 'equals.'

	♠ Q976 ♡ Q108 ◊ A7 ♣ J654	
♠ J8 ♡ 9532 ◊ KQJ9 ♣ Q108	N W E S	♠ 2 ♡ A76 ◊ 108652 ♣ A972
	♠ AK10543 ♡ KJ4 ◊ 43 ♣ K3	

Figure 22

In *figure 22,* South is the declarer at a four spade contract. West opens the king of diamonds, won by dummy's ace. Two rounds of high trumps are led. Since there is only one heart, the ace, that could beat either the 10, jack, queen or king, it is immaterial which of these cards is led. Each of these cards (K, Q, J, 10) has the same trick taking potentiality if held by a partnership.

Equals may be defined as cards in a sequence held by one or both members of a partnership. The lowest cards of the sequence (equals) will be the equivalent in trick taking ability to the highest. If there are a sufficient number of equals present in the combined hands, it is again immaterial whether an equal is led or led towards. On the other hand, where there are not sufficient equals present to solidify the holding *(figures 18 and 20)* it is imperative that they be led towards, not from.

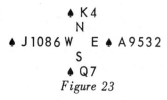

	♠ K4 N	
♠ J1086 W		E ♠ A9532
	S ♠ Q7	

Figure 23

In *figure 23,* both North and South have two spades apiece. Either the king or queen (which are equals) can be led since the remaining honor will win the second round of spades.

♠ Q 8 4
N
♠ 10 7 2 W E ♠ A 9 6 3
S
♠ K J 5

Figure 24

Figure 24 finds the king, queen and jack between the partnership. Since they are equals, the suit can be led from either North or South.

♠ J 4 3 2
N
♠ A 8 7 W E ♠ K 9 6
S
♠ Q 10 5

Figure 25

In *figure 25*, North-South hold the queen, jack and 10 between them. Since they are equals, any two of these cards can be used to drive out the adverse ace and king. In actual practice, the hand containing the fewer total number of cards (South in the above) will usually play its equals first so that later tricks can be won in the hand containing the greater number of cards. This permits capitalizing on the remaining cards of the suit. This is known as 'unblocking' and the retention of a high card or cards in a hand for purposes of placing the lead in that hand as 'entries' or 're-entries.' You will learn more about this in future lessons on the play of the hand.

QUIZ TWO

1 - Who can make the first bid?

2 - You did not bid at your first opportunity. Can you bid later?

3 - Define a rebiddable suit.

4 - Is ♠ A K Q J rebiddable?

5 - Can you rebid a poor (biddable) poor suit after partner has supported it?

6 - What is the poorest four card suit with which you can open the bidding?

7 - If you were the declarer and dummy held ♠ K Q 3 and you held ♠ 5 4 2, how would you attempt to win two tricks?

8 - Which cards in each combination are equals (a) K J; (b) J 10; (c) A K Q ?

9 - What is your opening bid, if any, on each of the following hands? How many points do you hold in each?

(a)	(b)	(c)
♠ K J 8 4 3	♠ Q J 10 8 6	♠ 9 8 7 4 3 2
♡ A 10 9	♡ K Q J 8	♡ A Q J
◇ A 5	◇ Q J 9	◇ K Q 5
♣ 8 7 6	♣ 4	♣ 7

(d)	(e)	(f)
♠ A 9 8 7	♠ A Q J 10 8	♠ K Q 9 5 4
♡ A 7 4	♡ K J 10	♡ K
◇ A 6 3	◇ 4	◇ A Q J
♣ 9 6 2	♣ Q 8 7 6	♣ 7 5 4 3

(g)	(h)	(i)
♠ A K 4 3	♠ A J 9 7 4	♠ A 5
♡ 9 7 2	♡ A	♡ 8 7 6
◇ 8 6 5	◇ A 7 5 4	◇ A K J 5 3
♣ A 5 2	♣ Q J 7	♣ 10 7 2

ANSWERS TO QUIZ TWO

1 - The dealer.

2 - Yes.

3 - Any five card suit headed by two or more of the top four honors of that suit; any six card or longer suit regardless of high cards.

4 - No.

5 - Yes.

6 - It must include at least three points in high cards as the king or queen-jack.

7 - Lead twice towards the king-queen from your hand.

8 - The J 10 in (b); the A K Q in (c).

9 - (a) one spade - 13 points
(b) one spade - 14 points
(c) one spade - 14 points
(d) pass - 12 points
(e) one spade - 15 points
(f) one spade - 16 points
In (f), one point was subtracted from the high card value of the king since it was singleton.
(g) pass - 11 points
(h) one spade - 18 points
(i) one diamond - 13 points

LESSON TWO HANDS

1.

	North	
	♠ 943 ♡ KQJ109 ◊ K6 ♣ AK2	
West ♠ 10762 ♡ 64 ◊ AJ10 ♣ QJ74	N W E S	**East** ♠ AJ8 ♡ 875 ◊ Q98 ♣ 10985
	♠ KQ5 ♡ A32 ◊ 75432 ♣ 63	

North dealer, neither side vul.

North	East	South	West
1 ht.	pass	2 hts.	pass
3 hts.	pass	4 hts.	pass
pass	pass		

Play the North hand at four hearts. East leads the club 10.

2.

	North	
	♠ AJ10 ♡ AQ86 ◊ 986 ♣ J87	
West ♠ 765 ♡ 752 ◊ 7432 ♣ AKQ	N W E S	**East** ♠ KQ432 ♡ K43 ◊ AK ♣ 542
	♠ 98 ♡ J109 ◊ QJ105 ♣ 10963	

East dealer, N-S vulnerable.

East	South	West	North
1 sp.	pass	1 n.t.	pass
2 sp.	pass	3 sp.	pass
4 sp.	pass	pass	pass

East is the declarer at four spades. South leads ◊Q.

3.

	North	
	♠ J8 ♡ 1063 ◊ QJ8765 ♣ AK	
West ♠ Q76 ♡ J542 ◊ A109 ♣ 1098	N W E S	**East** ♠ 5432 ♡ 987 ◊ K ♣ 76543
	♠ AK109 ♡ AKQ ◊ 432 ♣ QJ2	

South dealer,E-W vulnerable.

South	West	North	East
1 sp.	pass	2 dia.	pass
3 n.t.	pass	pass	pass

Play the South hand in three no trump. West will open the two of hearts.

4.

	North	
	♠ K7632 ♡ 5 ◊ Q1043 ♣ Q95	
West ♠ AQ5 ♡ AK6432 ◊ J8 ♣ K7	N W E S	**East** ♠ 4 ♡ Q108 ◊ A7652 ♣ J632
	♠ J1098 ♡ J97 ◊ K9 ♣ A1084	

West dealer, both vulnerable.

West	North	East	South
1 ht.	pass	2 hts	pass
4 hts.	pass	pass	pass

Play the West hand at four hearts. North will lead the three of diamonds.

SOLUTIONS TO LESSON TWO HANDS

1.
North declarer at four hearts.

Trick	E	S	W	N
1	♣10	♣3	♣7	**♣K**
2	♡5	♡2	♡4	**♡K**
3	♡7	♡3	♡6	**♡Q**
4	♣5	♣6	♣4	**♣A**
5	♣8	**♡A**	♣J	♣2
6	♢8	♢2	♢10	**♢K**
7	♡8	♢3	♠2	**♡J**
8	♠8	**♠Q**	♠6	♠3
9	♢9	♢4	**♢A**	♢6
10	♣9	♢5	♣Q	**♡9**
11	**♠A**	♠5	♠7	♠4
12	♢Q	♢7	♢J	**♡10**
13	♠J	**♠K**	♠10	♠9

North wins 11 tricks.

2.
East declarer at four spades.

Trick	S	W	N	E
1	♢Q	♢2	♢6	**♢K**
2	♣3	**♣Q**	♣7	♣2
3	♠8	♠5	♠10	**♠Q**
4	♣6	**♣K**	♣8	♣4
5	♠9	♠6	**♠A**	♠2
6	♢5	♢3	♢9	**♢A**
7	♣9	♠7	♠J	**♠K**
8	♣10	**♣A**	♣J	♣5
9	♡9	♡2	♡6	**♡K**
10	**♡10**	♡5	♡8	♡3
11	♢J	♢4	♢8	**♠3**
12	♡J	♡7	**♡Q**	♡4
13	♢10	♢7	♡A	**♠4**

East wins 10 tricks.

3.
South declarer at 3 no trump.

Trick	W	N	E	S
1	♡2	♡3	♡7	**♡Q**
2	♢9	♢J	**♢K**	♢2
3	♡4	♡6	♡9	**♡K**
4	♢10	**♢Q**	♣3	♢3
5	**♢A**	♢5	♠2	♢4
6	♡5	♡10	♡8	**♡A**
7	♣8	**♣K**	♣4	♣2
8	♣9	**♢8**	♠3	♠9
9	♣10	**♢7**	♠4	♠10
10	♡J	**♣A**	♣5	♣J
11	♠6	♠8	♠5	**♠K**
12	♠7	♠J	♣6	**♠A**
13	♠Q	♢6	♣7	**♣Q**

South wins 11 tricks.

4.
West declarer at four hearts.

Trick	N	E	S	W
1	♢3	**♢A**	♢9	♢8
2	♠7	♠4	♠8	**♠A**
3	♠2	**♡8**	♠9	♠5
4	♣5	♣2	♣4	**♣K**
5	♠K	**♡10**	♠10	♠Q
6	♡5	**♡Q**	♡7	♡2
7	**♣9**	♣3	♣8	♣7
8	♠3	♢2	♠J	**♡3**
9	♠6	♢5	♡9	**♡A**
10	♢4	♢6	♡J	**♡K**
11	♢Q	♢7	**♢K**	♢J
12	♣Q	♣6	♣A	**♡4**
13	♢10	♣J	♣10	**♡6**

West wins 11 tricks.

NOTE - Cards winning tricks are underlined.

COMMENTS ON LESSON TWO HANDS

With hand one, there are three important things for North, the declarer at four hearts, to notice. First, if the opponents' five trumps are divided as evenly as possible, three to one defender and two to the other, it will be necessary for North to lead three rounds of trumps. Since dummy, South, had only three trumps originally, that hand would be left trumpless. Notice that originally South held only two clubs, North had three. By leading only two rounds of trumps, declarer leaves one trump in the dummy and is able, after cashing his remaining high club, to trump the otherwise losing deuce of clubs in the dummy. Trumping with the ace of hearts is a simple precaution against the slight possibility of being over-trumped had West only two clubs originally and three trumps. Since the trumps held by North-South are 'solid' from the ace to the nine-spot, the ace can be used for trumping without the loss of a trick. The two remaining factors for declarer to note are that in order to take two tricks with the king and queen of spades, it was necessary to lead twice *towards* those cards and once *towards* the king of diamonds.

In hand two, West's only high cards, the ace-king-queen of clubs, must serve as three separate and distinct entries for the purpose of leading *three times* towards first, the king and queen of spades and lastly, the king of hearts. If East errs in playing two or more of dummy's high clubs on successive tricks, the contract is doomed since he (East) will be unable to return to the dummy the necessary three times.

Hand three again demonstrates the need of leading towards strength. Declarer will lead *twice towards* dummy's diamonds. The ace and king of clubs furnish the necessary re-entries to dummy for utilization of the remaining diamonds, once established as winners.

In hand four, notice dummy's (East's) singleton spade. Hence no finesse (see lesson three) is necessary. After winning the first trick with the ace of diamonds, dummy's four of spades is led to the ace and the five of spades is trumped with the eight of hearts. A club is led towards the king and subsequently, the queen of spades is trumped with the 10 of hearts, not with the queen! Since the ace-king-queen of hearts may (and will, in this case) be required to capture the missing jack, the trumping of losers should ordinarily be accomplished with trumps that can be spared rather than with high trumps that are required for capturing purposes.

Lesson III

PART ONE

Responses

PART TWO

Finesses

LESSON THREE

PART ONE

RESPONDING TO OPENING BIDS OF ONE IN A SUIT

Your partner has opened the bidding with a bid of 'one of a suit' as 'one club' or 'one diamond' or 'one heart' or 'one spade.'

Any bid you might make in answer to his opening bid is known as a 'response.'

The first bid made at the table is known as the 'opening bid.' But the fact that the opening bid was, let's presume, one spade, doesn't necessarily confine that player to merely bidding spades. He may later show some other suit or suits or even bid no trump when it again becomes his turn to bid.

Next, the highest bid at the table (numerically) determines the trump suit or no trump for that particular hand. If there are two or more bids of the same number but in different suits, then suit rank determines the higher or highest bid.

The declarer (who plays both his cards and those of dummy) is the member of the winning pair of bidders who *first* bid the final trump suit, regardless of which partner bid the greatest number of that suit. For example, if you sat South and opened the bidding with one spade and your partner, North, bid four spades, you would become the declarer.

Thus a partnership may bid several suits before a final choice is made and it is this accurate exchange of information which determines the ultimate contract.

The fact that one side has bid a suit does not prevent the other side from bidding the same suit. This sometimes happens and there are several reasons for it. One reason would be that the second side to bid the suit actually had better and more cards in it than the former. For example, let us imagine that South opened the bidding with 'one club.' Later, West bid 'two clubs' which became the final contract. It is West who is the declarer since he was the first person *of his side* to bid the final trump suit even though he was not the first person at the table to bid the club suit.

Another reason for bidding a suit first bid by the opponents is to show possession of the ace or void of that suit as a bid compelling the partnership to reach a game or possibly a slam contract.

As to doubles, here we have something else. There are two basic types of doubles - informatory and penalty. In addition, the double may be used to direct an opening lead of a specific suit from partner. The penalty double is also known as the 'business' double. Any player, *when it is his turn to bid,* may say the word 'double.' *after a player on the other side has made the last bid.* This means that the player saying 'double' feels that the opponents cannot fulfill their contract and the doubler wishes to increase the penalty the opponents will pay for non-fulfillment. An informatory double commands the doubler's partner to bid his best suit and shows a powerful hand, usually strong in everything but the doubled suit, by the doubler. We will learn how to distinguish one type from the other in Lesson 12.

CHOICE OF RESPONSE

The first thing you should know is that you don't have to respond to an opening bid of one of a suit. If you do, any bid you make after partner opens the bidding is entirely voluntary.

You will hear some incorrectly schooled players say, "I made a courtesy response, partner" or "I always keep one bids open."

Nothing could be more incorrect. Courtesy is extended among the players, not between inanimate pasteboard cards. One does not bid out of courtesy to a partner - a bid is made because you think you can win tricks.

Another common error of beginners is that they bid from 'fright.' Let us say that their partner opens the bidding with one spade. They have a very weak hand on which they should pass but it includes a singleton spade or even a void in spades. They are panicked into bidding 'two hearts' or 'two clubs' or whatever the suit may be - not because they have the values for the bid but rather because they are afraid that their partner can't make one spade because of their lack of spades. In other words, they're bidding from weakness, not strength.

What they lose track of is that partner will rightfully construe any response as showing strength and rebid accordingly. One moment later, they're too high, doubled and penalized. If North lacks support for his partner's suit, there is no assurance that partner has supporting cards for his (North's) suit.

It is true that there are certain bids where the partner of the opening bidder *must* bid. The principal case would be the opening bid *of two of a suit* which forces both partners to continue bidding until at least a game contract is reached. Bids of this nature will be discussed in Lesson 10.

TYPES OF RESPONSES

There are five possible types of responses you can make.

1 - A raise of partner's suit.

2 - Showing a new suit.

3 - Bidding no trump.

4 - A pass.

5 - A penalty double of an opponent's bid.

RAISING PARTNER'S SUIT

Suppose your partner opened the bidding with 'one heart' and you wished to support that suit. You could bid 'two hearts' which would contract for eight tricks or 'three hearts' which would obligate your side to win nine tricks or even bid four, five, six or seven hearts.

What I am trying to show is that the raise of partner's suit can vary from a little raise to a big one.

To raise partner's suit, one requisite is supporting cards in the suit, itself. It would be silly to raise partner's opening one heart bid to, let us say, two hearts, with one little heart in your hand even though you had strength elsewhere. The opponents could very well have more hearts (trumps) than your side.

So the first requirement is what we call 'adequate trump support.' That may be defined as enough trumps held by the responder which, added to the known four or more cards of the suit shown by the opening bidder, gives his side a majority of that suit in total cards.

Figure it out for yourself. There are 13 cards of a suit. Seven would give you a majority. Your partner is known to have four. Four from seven means you must have three cards of your partner's suit for the majority.

Until our partner rebids his suit *before* you have supported it, *we must assume it to be only four cards in length.* I cannot stress this point too strongly.

Suppose you held only two cards of your partner's suit. If his suit is only four cards long, then the combined hands would have a total of only six cards of the suit and the opponents, seven, the one thing you are trying to avoid. So rather than support (raise) your partner with two cards of his suit, you will try to find some other bid, if possible.

(a)

North, Partner, Dealer	East	You, South	West
1 spade	pass	2 clubs	pass
2 spades			

In bidding sequence (a), your partner has rebid his spade suit without any indication of support in spades from you.

What does that show?

Why, at least a five card suit headed by two or more of the top four honors of that suit or possibly a still longer suit. Armed with the knowledge that your partner has at least five cards of his suit, how many cards would you now need for support to have numerical superiority?

The answer is easy - *two!* So for every time your partner rebids his suit before you have supported it, you as responder will correspondingly need one less card to support that suit. In other words, if partner shows a five card suit, you need but two cards of that suit to give your side the majority.

But support requirements for a raise of partner's suit are not merely a matter of numbers. Your partner may have opened the bidding with a weak biddable suit such as four cards headed by the queen-jack or king. If you support his suit with three low cards, while your side will hold a combined total of seven cards of the suit, the opponents' six cards will include most of the big ones. What little advantage your side will have in numbers will be more than offset by the larger size of the opponents' cards.

Hence, if you do support with only three cards of partner's suit, these three cards should include either the ace or the king or the queen or, in a pinch, the jack and 10 with a low card. These are minimums. *If you have stronger supporting cards for your partner's suit, so much the better.*

Holding four or more cards of partner's suit, it is not necessary to have a high card of that suit to raise partner's suit. Quantity makes up for lack of quality.

MINIMUM TRUMP SUPPORT FOR PARTNER'S UNREBID SUIT

Axx, Kxx, Qxx, J10x or any four or more small cards. *

* *An x denotes any card lower than a 10.*

	♠ 5432	
	N	
♠ QJ10 W		E ♠ 98
	S	
	♠ AK76	

Figure 26

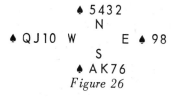

Look at *figure 26.* Sitting North, you can support your partner's spade bid with your four spades, notwithstanding they are the lowest spades in the deck. Even though your partner possesses but a four card suit and the opponents (East and West) hold the queen, jack, 10 and nine between them, they are able to win only one trick in the suit since the combined total of your partnership cards insures that the opponents' holdings be short in length, that their cards normally fall together when the suit is led.

Let me stress the fact that even a high doubleton as AK or AQ does not constitute trump support for an unrebid suit. Never raise your partner's suit with less than normal trump support until his rebids have indicated his suit to be rebiddable.

COUNTING POINTS TO RAISE PARTNER'S SUIT

WITH TRUMP SUPPORT

COUNT EACH	VALUE IN POINTS
Void	5
Singleton	3
Doubleton	1

Count high card points exactly as for opening the bidding.
Subtract one point if your distribution is 4-3-3-3.
Subtract one point if holding only three cards of partner's suit.

THEN TOTAL YOUR POINTS

REQUIREMENTS FOR RAISING PARTNER'S SUIT

POINTS	*MINIMUM NUMBER OF CARDS*	*RAISE TO*
6 to 12 *	3	2 (single raise)
13 to 16 **	4 (with jack or better)	3 (double raise)
11 to 14 ***	5	4 (triple raise)

FOOTNOTES

* *The single raise usually shows from six to nine points. Holding 10 to 12 points, a temporizing bid in another suit, followed by a single raise of partner's suit, is preferred to best describe the hand.*

** *With 17 points or more, the hand is too strong for the double raise. Try to find an alternate bid as showing a new suit, later jump raise partner's suit.*

*** *Not more than nine high card points.*

Let me explain what is meant by single, double and triple raises.

	PARTNER, OPENER	YOU, RESPONDER
THE SINGLE RAISE		
	1 heart	2 hearts
THE DOUBLE RAISE		
	1 heart	3 hearts
THE TRIPLE RAISE		
	1 heart	4 hearts

A single raise by responder from 'one' to 'two' shows a comparatively weak hand with six to 12 points and trump support. The average single raise will be based on six to nine points.

Let's suppose the opening bid was made with 13 points and a rebiddable suit. After a single raise, the total number of points would be anywhere from 19 to 25. Since 26 points are usually needed to make a game in the heart (major) suit, it is obvious that the partnership does not have sufficient strength to bid and make a game. Accordingly, the opening bidder can (and should) pass his partner's single raise when holding a minimum opening bid. Of course, if the opening bidder holds, let us say, 20 points, he knows his side can make a game and should bid it.

What I am driving at is that a single raise can and often should be passed by the opening bidder when it is his turn to bid again. Bids that can be passed by partner are known as *non-forcing*.

A double raise in a major as one heart by the opening bidder and a raise to three hearts by his partner when the latter hasn't previously passed is *forcing to game*. By that I mean both partners must continue bidding until at least a game contract has been reached.

As you will learn, there are several kinds of forcing bids. One type is known as *forcing to game*, where both partners after a forcing to game bid must keep on bidding until a game contract has been reached. The double raise in a major suit shown in the preceding paragraph is one example of a forcing to game bid.

Another type is called *forcing for one round*, where the partner of the last bidder must bid at least once more. Lastly, there is the *semi-forcing* bid, where the bid requests partner, with any extra values not already shown, to bid again; otherwise, pass.

As already stated, the double raise in a major suit, hearts or spades, is forcing to game. The probability is that the final contract will be played in the agreed and raised suit, but there is always the possibility that the partnership may find another suit they like even better, or play the hand at three no trump, deciding that winning nine tricks in no trump will be easier than 10 tricks in the major suit. But the point is this - *game must be reached in the bidding!*

Well, what about the double raise in a minor as - 'one club'-'three clubs?'

That bid is only *semi-forcing* and the opening bidder, with a minimum opening, may pass the raise. Since the bidding and making of a game in a minor requires the winning of 11 tricks (as against 10 in a major and nine in no trump) more strength is needed. Twenty-nine points will usually be needed to produce the minor suit game. Following a double raise in a minor, where the total point count of the combined hands may be 26 to 28 points, three no trump may be makeable if holding the right type of hand where 11 tricks in a minor cannot be won. You will learn more about this when you study rebidding.

Next, why does a jump from 'one' to 'four' show less strength than from 'one' to 'three?' That usually puzzles newer players.

Notice in our table on page 63 the double raise is shown as stronger than the triple raise. The former shows 13 to 16 points; the triple raise indicates 11 to 14 points with a maximum of nine points in high cards.

In other words, the triple raise shows a hand weaker in high cards but stronger in distribution than the double raise. The reason for jumping the bidding rapidly and higher with the hand, weaker in high cards but stronger in distribution, is to make it difficult for the other side to bid. Bids of this sort are known as '*pre-emptive*' or '*shut-out*', Let me give you an example .

Suppose your partner opened the bidding with one heart - the next player passes and you hold -

♠ 2 ♡ K76432 ◊ A5432 ♣ 9

Your hand totals 13 points, seven in high cards, six points for distribution since each singleton is worth three points in raising partner's suit. Your hand would be wonderful in support of your partner's heart suit but if the opponents played a spade or club contract, your hand would have little defensive value.

You could count on taking a trick with the ace of diamonds but due to your length in hearts and the fact that partner is known (from his bid) to have four or more hearts, one opponent has at best a singleton heart. So your king of hearts cannot win a second heart trick, defensively. The idea, then, is to get the bidding so high at once, with these defenseless hands, that it will be difficult or impossible for the opponents to enter the bidding safely or exchange information effectively. And if they do bid at the four or five level, your partner may very well be able to double and penalize them.

Yet while weak defensively, your hand has tremendous offensive value. So with hands of this type, we try to shut the opponents out of the bidding.

The jump raise from 'one' to 'four' is usually concerned with the major suits. The equivalent raise, from one to four in a minor, is seldom made since it precludes a possible three no trump rebid by the opening bidder. There are some hands, however, where the bidding goes - 'one club' by a player - 'five clubs' for the same reasons previously stated - a shutout bid on a hand with tremendous trump support and little defensive strength. As a rule, however, the jump to five of a minor is never made on a hand that could be played successfully at three no trump where only nine tricks are needed for game against 11 in the minor.

EXAMPLES OF RAISING PARTNER'S SUIT

Partner Has Opened With One Heart

HAND	POINTS H.C.	POINTS DIS.	TOTAL	RESPONSE
(a)				
♠ 1083	0	0		
♡ K543	3	0		
◇ Q76	2	0		
♣ J84	1	0		
	6	0	6	
Less 1 for 4-3-3-3			-- 1	
			5	Pass
(b)				
♠ 3	0	3		
♡ Q82	2	0		
◇ A9543	4	0		
♣ 5432	0	0		
	6	3	9	
Less 1 for 3 trumps			— 1	
			8	2 hearts
(c)				
♠ 7	0	3		
♡ KJ86	4	0		
◇ 52	0	1		
♣ J98743	1	0		
	5	4	9	2 hearts
(d)				
♠ KQ	5	1		
♡ 876543	0	0		
◇ 654	0	0		
♣ 109	0	1		
	5	2	7	2 hearts
(e)				
♠ 4	0	3		
♡ KQ108	5	0		
◇ AJ95	5	0		
♣ Q862	2	0		
	12	3	15	3 hearts

EXAMPLES OF RAISING PARTNER'S SUIT

Partner Has Opened With One Heart

HAND	POINTS H.C.	POINTS DIS.	TOTAL	RESPONSE
(f)				
♠ A Q	6	1		
♡ J 9 5 4 3	1	0		
◇ K Q 10	5	0		
♣ 5 3 2	0	0		
	12	1	13	3 hearts
(g)				
♠ 3 2	0	1		
♡ J 7 6 5	1	0		
◇ A Q J 9	7	0		
♣ K J 7	4	0		
	12	1	13	3 hearts
(h)				
♠ void	0	5		
♡ A J 9 8 7 6	5	0		
◇ 1 0 9 8	0	0		
♣ Q 6 4 3	2	0		
	7	5	12	4 hearts
(i)				
♠ Q	2	3		
♡ 1 0 8 7 6 5	0	0		
◇ A	4	3		
♣ 9 8 7 6 4 2	0	0		
	6	6	12	
Less 1 for the singleton ♠ Q			-- 1	
			11	4 hearts
(j)				
♠ 5	0	3		
♡ K J 8 6 4	4	0		
◇ K J 5 4 3	4	0		
♣ 8 2	0	1		
	8	4	12	4 hearts

EXAMPLES OF RAISING PARTNER'S SUIT

Partner Has Opened With One Club

HAND	POINTS H.C.	DIS.	TOTAL	RESPONSE
(k)				
♠ 743	0	0		
♡ Q2	2	1		
◇ 10542	0	0		
♣ A987	4	0		
	6	1	7	2 clubs
(l)				
♠ Q83	2	0		
♡ 64	0	1		
◇ K32	3	0		
♣ QJ1076	3	0		
	8	1	9	2 clubs
(m)				
♠ A	4	3		
♡ 765	0	0		
◇ 1083	0	0		
♣ J95432	1	0		
	5	3	8	2 clubs
(n)				
♠ K10	3	1		
♡ Q76	2	0		
◇ 432	0	0		
♣ AQJ72	7	0		
	12	1	13	3 clubs
(o)				
♠ 4	0	3		
♡ Q76	2	0		
◇ A432	4	0		
♣ KQJ86	6	0		
	12	3	15	3 clubs

EXAMPLES OF RAISING PARTNER'S SUIT

Partner Has Opened With One Club

HAND	POINTS H.C.	POINTS DIS.	TOTAL	RESPONSE
(p)				
♠ K J	4	1		
♡ 86	0	1		
◇ 542	0	0		
♣ A K 10862	7	0		
	11	2	13	3 clubs
(q)				
♠ Void	0	5		
♡ 43	0	1		
◇ Q 109	2	0		
♣ Q J876543	3	0		
	5	6	11	4 clubs
(r)				
♠ 8	0	3		
♡ 6	0	3		
◇ 543	0	0		
♣ K Q 1098654	5	0		
	5	6	11	4 clubs
(s)				
♠ 2	0	3		
♡ 7	0	3		
◇ A J 94	5	0		
♣ J 1098765	1	0		
	6	6	12	5 clubs
(t)				
♠ A 32	4	0		
♡ Void	0	5		
◇ 65	0	1		
♣ K 8765432	3	0		
	7	6	13	5 clubs

SHOWING A NEW SUIT

After your partner has opened the bidding with 'one of a suit,' you may have some other suit of your own that you would like to show. For example, let's say your partner opened the bidding with one heart and you held either hand (a) or (b).

(a)	(b)
♠ KJ876	♠ 54
♡ 3	♡ K9
◇ 7654	◇ Q87
♣ A109	♣ AQ10543

On (a) you would respond 'one spade;' on (b) you would say 'two clubs.'

The first thing you should notice is that with (a) you could show your suit at the one level. In other words, to show your suit, it wasn't necessary to increase the contract.

But on (b), in order to show the club suit, you had to bid 'two' over your partner's bid of one.

Common sense will tell you that the more you bid, the greater the number of high cards, trumps or both will be required to fulfill that contract.

There is one more point. The partner of the opening bidder, to show a new suit, *needs considerably less than opening bid requirements*. It is highly possible that the responder may have a hand stronger than that of partner. But usually, he has less.

In both cases shown above, there was one point in common - when the responder showed his suit, he bid it as cheaply as possible. In other words, with hand (a), over an opening one heart bid, the fewest number of spades responder needed to bid was 'one,' since spades outrank hearts. When the suit was clubs, since clubs are lower ranking than hearts, it was necessary to go to the two level, but still, the bid of two clubs was the fewest number of clubs that could be bid over one heart.

These are known as 'minimum responses.'

RESPONDER'S REQUIREMENTS TO SHOW A NEW SUIT

POINTS NEEDED	TYPE OF SUIT
AT THE ONE LEVEL	
6 or more	Any
AT THE TWO LEVEL	
10 or more	Four card suits should contain at least the queen; any five card or longer suit may be bid.

HOW TO COUNT POINTS TO SHOW A NEW SUIT BY RESPONDER

To show a new suit in response to your partner's opening bid, count and total your points *exactly the same as though you were opening the bidding*. See page 36.

HANDLING THE WEAK FOUR CARD SUIT

Virtually all top players, writers and authorities recommend responding with *any* four card or longer suit at the *one level* with six or more points.

In the early days of bridge, a response of 'one no trump' was the all-embracing response to show weak hands with weak suits lacking supporting cards for partner's suit.

This is as obsolete as the dodo!

Modern bidding is designed that the early rounds of bidding, the levels of 'one' and 'two', be used to find the suit or suits in which the partnership holds the greatest number of cards for a possible and eventual trump suit. Thus each partner shows suits, even though they may be weak ones, in the hope of finding a total of seven, eight or more cards of that suit between the combined partnership hands. If a 'fit' cannot be found, then no trump *can* be bid or the hand played in the best possible suit.

"Suppose I bid a spade holding ♠ 9765 ♡ A2 ◇ Q876 ♣643 after my partner opens with 'one heart' and he leaves me there?" you ask.

He can't !

Do you remember that I stated earlier that the bid of a new suit by responder, providing he has not already passed, is *forcing for one round*. Your partner *must* bid again. If he has good support for your suit, he'll show it by raising your suit and you've found the right suit. If he lacks support for your suit, he'll make some other bid.

"What if my partner thinks my suit better than it is,?" you add.

He *must* regard any suit you show as not rebiddable until you rebid it. You have no worry on that score.

One-over-one bidding offers tremendous advantages. It permits finding partnership 'fits' where both partners have weak holdings in the same suit.

Next, keeping the bidding at low level permits cheap and convenient rebidding by both partners, allowing still other suits to be shown safely. Lastly, bidding a shaded suit will frequently deter an opponent from leading that suit - an opening lead that might have been made before you bid the suit. It is to your advantage to steer the opponents' attack away from your weak suits. When you bid a shaded suit, the opponents do not know that it is weak. *Only you do!*

As an easy rule to remember -

Don't respond with one no trump if you have any suit of four cards or more that can be shown at the one level.

Engrave these words on your bridge subconciousness in letters of fire !

When it is necessary to bid 'two' in order to show a new suit as a response, a four card suit should seldom be shaded below that headed by a queen. For one thing, the fact that you have been able to bid your suit at the two level automatically leads your partner to expect something a little better than a straggly four-carder. The only occasions for shading four-carders at the two level is a tremendous 'fit' for partner's suit where you don't have quite enough for an immediate double raise (from one to three of the same suit) and too much for a single raise. This will be discussed later in this lesson under the heading, 'Temporizing Bids.'

THE SINGLE JUMP RESPONSE IN A NEW SUIT

By a 'single jump response in a new suit,' I mean that after your partner has opened the bidding with one of a suit, you have responded by bidding *one more than was necessary* to show your suit.

Case A

North, Partner, Opener	East	You, South	West
1 heart	pass	2 spades	

Case B

1 heart	pass	3 clubs	

In the above, we have two examples of single jump responses in new suits. In case A, you could have bid 'one spade' (instead of two) since, being higher-ranking than partner's heart suit, one spade would have been sufficient. In case B, you bid 'three clubs,' even though two clubs would have superseded one heart.

Why ?

Well, every now and then, after your partner opens the bidding with one of a suit, you will be fortunate enough to hold a hand so powerful that you know the combined hands can make a game, possibly a slam. By jumping the bidding *one more than necessary in a new suit,* you tell your partner that the bidding *must continue until at least a game contract has been reached.*

Hands of this type, containing 19 points or more, are shown *by responder bidding one more than necessary in a new suit.* Do not confuse the single jump raise in partner's suit with the single jump to a new suit.

Case C

North, Partner, Opener	East	You, South	West
1 heart	pass	3 hearts	

The bidding in case C illustrates a single jump *in the same suit.* Requirements for the single jump raise are 13 to 16 points; a single jump in a new suit as cases A and B require 19 points or more.

Let me give some specific examples of single jump responses in new suits. Let's suppose your partner has opened the bidding with one heart. You hold any of the following hands:

(a)	(b)	(c)	(d)
♠ A K J 8 6	♠ A	♠ A Q J 10 9 8	♠ 7 4
♡ Q J 10 8	♡ J 8	♡ 5	♡ K J 6
◊ A Q 7	◊ A K Q J 9	◊ A K J	◊ A K Q 5 4 3
♣ 2	♣ K Q J 10 8	♣ K Q 6	♣ A 2

On (a), holding 19 points, you would respond "two spades."

On (b), with 24 points, your response is "three diamonds." Later, you will show the club suit.

With (c), you have 22 points. You would bid "two spades."

With (d), you hold 19 points and would bid "three diamonds."

"What's the idea,?" you ask.

Why bid 'two spades' on hands (a) and (c) when one spade would have been sufficient? Similarly, to show the diamond suits on hands (b) and (d), that could have been accomplished by bidding 'two diamonds.' Why bid 'three?' Why bid more than necessary.

The answer is that after your partner has opened the bidding and your hand is so strong as to make game a certainty and slam a strong probability, you indicate that fact by bidding *one more than necessary in a new suit.* This is known as a *forcing to game bid.*

This bid (of one more than necessary in a new suit) is made whenever your hand, as responder, contains 19 or more points

AND

1 - A good 'fit' for partner's suit or,
2 - A solid or semi-solid suit of your own or,
3 - A combination of both.

"Well, why don't you just jump to game in these examples instead of fooling around? Why didn't you bid 'four hearts' on (a) or 'five diamonds' on (b) and (d) or 'four spades' on (c)?"

I'll tell you why.

Holding any of these hands, it should be apparent, after partner opens the bidding, that your side holds all or almost all of the high cards in the deck. The question then becomes not whether your side can make a game (which is obvious) but rather, can your side win 12 tricks for a small slam or 13 tricks for a grand slam.

Had you jumped directly to game on any of these hands, your partner could very well (with a minimum opening bid) pass and you will be playing the hand in a game contract instead of a slam.

So with a single bid, of one more than necessary in a new suit, you tell your partner that you are very strong, that game is certain even though he may have opened the bidding with a minimum hand and that both you and your partner must keep on bidding until you have done one of two things; either bid a game or slam, or doubled the opponents for an equivalent (to game) penalty.

There is an important proviso that I would like to emphasize. I mentioned that a *MUST* for the single jump in a new suit was, in addition to the necessary 19 or more points, a good 'fit' with partner's suit or a solid or semi-solid suit of your own or both.

There is an old pinochle expression that 'aces killed more people than bullets.'

What it means is that inexperienced players, holding lots of high cards, get in trouble.

Nothing could be sillier than making a forcing-to-game response without holding *either good supporting cards for partner's suit or an excellent suit of one's own.* If the responder doesn't have the slightest idea as to the eventual trump suit and if the hand is a misfit, there is a great possibility that the contract may wind up in the wrong spot or get too high for makeability and be defeated.

(e)
♠ A Q 4 3
♡ 2
♢ A K 6 5
♣ K J 3 2

Let me give you an example of what I mean. Suppose, holding hand (e) to the left, you hear your partner open with 'one heart.' Your hand, as a spade response, totals 19 points, 17 in high cards, two for distribution.

Should you bid 'two spades?'

No!

You lack both a 'fit' for partner's heart suit or a good suit of your own. On hands that at first glance appear to be 'misfits,' take it easy until you find out where the hand is going to play. Then - step on the gas by making a single jump bid in a new suit (which is forcing to game) or bid game at once.

What should you bid on hand (e)?

The answer is - one spade.

"Suppose I bid one spade," you enquire, "and then my partner passes."

He can't!

Your one spade response compels your partner to bid.

And that brings us to what is known in all bidding systems as

THE FORCING PRINCIPLE

The bid of any new suit by a responder who has not previously passed forces the opening bidder to rebid.

(1)		(2)	
OPENER	PARTNER	OPENER	PARTNER
1 club	1 heart	1 diamond	2 clubs

You will notice in both of the above examples, the partner, as responder, showed his suit as cheaply as possible. In the first example, the minimum number of hearts partner could bid was 'one'; in the second example, 'two clubs' was the fewest number of that suit to outrank the 'one diamond' opening bid.

The bidding of new, higher-ranking suits at the one level as in the first example is aptly known as 'one over one' bidding and is an integral part of every modern bidding system. Later on, in your lessons on rebidding, you will learn how it is frequently possible for a partnership to show all four suits, still remain at the one level of bidding.

RESPONSES WHICH OPENER MAY PASS

It stands to reason that there are some responses or times that do not compel the opening bidder to bid again.

1 - If responder previously failed to open the bidding.
2 - If the response was a single raise of opener's suit.
3 - A jump to game in partner's suit (shut-out).
4 - A jump to game in a new suit (shut-out).
5 - A response of one no trump.
6 - A response of three no trump.
7 - With a weak hand if right hand opponent bids.

Let's study these situations in the order listed.

1 - RESPONDER HAS PREVIOUSLY PASSED

If, as a responder, you previously failed to open the bidding and passed, you denied holding 13 or more points. If your partner now opens the bidding with a minimum 13 to 14 point hand, he may feel game unlikely and is at liberty to pass any response you might make.

For example, the bidding has been:

YOU, NORTH, DEALER	EAST	SOUTH, PARTNER	WEST
Pass	Pass	1 heart	Pass
1 spade	Pass		

Had you not passed, your partner would be obligated to rebid over your spade response. In this case, if he has a minimum hand, he may pass.

This does not mean he should pass, either in this or in the other non-forcing situations where he does not have to rebid. *It merely means he may pass.* Any rebid on his part would be entirely voluntary and show additional values which could be an extremely long suit, extra high cards, a new suit or excellent supporting cards for partner's suit.

2 - THE SINGLE RAISE OF PARTNER'S SUIT

Suppose the bidding had proceeded:

YOU, OPENER	PARTNER, RESPONDER
1 heart	2 hearts
?	

The single raise by partner shows a weak to medium strength hand - from six to 12 points. *It should again be pointed out that with 11 or 12 points, responder will usually find an alternative, temporizing response.* If you have opened the bidding with a minimum 13 point hand, the combined point count between the partnership will total from 19 to 25, short of the 26 points needed for game in a major suit. There is no point in further bidding on your part since game is unmakeable.

3 - A JUMP TO GAME IN PARTNER'S SUIT

This bid has been described at length on pages 63 through 66. Since responder's hand is weak in high cards but powerful in distribution, there is no purpose in the opening bidder making another bid (once game has been reached) unless he thinks he can make a slam or has been forced higher by an opponent's bid.

4 - A JUMP TO GAME IN A NEW SUIT

(f)
♠ KQJ109876
♡ 32
◊ 2
♣ 54

Pretend the bidding has been -

YOU	PARTNER
1 heart	4 spades

The reasoning behind the pre-emptive or shutout bid in a new suit is similar to that behind the jump raise to game in partner's suit previously described.

With spades trumps, hand (f) will win lots of tricks; defensively, the hand is practically worthless. So the jump to game accomplishes two things; it makes it difficult or impossible for the opponents to enter the bidding; second, it tells partner that the hand is good for nothing but to be played in that suit. He then passes unless his opening bid is so tremendous that he feels a slam makeable.

Be sure you understand the difference between the immediate jump to game in a suit (cases three and four) which are weak based largely on long suits or distribution and the bid of only one more than necessary in a new suit which shows 19 points or more and is forcing to game.

5 - A RESPONSE OF ONE NO TRUMP

While no trump responses will be discussed at length on future pages of this lesson, briefly, a response of one no trump to partner's opening bid of one of a suit shows the following:

1 - Six to 10 points in high cards. *Do not count any points for distribution.* The high card strength must be distributed between at least two suits. In other words, all of your strength is not in one place.

2 - No suit of four or more cards that can be shown at the one level.

3 - The hand does not contain a singleton or void of an unbid suit and preferably, should not have a singleton or void of partner's suit.

4 - Trump support for partner's (unrebid) suit is lacking.

6 - A RESPONSE OF THREE NO TRUMP

Unlike an immediate jump to game in a suit which shows a hand powerful in distribution but weak in high cards, an immediate jump response of three no trump shows a very powerful hand with 16 or 17 high card points. Since game has been reached, the opening bidder need not bid again unless he feels slam to be makeable or that the hand will play better in a suit.

7 - NOT REBIDDING A MINIMUM OPENING BID AFTER RIGHT HAND OPPONENT'S OVERCALL

YOU,SOUTH, OPENER	WEST	NORTH,PARTNER	EAST
1 heart	pass	1 spade	2 clubs

You have previously been told (pages 72 and 76) that when neither partner has previously passed, any bid of a new suit by responder forces the opening bidder to rebid at least once.

Yet in the above bidding sequence, where your partner has shown a new suit (spades) and you have opened the bidding and neither partner has previously passed, you now do not have to rebid at this point with a minimum hand.

Why? Why does your right hand opponent's overcall permit you to pass when without it, you would have been forced to rebid?

The answer is - you, the opening bidder, no longer need to rebid in order to give your partner another chance to bid. Your right hand opponent's overcall has done that for you. Now, your pass eloquently describes a weak opening bid and, thanks to the opponent's overcall, your partner will have further opportunity to show any other suits and any additional values he may hold. In addition, your partner is afforded a possible opportunity to make a penalty double.

Examine the previous bidding sequence. Notice that even if you pass, your partner is going to get another chance to bid. The two club overcall keeps the bidding alive. Since the bidding is not concluded until the last bid has been followed by three passes, realize that even if you pass over 'two clubs' and so does West, there have still been only two passes and your partner still has another chance to bid if he so desires.

Any kind of rebid by opener at this point (over right hand opponent's overcall) is entirely voluntary. The bridge term for a voluntary bid or rebid over a bid by an opponent is the word '*free*.' So, if after opening the bidding, you made a 'free' rebid over your right hand opponent's overcall, you are showing additional values of one sort or another. Nothing more eloquently describes a weak hand than a pass!

EXAMPLES OF SHOWING A NEW SUIT

1 - Your partner has opened the bidding with one club and the next player passes. You hold the following hands:

(a)	(b)	(c)	(d)
♠ KJ876	♠ 2	♠ 83	♠ J432
♡ 32	♡ J87654	♡ QJ109876	♡ 43
◊ 865	◊ Q86	◊ AQJ	◊ AK2
♣ A104	♣ 432	♣ 2	♣ 5432

(e)	(f)	(g)	(h)
♠ AJ976	♠ 4	♠ 97654	♠ 843
♡ AQJ8	♡ AQJ10987	♡ 32	♡ AQ62
◊ AK4	◊ AKQ4	◊ AQ5	◊ 973
♣ 2	♣ 3	♣ J32	♣ 1052

YOUR RESPONSE SHOULD BE

(a) One spade. Nine points.

(b) Pass. The hand, with only three high card points and a five point total, is too weak for a response, even with a six card suit.

(c) One heart, not two, three or four hearts. You have a total of 13 points.

(d) One spade. Don't be afraid to show weak four-carders.

(e) One spade, not two. With your singleton of partner's club suit, the hand shapes up as a misfit. Despite your 21 points, take it easy until a 'fit' has been established.

(f) Two hearts. Here, despite the lack of club 'fit,' your suit is sufficiently solid so that you know the hand can play in hearts without trump support from partner.

(g) One spade. Eight points.

(h) One heart. Six points.

EXAMPLES OF SHOWING A NEW SUIT

2 - Your partner has opened the bidding with one heart and the next player passes. You hold the following hands:

(i)	(j)	(k)	(l)
♠ 987654	♠ 87	♠ 543	♠ KQJ98765
♡ 2	♡ J4	♡ 863	♡ 32
♢ K109	♢ AQJ54	♢ K432	♢ 2
♣ 432	♣ K1098	♣ K43	♣ 75

(m)	(n)	(o)	(p)
♠ AJ976	♠ 432	♠ 8765	♠ 432
♡ AQJ8	♡ 2	♡ 7	♡ J8
♢ AK4	♢ AJ765	♢ A432	♢ AJ87
♣ 2	♣ J432	♣ KJ52	♣ AQ106

YOUR RESPONSE SHOULD BE

(i) Pass.

(j) Two diamonds.

(k) One no trump (see following page).

(l) Four spades.

(m) Two spades. Here your 21 points, plus the 'fit' for partner's heart suit, makes the jump response correct. Contrast this bid with the situation on hand (e).

(n) Pass. Only eight points and the possible two diamond response requires 10. The hand is further weakened by the apparent misfit.

(o) One spade. Here, with 10 points, the one spade response, though on a shaded suit, offers the easiest possible response.

(p) Two clubs. With 13 points, certainly a response is in order. The question of which suit should be bid first (from two or more suits) will be discussed in Lessons Four and Five.

NO TRUMP RESPONSES

Thus far, in considering responses you might make to your partner's opening bid of one of a suit, we have discussed two groups of responses. These were:

1 - Raises of his suit;
2 - Bidding a new suit.

Now, let's analyze a new group - responses of one or more no trump.

HOW TO COUNT POINTS FOR NO TRUMP RESPONSES

1 - Count high card points exactly as for suit bids and responses.

2 - Do not count any points for distribution.

A RESPONSE OF ONE NO TRUMP

REQUIREMENTS

Six to 10 high card points.

The high card points are divided between at least two suits. In other words, all your eggs aren't in one basket!

No singleton or void of an unbid suit and preferably not in partner's suit, either.

By now, the reader's bridge sense should infer that when the response is one no trump to an opening bid of one of a suit, the responder DENIES two things -

1 - Lack of trump support for partner's unrebid (at that point) suit.

2 - Lack of a new suit that can be shown as a response. This could be due to one or both of the following reasons: you don't hold six or more points and a four card or longer suit that can be shown at the one level; if it's necessary to show your suit at the two level, you lack 10 or more points.

I have already stressed the fact that *any* suit of four or more cards can be shown at the one level. It is only when you *can't* show a suit conveniently or support partner's suit that you should respond with a bid of one no trump.

RESPONSES OF TWO NO TRUMP

REQUIREMENTS

1 - 14 to 15 points in high cards.

2 - Do not count any points for distribution.

3 - At-least two cards (doubleton) of partner's suit.

4 - No singletons or voids.

5 - The hand contains one or more stoppers in all unbid suits.

The hand may contain a biddable suit (usually a minor). The *immediate* response of two no trump is *forcing to game*, i.e., the partnership must continue bidding until a game contract has been reached.

RESPONSES OF THREE NO TRUMP

REQUIREMENTS

1 - 16 to 17 points in high cards.

Remainder of requirements are identical with responses of two no trump.

WHAT EACH BID MEANS

A one no trump response shows a minimum hand, denies holding a four card or longer suit that could be shown at the one level and also denies good trump support for partner's suit.

A jump response of two no trump is forcing to game, shows an ability to play the hand in no trump if also agreeable to partner, the opening bidder.

A jump to three no trump indicates a tremendous hand. *It is not a shutout or pre-emptive bid* since it has so much high card strength. The opening bidder need not rebid since game has been reached. However, if the opening bidder's hand is strongly distributional with singletons or voids, he may feel it better to play the hand in a suit contract. Further, if the opening bidder has an extra-strong hand, coupled with the knowledge that his partner has 16 or 17 points in high cards, may bid higher in an effort to reach a slam contract.

HANDS ILLUSTRATING NO TRUMP RESPONSES

Your partner has opened the bidding with one diamond. The next player passes. What is your response with each of the following hands ?

(a)	(b)	(c)	(d)
♠ J86	♠ Q108	♠ AQ4	♠ J97
♡ K95	♡ A63	♡ 976	♡ 543
◇ 432	◇ 952	◇ 54	◇ K2
♣ Q432	♣ J643	♣ 86543	♣ K6543

(e)	(f)	(g)	(h)
♠ KJ9	♠ AJ3	♠ KQ	♠ K43
♡ A108	♡ AQ2	♡ AJ10	♡ K109
◇ Q43	◇ 5432	◇ J876	◇ AQ7
♣ KJ43	♣ QJ10	♣ QJ98	♣ K765

(i)	(j)	(k)	(l)
♠ AJ10	♠ KJ10	♠ AQ	♠ K108
♡ K2	♡ AJ8	♡ Q43	♡ AQ
◇ KJ65	◇ Q32	◇ KJ43	◇ Q43
♣ KQ43	♣ KQJ9	♣ AJ87	♣ AJ976

YOUR RESPONSE SHOULD BE

(a) One no trump.
(b) One no trump.
(c) Pass. Six points but all of it in one suit, spades.
(d) One no trump - the 10 points for 'two clubs' are lacking.
(e) Two no trump - 14 points.
(f) Two no trump - 14 points.
(g) Two no trump - 14 points
(h) Two no trump - 15 points.
(i) Three no trump - 17 points.
(j) Three no trump - 17 points.
(k) Three no trump - 17 points.
(l) Three no trump - 16 points.

RESPONDING AFTER AN OPPONENT BIDS

Thus far, in studying responses, we have been in the happy position of hearing our partner open the bidding with one of a suit, the next player (opponent) pass and our only problem was which, if any, response to make.

Frequently the opponents bid. They hold 13 cards apiece, exactly as do you and your partner. If they happen to hold high cards and good suits, they're going to enter the bidding. You will learn more about this in Lesson Eleven on Defensive Bidding. For the present, however, your problem will be - *"What effect does the opponent's bid (overcall) have on my possible response?"*

1 - Any response you make over an intervening bid (when you could have passed) is known as a *free* response.

2 - Any minimum free response - these are responses of (a) a new suit at the one level; (b) a new suit at the two level; (c) a single raise of partner's suit; (d) a response of one no trump - require TWO MORE points than as if the opponent had not bid.

In other words, to show a new suit at the one level (over an intervening bid) shows a minimum of eight points instead of six; a free single raise or a free response of one no trump similarly require at least eight points and showing a new suit at the two-level requires 12 points instead of 10.

3 - Requirements of all other responses (which show greater strength) remain the same.

4 - A four card suit shown as a free response should include at least the queen; a five card suit preferably the jack or better.

5 - If you have a singleton or void in your partner's suit and the suit you contemplate bidding is far from solid, it is usually better to pass with a minimum eight or nine points rather than bid. Remember, if your partner similarly lacks supporting cards for your suit, you're heading for trouble, since you're forcing him to bid again.

6 - Any no trump response, whether of one, two or three, after an opponent bids a suit, MUST include at least one taking trick in the bid suit.

7 - The penalty double. Holding six or more high card points plus length or taking tricks in the opponent's bid suit, it is frequently better and more profitable to make a penalty double

than to show a new suit or bid no trump. This is particularly true if you have a void, a singleton or worthless doubleton of partner's suit so that a 'fit' is lacking and the probable penalty appears more lucrative than a doubtful game. Doubles are fully covered in Lesson Twelve.

Don't be afraid to pass 'minnies.' You can always enter the bidding later if your partner rebids and if he passes, be happy you've stayed out of trouble.

RESPONDING AFTER HAVING PREVIOUSLY PASSED

Suppose the bidding had been -

YOU,SOUTH	WEST	NORTH,PARTNER	EAST
pass	pass	One heart	pass
?			

If you bid at this point, the first thing your partner knows is that you don't have 13 or 14 points, otherwise, you'd have opened the bidding. So if he has a minimum opening bid and no apparent probability of game, he may pass your response.

Summarized, after you originally passed, ANY response by you is NOT forcing. The only exception is the cue-bid of the opponent's suit - in other words, bidding the same suit bid by the opponent which will be explained at length in another lesson.

Yet there are many hands where a player hasn't quite enough to open the bidding, yet once partner opens, there is a certainty or strong probability of game. If game is certain, responder should bid it at once. If game is probable, the strongest possible bid should be made commensurate with the strength of the hand. Holding an excellent fit for partner's suit, a strong raise of that suit, as from one to three, is far better than showing a new suit. The former may evoke another bid from partner; the bid of a new suit could readily be passed by a player who has opened a near 'minnie.'

♠ AK54
♡ J876
◊ 3
♣ J542

With the bidding above, you hold the hand shown at the left. In support of partner's heart suit, it contains 12 points, nine in high cards and three points for the singleton *(when supporting partner's suit).*

Your response should be three hearts.

Referring to the table of requirements for suit raises on page 63, you will see that the double raise (from one to three of a suit) which is forcing to game requires 13 to 16 points. But since you've previously passed, now the double raise is no longer forcing and your partner may pass with a minimum opening bid. Further, having passed and with a good fit for partner's suit, you are permitted a slight s-t-r-e-t-c-h in making a raise with 11 or 12 points that would normally require 13 to 16 points.

"Why didn't you respond with one spade," someone may ask, **"then later support hearts?"**

There may be no 'later.' Since you passed originally, your spade response no longer compels your partner to rebid.

♠ KQJ87
♡ Q43
◇ K109
♣ 62

Let's take another case. Suppose you have passed, holding the hand to the left and your partner now opens the bidding with one heart. For a spade response, you hold 12 points, 11 in high cards, one in distribution.

You should respond with 'two spades' which portrays your hand beautifully.

Since you've bid one more than necessary, does your partner have to rebid?

No!

You've previously passed, remember? But since you've shown a near-opening bid, your partner can visualize a game with even the slightest of extra values.

On the other hand, let's suppose, after you've previously passed and partner opens with one heart, you hold the hand shown to the left. Again we have 12 points, nine in high cards and three in distribution.

♠ AK432
♡ 2
◇ Q5432
♣ 76

Should you respond with two spades, to show the near opening bid?

No!

Why not?

Because so far as you are concerned, the hand is a misfit and unless partner can voluntarily make some constructive rebid over one spade, you don't want to get too high. The difference between this hand and that above it is that the latter contained a substantial supporting fit with partner's heart suit in three cards headed by the queen so that you were prepared and willing to hear your partner rebid his heart suit. Here, with a singleton heart, that's the last thing you want to hear.

In other words - with a fit with partner's suit, you're permitted slight liberties after first passing; with a misfit, tread carefully!

A jump response in no trump, by a player who has previously passed, is frequently used to show near opening bid values, at least a partial fit with partner's suit, stoppers in all unbid suits, the probability of game with 11 or 12 points in high cards.

♠ KJ98
♡ Q4
◇ AJ7
♣ J1087

Let's again assume you've passed originally holding the hand to the left and your partner opens the bidding with one heart. You hold 12 points in high cards.

Of course, you could bid one spade. Had you not previously passed, that bid would have compelled your partner to bid again. Since you've previously passed, a one spade bid is no longer forcing and a jump to two trump is probably the most descriptive bid available. The reason for not bidding two spades is that the jump in a new suit is generally reserved for showing a good five card or longer suit.

The use of the jump response by a responder who has previously passed is common practice among good players.

WHICH RESPONSE SHOULD YOU MAKE?

By this time, the reader will be aware that there are some hands on which you have a choice of possible bids. For example, let's suppose your partner has opened the bidding with one heart and you hold hand (a) to the left.

(a)
♠ AQ43
♡ KJ75
◇ 7543
♣ 8

Should you bid one spade or raise partner's hearts?

On other hands, after your partner opens the bidding, the response is clear cut and you will have no choice. Suppose, over partner's one heart opening, you hold the following hands:

(b)	(c)	(d)
♠ AKQ43	♠ J6	♠ 2
♡ 2	♡ J8	♡ AJ76543
◇ 5432	◇ AKJ765	◇ 4
♣ 765	♣ 432	♣ QJ98

On hand (b) you would bid one spade; on (c), two diamonds; with (d), four hearts. There is no possible choice. There is only one possible bid.

But it is with hands such as (a) where there is a choice of responses that the new player may be puzzled as to which bid to make - bid a spade or support hearts?

The best advice I can give is -

If the hand is worth two or more bids, show your own suit first, later support partner's suit; if the hand is weak and you're only going to make one voluntary bid, then by all means show the support for partner's suit and forget your own.

♠ A8765
♡ 5432
♢ 52
♣ 63

For example, let's say your partner opens the bidding with one heart, the next player passes and you hold the hand shown to the left. What do you bid?

If you respond one spade and you have a total of six points, what will you do if your partner rebids with two hearts? Surely you'd like to show your heart support?

But you don't have enough strength to make two bids.

So when you've only enough strength to make one response it's better to support your partner (if you can) than show a suit of your own.

RULE

1 - With 10 points or less, support partner's suit;

2 - With 11 or more points, first show your suit, then if advisable, support partner's suit.

Accordingly with hand (a), it would have been correct to first show your spade suit before supporting partner's hearts.

THE TEMPORIZING BID

There are certain hands that bridge players describe as 'borderline.' By that they mean the hands are just between fitting the requirements for two possible bids. For example, let's pretend that your partner dealt and opened the bidding with one spade and you hold the hand to the left. It contains 12 points, 11 in high cards, one for the doubleton.

♠ Q987
♡ 1093
♢ KJ98
♣ KQ

Here is a hand which is almost but not quite good enough for the jump raise to three spades which requires 13 to 16 points - you have 12.

Bridge players jokingly refer to hands of this type as worth a bid of two and a half spades, wishing that such a make-believe bid existed.

Rather than overbid, even slightly, with a three spade response, *if we haven't previously passed*, we bid some other suit, if present, as cheaply as possible. Since this is a one round force, our partner must rebid and at our next chance to bid, we give our partner a single raise in his suit if game has not already been reached.

As an example,

PARTNER, OPENER	YOU, RESPONDER
1 spade	2 diamonds
2 spades	3 spades

This is the equivalent of saying to partner, **"I didn't have enough strength to jump to three immediately but I could raise you from two spades to three spades."**

Temporizing permits the responder (and both partners, in later rebidding) to accurately portray hands that are *in-between* single and double raises.

Here are some easy hints for responder on temporizing.

1 - With a weak hand (6 to 10 points) and trump support for your partner's suit, raise his suit. Don't show your suit *unless it is a five card major or longer and your partner has opened with a minor suit.*

2 - Holding 11 or 12 points and support for partner's suit, see if you can't find a four card or longer suit which you can bid before later raising partner's suit.

3 - With 11 or 12 points and four cards of partner's suit, *if you have previously passed*, stretch your hand slightly and give the double raise. After all, your partner knows you're not too strong-you couldn't open the bidding.

4 - Don't temporize if you've previously passed. Your partner doesn't have to rebid and if he has a 'minnie,' you may find yourself playing the hand in your temporizing suit. It is better (in cases where you've previously passed) to support partner immediately with trump support in his suit since your first response could very well be your last!

PART TWO

FINESSES

Since you are learning to play at the same time you are learning to bid, the second part of this lesson is on 'finesses.' A finesse is the attempt to win a trick with an intermediate card when both your side and the opponents hold higher cards.

If you ask me how this could happen, it's because the finessing side plays after the opponent we hope holds the higher card or cards against which we are finessing.

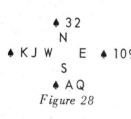

```
          ♠ 32
            N
♠ 109 W         E ♠ KJ
            S
          ♠ AQ
```

Figure 27

In *figure 27*, the deuce of spades is led from the North hand. East plays the jack and South finesses with the queen against the missing king. South hopes, as is the case, that East has the king and since South plays after East, the finesse will be successful and the queen will win that trick. Had East played the king, South would have won with the ace.

Finessing is the most common play you will use to gain tricks. A finesse has a 50 percent chance of success since half the times, the missing card will be to your right, the remaining half to your left.

```
        ♠ 32
          N
♠ KJ W        E  ♠ 109
          S
        ♠ AQ
```

Figure 28

Figure 28 is the same as *27* with one difference- the East-West hands have been transposed. Now, with the identical line of play - leading a low spade from the North hand, the queen will lose to the king.

Sometimes the bidding will yield definite clues as to the possible success or failure of an intended finesse. Suppose we were playing a hand with hearts trumps and the player to our left had bid and rebid spades during the auction. As South, we hold the ace-queen of spades. It's 10 to one that West, to our left, holds the king of his bid suit so that the finesse, if taken, must fail. In cases like these, good players try to avoid a probable losing finesse, resorting to what are known as end-plays, where an opponent is thrust unwillingly in the lead and forced ultimately to lead spades into your ace-queen.

There are different kinds of finesses. The most frequently

encountered (and the ones you should learn first) are those where you finesse against one and two missing cards. These are known as single and double finesses. The others can be learned gradually as the student's bridge ability increases. There are eight types of finesses. These are:

1 - The single finesse;
2 - The double finesse;
3 - The triple finesse;
4 - The deep finesse;
5 - The obligatory finesse;
6 - The backward finesse;
7 - The trump finesse;
8 - The free finesse.

THE SINGLE FINESSE

The single finesse is exactly what its name implies - a finesse against a single missing card. *Figures 27 and 28* are examples of single finesses against a missing king.

```
        ♠ A73
          N
♠ 1096 W     E ♠ Q842
          S
        ♠ KJ5
```

Figure 29

Here in *figure 29* we have another single finesse. Between the North-South partnership, we hold the ace, king and jack. The queen is missing. South's object is to win three tricks in the suit. The five is led, taken with the ace. The trey follows. East will play a low spade to each of these tricks since to interpose the queen would give the show away, remove all guess for South as to the whereabouts of that card. After East plays a low spade on the second round of that suit, South plays the jack in a single finesse against the missing queen.

```
        ♠ 432
        ♡ A2
          N
♠ 5    W      E ♠ J986
♡ KQ86          ♡ 9
          S
        ♠ AKQ10
        ♡ 5
```

Figure 30

Let me give additional examples. In *figure 30*, South has the lead in a three no trump contract. The ace and king of spades are played, West discarding a heart on the second spade. It is now a simple matter for South to lead his lone heart, take the trick with the ace. The last spade is led from the North hand, South playing the 10 third-hand over East's nine in a single finesse against East's nine. The finesse is certain to succeed since West is known not to hold any more spades.

♠ J842
N
♠ 9765 W E ♠ Q10
♡ AQ
S
♠ AK3
♡ J

Figure 31

Finesses, whether single or other types, can and often are taken against low cards when necessary. In *figure 31* South has the lead. The contract is no trump. South plays the king of spades on which East drops the 10. On the lead of the ace, East follows with the queen. It should be obvious that East is not dropping the queen because he wants to - it is a matter of following suit. West, therefore, is marked for the remaining spades, the nine and the seven. All that remains for South to do is lead his three of spades, play dummy's eight after West's seven in a winning single finesse against West's nine.

♠ A43
N
♠ K98 W E ♠ 765
S
♠ QJ10

Figure 32

Now for a more advanced type of single finesse. Examine *figure 32* and compare it with *figures 27 and 28.* In *figures 27 and 28,* we took the single finesse against the missing king but in these earlier examples, both the ace and queen were in the same hand. In *figure 32,* the ace and queen are in opposite hands (of the partnership) yet the same finesse against the king is possible. South leads any of his equals, as the queen. If West plays low, the trey is played from dummy.

♠ AJ4
N
♠ K98 W E ♠ 765
S
♠ Q103

Figure 33

In *figure 33,* the high cards between the partnership are more widespread, yet the identical finesse against the king can be taken.

♠ AK2
N
♠ Q98 W E ♠ 765
S
♠ J103

Figure 34

In *figure 34,* South, by leading the jack of spades, can take the single finesse against the missing queen.

I would like to emphasize an important point. Whenever a high card (usually an honor) is led that the opponents can cover with a higher card *(figures 32, 33 and 34)*, it is necessary that the declarer or dummy have the card or cards directly beneath that led. In *figures 32 and 33*, South can afford to lead the queen. If West covers with the king, forcing dummy's ace, it is all to South's advantage since the jack and 10, now the highest remaining cards of the suit, are in South's possession.

A similar situation exists in *figure 34*. It is immaterial to South whether West covers the jack with the queen. If he does, the king or ace wins. The 10 spot will move up from fifth to second place in the spade suit. And the 10 is in the South hand!

So your rule, when leading an honor or high card which can be covered, is always to have the card, in your hand or dummy, beneath the card you plan to lead. That way, the card that will be promoted belongs to you and not to an opponent. Possession of the next two or three cards in rank below the card being led makes leading a coverable honor even sounder, since it gives your side still further high card promotions.

♠ A 4 3
N
♠ K 8 7 W E ♠ J 10 5
S
♠ Q 9 6

Figure 35

As an example of WHAT NOT TO DO, look at *figure 35*. Here South, in a mistaken idea that he is taking a finesse, leads the spade queen. West covers with the king. Dummy's ace wins. The cards that have been promoted to number one and two rank in the suit, the jack and 10, belong to the defenders. All South succeeded in doing was promoting the other side's cards.

♠ A 4 3
N
♠ J 10 5 W E ♠ K 8 7
S
♠ Q 9 6

Figure 36

In *figure 36*, we have transposed the East-West cards of the preceding example. If South (IN ERROR) leads the queen, East will win with the king. West's jack has been promoted from fourth to second place in the suit.

Correct technique in *figures 35 and 36* is to lead a low card from the North hand. If the lead is in the South hand, a low spade is first led by South and won with dummy's ace. The low card is then led from the North hand *towards the queen.*

In the event of East playing a low card, the queen is played by South. If East has the king *(figure 36)*, the queen will win. If the East-West cards lie as in *figure 35*, the queen will lose. We have a 50 percent chance of winning a trick with the queen by leading towards it whereas by leading the queen (without holding the jack) we have no chance whatever of winning a second trick in the suit against correct defensive play. This is exactly in accordance with the principles of leading up to strength outlined in Lesson Two.

If possible, a high card (when it can be spared from two or more equals) should first be played before taking a single finesse. This play safeguards against the missing card being singleton .

The first round play of an ace (or king) from an ace-king combination is particularly common in single finesses against missing queens. Further, the greater the number of cards held in a suit by the combined partnership, the fewer cards will be held in that suit by the opponents and the greater the likelihood that a missing card can be alone or so thinly protected that it can be captured and a finesse would be unnecessary.

	♠ 1043 ♡ J87 ♢ KJ108 ♣ A75	
♠ Q ♡ AK1092 ♢ 743 ♣ Q1092	N W E S	♠ 8765 ♡ Q65 ♢ A95 ♣ 864
	♠ AKJ92 ♡ 43 ♢ Q62 ♣ KJ3	

Figure 37

South, in *figure 37*, is the declarer at four spades. Three rounds of high hearts find South trumping the third round with a low spade. South has two possible finesses, both against missing black queens. To protect himself against the trump queen being singleton, declarer first plays the spade king. Sure enough, the queen falls. The ace of diamonds is forced out, the opponents' trumps drawn and South's losing three of clubs is eventually discarded on dummy's last diamond, making the club finesse unnecessary.

This play of a higher honor, before taking a finesse, is known as a 'safety play.' Had the queen not fallen singleton, South, in all probability, would have taken the finesse against that card the next time spades were led.

	♠ AK4 ♡ 3	
♠ Q987	N W E S	♠ 653 ♡ 4
	♠ J102 ♡ 7	

Figure 38

In *figure 38*, the contract is no trump. South's first play is the deuce of spades to dummy's king. When the safety play fails to drop the queen, South returns to his hand via the heart seven. The spade jack is led in a conventional single finesse against the missing queen.

	♠ A43	
♠ K98	N W E S	♠ 765
	♠ QJ10	

Figure 39

In *figure 39*, South has the lead. He cannot afford to play the ace of spades initially in the slim hope of catching a lone king, since with the ace gone, there is no card left capable of capturing the king. The finesse, then, must be taken then and there.

For reasons of retaining trump control or scarcity of entries to one hand or the other, it is sometimes necessary to omit the safety play of playing the ace or king first before finessing against a missing queen.

	♠ 4 ♡ 102 ♢ KQJ43 ♣ A5432	
♠ KQJ98 ♡ Q76 ♢ 105 ♣ KJ9	N W E S	♠ 1076 ♡ 43 ♢ 9876 ♣ Q1087
	♠ A532 ♡ AKJ985 ♢ A2 ♣ 6	

Figure 40

In *figure 40*, South is playing a six heart contract. West opens the king of spades and South wins with the ace. It looks as though South could afford the safety play of first playing the king of hearts. If the queen doesn't drop, declarer can now enter dummy with the ace of clubs, still finesse against the queen of hearts.

But in this case, the safety play is a luxury South cannot afford since West, on winning with the queen of hearts, can cash setting spade tricks since both of dummy's trumps have been played. The trump finesse, then, must be taken immediately so that if it loses, dummy will retain a trump as protection against the missing spade suit.

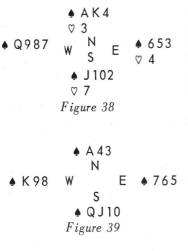

After losing the first round of hearts to West's queen, declarer will regain the lead - pull trumps and discard his losing spades on dummy's diamonds.

West	North / South	East
	♠ A4 ♡ 8532 ◇ J106 ♣ Q432	
♠ QJ1065 ♡ Q7 ◇ 543 ♣ J97	N W E S	♠ 832 ♡ J964 ◇ Q72 ♣ K105
	♠ K97 ♡ AK10 ◇ AK98 ♣ A86	

Figure 41

South is playing a three no trump contract in *figure 41.* West opens the spade queen, dummy's ace winning. Since with the ace of spades gone, dummy has no further cards of entry to permit a diamond finesse after first taking the safety play in that suit. Accordingly, the finesse against the queen of diamonds must be taken immediately by leading the jack of diamonds and hoping that East holds the queen.

THE TWO-WAY FINESSE

West	North / South	East
	♠ AJ4	
♠ ?	N W E S	♠ ?
	♠ K109	

Figure 42

A two-way finesse is a single finesse which can be taken in either direction and usually against a missing queen. For the play to be workable, each of the two partnership hands contains a card with capturing power. In *figure 42*, the ace is in the North hand with the jack and the king is in the South with the 10.

Which way to finesse is purely a guess. The opponents' bidding and previously played cards may have furnished some information. For instance, if the defenders hold a total of two queens between them and the defender to the left of declarer has played one of these queens, there is a strong mathematical possibility that the other defender holds the remaining queen. If possible, the ace or king should first be played as a safety measure against the possibility of a singleton queen.

	♠ A 4 3 2	
	N	
♠ ? W		E ♠ ?
	S	
	♠ K J 10 9	

Figure 43

In *figure 43* we have a two-way finesse against the missing queen. Since some players are avid 'coverers of honors,' it is possible to take advantage of that fact. South leads the jack.

If West is one of the 'eager beaver coverers,' he will break his wrist in his hurry to cover the jack with the queen. If he fails to cover, it's a safe assumption that he doesn't have the queen so we go up with dummy's ace and take the finesse in the other direction.

This is not always true since a shrewd defender, sitting West, could analyze the position and refuse to cover and South would still be guessing which defender holds the queen. It should be pointed out that South can afford to have West cover the jack since in this case, all the key cards that will be promoted by the cover are held by North and South.

DOUBLE FINESSES

The name 'double finesse' is descriptive of a finessing situation against two missing cards. In *figure 44*, the defenders sitting East-West hold the king and jack among their spades. The lead being with South, the six is led. West plays the five. The 10 is played from dummy. South's hope is that West holds both king and jack (as is the case) so that the 10 will win the trick.

	♠ A Q 10 ♡ 3	
	N	
♠ K J 5 ♡ 8	W E	♠ 9 4 3 2 ♡ void
	S	
	♠ 8 7 6 ♡ Q	

Figure 44

Returning to his hand via the heart queen, South leads another low spade, dummy's queen wins over West's jack. Even if one of the double finesses loses, the remaining finesse can still be tried.

West		North / South		East
		♠ A Q 10 ♡ 3		
		N		
♠ K 5 2 ♡ 4	W		E	♠ J 8 7 ♡ 2
		S		
		♠ 6 4 3 ♡ Q		

Figure 45

In *figure 45*, the first round finesse of the 10 loses to East's jack. South wins the heart return, now successfully finesses with dummy's queen against West's king.

Another commonly encountered double finesse is shown in *figure 46*. South has the lead in a no trump contract. A heart is led and won in dummy. The deuce of spades follows. Should East play the nine, South plays the 10, hoping that East also holds the queen and jack. Should East play an honor, South wins, re-enters dummy and takes the single finesse against East's remaining honor.

West		North / South		East
		♠ 4 3 2 ♡ K Q		
		N		
♠ 8 7 6 ♡ J 10	W		E	♠ Q J 9 ♡ 6 5
		S		
		♠ A K 10 ♡ 8 7		

Figure 46

West		North / South		East
		♠ J 10 9 ♡ A K		
		N		
♠ K 8 4 ♡ Q 2	W		E	♠ Q 7 6 ♡ J 8
		S		
		♠ A 5 3 ♡ 10 4		

Figure 47

Sometimes double finesses are taken against two missing cards when declarer can capture only one of them. South's object *in figure 47* is to win four of the remaining five tricks. In other words, he must avoid, if possible, losing two spade tricks. A heart is won in dummy. The spade jack is led. If East plays a low card, so does South. West wins with the king. Dummy regains the lead with a high heart and the 10 of spades is led. This time the play is reduced to a single finesse against the queen.

It must again be emphasized that when high cards are led from the North hand for the two finesses in *figure 47*, each time the North-South partnership held the card beneath that led. In other words, the card that could be promoted (by a cover of the led card) was held by North-South. When the jack was led, North held the 10. Similarly, the lead of the 10 found North holding the nine. Give the defenders the nine-spot and see what happens if East covers with the queen.

	♠ 432	
	♡ AK	
	◇ 62	
♠ K9	N	♠ Q65
♡ J10	W E	♡ Q9
◇ Q87	S	◇ 54
	♠ AJ1087	
	♡ 65	

Figure 48

Figure 48 is a variation of *47*. South's object is to hold the spade losers to one. Dummy is entered via a high heart and a spade is led. The 10 is played third-hand over East's five. West wins with the king. South trumps the diamond return. A heart is won in dummy and a second spade finesse taken with the jack. The ace now drops the queen.

	♠ KJ8	
	♡ 43	
	N	
♠ Q72	W E	♠ A54
♡ J10		♡ 85
	S	
	♠ 1093	
	♡ AK	

Figure 49

When the declarer's and dummy's holdings include the king and jack, and the defenders hold the ace and queen, double finesses can be taken against the latter combination. A trick must be lost to the ace, of course, but if the queen is 'right,' that is, in front of the king, it is frequently possible to avoid losing a second trick in the suit. In *figure 49*, the 10 is led by South, who can afford the lead of that card since if it is covered, he has the nine in his possession.

	♠ K76	
	♡ 43	
	N	
♠ Q72	W E	♠ A85
♡ J10		♡ 65
	S	
	♠ J109	
	♡ AK	

Figure 50

In *figure 50*, South leads the jack. A low card is played from dummy if West fails to cover.

	♠ KJ4	
	♡ 43	
	N	
♠ 1098	W E	♠ AQ2
♡ J10		♡ 65
	S	
	♠ 765	
	♡ AK	

Figure 51

In *figure 51*, both spade finesses are 'wrong' and the ace-queen of spades lies over the king-jack. Of course, were the East-West hands reversed, both finesses would have succeeded. In fact, if West had either the ace or the queen, one of the two finesses would have succeeded.

THE TRIPLE FINESSE

The 'triple finesse' is a finesse against three missing cards. In *figure 52*, spades are trumps. West opens the king of diamonds. The suit is continued, South trumping the third round. Success in making four spades hinges in holding the heart losers to one. After the second round of trumps has been won in the South hand, the deuce of hearts is led. Dummy's nine is played after West's seven in a finesse against the missing king, queen and 10. South hopes, as is the case, that West holds some of these cards. The nine of hearts is captured by the king. South later leads a heart, playing the jack over West's 10 to win two heart tricks.

	North	
	♠ Q1082 ♡ AJ9 ◊ 7432 ♣ KJ	
West ♠ 74 ♡ Q107 ◊ KQ108 ♣ 10964	N W E S	**East** ♠ 6 ♡ K653 ◊ AJ6 ♣ Q8753
	♠ AKJ953 ♡ 842 ◊ 95 ♣ A2	
	South	

Figure 52

In *figure 53*, we have a West who bid spades during the auction. Accordingly, needing four spade tricks, we plan to triple finesse against West for the missing king, jack and nine. A low spade is led by South, dummy covering whatever card West plays. The process is repeated.

	North	
	♠ AQ108 ♡ 43	
West ♠ KJ96 ♡ J10	N W E S	**East** ♠ 43 ♡ 9876
	♠ 752 ♡ AK5	
	South	

Figure 53

Do not regard double and triple finesses as rare plays. They are quite commonplace.

THE DEEP FINESSE

The 'deep finesse' is really a ducking play and not a finesse at all. It usually arises when a trick must be lost in a specific suit and it is more advantageous to declarer to lose it on an early round than later.

	♠ J 96 ♡ Q 84 ◇ AK752 ♣ 52	
♠ Q1082 ♡ KJ95 ◇ J4 ♣ J87	N W E S	♠ A73 ♡ 1076 ◇ Q108 ♣ 10964
	♠ K54 ♡ A32 ◇ 963 ♣ AKQ3	

Figure 54

In *figure 54*, the contract is three no trump played by South. West opens the deuce of spades. East takes the ace, returns the seven. South plays the five. The spade king is knocked out on the third round. South leads the trey of diamonds. Over West's four, dummy takes the deep finesse of playing the five or seven from the dummy.

East will obviously take the trick. South takes the ace of whatever suit East returns. The ace and king of diamonds capture the outstanding cards of that suit. Dummy's remaining low diamonds are now winners.

Advantage of the deep finesse is that it permits retention of a card of entry to an otherwise re-entryless hand while giving up a trick which would have to be lost in any event.

THE OBLIGATORY FINESSE

Success of the obligatory finesse depends upon a defender originally holding only two cards *including* a missing higher honor.

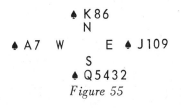

	♠ K86	
♠ A7	N W E S	♠ J109
	♠ Q5432	

Figure 55

This finesse is really a type ducking play and generally occurs when the declarer and dummy have a total of eight cards of the suit between the combined hands. South leads the deuce, West plays the seven. Dummy's king wins. The six is returned. Though East plays the jack or 10, South *must refuse to play the queen!* This is the obligatory finesse.

The reason for South's play should be apparent. West is marked for the ace from East's inability to capture the king. Playing the queen would find West playing the ace.

But West was going to play the ace, anyhow! South didn't have to play the queen to force the ace. The latter card was now alone. Moreover, the moment South released the queen, East's last card became the highest remaining card of the suit.

Had West three cards of the suit originally, as AJ7, two tricks must be lost by South whether South plays the queen to the second round of spades or plays a low card. On the other hand, if West started with a doubleton ace, only one spade trick need be lost if South employs the obligatory finesse since the queen is retained to capture East's last card.

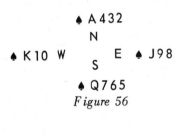

♠ A432
N
♠ K10 W E ♠ J98
S
♠ Q765

Figure 56

In *figure 56*, we have another obligatory finesse. South leads a low spade, wins with dummy's ace over West's 10-spot. The deuce is returned, South ducking East's nine spot. Since the king was originally doubleton, only one trick need be lost. The reasoning behind the play is the same as in *figure 55*.

THE BACKWARD FINESSE

♠ A43
N
♠ Q76 W E ♠ 1052
S
♠ KJ9

Figure 57

The backward finesse involves leading a high card that can be covered so that the card directly beneath that led and held by the other defender, can be finessed against in the other direction.

This play usually occurs when the opponents' bidding has apparently located the higher, missing honor (in this case, the queen) and the main hope of not losing a trick in the suit is to find the other, lower card in the opposite defender's hand.

Let's presume that South is playing the hand after West, in an earlier stage of the bidding, had bid 'no trump.' In all probability, West holds the queen of spades. The location of the 10 of spades is unknown.

In order to take the backward finesse, South leads the jack. If West refuses to cover, a low card is played from the North hand; if West covers, the ace wins. A low spade is played from dummy and the nine-spot played over East's five.

For the backward finesse to be successful, it is vital that the hand taking the second finesse as South in *figure 57* has the cards above and below the missing card being finessed against on the second round as the jack and nine with the missing 10. It should also be pointed out that if West held ♠ Q10x, no amount of finessing would shut him out of a trick, as long as he covered the jack with the queen.

THE TRUMP FINESSE

In playing suit contracts, a void in a side suit gives the declarer or dummy the happy ability to trump a high card held by a defender or to discard a loser on that suit if the adverse high card isn't played.

The ability to capture a missing high card by reason of trumping ability, thus setting up as winners the remaining cards of that suit, is known as a 'trump finesse.' It has nothing to do with a finesse when leading trumps.

	♠ KJ9 ♡ A42 ♢ AQJ109 ♣ J4	
♠ 52 ♡ KQ1098 ♢ 743 ♣ K65	N W E S	♠ 43 ♡ J76 ♢ K852 ♣ A1097
	♠ AQ10876 ♡ 53 ♢ 6 ♣ Q832	

Figure 58

In *figure 58,* South is the declarer at four spades. West opens the king of hearts. Dummy's ace wins. Two rounds of trumps are led. The ace of diamonds is cashed. The queen of diamonds follows. Declarer now takes repeated finesses against East's king of diamonds just as though he held the diamond ace. The ability to trump the king when (and if) it appears gives South that ability.

If East plays the king of diamonds, South trumps. If East does not cover the queen, South discards his losing heart.

The trump finesse has a very great advantage over conventional single and double finesses. Had South, in *figure 58*, won the second spade in his hand, then led the six of diamonds and taken the single finesse against the missing king by playing the queen. East would win with the king. The defense could now take a heart trick and two clubs which, with the king of diamonds, defeats the contract. With the trump finesse, even though it might fail *(as it might have had West the diamond king in figure 58)*, South has simultaneously gotten rid of a losing card. In other words, it's 'trick for trick.' Moreover, the trump finesse permits repeated finesses whereas the conventional single finesse would only permit the play being made once where the finessing player holds a singleton.

Sometimes an opponent may 'show out' on an early round of a suit, making the trump finesse marked. This will usually happen against missing queens and jacks.

	♠ 86 ♡ Q10 ◇ AKJ1074 ♣ A32	
♠ QJ1097 ♡ 942 ◇ 5 ♣ 10854	N W E S	♠ K532 ♡ 53 ◇ Q986 ♣ QJ9
	♠ A4 ♡ AKJ876 ◇ 32 ♣ K76	

Figure 59

South, in *figure 59*, is the declarer at six hearts. West opens the queen of spades. South wins with the ace, leads three rounds of high trumps. The ace and king of diamonds are cashed. When West shows out on the second round, it is a simple matter to lead the jack of diamonds from the dummy and take the trump finesse against the queen.

THE FREE FINESSE

A 'free' finesse is when an opponent leads a suit and an intermediate card is played second hand from the dummy or declarer's hand in the hope of winning that trick. If the defender sitting third hand can play a higher card than that played second-hand, the fourth-hand player posseses a *still higher card* capable of winning the trick.

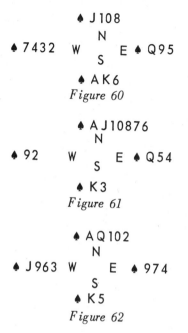

♠ J 10 8
N
♠ 7 4 3 2 W E ♠ Q 9 5
S
♠ A K 6

Figure 60

In *figure 60,* West leads a spade. The jack or 10 is played from dummy. This is a typical free finesse since if the jack is covered by the queen, South can still win the trick with the king or ace. Had West the queen, North's card would have won the trick.

♠ A J 10 8 7 6
N
♠ 9 2 W E ♠ Q 5 4
S
♠ K 3

Figure 61

Figure 61 presents another free finesse. Against a heart contract by South, West opens the nine of spades, hoping for a third round ruff. Dummy plays the jack or 10 and again the jack must win the trick or the king can capture the queen.

♠ A Q 10 2
N
♠ J 9 6 3 W E ♠ 9 7 4
S
♠ K 5

Figure 62

Here in *figure 62,* we have an example of a free finesse against the jack. West opens the trey and the 10 is played from the dummy.

The main point about the free finesse is that the trick cannot be lost - if the first card played doesn't win the trick - the second card can and will.

FINESSING IN GENERAL

It stands to reason that the more cards of a suit held by a partnership, the fewer cards (of that suit) remain to be held by the opponents. In most of these cases, the card or cards held by opponents is either thinly guarded or alone so that it may be captured without the need of a finesse.

♠ J 10 9 8 7
N
♠ K W E ♠ void
S
♠ A Q 6 5 4 3 2

Figure 63

With 12 spades in the North-South partnership in *figure 63,* it isn't necessary to finesse against the missing king. Simple counting will show the king to be alone and that it must fall when the ace is played.

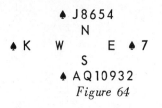

	♠ J8654	
	N	
♠ K W		E ♠ 7
	S	
	♠ AQ10932	

Figure 64

Similarly, in *figure 64*, with 11 cards of the suit between the partnership, there is a great likelihood that the two missing cards may be split between the two defenders. Hence, the king will be alone and the ace will 'pick it up.' Of course, the opponents' bidding will often furnish supplementary clues. If one opponent, with a dearth of high cards, has supported his partner's suit aggressively, he may be presumed to have a void or singleton or some distributionary values; on the other hand, if an opponent has bid no trump, it is likely that he has a missing high card. These rules are not rigid but they do apply in general.

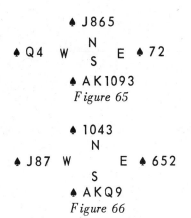

	♠ J865	
	N	
♠ Q4 W		E ♠ 72
	S	
	♠ AK1093	

Figure 65

Identical reasoning, with nine cards (or even eight) of a suit between the partnership, will frequently influence the declarer into refusing a finesse for a missing queen and playing for the 'drop' instead.

This reasoning would also apply to holding seven cards between the partnership lacking the jack of a suit as in *figure 66.*

	♠ 1043	
	N	
♠ J87 W		E ♠ 652
	S	
	♠ AKQ9	

Figure 66

FINESSING HINTS

The greater the number of cards in a suit held by a partnership, the greater the possibility that a missing card may be thinly guarded, fall under high cards, obviating the need of a finesse. In other words, see if the missing card can be captured.

Before finessing, see if there isn't a safer method of play offering a better chance of success than the 50 percent probability furnished by the finesse. This could be discarding the potential losing card on a winner from the opposite hand, an end-play (where an opponent is forced to lead the suit to you) or one of the advanced plays you will meet later.

If you can afford a safety play on the first round against a missing queen, do so.

FINESSE TABLE

YOU LACK	*NUMBER OF CARDS IN COMBINED HANDS*	*TACTICS*
King	11 or more	Play ace-do not finesse
"	10 or less	Finesse
Queen	10	First play ace or king. If both defenders follow, play for the drop
"	9	As above
"	8 or less	Finesse
Jack	8 or more	Play for the drop.
"	7	As above
"	6	Toss-up

TABLE OF PROBABILITIES

YOU AND PARTNER HOLD	*REMAINING CARDS WILL SPLIT*	*%*
6 cards of a suit	4 - 3	62
	5 - 2	31
	6 - 1	7
	7 - 0	0.4
7 cards of a suit	4 - 2	48
	3 - 3	36
	5 - 1	15
	6 - 0	1
8 cards of a suit	3 - 2	68
	4 - 1	28
	5 - 0	4
9 cards of a suit	3 - 1	50
	2 - 2	40
	4 - 0	10
10 cards of a suit	2 - 1	78
	3 - 0	22
11 cards of a suit	1 - 1	52
	2 - 0	48

QUIZ THREE

1 - What is the minimum number of cards of your partner's suit you must hold in order to support his suit before it has been rebid?

2 - Your partner is the dealer and opens the bidding with one heart. What is your response with each of the following hands?

(a)	(b)	(c)	(d)
♠ J743	♠ 6	♠ AK743	♠ KJ7
♡ AK	♡ J109	♡ 2	♡ Q2
◇ J1032	◇ A5432	◇ KQ6	◇ A1086
♣ 542	♣ 10876	♣ AJ42	♣ KJ97

(e)	(f)	(g)	(h)
♠ 76	♠ KQ	♠ 96	♠ 3
♡ 84	♡ 6	♡ Q864	♡ 108643
◇ A5432	◇ AKJ1098	◇ AQJ9	◇ AQ752
♣ 9532	♣ KQJ2	♣ J43	♣ 65

(i)	(j)	(k)	(l)
♠ Q43	♠ A843	♠ A864	♠ AKJ6
♡ 2	♡ QJ86	♡ A97	♡ KJ10
◇ Q7652	◇ 2	◇ J52	◇ AQ109
♣ Q1082	♣ K1074	♣ 632	♣ K2

3 - You deal and pass. The next player also passes and your partner opens the bidding with one heart. What is your response with each of the following hands?

(m)	(n)	(o)	(p)
♠ KJ1098	♠ AQJ7	♠ AJ8765	♠ Q109
♡ Q4	♡ K1098	♡ 2	♡ J8
◇ KJ97	◇ 7643	◇ Q742	◇ AJ87
♣ 63	♣ 2	♣ J6	♣ KJ92

4 - Your partner as dealer opens the bidding with one club. The next player passes. What is your response with each of the following hands?

(q)	(r)	(s)	(t)
♠ J1065	♠ KQ4	♠ K2	♠ Q6
♡ 42	♡ AJ10	♡ Q874	♡ A10
◇ 653	◇ K76	◇ A65	◇ 876
♣ KQ108	♣ K1098	♣ KJ73	♣ KQJ876

5 - Your partner deals and bids one diamond. The next player overcalls with one heart. With both sides vulnerable, what is your response with each of the following hands?

(u)	(v)	(w)	(x)
♠ KQJ9	♠ AJ86	♠ K74	♠ 643
♡ AJ987	♡ 1052	♡ Q96	♡ 9753
◇ 85	◇ K63	◇ K82	◇ 5
♣ Q4	♣ 542	♣ Q1062	♣ AQJ54

6 -

♠ AQ
N
W E
S
♠ 32

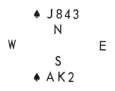

You are South in the accompanying diagram. The lead is in your hand. How would you play to win two tricks?

7 -

♠ K543
N
W E
S
♠ Q762

You are South, playing the accompanying spade suit. You lead the deuce from your hand. West plays the eight and you play the king from dummy (North) which wins, East playing the nine. You now lead the trey from dummy. East plays the 10. What card do you play? Why?

8 -

♠ J843
N
W E
S
♠ AK2

You are South, playing the diagrammed spade suit. You first lead the king of spades on which West plays a low spade and East the nine. When you play the ace of spades, West again follows with a low spade and East drops the queen. Since it is assumed that you need four tricks in the spade suit to complete your contract, how do you continue playing the suit?

9 -

♠ 10 8 7 6 5
N
W E
S
♠ A K J 4 3 2

You are South and spades are trumps. The lead is in the North hand. You play the five of spades and East follows with the nine. What card do you play from your hand? Why?

10 -

♠ A 4 2
N
W E
S
♠ Q 5 3

How do you plan to win two tricks with the diagrammed combination? The lead can be in either hand.

11 -

♠ A Q 10
N
W E
S
♠ 4 3 2

The lead is in the South hand. It is assumed that the South hand has re-entries in other suits so that you can return to that hand as often as you wish.

How do you plan to try to win three spade tricks? For you to win three tricks, which opponent must have what high cards?

12 -

♠ A J 10
N
W E
S
♠ 4 3 2

In question 12, you need to win two tricks with the given combination. The lead is in the South hand which contains re-entries elsewhere.

How do you plan the play? How must the adverse high cards be distributed for you to win two tricks?

ANSWERS TO QUIZ THREE

1 - Three cards including the queen or higher card; or three cards including the jack and 10; or any four or more low cards.

2 - (a) one spade; (b) two hearts; (c) one spade - the lack of fit with partner's heart suit and the lack of solidity of the spade suit makes one spade a better response than two spades, despite the 19 points; (d) two no trump; (e) pass (f) three diamonds; (g) two diamonds - a temporizing response; (h) four hearts; (i) pass; (j) three hearts is preferable to one spade; (k) two hearts; (l) two spades.

3 - (m) two spades; (n) three hearts; (o) one spade; (p) two no trump.

4 - (q) two clubs; (r) three no trump; (s) one heart; (t) three clubs.

5 - (u) double; (v) one spade; (w) one no trump; (x) pass.

6 - Lead low towards the ace-queen and play the queen third-hand over any low spade played by West.

7 - Any spade except the queen. West is marked for the ace. Your hope of losing only one trick in the suit is that West originally held a doubleton ace and that it is now alone on the second round.

8 - Lead the deuce and play dummy's eight if West plays a low card. West is marked for an original holding of four cards headed by the 10.

9 - The king or ace. No finesse is necessary since counting reveals that the opponents hold a total of two spades. The queen must fall under the ace and king.

10 - Lead a low card from the North hand towards the queen, hoping that East has the king.

11 - Lead twice toward the North hand. In order to win three tricks, West must hold both the king and jack.

12 - Lead twice toward the North hand. The king and queen of spades must be divided between the two defenders or West must have both of these missing honors.

LESSON THREE
HANDS

1.

	North	
	♠ 6542 ♡ A872 ◇ J6 ♣ KQJ	
West ♠ 9 ♡ 1093 ◇ AKQ95 ♣ 7432	N W E S	**East** ♠ K108 ♡ Q54 ◇ 10872 ♣ 865
	♠ AQJ73 ♡ KJ6 ◇ 43 ♣ A109	

South dealer - The bidding

South	West	North	East
1 sp.	pass	2 hts.	pass
3 hts.	pass	3 sp.	pass
4 sp.	pass	pass	pass

Play the hand at four spades. West wins two diamonds, then leads the deuce of clubs.

2.

	North	
	♠ KQJ7 ♡ A65 ◇ J106 ♣ 1086	
West ♠ A84 ♡ KJ10983 ◇ AQ5 ♣ 5	N W E S	**East** ♠ 2 ♡ Q74 ◇ 9832 ♣ AJ432
	♠ 109653 ♡ 2 ◇ K74 ♣ KQ97	

West dealer - The bidding

West	North	East	South
1 ht.	pass	2 hts.	pass
3 hts.	pass	4 hts.	pass
pass	pass	pass	

Play the hand at four hearts. North's opening lead is the king of spades.

3.

	North	
	♠ K764 ♡ AQ42 ◇ AJ10 ♣ QJ	
West ♠ J102 ♡ K987 ◇ Q63 ♣ 1075	N W E S	**East** ♠ A9 ♡ 1053 ◇ K952 ♣ K982
	♠ Q853 ♡ J6 ◇ 874 ♣ A643	

North dealer - The bidding

North	East	South	West
1 sp.	pass	2 sp.	pass
3 hts.	pass	4 sp.	pass
pass	pass		

North is declarer at four East opens the club two-spot.

4.

	North	
	♠ Q2 ♡ K73 ◇ KJ86 ♣ 8643	
West ♠ A65 ♡ A942 ◇ 432 ♣ K75	N W E S	**East** ♠ J10987 ♡ J105 ◇ AQ10 ♣ A2
	♠ K43 ♡ Q86 ◇ 975 ♣ QJ109	

East dealer - The bidding

East	South	West	North
1 sp.	pass	2 hts.	pass
3 hts.	pass	3 sp.	pass
4 sp.	pass	pass	pass

East, declarer at four spades. South opens the club queen.

SOLUTIONS TO LESSON THREE HANDS

1.

South declarer at four spades.

Trick	W	N	E	S
1	♢K	♢6	♢2	♢3
2	♢Q	♢J	♢7	♢4
3	♣2	♣J	♣5	♣9
4	♠9	♠2	♠8	♠J
5	♡3	♡A	♡4	♡6
6	♣3	♠4	♠10	♠Q
7	♢5	♠5	♠K	♠A
8	♣4	♣Q	♣6	♣10
9	♡9	♡2	♡5	♡J
10	♡10	♡7	♡Q	♡K
11	♣7	♣K	♣8	♣A
12	♢9	♠6	♢8	♠7
13	♢A	♡8	♢10	♠3

South wins 11 tricks.

2.

West declarer at four hearts.

Trick	N	E	S	W
1	♠K	♠2	♠3	♠A
2	♠7	♡7	♠5	♠4
3	♣6	♣A	♣9	♣5
4	♣8	♣2	♣Q	♡8
5	♠J	♡Q	♠6	♠8
6	♢6	♢2	♢4	♢Q
7	♡A	♡4	♡2	♡K
8	♠Q	♣3	♠9	♡3
9	♡5	♣4	♠10	♡J
10	♡6	♢3	♣7	♡10
11	♣10	♢8	♣K	♡9
12	♢10	♢9	♢7	♢A
13	♢J	♣J	♢K	♢5

West wins 11 tricks.

3.

North declarer at four spades.

Trick	E	S	W	N
1	♣2	♣3	♣10	♣J
2	♠9	♠Q	♠2	♠4
3	♠A	♠3	♠10	♠6
4	♡10	♡J	♡K	♡A
5	♡3	♡6	♡7	♡Q
6	♡5	♠5	♡8	♡2
7	♢K	♢4	♢3	♢10
8	♢2	♢7	♢Q	♢A
9	♢5	♠8	♡9	♡4
10	♣8	♣A	♣5	♣Q
11	♣9	♣4	♣7	♠7
12	♣K	♣6	♠J	♠K
13	♢9	♢8	♢6	♢J

North wins 11 tricks.

4.

East declarer at four spades.

Trick	S	W	N	E
1	♣Q	♣5	♣3	♣A
2	♠3	♠5	♠Q	♠J
3	♣9	♣K	♣4	♣2
4	♢5	♢2	♢6	♢10
5	♠4	♠6	♠2	♠10
6	♠K	♠A	♣6	♠7
7	♢7	♢3	♢8	♢Q
8	♡Q	♡A	♡7	♡J
9	♡6	♡2	♡3	♡10
10	♢9	♢4	♢J	♢A
11	♡8	♡4	♣8	♠9
12	♣10	♡9	♢K	♠8
13	♣J	♣7	♡K	♡5

East wins 11 tricks.

COMMENTS ON LESSON THREE HANDS

In hand one with no losing cards to trump in the dummy, declarer immediately leads trumps after winning the first club in the dummy. East should play his lowest spade, the eight. Many new players, as defenders in this position, would (erroneously) play the king. The play of a high card by a defender, particularly playing second-hand, should have a valid reason as some expectancy of taking a trick or promoting a *probable* trick for partner. On the first lead of trumps from the dummy, declarer will finesse against the missing king by playing the jack or queen. After this trick, note that there are still two spades, the king and 10, remaining in the defenders' combined hands and since there is no certainty that they are divided one apiece, declarer can re-enter dummy by playing the ace of hearts and repeat the spade finesse. After the second round of spades, East's king is known to be alone and may be captured by laying down the ace. A second point to be noted is that in finessing against the missing queen of hearts, declarer leads a low heart from dummy *towards* the king-jack. To lead the jack towards the ace would be fatal since in order to lead an honor for a finesse, it is necessary to have the card directly beneath, in rank, the led card, viz., the 10 in this case.

Hand two illustrates another case of deferring trump leads until *after* declarer has trumped the four and eight of spades in dummy. Cashing the ace of clubs, then trumping a club affords declarer a positive reentry to his hand for the purpose of trumping the remaining spade. To attempt the diamond finesse early could be fatal if it failed since the defenders could switch to trumps, preventing the trumping of the losing spades in the dummy.

On hand three, a common error of new students is in attacking the heart suit, either to lead a low heart from North towards dummy's jack or to lead the queen from the North hand. Both are completely incorrect since they permit the defender sitting West to capture, undeservedly, a trick with the king. By leading a heart from the dummy towards the ace-queen and taking the finesse, declarer avoids losing a trick to the king and can subsequently trump both losing low hearts in the dummy. The hand furnishes an excellent example of an obligatory finesse. Do not make the error of immediately cashing the ace of clubs at trick two. This card will be needed for the subsequent heart finesse, should the opponents not lead hearts. Trumping low hearts will provide entries (to dummy) for the double diamond finesse.

Hand four. With no losers to be trumped in the dummy, declarer will lead trumps immediately. In order to finesse against the missing king-queen of spades, trump leads must come from the East hand *towards* the ace. Hence, the first club lead should be taken in the East hand since that is where you want the lead to be.

Lesson IV

Choice of Suit
by
The Opening Bidder

LESSON FOUR

CHOICE OF SUIT BY OPENER

Up to the present, the reader's problem in deciding whether to open the bidding was guided solely by two factors - did the hand have 13 or more points and a biddable suit? If both were present, he opened the bidding; otherwise, he passed. It was as simple as ABC.

But a hand of 13 cards may frequently include two or three suits of four cards each or longer. Thus there is a problem, not only whether to bid but *which suit to bid first.*

Modern bidding is based on three key points -

1 - The opening bidder promises *to bid again* to any response which is less than game in order to permit partner to show possible additional values unless partner's first response was weak and limited the amount of strength present. These weak responses are:

(a) One no trump - maximum of 10 points;

(b) Single raise of partner's suit - maximum, 12 points;

(c) Jumps of *more than one in a new suit* as a shut-out. Shows a long solid or semi-solid suit and a hand weak in high card strength.

2 - From two or more suits, the opener will select as his first choice, the suit that will best portray, in later possible rebidding, the comparative lengths of suits to be shown and the strength of the hand as a whole.

3 - The first suit chosen will be the suit that will make it as easy as possible for both the opening bidder and his partner to rebid. This is known as the principle of preparedness or anticipation. Another term could be 'looking ahead.'

In the swaddling clothes days of bridge, there were two basic rules which governed the opening bidder's decision as to which of two or more suits to bid first. Number one was to bid the suit higher in rank first if the suits were of equal length. The second rule was always to bid the longer suit first.

While to some extent these rules still apply in spirit, there are so many exceptions that they can scarcely be called 'rules' any longer.

1 - HOLDING TWO TOUCHING SUITS OF EQUAL LENGTH

RULE - Always bid the HIGHER in rank first.

Before proceeding, it might be well to refresh the student's memory as to what is meant by the term 'touching.'

Suits, you will remember, have rank in relation to each other. Suit rank played a determining role in the selection of partners where two or more players 'cut' the same sized card and also in bidding where a bid of 'three spades,' let us say, is higher than a bid of three hearts, diamonds or clubs. Suits rank as follows:

1 - Spades
2 - Hearts
3 - Diamonds
4 - Clubs

Suits that are neighbors in rank are said to be touching. Thus hearts touch both spades above and diamonds below; diamonds touch hearts and clubs; spades touch hearts and clubs touch diamonds.

♠ AQJ8	♠ 64	♠ 3
♡ AK64	♡ 10	♡ AJ876
◇ 85	◇ A6543	◇ KQJ98
♣ 1098	♣ AK1098	♣ K2
Bid one spade	Bid one diamond	Bid one heart

Note that in the first two of the three examples, the lower ranking suit is considerably the stronger. Yet the higher ranking suit is the correct choice in all three cases.

Why?

ANSWER - By opening the bidding with the higher ranking of two suits, you enable your partner to express a preference without increasing the contract.

Suppose, holding the first of the three hands, the complete partnership holdings were:

YOU, OPENER	PARTNER, RESPONDER
♠ A Q J 8	♠ 10 7 5
♡ A K 6 4	♡ J 2
◇ 8 5	◇ K 10 6 2
♣ 10 9 8	♣ K J 6 2

If you opened the bidding with one spade and there had been no intervening bid by the opponents, the bidding could proceed:

YOU	PARTNER
One spade	One no trump
Two hearts	

Since your partner holds a greater number of spades than hearts, he can return you to your first suit, spades, by bidding 'two spades' *without increasing the number of tricks your side must win to fulfill the contract.*

Let's suppose that the hand had been opened incorrectly with one heart. The partner holds the same hand and the bidding now proceeds:

YOU	PARTNER
One heart	One no trump
Two spades	Three hearts !

Note that when the suits were opened in the opposite order of rank, your partner had to increase the contract to 'three' in order to indicate which suit he liked the better. With your weak hand, this would be fatal.

In bridge, telling one's partner which of his suits you prefer is termed 'expressing a preference.' When preference is shown as cheaply as possible, it *does not show good supporting cards* for the preferred suit - merely that more cards are held in that suit than another!

A MATTER OF PREFERENCE

I would like to emphasize that a preference is based on the number of cards held in each of partner's suits, not the size of these cards. For example, if my partner had opened with one spade, later bid two hearts over my response of one no trump and I held - ♠ 863 ♡ AQ ◇ K1086 ♣ J632

I would give a spade preference by bidding 'two spades' since I held three spades as against two hearts, even though the latter were larger. With the same number of each, then size becomes the determining factor in expressing a preference.

When one's partner has bid two or more suits, it stands to reason that you may hold approximately the same number of cards in each of his suits or you may have far better support, numerically, for one of his suits than another.

For example, let's suppose your partner has opened the bidding with one spade and over your two club response, has rebid with two hearts. You hold each of the following hands:

(a)	(b)	(c)
♠ J86	♠ 9864	♠ Q1087
♡ K2	♡ 2	♡ A2
◇ 743	◇ 7653	◇ Q7
♣ AQ986	♣ AKQ8	♣ AQJ98

With (a) you would rebid two spades; with (b) three spades and with (c), four spades.

Where a preference is given as cheaply as possible as in (a), it is known as a 'simple preference'; where the bidding is jumped simultaneously with the preference as in (b) and (c), it is known as a jump preference.

The jump preference, in effect, says to partner, "I like this suit far better than the other." In other words, it shows a decided liking for the supported suit. Further, since the contract has been raised, the jump preference promises additional values over and above those needed for any previous bid. The subject of preferences in rebidding will be fully discussed in Lesson Seven.

Bidding one's suits in the proper order facilitates partner's responses in every situation.

CHOICE OF TWO SUITS OF EQUAL LENGTH

FROM TWO FIVE CARD OR SIX CARD SUITS -

RULE - Bid the higher in rank first, regardless of which is the stronger. Whether the suits touch or not has no bearing.

(d)	(e)	(f)	(g)
♠ AJ643	♠ 103	♠ A87654	♠ 2
♡ 103	♡ KJ1087	♡ KQJ987	♡ K10987
◇ AK862	◇ 4	◇ void	◇ AQJ64
♣ 3	♣ AQJ98	♣ 3	♣ A2
One spade	One heart	One spade	One heart

So far, so good. Nothing really complicated there. It is in the bidding of hands containing four card suits or suits of unequal lengths that we find apparent contradictions. If, in studying this text, the student will reason along with the author and his teacher, reasons for each selection will soon be apparent.

THE BIDDING OF FOUR CARD SUITS

TWO FOUR CARD SUITS THAT TOUCH

RULE - Bid the higher in rank first.

(h)	(i)	(j)
♠ AKJ6	♠ AQ	♠ K10
♡ AQ105	♡ AJ64	♡ 876
◇ 65	◇ KQ63	◇ AQ43
♣ J87	♣ 1032	♣ AQ102

This follows the standard practice that with touching suits of equal length, the higher-ranking is bid first.

TWO FOUR CARD SUITS, BOTH BLACK

RULE - With four clubs and four spades, bid the club suit first

(k)	(l)
♠ AKJ6	♠ KQJ6
♡ 1087	♡ A2
◇ 62	◇ K109
♣ AQ109	♣ AQJ2
One club	One club

REASON - Suppose, with hand (k), you opened the bidding with one club and the bidding proceeds:

YOU	PARTNER
One club	One diamond (supposed response)
One spade	

Had you *incorrectly* opened with one spade, we would have:

YOU	PARTNER
One spade	Two !! diamonds
Three !!! clubs	

By opening with one club, the partnership was able to show thrée suits, still remain at the one level of bidding. With the opening bid of one spade, the partner was forced to bid 'two' to show his suit and you were compelled to bid 'three' in order to show your second suit.

If you have a weak opening bid as (k), common sense dictates that you would like to show both of your suits but that it must be accomplished economically and safely until partner's bidding has indicated sufficient strength or supporting fit to warrant the higher contract.

If the partner (responder) is weak, the choice of the club suit makes his response far easier. *Try bidding over a spade and see how much more difficult it is than over a club.* There are many hands where the responder holds from six to nine points and could have bid 'one' of his suit had you opened with one club but couldn't bid 'two' if you opened with a spade since the necessary 10 or more points were lacking. In these cases, partner's response would probably be one no trump, and the possibility of finding the best suit is appreciably diminished.

As long as your two four card suits are clubs and spades, *open with the club suit!!!* If your hand is weak, the club opening makes your possible rebid easier and cheaper. If partner's hand is weak, his response is made easier.

FOUR CARD SUITS OF DIFFERENT COLORS, NOT TOUCHING

Hearts and diamonds are red - clubs and spades are black. Take one four card suit of each, put them in the same hand and you'll have a hand containing two four-carders of different colors.

Remember our order of suit rank that determined touching suits?

1	2	3	4
SPADES	HEARTS	DIAMONDS	CLUBS

In the listing above, you will observe the number above each suit. Select two even numbers or two odd numbers and you will have the only two possible combinations of suits of different colors that do not touch.

Simple, isn't it?

Since you hold two four card suits, your remaining five cards must be divided 3 - 2. If they were divided 4 - 1 or 5 - 0, then you would have a third suit of four or more cards.

RULE - Open the bidding with the suit ranking beneath your doubleton.

REASON - It is only logical to suppose that your partner will have the most cards in the suit where you hold the fewest. Let's suppose you were fortunate enough to be dealt a hand with 10 spades. That would leave only three spades to be divided between the remaining three players. If each of these three players *(including your partner)* holds his share, each will have one spade. This is what bridge-players term *'normal expectancy.'*

Conversely, let's suppose you're dealt a hand containing only one spade. This leaves 12 spades to be divided between the other three players and your partner's normal expectancy should be four spades.

Boiled down, you can normally expect your partner to hold the greatest number of cards in the suit where you have the fewest and vice-versa. By opening the bidding with the suit beneath your doubleton, you simplify partner's expected response.

EXAMPLES

♠ AQ108
♡ 63
♢ AQ64
♣ 1082

With the accompanying hand to the left, open the bidding with one diamond. Over the anticipated heart response, rebid with one spade.

♠ 874
♡ AK54
♢ 62
♣ AJ87

Here we open with a club, expecting our partner to bid a diamond over which we will rebid one heart.

1 - Always anticipate what partner's most likely response will be and choose your bids accordingly, making it easy for him to respond and you to rebid.

2 - The bid of a second suit at the one range by the opening bidder *does not* show any additional values in the opening bidder's hand in excess of opening bid requirements.

For example, I have opened the bidding with a club in the second example. My partner has responded with one diamond and I have rebid with one heart. My heart bid does not show any more strength than that already promised by my opening bid of one club. The heart rebid merely indicates four or more hearts and is an effort to explore the hand looking for a 'fit' between the partnership.

THREE FOUR CARD SUITS

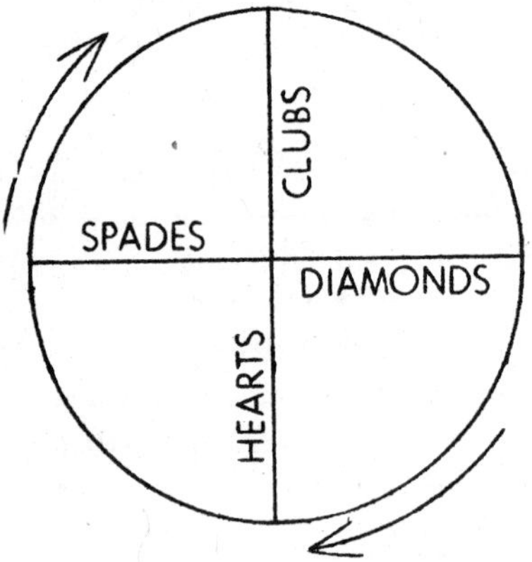

Your choice of which suit to bid first will be made very simple if you remember an easy *RULE - Open the bidding with the suit ranking beneath your singleton.*

By inspecting the wheel in the accompanying diagram, you will see that it has four spokes, each representing a suit. The wheel turns clockwise as do the arrows along its perimiter. Thus diamonds are below hearts, hearts below spades, clubs below diamonds and everything is the same as before with the somewhat new proviso that spades are below clubs.

EXAMPLES OF CHOICE

♠ 8	♠ KQ64	♠ KJ108	♠ K1086
♡ KQ75	♡ 8	♡ KQ76	♡ AQ76
◇ AJ108	◇ QJ76	◇ 5	◇ AQ43
♣ KQ65	♣ AQJ9	♣ AJ54	♣ 2
One heart	One diamond	One club	One spade

In the above cases, you have been singularly fortunate that all of the suits shown have been good, biddable four-carders. Every now and then, you will find that the suit beneath the singleton does not meet the biddability requirement that the four card suit contains at least three points in high cards but that the other suits do meet biddability requirements.

What suit do you bid, then?

ANSWER - If the suit beneath the singleton is not too far below biddability standards, bid it nevertheless. I would set a four card suit headed by the jack as the absolute minimum. Later, of course, the second or third suit shown by the partnership can be headed by literally nothing as long as it contains four or more cards. Biddability, as stated in the second lesson, applies only to the first suit bid by the partnership.

If the suit ranking beneath the singleton is completely 'broke' as 6432 and the hand contains the values for an opening bid, open the bidding with the suit beneath your normal choice.

EXAMPLES

♠ 8	♠ AK65
♡ 8432	♡ 7
◇ AKJ6	◇ 7543
♣ AQ107	♣ AQ109
One diamond	One club

No text on bidding could possibly hope to cover the billions of combinations possible with a deck of 52 cards. No rules can be absolutely rigid. When the opening bidder has a choice between bidding a suit slightly beneath minimum biddable requirements or opening with the wrong suit, choose the shaded suit as the lesser of the evils. *It is far better* to select the shaded suit and give yourself an easy, prepared rebid than to select a suit merely because it has high cards and later find yourself in an awkward dilemma for rebids.

CHOICE OF TWO SUITS OF UNEQUAL LENGTH

The problem of which suit to bid first, one being longer than the other, is determined by three factors. These are:

1 - Which suit is the longer;
2 - Relative rank of the suits;
3 - High card strength of the entire hand.

The order in which suits are bid, with subsequent rebids, form one of the fascinating features of modern bidding. Done with precision, it is as though each successive bid painted with accurate brush strokes, an exact picture of the bidder's holding.

A FIVE CARD AND A FOUR CARD SUIT

If the five carder is higher in rank, bid it first.

(a)

♠ A 10 8 7 6	♠ 7 6
♡ A K Q 5	♡ K J 10 8 7
◊ J 2	◊ 3 2
♣ 8 7	♣ A K Q J
One spade	One heart

Note in the above, the question of which suit to bid first is not guided by which suit is the stronger but purely by length and rank. Always bid the longer first, if higher ranking.

If the five card suit is lower in rank and the suits are not touching, it should be bid first.

(b)

♠ A J 10 9	♠ A Q J 10
♡ 6 5	♡ 7
◊ A Q 7 6 5	◊ J 3 2
♣ J 2	♣ A Q 10 8 7
One diamond	One club

If the five-carder is lower in rank and the suits touch -

1 - With less than 18 points, treat the suits as though they were equal in length and bid the higher-ranking suit first.

2 - With 18 or more points, bid the longer, lower-ranking suit first.

(c)

♠ A Q 10 8	♠ A Q J 8
♡ K Q 7 6 5	♡ K Q 10 8 7
◊ 7 4	◊ K 4
♣ 8 2	♣ A 2
One spade	One heart

This sharp cleavage calls for more than a word of explanation. In the first two cases (a), where the five card suit was higher in rank; in (b), where the five card suit was lower in rank and not touching, an easy rebid for the opening bidder was always available for any possible response by partner.

Supposing, holding the first hand in (a), the bidding had been-

YOU	PARTNER
One spade	One no trump
Two hearts	

♠ A 10 8 7 6
♡ A K Q 5
◇ J 2
♣ 8 7
Repeated for convenience

Now your partner can readily express his preference by either passing two hearts or by taking you back to your original suit, spades, by bidding 'two spades.' In either event, you had an easy second bid and if your partner had a weak hand, he had an easy rebid, too.

In (b), the first hand is shown to the left. If the bidding went-

♠ A J 10 9
♡ 6 5
◇ A Q 7 6 5
♣ J 2
Repeated for convenience.

YOU	PARTNER
One diamond	One heart
One spade	

Again, you have an easy rebid. With your weak hand, you have kept the bidding low, yet have been able to show both of your suits and still contract for only seven tricks. This is in line with our previously discussed principle of preparedness.

Had your partner responded with 'two clubs' in the last bidding example instead of 'one heart' as -

YOU	PARTNER
One diamond	Two clubs
Two diamonds	

Your rebid should be two diamonds rather than two spades. You cannot afford to show your second suit, spades, since now your partner to show a preference for your first suit, diamonds, *he must increase the bidding to 'three.'* You are contracting for nine tricks with a weak hand and a doubtful expectancy of winning them if your partner is weak. So, while you would like to show both your suits - you can't afford to show a second suit *with a weak hand if partner's preference for the first suit will increase the bidding to the three level.*

It is true that there are cases where the longer suit may be bid first with the expectancy of bidding the shorter, higher ranking suit later at a higher level. Since in these cases the suits are bid in the reverse order of rank, they are known as 'reverses' and are fully discussed in the next few pages.

♠ AQ108
♡ KQ765
◇ 74
♣ 82
Repeated for convenience.

In the third set of bidding examples (c), you had two hands with similar distribution, 5-4, in touching suits but varying in high card strength. The first is shown to the left.

Here you would like to bid your longer heart suit first, naturally. Let's suppose you do as:

YOU	PARTNER
One heart	One no trump
Two spades ?	Three hearts ?

Again your partner's preference for your first suit forced the bidding to the three level and you can't afford that luxury with your weak hand. There are two things you would like to do on this and other two-suited hands. These are:

1 - Show both suits;
2 - Bid the longer suit first.

But you can't make bricks without straw, and with only five and four card suits, and little high card strength, you may not be able to win nine tricks. Accordingly, with 13 to 17 point you can't afford to bid more than you are reasonably certain of making until partner has evidenced, through his bidding, the necessary additional high cards or supporting fit.

So with 5-4 distribution, where the suits touch, where the shorter suit is the higher-ranking and the hand is weak, *we treat the suits as though they were of equal length and bid the higher-ranking suit first.*

The reader may ask, **"How will my partner know my second suit is longer, since I bid them exactly as though they were touching suits of equal length?"**

The answer is - **"He won't."** He may think your suits are equal in length.

BUT - which would you say is the more important - to be able, with a weak hand, to show both suits safely or to show the relative length of each and get too high in the process.

It would be nice, of course, always to bid our longer suit first but sometimes, it's a luxury we just can't afford.

♠ AQJ8
♡ KQ1087
◊ K4
♣ A2
Repeated for convenience

Let's take the second hand from (c) on page 128. Now, even if partner has very little, you can afford to play a nine trick contract or even a game contract because your hand is so powerful. Here you can afford to show the relative length of your suits, even though it would invite a preference that could increase the contract. The bidding would go -

YOU	PARTNER
One heart	One no trump
Two spades	

TOUCHING SIX AND FIVE CARD SUITS

A hand containing two touching suits, one of six cards, the other of five - should be bid similarly to touching five-four combinations with slightly lessened requirements for reversing.

RULE - If the six-carder is higher in rank, bid it first. If the six-carder is lower in rank, bid it first only with 16 or more points.

♠ A108765	♠ AQ876	♠ 8	♠ KQJ87
♡ AK1087	♡ KQ7654	♡ AJ1087	♡ AQ6543
◊ 3	◊ 5	◊ KQ10876	◊ A
♣ 2	♣ 4	♣ 3	♣ 7
One spade	One spade	One heart	One heart

It is far better, with weak hands, to show both suits easily even though it may mean fibbing a little over the comparative length of both suits than to give a precise picture of your distribution and as a consequence, tangling yourself up in future rebidding and mis-stating the strength of the entire hand.

SIX AND FIVE CARD SUITS, NOT TOUCHING

RULE - Bid the six card suit first

A SIX AND A FOUR CARD SUIT

RULE - Bid the six card suit first

SEVEN-SIX, SEVEN-FIVE AND SEVEN-FOUR

RULE - Bid the seven card suit first.

REVERSE BIDDING

On earlier pages of this lesson, I have mentioned the terms 'reverse bidding' and 'reverses.

♠ AJ876
♡ AJ876
◇ A2
♣ 3

Until now, you have been taught to bid two or more suits in the same hand in the most convenient and natural manner. Holding the hand to the left, you would open the bidding with one spade, the higher-ranking of the two suits. They are touching and of equal length.

But let's suppose, on the other hand, you heard your partner open the bidding with one heart. Later, over your response of two clubs, your partner's next bid is two spades.

He's not bidding naturally, is he? If his suits were of equal length, he would have first bid one spade.

So the fact that he bid them in backward order, hearts before spades, should tell you something.

That 'something' is that the suits are NOT OF EQUAL LENGTH! In other words, partner bid the longer suit first, regardless of suit rank.

That's a reverse bid!

The requirements for a reverse are:

1 - The first bid suit is longer than the second;
2 - The first bid suit is lower-ranking than the second;
3 - The hand itself is very strong (minimum of 18 points with 5-4 distribution, 16 points with 6-5).
4 - The second suit bid by opener is shown at a higher bidding level than the first.

Let's take an example of normal, routine bidding.

YOU	PARTNER
One spade	One no trump
Two hearts	

If your partner has a weak hand and likes hearts better than spades, he can pass; if he likes spades better, all he has to do is bid two spades. Either way, he could express a preference without increasing the contract.

Yet - suppose we reversed the bidding so that it went:

YOU, OPENER	PARTNER, RESPONDER
One heart	One no trump
Two spades	

Note now that partner, to express a preference for your first suit, hearts, must increase the contract from 'two' to 'three.'

Since reverse bidding may very well obtain a preference from partner that will force the bidding to the three level, it stands to reason that a reverse not only requires more strength than the conventional 13 point opening but better suits as well.

HOW TO RECOGNIZE REVERSE BIDDING

To reverse the bidding, *the second suit must be shorter than the first suit and the second suit must be bid at a higher level than the first bid suit.* Case (a) illustrates a reverse.

(a)

YOU	PARTNER
One diamond	One spade
Two hearts	

But this is not:

(b)

YOU	PARTNER
One diamond	One heart
One spade	

"Why not,?" you ask. "My spade suit is shorter and higher ranking than my first suit, diamonds."

True. But it wasn't shown at a higher level than the first suit. They were both shown at the one level. You're not reversing in (b). You're bidding normally, using the principle of preparedness, in order to show both suits conveniently and cheaply.

With the bidding in sequence (b), you could hold any of the following hands:

(c)	(d)	(e)	(f)
♠ AJ87	♠ AQ65	♠ J876	♠ K987
♡ K2	♡ 3	♡ A4	♡ 2
◇ AJ432	◇ AQ52	◇ KQJ9	◇ AQ5432
♣ K2	♣ K1098	♣ AQ4	♣ A2

In the case of hand (f), it is far better to show the spade suit at the one level than rebid with two diamonds. It is more valuable (and certainly cheaper) to show your partner a second suit than to show the first suit to be rebiddable and suppress the second suit.

However, had your partner responded with two clubs instead of one heart in bidding sequence (b), your correct rebid with hand (f) would be two diamonds, not two spades since as you will discover, the hand is not strong enough to immediately reverse the bidding.

But the important thing to remember is this - *showing a second, higher-ranking suit at the one level is not a reverse.*

REQUIREMENTS TO REVERSE THE BIDDING

DISTRIBUTION	TOTAL POINTS REQUIRED MINIMUM
5 - 4	18
6 - 5	16
6 - 4	16

♠ A432
♡ A5432
◊ A4
♣ A5

In all cases involving a reverse, the suits themselves should have some solidity and body. To reverse the bidding holding the hand to the left with the following bidding would be highly dangerous.

YOU	PARTNER
One heart	Two clubs
?	

I prefer a rebid of two no trump rather than two spades due to the lack of solidity of the suits.

♠ AKJ6
♡ AK1097
◊ J2
♣ 95

However, had your hand been that shown to the left, then a two spade rebid would be correct.

AN IMMEDIATE REVERSE TO THE TWO LEVEL

When the opening bidder bids a second suit that is higher ranking than his first suit and the second suit is shown at the two-level, the bidding sequence indicates the following:

1 - That the first bid, lower-ranking suit is longer than the second;

2 - That the opener's hand is sufficiently strong to invite a preference that could carry the bidding to the three level.

Here is an example -

YOU	PARTNER
One diamond	Two clubs
Two spades	

By an immediate reverse is meant that the second, higher-ranking suit is the opening bidder's first rebid.

Let's see what the reverse accomplishes..

First, it establishes the first bid suit as being rebiddable, of five cards or longer, without the suit ever having been rebid.

How is that accomplished?

Simply.

You see, the moment a player reverses the bidding, he shows that the first suit is longer than the second. Since the second must be at least four cards in length, the first suit to be longer must be at least five cards in length.

Second, the opening bidder's hand, in order to reverse, must meet the minimum point count requirements shown on page 134. *You CANNOT reverse the bidding merely because you have two suits of unequal length or because you have a strong hand. BOTH conditions must be present to justify a reverse. One alone will not do!*

(a)
♠ KQ108
♡ AQ765
◇ J7
♣ AQ

Hand (a) to the left can be reversed. The bidding should be opened with one heart and the spade suit shown as the rebid. The hand contains a five card suit, a higher-ranking four card suit and 20 points.

(b)
♠ KQ108
♡ AQ765
◇ J7
♣ 43

With hand (b), you would open the bidding with one spade, later, if possible, show the heart suit. The hand is not strong enough to reverse and your object is to show both suits without getting too high in the process, unless partner shows a strong hand.

It is not necessary that the suits be touching to reverse.

(c)

	OPENER	PARTNER
♠ K 10		
♡ A Q J 8	One club	One spade
◊ J 5	Two hearts	
♣ A Q 7 6 5		

Hand (c) and the accompanying bidding illustrate reverse bidding with a hand containing non-touching suits.

(d)

♠ K 10
♡ K J 9 8
◊ 7 6
♣ A Q 7 6 5

Holding hand (d), our opening bid would be one club. Should partner respond with one spade, our rebid would be two clubs. The hand is not strong enough to reverse. Had partner responded with one diamond, our rebid would have been simple - one heart. This, as was explained on pages 133 and 134, is not a reverse - simply normal *one-over-one* bidding by the opening bidder showing four or more hearts in the opening bidder's hand.

The strength of an opening bid can vary from a bare minimum 13 points to a hand with 20 points or more. It is a player's first rebid (his second bid) which best portrays his hand and you will learn about rebidding in Lessons Six and Seven.

THE SEMI-FORCING PRINCIPLE OF REVERSES

There are several types of bids - so far as making one's partner bid or bid again.

The first is any bid *which is forcing to game*. This is a bid which says, **"Partner, you must keep on bidding with me until our side has reached a game contract."**

The second type is *forcing for one round*. This is a bid to which partner *must* respond at least once.

The third type is known as *semi-forcing*. This is a bid which shows great strength and *strongly invites* partner to bid or bid again with any values in excess of those which may have already been shown by previous bids. Reverses are semi-forcing. They may be passed by a weak partner.

The fourth and last type is *non-forcing*. These are bids which show little strength and, if partner is weak, can be passed.

You can see the reason for needing strong hands and good suits to reverse the bidding. Since reverses are semi-forcing, there is a great likelihood that partner will bid again and if you don't have the values promised by the reverse, the result will be that you'll have bid more than you can make.

SUBSEQUENT (LATER) REVERSES AT THE TWO LEVEL

By a subsequent reverse, I mean that the opening bidder didn't reverse the bidding at his first opportunity to rebid but he did so at his second chance to rebid. For example -

(e)	YOU	PARTNER
♠ 3	One club	One spade
♡ KJ62	Two clubs	Two diamonds
◊ Q64	Two hearts	
♠ AKJ98		

Later reverses do not show the 16 or 18 points required for immediate reverses but, rather, secondary suits which can be shown cheaply without increasing the contract.

You see, partner's two diamond bid is forcing on you to bid again (as you will discover in Lessons Six and Seven on rebidding). Therefore, you must make another bid.

There's no advantage to rebidding 'three clubs.' You've already told your partner with your two club rebid that your club suit is rebiddable. It isn't good enough to be twice-rebiddable. Two no trump would be a bad bid since you hold a singleton of partner's spade suit and the hand lacks the necessary high card strength for that bid.

Since you can't pass, the alternatives are between a bid of two hearts and a raise to three diamonds. You can see that you can bid two hearts, still leave room for a three diamond bid later, if desired. Moreover, knowing that you hold hearts may be the very thing partner needs to hear in order to bid no trump safely.

SUBSEQUENT (LATER) REVERSES AT THE THREE LEVEL

The later reverse to the three level is similar to its predecessor, the later reverse to the two level, in that it does not show the high card values of an immediate reverse but rather, is an attempt to find a fit in a later suit or show some previously undisclosed suit in an effort to reach a better or higher contract.

This bid will usually show 6 - 4 distribution and from 15 to 17 points.

(f)	YOU	PARTNER
♠ K7	One club	One spade
♡ AJ108	Two clubs	Two no trump
◊ 5	Three hearts	
♣ AQ9754		

The three heart rebid is constructive, evinces a cautious desire in possibly reaching a game contract. It explores the possibility of partner having a four card heart holding or a rebiddable spade suit or a club fit or enough diamond stoppers plus additional high cards to make three no trump a desirable contract.

I might add at this point that when a hand shapes up as a misfit, and many hands do, discretion is the better part of valor. It is often better, when a player has already shown his entire values in the earlier bidding stages, to pass, even though he is unable to support any of partner's suits, rather than fumble around showing new short suits at higher levels in the faint and remote hope of finally hitting pay-dirt.

First, you can easily go from bad to worse. Next, you may get doubled whereas the lower bid by your partner has not been doubled. Third, your partner may very correctly construe additional voluntary rebids by you as signs of extra, undisclosed strength whereas you are merely trying to escape from what you consider a bad contract.

Actually, what you may consider a bad contract could possibly be the best one for the combined hands.

REVERSING WITH A THREE-SUITER

There are two types of three-suited hands. The first, discussed on pages 126 and 127, are hands containing three suits, each of four cards. A reverse would be impossible with this type of hand since, to reverse, one suit must be longer than the other.

The other type of three suiter has a 5 - 4 - 4 suit pattern.

RULE - Open in all cases with the five-carder. If you can rebid at the one level with one of your four card suits, do so. If both four card suits can be shown at the one level as a rebid, bid the cheaper. A reverse to the two level as a rebid would promise a minimum of 18 points.

(a)
♠ KQ86
♡ KJ72
◇ void
♣ AJ976

Open (a) with one club. If partner responds with one diamond, rebid with one heart. If partner bids a heart or a spade, raise to three of that suit.

(b)
♠ void
♡ KJ109
◇ AJ1086
♣ KQ64

Open (b) with one diamond. If partner bids one spade, rebid with two clubs. Don't reverse by bidding two hearts. Above all, don't bid two no trump 'because you have everything else stopped.' Voluntary rebids of two no trump show that the hand 'fits,' rather than a misfit.

(c)
♠ void
♡ AQJ9
◇ AJ1086
♣ A987

Again you open with one diamond and partner bids one spade, hitting your void. Even though your hand totals 19 points, more than enough for a reverse to two hearts, two clubs is the correct rebid.

Let me show you why. The moment your partner bid spades, the hand became a misfit. Therefore, you should be careful not to get too high. Your partner, with a weak hand, can pass two clubs. On the other hand, if you reverse the bidding with two hearts, he will probably bid again since the reverse is semi-forcing.

Unless pretty well assured that game is makeable, don't make a forcing or semi-forcing rebid until you know in what suit the partnership hands will play.

IN RETROSPECT

To cheer you up, let me tell you that this lesson on 'Choice of Suit' is the most difficult of the course. It contains many apparent contradictions and exceptions.

But basically - it boils down to one thing - you bid in proportion to your high cards and suit lengths just as though, in entering a department store, you purchase according to the money in your purse.

QUIZ FOUR

1 - What is meant by the principle of preparedness?

2 - Does showing a second suit at the one level by the opening bidder show any values in excess of those already promised by the opening bid?

3 - With three four card suits, all biddable, how would you select the correct suit for the opening bid?

4 - Can you reverse the bidding with suits of equal length?

5 - What is your opening bid with each of the following hands?

(a)	(b)	(c)
♠ KJ109	♠ A	♠ J10987
♡ AKJ7	♡ QJ1074	♡ AQJ107
◇ 864	◇ 86	◇ AK
♣ A3	♣ KQ1098	♣ 3
(d)	**(e)**	**(f)**
♠ AKJ9	♠ 83	♠ KJ86
♡ 87	♡ KQ109	♡ 2
◇ 1094	◇ Q109	◇ KJ109
♣ KQJ5	♣ AK64	♣ AQ109
(g)	**(h)**	**(i)**
♠ KQ109	♠ AJ64	♠ AK43
♡ AJ107	♡ 2	♡ KQ752
◇ A1086	◇ 7543	◇ J8
♣ 2	♣ AK109	♣ 64
(j)	**(k)**	**(l)**
♠ J	♠ KQ84	♠ AJ8765
♡ KQJ9	♡ AQ543	♡ 2
◇ AQ872	◇ void	◇ void
♣ AQ4	♣ KJ76	♣ KQJ976

ANSWERS TO QUIZ FOUR

1 - Selecting, from two or more suits, for the opening bid the suit which will make it as easy as possible for partner to make his anticipated response and facilitate opener's most likely rebid.

2 - No.

3 - The suit ranking beneath the singleton.

4 - No.

5 - (a) One spade; (b) one heart; (c) one spade; (d) one club; (e) one heart; (f) one diamond; (g) one spade; (h) one club; (i) one spade; (j) one diamond; (k) one heart; (l) one spade.

LESSON FOUR
HANDS

1.

North: ♠ 8643 ♡ 52 ◇ AQ3 ♣ AK52

West: ♠ K7 ♡ AJ7 ◇ K542 ♣ QJ109

East: ♠ J52 ♡ 1094 ◇ J1096 ♣ 876

South: ♠ AQ109 ♡ KQ863 ◇ 87 ♣ 43

South dealer - The bidding

South	West	North	East
1 sp.	pass	2 cl.	pass
2 hts.	pass	4 sp.	pass
pass	pass		

Opening lead, queen of clubs.

2.

North: ♠ A8 ♡ KJ109 ◇ 10987 ♣ QJ10

West: ♠ Q752 ♡ 43 ◇ AKJ5 ♣ K86

East: ♠ J1094 ♡ Q876 ◇ Q4 ♣ A32

South: ♠ K63 ♡ A52 ◇ 632 ♣ 9754

West dealer - The bidding

West	North	East	South
1 dia.	pass	1 ht.	pass
1 sp.	pass	2 sp.	pass
pass	pass		

Opening lead, queen of clubs.

3.

North: ♠ AJ1074 ♡ KQ10852 ◇ A ♣ 2

West: ♠ Q52 ♡ J976 ◇ K1083 ♣ Q5

East: ♠ K3 ♡ 3 ◇ J6542 ♣ K9743

South: ♠ 986 ♡ A4 ◇ Q97 ♣ AJ1086

North dealer - The bidding

North	East	South	West
1 ht.	pass	2 cl.	pass
2 sp.	pass	3 cl.	pass
3 sp.	pass	4 sp.	pass
pass	pass		

Opening lead, diamond four.

4.

North: ♠ A5 ♡ K7 ◇ KJ76 ♣ 96432

West: ♠ J3 ♡ J9 ◇ AQ10532 ♣ K105

East: ♠ KQ1084 ♡ AQ10542 ◇ void ♣ AJ

South: ♠ 9762 ♡ 863 ◇ 984 ♣ Q87

East dealer - The bidding

East	South	West	North
1 ht.	pass	2 dia.	pass
2 sp.	pass	2 no tr.	pass
3 sp.	pass	4 hts.	pass
pass	pass		

Opening lead, club seven.

SOLUTIONS TO LESSON FOUR HANDS

1

South declarer at four spades.

Trick	W	N	E	S
1	♣Q	♣K	♣6	♣3
2	♡A	♡2	♡4	♡Q
3	♣9	♣A	♣7	♣4
4	♠K	♠3	♠2	♠9
5	♣J	♣2	♣8	♠10
6	♡7	♡5	♡9	♡K
7	♡J	♠8	♡10	♡3
8	♠7	♠4	♠5	♠Q
9	♢2	♠6	♠J	♠A
10	♢4	♢3	♢6	♡8
11	♢5	♣5	♢9	♡6
12	♢K	♢A	♢10	♢7
13	♣10	♢Q	♢J	♢8

South wins 11 tricks. West is squeezed at trick 11.

2

West declarer at two spades.

Trick	N	E	S	W
1	♣Q	♣A	♣4	♣6
2	♠A	♠J	♠3	♠2
3	♣J	♣2	♣5	♣K
4	♢7	♢Q	♢2	♢5
5	♢8	♢4	♢3	♢K
6	♢9	♣3	♢6	♢A
7	♠8	♠10	♠K	♠5
8	♢10	♠4	♠6	♠Q
9	♡J	♡6	♣7	♢J
10	♣10	♠9	♣9	♣8
11	♡10	♡7	♡5	♡3
12	♡9	♡8	♡A	♡4
13	♡K	♡Q	♡2	♠7

West wins nine tricks.

3.

North declarer at four spades.

Trick	E	S	W	N
1	♢4	♢7	♢8	♢A
2	♣3	♣A	♣5	♣2
3	♠K	♠9	♠2	♠4
4	♢2	♢9	♢10	♠10
5	♡3	♡A	♡6	♡2
6	♠3	♠8	♠5	♠7
7	♣4	♡4	♡7	♡Q
8	♣7	♠6	♡9	♡5
9	♣9	♣6	♣Q	♠J
10	♢5	♣8	♠Q	♠A
11	♢6	♢J	♡J	♡K

North claims the remaining two tricks, winning 12 tricks.

4

East declarer at four hearts.

Trick	S	W	N	E
1	♣7	♣K	♣2	♣J
2	♡6	♡J	♡K	♡A
3	♡3	♡9	♡7	♡2
4	♢4	♢2	♢J	♡4
5	♡8	♢3	♣3	♡Q
6	♠2	♠J	♠A	♠4
7	♣8	♣10	♣4	♣A
8	♠6	♠3	♠5	♠K

East claims the balance, winning 12 tricks.

COMMENTS ON LESSON FOUR HANDS

Hand one. The success or failure of most two-suited hands hinges upon the development into tricks of the second (non-trump) suit, usually described as the 'side suit'. Accordingly, after winning the opening club lead in the dummy, a heart is led from that hand (towards strength, of course) and the king or queen played. On winning with the ace, West will continue clubs, dummy winning. A trump is led and the double finesse taken. On winning with the king of spades, West leads a third club, forcing declarer to trump. After cashing his remaining high heart, a heart is trumped in dummy. With both adverse hearts falling, South's remaining hearts are 'good'. Trumps are 'pulled' and when the hearts are cashed, West will be squeezed, being unable to retain the fourth club and protect the king of diamonds. Dummy will keep whichever suit West discards.

Hand two. On winning the first club and leading a trump, the latter won by a defender, a second club lead forces out declarer's remaining high club. To lead a second round of trumps would permit the defenders to cash a club trick. Hence, before yielding the lead to the defenders, declarer leads three rounds of high diamonds beginning with dummy's queen and discards dummy's losing club. When the defenders regain the lead with a trump, their potential club trick has vanished. To the reader who asks "Suppose a defender had trumped the third diamond,?" the answer is that first, with seven diamonds known to be held by the defenders, that possibility is rather unlikely and second, even if it were to happen, declarer has simultaneously disposed of a losing club so that he's lost nothing - it's trick for trick.

In hand three, North's bidding has indicated six hearts and five spades. South can count a total of eight cards between the partnership in either suit and his preference is based on the fact that his three spades permit the trumping of a third (and possible losing) round of hearts, not true if the latter suit were trumps. Notice that before 'pulling' the last trump, declarer tests the trump suit to see if it will 'break' before leading the third round of trumps. Most important of all, declarer has led two rounds of trumps before playing the second round of the side-suit, hearts.

Hand four stresses the importance of playing carefully to the first trick. In order to finesse against the missing king of hearts, declarer must be able to enter dummy's hand, that of West. By winning the opening club lead with the king, this purpose is accomplished. Had East, the declarer, won the first club with the jack in his hand, his ace of clubs blocks that suit and without a diamond in his hand, he cannot use dummy's ace.

Lesson V

PART ONE

Choice of Suit by Responder

PART TWO

Leads—Defensive Play

LESSON FIVE

PART ONE

CHOICE OF SUIT BY RESPONDER

What has already been written about the opening bidder anticipating his partner's most likely response, his own rebid, and selecting, from two or more suits, his first bid applies in even greater measure to his partner, the responder.

In this respect, both partners think alike. Each is naturally desirous of bidding the longest suit first, and of keeping the bidding at a safe (and low) level, until the bidding discloses that the combined hands contain enough points to bid higher and win a correspondingly greater number of tricks.

CHOOSING BETWEEN TWO FOUR CARD SUITS, BOTH OF WHICH CAN BE SHOWN AS A RESPONSE AT THE ONE LEVEL

RULE - Bid the cheaper first!

(a)
♠ KJ107
♡ Q87
◇ K1098
♣ KQ

Let's suppose you hold hand (a) and your partner opens the bidding with one club.

(b)
♠ A98
♡ KJ109
◇ J4
♣ A1098

Partner's hand is shown as (b) to the left.

The bidding will proceed:

PARTNER	YOU
One club	One diamond
One heart	One spade
One no trump	Three no trump

What should be extremely interesting to the reader is that the partnership was able to make four bids in the first two rounds of bidding, *show all four suits and still remain at the one level!*

Some student may inquire at this point, **"Well, after partner discovered that you held diamonds and spades, and since he**

had hearts and clubs, why didn't he bid a game at once instead of bidding only one no trump?"

The reason is that your partner didn't have the necessary high card values for a three no trump rebid. After all, he had the barest of opening bids - 13 high card points plus one point for the doubleton diamond. He not only opened the bidding with this minimum hand but found a second bid of one heart, a third bid of one no trump.

Now, here's the point to realize. Your partner's second bid of one heart and his next bid of one no trump were forced. *In other words, he HAD to bid again, since every time you bid a new suit, he was again compelled to bid.*

So opener's second bid, of one heart, promised no extra values in excess of opening bid requirements except showing four or more hearts as well as a club suit. The one no trump rebid is similarly wrung out of the opening bidder. Your one spade bid forced him to bid again and all he's doing now is saying, **"I'm rebidding because your spade bid makes me bid again. I have no more suits to show, my suits aren't rebiddable. I don't have support for your suits, and believe me, I have a weak hand."**

The great advantage of responding with the cheaper of four card suits is demonstrated in the following bidding sequence.

NORTH, OPENER	SOUTH, YOU	NORTH	SOUTH
♠ J43	♠ A1097		
♡ Q654	♡ K987	One club	One heart
◊ A7	◊ 832	Two hearts	Pass
♣ AK62	♣ 75		

So, by bidding the cheaper of the two four card suits, in this case, hearts, your partner, who opened the bidding, would give you an immediate raise and you have instantly found the best suit fit between the partnership hands.

You see, it isn't so much which partner has the longest suit but, rather, which suit contains the greatest number of cards *between the combined partnership hands.* After receiving partner's raise to two hearts, you would then pass when next it is your turn to bid, since there is little or no chance of game and you are content to play the hand for a part score.

Now let's see what would have happened had you responded incorrectly with a spade (instead of a heart) with the foregoing hands.

NORTH, OPENER	SOUTH, YOU
One club	One spade
One no trump	Pass

Note that when you bid a spade, the heart suit was effectively blocked out of the bidding, since North lacked both sufficient high card strength and distribution to reverse the bidding by bidding two hearts. Since you have a weak hand, you cannot find a second bid and must pass your partner's one no trump rebid. Accordingly, hearts, the partnership's best suit, would never be shown.

Let's analyze some other possible bidding situations. Supposing you held the same hands shown on page 148, but we transposed the heart and spade suits in your partner's hand so that we'd now have -

NORTH, OPENER	SOUTH, YOU	NORTH	SOUTH
♠ Q654	♠ A1097		
♡ J43	♡ K987	One club	One heart
◊ A7	◊ 832	One spade	Two spades
♣ AK62	♣ 75	Pass	

Thus by bidding the lower-ranking of two four-carders, it is an extremely simple matter to find a fit between the partnership. Using this method, exact inferences can be drawn regarding partner's suits or lack of them. Let us say you are South, hold-

	SOUTH, YOU	NORTH, PARTNER
♠ KJ7		
♡ AQ72		
◊ J3	One club	One spade
♣ A1082		

You will be absolutely correct in inferring that from partner's inability to bid either one diamond or one heart, he cannot have four cards of either suit *if his spade suit is four cards in length.*

The reason is clear - had your partner four diamonds or four hearts *and four spades*, he would have bid a red suit first.

The entire mechanics of responding and rebidding with two or more four card suits, **'A suit skipped is a suit denied.'** In other words, when partner bids one spade over one club, assuming he has a four card spade suit, he denies holding four hearts or four diamonds.

WARNING - In the foregoing bidding example, it is possible that partner held four diamonds or four hearts with FIVE or more spades. This possibility is discussed on following pages.

This method of 'bidding up the ladder' in responding with two or more four card suits is designed to find a fit between the partnership when there may not be enough high cards to bid all suits. So if a suit is skipped in responding or rebidding, it is generally safe to assume that four cards of that suit are lacking; or if a suit skipped in earlier bidding is shown later, assume that the first suit shown is at least five cards in length.

For example -

PARTNER, OPENER	YOU, RESPONDER
One diamond	One heart
Two clubs *	

* *Practically denies holding four spades.*

(a)

♠ K987
♡ K987
♢ Q54
♣ 32

(b)

♠ AJ108
♡ KQ76
♢ J2
♣ 1083

Let's call the accompanying responder's hands (a) and (b).

On hand (a) with the preceding bidding, you would simply bid two diamonds telling your partner that you like diamonds better than clubs.

With hand (b), there is no question of the fact that you have enough high card strength to warrant a second bid. Is a two spade rebid in order?

Definitely not!

Your partner can't hold four spades or he would have shown them over your response of one heart. The heart suit is not rebiddable, nor have you support for either of partner's suits. But you can and should bid *two no trump* since you have the only unbid suit, spades, well protected; 11 high card points; and your best chance of making a game apparently is in no trump.

RESPONDING WITH TWO FOUR-CARDERS, ONE THAT CAN BE SHOWN AT THE ONE LEVEL, THE OTHER AT THE TWO LEVEL.

RULE - Bid the cheaper!

(c)
♠ QJ109
♡ QJ109
◇ 5
♣ KQ87

(d)
♠ KQ65
♡ QJ109
◇ KJ76
♣ 3

Your partner opened the bidding with one diamond and you hold hand (c). Respond with one heart. It's cheaper than either one spade or two clubs:

Let's suppose your partner opened the bidding with one club and you hold hand (d). Respond with one diamond. It's your cheapest response.

RESPONDING AT THE TWO LEVEL WITH TWO FOURS

RULE - Bid the cheaper but only with 10 or more points. With six to nine points and balanced distribution, bid one no trump.

For example, your partner has opened the bidding with one spade and you hold each of the following hands.

(e)	(f)	(g)
♠ 82	♠ KJ8	♠ J5
♡ AQ75	♡ K1098	♡ A1096
◇ J92	◇ J10	◇ 1042
♣ KQ63	♣ Q743	♣ Q962
Bid two clubs	Bid two clubs	Bid one no trump

RESPONDING WITH TWO FOURS AND A FIVE CARD SUIT

RULE - If the five-carder can be shown at the one level, it should be bid first regardless of rank or high card strength.

If it is necessary to go to the two level in order to show your five card suit, the hand should contain 10 points or more. It's the old, old story of bidding what you can afford and if you don't have 10 points but have six to nine, you show the suit or suits that can be shown at the one level.

Should your void be in your partner's suit, then you should literally tread on eggs and bid carefully. For one thing, the hand looms up as a misfit. Make a one over one response with six or more points but to enter the two level, even with a five card suit, you should have a trifle more than the normal minimum requirements - at least 12 points rather than 10.

For example, your partner has opened with one diamond. You hold each of the following hands in response -

(h)	(i)	(j)	(k)
♠ Q1087	♠ KJ54	♠ 108432	♠ 10987
♡ void	♡ Q643	♡ 9764	♡ KQ52
◇ 6432	◇ void	◇ void	◇ void
♣ KJ954	♣ Q10876	♣ A875	♣ AJ1086
One spade	One heart	One spade	Two clubs

RESPONDING WITH TWO FIVE CARD SUITS

In responding with two five card suits, the higher-ranking is bid first. Later, the second suit can be shown if desirable. *This is the opposite* of responding with four card suits where the cheaper suit is shown first.

Example - Your partner has opened the bidding with one diamond and you hold the following hands -

(c)	(d)
♠ K10876	♠ 54
♡ KQ743	♡ J8765
◇ J2	◇ 7
♣ 3	♣ KQ1076

With (c), your response is one spade; with (d), one heart. Should partner rebid 'two diamonds,' you can rebid two hearts with (c), pass with (d). A second bid of three clubs on (d) would be risky in view of the apparent misfit and that the overall strength of the hand does not warrant a second voluntary bid.

However, had partner's rebid been one no trump, a second response would be justified on both hands, since because of the unbalanced distribution, the combined hands will probably play better in a suit contract than in no trump.

The reason for bidding the higher-ranking suit first with two five-carders is that the extra playing strength afforded by the aggressive distribution (two five-carders) permits you usually to show the second suit, and since your suits are five cards in length, they need far less bolstering in the way of trump support. Four card suits, on the other hand, must be bid cheaply and at low levels until a fit is found or a safe contract assured.

RESPONDING WITH A FIVE AND A FOUR CARD SUIT

RULE - If both suits can be shown at the one level, the five-carder is bid first.

Example - Your partner has opened with one diamond. You hold the following hands.

(e)	(f)
♠ K10876	♠ K1087
♡ AJ54	♡ AJ543
◊ J8	◊ J8
♣ 43	♣ 43
One spade	One heart

RULE - If the five carder can be shown at the one level but it is necessary to bid two in order to show the four-carder, bid the five card suit first.

Example - Your partner has opened the bidding with one diamond and you hold the following hands -

(g)	(h)
♠ K9743	♠ Q2
♡ 3	♡ 108762
◊ J74	◊ 53
♣ AQJ9	♣ AK43
One spade	One heart

RULE - If the four-carder can be shown at the one level but it is necessary to bid two in order to show the five-carder -

1 - Bid the five-carder first with 10 points or more;

2 - Bid the four card suit first with six to nine points.

Example - Your partner has opened the bidding with one diamond and you hold the following hands -

(i)	(j)
♠ KJ87	♠ Q1065
♡ J6	♡ 87
◊ 43	◊ 43
♣ AK742	♣ A8765
Two clubs	One spade

Here we meet our old friend, the reverse. You will remember that when the opening bidder had 16 or 18 points or more, he could open the bidding with a lower-ranking, longer suit before bidding the shorter, higher-ranking suit at an increased level.

The responding hand can also reverse the bidding to show the first bid, lower-ranking suit to be longer than the second bid suit but responder's requirements are greatly lessened from that of the opening bidder.

The responder can reverse the bidding with 12 points or more, providing his first bid suit is BOTH lower-ranking and longer than his second suit. Obviously, for him to make such a strength showing rebid, there should be a strong probability of game.

With hand (i), the clubs are bid first since, as a rebid, you can later show the spade suit. This paints an accurate picture of your hand, telling partner that the club suit is longer than the spade suit and that you hold 12 points or more.

A reverse by a responder who has not previously passed is forcing upon opener to rebid at least once more. It is not an absolute force to game although highly invitational.

RESPONDING WITH SIX - SIX

RULE - Bid the higher-ranking suit first.

RESPONDING WITH SIX - FIVE

RULE - Always bid the six-carder first if higher in rank.

Example - Over partner's one diamond bid, respond -

(k)	(l)
♠ 1087654	♠ 5
♡ AJ1087	♡ J85432
◇ 2	◇ 7
♣ 3	♣ AQJ109
One spade	One heart

RULE - If the six-carder is lower in rank, it should be bid first only with 10 points or more.

Example - Responding to one diamond -

(m)	(n)
♠ Q7543	♠ QJ765
♡ 3	♡ 3
◇ 2	◇ 2
♣ K108765	♣ AQJ876
One spade	Two clubs

RESPONDING WITH SIX - FOUR

RULE - The six card suit should always be bid first if it can be shown at the one level. If it is necessary to bid 'two' in order to bid the six-carder, 10 points or more must be present.

With six to nine points, when we can show the four-carder at the one level but it is necessary to bid 'two' in order to show the six-carder, the four card suit is bid.

(o)	(p)	(q)	(r)
♠ A76543	♠ K876	♠ QJ109	♠ Q1098
♡ K1076	♡ AJ9765	♡ 3	♡ 5
◇ 6	◇ 4	◇ 95	◇ 65
♣ 87	♣ 65	♣ AQJ765	♣ K76543
One spade	One heart	Two clubs	One spade

It's the old, old story of purchasing according to the money in your purse. In the last hand, you don't have enough money to bid two clubs. You can eke out enough to bid one spade, even though it means bidding the shorter suit first.

It's all you can afford!

THINGS TO REMEMBER

1 - Make the response best fitted to your purse. Try to show the longer of two suits first, and the relation of each suit to the other in terms of length and rank, but if your hand has only six to nine points, don't enter the two-level of bidding.

2 - The fit between the partnership hands is of utmost importance in the bidding. When you lack support for partner's suit or suits and he apparently has none for yours, the better part of valor is not to rebid minimum hands. Don't bid merely because you don't like your partner's suits.

3 - The fact that you possess two or more suits does not mean that you should show them all. You may not have enough strength to find a second bid. With touching four-card suits in responding, usually only the lower-ranking is shown. If partner, in rebidding, skips the touching higher-ranking suit you hold, it is safe to assume that in over 90 percent of these cases, lacks holding four cards of the skipped suit.

4 - The higher the level to which you force the bidding, the greater the number of tricks are required to fulfill the contract, and correspondingly, the more strength you must have.

5 - Every time you bid voluntarily, you guarantee the strength indicated by that bid; every time you rebid, you show added strength. You can't bid the same cards over and over again!

PART TWO

LEADS AND PLAYS BY THE DEFENDERS

Defense is the play of the cards by the side that did not win the auction.

Basically, there are two types of defensive tactics; against suit (trump) contracts; and against no trump.

Against suit contracts, the defenders try to take their tricks before the declarer and dummy can trump them; or before the declarer and dummy can get rid of their losing cards by discarding them on winning cards in other suits.

Thus, it is a race between the defenders, who try to take tricks, and the other side, which tries to avoid losing these tricks. But in this race, there is an important proviso for the defenders - in their hurry to win tricks, they must try to avoid creating winning tricks for the other side. For instance, it would be bad policy to hurriedly lead the ace of spades if by so doing we made winners out of the opponents' king, queen and jack.

Defending against no trump is an entirely different matter. Here, since cards cannot be trumped, the defenders attempt to create winners out of low cards. So the defenders will usually begin by leading from long suits, trying to push out the declarer's high cards in that suit so ultimately, the defender's remaining cards have become established as winners. By retaining their high cards, the defenders hope to regain the lead a sufficient number of times first to establish lower cards as winners and later, to capitalize on them. High cards used for gaining the lead are known as 'entries.'

In defending hands, years of constant experimentation have developed the best methods of handling commonly recurring situations. Conventions (which are merely understandings between partners) have grown up so that the play of a specific card may carry a great deal of meaning and significance. Literally, *the cards talk*, and the play of one card may carry one message while the play of another card may tell still an entirely different story.

SEQUENCE LEAD TABLE

HOLDING	NO TRUMP — With side entry 1st lead	NO TRUMP — With side entry 2nd lead	NO TRUMP — Without entry 1st lead	NO TRUMP — Without entry 2nd lead	SUIT 1st lead	SUIT 2nd lead
AKQJ or more	A	J	A	J	K	J
AKQxxx	A	K	A	K	K	Q
AKQxx	K	Q	K	Q	K	Q
AKQx or AKQ	K	Q	K	Q	K	Q
AKJxxxx	A	K	A	K	K	A
AK10xxxx	A	K	A		K	A
AKJ10xx	A	K	J		K	A
AKJxxx	A		4th best		K	A
AKJxx	K		4th best		K	A
AQJxxxx	A	Q	Q		avoid	
AQJxxx	A	Q	Q		avoid	
AQJxx	A	Q	Q		avoid	
AQ109x	10		10		avoid	
AJ10x or more	J		J		avoid	
A109x or more	10		10		A	10
AKx	K	A	K	A	K	A
AK alone	Avoid		avoid		A	K
KQJ or more	K	J	K	J	K	J
KQ10 or more	K		K		K	
KQxxxxx	K	4th best	4th best		K	
KQxxxx	K		4th best		K	
KQ9xx	K		4th best		K	
KQxxx	4th best		4th best		K	
KQxx	4th best		4th best		K	
KQ or KQx	K	Q	K	Q	K	Q
KJ10x or longer	J		J		J	
K109x or more	10		10		10	
K98x or more	9		9		9	
QJ10x or more	Q	10	Q	10	Q	10
QJ9x or more	Q		Q		Q	
QJxx or QJxxx	4th best		4th best		Q	
QJ alone	avoid		avoid		Q	
Q109x or longer	10		10		10	
Q98xx	9		9		9	
J109x or longer	J		J		J	
J108x or longer	J		J		J	
J10xx or longer	4th best		4th best		J	
J10x	J		J		J	
J98x or longer	9		9		9	
1098x or longer	10		10		10	

Note - x denotes any card lower than a 10.

THE HANDLING OF SEQUENCES

What is a sequence?

A sequence is two or more cards of the same suit in a row. The ace and king of spades form a two card sequence; KQJ of hearts would be a three card sequence; QJ1098 of diamonds are a five card sequence. The more cards that are in a sequence, the better - a bridge player would say "**the more solid.**"

LEADING - The top card of the sequence is the correct lead in every case but one. From KQJ, we first lead the king; from QJ10, we choose the queen; from J109, the jack. The only exception is a sequence containing *the ace, king and any one or more cards in which case the king is led first.*

So the opening lead of a king can show two possible holdings; either the leader holds AKx or KQx or longer. Usually the partner will see one of the complementary cards in the led suit. In *figure 67*, you are East, defending against South's four heart contract. Your partner leads the king of spades. Since the queen is in dummy, partner is known to hold the ace *and one or more spades.*

♠ Q43
N
♠ K (led) W E ♠ J86
S

Figure 67

In *figure 68*, you are again East defending against South's four heart contract. With the ace of spades in the dummy, partner is known to hold the queen.

♠ A43
N
♠ K (led) W E ♠ 752
S

Figure 68

It should be pointed out that there will be times when your partner will lead the king and neither the queen or ace will be in the dummy or in your hand. In these cases, the ambiguity will usually be clarified when the suit is led a second time and frequently the bidding will afford clues as to the locations of missing high cards.

Let's see what inferences can be drawn from the leads in *figure 69*. You are East, South is playing a four heart contract. Your partner opens the ace of spades and follows with the king of that suit. Since if he held the ace, king and one or

♠ J52
N
♠ A (first lead W E ♠ 10876
♠ K (second lead)
S

Figure 69

more spades, he would have first led the king, the answer should be crystal-clear - *your partner does not have the 'one or more spades.'* The ace and king are your partner's only spades and the lead of the ace, followed by the king of that suit, is the conventional manner of showing a two-card (doubleton) holding.

PLAYING FROM a sequence, the reverse of the foregoing is true. When a suit is led by another player, the defender with a sequence tries to win the trick as cheaply as possible. In other words, he attempts to take the trick with the bottom card of the sequence. Let's suppose we sit East in the accompanying diagram and the deuce is led from dummy, North. The underlined card is the card we should play from each of the following sequences.

	2 (led)	
	N	
W		E
	S	

Figure 70

AKQJ<u>10</u> QJ10<u>9</u> K<u>Q</u>87 KQ<u>J</u>65 J<u>10</u>4

THE INTERIOR SEQUENCE

An interior sequence is a sequence with a still higher card or cards not in sequence. For example, take KJ109. The J109 form a three card sequence. The king is not in sequence, since there is a gap between the king and the jack. The queen, the card necessary to complete the sequence, is missing.

In playing or leading from an interior sequence, the choice of the card to be led or played is based upon the sequence itself *and not on the higher card or cards not in sequence.* First, we'll underline the card that should be led from typical interior sequences.

LEADING -

K<u>J</u>1098 Q<u>10</u>987

PLAYING -

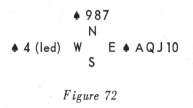

♠ K98
N
♠ 4 (led) W E ♠ AQJ10
S

Figure 71

In general, the question of which card should be *played* from an intermediate sequence in the absence of the missing intermediate cards necessary to complete the sequence depends on dummy's holding and your own in the led suit. For example, you are defending against an adverse contract in *figure 71* and your partner leads the four of spades. The eight is played from dummy. You should play the 10, the bottom card of the sequence. The 10 actually has the same capturing power as the ace since the king, the card needed to complete the sequence, remains unplayed in the dummy.

♠ 987
N
♠ 4 (led) W E ♠ AQJ10
S

Figure 72

Let's change the North hand to resemble that in *figure 72.* Again you are East and your partner leads the four of spades. Since the location of the missing king is unknown, you play the card most likely to win the trick, obviously the ace.

The new player will generally have two problems as to which card to play from an intermediate sequence. The first problem is - *should a card from the sequence or one of the higher cards not in sequence be played first?* The second problem is - *if we play from the sequence, which card do we play first?*

Let's answer these in order. First, the question of whether to play from the intermediate sequence or one of the higher cards not in sequence is determined by two factors - which card is most likely to win the trick and what missing (from the sequence) cards are in dummy. In *figure 72* you played the ace since there was no assurance a lower card would win the trick.

When, however, it is decided to play a card from the sequence as in *figure 71,* the bottom of the sequence is played exactly as from any other sequence.

WHY THE NO TRUMP COLUMN IS DIVIDED INTO TWO COLUMNS, WITH AND WITHOUT ENTRY

In defending against no trump, you may sometimes be on lead holding a powerful suit as ♠ AKJ1086 with no other high cards in your hand. Since you hold a six card suit, there will be seven cards of the suit held by the remaining three players. The most probable distribution of these seven cards is 3 - 2 - 2.

	♠ 32 ♡ Q8 ♢ KJ109743 ♣ KJ	
♠ AKJ1086 ♡ 743 ♢ 5 ♣ 863	N W E S	♠ 54 ♡ J9652 ♢ A6 ♣ 7542
	♠ Q97 ♡ AK10 ♢ Q82 ♣ AQ109	

Figure 73

South, declarer at three no trump.

Having bid no trump, it is more than likely that the declarer holds the three cards headed by the queen.

Let's pretend you are West in *figure 73*. If you first cash the king and ace of spades, it will be necessary to lead a third round to force out the queen. Your remaining three spades will take tricks when and if you regain the lead.

But you can't regain the lead! Once your two high spades were played, you no longer held a high card with which to recapture the lead. To make matters worse, your partner, on gaining the lead with the ace of diamonds, will not have a spade to return. He was forced to play both of his spades when you led the king and ace.

The important things, then, are - first, when all of your high cards are in the suit you are attempting to establish, that the high cards be retained to serve as later re-entries in addition to their capturing power; secondly, that when it is hoped that partner can capture a trick during the play so that on gaining the lead, partner will have one or more cards of your suit to return.

Hence West, with no high card of re-entry outside of the spade suit he is attempting to establish, must keep these high cards as future re-entries. Accordingly, West should open the jack of spades. South wins with the queen. Sooner or later, South must lead a diamond, having only eight tricks - four clubs, three hearts and one spade - without that (diamond) suit. East wins with the ace, returns his remaining spade and the hand is beaten. When West played two rounds of spades, South was able to win an over-trick.

	♠ 32 ♡ Q8 ◇ KJ109743 ♣ KJ	
♠ AKJ1086 ♠ 743 ◇ A ♣ 863	N W E S	♠ 54 ♡ J9652 ◇ 65 ♣ 7542
	♠ Q97 ♡ AK10 ◇ Q82 ♣ AQ109	

Figure 74

Let's transpose the ace and five of diamonds so that the hand resembles *figure 74*.

As West, you are again on lead against South's contract of three no trump. But this time, since you also hold a positive card of re-entry - the ace of diamonds, you should play your ace and king of spades. This affords you the additional possibility of capturing the missing queen. If the latter card falls, you will be able to win six spade tricks - if it doesn't, you will lead a third round of the suit to be taken by South's queen. Later, when diamonds are led, you can be absolutely certain of regaining the lead with the ace of diamonds to cash your remaining spades.

Be sure that when you release the high cards in the suit you are attempting to establish, that the outside re-entry cards are positive - that is, that they are certain of winning a trick.

An ace is a positive re-entry; a guarded king behind *(to the left of)* the bidder of that suit is usually a positive re-entry. However, if you hold the king of a suit which has been bid to your left *(you are in front of the bidder)*, the capturing power of that king is decidedly diminished. Queens and jacks are far from being positive re-entries.

RECOMMENDED LEADS AGAINST SUIT CONTRACTS WHEN PARTNER HAS NOT BID

This and subsequent lead tables are based upon what leads will be best most of the time. Obviously, there will be times where a lead, rated lower in the order of preference, will prove more effective than one with a higher rating. Inferences drawn from the bidding will be of immeasurable assistance in determining which suit to lead. But the important thing to remember is this - no lead is the best lead all of the time!

1 - A sequence. The stronger and more solid the sequence, the more desirable the lead. Examples - K from AKQ, K from KQJ or Q from QJ109, etc.

2 - Leads from intermediate sequences headed by the queen, sometimes the king but never the ace.

3 - Trumps, particularly when the bidding has indicated that dummy has ruffing power or that a cross-ruff is imminent.

4 - Fourth best from a four card or longer suit which may be headed by any card except the ace or a sequence.

5 - Ace from a four card or longer suit.

6 - Three card worthless holdings of unbid suits. The bottom card should be led first.

7 - Singletons, *when holding a high trump and not more than a total of three trumps.*

8 - Doubletons, with the same conditions as number seven.

RECOMMENDED LEADS AGAINST SUIT CONTRACTS AFTER PARTNER HAS BID

In general, the opening leader will achieve the best results by opening the suit bid by partner, particularly if the suit was bid *as an opening bid* marking it to be biddable. Hence, it must contain high cards that can win tricks or quickly be developed into tricks.

If, however, partner's suit has been bid as a response or under compulsion, beyond being of four or more cards, the suit may be completely lacking in high cards. To lead that suit then would be a waste of time and jeopardize a possible potential winning card of that suit in the leader's hand.

I would like to emphasize that it is *not mandatory* to lead partner's bid suit. Every now and then the opening leader may have a sound lead of his own. Accordingly, this section dealing with leading partner's suit against trump contracts will be divided into two portions: the first will describe what card to lead of partner's suit; the second, when it may be better not to lead it.

LEADING PARTNER'S SUIT

1 - With two cards, open the higher.

2 - With three cards. If headed by the ace or a sequence, open the ace or, the top of the sequence, respectively. From three worthless cards or three cards headed by an honor (other than the ace) or three cards including two honors not in sequence (excluding the ace), lead the bottom card.

3 - With four or more cards, open the fourth-best unless:

(a) the suit is headed by the ace in which case the ace is led;

(b) the suit is headed by a sequence of two or more touching honors in which case the top of the sequence is led.

EXAMPLES

It is assumed that your partner opened the bidding with one spade and you are on opening lead against an adverse four heart contract. Each of the following combinations represents your spade holding. The correct choice of opening lead is underlined in each case.

(a)	(b)	(c)	(d)	(e)
<u>J</u> 2	<u>A</u> 8 2	<u>Q</u> J 7	K J <u>6</u>	K 7 <u>5</u>

(f)	(g)	(h)	(i)	(j)
9 5 <u>3</u>	<u>A</u> J 8 5	<u>K</u> Q 4 2	9 6 4 <u>3</u>	Q 10 8 <u>6</u>

WHEN NOT TO LEAD PARTNER'S SUIT

1 - When holding a sequence containing the ace and king or a sequence at least three cards in depth as KQJ that will quickly either take a trick or develop a trick without cost.

2 - A trump lead may be desirable when trumps can be led without jeopardizing a trump trick in the leader's hand and the bidding has indicated dummy to hold extreme ruffing value which can be cut down by trump leads.

3 - A singleton may be led providing that the leader holds a maximum of three trumps containing at least the ace, king or queen. The singleton preferably should be in an unbid suit, rarely in dummy's bid suit and *never* in declarer's side suit.

LEADING PARTNER'S BID SUIT AGAINST NO TRUMP

1 - With two cards, open the higher.

2 - With three worthless cards, open the lowest card. With three cards headed by an honor *(including the ace)*, open the lowest card. The reason is that your honor may capture one of declarer's high cards in that suit.

♠ 73
N
♠ Q62 W E ♠ A9854
S
♠ KJ10

Figure 75

In *figure 75*, East, your partner, has bid spades. South is playing a no trump contract. As West, you open the deuce. Partner will play the ace, return the five, and your queen will capture South's jack. Note that had you originally led the queen, South would have won two spade tricks instead of one.

♠ 65
N
♠ K84 W E ♠ AJ1073
S
♠ Q92

Figure 76

In *figure 76*, South is playing a no trump contract. East has bid spades. West leads the four. East takes the ace, returns the jack and South's queen is trapped.

♠ 87
N
♠ AJ6 W E ♠ K5432
S
♠ Q109

Figure 77

In *figure 77*, East has again bid spades with South the declarer at no trump. West will open the spade six. East plays the king, returns the trey and South's queen will be caught.

3 - From a sequence in partner's bid suit, lead the top of that sequence. Examples - king from KQxx, queen from QJx, etc.

4 - From any four or more cards of partner's bid suit, open the fourth-best unless the suit is headed by a sequence, in which case the top of the sequence is led.

NOTE - After one's partner has bid and the opponents wind up playing the hand in no trump, the best results will usually be achieved by leading partner's suit. It may be, as in the case of an overcall, that the suit was bid primarily to direct the opening lead. Sometimes, however, the opening leader may have a *sound* opening lead of his own. This will usually be a *solid or virtually solid suit of his own at least four cards in length plus a positive re-entry.*

By no means let the fact that the opponents have bid no trump after your partner has bid a suit dissuade you from leading his suit. Your partner is the player to believe, not the opponents.

CHOICE OF LEADS AGAINST NO TRUMP WHEN PARTNER HAS NOT BID

1 - Solid sequences as KQJxx, QJ10xx, etc.

2 - Top of interior sequences as jack from KJ109x, etc.

3 - Fourth-best from four or more cards.

4 - Short, worthless suits. By short I mean of less than four cards. You will usually make this lead when the suit you ordinarily would have led has been bid by an opponent. You are now trying to 'hit' the suit partner would have opened, had he been on opening lead. Another reason for a possible short suit lead is that your only suit of four or more cards is absolutely worthless, and the hand is completely devoid of high cards for possible re-entries. Again, your hope is to lead the suit you think your partner would have opened. In this regard, it is far better to open from a three card holding than a doubleton since it permits you to continue leading the suit an additional time. Do not open a singleton of an *unbid* suit.

OPENING LEADS AGAINST SUIT CONTRACTS THAT ARE *UNSOUND* AND SHOULD BE AVOIDED

1 - Leads of side-suits bid by the declarer.

2 - Leads of singleton trumps.

3 - Underleads (leading away) from aces.

4 - Leading aces from ace-queen or ace-jack combinations.

5 - Suits *rebid* by the eventual dummy.

6 - Singletons or doubletons without a high trump or with four or more trumps.

7 - Leads of doubleton honors as queen from Qx, etc. in unbid suits.

8 - Leads of aces from three card suits.

9 - Leads from three card suits headed by the queen.

10 - Underleads of kings. *Note - this lead is ordinarily unsound but there are cases, as where the opponents have shown strength in the remaining three suits, that the lead of the fourth suit containing the king is practically obvious.*

THE RULE OF ELEVEN

The ‘Rule of Eleven’ is the only thing in bridge to which ‘*always and ever*’ can be applied. Mathematically precise, it applies to any lead when the card led is the fourth-highest (fourth from the top) of a suit. Holding the king, jack, eight, six and four, the six-spot would be the fourth-best.

The advantage of the Rule of Eleven is that after a player has led the fourth-best card of a suit, his partner can tell exactly how many cards the declarer (the closed hand) has higher than the led card. The opening leader's partner simply subtracts the number of spots on the led card from 11.

Let's say, for example, the six was opened. The difference between six and 11 is five. That means there are five cards of that suit higher than the six which are not in the opening leader's hand. The partner now looks around for those five cards. Perhaps he sees two of them in the dummy and one of them in his own hand. That accounts for three of the five higher cards known not to be in the opening leader's hand. The remainder, two, must be in the declarer's hand.

The declarer can also employ the Rule of Eleven through similar steps. He will subtract the ‘spots’ on the led card from 11. The difference represents the number of cards higher than that led not in the leader's hand. Let's call that ‘a’. The declarer looks at his own hand and the dummy and totals the number of cards in that suit higher than that led. Let's call that total ‘b.’ Subtracting ‘b’ ’from ‘a’ yields the exact number of cards held by the leader's partner (in that suit) that are higher than the led card.

♠ K63
N
♠ Q1087 W E ♠ AJ94
S
♠ 52
Declarer
Figure 78

Figure 78 illustrates use of the Rule of Eleven by the defenders. West opens his fourth-best, the seven. East subtracts seven from 11, leaving four. Therefore there are four cards higher than the seven not in the leader's hand. One of the four, the king, is in the dummy. The remaining three, the ace, jack and nine, are with East. South, therefore, does not hold a spade higher than the seven.

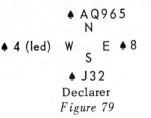

♠ AQ965
N
♠ 4 (led) W E ♠ 8
S
♠ J32
Declarer
Figure 79

In *figure 79*, we see the employment of the Rule of Eleven by the declarer. West opens the four. Subtracting four from 11 leaves seven. Of these seven, dummy has five cards capable of beating the four. East has shown one higher, the eight, and South has the seventh, the jack. South, the declarer, can place the king, 10 and seven in West's hand just as surely as though he had looked in that hand.

The opening lead of the fourth-best is employed against both no trump and suit contracts. The fourth-best card can be led *after another suit has previously been played, but you cannot lead the fourth-best and expect your partner to decipher it after previously having led a low card of that suit.*

The Rule of Eleven is invaluable in spotting short suit leads since if the resulting figure, after subtraction from 11, does not jibe with dummy's and defender's holdings in the suit, the lead is marked as unorthodox and not fourth-best.

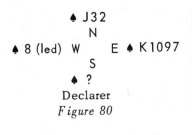

♠ J32
N
♠ 8 (led) W E ♠ K1097
S
♠ ?
Declarer
Figure 80

In *figure 80*, West opens the spade eight. To East, can the lead be fourth-best? Hardly! Eight from 11 leaves three cards higher not with West. But East sees four - the jack in the dummy and three in his hand. The lead, then, is not fourth-best but from a three card or shorter holding.

SHOWING FIVE CARD AND LONGER SUITS BY LEADER

After originally leading the fourth-best of any suit, the lead or play of a lower card by the leader would show five cards in the suit. The later play or lead of a still lower card would indicate that a six card suit was originally present. In *figure 81*, West originally leads his fourth-best, the five-spot. Later, he leads or plays the trey to show fifth-best, and at some future point, plays the deuce to show sixth-best.

N
♠ J86532 W E
S
Figure 81

Notice that in leading or playing from a six card or longer suit, where the fourth-best is first led, the next play is the fifth-best, not the sixth-best. In *figure 81*, leading the five, later leading the deuce would completely deny holding the trey or four-spot, show only a five card suit. After the fourth-best, go down the line.

FOUR AND FIVE CARD SHOWING BY LEADER'S PARTNER

A defender leading a suit naturally would like to know the number of cards (of that suit) held by the declarer. This is frequently possible, particularly where the leader's partner holds four or more cards of the suit in question.

Let's start quite simply. Pretend you are West and lead a spade from a four card suit. Dummy's hand, on being exposed, shows two spades. At this point, six of the 13 spades in the deck are located. Now let's take a giant step forward and suppose that your partner, in returning the suit, indicates that he, too, holds four spades. Our known total has grown to 10 - four spades in our hand, two in dummy, four in partner's hand. By subtracting 10 from 13 it is apparent that South started with three spades.

RULE - In returning partner's led suit from an original holding of four or more cards not headed by a sequence, return the card that was your original fourth-best.

	♠ K98 ♡ 3 ◇ K632 ♣ A9876	
♠ J65 ♡ K10872 ◇ J975 ♣ 4	N W E S	♠ Q732 ♡ Q654 ◇ Q4 ♣ K52
	♠ A104 ♡ AJ9 ◇ A108 ♣ QJ103	

Figure 82

Against South's three no trump contract in *figure 82*, West opens his fourth-best heart, the seven. East's queen is taken by the ace, the queen of clubs led by South for the finesse and East wins with the king.

East returns the **four** of hearts. South will probably play the nine and West wins with the 10.

At this point, West should know that the jack of hearts is in the South hand, that it is now all alone, and will drop when the king is led.

Why ?

First, had East's hearts been headed by a sequence containing both the queen and jack, he would have played the bottom of the sequence. The play of the queen completely denied possession of the jack, marking the latter card with declarer.

Next, when East returned his partner's suit, he led the card which was originally his fourth-best. Since the possible fifth and sixth-best cards (the trey and deuce) were in dummy and West's hands respectively. East could have no more than four hearts. Adding East's known four hearts to West's five and dummy's one adds up to 10, leaving three hearts for South. Since two of those three hearts, the ace and nine, have been played, the remaining card, known to be the jack, must now be alone.

A reader may ask, **"Well, wouldn't East have led the same way if his heart holding were originally a doubleton , as Q4?"**

True, but then South originally would have had five hearts resembling ♡ AJ965, and would have undoubtedly bid that suit during the auction. The fact that hearts were never mentioned by South yields a supplementary clue.

With five or more cards in the suit led by partner against no trump, bear in mind that the opening lead may have been from a four card suit. Hence in returning your partner's lead, you should try to show him that you may have more cards in the suit than he has so that he can get out of your way.

	♠ 3	
	N	
♠ AJ74	W E	♠ KQ652
	S	
	♠ 1098	

Figure 83

In *figure 83*, West opens the four of spades against South's no trump contract. The four is just like the deuce in limiting West to a four card holding, since the trey is in the dummy and East has the deuce.

East wins the first trick with queen, returns the five (originally his fourth-best). West wins with the jack, cashes the ace on which East plays the deuce, his fifth-best. The seven is led and is overtaken by East who cashes his fifth spade. Had East incorrectly led the king of spades after winning the first trick with the queen, the defense would have won only four spade tricks instead of five.

Usually, however, it is the leader of the suit who possesses the greater length in the led suit, and if he has a five card or longer suit, his partner must be careful to get out of his way when holding fewer cards of the suit than the leader. This is particularly true when the partner holds three or four cards (of the suit) including some high cards that could block the smooth 'running' of the suit. Getting high cards out of partner's way is known in bridge as 'unblocking.'

On page 169, I gave as a rule that when holding four or more cards of partner's led suit, we returned the card originally fourth-best unless the four or more cards contained a sequence. Let's see what we should do returning partner's suit from sequences .

RULE - When returning partner's lead from four or more cards -

(a) if you originally held only a two-card sequence and one card of that sequence was played to the first lead, return the card originally your fourth-best;

(b) if, after playing to the first lead of the suit, a sequence of two or more cards still remains, return the top of the remaining sequence.

Figure 83 is an example of case (a) - returning fourth-best when a sequence no longer remains in the hand returning the lead.

♠ 3
N
♠ K8742 W E ♠ Q1095
S
♠ AJ6

Figure 84

In *figure 84*, we have an example of case (b) - returning partner's led suit from a sequence. West opens the four. The queen is taken by the ace. When East gains the lead, he returns the 10, top of the sequence, not the five, even though the latter card was originally fourth-best.

Had East *incorrectly* returned the five, South could play the six, and West would win with the seven. West's king will drop the jack, but East's 10 will now block West's fifth card in the suit from taking a trick.

With the return of the 10, should South cover with the jack, West will win with the king and return the deuce - his fifth-best. East wins with the nine, returns the five. West overtakes with the seven and cashes the eight to win all five spade tricks.

Had South not played the jack on the 10, the latter card wins and the nine follows to further unblock the suit. West will capture the jack with the king and cash his two remaining spades.

FURTHER EXAMPLES OF UNBLOCKING

When suit is led by partner -

HOLDING	FIRST PLAY	THEN RETURN
A 10 9 2	A	10
J 10 9 6	9	J
K J 10 8	K	J
Q 10 9 4	Q	10
K Q J 2	J	K

ENCOURAGING AND DISCOURAGING SIGNALS

Previous pages of this section on Defensive Play have demonstrated how the lead or play of one card can show the presence or absence of another. Equally important is the manner in which one defender tells his partner which suit to lead or not to lead.

The simplest and easiest understood 'come-on' signal is the playing of an unnecessarily high card, usually the seven-spot or larger, to tell partner to continue leading that suit, or to lead that suit when he wins a trick. Conversely, a small card (six or less) would inform partner not to lead that suit.

	North	
	♠ Q J 5 ♡ 8 3 2 ♢ A Q 7 6 5 ♣ 5 4	
West ♠ 4 3 ♡ A 10 ♢ 10 9 4 ♣ A Q 10 8 7 6	N W E S	**East** ♠ 8 2 ♡ K Q 9 7 4 ♢ 8 3 2 ♣ J 9 3
	♠ A K 10 9 7 6 ♡ J 6 5 ♢ K J ♣ K 2	

Figure 85

South, in *figure 85*, is the declarer at four spades. West's opening lead is the heart ace. East drops the nine. While the seven-spot could also be read as a come-on, the nine being the higher card is more emphatic. In signalling, play the highest card you can spare.

With a heart continuation, the hand can be beaten two tricks, the defenders winning two clubs and three hearts.

```
              ♠ QJ52
              ♡ 83
              ◇ KQJ87
              ♣ 106
♠ 43            N         ♠ A6
♡ A10       W       E     ♡ J9762
◇ 965                     ◇ 1043
♣ 975432        S         ♣ AK8
              ♠ K10987
              ♡ KQ54
              ◇ A2
              ♣ QJ
```

Figure 86

In *figure 86*, the contract is once more four spades by South. West makes the same opening lead as in the preceding hand, the ace of hearts.

But does East want the suit continued?

Obviously not !

So he plays the lowest heart he can, the deuce, which tells partner not to lead the suit again. Since there is nothing to be gained by attacking dummy's almost solid diamond suit, the shift has to be to the club suit, which enables the defenders to defeat the hand.

THE ECHO

Just as two heads are better than one, a two card signal cannot be misinterpreted while the play of one card (as a signal) may be misunderstood, particularly if the declarer conceals some of the missing lower cards. An echo is the play of a high card, followed by a lower card, by the player not on lead.

```
              ♠ Q7
              ♡ Q54
              ◇ KQJ10
              ♣ KQJ10
♠ J82           N         ♠ 106
♡ AK763     W       E     ♡ 98
◇ 42                      ◇ 98763
♣ A42           S         ♣ 9876
              ♠ AK9543
              ♡ J102
              ◇ A5
              ♣ 53
```

Figure 87

West, in *figure 87*, opens the king of hearts against South's four spade contract. East plays the nine and South falsecards by dropping the jack, the eight is played by East to complete the echo. This high-low shows a desire for a third round continuation which in this case could only be the ability to trump, despite South's attempt to becloud the issue by dropping the jack.

Similarly, a low card followed by a higher card says "stop."

THE LAGRON ECHO

Every now and then, your partner will lead a card, *knowing that you can win that trick.* In almost all of these cases, you have previously echoed and can win the third round by trumping. After trumping, you will be confronted with the problem of which suit to lead next.

Figure 87 furnishes an excellent example. You sit East. Your partner has led the king of hearts, followed by the ace, on which you have played the nine and eight, respectively. He now leads the three of hearts which you trump.

HE HAS SIGNALLED YOU TO LEAD A CLUB - *HOW ?*

Dummy's holdings are identical in both minors. Ordinarily, you would have to guess which suit to return. The Lagron Echo makes it open and shut.

1 - There are four suits in the deck.

2 - Since you are trumping one suit (of which you are void), there are only three remaining suits that you can lead.

3 - Of these three suits, one is trump, so we will eliminate the trump suit from consideration.

4 - Of the two remaining suits, one is higher in rank than the other.

5 - If your partner leads a low card (for you to trump), usually the six or lower, *he wants you to return the lower-ranking suit;* if he leads a high card (for you to trump), *he requests the return of the higher-ranking suit.*

Simple, isn't it? You should master it within 30 seconds. Your partner on the preceding hand led the trey of hearts for you to trump, because he wished you to return the lower-ranking of the remaining suits, clubs. Had he desired a diamond return, he would have led the seven of hearts, a high card, for you to trump.

THE LAVINTHAL ECHO

The Lavinthal Echo is named after Hy Lavinthal, its inventor, of Camden, New Jersey. In fact, in eastern circles, he is also given credit for what I have just described as the Lagron Echo.

In the Lavinthal Echo, it is the size of the card *played* by the defender *not on lead* that indicates the desired suit switch. This will usually occur when a continuation of the originally led suit is undesirable, either because dummy has a singleton of the led suit and plenty of trumps, or because dummy has the remaining high cards of that suit.

West	North / South	East
	♠ K765 ♡ Q1087 ◇ 5 ♣ K765	
♠ J104 ♡ 32 ◇ AKJ96 ♣ 842	N W E S	♠ AQ8 ♡ 95 ◇ Q10432 ♣ 1093
	♠ 932 ♡ AKJ64 ◇ 87 ♣ AQJ	

Figure 88

In *figure 88*, South is the declarer at four hearts. West opens the king of diamonds on which partner drops the 10 of diamonds.

What could East's reason be for the play of an unnecessarily high card, in view of dummy's singleton?

The answer is that East is signalling for a shift to the higher-ranking of the two remaining suits.

NEGATIVE DISCARDS

West	North / South	East
	♠ AQ8	
♠ ?	N W E S	♠ KJ2
	♠ ?	

Figure 89

During the play of the hand, a defender might wish to indicate to partner a desire to have a certain suit led. However, the defender's cards may be such that he cannot afford the discard of a high card as a 'come-on' signal since it would cost a trick. *Figure 89* illustrates just such a case.

For East to discard the jack of spades as a signal to partner to lead that suit would cost a spade trick; the discard of the deuce would tell partner not to lead spades.

The trick in these cases *(when you want a suit led but can't afford the discard of a high card as a signal)* is to discard low, discouraging cards in the suits you don't want led. By negative inference, your partner will realize that if you don't want suits (a) and (b), you must want suit (c).

DEFENSIVE FINESSING

A finesse has been described as an attempt to win a trick with an intermediate card by playing after an opponent with a higher card or cards capable of winning the trick.

A defender, too, can take a finesse. In some cases he knows his finesse must succeed, since the missing, finessed against card is in plain sight in the dummy.

♠ Q65
N
♠ 2 (led) W E ♠ AKJ
S

Figure 90

In *figure 90*, West leads the deuce of spades. Dummy, North, plays the five; East, the jack.. The finesse must win since the only card capable of beating the jack, the queen, is in the dummy.

♠ J97
N
♠ 2 (led) W E ♠ KQ108
S

Figure 91

Again *(in figure 91)*, the deuce is led. Dummy plays the seven. Your correct play is the eight, since with the jack-nine in dummy, the eight is the equal of the king.

♠ 843
N
♠ AQ W E ♠ 2 (led)
S
♠ J (played)

Figure 92

In *figure 92*, we have a different situation. East leads the deuce. South, declarer, plays the jack. West will win the trick with the queen. West knows that his queen must win the trick since the dummy, yet to play, doesn't have the king, and South's jack has been captured.

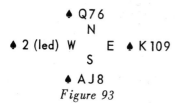

	♠ Q76	
	N	
♠ 2 (led) W		E ♠ K109
	S	
	♠ AJ8	

Figure 93

In *figure 93*, I have illustrated a less common, but nevertheless, frequent type of defensive finesse. After West leads the deuce, dummy, north, plays the six. East should play the nine. Inspection will show that while South will win with the jack, he will be limited to two tricks in the suit, whereas had East played the king, North-South had three tricks in the suit with the ace, jack and queen.

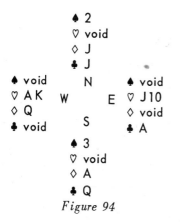

RUFF AND SLUFF

	♠ 2 ♡ void ◊ J ♣ J	
♠ void ♡ AK ◊ Q ♣ void	W N E S	♠ void ♡ J10 ◊ void ♣ A
	♠ 3 ♡ void ◊ A ♣ Q	

Figure 94

The expression, 'ruff and sluff,' means to lead a suit of which both players of the other side are void, permitting them to trump in one hand, discard a loser from the other. Together with voids, one or more trumps must be present in both hands.

Examine *figure 94*. West has the lead. South is playing the remaining cards of a spade contract. Both North (dummy) and South (declarer) are void of hearts. If West leads a heart, he gives the opponents a sluff and ruff, since one hand can trump, and the other discard the losing club. Note that a diamond lead from West would have preserved the defenders' club trick.

In 99 percent of cases, giving the declarer a ruff and sluff costs the defenders a trick. *Try to avoid it!*

FALSECARDING

Falsecarding is the act of playing a higher card for the purpose of misleading the opponents as to the location of a lower card or other cards. A simple example of a falsecard would be capturing a trick with the ace when holding the ace, king and queen of the led suit.

Falsecarding by the declarer is common practice. After all, if by playing his cards in a deceptive manner, he can fool his opponents, well and good. The declarer is under no obligation to tell his opponents what cards he holds. Further, it doesn't matter if the dummy is fooled by declarer's falsecards since the dummy *doesn't have the slightest thing to say about the play of his cards.* It is because of declarer's frequent throwing up a smoke screen by falsecarding that the defenders must be accurate and precise in their signals and discards to each other.

The defenders, on the other hand, *should avoid falsecarding.*

♠ 854
N
♠ K763 W E ♠ QJ2
S
♠ A109

Figure 95

A case in point is shown in *figure 95.* West opens the three of spades against south's contract in either suit or no trump. *(The principle is the same in both types of play).* The correct play by East is the jack. When declarer is compelled to play the ace in order to capture the jack, it is quite obvious to West that his partner must have the queen - otherwise, why would declarer play the ace and make West's king a winner?

Had East *incorrectly* first played the queen, South would win with the ace. But here's the big difference. West will place the jack as being in the declarer's hand since the correct play from a sequence is the *bottom* card of the sequence as shown on page 159. Hence East's misguided falsecard has fooled partner into believing that declarer holds the jack of spades.

There will be a very small minority of times where a falsecard by a defender *cannot mislead partner and may lure the declarer into a losing line of play.* However, this requires a great deal of experience and the student is advised, in the early stages of his bridge development, to play his cards as a defender 'straight down the middle.'

HOLDUPS

A holdup may be described as the refusal to play a winning card to the currently led trick in order to capture a later trick of that suit with the self-same winning card. The primary purpose of holding up is to wait with the winning card until one of the opponents is void of the led suit and can no longer lead it.

	♠ 106 ♡ Q63 ♢ KQ10982 ♣ 42	
♠ J9754 ♡ A72 ♢ 765 ♣ Q9	N W E S	♠ K83 ♡ 10854 ♢ A4 ♣ J865
	♠ AQ2 ♡ KJ9 ♢ J3 ♣ AK1073	

Figure 96

Figure 96 is a case in point. South is declarer at three no trump. West opens the five of spades. Dummy plays the 10, East the king and South wins with the ace. The jack of diamonds is led by by declarer. East refuses to take the trick with his ace. This is an example of a hold-up by a defender. A second diamond follows, East winning with the ace. Note that South no longer has a diamond and cannot lead that suit again from his hand. Dummy's remaining four diamonds, although established as winners, are virtually marooned in the absence of a positive re-entry in that hand.

Had East captured the first round of diamonds, declarer would have made his three no trump contract with ease, winning five diamonds, two spades and two clubs. With the hold up, declarer will no longer retain a diamond to use the remaining cards of that suit and the hand will be defeated through East's returning a spade after winning with the diamond ace and the defenders winning three spades, one diamond and one heart.

Holdups are also frequently employed by the declarer for the same purpose, viz., to exhaust one defender of the suit led by his partner. They are used principally in hands played in no trump since in suit contracts, the longer a player waits to play a winning card, the greater the danger of it being trumped.

QUIZ FIVE

1 - Your partner has opened the bidding with one club. The next player passes. What is your response with each of the following hands?

(a)	(b)	(c)	(d)	(e)	(f)
♠ AJ87	♠ KQ43	♠ K432	♠ AJ953	♠ KQ86	♠ A5432
♡ Q4	♡ KQ43	♡ K432	♡ 6	♡ K10742	♡ J6
◇ Q876	◇ J8	◇ K432	◇ AJ953	◇ J8	◇ KQJ10
♣ 1052	♣ 1076	♣ 2	♣ 104	♣ 42	♣ 52

2 - Your partner deals and bids one heart. The next player passes. What is your response with each of the following hands?

(g)	(h)	(i)	(j)
♠ Q865	♠ 543	♠ AJ43	♠ 876532
♡ 2	♡ J	♡ 107	♡ A
◇ A5432	◇ Q752	◇ KQ1075	◇ KJ9765
♣ 1054	♣ J10643	♣ J2	♣ void

3 -

♠ K84
dummy

♠ 6 (led) ♠ AJ93

South ?

Your partner, West, has led the six of spades. Assuming the lead to be fourth-best, how many spades does South, the declarer, have capable of beating the six?

4 -

♠ J962
dummy

♠ K (led) ♠ Q1087

Your partner, West, has led the king of spades. Assuming you wish a continuation, which spade do you play ?

5 -

♠ J962
dummy

♠ 3 (led) ♠ Q1087

Your partner opens the trey of spades. Dummy plays the deuce. Which spade do you play?

6 -

♡ Q96
dummy

♡ 8 (led) ♠A1054

Your partner opens the eight of hearts. Dummy's holding as well as your own is shown. Is partner's lead fourth-best?

7 -

	♠ Q42	
	dummy	
♠ 5 (led)		♠ K63

Assuming your partner's lead of the spade five to be fourth-best, how many spades did he have originally?

8 -

	♠ Q76	
	dummy	
♠ K, then A		♠ 8, then 2
(led)		(played)

South is playing a four heart contract. West opens the king of spades on which you play the eight as the start of an echo. The ace is continued on which you drop the deuce. South respectively played the three and five of spades. Your partner now leads the 10, which you trump, South dropping the jack. Your partner has asked you to return which suit ?

9 -

♠ KQJ10
♡ 10987
◊ AKQJ
♣ QJ

From the sequences to the left, indicate in one column the card you would lead from each. In a second column, show the card you would play if the suit were led by another player.

ANSWERS TO QUIZ FIVE

1 - (a) One diamond; (b) one heart; (c) one diamond; (d) one spade; (e) one heart; (f) one spade.
2 - (g) One spade; (h) pass; (i) two diamonds; (j) one spade.
3 - None.
4 - The eight, not the seven or 10. Playing the 10 could cost a trick.
5 - The seven, bottom of the sequence. Here you are following suit as opposed to signalling in question four.
6 - No. There are four cards higher than the eight in sight. If the eight were fourth-best, there would only be three outstanding higher cards.
7 - He originally held exactly four spades since all lower spades (that possibly could have been fifth and sixth-best) as the four, trey and deuce are in the dummy or in your hand.
8 - Partner's lead of the high card, the 10 of spades, for you to trump, calls for you to return the higher-ranking of the two side-suits, in this case, diamonds.
9 -

FROM	LEAD	PLAY
♠ KQJ10	K	10
♡ 10987	10	7
◊ AKQJ	K	J
♣ QJ	Q	J

LESSON FIVE
HANDS

1.

	North	
	♠ J952 ♡ AK1076 ♢ Q108 ♣ 3	
West ♠ Q103 ♡ 54 ♢ AKJ97 ♣ Q84	N W E S	**East** ♠ 84 ♡ QJ9 ♢ 6532 ♣ 10765
	♠ AK76 ♡ 832 ♢ 4 ♣ AKJ92	

South dealer, neither side vul.

South	West	North	East
1 cl.	1 dia..	1 ht.	pass
1 sp.	pass	3 sp..	pass
4 sp.	pass	pass	pass

West opens the diamond king.

2.

	North	
	♠ QJ1063 ♡ 532 ♢ J2 ♣ AJ8	
West ♠ AK9 ♡ Q4 ♢ K964 ♣ K1074	N W E S	**East** ♠ 74 ♡ KJ1098 ♢ A107 ♣ Q53
	♠ 852 ♡ A76 ♢ Q853 ♣ 962	

West dealer, N-S vulnerable..

West	North	East	South
1 dia.	pass	1 ht.	pass
1 no.tr.	pass	2 no tr.	pass
3 no tr.	pass	pass	pass

You select North's lead!

3.

	North	
	♠ Q53 ♡ AQ10 ♢ K76 ♣ AK54	
West ♠ 9 ♡ KJ642 ♢ 542 ♣ Q1087	N W E S	**East** ♠ K10764 ♡ 53 ♢ Q103 ♣ J93
	♠ AJ82 ♡ 987 ♢ AJ98 ♣ 62	

North dealer, E-W vulnerable

North	East	South	West
1 cl.	pass	1 dia.	pass
2 no tr.	pass	3 no tr.	pass
pass	pass		

East leads the spade six.

4..

	North	
	♠ K105 ♡ K98 ♢ K1063 ♣ Q107	
West ♠ 963 ♡ J2 ♢ A854 ♣ K632	N W E S	**East** ♠ AJ874 ♡ AQ543 ♢ 2 ♣ J8
	♠ Q2 ♡ 1076 ♢ QJ97 ♣ A954	

East dealer, both vulnerable.

East	South	West	North
1 sp.	pass	1 no tr.	pass
2 hts.	pass	2 sp.	pass
pass	pass		

South leads the diamond queen.

SOLUTIONS TO LESSON FIVE HANDS

1.

South declarer at four spades.

Trick	W	N	E	S
1	♢K	♢8	♢2	♢4
2	♡5	♡K	♡9	♡2
3	♣4	♣3	♣5	♣K
4	♣8	♠2	♣6	♣2
5	♠3	♠5	♠4	♠K
6	♠10	♠9	♠8	♠A
7	♣Q	♡6	♣7	♣A
8	♠Q	♡7	♣10	♣J
9	♡4	♡A	♡J	♡3
10	♢7	♢10	♢3	♠6
11	♢9	♡10	♢5	♣9

South wins 11 tricks, trumping the eight of hearts in the dummy and the queen of diamonds in his own hand.

2.

West declarer at 3 no trump.

Trick	N	E	S	W
1	♠Q	♠4	♠5	♠9
2	♠J	♠7	♠2	♠K
3	♡2	♡8	♡6	♡Q
4	♡3	♡9	♡A	♡4
5	♠3	♣3	♠8	♠A
6	♢2	♢A	♢3	♢4
7	♡5	♡K	♡7	♣4
8	♣J	♡J	♣2	♣6
9	♣8	♡10	♣6	♢9
10	♣A	♣5	♣9	♣K

North cashes his two spade tricks, concedes the last trick to West's king of diamonds.

3.

North declarer at three no trump.

Trick	E	S	W	N
1	♠6	♠2	♠9	♠Q
2	♠4	♠8	♡2	♠3
3	♡3	♡7	♡4	♡10
4	♢3	♢8	♢2	♢K
5	♢10	♢J	♢4	♢6
6	♡5	♡8	♡6	♡Q
7	♠7	♠J	♣7	♠5
8	♠10	♠A	♢5	♣4
9	♢Q	♢A	♡J	♢7

North wins the remaining four tricks with dummy's fourth diamond, the ace of hearts, and the ace-king of clubs. North wins 13 tricks.

4.

East declarer at two spades.

Trick	S	W	N	E
1	♢Q	♢A	♢6	♢2
2	♡6	♡J	♡K	♡A
3	♡7	♡2	♡8	♡Q
4	♡10	♠3	♡9	♡3
5	♠Q	♠6	♠5	♠4
6	♢7	♢4	♢K	♠7
7	♣4	♣K	♣7	♣8
8	♠2	♠9	♠10	♠J
9	♣5	♣2	♠K	♠A

East takes his two hearts and remaining spade, concedes a club to win 11 tricks and make five spades.

COMMENTS ON LESSON FIVE HANDS

Hand one - Had West led the ace of diamonds at the second trick and disregarded his partner's discouraging play of the deuce, the declarer would have had a much easier time to make five spades since after trumping the ace of diamonds, declarer's third (and losing) heart can be discarded on dummy's queen of diamonds.

It is safe to say that in the play of a two-suited hand, the success or failure of the contract will usually hinge upon the development, into tricks, of the side-suit. The student should notice how the declarer's first step is to trump away the queen of club *before* pulling trumps and the manner in which declarer's high trumps served as re-entries to his hand in addition to their capturin g power.

Hand two - This hand is intended to illustrate the tremendous superiority of the sequence lead over the fourth-best. Where North correctly opens the queen of spades, West will be held to two spade tricks, and later, defeated.

Had North opened the fourth-best spade, West would have been able to win the first trick with the nine, then win three spade tricks instead of two.

There are two other plays that the student should observe. The first is West's refusal to win the first spade and South's refusal to capture the queen of hearts. These are examples of 'hold-ups' as described on page 179 and are intended to exhaust the leader or his partner of the led suit.

The other play I hope you noti ced was North's 'high-low' with the jack and eight of clubs to show his partner the location of the re-entry for the now set-up spade suit.

Hand three - Note how declarer (North) used the rule of 11 in counting East's spade holding. Since West was marked for having only one spade higher than the six, that card was the nine, and once it was played, West could no longer capture dummy's eight.

Hand four - The hand is very lucky to make game, since every card is 'right.' Notice East's triple finesse in the trump suit against the missing king, queen and 10-spot.

Lesson VI

PART ONE

Opener's Rebids

PART TWO

The Management of Trump Suits

LESSON SIX
PART ONE

REBIDS BY THE OPENING BIDDER

By now, the student should be familiar with the more common bridge terms. The first bid at the table is known as the 'opening bid.' The answering bid by opener's partner is termed the 'response.'

We are going to discuss the *second* bid by the opening bidder. This is known as a *rebid.* The term describes any subsequent bid made by a player who has already bid. Thus, the second, third, fourth or subsequent bid by any player is a rebid.

Having opened the bidding, your possible rebid depends on three things -

1 - Your hand,
2 - Your partner's response,
3 - What the opponents do.

COUNTING POINTS FOR THE REBID

It is only natural that the value of a player's hand will change according to his partner's bids and those of the opponents. If the best suit in your hand is spades and you hear an opponent bidding spades, the playing strength of your hand lessens accordingly.

Let's suppose you have opened the bidding with one spade. Your partner responds with 'two hearts.' When you opened the bidding, you evaluated your distribution on a 3 - 2 - 1 basis. But if you intend to support (raise) your partner's heart suit, providing you hold adequate trump support for his suit, you should revalue your distribution as five points for a void, three points for a singleton and one point for a doubleton.

Similarly, if your rebid is to be in no trump, you can count *only high card points*. Distributional values, which are really nothing more or less than a measure of the ability to trump, cannot be counted in bids and rebids of no trump since in the latter contract, there is no such thing as trumping.

Don't forget, if you intend to raise partner's suit, to subtract one point for 4 - 3 - 3 - 3 distribution and / or for only three cards of his suit.

TO MAKE	IF AGREED SUIT IS	COMBINED POINTS BETWEEN PARTNERSHIP - MINIMUM
Game	Major	26
,,	No trump	26
,,	Minor	29
Small slam	Any	33
Grand slam	Any	37

ON FITS AND MISFITS

The above figures will hold true *most of the time*. Occasionally, you will meet a hand where game or slam is made with considerably less than the above. This will be due to tremendous trump fits, and long suits in distributional hands.

On the other hand, where there is no fit between the partnership, and neither partner has been able to support his partner's suit, 26 points may not be enough to produce a game in either a major suit or no trump.

As a general rule, when you have a singleton of your partner's suit, and he has been unable to support your suit, *add two points* to the requirements for game and slam.

In other words, a supporting fit can be as important as aces and kings.

RESPONSES OPENER MAY PASS

1 - Partner, before responding, previously passed.
2 - Partner passed after you opened and the opponents bid.
3 - Partner makes a weak response -
    (a) - one no trump;
    (b) - single raise, as from one heart to two hearts;
    (c) - pre-emptive (shutout) jump as from one to four hearts or from one club to four spades.
4 - Your right hand opponent bids after your partner has responded and you hold a minimum opening bid.

THE DIFFERENT KINDS OF JUMPS TO GAME

It stands to reason that once the bidding has reached a game contract, there is no point in further *voluntary* bidding unless sufficient values have been shown to warrant contracting for a slam with its attendant bonus.

You will hear, from some of your friends, that an immediate jump to game is a 'shutout' intended to close out the bidding. This is far from always being true.

First, any direct jump to game in no trump as you, one heart - partner, three no trump - shows an extremely powerful hand by responder and if your opening bid has 17 points or more, you should bid again since a makeable slam is quite probable. In other words, a jump to game in no trump is anything but a shutout.

It is where the jump to game is *in a suit* that the greatest misunderstanding lies. The following rule should be of assistance.

RULE - If the jump to game (in a suit) is a player's first bid, it is a shutout, showing a hand with a long suit or distributional values - that is weak in high cards.

When the jump to game is made as a player's second or subsequent bid, it shows great strength since it promises the makeability of game even if partner has a minimum.

EXAMPLES

Case A		Case B	
Opener	Responder	Opener	Responder
One heart	Four hearts	One heart	One spade
		Four spades	

WHEN THE OPENING BIDDER SHOULD REBID

1 - His partner (who has *not* previously passed) responds by bidding a new suit.

2 - The combined point count shows game to be makeable.

3 - There is a probability of game if responder has the maximum values shown by his response.

4 - Responder has bid one no trump and the opening bidder has a two-suited hand that will play better in a suit than in no trump.

♠ AQ876 ♡ KQ532 ◊ 2 ♣ 43

You have opened the bidding with the above hand with one spade. Your partner responds with 'one no trump.' Your rebid would be 'two hearts.'

5 - The combined point count, after partner's response, shows a slam to be makeable.

6 - Responder makes a forcing-to-game response. This can be a response of *one more than necessary in a new suit or in no trump.*

EXAMPLES

CASE C			CASE D	
YOU	PARTNER		YOU	PARTNER
One club	Two hearts	*or*	One heart	Two no trump

7 - Partner gives a double-raise in opener's major suit as in case (e). This bid, by a partner who has not previously passed, is forcing to game. The double-raise in a minor, shown in case (f), is semi-forcing, i.e., highly invitational.

EXAMPLES

CASE E		CASE F	
YOU	PARTNER	YOU	PARTNER
One spade	Three spades	One club	Three clubs
Forcing-to-game		*Semi-forcing*	

8 - Penalty doubles. Whenever your right hand opponent overcalls after your partner has responded, and you feel that because of the strength shown by partner's bid plus that in your own hand, the opponent cannot win the tricks necessary to complete his contract, you should double for penalty *provided* that the penalty will be equal or superior to the points your side would have scored in an alternative contract.

WHEN PARTNER HAS PREVIOUSLY PASSED

I have stated that the opening bidder is not compelled to rebid to his partner's response if the partner earlier was unable to open the bidding. However, if a partner who has previously passed does respond - should opener feel, with the strength shown by partner's response that there is a likelihood of game or a possibility of reaching a better contract, then the opening bidder can and should rebid.

WHEN SURE OF MAKING A GAME

The following words are among the most important in this text, and I wish the student to read and re-read them until they are understood perfectly.

When you have opened the bidding and your partner's response in combination with your hand indicates that your side can make a game, *show that fact immediately*. Whether the makeable game is in your suit or in partner's suit or in no trump isn't the important thing. What is important is to tell your partner that your side can make a game and that the bidding *must* continue, no matter how weak he may be, until at least game is reached.

There are two ways to accomplish this. The first (and most direct) is to jump directly to game.

CASE G

YOU	PARTNER
One heart	One spade
Four hearts	

CASE H

YOU	PARTNER
One heart	One spade
Four spades	

The other method is to make a rebid which is *absolutely forcing to game*. Either partner can insure that the bidding will continue to a game contract by bidding *one more than necessary in a previously unbid (new) suit.*

The only time, after a forcing-to-game bid, you need not continue bidding to game, is when an opponent interjects a bid which has been doubled for penalty.

CASE I

YOU	PARTNER
One heart	One spade
Three clubs	

CASE J

YOU	PARTNER
One spade	One no trump
Three hearts	

It is not necessary to jump more than one level of bidding in order to make a forcing-to-game bid. There is a tendency among new players to think that the higher the jump, the stronger the hand. *This is not true.* A single jump in a new suit shows an extremely strong hand with game probability; a jump of more than one level *in a new suit* is intended as a shutout and shows a hand with an extremely long suit that is weak in high cards.

In addition, once one player has made a single jump in a new suit as a forcing-to-game bid, neither partner need jump again since now the bidding *must* continue until game is reached.

The student may ask, "Well, if you're so sure about being able to make a game, why didn't you bid it at once instead of fooling around with jumps in other suits?"

The reason jump forces are used far more often than direct jumps to game is that the former wastes only one round of bidding (the jumped round), still leaves room for additional exchange of information before game is reached. It is in these extra rounds of bidding that the partnership can ascertain the best suit, whether the hand should play in no trump, whether the partnership can safely contract for slam or stop at game.

When the first round of bidding indicates 26 or more points between the partnership and you have a major suit fit or think the combined hands will play in no trump, bid a game at once or make a forcing-to-game rebid. The same reasoning applies to minor suit fits with 29 points or more. Your partner, who may have responded with a minimum, would probably pass a non-forcing rebid on your part.

While a jump response of two no trump is forcing to game, the same bid, as a rebid, is only semi-forcing.

CASE K		CASE L	
YOU	PARTNER	YOU	PARTNER
One club	Two no trump	One club	One spade
		Two no trump	
Forcing		*Semi-forcing*	

Be certain you understand the difference between the forcing to game response of two no trump (case k) and the rebid of two no trump (case l) which is semi-forcing.

THE DIFFERENCE BETWEEN FORCING AND SEMI-FORCING BIDS

A jump bid of *one more than necessary in a new suit* by either partner, after one partner opened the bidding, is forcing to game, and indicates slam possibility.

A jump rebid *in a previously bid suit* is only semi-forcing.

CASE M		CASE N	
YOU	PARTNER	YOU	PARTNER
One heart	One spade	One heart	One spade
Three hearts		Two hearts	Three spades

Both your three heart rebid in case (m) and partner's jump rebid of three spades in case (n) are only semi-forcing since the jumps were made in the same suit previously bid by that player.

A semi-forcing bid may be passed by a partner who has already shown the full extent of his values. Remember - to be forcing to game, the bid must be a *single* jump *in a new suit.*

THE IN-BETWEEN HANDS

There are three responses that can be made with as little as six points. These are - (a) the bid of a new suit at the one level; (b) the single raise of opener's suit; (c) a response of one no trump.

On many hands, a game can be bid and made if the responder has a little more than the minimum, say, nine points instead of the required six. In order to explore this possibility, the opening bidder, with 17 to 19 points, should make a second bid. This rebid will be either non-forcing or semi-forcing so that a responder, with a minimum hand, can pass.

RULE FOR OPENER'S REBIDS
(Following a minimum response)

IF YOU HAVE OPENED WITH	AND PARTNER RESPONDS	YOU SHOULD
13 to 16 points	One no trump	Pass unless hand is distributional, then show a second suit or a rebiddable suit.
	Single raise	Pass
	New suit	You must rebid.
17 to 19 points	Any of the above	Make another bid.
20 or more	Any of the above	Bid a game or make a bid that is forcing to game.

SUPPORTING PARTNER VS. REBIDDING ONE'S OWN SUIT

One of the most frequently asked questions is "**When it's my turn to rebid, should I first show my suit to be rebiddable or raise my partner if I have support for his suit?**"

In general, it is more constructive to support partner's suit than to make a simple rebid of one's own suit. Raising partner's suit shows a fit and a willingness to reach a higher contract, whereas a simple minimum rebid by the opening bidder of his suit is a semi-signoff showing a rebiddable suit and a maximum of 16 points. The choice becomes more difficult, even to experienced players, when the selection lies between rebidding a major suit or supporting partner's minor suit response.

BIDDING A SECOND SUIT VERSUS SHOWING THE FIRST SUIT TO BE REBIDDABLE

Modern bidding methods, as explained in this text, make it easy to show second suits and rebiddable suits cheaply and safely. But if you can't show both features cheaply and safely - if the price is too high for safety - you may have to suppress one feature or the other. In other words, showing all of your features is a luxury you just can't afford.

With a weak hand where showing the second suit will increase the contract, it is better to forget the second suit and simply show the first bid suit to be rebiddable; if the second suit can be shown without increasing the contract, by all means bid it; but if showing the second suit requires increasing the contract, be sure you have a strong hand, preferably 17 points or more.

Suppose you hold -

♠ AQJ64 ♡ 9 ◇ A10876 ♣73

CASE O		CASE P	
YOU	PARTNER	YOU	PARTNER
One spade	Two clubs	One spade	Two hearts
Two diamonds		Two spades	

OPENER'S REBIDS TO A ONE OVER ONE RESPONSE

After you open the bidding with one of a suit, the most frequent response you will hear from partner will be a bid of 'one' of a higher ranking suit. In other words, let's say that you've opened the bidding with one club, and your partner responds with one heart.

The first thing you must remember is that if your partner hasn't previously passed, *you must bid at least once more.* Now we'll examine the various types of rebids and see what each would indicate and require.

A REBID OF ONE NO TRUMP

YOU	PARTNER	YOUR HANDS (a)	YOUR HANDS (b)
(a)			
One club	One diamond	♠ A43	♠ Q108
One no trump		♡ J87	♡ J2
(b)		◇ 432	◇ AK654
One diamond	One heart	♣ AKJ9	♣ K92
One no trump			

Non-Forcing.

(a) Denies four hearts or four spades or good diamond support, indicates a minimum hand with possibly a rebiddable club suit. 13 to 16 points, balanced or semi-balanced distribution.

(b) Denies four or more spades, shows 13 to 16 points, lacks heart support, may have rebiddable diamond suit or a secondary club suit. Balanced or semi-balanced hand.

Try not to rebid one no trump with any singleton, whether in partner's suit or elsewhere, even if the singleton is an ace or a king.

Do not rebid one no trump if you can show a second suit, no matter how weak, at the one level.

It is entirely possible to rebid one no trump when holding a rebiddable suit if rebidding that suit causes the bidding to go one step higher. With a minimum hand as (b), the opener might prefer to play for seven tricks in no trump rather than eight in his suit so he conceals the fact that the suit is rebiddable, makes the cheaper rebid of one no trump.

A JUMP REBID OF TWO NO TRUMP

YOU	PARTNER	YOUR HANDS (c)	(d)
One club	One diamond	♠ A 10 9	♠ K 2
Two no trump		♡ A K 8	♡ A Q 8
		◊ J 3 2	◊ K J 5
SEMI-FORCING		♣ A K 7 6	♣ A J 4 3 2

Shows 18 to 19 high card points in the opening bidder's hand. As in all no trump bids and rebids, no points are counted for distribution. The hand should not contain any singletons or voids and high cards capable of taking a trick must be present in all unbid suits. Ordinarily, the jump rebid in no trump will deny the presence of any higher-ranking suit of four or more cards that could be shown at the one level as four hearts or four spades in the above examples.

A JUMP REBID OF THREE NO TRUMP

YOU	PARTNER	YOUR HAND (e)
One club	One diamond	♠ A Q
Three no trump		♡ K 10 9
		◊ K Q 5
		♣ A K 4 3 2

Indicates 20 - 21 high card points in the opening bidder's hand. The remainder of the requirements are similar to those of the rebid of two no trump.

Since this rebid shows a tremendously strong hand, it is under no circumstances a shutout or signoff. Responder, with 12 points or more, should realize that a slam may be makeable and continue bidding in these cases.

SHOWING A SECOND SUIT AT THE ONE LEVEL

YOU	PARTNER	YOUR HANDS (f)	(g)
One club	One diamond	♠ A Q 10	♠ A Q 10 8
One heart		♡ K 7 6 2	♡ K 7 6 2
		◇ 3 2	◇ 8
		♣ A J 6 2	♣ A J 6 2

Indicates four or more hearts (in these examples), no more strength than the 13 points originally required for the opening bid. Of course, the hand *could have more* than 13 points, but the point I'm making is that the rebid of the second suit promises no additional values over the opening bid.

One-over-one bidding leaves room for the responder to show a possible four card spade holding on the way up *and it applies only in responding and rebidding - not in the original choice of which suit to bid first.*

NOT FORCING - Responder may pass the second suit though he will usually try to keep the bidding alive over any new suit.

SINGLE RAISE OF PARTNER'S SUIT

YOU	PARTNER	YOUR HAND (h)
One diamond	One spade	♠ Q 5 2
Two spades		♡ 6 4
NOT-FORCING		◇ A K 10 9
		♣ A 10 8 6

Indicates 13 to 16 points, trump support for partner's suit, and a comparatively minimum hand.

DOUBLE RAISE OF PARTNER'S SUIT

YOU	PARTNER	YOUR HAND (i)
One diamond	One spade	♠ K J 8 7
Three spades		♡ 3
		◇ A Q 10 9 8
SEMI-FORCING		♣ A J 5

Indicates 17 to 19 points, at least four trumps including the jack or better, usually some ruffing value in a side suit, game probability if partner has eight or more points.

If the double raise is in a minor suit as with hand (j), it will deny four hearts or four spades in the opening bidder's hand and be strongly invitational to responder to bid three no trump with some high cards in the unbid suits and eight or more points.

YOU	PARTNER	YOUR HAND
One club	One diamond	(j)
Three diamonds		♠ A 3
		♡ J 3
		◇ K J 8 4
SEMI-FORCING		♣ A K J 10 8

TRIPLE RAISE OF PARTNER'S SUIT

YOU	PARTNER	YOUR HAND
One diamond	One spade	(k)
Four spades		♠ A J 9 6
		♡ 8
		◇ A Q J 7 6
		♣ K Q 10

A POWERFUL REBID

This jump from one to four in responder's suit is invariably made in a major suit, rarely in a minor, since a raise to four clubs or four diamonds would preclude playing a possible three no trump contract which might have been easier to produce.

It should be emphasized that the immediate raise of partner's response to game-level is *a very strong bid that shows an extremely strong hand with 20 points or more and is anything but a shutout.* With 13 points or more, the responder should make a slam try.

It is the immediate jump to game *by responder as his first bid* that is intended as a shutout to show a hand powerful in distribution and weak in high card strength. This bid is described on pages 63 through 66.

MINIMUM REBID OF ORIGINAL SUIT

YOU	PARTNER	YOUR HAND (l)
One diamond	One heart	♠ A 7 4
Two diamonds		♡ 2
		◇ K Q J 9 8 7
		♣ Q J 3

NON-FORCING

Indicates a minimum hand with a rebiddable suit, no other suit that can be shown at the one level. Denies good support for partner's suit and from 13 to 16 points.

SINGLE JUMP REBID OF ORIGINAL SUIT

YOU	PARTNER	YOUR HAND (m)
One heart	One spade	♠ A 2
Three hearts		♡ A K 9 8 7 6
		◇ A J 3
		♣ 6 2

SEMI-FORCING

Indicates 17 to 19 points with a six card or longer suit or an exceedingly staunch five-carder. Usually some fit with partner's suit, even though partial, is present.

Unless opener's suit is solid or semi-solid, the jump rebid should not be made with a singleton or void of responder's suit with less than 18 points since the hand may be a misfit.

JUMP REBID TO GAME IN ORIGINAL SUIT

YOU	PARTNER	YOUR HAND (n)
One heart	One spade	♠ K 2
Four hearts		♡ A K J 10 9 8 7
		◇ A Q 3
		♣ 2

Indicates 20 or more points in the opening bidder's hand, plus a solid or practically solid suit of six cards or longer.

SHOWING A NEW, LOWER-RANKING SUIT AT THE TWO LEVEL

It stands to reason that whenever the opening bidder, in order to show a second suit, must increase the bidding level, he should have a little more strength than that already promised by his opening bid. This 'little more strength' can be in distributional values or perhaps in high cards. The hand will usually contain 14 to 17 points with no assurance of game at this point.

(o)

♠ 86
♡ A Q 10 8 7
◇ 7
♣ K Q 8 5 4

Open with one heart. If partner bids one spade, rebid with two clubs. Had partner bid two diamonds, you would have bid two hearts.

(p)

♠ 10 9 8
♡ 6 5
◇ A Q 10 9
♣ A K Q J

Open the bidding with one diamond. Over partner's response of one heart or one spade, rebid with two clubs.

SHOWING A NEW, HIGHER-RANKING SUIT AT THE TWO LEVEL

This has been adequately discussed under 'Reverses' on pages 132 through 137.

REBIDS BY OPENER TO A RESPONSE OF ONE NO TRUMP

You have opened the bidding with one of a suit and your partner has responded with one no trump.

What has been said about rebidding after receiving a one over one response applies, in great measure, to rebidding after partner's one no trump response.

Both responses can be made with as little as six points. But there the similarity ends.

First, the response of one no trump is based on high cards only. In other words, *all of the six or more points is in aces, kings, queens and jacks - no points are counted for distribution.* Second and even more important, the one no trump reponse places a ceiling on responder's hand of 10 points. The opening bidder is aware that his partner holds from six to 10 points, all of it in high cards.

The one over one response (of a new suit) can show from six points *upwards - the hand could have 10 - 15 or even more!* The responder will show these extra values in possible subsequent rebids.

But when the response has been one no trump, the responder has usually told his whole story with the one bid. Further, it is a simple matter for the opening bidder to add the figures 'six to 10' to his own points and see if the total is 26 - if game is makeable or not.

There are really only two reasons for rebidding after receiving a one no trump response. The first is that you feel a game to be makeable in which case you will either jump directly to game or make a forcing to game rebid by bidding one more than necessary *in a new suit;* the other reason is that the hand, being distributional with singletons and long suits, will play better in a suit contract than in no trump.

With these things in mind, let's take stock and see what our partner's hand, after his one no trump response, looks like.

For one thing, we've already established that he has from six to 10 high card points. Secondly, he should preferably hold at least two cards in your suit, since responding one no trump with a singleton of partner's suit is unsound practice, a bid that good players try to avoid.

Third, partner lacks good supporting cards for your suit since with them, he would have raised your suit in preference to responding, with one no trump. Of course, remember this - your partner *must* assume your suit is not rebiddable since it has not been rebid.

Fourth and a very important fourth - your partner lacks four or more cards of any higher-ranking suit that could have been bid at the one level.

THE PASS

When you have opened the bidding holding a minimum hand and your partner has responded with one no trump, you should pass unless your hand is unable to play satisfactorily in that contract. A void suit (and sometimes a singleton) will unfit your hand for no trump play.

Don't be afraid to pass your partner's one no trump when you have opened with from 13 to 16 points, even though your hand may contain a second suit you haven't yet shown. With a weak two-suiter, say both suits of four cards each, or perhaps one of five cards and the other of four, showing the second suit would force you to the two level. That means that you would need eight tricks to fulfill the contract. At one no trump, your side only needed seven!

Moreover, if you do rebid, your partner may also bid again, thinking you have extra values and then you're still higher in the bidding.

THE PASS FOLLOWING AN INTERVENING BID BY RIGHT HAND OPPONENT

If you have opened a minimum or near minimum hand (13 to 16 points) and after your partner's one no trump response, should your right hand opponent now overcall, pass !

Should you make another bid at this point, you show extra values.

With strength in the opponent's suit and the belief that he cannot win enough tricks to fulfill his contract, you should double for penalty.

A 'free' rebid at this point would show 17 points or more.

THE MINIMUM REBID OF THE SAME SUIT

Suppose you opened the bidding with one heart and your partner responded with one no trump. The fewest number of hearts you can bid in order to return to hearts from no trump would be a bid of two hearts. That's a minimum rebid.

The minimum rebid after a response of one no trump would show a rebiddable suit of five cards or more and from 13 to 16 points and indicates an unwillingness to play the hand in no trump.

A SEMI-SIGNOFF

SINGLE JUMP REBID OF ORIGINAL SUIT

Let's assume you opened the bidding with one heart and your partner responded with one no trump. You now rebid 'three hearts, one more than necessary - in the very same suit with which you opened the bidding.

You have shown a strongly rebiddable suit, probably of six cards or longer and from 17 to 19 points. There is a probability of game if partner has a maximum response.

(q)
♠ 7 4
♡ A Q J 10 8 7
◇ K Q J
♣ K 2
SEMI-FORCING

THE BID OF A NEW, LOWER-RANKING SUIT

Suppose you opened the bidding with one heart on the following hands and your partner responded with one no trump.

(r)	(s)	(t)
♠ J 8	♠ 8 4	♠ 3
♡ A K 6 5 4	♡ A Q 10 9 8	♡ A J 9 7 5 4
◇ A Q 8 7	◇ 2	◇ A J 8 6 5
♣ 4 3	♣ K Q 4 3 2	♣ 4

Your rebids should be -

(r) two diamonds; (s) two clubs; (t) two diamonds.

Showing a second, lower-ranking suit as a minimum rebid indicates from 13 to 17 points in the opening bidder's hand and is semi-constructive. It shows some additional values, either in high cards or in distribution, a desire to play the hand in a suit rather than in no trump.

NON-FORCING

STRENGTH-SHOWING REBIDS

If you have opened the bidding with 20 points or more, the six or more points guaranteed by partner's one no trump response are all you need to make a game.

(u)	(v)
♠ A K J 10 8 7	♠ A K J 8 7
♡ K J 8	♡ A Q 10 9 8
◇ Q 4	◇ K 2
♣ A 2	♣ 3

Holding hand (u) you have opened the bidding with one spade. Your partner responds with one no trump. You should now rebid with four spades. Your 20 points, plus partner's known six or more, virtually insure the major suit game.

Hand (v), with 20 points, in combination with the six to 10 points promised by partner's response of one no trump, should similarly be bid to a game contract. However, there is a question of whether the hand should play in spades or hearts or possibly in no trump. This question can be resolved by making the forcing-to-game rebid of 'three hearts,' a bid of one more than necessary in a new suit. Partner's raise or preference will be the determining factor.

REBIDDING AFTER OPENER'S SUIT HAS BEEN RAISED

We will suppose that you have opened the bidding with one heart. Your partner has made one of the three following bids.

A - Two hearts;
B - Three hearts;
C - Four hearts

Looking at our table of responses on page 63, you will see that the single raise from one to two hearts can be made with from six to 12 points; the double raise, as from one heart to three hearts, shows a strong hand of from 13 to 16 points and is forcing to game; the triple raise from one heart to four hearts indicates 11 to 14 total points with a maximum of nine points in high cards and is pre-emptive.

First, let's consider possible rebidding after receiving a single raise from one to two hearts. We've stated that this raise can show from six to 12 points.

There are only two possible valid reasons for a rebid by you. The first is that you think your side can make a game; the other, you have been 'pushed' higher by an opponent's bid.

Let's suppose the opponents didn't bid and you hold 14 or 15 points. You could say to yourself, "**If my partner has 11 or 12 points, we can make a game.**"

But stop and think. While it is possible that he does have 11 or 12 points, it is most unlikely.

Why?

Because with from 10 to 12 points and a maximum raise, your partner, if he has not previously passed, will usually attempt to bid some other suit before supporting your suit. This will give him an opportunity to make two bids on hands which are almost, but not quite, worth a double raise. This is the way a bridge-player would jokingly describe a hand worth a bid of 'two and a half hearts,' a bid, of course, that doesn't exist. These are known as 'temporizing bids' and were mentioned in a footnote on page 63.

So we should assume that he has from six to nine points. Accordingly, to make a voluntary rebid, you should have a minimum of 17 points. On the other hand, with 20 or more points, you should contract for game.

If, after your partner's single raise, your right hand opponent 'sticks in' a bid, you have a golden opportunity to show a weak opening bid by passing.

Nothing is more eloquent of weakness than a pass. If your partner has only been able to give you a single raise and your right hand opponent now bids, you should ordinarily pass with 13 to 16 point opening bids. With 17 to 19, you can make a 'free' rebid and with 20 or more points, get to game.

An alternative is when you feel a game to be unmakeable but if your right hand opponent bids what happens to be your other suit and you feel that the opponent cannot possibly win the tricks necessary to fulfill his contract, a penalty double will be more lucrative than any other result your way of the cards.

(w)
♠ A 2
♡ K Q J 8 7
◇ K J 10 8 6
♣ 4

For example, let's suppose that you have opened the bidding with one heart with hand (w). Your partner raises you to two hearts after which your right hand opponent overcalls with three diamonds. While your hand totals 17 points, so that a three heart bid would be in order, it is apparent that against your hand, it would be impossible for an opponent to win nine tricks with diamonds as trumps. You should double for penalty.

The question of when to double for penalty and when to rebid is not always so clear cut. Sometimes even the expert may ponder, particularly when the decision is close.

If the student will bear in mind that any time he rebids when he doesn't have to bid, he's showing extra strength, he will avoid overbidding, disastrous penalties, and the consequent shaking of partnership morale!

Should your partner have given you a strength showing double-raise from one heart to three hearts, that is forcing to game, and you *must* rebid, even if you opened with a bare 13 points. Whether you rebid your raised suit, or show another suit depends upon the type of hand you hold. With that bidding, let's pretend that you hold each of the following hands -

(x)	(y)	(z)
♠ A J 5	♠ 2	♠ A Q 4 3
♡ K Q 10 9	♡ A K J 5 4	♡ A Q 10 9 8
◇ Q 10 9 8	◇ K J 9 8	◇ K J
♣ K J	♣ J 5 2	♣ Q 4
Rebid three no trump. If partner's hand is unbalanced, he will now bid four hearts.	Rebid four hearts.	Rebid with three spades. Partner cannot pass.

Now, let's suppose your partner raised your opening bid of one heart to four hearts. That shows a hand weak in high card values, but strong in playing strength.

The opening bidder, with less than 20 points, should pass and be happy he's in game. With 20 points or more, the possibility of slam should be explored.

IF THE RAISED SUIT IS A MINOR

In all of the preceding bidding examples, we supposed that the opening bid was one heart and that partner raised it to two hearts, three hearts or four hearts.

Suppose the opening bid had been one club or one diamond, and partner raised to two, three, four or even five of that suit.

The point count shown by responder is the same, minor as major. There are, however, some important differences.

First, to make game in a minor, you need win 11 tricks instead of the 10 required in the major. Correspondingly, you should have a total of 29 or more points between the partnership instead of the 26 that will normally produce a major suit game. Bear this in mind.

However, there is one shortcut to game. That is the contract of three no trump which requires the winning of only nine tricks, and can usually be produced by 26 high card points. If you can make a game in no trump, and you have the requisite stoppers in the unbid suits, it will frequently be the easier contract to fufiill than the alternative game in the minor suit.

But remember one thing! The jump from one to three in a major suit is *forcing to game;* the single jump (double raise) in a minor is only *semi-forcing and can be passed* by an opening bidder with a minimum hand.

REBIDDING AFTER A TWO OVER ONE RESPONSE

You have opened the bidding with, let us say, one spade. Your partner now responds with two of a lower ranking suit, in this case, clubs.

First, we know that he has at least 10 points since that is the minimum requirement for showing a new suit as a response at the two level. So 16 points in the opener's hand, plus at least a partial fit or a good suit, will produce a game in a major suit or in no trump.

You should rebid normally at this point. If you have a minimum hand, you can show this fact by making a minimum rebid. Perhaps you have a second suit to show, or think you can make a game. Perhaps you'd like to support your partner's suit. Lastly, you may wish to bid no trump.

It depends on your hand! And the rebid tells the story!

In each of the following hands,. you have opened the bidding with one spade and your partner responded with two clubs.

(a)	(b)	(c)
♠ AQJ84	♠ AJ8763	♠ AKJ987
♡ KJ986	♡ Q2	♡ 5
♢ K10	♢ AQ	♢ KQJ
♣ 2	♣ 643	♣ 876
Rebid two hearts	Rebid two spades	Rebid three spades

(d)	(e)	(f)
♠ AQJ109	♠ AQ107	♠ AKJ8
♡ KQ1098	♡ KJ8	♡ AJ10
♢ void	♢ A42	♢ K42
♣ KJ8	♣ Q109	♣ A87
Rebid three hearts	Rebid two no trump	Rebid three no trump

OPENER'S REBIDS FOLLOWING A JUMP FORCE

You have opened the bidding with one of a suit, and your partner has made a jump force (bid one more than necessary) in a new suit.

What do you do now?

In order of preference:

1 - Show a second, biddable suit if present;
2 - Rebid a rebiddable suit;
3 - Support your partner's suit with adequate trump holdings.
4 - Bid the minimum number of no trump with a minimum 13 to 16 point hand lacking any of the above.

In all of the following, it is presumed that you have opened the bidding with one spade, and your partner bid three diamonds.

(g)	(h)	(i)
♠ AK654	♠ AK432	♠ KQJ92
♡ AJ765	♡ J98	♡ Q10
♢ J2	♢ A54	♢ 82
♣ 3	♣ 87	♣ AK43
Bid three hearts	Bid three spades	Bid four clubs

(j)
♠ A K Q J 10 8
♡ 8 2
♢ 7 5
♣ A 4 3
Bid *four* spades. This is the one exception to jumping after a jump response. It shows a solid or semi-solid suit.

(k)
♠ A J 8 7
♡ K Q 10 9
♢ A 4 3 2
♣ 3
Bid three hearts. If partner raises the spade suit, you now show the diamond fit.

(l)
♠ A K Q 8
♡ A 4 3
♢ K J 5
♣ 4 3 2
Raise to four diamonds.

(m)
♠ A 8 7 6 5
♡ K Q 3
♢ 8 2
♣ K J 9
Bid three no trump to show that you have opened a minimum hand.

(n)
♠ K Q 8 6
♡ K 5 3
♢ 4 3 2
♣ A Q 2
Bid three no trump. Again you show the minimum character of the opening bid.

It should be empasized that the rebid of the minimum number of no trump to indicate a scant opening bid does not necessarily show a desire on the part of the opening bidder to play the hand in no trump. It is merely a means of telling partner that you have little or nothing in excess of the values already promised by your opening bid, that your suit in most cases is not rebiddable, that you lack good support for partner's suit, have no other suit to show, and that you want to put the brakes on the bidding before you get too high. In other words, you're obligated because of partner's jump force to continue bidding until a game contract has been reached, but you do want to tell your partner that you have a minimum opening bid.

Now, presuming you have opened the bidding with one club, and your partner has responded with two spades, let's see what your rebid should be with each of the following hands.

(o)
♠ A J 8
♡ K 10 9 8
♢ A Q
♣ A J 8 7

(p)
♠ Q 2
♡ A J 8 7
♢ J 3
♣ A K J 9 7

(q)
♠ J 8 3
♡ K Q 5
♢ 4 3
♣ A Q J 8 7

(o) Support your partner by raising him to three spades. To reverse the bidding by bidding 'three hearts' would give partner the false impression that the club suit is longer than the heart suit which certainly is not true.

(p) Three hearts. Here both your distribution and high card holding justify the reverse bid.

(q) Two no trump. The important thing is first to tell partner that you have opened a minimum hand. The fact that the club suit is rebiddable can, if desired, be shown later.

REBIDS FOLLOWING A TWO NO TRUMP RESPONSE

The student will or already has discovered that the bid of two no trump can be used in a lot of different ways. When made as the first response by opener's partner who has not previously passed, it is forcing to game. For example -

YOU, OPENER	PARTNER, RESPONDER
One heart	Two no trump

You must continue to game!

Thus your next bid is forced, and what you do depends entirely on the type of hand you hold. With the preceding bidding, let's pretend that you hold the following hands -

(r)	(s)	(t)
♠ A 8 7	♠ 4	♠ K 2
♡ A J 10 9	♡ A K 8 7 6	♡ A Q 7 6 5
◇ K Q 3	◇ K Q 7	◇ K Q 10 9 8
♣ 10 8 7	♣ 8 5 4 3	♣ 3
Rebid three no trump.	Rebid three hearts.	Rebid four diamonds

Do not, under any circumstances, pass or fail to continue bidding until a game contract has been reached, or an opponent's bid has been doubled for penalty.

REBIDDING WHEN PARTNER'S RESPONSE HAS ALREADY PLACED YOU IN GAME

There are four possible situations after you have opened the bidding with one of a suit and your partner's response has placed you in a game contract. These are -

1 - A jump from one of a minor to five of that suit, as from one club to five clubs.

2 - From one to four in a major suit as one heart - four hearts.

3 - From one of a suit to game in another suit, as one heart - four spades.

4 - From one of a suit to three no trump, as you, one heart; partner, three no trump.

The first three cases illustrate responses where responder's hands are *weak in high cards*, but long in suits and distribution. Therefore, there is no excuse for a possible rebid by the opening bidder that will get the partnership higher than a game contract unless he thinks there is a strong probability of slam.

In the fourth example, where partner's immediate response was three no trump, there are two possible reasons for a rebid by the opening bidder. The first reason is that he thinks a slam is possible. The responder has shown 16 or 17 high card points. If the opening bidder has 17 points or more, slam should be makeable.

The other reason is that the opening bidder feels that his hand will play better in a suit contract than in no trump. This may be due to the fact that opener's hand is unbalanced, or that he has a second suit worth showing, or that the hand is short of re-entries.

I hope you realize that the first three bidding cases - where the first response was an immediate jump to game *in a suit* - showed weak hands and were shutout bids; that the jump to *three no trump in the fourth case showed an extremely powerful hand, and was anything but a shutout.* The opener, with a powerful hand, should rebid and try to get to slam.

With the following hands, it is presumed that your partner has bid three no trump in response to your opening bid of one heart.

(u)	(v)	(w)
♠ void	♠ 872	♠ 86
♡ AJ8764	♡ KQJ9743	♡ AQ1043
♢ KQ432	♢ A	♢ AJ9
♣ J8	♣ 32	♣ Q43
Rebid four diamonds.	Rebid four hearts.	Pass

REBIDDING IN BRIEF

If partner has made a weak response of one no trump or a single raise from one to two of your suit -

HOLDING POINTS	REBID
13 - 16	Pass a single raise. Rebid over one no trump only if the hand is distributional with a long suit or if you have other suits to show.
17 - 19	Make another bid, according to your hand.
20 or more	Bid a game or make a forcing to game rebid.

IF PARTNER HAS PREVIOUSLY PASSED

You may pass a response which normally would be forcing. Any rebid by the opening bidder is entirely voluntary.

ON MISFITS

If the hand is apparently a misfit - you may have a singleton or void of partner's suit - and he has apparently been unable to support your suit, add two points to the requirements for game.

ON FREE REBIDS

A free bid is a voluntary bid made after an opponent has bid. Any free rebid by the opening bidder shows additional values in excess of the opening bid. With a minimum hand, the opening bidder should pass an overcall by his right hand opponent.

PART TWO

THE MANAGEMENT OF TRUMP SUITS

No subject in bridge has been the source of more jokes and cliches than that of declarer leading trumps. Among them are: **'Many a child is walking the streets of London whose father failed to lead trump;'** another, also oddly enough of English origin, gives a tramp, on being aroused on a park bench by an English 'bobbie,' remarking, **'If I had it to do all over again, I'd've led trumps;** the third, far from always true, is - **'When in doubt, lead trumps.'**

As a general rule, the first suit to be led by the declarer should be the trump suit. But there are also many, many times where trump leads by the declarer should be deferred or not led at all. Naturally, knowing when to lead trumps or not to lead trumps comes with experience in the play of the cards. But it is possible to lay down general basic principles which will be illustrated on ensuing pages.

WHEN TO LEAD TRUMPS IMMEDIATELY

1 - Trumps should be led immediately by declarer when there is a danger that a defender can trump a high card held by declarer or dummy.

2 - When, after leading trumps, sufficient trumps will remain in dummy or declarer's hand or both (as the case may be) to insure trumping losing cards in side suits.

	♠ K J 8 ♡ K 7 4 ◇ A Q 10 8 7 ♣ Q 10	
♠ 6 5 4 ♡ A 8 6 5 3 2 ◇ 2 ♣ A J 2	N W E S	♠ 3 2 ♡ 9 ◇ J 9 4 3 ♣ 9 8 7 6 5 4
	♠ A Q 10 9 7 ♡ Q J 10 ◇ K 6 5 ♣ K 3	

Figure 97

In *figure 97*, South is the declarer at four spades, West having overcalled South's opening one spade bid with two hearts. The hand can be defeated with the opening lead of the ace of hearts, followed by another heart. East will trump and return a club. After winning with the ace, West leads another heart. Again East trumps, this time for the setting trick.

But not being clairvoyant, West opened the singleton diamond. South won with the king. Note that if South leads any suit but trump, the hand will be defeated. The contract will be assured by leading three rounds of trumps, then knocking out the heart ace and club ace. The hand will win 11 tricks. Here dummy's trumps did nothing but assist in the drawing of the adverse trumps.

In *figure 98*, South is again playing a four spade contract. The queen of hearts would be West's opening lead. After winning with the ace, South can afford two leads of high trumps since dummy will still retain three trumps to take care of South's three losing hearts.

	♠ K8742 ♡ 2 ♢ AJ953 ♣ K10	
♠ 10 ♡ QJ1076 ♢ Q82 ♣ QJ43	N W E S	♠ 95 ♡ K94 ♢ K107 ♣ A9865
	♠ AQJ63 ♡ A853 ♢ 64 ♣ 72	

Figure 98

WHEN NOT TO LEAD TRUMPS IMMEDIATELY

Oddly enough, there are more times when trump leads by declarer should be deferred than the contrary. These include -

1 - When losers must be trumped in dummy;

2 - When dummy's losers are trumped in declarer's hand and dummy's trumps become the master trumps. This is known as a *dummy reversal.*

3 - A cross-ruff;

4 - The need of trumps as later cards of re-entry.

5 - Discards (of losing cards) must be taken or obtained before the opponents are permitted to regain the lead in the trump suit in which they hold winning cards.

6 - The need of a trump 'policeman' in the dummy while setting up winning tricks in a side suit.

7 - Safety plays in side suits.

Rather an imposing list so we'll give an example of each.

	♠ 10 5 ♡ J 10 7 ◇ A K 3 2 ♣ Q 8 6 4	
♠ K J 9 8 ♡ Q 4 3 ◇ Q J 10 9 ♣ 7 5	N W E S	♠ A 7 4 3 ♡ 9 2 ◇ 8 7 6 ♣ J 10 9 3
	♠ Q 6 2 ♡ A K 8 6 5 ◇ 5 4 ♣ A K 2	

Figure 99

Figure 99 is an example of first trumping losers in dummy before leading trumps.

West opens the queen of diamonds. Dummy wins with the king. How should the hand be played?

If trumps are 'pulled' in the routine fashion of first leading the king, later taking a losing finesse to West's queen, the hand will go down one trick since three spades and one heart must be lost.

Correct technique after winning the first diamond is to lead a spade which is taken by a defender. No matter whether a trump is returned, South wins, leads a second spade. Now the third spade in declarer's hand can be trumped in the dummy.

What I want to point out that in *figure 99*, the dummy's trumps had a definite function, viz., to trump a spade. Not until that was accomplished could trumps be led.

	♠ J 10 9 ♡ A 8 6 4 ◇ K Q 2 ♣ A 7 4	
♠ 8 6 4 ♡ Q J 10 9 ◇ 10 7 3 ♣ J 10 8	N W E S	♠ 7 5 ♡ K 7 5 3 ◇ 9 6 4 ♣ Q 9 6 2
	♠ A K Q 3 2 ♡ 2 ◇ A J 8 5 ♣ K 5 3	

Figure 100

As a general rule, losing cards should be trumped in the dummy rather than the reverse.

But there is a type of hand *(figure 100)* where dummy's trumps are equal in size to those of declarer and at the start of play, declarer's trumps are usually longer than those of dummy. After trumping dummy's losers, declarer will have fewer trumps than dummy and the latter's trumps will be used for the purpose of 'pulling' those held by the opponents.

This play will be found highly useful to get rid of an apparently unavoidable loser in *declarer's hand.* It will not obviate a losing card from the dummy.

In *figure 100,* South is the declarer at a seven spade contract. If South, after receiving the queen of hearts opening, attempts to 'pull' three rounds of trumps, down he'll go! There is no place to jettison the losing club.

Correct play, after winning the first heart with the ace, is to lead a second heart, trump in South with a high spade. Dummy is entered with a diamond and another heart trumped with a high trump. The deuce of spades is led, won in the dummy and that hand's last heart led and trumped with South's remaining high spade. The three of spades follows and is won in the dummy with the 10. The jack of spades draws West's last trump, declarer simultaneously discarding the losing three of clubs. All of the remaining tricks are won with high diamonds and the ace and king of clubs.

	♠ Q J 10 8 ♡ 3 ◇ A 7 4 3 ♣ 9 6 5 2	
♠ 5 4 ♡ K J 8 7 ◇ Q 6 2 ♣ A K Q J	N W E S	♠ 3 2 ♡ Q 10 9 6 ◇ K J 10 9 8 ♣ 7 4
	♠ A K 9 7 6 ♡ A 5 4 2 ◇ 5 ♣ 10 8 3	

Figure 101

Figure 101 illustrates one of the best known types of trumping plays, the cross-ruff.

It is based on the need of winning tricks separately with dummy's and declarer's trumps by trumping back and forth.

If West, who will open the king of clubs against South's four spade contract, continues the suit, declarer will trump the fourth round.

Correct line of play is for South to cash the ace of hearts, then trump a heart in the dummy. The ace of diamonds is played and a diamond trumped by declarer. This process of trumping back and forth is continued until all three low hearts have been trumped in dummy and that hand's three losing diamonds have been trumped by declarer. Obviously, for declarer to lead even two rounds of trumps before beginning the cross-ruff dooms the contract. In playing a cross-ruff, the declarer should avoid leading *even one round of trumps* until the cross-ruff has been completed.

	North	
	♠ A K 6 4 3 2	
	♡ Q 10 9	
	◇ 3	
	♣ J 8 7	
West		**East**
♠ 10 9 8		♠ Q J 7
♡ 6 5 2		♡ 8 3
◇ K Q J 9		◇ 10 8 7 4
♣ K 9 5		♣ A 10 3 2
	South	
	♠ 5	
	♡ A K J 7 4	
	◇ A 6 5 2	
	♣ Q 6 4	

Figure 102

Figure 102 demonstrates the need of postponing trump leads when dummy's trumps are required as entries for the establishment of a side suit.

South is the declarer at four hearts. West opens the king of diamonds. Many players, on winning with the ace, would be in a hurry to trump some diamonds in dummy in order to use dummy's trumps as in *figure 99*. This is incorrect.

It should be pointed out that as a general rule, when there is a choice between two lines of play, one involving trumping losing cards in dummy; the other relating to the establishment of dummy's long suit as winning tricks on which declarer can discard losing cards, the latter is usually far preferable.

If South attempts to trump *even one diamond* in dummy, the spade suit can never be established since one defender will then have one more trump than the dummy. When dummy's trumps are to be used as entries, conserve them as though they were aces. In a way, they really are!

Correct technique, after winning the first trick with the ace of diamonds, is to lead the singleton spade and play dummy's ace. The deuce of spades is led and trumped with the king or ace of hearts. The four of hearts is led and taken by dummy's nine of that suit. The three of spades is trumped with South's remaining high honor and the seven of hearts is led to dummy's 10. The queen of hearts is led, with South following suit with the jack and West playing his last heart, the five-spot. The king, six and four of spades successively win tricks and at the finish, declarer concedes the last three tricks to make four hearts.

The discerning reader may have noticed that had declarer trumped only one spade (instead of two), he would have made an an extra trick since the six spades held by the opponents were divided evenly; however, the recommended line of play assured the contract even against the slightly more likely possibility of one defender holding four spades.

	♠ 832 ♡ 764 ◇ AQJ73 ♣ A4	
♠ 64 ♡ KQJ10 ◇ K105 ♣ 9653	N W E S	♠ J97 ♡ 953 ◇ 92 ♣ KJ1087
	♠ AKQ105 ♡ A82 ◇ 864 ♣ Q2	

Figure 103

Figure 103 is another example of delaying trump leads since high trumps are needed as re-entries for finessing purposes. The main difference between this and its predecessor, *figure 102*, was that in *102*, the trump entry was preserved in the dummy and here it is required in the declarer's hand.

Suppose South, after winning the opening king of hearts lead, were to lead his three high spades in order to capture the adverse trumps. This accomplished, he can now take the diamond finesse by leading low towards dummy, playing the jack third-hand. The finesse will succeed but how does our hapless declarer return to his hand to take another finesse? He can't and if he's the least bit careless, may go down.

Correct line of play would be for declarer to take *two rounds of high trumps* (to minimize the danger of an adverse ruff) and then take the diamond finesse. When it proves successful, declarer can return to his hand via the last high spade which has been left there for that purpose. Now, a second diamond finesse can be taken and with the king falling under the ace, two losing cards can be discarded on dummy's fourth and fifth diamonds to make an over-trick.

A good rule to follow is to lead the maximum number of trumps contingent with safety and re-entry requirements.

	North	
	♠ 643 ♡ AK3 ◇ KJ7 ♣ 9862	
♠ A2 ♡ QJ1098 ◇ A1086 ♣ J10	N W E S	♠ K5 ♡ 74 ◇ 9532 ♣ Q7543
	♠ QJ10987 ♡ 652 ◇ Q4 ♣ AK	

Figure 104

In *figure 104*, South, who is in a four spade contract, must get rid of a losing card before attempting to lead trumps.

West makes the opening lead of the heart queen. If declarer attempts to lead trumps at once, dummy's remaining high heart will be knocked out on the third trick and declarer will lose two spades, one diamond and one heart, going down one trick.

Thus, the heart loser must be obviated before even thinking of leading trumps and this can be readily accomplished by first playing the queen of diamonds to force West's ace. West will lead a second round of hearts, it is true, but the two high diamonds in dummy, immediately cashed, afford a place to jettison the losing remaining heart. In addition to the diamond trick already lost, declarer's only remaining losers are the missing ace and king of trumps and four spades will be made.

	North	
	♠ 72 ♡ A ◇ K1065 ♣ AQ7432	
♠ Q108 ♡ J1096 ◇ J72 ♣ J106	N W E S	♠ J93 ♡ KQ875 ◇ Q98 ♣ 95
	♠ AK654 ♡ 432 ◇ A43 ♣ K8	

Figure 105

The term 'trump policeman' was first coined by Frank K. Perkins of Boston, one of the nation's top bridge columnists and authors. It refers to the retention of a trump in the dummy when that hand is void in some side suit.

The trump, opposite the void, prevents the opponents from taking a trick in the void suit and effectively 'patrols that beat.'

As an example of a 'trump policeman,' let's look at *figure 105.* South is playing a hazardous six spade contract. Seven clubs is makeable. Against six spades, West opens the jack of hearts.

On taking dummy's ace, while needing an even division of the defenders' six spades, South doesn't dare play the ace and king of spades and then lead a third round of the suit since the defenders, on winning that trick, can cash two setting heart tricks.

Since declarer must lose one spade trick, even with a three-three split of the missing six spades, declarer will lead the deuce of spades from dummy (at trick two) and play a low spade from his hand *regardless of the size of the card played by East!* Whichever defender wins the trick doesn't matter. Dummy still retains a trump to prevent the defenders from taking a heart trick. Later, declarer bangs down the ace and king of spades, captures the remaining adverse trumps to make his small slam.

	♠ 865 ♡ Q42 ◇ AJ97 ♣ J108	
♠ 1094 ♡ J863 ◇ 654 ♣ AKQ	N W E S	♠ 73 ♡ 105 ◇ KQ1083 ♣ 9765
	♠ AKQJ2 ♡ AK97 ◇ 2 ♣ 432	

Figure 106

The seventh reason given on page 212 for postponing trump leads was 'A safety play in a side suit.' This play involves the retention of one trump in the dummy so that if a side suit does not divide evenly, an otherwise losing card can be trumped.

In *figure 106,* West will cash his three high clubs, then shift to a diamond, taken with dummy's ace. *Only two rounds of trumps are led* and are followed by the king, queen and ace of hearts in that order. If each defender follows to all three rounds of hearts, the suit is known to have 'split' and the last trump is 'pulled' prior to declarer cashing his fourth heart. When, as in the above, hearts do not 'break,' and since the same defender (West) holds both the one outstanding trump and four hearts, declarer's fourth (and otherwise losing) heart can be trumped with the third round of trumps led later. In the event that the defender with only two hearts held three trumps, it is what we term 'trick for trick.' By permitting a defender to score a trick with a trump which could have been captured, we regain that trick through the ability to trump our fourth heart which otherwise would have been a losing card.

TRUMP PLAYS THAT DECLARER SHOULD AVOID

The late Sidney Lenz, who during his life-time of more than 90 years, was unequalled as an author, outstanding bridge expert (Culbertson-Lenz matches), story-teller and constructor of bridge problems for magazines and theatre programs, once described the act of a declarer needlessly and fruitlessly frittering away his trumps by trumping worthless cards from the dummy, without accomplishing anything, as the **'Ostrich Coup.'**

West		East
	♠ 643 ♡ A752 ◇ Q108 ♣ K103	
♠ J105 ♡ KQJ86 ◇ AK ♣ J64	N W E S	♠ Q2 ♡ 1094 ◇ 432 ♣ Q9875
	♠ AK987 ♡ 3 ◇ J9765 ♣ A2	

Figure 107

The declarer should not trump worthless cards from the dummy for no other purpose than to take a few trump tricks. Of course, there are times where the declarer should trump a card or cards from the dummy voluntarily. Such cases would include the need of returning to his own hand by trumping, the establishment of a long suit in dummy as shown in *figure 102* or a cross-ruff as in *figure 101*. But in these cases, the trumping serves a useful purpose, viz., the development of *additional tricks*. Where trumping serves no specific purpose, the trump suit is weakened and and shortened to the point that declarer will frequently be unable to develop and capitalize upon tricks in the side suits.

Figure 107 is a case in point. South is playing a four spade contract after opening the bidding with one spade which West overcalled with two hearts. West will open the king of hearts which will be won with dummy's ace. If declarer makes the common error of immediately trumping a heart from the dummy, he will be defeated. The success of the hand pivots upon the declarer winning three diamond tricks. After trumping a heart, declarer will cash the ace and king of spades. He will then lead a low diamond. After winning with the king, West will lead the jack of spades, denuding dummy of its last trump and leaving declarer with only one trump, the nine-spot. Now West administers the coup de grace by leading the queen of hearts. *South* is forced to trump with his last trump, the nine-spot. When he leads the second round of diamonds. West wins and cashes his two remaining hearts to defeat the contract two tricks.

Let's see what would have happened if declarer hadn't wasted that one trump. After taking the ace of hearts, the ace and king of spades are cashed. The five of diamonds is led. West wins with the king, leads the jack of spades exactly as before, then leads the queen of hearts. South trumps with the eight of spades. The six of diamonds follows. West wins and leads the jack of hearts. *Declarer trumps with the nine of spades and wins the remainder of the tricks. And there's the difference between going down two and making the bid - that one extra trump!*

A common error, by the new player, to be avoided is the unsound practice of leading an extra round of trumps *when there is only one trump remaining between both defenders and that trump is the highest remaining card of the suit.*

When the play is made, it is usually prefaced by a remark as, **"Let's get out the big one."**

The play is a losing proposition for declarer for two reasons - first, it will generally take two trumps, one from dummy, the other from declarer's hand to give a defender a trick which is already his; the second reason is that it wastes something as valuable as high cards - namely, the element of time.

Please turn back to *figure 107* on the preceding page. Replay the hand by pretending that after winning the opening lead with the ace of hearts, declarer plays his two high spades and then makes the fatal error of a third round to force out West's jack. Time has now swung to the side of the defenders who can compel declarer to expend his two spades trumping hearts before he can establish the diamond suit.

Like almost everything else in bridge, there are exceptions. One such case would be where the dummy holds a long, solid suit without any re-entries and it is necessary to remove the defender's trump so that he can't trump that suit; another case would be to deliberately thrust a defender in the lead to force him to lead some other suit or suits. But these are exceptions.

QUIZ SIX

1 - You have opened the bidding with one heart and hold -

♠ KJ8 ♡ AK843 ◇ K109 ♣ 72

What is your rebid to each of the following responses? The opponents will not enter the bidding.

(a) One spade (b) Two hearts (c) One no trump
(d) Two clubs (e) Four hearts (f) Three clubs
(g) Two no trump (h) Three hearts

2 - The bidding has been -

You, South	West	North, Partner	East
One diamond	One heart	One spade	pass
?			

You hold - ♠ A4 ♡ K743 ◇ KQJ98 ♣ 73. What is your rebid?

3 - The bidding has been -

You, South	West	North, Partner	East
One heart	pass	One spade	pass
?			

You hold - ♠ AJ6 ♡ KQ765 ◇ A42 ♣ 42. What is your rebid?

4 - The bidding has proceeded -

You, South	West	North, Partner	East
One heart	pass	One spade	pass
?			

What is your rebid with each of the following hands?

(i)	(j)	(k)
♠ 2	♠ KQ64	♠ AK7
♡ AKJ1087	♡ AQ8765	♡ AQJ86
◇ A10	◇ A	◇ KQ109
♣ KJ97	♣ J2	♣ 3

(l)	(m)	(n)
♠ J5	♠ 72	♠ Q876
♡ AKQ107	♡ KQJ10843	♡ AK1054
◇ 4	◇ AQ	◇ 3
♣ AKJ108	♣ KQ	♣ A105

5 - The bidding has been -

Partner, North, dealer	East	You, South	West
Pass	pass	One heart	pass
One spade	pass	?	

What is your rebid with each of the following hands?

(o) ♠ Q109
♡ AK432
◇ QJ6
♣ 84

(p) ♠ 2
♡ AQ543
◇ KJ1087
♣ 54

(q) ♠ Q109
♡ AK432
◇ K87
♣ K2

6 - You have opened the bidding with one club. Your partner, who hasn't passed, responds with one diamond.
You hold - ♠ AJ87 ♡ Q542 ◇ 2 ♣ AKJ6
What is your rebid?

7 - In each of the following examples, only the North-South hands will be shown. You are South in each case. With the given lead and contract, how would you play each hand?

(a)
♠ 862
♡ 105
◇ K874
♣ A1053
N
S
♠ AK7543
♡ A62
◇ A53
♣ 2

The contract is four spades and West opens the queen of clubs. After winning with dummy's ace, do you lead trumps immediately? If so, how many rounds do you lead? What is your plan of play?

8 - (b)
♠ Q643
♡ A865
◇ 2
♣ K542
N
S
♠ AKJ95
♡ 3
◇ A943
♣ A63

Again the contract is four spades. West opens the king of hearts which is taken with dummy's ace. Do you lead trumps immediately? If so, how many rounds do you play? What is your plan of play?

9 -

♠ Q J 2
♡ A 8 7 5 4 2
◊ 3
♣ 10 7 2
N
S
♠ A K 8 7 6 5
♡ 3
◊ A 5 4
♣ A 6 3

The contract is six spades. West opens a low club and East plays the king which you capture with the ace. Do you lead trumps immediately? If you do, which hand first plays a high trump? How many rounds of trumps do you lead? How do you plan to avoid losing two club tricks?

ANSWERS TO QUIZ SIX

1 - (a) Two spades; (b) pass; (c) pass; (d) two hearts; (e) pass; (f) three hearts; (g) three no trump; (h) four hearts.

2 - Two diamonds.

3 - Two spades, not two hearts.

4 - (i) Three hearts; (j) four spades; (k) three diamonds; (l) three clubs; (m) four hearts; (n) three spades.

5 - (o) Pass. Your partner couldn't open the bidding. Accordingly, his one-over-one response is not forcing if you have a minimum opening bid; (p) two diamonds; (q) two spades.

6 - One heart, not one spade. In rebidding with four card suits, you rebid 'up the ladder.' It is cheaper to rebid with one heart than one spade.

7 - You should lead no more than one round of spades, winning with the king or ace. Your next play should be the ace of hearts, followed by a low heart. After winning the next trick, either by trumping the second round of clubs or capturing the trick with a high card, depending upon which suit is led by the defenders, trump your third heart in dummy. *Only then can you lead a second round of trumps.* If you played two high trumps before leading leading hearts, you will be defeated if one defender holds three trumps and removes dummy's last trump on winning a heart trick.

8 - You *do not lead trumps immediately.* The hand should be cross-ruffed but before cross-ruffing, cash the ace and king of clubs to prevent an opponent from discarding his cards of that suit during the cross-ruff.

9 - You *do not* lead trumps immediately. After winning the first trick with the ace of clubs, your first play should be to lead the singleton heart and plan on establishing dummy's heart suit by trumping the opponents' hearts. Dummy's high spades must be conserved as entries. Trumping a diamond immediately in dummy is wrong, wastes an entry and does nothing to obviate declarer's two club losers.

LESSON SIX
HANDS

Note - The student should bid these hands without consulting the 'par' bidding at the foot of this page. After reaching what he considers the correct final contract, compare the actual bidding with 'par.' In playing the hand, use the designated bidding and opening lead.

1.

North: ♠ Q543 ♡ J92 ◇ AQ107 ♣ 98

West: ♠ 962 ♡ K654 ◇ KJ52 ♣ Q6

East: ♠ K10 ♡ Q1083 ◇ 98 ♣ KJ743

South: ♠ AJ87 ♡ A7 ◇ 643 ♣ A1052

South dealer, neither side vul.

2.

North: ♠ J8 ♡ 8765 ◇ Q104 ♣ KQJ9

West: ♠ AK943 ♡ AJ43 ◇ 75 ♣ 62

East: ♠ 765 ♡ Q2 ◇ AJ863 ♣ 1083

South: ♠ Q102 ♡ K109 ◇ K92 ♣ A754

West dealer, N-S vulnerable.

3.

North: ♠ AQ1075 ♡ K10543 ◇ 10 ♣ A6

West: ♠ K98 ♡ J987 ◇ Q32 ♣ KJ10

East: ♠ 43 ♡ Q6 ◇ AJ87 ♣ 75432

South: ♠ J62 ♡ A2 ◇ K9654 ♣ Q98

North dealer, both sides vul.

4.

North: ♠ J3 ♡ AK732 ◇ 53 ♣ A986

West: ♠ 10654 ♡ Q54 ◇ KQ1098 ♣ 4

East: ♠ A987 ♡ 6 ◇ AJ7 ♣ KQ532

South: ♠ KQ2 ♡ J1098 ◇ 642 ♣ J107

East dealer, E-W vulnerable.

PAR

1.

South	West	North	East
1 cl.	pass	1 dia.	pass
1 sp.	pass	2 sp.	pass
pass	pass		

Opening lead - heart four.

2.

West	North	East	South
1 sp.	pass	1 no tr.	pass
2 hts.	pass	2 sp.	pass
pass	pass		

Opening lead - club king.

3.

North	East	South	West
1 sp.	pass	2 dia.	pass
2 hts.	pass	2 sp.	pass
3 sp.	pass	4 sp.	All pass

Opening lead - club three

4.

East	South	West	North
1 cl.	pass	1 dia.	1 ht.
1 sp.	pass	2 sp.	pass
pass	pass		

Opening lead - heart jack.

SOLUTIONS TO LESSON SIX HANDS

1.

South declarer at two spades.

Trick	W	N	E	S
1	♡4	♡9	♡10	♡A
2	♢2	♢10	♢9	♢3
3	♠2	♠3	♠10	♠J
4	♠6	♠4	♠K	♠A
5	♢5	♢Q	♢8	♢4
6	♢J	♢A	♣3	♢6
7	♢K	♢7	♡3	♠7
8	♡K	♡2	♡8	♡7
9	♠9	♠Q	♣4	♠8
10	♡5	♠5	♣7	♣2
11	♣6	♣8	♣J	♣A
12	♣Q	♣9	♣K	♣5
13	♡6	♡J	♡Q	♣10

South wins 10 tricks.

2.

West declarer at two spades.

Trick	N	E	S	W
1	♣K	♣3	♣7	♣2
2	♣Q	♣8	♣4	♣6
3	♣J	♣10	♣5	♠3
4	♢4	♢A	♢9	♢5
5	♡5	♡Q	♡K	♡A
6	♡6	♡2	♡9	♡J
7	♡7	♠5	♡10	♡3
8	♢10	♢3	♢K	♢7
9	♠8	♠6	♠2	♠K
10	♡8	♠7	♠10	♡4
11	♢Q	♢6	♢2	♠4
12	♠J	♢8	♠Q	♠A
13	♣9	♢J	♣A	♠9

West wins nine tricks.

3.

North declarer at two spades

Trick	E	S	W	N
1	♣3	♣8	♣10	♣A
2	♢A	♢4	♢2	♢10
3	♣2	♣9	♣J	♣6
4	♣4	♣Q	♣K	♠5
5	♡6	♡A	♡7	♡3
6	♢7	♢K	♢3	♡4
7	♡Q	♡2	♡8	♡K
8	♣5	♠2	♡9	♡5
9	♢8	♢5	♢Q	♠7
10	♢J	♠6	♡J	♡10
11	♠3	♠J	♠K	♠A

North wins 11 tricks, claims the remaining tricks with the two high trumps.

4.

East declarer at two spades.

Trick	S	W	N	E
1	♡J	♡4	♡7	♡6
2	♡10	♡5	♡2	♠7
3	♠2	♠4	♠J	♠8
4	♠Q	♠5	♠3	♠A

East wins nine tricks, states that he will now play the diamond suit, and that he will concede two tricks to the king of spades and the ace of clubs.

Lesson VII

PART ONE

Responder's Rebids

PART TWO

Subsequent Rebids by Opener and Responder

PART THREE

The Covering of Honors

LESSON SEVEN
PART ONE

RESPONDER'S REBIDS

The responder, like any other player at the table, must have a valid reason for making additional bids. These reasons could be any one or more of the following:

1 - The opening bidder has made a forcing rebid;
2 - Responder feels that his side can make a (yet unbid) game or slam;
3 - He holds additional, undisclosed values;
4 - To show a new suit, or to rebid an old one;
5 - To raise (support) partner's suit;
6 - To give a preference for one of partner's suits;
7 - The opponents have pushed the bidding one step higher.

Which rebid the responder selects depends entirely on his hand, and the number of points he holds. Where the combined point count indicates a makeable game, responder must force by either bidding one more than necessary in a new suit or by bidding a new suit at the three level which is forcing for one round.

The responder's hands will fall into four categories -

1 - Hands with less than six points;
2 - Hands with six to 9 points;
3 - Hands with 10 to 12 points;
4 - Hands with 13 or more points.

Since with less than six points, you would have passed your partner's opening bid, you will not be faced with a rebidding problem since you didn't bid earlier. Any subsequent bid or raise (of partner's suit) on your part would depend upon the subsequent trend of bidding, both by your partner and by the opponents. If you do bid later, your partner should be aware of the fact that you lack six points since ordinarily with this strength, you would normally have made a first round response.

Virtually all of your problems as responder, whether to pass or rebid, will be when you hold six to nine points and your partner, the opening bidder, has made a semi-forcing rebid. This would be a jump rebid or jump raise of a *previously bid suit* or a jump to two no trump, following a one-over-one response.

WITH SIX TO NINE POINTS

With six to nine points, you would have made one of the following responses:

1 - Bid a new suit at the level of one;

2 - Given partner a single raise;

3 - Bid one no trump.

Whether you make a second bid depends upon what your partner may do, what the opponents do and whether you have a minimum six or seven points or the maximum eight or nine for this bracket.

Let's suppose your partner has opened the bidding with one diamond to which you have responded with one heart. He now makes one of the five following possible rebids -

A - a new suit at the level of one;

B - a new suit (without jumping) at the level of two;

C - a rebid of one no trump;

D - a simple, minimum rebid of his own suit;

E - a single raise of your suit.

AFTER A NEW SUIT BY OPENER

x

CASE A		CASE B	
PARTNER	YOU	PARTNER	YOU
One diamond	One heart	One diamond	One heart
One spade	?	Two clubs	?

The first thing I would like to tell you is that while the bidding of a new suit by a responder (who hasn't previously passed) compels the opening bidder to rebid, the responder *is not compelled to rebid when the opening bidder shows a second suit as cheaply as possible.*

Cases A and B are examples. In A, if you have a weak hand and like spades better than diamonds, you should pass; in B, if you prefer clubs to diamonds, you may similarly pass.

This is termed 'expressing a simple preference' and in the foregoing, you were able to express that preference by passing. But let's suppose you liked partner's first suit better than his second. In these cases, you would bid 'two diamonds' in both A and B and again you are expressing a simple preference.

Usually, however, the responder will *try to find another bid* whenever the opening bidder bids a second suit. This could be a rebid of one no trump in Case A which would deny supporting cards for either of opener's suits and a maximum of nine or 10 points in responder's hand. It is possible that the responder has a rebiddable suit of his own and wishes to show that fact as by rebidding 'two hearts' in Case A. Still another possibility is that the responder, too, may wish to show a second suit as by bidding 'two clubs' in Case A.

Let's pretend that with the bidding in case A, you hold each of the following hands and see what your rebids would be -

(a)	(b)	(c)
♠ J107	♠ 8	♠ 83
♡ KJ643	♡ Q10762	♡ Q1098
◊ 62	◊ K75	◊ K2
♣ Q104	♣ Q743	♣ Q9876
Pass	Two diamonds	One no trump

(d)	(e)	(f)
♠ 42	♠ 5	♠ 8743
♡ KQJ876	♡ Q10762	♡ KJ97
◊ 73	◊ 2	◊ 2
♣ 543	♣ QJ9764	♣ Q1096
Two hearts	Two clubs	Two spades

AFTER A REBID OF ONE NO TRUMP BY OPENER

A rebid of one no trump by the opening bidder indicates a minimum, 13 to 16 point opening bid. If the responder holds only six to nine points, game is impossible since the needed 26 points for game can't possibly be present. Any rebid by the responder is simply indicative of a desire to play the hand in a suit contract rather than in no trump. Let's suppose the bidding had gone as in Case C. The correct rebid is indicated beneath each example hand.

CASE C

PARTNER	YOU
One diamond	One heart
One no trump	

(g)
♠ KJ98
♡ KJ98
◊ 32
♣ 432
Pass !

With hand (g), you correctly responded with one heart to your partner's opening bid of one diamond. Should you now bid 'two spades?' Decidedly not! The bidding has disclosed two very important things: first, that the partnership doesn't have enough strength for game; second, that your partner doesn't have four spades since had he held them, he would have bid one spade over your response of one heart.

Returning to hands (a) to (f) with the bidding in Case C, you should pass with (a), bid two diamonds with (b), pass with (c), bid two hearts with (d), two clubs with (e) and pass with (f).

NOTE - Where the opening bidder's rebid is 'one no trump,' subsequent bids of new suits at minimum level by responder are not forcing.

In other words, having rebid 'one no trump,' the opener may (and probably will) pass the rebid of two clubs in (e). Of course, a bid of one more than necessary in a new suit compels the partner to continue bidding until at least game is reached, *regardless of the nature of that player's earlier bid.* With hand (e), were the hand stronger and the suits more powerful, a rebid of three clubs would have compelled partner to continue to game, despite the fact that he indicated a weak opening bid by his earlier rebid of one no trump.

AFTER A SIMPLE,MINIMUM REBID BY OPENER

CASE D		(h)
OPENER	YOU	♠ K4
One diamond	One heart	♡ Q10876
Two diamonds		◇ 432
		♣ Q83
		Pass

Ordinarily, after making a one-over-one response with six to nine points and hearing your partner make a simple, minimum rebid of the same suit with which he opened, you should pass. Since the opening bidder's rebid indicates from 13 to 16 points, game is usually not makeable and the only reasons responder might have for rebidding is the desire to play the hand in a rebiddable suit as in hand (d) or to show a second suit as (e).

There are two points that should be emphasized. The first is that you shouldn't bid a second suit at the two level or higher merely because you don't like your partner's suit. He may not like yours, either. Remember that additional voluntary rebids show additional strength *and are never made for the purpose of rescuing partner from what you consider to be a bad contract.* The second point is that when your partner rebids his suit, the bidding is now at the two-level. That means that you'd have to bid at least 'two' in order to show a second suit. That rebid would require at least 10 points in the responder's hand and you have only six to nine points.

The discerning reader will have noticed that with hand (e) on page 231, the recommended rebid by responder was 'two clubs' despite the fact that the hand totaled only nine points. But there is a substantial difference. Here, on page 231, the opener's rebid was one no trump which indicated a somewhat balanced hand. Accordingly, responder knew that if he didn't find supporting cards in one of his suits, he was almost certain to find them in the other suit. Lastly, and this is the most important reason of all - after the opening bidder rebid 'one no trump,' *any new suit shown by responder did not compel him to bid again.* This is not true in other rebidding situations where the bidding of a new suit by the responder compels the opening bidder to bid again. Further, when the best the opening bidder can do is to rebid the same suit as cheaply as possible, there is no guarantee that he will hold supporting cards in one of the remaining suits.

If the hand appears to be a misfit, discretion is the better part of valor. You'll never 'go down' 800 points if you pass; you will if you bid too much on misfit hands.

AFTER RECEIVING A SINGLE RAISE

CASE E

OPENER	YOU
One diamond	One heart
Two hearts	

The single raise of responder's suit by the opening bidder, shown in Case E, indicates a minimum 13 to 16 point opening bid. Since you have only six to nine points, game should be unmakeable and you should pass. Hands (a) through (h) are cases in point.

RESPONDING TO SEMI-FORCING BIDS WITH SIX TO NINE POINTS

A semi-forcing rebid is any bid, although usually a non-forcing jump rebid, which holds promise of game if the partner has some slight additional values over those already shown. There are three possible non-forcing rebids that the opening bidder can make after opening the bidding with one of a suit.

The first case would be a jump rebid of 'two no trump' following partner bidding a new suit at the one level. This bid, together with illustrative hands, is described on page 195, and guarantees 18 or 19 high card points in the opening bidder's hand..

CASE F

OPENER	YOU
One diamond	One spade
Three spades	

The second situation is where the suit shown by responder at the one-level is double-raised by the opening bidder as in Case F. The opening bidder promises 17 to 19 points in support of spades and this is fully described on pages 196 and 197.

CASE G

OPENER	YOU
One heart	One spade
Three hearts	

The third case would find the opening bidder making a jump rebid in his originally bid suit as shown in Case G. The rebid promises 17 to 19 points and is described on page 198.

There are three possible responses that can be made with as little as six points. These are:

1 - Showing a new suit at the one-level;

2 - A response of one no trump;

3 - A single raise of opener's suit.

What remains now is merely a matter of simple arithmetic to determine whether the partnership holds the 26 points needed for game. Since the opening bidder, through his semi-forcing rebid, has shown 17 to 19 points in the case of a jump suit rebid and 18 or 19 high card points for a jump rebid of two no trump, game is virtually certain if the responder holds eight or nine or more points.

Accordingly, the responder, after opener's semi-forcing rebid, *should continue bidding until game is reached with eight points or more and should pass with only six or seven points.* The nature of responder's rebids, of course, will depend upon the hands themselves. On some, it will be advisable to raise partner's suit; on others, for the responder to rebid his own suit or to show a possible second suit; lastly, perhaps the responder may wish to bid no trump (after previously having bid a suit) or raise partner's jump rebid of two no trump. It should be remembered that in bidding or supporting no trump, only points for high cards are counted.

REBIDDING WITH SIX TO NINE POINTS AFTER OPENER HAS MADE A FORCING REBID

CASE H

PARTNER	YOU
One heart	One no trump
Three clubs	

When, following a response which can be made with as little as six points, your partner makes a forcing-to-game rebid of *one more than necessary in a previously unbid suit,* he has shown a minimum of 20 points since you have promised only six. Since he has indicated game to be certain, you are compelled to continue bidding until a game contract has been reached. The future rounds of bidding, based on his hand and yours, should determine the best final contract.

REBIDDING WITH SIX TO NINE POINTS AFTER OPENER HAS JUMPED TO GAME

CASE I

PARTNER	YOU
One heart	One no trump
Three no trump	

CASE J

PARTNER	YOU
One heart	One spade
Three no trump	

CASE K

One heart	One spade
Four hearts	

CASE L

One heart	One spade
Four spades	

With the bidding in Case I, any further bidding by you would be unthinkable. Your response of one no trump indicated six to 10-high card points in a balanced or semi-balanced hand. Your partner holds the needed missing strength and is desirous of playing the hand in no trump. Bidding a suit, not previously shown, at this point would be ridiculous. Common sense will tell you that if a suit isn't worth showing at the one-level, it shouldn't be bid at the four-level, particularly when it disturbs what partner has already determined to be the best contract.

(i)
♠ KJ108762
♡ J2
◇ J83
♣ 4

Case J affords the responder some discretionary power in determining the final contract. Holding a hand similar to (i) at the left, the responder should realize that the extremely long spade suit will win a lot of tricks if that suit becomes trump. On the other hand, if the hand is played in no trump, the spade suit, even if it could be set up, might not be available to win tricks since the hand apparently lacks any positive card of re-entry. Lastly, the singleton club could prove to be an Achilles' heel in no trump. A four spade rebid by responder would be correct.

With the bidding in Case K, the responder should ordinarily pass. The opening bidder has stated, through his bidding, his belief that he can make four hearts. Obviously, his heart suit is virtually solid and requires no bolstering. For the responder to now bid four spades could only be based on an extremely long suit of at least seven cards in a hand devoid of much high card strength - a hand that will win tricks with responder's suit as trump and be valueless to partner as the dummy. I would again like to emphasize that the responder should think long and hard before taking out partner's jump rebid to game.

In Case L, there is no excuse whatever to justify another bid by the responder. With only six to nine points, the responder should be happy to be in game - partner has shown tremendous supporting cards in spades - and the necessary points for slam are lacking.

RESPONDING TO AN INVITATION TO REBID

After you have responded either with one no trump or by giving your partner's suit a single raise to the two level, there are two possible ways in which he may *invite* you to rebid if you have the maximum values for your response.

CASE M		CASE N	
PARTNER	YOU	PARTNER	YOU
One heart	One no trump	One heart	Two hearts
Two no trump	?	Three hearts	?

The bidding sequences shown as Cases M and N are not at all uncommon. In the former, the opening bidder is indicating 17 to 19 points, balanced distribution, high cards in other suits and a willingness to play the hand in no trump. The hand may very well contain a rebiddable suit as shown in hand (j) but

(j)	(k)
♠ K 10	♠ 4
♡ A K Q J 6	♡ A Q 10 8 3 2
◇ K 8 6	◇ Q J 7
♣ Q 9 7	♣ A Q 9

the important thing is that the opening bidder feels that game in no trump is more readily makeable than in a suit contract and that the rebiddable suit can be fully utilized in no trump. The responder should bid three no trump with nine or 10 high card points or with eight high card points and a readily-establishable five card or longer suit. With only six or seven points, the responder should pass. Under no circumstances should you bid a new suit at this point. That's the last thing the opening bidder wants to hear. Ordinarily, you should either bid three no trump or pass. However, there will be times when you will have hands containing three cards of the suit bid by your partner but lacking the queen or better to constitute 'normal trump support.' Hand (1) is a case in point. If the queen of spades was the queen of hearts, your correct response would have been two hearts rather than one no trump in Case M. After opener's rebid of two no trump, a bid of three hearts would describe the hand as having 'near' heart support since with valid trump support, you would have given an immediate raise in that suit. The three heart rebid indicates a willingness to play the hand in four hearts if the opener has a rebiddable suit and a partially unbalanced hand. Hands (j) and (1) will normally produce 10 tricks with hearts trump whereas a contract of three no trump is readily defeated if the opponents lead spades.

(1)
♠ Q 9
♡ 10 8 7
◇ Q J 10 9
♣ K 10 8 4

Hand (k) is illustrative of the opening bidder's hand in Case N. The voluntary (and invitational) rebid shows 17 to 19 points, asks partner to bid 'four' with eight or nine or more points and to pass with less. There is one important corollary. The suit in Case N is a major, hearts. If the suit had been a minor, as clubs or diamonds, the invitational rebid to the three level by opener of the minor suit requests responder to rebid 'three no trump' holding nine or 10 well-scattered high card points and balanced or semi-balanced distribution. Under no circumstances would the opener's rebid to three of a minor invite a jump to five of that suit since the bidding has indicated that the 29 or more points necessary to produce a minor suit game are lacking.

WITH 10 TO 12 POINTS

Apart from the difference in strength between six to nine points and 10 to 12 points, there is an even more important variance in the responder's tactics. With only six to nine points, the responder will *usually bid only once* unless his partner, the opening bidder, makes a forcing, semi-forcing or invitational rebid or bids a second suit to which responder indicates a preference for the first bid suit. I might add that this expressing a preference as cheaply as possible, as by bidding 'two hearts' over 'two diamonds' is known in bridge as a *simple preference and promises no extra strength over and above that already shown - merely a liking of one suit over another, generally by virtue of holding a greater number of cards in the former.*

But the responder with 10 to 12 points should bid at least once again, even if the opening bidder's rebid has indicated a minimum 13 to 16 point opening bid. The reason is that there is still a strong possibility that the combined hands hold a total of 26 points.

Holding 10 to 12 points, the responder's tactics should be -

IF OPENER'S REBID WAS	*YOU SHOULD*
Minimum This would be a rebid of one no trump or a simple rebid by the opening bidder of his original suit or a single raise of your (responder's) suit.	*Bid once more*
Semi-forcing Semi-forcing rebids by the opening bidder show 17 to 19 points and include single jump rebids by opener of his original suit, single jump raises of responder's suit or a jump rebid to two no trump following a one-over-one response. Invitational rebids, as described on pages 236 and 237, fall in this category.	*Get to game*
Forcing-to-game This is the bidding of one more than necessary in a previously unbid suit.	*Get to game*
Jump to game	*Pass*

WITH 13 OR MORE POINTS

It is primarily the responsibility of the responder, when holding 13 or more points, to insure that the partnership reach at least a game contract after the partner has opened the bidding. The reason should be obvious - the opener is known to have at least 13 points from the very fact that he opened the bidding but the responder is *not known* to have 13 or more points, particularly if his first response could have been made with as little as six points. You will discover that it is a player's first rebid, rather than his first bid, that best describes his hand.

There is a cardinal principle of bidding. When a player makes a bid, and it doesn't matter whether it's an opening bid or a response or a bid after the other side opened the bidding (which you will meet later in these lessons), *it is assumed that the bid shows the minimum values required. It is by rebidding that additional values are shown.*

This is particularly true when the responder's first response was the one-over-one showing of a new suit. This bid could have been made with as little as six points, as already stated. Hence, the opening bidder must assume no more than six points in the responder's hand. When the responder holds 13 or more points, he must apprise the opening bidder of that fact. In other words, the opening bidder must be informed that there are enough values between the partnership to insure a game.

As in the case of the opening bidder's rebids (page 190), there are two methods of indicating that a game is makeable: the first is that the *rebid* jump directly to game; the second, that the responder bid one more than necessary in a previously unbid suit.

CASE O		CASE P	
OPENER	YOU	OPENER	YOU
1 diamond	1 heart	1 diamond	1 heart
1 spade	4 spades	2 clubs	4 hearts

CASE Q		CASE R	
OPENER	YOU	OPENER	YOU
1 diamond	1 heart	1 club	1 spade
2 clubs	3 no trump	1 no trump	3 hearts

Again I would like to stress that *when the jump to game is made as a player's rebid, it shows a tremendously strong hand (page 189).* It is when the jump to game is a player's *first* bid that the hand is marked as weak in high cards although powerful distributionally.

THE POSSIBILITY OF SLAM

But with 13 or more points, in addition to the almost certainty of game, there is the strong probability of slam if the combined hands contain a total of 33 or more points and some degree of supporting suit 'fit.'

Goren, in one of his many excellent books, expressed this very succinctly, stating, "**An opening bid facing an opening bid equals game; an opening bid facing an opening bid plus a jump raise by the opening bidder of responder's suit equals slam.**"

What this means is that if both partners have 13 points or more, game is makeable; if the responder has 13 points or more and the opening bidder has shown 17 points or more through a jump raise or jump rebid, it is highly probable that the combined hands hold the 33 or more points needed for slam and that possibility should be explored by the responder.

With 19 points or more in the responder's hand opposite partner's opening bid, there is almost a definite certainty of slam *providing the hand is not a misfit.* I cannot emphasize this too strongly. It takes more than a few swallows to make a summer - it takes more than an arbitrary number of points to win a given number of tricks when the hand is a misfit, when neither partner cannot support the other's suit, without long suits and without the supporting trumps necessary to take care of one's losing cards in side suits.

THE VARIOUS MEANINGS OF TWO NO TRUMP

Certain bids draw their meanings from the circumstances under which they are used. In other words, the preceding bids will determine or affect the meaning of a subsequent bid.

The bid of *two no trump falls in that category.* When employed as an opening bid, it denotes a very strong hand with from 22 to 24 high card points; conversely, when made as a response to an opening forcing-to-game bid of two of a suit, it denotes an extremely weak hand. We will meet these bids in future lessons.

But since we are currently dealing with rebids, I would like to review the use of two no trump as a response, as a rebid by the responder and as a rebid by the opening bidder.

CASE S

OPENER	RESPONDER

1 - A jump rebid of two no trump by opener is *not forcing.*
2 - An immediate jump response of two no trump by responder *is forcing to game.*
3 - Any rebid of two no trump by responder is *not forcing.*

CASE S

OPENER	RESPONDER	
One heart	One spade	The two no trump in Case S shows 18 or 19 high card points.
Two no trump		Since it is a rebid, *it is not forcing.*

CASE T

OPENER	RESPONDER	
One heart	Two no trump	Case T is *forcing to game.* Here the two no trump is an immediate response.

CASE U

OPENER	RESPONDER	
One club	One heart	*Not forcing,* since the two no trump was a rebid, not an immediate response.
One spade	Two no trump	Used as a rebid by responder, it shows 11 to 13 high card points.

PREFERENCE BIDDING BY RESPONDER

On many hands, your partner will bid two suits; on a few, three suits. In a few cases, your own suit will be sufficiently strong that you prefer it as trump, and will rebid it, despite the fact that partner, by bidding other suits, has tacitly denied support for yours. For example -

(m)

♠ 84
♡ KQJ975
◊ 643
♣ 52

CASE V

OPENER	YOU, RESPONDER
One club	One heart
One spade	Two hearts

Certainly with hand (m) you would prefer to play the hand in hearts rather than either black suit, even if your partner has only one or two hearts. Your suit is that good.

But this is the exception rather than the rule. It is seldom that your suit will be that good, that long and that solid.

As a general rule, it is much better to tell partner which of his suits you prefer. Or, if you don't like any of his suits and have some high card strength in the unbid suit, you may prefer to bid no trump if the necessary values are present.

But what I want to impress, most of all, is that in giving a preference, do it to the hilt! Be sure to let your partner know whether you like one suit a lot better than another or whether yours is simply a luke-warm preference.

CASE W

(n)	OPENER	YOU, RESPONDER
♠ 1086	One spade	Two clubs
♡ J2	Two hearts	Two spades
◊ J73		
♣ AQJ98		

Holding hand (n) with the above bidding, your two spade rebid would be the luke-warm variety of preference.

CASE X

(o)	OPENER	YOU, RESPONDER
♠ KJ8	One spade	Two clubs
♡ 3	Two hearts	Three spades
◊ 10864		
♣ AQ1086		

Example (o) is an example of a jump preference. You are saying, "**Partner, I like spades lots better than hearts. My jump rebid shows a little more than the 10 points already promised by my two club bid. If you have even a little better than a minimum opening bid, we can make a game.**" This rebid is semi-forcing.

CASE Y

(p)	OPENER	YOU, RESPONDER
	One spade	Two clubs
♠ KJ87	Two hearts	?
♡ 3		
◊ K64		
♣ AQ876		

In Case Y, I have deliberately omitted your rebid with hand (p) to permit you to make what you consider to be the correct rebid.

Answer to Case Y. Your rebid should be four spades and nothing else. You hold 16 points in support of partner's spade suit so that game is certain. Three spades would be an incorrect underbid which partner, with a minimum opening bid, could pass.

CASE Z

OPENER	RESPONDER
One spade	Two clubs
Two hearts	Two no trump

Case Z shows, by your rebid, that you think game is makeable, and that you feel it better to play the hand in no trump. You deny excellent support for either of partner's major suits and guarantee some high card strength in the unbid diamond suit.

I might add that if one or both of your partner's suits are minors, you will frequently prefer to play the hand in no trump rather than a suit even though you may hold a very fine supporting 'fit' for these suits. The preference for no trump over the minor suit contract is based on the dual reasoning that, first, nine tricks will be easier to win in no trump than 11 in a minor; second, the scoring value of no trump is far greater than the alternative minor, something that will be of great importance when you encounter duplicate (tournament) bridge in your future bridge careers.

When partner has bid both major suits, the desire to play the hand in no trump is usually not present, since the ability to trump losers when played in a suit contract will more than offset the no trump's nine trick contract as against the 10 needed for the major suit game.

CASE A

OPENER	RESPONDER
One spade	Two clubs
Two hearts	Pass !

It is possible (and frequently desirable) to give a preference by passing as in Case A. The first thing for you to remember is that showing a second suit by by the opening bidder at minimum level *is not forcing*. The opening bidder couldn't guarantee that a game was makeable since in that event he would have made a forcing rebid of one more than necessary in a new suit or jumped directly to game.

Therefore, the opening bidder is feeling out the hand carefully, trying to find out the best suit between the partnership for the trump suit, and if you have a minimum hand and like his second suit better than his first, pass. A typical hand would be that shown to the left - which is the same hand shown as (n) on page 242 except I have transposed the spades and hearts.

(q)
♠ J2
♡ 1086
◊ J73
♣ AQJ98

A REBID OF A NEW SUIT BY RESPONDER

CASE B

OPENER	RESPONDER
One heart	One spade
Two clubs	Two diamonds

The bid of a new suit by a responder who has not yet passed is absolutely forcing upon the opening bidder to rebid. While the bid of a second suit by responder is not forcing to game, it carries an inference of strength, since without the possibility of game, there would have been little point in responder bidding again.

To the student who may ask, **"Why didn't responder bid no trump himself since he held spades and diamonds, and his partner showed hearts and clubs,?"** I would like to answer that perhaps responder didn't want to play the hand in no trump with a highly distributional two-suiter. If responder did wish to play the hand in no trump, he may have felt that the hand would play better from the other side of the table. In other words, the opening lead would have come up to his partner's cards, not through them. Frequently this is the reason for making one player or the other the declarer.

CASE C

OPENER	RESPONDER
One heart	One spade
One no trump	Two diamonds

The only time a new suit bid by a responder who has not previously passed is not forcing upon the opening bidder to rebid is when the latter's rebid had been one no trump. The opening bidder may pass the two diamond rebid in Case C if he likes diamonds better than spades. He has already indicated a minimum opening bid with the one no trump rebid.

Had the responder felt a game makeable in Case C, he should have rebid with three diamonds, which, being one more than necessary in a new suit, couldn't be passed. In this respect, I would like to point out that once a player jumps in a new suit, it is not necessary for either partner to jump again, since the partnership is now committed to continue bidding until at least game is reached.

RESPONDER'S REBIDS AFTER OPENER'S REVERSE

What should you do as responder, after your partner, who opened the bidding, reverses as his rebid?

The first thing for responder to remember is that the first suit shown by the opening bidder *is longer than his second.* Any preference for one suit over the other must be based on that logic. The first suit is known *to be at least one card longer.* Thus, responder, in helping to select the final trump suit, must take an imaginary count of both suits bid by his partner.

The estimated number of cards in each of opener's suits are added by responder to his holdings in those suits. The preference is given to the suit in which the greater estimated total is held.

Where the bidding has indicated the number of cards held by the partnership to be the same in both suits, the responder, rather than the opening bidder, will usually play the determining role in selecting the trump suit. This will usually involve situations where the partnership holds a total of either seven or eight cards in each of two suits.

When the combined totals are seven cards, the opening bidder will usually have five cards of his first suit and four cards of his second. In order to bring the total up to seven, the responder will hold two cards of partner's first suit and three cards of the second suit. In these cases, the responder should give a preference for the first suit - the suit in which the opening bidder is known to have five cards. The second (and far more infrequent situation) is where the opening bidder, through his reverse and subsequent rebid, has shown six cards of his first suit and five of his second and the responder holds a singleton of the first bid suit and a doubleton of the latter.

When, as responder, you hold two cards of the suit in which partner is known to hold five cards and you hold three cards of partner's four card suit, express the preference for the five card suit; when partner has shown six-five and you hold one and two cards respectively, show the preference for the suit in which you have the doubleton.

With eight cards in two suits between the partnership, the opening bidder will usually have five cards in his first suit and four in his second or six cards in his first suit and five in his second. Correspondingly, in the first case, responder will have three cards of opener's five-carder and four cards of the four card suit - the preference should be for the suit in which the responder holds four cards.

As the student's experience grows, he will discover that when the hand is played with a four-four trump suit, it will win at least one more trick than if played with the five-three trump suit. The reason for this apparent phenomena is that the five card suit, when utilized as a side-suit, affords discards of the other hand's losers plus the additional trumping value afforded by the possession of four trumps in each of the partnership hands.

Where the opening bidder has shown six-five and the responder holds two cards of the former and three cards of the five card suit, the preference is given to the latter. This permits the longer suit to be used as a side-suit for discarding purposes with the further advantage that a possible loser in the longer suit can be trumped in the dummy as with hand three on page 142.

REVERSE BIDDING BY THE RESPONDER

The responder, in rebidding, may reverse exactly as did the opening bidder. Both reverses show the same things - that the first suit is longer than the second, higher-ranking suit, and that the hand is strong enough to withstand a preference that might place the contract one zone higher.

Only the required strength differs. The opening bidder needed a minimum of 16 or 18 points to reverse; the responder needed but 12.

A reverse by responder is *absolutely forcing upon opener to rebid* if the responder has not previously passed. This is true even if the opening bidder has indicated a minimum hand by his rebid. Responder's reverse is not 100 percent forcing to game, although strongly invitational to that contract.

PART TWO

LATER REBIDS BY OPENER AND RESPONDER

On pages 148 and 196, I stated that the bid of a new suit at the one level by the opening bidder as a rebid showed no values in addition to the 13 points promised by the opening bid - that the bid merely showed four cards or more of the new suit.

CASE A

PARTNER	YOU
One club	One diamond
One heart	

The one heart rebid shows four or more hearts, nothing extra in high cards.

Now, let's go one step further.

CASE B

PARTNER	YOU
One club	One diamond
One heart	One spade

By rebidding with one spade, you are forcing your partner to bid again. This may get the contract higher. Accordingly, since the opening bidder may be rebidding with the same 13 or 14 points with which he opened the bidding, you as responder should have a little extra in high cards or in distribution for each time you find another bid.

(a)	(b)
♠ Q 10 9 8	♠ Q 10 9 8
♡ J 2	♡ J 4 3
◇ A Q 3 2	◇ K 7 6 5 4
♣ 8 7 6	♣ 2

With the bidding in Case A, as responder, you should rebid 'one spade' holding hand (a) and pass opener's one heart rebid holding hand (b).

Let's carry our bidding sequence one step further.

CASE C

PARTNER	YOU
One club	One diamond
One heart	One spade
One no trump	

Examining each of partner's bids -

1 - The one club bid promised 13 or more points.

2 - The one heart rebid is *forced*, shows four or more hearts and promises no additional values over the original 13 points.

3 - The one no trump rebid was also *forced* (this time by your one spade rebid), also promises nothing in excess of 13 points.

THE ORDER OF REBIDDING SUITS TO SHOW DISTRIBUTION

The length of a player's suit or suits is shown by his rebids of those suits, or his failure to rebid them. The order in which two or more suits are bid can paint a very accurate picture of distribution.

1 - Any suit, until rebid, is considered to be only four cards in length. The only exception is when the first suit in a reverse, though it has never been rebid, is marked as longer than the second by the rebid.

CASE D

OPENER	RESPONDER
One heart	One spade
Two clubs	

In Case D, the responder must assume that both suits bid by the opener, hearts and clubs, are only four cards long until they are rebid.

CASE E

OPENER	RESPONDER
One heart	Two clubs
Two spades	

In Case E, the heart suit is known to be rebiddable, since the opener has reversed the bidding.

2 - Holding two five card suits, the higher-ranking is bid first, the lower-ranking suit shown at the next opportunity. The lower-ranking is then rebid as in Case F. This permits partner to express a preference without increasing the contract.

CASE F

OPENER	RESPONDER
One spade	Two clubs
Two hearts	Two no trump
Three hearts	

3 - With suits of unequal length, bid the longer first in most cases. If the shorter suit is of five or more cards, bid and rebid it before rebidding the longer. This will be particularly true in cases where you have reversed the bidding with six-five.

CASE G

OPENER	RESPONDER
One heart	Two clubs
Two spades	Two no trump
Three spades	

Notice, in Case G, how rebidding the higher ranking suit, spades, marks it for at least five cards. Hence hearts, known to be still longer from the reverse, must be six cards in length.

4 - With six-four, rebid the six card suit first before showing the four-carder, *unless the latter can be shown at the one-level as a rebid.*

(c)

OPENER'S HAND
♠ 8
♡ A Q 3 2
◊ 6 5
♣ A Q 6 5 4 3

After opening the bidding with one club holding hand (c), the opening bidder would, after a response of one spade, rebid with two clubs; however, had the response been one diamond, *the opener's rebid should be one heart.*

5 - In rebidding or responding with four card suits, one bids '*up the ladder*,' in other words, the cheaper suit first.

THE KEY TO REBIDDING

1 - If one partner has previously passed, any bid otherwise forcing is not forcing, and may be passed. The only exception is an immediate cue-bid of the opponents' last bid suit.

2 - One-over-one bidding by responder forces the opener to rebid; one-over-one by opener may be passed by the responder.

3 - A free rebid shows additional values; forced rebids do not.

4 - A rebid which forces the bidding into the two-level requires additional strength over a rebid that can be made at the one-level.

5 - Don't bid or rebid merely because you don't like your partner's suits. He may not like yours, either.

6 - A rebid of two no trump shows at least a partial fit with partner's suit or suits; it is not bid to escape from badly fitting suits or suit.

PART THREE

THE COVERING OF HONORS

The expression, 'covering an honor with an honor,' refers to playing a card higher than a high card led by the other side, not in the hope of taking a trick but in the hope of promoting in trick taking value, a lower card that you or your partner may hold.

♠ A432
N
♠ KJ7 W E ♠ 1086
S
♠ Q95

Figure 108

A basic case is illustrated in *figure 108*. South, the declarer, leads the queen of spades. By covering with the king, the ace is forced to win the trick.

What card has been promoted to first place in the spade suit?

Why, the jack!

And you have it!

♠ A432
N
♠ K76 W E ♠ J108
S
♠ Q95

Figure 109

In *figure 109*, I have transposed some of the East-West cards. Should West cover or not? He doesn't have either the jack or 10, the cards that would be promoted by the cover, nor does he know who has them.

Since you, unlike West, can see all 13 cards of the suit, and that by covering you will promote your partner's jack and 10, you should cover the queen with the king. In this manner, the declarer will win only one trick, the ace. Had you not covered the queen with the king, declarer could have played the deuce on the queen and won the first trick with the latter card, then would win a second trick with dummy's ace.

THE ERROR OF LEADING THE QUEEN

No good bridge player would lead the queen in figures 108 and 109 from the South hand unless his side also held the jack, or 10 and nine, in combination with the queen. It stands to reason that if lower cards can be promoted in value by covering a card led by the declarer, they should be cards held by the declarer or dummy and certainly not by the opponents.

The correct way to try to win two tricks with the combinations shown in *figures 108 and 109* is to lead a low card from the North hand towards the queen, hope that East holds the king. See *figures 35 and 36*, page 95.

WHEN AND WHEN NOT TO COVER

The best advice I can give you, when you are a defender, on when to cover an adverse led honor is "cover when your side has or believe has one or more of the cards that will be promoted by the cover." In other words, you cover when you think you can gain by covering and you don't cover when it is obvious that you have nothing to gain and everything to lose by covering.

In *figure 108*, you held the jack. It was a simple matter to cover the queen with the king and promote your jack.

In *figure 109*, your partner held both the jack and 10. Here by covering the queen with the king, you promoted his cards.

	♠ QJ10987	
	N	
♠ 65	W E	♠ K43
	S	
	♠ A2	

Figure 110

In *figure 110*, the queen of spades is led from the North hand which is the dummy. Should you, East, cover with the king?

Well, hardly !

Stop and think. All of the cards that will be promoted in value as the jack, 10, nine, eight, etc., belong to the opponents. Moreover, in the case illustrated above, East's king is better protected than South's ace and it (the king) cannot be caught by finessing. Here the cover is not only futile - it's suicidal.

BETWEEN GOOD AND BAD PLAYERS

As has been pointed out, leading the queen towards the ace, minus supporting cards, as in *figures 35, 36, 108 and 109*, is the incorrect way to play the combination. I have only given these examples to demonstrate the effects of covering. The correct way to play these cards is to lead a low card towards the queen.

Let me give you a little tip. When an experienced player leads a card that may be covered for a finesse, you can bet your bottom dollar that he's equipped to have you cover. On the other hand, a careless player may lead an unsupported card.

So, if in an apparent finesse, a good player leads a high card that you can cover, beware the Greeks bearing gifts and ask yourself these questions - **Do I have any cards that will be promoted if I cover? Does my partner?** If you think the answer is **'yes'** in either case, then cover.

I realize that the younger player cannot reach decisions whether or not to cover as rapidly as his more experienced brother. That is only natural. But nothing is more revealing than hesitation by a player over whether to cover. He might as well tell everybody at the table he holds that particular card and doesn't know what to do with it.

Try to play each of your cards at the same rate of speed. Above all, if a high card is led in what is obviously a finesse and you are unable to cover, do not hesitate as though to convey the impression that you are pondering whether or not to cover. That is unethical, which is a polite way of saying **'cheating.'**

In the following paragraphs, I will illustrate some common covering situations.

```
          ♠ A432
             N
♠ K106  W         E  ♠ 875
             S
          ♠ QJ9
```

Figure 111

In *figure 111*, South leads the queen. West covers with the king. The ace wins. Sooner or later, depending on whether South finesses against the missing 10, West must win a trick with that card.

Now we're assuming that South is a good player so that he wouldn't have led the queen without the jack. Notice that in *figure 111* we could have played the six on the lead of the queen,, later covered the jack with the king to win the self-same trick with the 10.

```
          ♠ A432
             N
♠ K87   W         E  ♠ 1065
             S
          ♠ QJ9
```

Figure 112

Let's change *figure 111* to resemble *figure 112*. In the latter, South again leads the queen. West covers with the king. The ace wins. East's 10 is now finessable so East-West win no tricks.

♠ J86
N
♠ 1032 W E ♠ Q54
S
♠ AK97
Figure 113

In *figure 113*, the jack is led from the North hand. East's cover with the queen promotes West's 10 to second place in the suit by compelling South to play the ace or king to take the trick.

♠ J108
N
♠ K654 W E ♠ Q97
S
♠ A32
Figure 114

The jack is led in *figure 114*. East should not cover since the 10 is in the dummy. Accordingly, East will play the seven, South the deuce, and West will win with the king.

Now watch what happens. When the suit is again played, the card played by East depends upon the card led from the dummy. If North leads the 10, East will cover with the queen, forcing South's ace. East's nine has been promoted to first place in the suit!

Had dummy, North, played the eight (instead of the 10) on the second round of spades, East's nine would have forced the ace, leaving the queen to win the third round of the suit.

By refusing to cover the first honor from a two card sequence, but covering the second, East helped his side win two tricks. Had East covered the jack on the first round, his side would have taken only one trick with the same cards. The play, with cards winning tricks underlined, would have gone as follows -

N	E	S	W
♠ J	♠ Q	♠ A	♠ 4
♠ 8	♠ 7	♠ 2	♠ K

Dummy's 10-spot is now the highest card!

♠ 1032
N
♠ K987 W E ♠ Q65
S
♠ AJ4
Figure 115

In *figures 115* and *116*, we meet a new type of covering situation. Most of the cards involved in the cover are not visible to the player making the cover. In *figure 115*, the 10 is led from the dummy, North. East covers with the queen. South wins with the ace, but North-South can now win only one trick in the suit. Note that had East not played the queen on the 10, South would have played the four and West would take the trick with the king. At some later point, a low spade would be led from the dummy. With the king played to the first trick, South's ace-jack brackets East's queen, gives North-South two tricks in the suit.

	♠ 1032	
	N	
♠ Q987	W E	♠ K65
	S	
	♠ AJ4	

Figure 116

	♠ AJ1086	
	N	
♠ K4	W E	♠ 9532
	S	
	♠ Q7	

Figure 117

In *figure 116*, I have merely transposed the king and queen of spades. The principle behind covering the 10 with the king is identical to *figure 115*.

South leads the queen of spades in *figure 117*, and West covers with the king. Notice how the cover promotes East's nine-spot so that the nine can win the fourth round of that suit. Had West not covered the queen, North-South would have won all five spade tricks.

There are additional instances where the defender sitting second hand should not cover. One such case is illustrated in *figure 118* where the bidding has indicated that partner at most has a singleton which must fall on the first round of the suit. Therefor, partner can have no promotable cards for later rounds.

	♠ Q743	
	N	
♠ A	W E	♠ K5
	S	
	♠ J109862	

Figure 118

In *figure 118*, South has bid and rebid spades. Dummy leads the queen. Should East cover? **No!**

South's spade rebid marked him for five or six spades, so West can't have enough spades to promote, I might add that enticing a cover, as in *figure 118*, is a common device employed by shrewd declarers to trap two opposing high cards into falling simultaneously.

West		North / South		East
		♠ J7432 ♡ AKJ8 ◇ 5 ♣ Q43		
♠ void ♡ 107643 ◇ KJ94 ♣ J1098	W	N S	E	♠ K5 ♡ 95 ◇ 1087632 ♣ K76
		♠ AQ10986 ♡ Q2 ◇ AQ ♣ A52		

Figure 119

Figure 119 gives another example of when not to cover. Let's say the bidding was -

South	North
One spade	Two hearts
Three spades	Six spades

Your partner, West, opens the jack of clubs. The queen is played from the dummy. The king covers and the ace wins. The ace of diamonds is cashed and the queen of diamonds is trumped in the dummy in order to place the lead in that hand. The jack of spades is then led.

Should you cover with the king ?

No !

South, by his jump rebid in spades, has at least five cards of that suit, and probably six as is the case. He doesn't know whether the two outstanding spades will divide evenly - one to each defender - or whether one defender has both spades. If you play the five spot when the jack is led, the declarer may very well guess wrong and play his ace, expecting the two missing spades to be 'split.' If he guesses incorrectly, you'll beat the hand.

COVERING HINTS IN GENERAL

1 - Cover when you think your side can gain by the cover.

2 - Do not cover a card from a sequence in dummy until the last card of the sequence is led. This naturally presupposes that you hold sufficient additional cards with your honor affording you the option of covering or playing a low card.

3 - If your honor is originally doubleton, and there is a possibility that partner may hold a card that might be promoted by covering, cover the first round of the led sequence. Since you must play your honor by the second round, you might just as well cover the biggest card you can with it.

4 - Poor players lead unsupported cards; good players don't.

5 - If you don't have a card that can be promoted by the cover, your partner may have.

QUIZ SEVEN

1 - The bidding has been -

South, Partner, Opener	West	You, North	East
One club	Pass	One diamond	Pass
One heart	Pass	?	

What is your rebid with each of the following hands?

(a)	(b)	(c)
♠ 10743	♠ AJ9	♠ J876
♡ Q8	♡ K82	♡ 1052
◇ K10752	◇ QJ108	◇ A5432
♣ K3	♣ J63	♣ 2

(d)	(e)	(f)
♠ Q107	♠ A543	♠ A2
♡ Q643	♡ Q876	♡ KQ107
◇ K873	◇ K1052	◇ KJ98
♣ 42	♣ 3	♣ 432

2 - The bidding has been -

South, Partner, Opener	West	You, North	East
One spade	Pass	Two clubs	Pass
Two hearts	Pass	?	

What is your rebid with each of the following hands ?

(g)	(h)	(i)
♠ 876	♠ A6	♠ A87
♡ AJ	♡ Q54	♡ 2
◇ 654	◇ 105	◇ A843
♣ KQ432	♣ KJ7632	♣ KJ652

(j)	(k)	(l)
♠ A8	♠ Q8	♠ KJ73
♡ J6	♡ J6	♡ A2
◇ KJ98	◇ AQJ8	◇ Q
♣ K9876	♣ KQ876	♣ KQJ876

3 - The bidding has been -

South, Partner, Opener	West	You, North	East
One heart	Pass	Two clubs	Pass
Two spades	Pass	?	

What is your rebid with each of the following hands?

(m)	(n)	(o)
♠ Q2	♠ 75	♠ J6
♡ Q2	♡ 75	♡ J109
◇ J864	◇ QJ107	◇ A3
♣ AK1074	♣ AK1094	♣ AQJ862

4 - The bidding has been -

You, South, Opener	West	North, Partner	East
One club	Pass	One heart	One spade
Pass	Pass	Three dia.	Pass
?			

What is your rebid with each of the following hands ?

(p)	(q)	(r)
♠ K 10 6	♠ Q 5 2	♠ A 5
♡ J 4	♡ K 7 3	♡ 10 7
◇ K 10 3	◇ 7 4	◇ K 7 4 3
♣ A Q J 7 6	♣ A K J 9 8	♣ A Q 6 5 4

ANSWERS TO QUIZ SEVEN

1 -
(a) One spade; (b) two no trump; (c) pass; (d) two hearts; (e) three hearts; (f) four hearts.

2 -
(g) Two spades; (h) three hearts; (i) four spades; (j) two no trump or three diamonds; (k) three diamonds; (l) five spades - *since slam bidding has not yet been discussed, a rebid of four spades will be considered correct.*

3 -
(m) Three hearts; (n) Three no trump; (o) four hearts - *later in your instruction, you will see the merit of a temporizing cue-bid of three diamonds.*

4 -
(p) Three no trump; (q) three hearts; (r) four diamonds.

LESSON SEVEN
HANDS

Since each of Lesson Seven's hands is intended to illustrate when and when not to cover honors, the bidding and early play is given in each case. The card winning each trick is underlined. Where a question mark appears, the student is to make the decision as to which card should be played.

1.

North: ♠ Q2 ♡ KQ732 ◊ 2 ♣ AJ1075

West: ♠ 103 ♡ AJ4 ◊ Q7653 ♣ K98

East: ♠ K98 ♡ 1095 ◊ J1094 ♣ Q62

South: ♠ AJ7654 ♡ 86 ◊ AK8 ♣ 43

South dealer, N-S vulnerable.

South	West	North	East
1 sp.	pass	2 hts.	pass
2 sp.	pass	3 cl.	pass
3 no. tr.	pass	4 sp.	pass
pass	pass		

2.

North: ♠ AQ10876 ♡ A2 ◊ KQJ ♣ 72

West: ♠ K2 ♡ 6543 ◊ 10987 ♣ A85

East: ♠ void ♡ QJ1087 ◊ 6432 ♣ 9643

South: ♠ J9543 ♡ K9 ◊ A5 ♣ KQJ10

North dealer, E-W vulnerable.

North	East	South	West
1 sp.	pass	2 cl.	pass
3 sp.	pass	6 sp. *	pass
pass	pass		

THE PLAY

Hand 1:

West	North	East	South
◊5	◊2	◊9	◊K
♡4	♡Q	♡5	♡6
	♠Q	?	

Hand 2:

East	South	West	North
♡Q	♡K	♡3	♡2
	♠J	?	

FOOTNOTE

* *There are far better and more accurate slam bidding methods than the jump to six shown in hand two. These better methods will be shown in Lesson Thirteen.*

3.

	North	
	♠ 64 ♡ K762 ♢ J1095 ♣ 1042	
West ♠ AKQJ105 ♡ A43 ♢ 43 ♣ 65	N W E S	**East** ♠ 873 ♡ J105 ♢ Q72 ♣ AK98
	♠ 92 ♡ Q98 ♢ AK86 ♣ QJ73	

West dealer, neither side vul.

West	North	East	South
1 sp.	pass	2 cl.	pass
3 sp.	pass	4 sp.	pass
pass	pass		

4.

	North	
	♠ KJ76 ♡ K82 ♢ Q93 ♣ 952	
West ♠ 92 ♡ 104 ♢ AJ8764 ♣ K107	N W E S	**East** ♠ A10843 ♡ AJ7 ♢ 105 ♣ AQJ
	♠ Q5 ♡ Q9653 ♢ K2 ♣ 8643	

East dealer, both sides vul.

East	South	West	North
1 sp.	pass	2 dia.	pass
2 no tr.	pass	3 no tr.	pass
pass	pass		

THE PLAY

Hand 3:

North	East	South	West
♢J	♢2	♢8	♢3
♢10	♢7	♢6	♢4
♢5	♢Q	♢K	♠5
♠4	♠3	♠2	♠A
♠6	♠7	♠9	♠K
♣2	♣K	♣7	♣5
	♡J	♡ ?	

Hand 4:

South	West	North	East
♡5	♡4	♡K	♡A
♢ ?			♢10

COMMENTS

1 - East must cover with the king. His only hope of winning a trump trick is that his partner holds the 10. Notice that if East covers, he will win the third round of spades with the nine; if he fails to cover, his side will not win a spade trick.

2 - Covering would be senseless. The bidding has indicated partner to hold few, if any, spades. Covering will only solve declarer's problem as to finesse or play for the 'drop.'

3 - South should not cover the jack with the queen since the 10 remains in dummy. Covering will give declarer two tricks since after winning with the ace, a low card can be led towards dummy's 10.

4 - South must cover with the king. This gives the defense two diamond tricks, playing the deuce but one trick.

SOLUTIONS TO LESSON SEVEN HANDS

1.

South declarer at four spades.

Trick	W	N	E	S
1	◇5	◇2	◇9	◇K
2	♡4	♡Q	♡5	♡6
3	♠3	♠Q	♠K	♠A
4	♡A	♡2	♡9	♡8
5	♣9	♣A	♣6	♣3
6	♡J	♡K	♡10	♣4
7	♣8	♣5	♣2	♠4
8	◇3	♠2	◇4	◇8
9	♣K	♣7	♣Q	♠5
10	♠10	♡3	♠8	♠J
11	◇6	♡7	◇10	◇A
12	◇7	♣10	♠9	♠6
13	◇Q	♣J	◇J	♠7

South wins 11 tricks.

2.

North declarer at six spades.

Trick	E	S	W	N
1	♡Q	♡K	♡3	♡2
2		♠J	♠2	♠?

After West correctly refuses to cover the jack of spades with the king, success or failure of the slam contract hinges on whether the declarer takes the finesse or plays for the 'drop.'

There is a strong probability that without the cover, declarer will guess 'wrong;' covering removes all doubt!

3.

West declarer at four spades.

Trick	N	E	S	W
1	◇J	◇2	◇8	◇3
2	◇10	◇7	◇6	◇4
3	◇5	◇Q	◇K	♠5
4	♠4	♠3	♠2	♠A
5	♠6	♠7	♠9	♠K
6	♣2	♣K	♣7	♣5
7	♡K	♡J	♡8	♡3
8	♣4	♣A	♣3	♣6
9	♡2	♡5	♡9	♡A
10	◇9	♠8	◇A	♠Q
11	♣10	♣8	♣J	♠J
12	♡6	♡10	♣Q	♠10
13	♡7	♣9	♡Q	♡4

West wins nine tricks.

4.

East declarer at 3 no trump.

Trick	S	W	N	E
1	♡5	♡4	♡K	♡A
2	◇K	◇4	◇3	◇10
3	♡3	♡10	♡2	♡7
4	♣3	♣7	♣2	♣Q
5	◇2	◇J	◇Q	◇5
6	♡Q	♠2	♡8	♡J
7	♡9	◇6	♠7	♠3
8	♡6	◇7	♣5	♠4
9	♠Q	♠9	♠6	♠A
10	♣4	♣10	♣9	♣A
11	♣6	♣K	◇9	♣J
12	♣8	◇A	♠J	♠8
13	♠5	◇8	♠K	♠10

East wins eight tricks.

Lesson VIII

No Trump

PART ONE

Bidding

PART TWO

Play of the Cards

LESSON EIGHT

PART ONE

NO TRUMP BIDDING

In your very first lesson, I described no trump as the leveling off of all four suits to equal trick-taking status. In no trump, cards win tricks solely in the order of their rank, in that suit, when played. The deuce of spades would win a trick if led, providing no other player had a spade. Even the ace of another suit couldn't capture the spade deuce in no trump.

This lesson will be concerned with opening bids of one or more no trump, together with raises and takeouts to suit contracts, and the play of the hand in no trump.

It should be pointed out that the fact that the bidding has opened with no trump does not preclude the final contract being played with a suit as trump exactly as an opening bid in a suit had no bearing on whether the final contract was played in that suit, or in another suit, or in no trump.

HOW PLAY IN NO TRUMP WORKS

In a suit (trump) contract, most of the tricks won in any suit are usually taken with high cards as aces, kings and queens. It is rare that any suit can be played three times without the third round being trumped by one or more players. In a suit contract, the lower cards that can win the fourth and fifth rounds as jacks, 10's and nines have little immediate trick taking value other than their abilities to bolster and reinforce still higher cards.

Just the reverse is true in no trump!

Since in no trump, cards in the led suit win tricks purely in the order of their rank in the led suit, a jack will win a trick if the ace, king and queen of that suit have been expended. Similarly, a deuce or trey, as already mentioned, will win a trick if led and all higher cards are gone.

No trump play, then, is a matter of development of low cards into winners, both by offense and defense.

STAYMAN

Later in this book, in Lesson XVI, you will find a resume of what has become known as "The Stayman Convention."

This method of no trump bidding, together with exceedingly accurate responses, was originated some years ago by two top New York players, George Rapee and Samuel Stayman. Almost every good player throughout the world today uses this method which, through authorship of books on the subject by Stayman, bears the latter's name..

Since most of the players you will meet use so-called standard methods of no trump bidding, this lesson will be devoted to describing those methods. In that way, you will be able to sit down and play bridge with everyone and they will understand your bids and you will understand theirs.

By the time you reach the 16th lesson, you will have become sufficiently proficient to master Stayman. At this point you will find yourself using this method exclusively with all of your partners that are familiar with it. For the present, our no trump bidding will follow conventional patterns.

REQUIREMENTS FOR AN OPENING BID OF ONE NO TRUMP

1 - 16 to 18 points in high cards - no more, no less!

2 - Distribution. The hand should be 4-3-3-3 or 4-4-3-2, rarely 5-3-3-2 if the five card suit is a minor and the hand contains tenaces.

3 - Stoppers. Stoppers in at least three suits with a potential stopper in the fourth suit.

A 'stopper' is a high card that will win a trick if the lead comes up to that card from the player to the left. For example, let's suppose South holds ♠K2. With West, to the left, leading a spade, the protected king must win a trick regardless of the location of the missing ace. Minimum stoppers are Kx, Qxx, Jxxx. It can be seen that each of these combinations will win a trick if repeatedly led up to. Of course, when you get down to Jxxx, you're cutting it pretty fine.

The ace, of course, is a sure stopper. An ace-king or ace-queen combination would be a double stopper. Then there are what we call 'potential stoppers.'

(a)
♠ J72
N
W E
S
♠ Q5

(b)
♠ Q2
N
W E
S
♠ J63

South's holdings in each of the following examples are potential stoppers. Notice how, when reinforced with a card of that suit in the dummy, a trick is insured in the suit when led by the opponents.

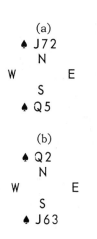

The advantage of stoppers is that they prevent the other side from winning an uninterrupted flow of tricks in a suit. Looking at (a) and (b), you can see that if you were playing the hands with the above spade suits, the defenders could win the first and second rounds with the ace and king of spades, but if you play a low card from the North and South hands when the opponents play the ace and king, you must win the third round.

Do not make a common beginner's error in (a) and (b) of playing a high card from the dummy to 'force' a bigger card from the opponents. If you do, you will throw away your stopper as in *figure 120.*

♠ Q2
N
♠ A10854 W E ♠ K97
S
♠ J63

Figure 120

Let's pretend you are South, playing a no trump contract. West opens his fourth-best spade, the five-spot. Your correct play of the North-South cards would be -

CORRECT PLAY

W	N	E	S
♠5	♠2	♠K	♠3
♠A	♠Q	♠9	♠6
♠4		♠7	♠J

INCORRECT PLAY

W	N	E	S
♠5	♠Q	♠K	♠3
♠A	♠2	♠9	♠J
♠10		♠7	♠6

Note, that in the correct version, by playing the deuce from the dummy to the opening lead, North-South were bound to win a spade trick. Had East played the nine of spades to the opening lead (this is termed a defensive finesse), South would have captured the first trick with the jack.

But when South (in error) released dummy's queen, the king won the trick. When East returned the nine, South's jack was trapped. If South played the jack on the second round of the suit, West would win with the ace. If South played the six of spades under East's nine, the third round of the suit would find East leading the seven, South playing the jack, and West winning with the ace. Either way, after dummy's queen was played, North-South had tossed away their spade stopper.

COUNTING POINTS FOR NO TRUMP

As has been previously stated, count only points for high cards when bidding no trump. Award no points for distribution.

(a)	(b)	(c)
♠ A 8 6	♠ K 10 7 6	♠ K 2
♡ A 9 4	♡ A J	♡ K Q 2
◊ K 10 7 3	◊ K J 9 2	◊ A 10 3
♣ A J 8	♣ A Q 3	♣ A J 9 7 5
16 points	18 points	17 points

RESPONSES TO ONE NO TRUMP

The first thing for the responder to do, after his partner has opened the bidding with one no trump, is to add his points to the 16 to 18 points promised by the opening bid. If the responder contemplates an eventual suit contract, he should count points for both distribution and high cards; if the response or final contract is to be in no trump, only high card values are counted.

After totaling the points in the combined hands, it will usually be apparent to the responder whether game is or is not makeable. Then too, there is the question of whether the combined hands will play better in a suit contract or in no trump. If the responder's hand contains a long suit, together with a singleton or void, or responder holds two suits with one suit of at least five cards, the suit contract will frequently produce more tricks than if the hand is played in no trump.

One point I want to make clear. *You do NOT have to respond to an opening bid of one no trump.* If you are 'busted,' you should pass. An opening bid of one no trump is *NOT* forcing.

THE PASS

Of course, the weakest response you can make following partner's opening one no trump bid is to pass.

RULE - Pass with less than eight high card points unless -

1 - You have a six card or longer suit;
2 - You have two suits, one of which is at least five cards;
3 - You have a five card suit and a singleton;
4 - Your hand contains a void.

(d)	(e)	(f)	(g)	(h)
♠ Q643	♠ 106542	♠ Q108	♠ 32	♠ Q8432
♡ KJ8	♡ K6	♡ 6432	♡ 873	♡ K76
◊ 1062	◊ 843	◊ J965	◊ J8654	◊ 63
♣ 987	♣ 863	♣ K3	♣ 432	♣ 432

As responder, you should pass partner's opening one no trump bid with each of the above hands.

THE TAKEOUT TO TWO OF A SUIT

Bidding two of a suit after partner has opened with one no trump says, "**Partner, I don't think we can make a game. I think the hand will play better in my suit than in no trump. Please pass my response and let me play the hand in my suit in the part score contract *unless* you have a maximum 17 or 18 point no trump and excellent supporting cards in my suit in which it's safe to give my suit a single raise to the three-level.**"

Now for a few words of caution and I've started this paragraph in italics for emphasis. The average partner you will meet won't know that your response of two in a suit is a signoff. Most of them will look at the same hand, with its 16 to 18 points, and want to show it all over again, forgetting that their first bid completely described the hand's full strength.

So, they'll rebid, and that rebid is usually two no trump, sometimes even three no trump. If they do bid two no trump and you try to sign off again by bidding three of your suit, the no trump bidder will incorrectly take your rebid as showing added strength rather than a desire to get out of no trump into a suit, less than game, contract. So the opening bidder will find still another bid which will usually be three no trump or possibly a raise of your suit to an unmakeable four or five level. By this time the opponents begin doubling for profitable penalties.

There is a bridge anecdote about a similar situation. After an opening bid of one no trump, responder bid two spades. The opening bidder then bid two no trump. Responder bid three spades, and opener correspondingly bid three no trump. Responder bid four spades, and opener rebid four no trump whereon the responder then bid seven no trump.

When asked why he bid seven no trump with a hand so weak that originally warranted only a two spade response, the answer was **"I knew we were going there eventually and I wanted to save three rounds of bidding!"**

So with a partner that 'won't let go,' it's better to pass with a weak hand, even though you know the combined hands would play better in a suit contract than in no trump. But we will suppose your partner can recognize a signoff, and credits you for knowing what you are doing.

TO SHOW A SUIT AT THE TWO LEVEL

Any bid of two of a suit, in response to an opening bid of one no trump, *guarantees that the suit is at least five cards in length.* Never take out partner's no trump into two of a suit when the suit is only of four cards, particularly if the hand is weak. If your hand, as responder, is so weak that you don't think the partnership can win seven tricks in no trump, how would you expect to win *eight* tricks with a weak hand and only a four card trump suit?

REQUIREMENTS -

With a six card or longer suit and an unbalanced hand containing a singleton or two worthless doubletons, the response of two of a suit may be made without any high cards whatever.

With two five card suits, the hand should contain a minimum of three high card points.

With a five card and a four card suit, the hand should have a minimum of four high card points.

In no case should the response of two of a suit be made with more than seven high card points.

(i)	(j)	(k)
♠ 965432	♠ 62	♠ 74
♡ 86	♡ QJ987	♡ 108
◇ J43	◇ Q743	◇ Q87643
♣ 62	♣ 85	♣ 752

Respond two spades with (i); two hearts with (j); two diamonds with (k).

THE RAISE TO TWO NO TRUMP

The raise to two no trump says, 'Partner, I think we can make a game if you have a maximum opening no trump of 17 or 18 points. If you have a minimum 16 pointer, then pass.'

This raise (to two no trump) can be made on a variety of hands ranging from scattered strength throughout the hand with only four card suits to hands containing five card or longer suits that can be utilized in no trump play.

REQUIREMENTS -

Eight or nine high card points and a balanced or semi-balanced hand with no voids or singletons. Where the responder's hand contains a solid or semi-solid five card or longer suit that can be 'run' in no trump, the raise to two no trump may be shaded one point to a minimum of seven high card points.

EXAMPLES OF RAISES TO TWO NO TRUMP

(l)	(m)	(n)	(o)
♠ Q74	♠ Q7	♠ J108	♠ 92
♡ K109	♡ AQ432	♡ 765	♡ KJ9
◇ QJ76	◇ 842	◇ KQJ76	◇ QJ10865
♣ 1083	♣ J109	♣ 104	♣ 73

While in some cases with the above hands in the event of the opening bidder rebidding to three no trump, the combined partnership point count may not quite total 26 points, particularly where responder's raise is partially based on holding an establishable suit, game is so highly probable that it should be bid.

Moreover, the reader should by now appreciate that the figure of 26 points normally needed to produce a game in no trump or a major suit *is the average* and doesn't always hold true. On some hands, where the partnership holds a long suit that can be 'run' in no trump or where there are tremendous trump 'fits' combined with highly unbalanced distribution permitting the trumping of adverse aces and kings, game can (and is) frequently made with less than 26 points.

On the other hand, without benefit of long suits to 'run' or a good supporting trump 'fit,' I have seen hands with 28 or more points go down to defeat in game contracts where the defenders held the long suits, finesses didn't 'work' and suits didn't 'break.'

THE RAISE TO THREE NO TRUMP

The bid of three no trump, in response to an opening bid of one no trump, indicates 10 to 14 high card points in the responder's hand and denies slam probabilities. The raise can be made on a hand containing scattered strength and no long suit, or the hand may have a long suit or suits that can be utilized in no trump.

As with the raise to two no trump, the responder may shade his minimum requirements one point to nine points if holding a five card or longer solid or semi-solid suit that would be readily establishable.

Again, count high card points only!

EXAMPLES OF RAISES TO THREE NO TRUMP

(p)	(q)	(r)
♠ A43	♠ Q5	♠ AK42
♡ 104	♡ AQJ87	♡ J87
◇ KQ10987	◇ K102	◇ K76
♣ 92	♣ 874	♣ Q53

THE JUMP TO THREE OF A SUIT

A jump, by responder, to three of a suit is *forcing to game*. While it shows that game is makeable, the jump suit takeout does not necessarily mean that the final contract is to be in that suit.

The opener or his partner may prefer to play the hand in no trump or still another suit for various reasons. First, opener's no trump may include tenaces and the combined hands will play more advantageously with the opening lead coming up to, not through, those tenaces. Next, there may be a better fit in a second suit yet to be shown. Third, the partnership may feel nine tricks in no trump easier to win than 10 or 11 in a suit.

It is the exchange of information between the partnership that determines the final contract.

REQUIREMENTS -

1 - A minimum of 10 points. In responding in a suit, both high card points and distributional points are counted.

2 - The hand contains a suit of five cards or more, generally a major, or two or more suits, at least one of which is five cards

or longer. With a balanced hand or where the long suit is a minor and 10 to 14 points, the raise to three no trump is usually preferable to the jump suit takeout. With 15 points or more, the jump takeout to three of a suit should be employed to explore the probability of slam.

(s)	(t)	(u)
♠ K72	♠ AQ 10876	♠ KJ876
♡ AKJ76	♡ 5	♡ Q10643
◇ 7632	◇ QJ8	◇ A73
♣ 4	♣ 654	♣ void

(s) Three hearts.

(t) Three spades.

(u) Three spades. If partner raises to four spades, pass. If partner rebids with three no trump, you now bid four hearts. Note that with two five-carders, the higher-ranking is bid first, exactly as for opening bids and responses.

JUMPS TO GAME IN A SUIT

You will remember that a takeout to two of a suit was a signoff, telling the opening bidder to pass. The same is true when the responder's bid is an immediate jump to game in a suit, as by bidding four spades or five clubs, let us say, after partner's opening bid of one no trump.

This response can be made on a hand containing *no high cards whatever* to hands with a maximum of seven high card points. The hand will contain an extremely long suit, usually seven cards or longer.

The jump to game (following the no trump opening) merely shows a desire to play a game contract in the bid suit *and to stop bidding right there. It is a complete signoff!* It is by no means either strength-showing, or is it slam invitational. The opening bidder should pass the response!

(v)	(w)	(x)
♠ void	♠ 10	♠ 97
♡ 98765432	♡ AJ10987	♡ 3
◇ 876	◇ J987	◇ KJ9765432
♣ 53	♣ 62	♣ 2

Respond four hearts with (v) and (w); five diamonds with (x).

SLAM TRIES

When your partner opens the bidding with one no trump, you know that he has 16 to 18 high card points. By adding your points to these figures, if the total is at least 33, you should be able to make a small slam; if the total is 37, a grand slam.

The simplest way to ascertain whether the no trump bidder has a minimum 16 points or a maximum 17 to 18 points is for the responder to bid three of his suit. If the opener rebids with three no trump, he is indicating a minimum 16 point no trump. There are two ways for the no trump bidder to show a 17 or 18 point no trump: the first is for the opening bidder to bid three of a higher ranking suit as his rebid, as by bidding three spades over three hearts; the second method is for the opener to raise responder's suit takeout from three to the four level.

If you, as responder, can count 33 or 37 points in the combined hands, you can jump to six or seven no trump at once. This, of course, makes it impossible to probe for a suit fit.

You can now see why the jump takeout to three of a suit is better (and more accurate) than 'hopping' directly to slam in no trump, since in the former the possibility of finding a suit fit is explored before decision as to the best final contract.

Avoid an immediate response of four no trump after your partner has opened the bidding with one no trump. The four no trump bid, used in this situation, is neither fish or fowl - it is *not a forcing bid where the preceding bidding has been exclusively in no trump.* The opening bidder can (and should) pass. He told you his entire story with his opening bid.

REBIDS BY THE NO TRUMP OPENER

You have opened the bidding with one no trump and -

1 - Your partner passed.

You may not have a chance to bid again unless the opponents reopen the bidding. In that case, I advise extreme caution on your part since your partner, by his pass, warned you that he neither had eight points or an extremely long suit. Remember, too, that any double on your part after first opening the bidding with no trump *is always for penalty.*

2 - Your partner has bid two of a suit.

In 90 percent of these cases you should pass. If, however, your hand contains aggressive support for your partner's suit with a full 17 or 18 high card points, you should give him a single raise in his suit, whether major or minor, to the three level. By aggressive support, I mean that if the no trump opener holds three cards of partner's suit, that they include at least one of the suit's top three honors.

CASE A

YOU	PARTNER
One no trump	Two spades
Three spades	

CASE B

YOU	PARTNER
One no trump	Two clubs
Three clubs	

In Case A, your rebid says that you have help for partner's suit, possibly a doubleton in a side-suit to afford some ruffing value, and tells partner that even though you know he is weak you have enough strength to insure the makeability of the three spade contract. Now - if he has eight or nine points, he can try for game. With less, he would pass.

In Case B, you again show your 17 to 18 points plus the strong fit for partner's suit. But here the message is slightly different due to partner's suit being a minor. While your rebid states that sufficient cards are present to win nine tricks, you also inform him that you hold the right supplementary cards in his suit to permit you to run his suit in no trump, even if his holding isn't solid. In other words, your cards solidify his suit so that it can be run *in no trump*. Thus you tell him that his minor suit can now provide five or more tricks played in no trump. If he has anything extra, as an extra king or queen, he should now bid three no trump. *By no manner of means is this raise to three of a minor asking partner to bid five of that suit!*

Under no circumstances should the no trump bidder rebid with two no trump after receiving a response to two of a suit. That's like telling your partner he doesn't know what he's doing.

3 - Your partner raised to two no trump.

If you have opened the bidding with a 16 point no trump and your partner raises you to two no trump, you should pass. You told your story with your first bid and your partner has similarly told his story. If partner had more than eight or nine points, he would have raised to three no trump or jumped in a suit.

With 17 or 18 points, after receiving a raise to two no trump, the opening bidder should simply bid three no trump without further ado. Do not, at this point, bid a suit at the three level. The bid will be misunderstood by the average partner you will encounter. Later, in Lesson 16, you will become familiar with the Stayman Convention which is designed to discover when each member of the partnership holds four or more cards of the same major suit after the bidding has opened with one or more no trump.

4 - Your partner has jumped to three of a suit.

By jumping to three of a suit after you opened the bidding with one no trump, your partner has shown 10 or more points and a good suit of five cards or longer. If your partner has 16 points or more, he will wish to explore the probability of slam.

It is now up to the opening no trump bidder, following the jump suit takeout, to describe his hand more fully. This can be done in three ways. In order of preference, they are -

A - Bid a new suit of four or more cards if it can be shown at the three level. If two suits are present, both of which can be shown at the three level, bid the cheaper.

(e)	CASE E	
♠ KJ3	OPENER	RESPONDER
♡ AJ10	One no trump	Three clubs
◊ KQ75	Three diamonds	
♣ K98		

(f)	CASE F	
♠ QJ87	OPENER	RESPONDER
♡ KQ63	One no trump	Three clubs
◊ AQ3	Three hearts	
♣ K98		

B - Support partner's suit by giving him a single raise (if the suit is a major) and you have adequate trump support, probably a doubleton somewhere in the hand, and feel game in the major will be easier to make than in no trump. If partner's suit is a minor, remember that the moment you raise that suit to the four level, you can no longer back-track to three no trump. Therefore, unless you feel a minor suit slam probable, it will usually be better to play minor suit hands for nine tricks in no trump rather than for 11 tricks in the minor.

OPENER'S HANDS

(g)	CASE G	
	OPENER	RESPONDER
♠ A J	One no trump	Three hearts
♡ K 6 4 3	Four hearts	
◇ A Q 10 8		
♣ Q 4 3		

(h)	CASE H	
	OPENER	RESPONDER
♠ A J 7	One no trump	Three hearts
♡ Q 5 2	Three no trump	
◇ K J 8 7		
♣ A J 8		

(i)	CASE I	
	OPENER	RESPONDER
♠ A J 9	One no trump	Three diamonds
♡ A J 8	Three no trump.	
◇ Q 10 9		
♣ K J 8 7		

C - Rebid three no trump with only neutral support for partner's suit, balanced distribution, and no suit that can be shown at the three level. Cases H and I.

5 - Partner has jumped to four or five of his suit.

The opening no trump bidder must pass!

6 - Rebidding after a raise to three no trump.

If the bidding resembles Cases J and K, there is no rhyme or reason for any possible rebid by responder in J, and none for the opening bidder in K.

CASE J		CASE K	
OPENER	RESPONDER	OPENER	RESPONDER
One no trump	Two no trump	One no trump	Three no trump
Three no trump			

The responder, however, will sometimes disturb opener's three no trump rebid by rebidding his suit or by showing a second suit. If either of these bids do not contract for game, *the bidding must resume and continue until a game contract has again been reached.*

CASE L		CASE M	
OPENER	RESPONDER	OPENER	RESPONDER
One no trump	Three hearts	One no trump	Three diamonds
Three no trump	Four clubs	Three no trump	Four diamonds

Both of responder's rebids, that of four clubs in Case L, and that of four diamonds in Case M, are absolutely forcing upon the opening bidder to reach another game contract. In Case L, the responder is showing a powerful two-suiter and is asking for a preference which may wind up in a game contract of four hearts or five clubs or possibly slam.

In Case M, responder shows that he would prefer to bid higher. He might prefer a final diamond contract, or perhaps be probing the hand further for a possible slam.

Either way, once a game contract is voluntarily disturbed, game must be reached again. This is true in all bidding situations, whether after an opening bid of no trump or of a suit.

RESPONDER'S REBIDS

Responder's rebids fall into three possible patterns.

CASE N

OPENER	RESPONDER
One no trump	Two no trump
Three no trump	

You must pass. For heaven's sake, don't start showing new suits at this point.

CASE O

OPENER	RESPONDER
One no trump	Three of a suit
Three of a higher-ranking suit	

Your course of action depends on your hand. If you can show still another suit at the three level, do so. But remember, there's no point in getting past game unless you're pretty sure you can make a slam.

CASE P

OPENER	RESPONDER
1 no trump	2 of a suit
3 of the same suit	

This is the most common rebidding situation that will confront the responder. Despite the signoff of two of a suit, the opening no trump bidder shows a willingness to continue to game. For his rebid, the opening bidder shows a full 17 or 18 points, plus an excellent supporting fit for responder's suit. If the responder has eight or nine points and a good suit, he should bid three no trump if his suit is a minor; bid four if his suit is a major with an unbalanced hand. In some rare cases where the suit is a major and the hand is balanced, viz., no voids or singletons, responder may prefer rebidding three no trump if his suit can be run in that contract and nine tricks in no trump appear easier to win than 10 tricks in the major suit.

OPENING BIDS OF TWO NO TRUMP

Opening bids of two no trump show 22 to 24 high card points, double stoppers in three suits with the fourth suit at least singly stopped. The distribution can be 4-3-3-3, or 4-4-3-2, or even 5-3-3-2 or 6-3-2-2. In these latter cases, where the hand contains a five or six card suit, it is almost invariably a minor, though in very rare cases it can be a solid major that can be run in no trump. Under no circumstances may the hand contain a singleton, even were that singleton the ace.

EXAMPLES OF OPENING TWO NO TRUMP BIDS

(j)	(k)	(l)
♠ K Q J	♠ A Q	♠ K J 9 8
♡ A J 10	♡ K J 10	♡ A Q J 7
◇ K Q 4 3	◇ A K Q J 6	◇ A J 10
♣ A Q 2	♣ K 8 7	♣ A K

RESPONSES TO TWO NO TRUMP BIDS

The responder, following an opening two no trump bid, should find a bid with three or more high card points or with ANY one or more of the following-

1 - Three or more high card points,
2 - A six card or longer major suit,
3 - Two five card or longer suits.

Responder, with a weak hand and an establishable five card or longer suit, should prefer the raise to three no trump over merely bidding three of his suit, particularly if the suit is a minor.

A jump response from two no trump to game in a suit, as by bidding four hearts or five clubs, is a signoff, exactly as in responding to opening bids of one no trump. (Page 275).

Remember, any response to an opening two no trump bid is forcing to game, but an opening bid of two no trump *is not forcing*. Partner, with no high cards and lacking a long suit, can and should pass the opening two no trump bid.

OPENING BIDS OF THREE NO TRUMP

An opening bid of three no trump shows 25 to 27 high card points. The hand will usually be able to win eight tricks single-handed. Distribution requirements are identical to those given for opening bids of two no trump.

RESPONSES TO OPENING BIDS OF THREE NO TRUMP

Eight or more high card points in responder's hand are usually enough to give the combined hands a good play for slam, particularly if responder's hand contains an establishable suit of five cards or longer.

A takeout to four of a suit, such as bidding four hearts, is a signoff, showing the desire to play the hand in a suit contract rather than in no trump. Opener should then pass. It is rare that responder will take out the opening no trump into a minor suit without slam probabilities, since in most cases, if the hand will only produce five clubs or five diamonds, it will make three or more no trump with far less effort.

PENALTY DOUBLES OF OVERCALLS AFTER NO TRUMP BIDS

It is very seldom that the opponents will overcall after your side has opened the bidding with one no trump. The reason is-it's too dangerous! Against the known 16 to 18 points in high cards, there is little chance of making a game and a good probability of being penalized.

However, on certain hands, particularly those containing long suits and distributional features, the adversaries may overcall, particularly to indicate the suit desired to be led to their partners.

You are now concerned with what to do when they overcall.

First - After an opening one no trump bid, any double by either the opening bidder or his partner is for penalty.

Second, if game your way appears doubtful and you are certain that the opponent cannot fulfill his contract, then you should double the overcall and collect the penalty. You can't beat a sure profit !

Third - Figure a non-vulnerable game as worth 300 points in addition to the points for tricks won. For example, bidding and making four hearts, not vulnerable, would be estimated at 300 points for the non-vulnerable game plus the 120 points below the line. The 300 points, of course, are intangible. They are an approximate valuation of the value of the first game towards the rubber bonus. Similarly, the intangible value of a game when vulnerable is worth around 500 points. If your side is able to make a game, any penalty you accept by doubling in lieu of the game should be at least the latter's equivalent in value.

There are times, however, when you have bid as high as your side's cards warrant and the opponents bid still higher as a sacrifice. In these cases, the sacrifice may very well be less than the score your side would have received had your side played the hand. Nevertheless, it is far better to accept the penalty rather than overbid and be penalized yourself. *Never permit sacrificial bidding by the opponents to push you into an unmakeable contract!*

If you think your side can make a slam, you should be wary of accepting a penalty less in value than your combined scores for tricks, game and slam.

Fourth - On close hands, where the partner of the opening no trump bidder is faced with the problem of whether or not to double, a penalty double of an overcall can be made with as little as four high card points plus either a sure trick in the opponent's bid suit or four cards of that suit.

SUMMARIZED

In bidding no trump, whether opening, raising, or rebidding, count only high card points.

A one no trump opening bid shows 16 to 18 high card points.
A two " " " " " 22 to 24 " " "
A three" " " " " 25 to 27 " " "

PART TWO

PLAY OF THE CARDS IN NO TRUMP

The essential difference between no trump and suit (trump) play is that in the former, low cards as deuces and treys win tricks if no player has a higher card of that suit; in trump contracts, these low cards could be trumped.

Sometimes you will hear a player remark during a hand being played in a suit contract, "**Why, this is going to play in no trump.**" By that is meant that all of the trumps in all four hands have been expended and from that moment on, in a now trumpless hand, the play would continue as though it were in no trump, even though the hand was being played in a suit contract.

Both sides, defenders and declarer alike in no trump, will attempt to convert low cards into winners. Naturally, they will attack the suits in which they have the greatest number of cards which is the same as saying 'their longest suits.' There are a few exceptions as when the long suit has been bid by the other side or when needed tricks can be developed quicker in shorter suits but in 95 percent of cases, it is the suit with the 'mostest developable' cards that both defenders and declarers will lead in the hope of establishing low card winners.

To achieve this result - establishing low cards as winners - both sides need the same things - establishable suits of four or more cards and the ability, through high cards in the led suit or elsewhere in the hand, first to force the other side to take their high cards in the led suit and later, additional high cards with which to regain the lead in order to 'cash' the now established low winning cards.

Thus while in suit contracts, the defender on lead will usually attempt to cash his aces, kings and queens before they can be trumped; against no trump contracts, these cards are conserved as re-entries in order to keep regaining the lead and driving out the declarer's and dummy's high cards (stoppers) in the suit the defenders are attempting to establish.

The defenders have one great advantage on their side - the time element. To them belongs the opening lead, the first shot fired, as it were. This affords them the first attack on declarer's stoppers. On the other hand, declarer usually has the heavier weapons. That is only natural since his side won the auction indicating possession of most of the high cards.

So both sides have the same objectives - to establish low cards in long suits into winning tricks and to prevent the other side from doing the same.

THE HOLD-UP

The main weapon declarer has to prevent the defenders from establishing or capitalizing on their suit is known as the 'hold-up.' It was previously described, from a defender's point of view, in *figure 96* on page 179. When employed by the declarer, it is the refusal, by declarer, to win an early round of the suit opened by the left hand defender until the declarer feels that the other defender no longer has any more cards of that suit or that a continuation of the suit by the left hand opponent would give the declarer additional stoppers.

	North	
	♠ 72 ♡ A53 ◇ AJ10987 ♣ 75	
West ♠ QJ1053 ♡ K92 ◇ 6 ♣ J832	N W E S	**East** ♠ K94 ♡ 10876 ◇ K43 ♣ Q109
	♠ A86 ♡ QJ4 ◇ Q52 ♣ AK64	
	South	

Figure 121

In *figure 121,* South is the declarer at three no trump. West opens the queen of spades and East plays the encouraging nine-spot.

Does South win the trick with the ace? Well, hardly! South's hope of winning the necessary nine tricks hinges on establishing the low cards in dummy's diamond suit as winners. In order to do that, he must take the diamond finesse which will lose to East's king. If South had captured the first spade with the ace, East, after gaining the lead with the king of diamonds, would cash the king of spades, then lead the four-spot. West would win the third round of spades with the 10 and cash his remaining two spades to defeat the contract.

Now South, if he were a bad player, might blame his failure on the fact that the diamond finesse didn't succeed. Actually, the cause was his failure to hold up. He should have refused to take his ace of spades until he felt as secure as possible that East no longer had any spades to lead in case the diamond finesse failed. That would have meant permitting the queen of spades to win the first trick, the king to win the second round and South taking the third round with the ace. Thereafter, East, on winning with the king of diamonds, will no longer have a spade to return to his partner.

Another case where the hold-up is advantageous to the declarer is when, after the opening leader has been permitted to win the first trick or tricks, a continuation would give declarer additional tricks. This will usually happen when the declarer has a tenace position in the led suit.

West	North / South	East
	♠ 73 ♡ J10986 ◊ A74 ♣ K52	
♠ KQ1094 ♡ 53 ◊ J1098 ♣ Q4	N W E S	♠ 865 ♡ A42 ◊ Q63 ♣ J1097
	♠ AJ2 ♡ KQ7 ◊ K52 ♣ A863	

Figure 122

In *figure 122*, South is again playing a three no trump contract. West opens the king of spades. If South takes the trick with the ace, then attempts to set up dummy's heart suit by knocking out that ace, East will win, return a spade through South's thinly guarded jack and the defense wins four spades and one heart, just enough to defeat the contract.

But - if South holds up on the opening lead and permits the king to win the first trick, West cannot continue the suit without giving South two spade tricks. Moreover, if West shifts to some suit (other than spades) at trick two, South now has time to knock out the ace of hearts with his spade stopper still intact.

This hold-up with the ace, jack and one or more cards of the suit is known as the 'Bath Coup,' presumably after the Earl of Bath who is supposed to have originated the play in the early days of whist.

A hold-up is frequently advisable, even with two stoppers of the adversely led suit, particularly when the declarer has two high cards (in the suit he hopes to establish) to drive out.

In *figure 123*, South is the declarer at three no trump. West opens the queen of spades. If declarer, lulled to a sense of false security by the presence of two spade stoppers, wins the first spade with the ace, then leads a diamond, he will be defeated. West will duck with the ace and East wins with the king, returns his remaining spade. It is now too late to put Humpty-Dumpty together again, even if South makes a belated (and futile) hold-up at this point. West will win and the king of spades will ultimately be forced out. The moment West gains the lead with the ace of diamonds, the remaining spades are cashed to set the contract.

	♠ K43 ♡ 82 ♢ QJ1098 ♣ AQ7	
♠ QJ1092 ♡ Q975 ♢ A2 ♣ 52	N W E S	♠ 75 ♡ 1043 ♢ K43 ♣ 98643
	♠ A86 ♡ AKJ6 ♢ 765 ♣ KJ10	

Figure 123

But had declarer held up on the opening spade lead, then won the second round, the contract would have been fulfilled since East, on winning with the diamond king, will not have a third spade to lead.

Figure 124 is closely akin to its predecessor in that declarer, with two adverse high cards to knock out, holds up on the first round of hearts, even though his ace-queen is a certain double-stopper since East has played the king on the opening lead of the five-spot by his partner.

	♠ A9764 ♡ 632 ♢ 65 ♣ KQ6	
♠ 532 ♡ J9754 ♢ K2 ♣ 542	N W E S	♠ KQ8 ♡ K10 ♢ A43 ♣ 109873
	♠ J10 ♡ AQ8 ♢ QJ10987 ♣ AJ	

Figure 124

The reason I have included this hand is because of a feeling common to most new players that the ace-queen are not two sure tricks. That is quite true but when the lead *comes up to* that combination or the king is played earlier, the ace-queen automatically become two tricks and a dual stopper. Thus with two high diamonds to knock out, the declarer should duck the first round (when East played the king) and win the second round with the ace or queen.

Since East started with a doubleton heart, he will not have a third card of that suit to return on winning a diamond trick with the ace.

WHEN NOT TO HOLD UP

It stands to reason that if there are times when a hold-up is in order, there are situations where the declarer in no trump should capture the opening lead. These are:

1 - When by winning the opening lead, declarer would have two stoppers; with a hold-up, only one.

2 - If holding up will jeopardize the trick-taking ability of a single stopper.

3 - When by permitting an opponent to hold the first trick, he could switch to another, more dangerous (to declarer) suit.

	♠ J2 ♡ Q10976 ◇ Q109 ♣ AJ3	
♠ K9753 ♡ A2 ◇ 652 ♣ 864	N W E S	♠ Q86 ♡ 543 ◇ KJ84 ♣ 752
	♠ A104 ♡ KJ8 ◇ A73 ♣ KQ109	

Figure 125

Figure 125 is an example of the first case, where holding-up would lose declarer's second stopper. West opens the five of spades, his fourth-best, against South's three no trump contract. Dummy plays *the deuce !* and East plays the queen. South should win with the ace, knock out the ace of hearts. West can play the spade king, capturing dummy's jack but South's 10-spot will win the third round.

Let's contrast this treatment with an incorrect hold-up. If the queen is permitted to win the first trick, East will return the eight-spot, the higher of his two remaining cards. If South plays the ace at this point, that's his one and only trick in the suit since West, on regaining the lead with the ace of hearts, can capture the 10-spot. Should South play the 10-spot at trick two, it is a simple matter for West to win with the king and lead the trey to knock out the now lone ace. Either way, after ducking the first spade trick, declarer will win only one spade trick; by capturing the first trick, he'll win two!

The key to the situation is possession of the guarded 10-spot. In *figure 125 and figures 126 through 130, inclusive*, the declarer can insure two tricks in the suit, if led by his left hand opponent, by first, playing a *low card* from the dummy on the opening lead and second, winning the first round of the led suit.

♠ 10x	♠ xx	♠ Qx	♠ Jx	♠ Qx
N	N	N	N	N
S	S	S	S	S
♠ AJx	♠ AJ10	♠ A10x	♠ A10x	♠ K10x
Figure 126	*Figure 127*	*Figure 128*	*Figure 129*	*Figure 130*

When the 10-spot is missing between the declarer's and dummy's hands and the dummy's honor is originally doubleton, it is usually advisable to play that honor to the opening lead in the hope that it will take the trick and leave declarer's remaining high card or cards intact as future stoppers.

♠ Qx	♠ Qx	♠ Qx	♠ Jx
N	N	N	N
S	S	S	S
♠ Axx	♠ Kxx	♠ AJx	♠ AQx
Figure 131	*Figure 132*	*Figure 133*	*Figure 134*

In all cases above *(figures 131 to 134, inclusive)*, West is presumed to have opened a low spade.

In the first three examples, we play the queen at once; in the fourth, the jack. Let's see why.

In *figure 131*, our only hope of taking two tricks in the suit is that West opened away from the king. In that event, the queen will win. On the other hand, if we incorrectly play dummy's low card to the opening lead, any intermediate card that East may play as the eight, nine or 10 may force the ace and the queen, now alone, will be a sitting duck for the defenders to pick off with the king.

In *figure 132*, any expectancy of taking two tricks is that West opened away from (underled) the ace originally. In that case, the queen will win. Our subsequent problem will be to keep East out of the lead so that he cannot lead through and capture our king.

♠ Q2

N

♠ K9764 W E ♠ 1053

S

♠ AJ8

Figure 133 (repeated in full)

With *figure 133*, I'll show all 13 cards of the led suit. West opens the six of spades. South's hope of taking three tricks in the suit is to play dummy's queen and hope that West has led away from the king. If this is the case, the queen will win and the possibility of winning three spade tricks hinges on keeping East from leading through the ace-jack. Had declarer played the deuce from dummy on the opening lead, the 10 would force the jack. Later, West (if he had the lead) could bang down the king, dropping the queen and force South, if he wanted to win the trick, to play the ace.

But by playing the queen on the first trick, we made it impossible for West to continue leading the spade suit without giving declarer two additional tricks in the suit - from the defenders' point of view, from the East hand. And that is what the declarer should attempt to prevent.

The identical reasoning applies to the play of the jack to the opening lead in *figure 134* in which the two equals, the queen and jack, have been transposed between the dummy and the declarer's hand.

Be certain you understand that it is only when dummy's high card is doubleton and can be captured *by either opponent* on the second round that it is played to the opening lead. Add a low spade to the dummy's holdings in *figures 131 through 134* and dummy's honor will be sufficiently protected that there is no need of playing dummy's honor to the opening lead.

The second case where the declarer should not hold up is when holding stoppers which, if not immediately utilized, later vanish in trick-taking ability. This will usually hold true when the opening lead is won by the declarer's right hand opponent as in *figure 135*.

	♠ 84 ♡ KQJ ♢ AQJ95 ♣ 732	
♠ AJ975 ♡ 43 ♢ K2 ♣ J865	N W E S	♠ Q102 ♡ 109865 ♢ 743 ♣ Q9
	♠ K63 ♡ A72 ♢ 1086 ♣ AK104	

Figure 135

South, after opening the bidding with one club, is the declarer in a three no trump contract in *figure 135*. The defenders have not bid. West makes the normal choice of openings, the seven of spades and East plays the queen.

Should South hold up with the king and permit East to take the first trick with the queen?

Well, hardly !

If the queen is (erroneously) permitted to win, East will return the 10 of spades and South's king is trapped by West's ace-jack combination which is now waiting to gobble up South's one-time stopper. Through holding up in this case, South will win no spades tricks-the defenders will win all five-and the hand will be defeated.

On the other hand, if South captures the queen with the king, he's one step ahead-he's taken a trick he otherwise would have lost had he held up. He can now count seven sure tricks-one spade, three hearts, one diamond and two clubs. Success of the contract, therefore, hinges on the diamond finesse against the missing king. If West has that card, South will win 11 tricks-five diamonds, three hearts, one spade and two clubs; if East has the king of diamonds, the finesse will fail and so will the contract as the defenders cash their remaining spades.

But even with the diamond finesse failing, there is still a grain of hope for the contract, as long as South captured the first trick, if the eight spades held by the defenders are evenly divided, viz., four to each. In this event, they can win only three spades and one diamond.

While in *figure 135*, the defenders' spades are split five-three, you will be surprised at the number of hands where a missing suit of eight cards will be divided four-four and had you captured the first trick, the opponents on regaining the lead can win only three tricks in the suit.

But the important thing for you to see is this - if the trick taking ability of your stopper is not affected by holding up and if the play is warranted, then hold up to exhaust one defender of his partner's suit. On the other hand, if ducking will jeopardize the capturing power of a card if played later, then by all means utilize it at once when it has its fullest value.

Let's transpose the spades from the previous example so that the suit now resembles *figure 136*. Against the self-same three no trump contract, West will lead the six of spades. East will win with the ace and return the jack.

	♠ 84	
	N	
♠ Q10765	W E	♠ AJ2
	S	
	♠ K93	

Figure 136

Now I hope you see the important difference between this example and its immediate predecessor. Once the ace of spades had been played, South's king became "high." With its capturing power the same whether played to the second round or the third and since the king can no longer be captured with ace gone, declarer can afford the luxury of holding up in case East held the missing king of diamonds of *figure 135*.

The third situation where the declarer should not hold up is when, if the defender is permitted to win the first trick, it is highly probable that the defenders will switch to an even more thinly-protected (and to the declarer, far more dangerous) suit.

	♠ 92 ♡ 76 ♢ AJ10976 ♣ KQ4	
♠ KJ83 ♡ A543 ♢ K32 ♣ 97	N W E S	♠ Q104 ♡ QJ1098 ♢ 8 ♣ 10652
	♠ A765 ♡ K2 ♢ Q54 ♣ AJ83	

Figure 137

Let's presume that West has opened the three of spades against South's three no trump contract in *figure 137*. East plays the queen.

South must win the trick since he cannot afford the luxury of the hold-up. Let's see why.

First, success or failure of the contract hinges on the location of the missing king of diamonds. Second, West is known to have only four spades from his opening lead of the trey and with the deuce in the dummy. Third and most important of all, declarer at worst can lose only three spade tricks but if East is permitted to hold the first trick, then leads a heart, South could (and would) lose five heart tricks if the ace of that suit is with West as is the case. Hence it is a case of the lesser of the evils.

With the dangerous heart switch imminent, declarer must win the first spade trick and base his hopes on the success of the diamond finesse.

SUIT ESTABLISHMENT

	♠ A 4 3 ♡ Q J 10 8 7 ◇ J 4 3 ♣ 10 9	
♠ Q J 10 9 8 ♡ A 5 4 ◇ Q 8 7 ♣ J 2	N W E S	♠ 7 6 ♡ 3 2 ◇ 10 9 6 2 ♣ K Q 6 5 4
	♠ K 5 2 ♡ K 9 6 ◇ A K 5 ♣ A 8 7 3	

Figure 138

One of the simplest types of suit establishment is shown in *figure 138*.

South is the declarer in three no trump and West opens the spade queen. South wins with the king, leads the king of hearts. If West correctly refuses to take the ace, the nine of hearts if led and if West again ducks, the six of hearts follows. The ace of spades furnishes a positive re-entry to dummy's two good hearts.

All this hand consisted of was forcing out the defenders' high card in the suit declarer was establishing. The important thing for the reader to notice is that the opening lead (of the spade queen) was won in the South hand, thus leaving the spade ace in the dummy as a re-entry for the heart suit. Re-entries should usually be conserved in the hand containing the suit to be established or in the hand with the fewer high cards.

	North	
	♠ AKQJ ♡ 87 ◊ 432 ♣ 10862	
♠ 108 ♡ J96543 ◊ K7 ♣ K43	N W E S	♠ 9743 ♡ K102 ◊ Q65 ♣ Q97
	♠ 652 ♡ AQ ◊ AJ1098 ♣ AJ5	

Figure 139

A solid suit which can be 'run' in no trump can also be used as a means of furnishing entries to an otherwise worthless hand so that finesses in other suits may be taken.

In *figure 139*, South is the declarer at three no trump. West opens the five of hearts and the king is taken by the ace. Dummy is entered via a spade. Note that if declarer immediately plays all four of dummy's spades, he will have only eight tricks - four spades, two hearts and the two minor aces. To fulfill the contract, a trick must be established. The easiest way is to finesse twice in the diamond suit by leading towards the South hand, hoping that the missing king and queen are divided between the defenders or that East has both of these cards.

Accordingly, after winning the first spade in dummy, a diamond is led from that hand. East will probably play low and the 10, nine or eight will force the king. South's remaining heart stopper is knocked out.

Dummy is re-entered with a second round of spades and another diamond finesse taken. When it succeeds, South's worries are over. Dummy's remaining spades are cashed with a club discarded on the fourth spade. The ace of diamonds drops the queen and a club is given up at the finish to make five no trump. The reader may ask, "After taking one diamond finesse, why didn't declarer run the remainder of dummy's spades before taking the second diamond finesse?"

North: ◇ 652

West: ◇ K — East: ◇ Q743

South: ♣ AJ1098

Figure 140

If the diamonds in *figure 139* resembled those in *figure 140*, it would have been necessary to take three diamond finesses to capture East's queen. For that reason, dummy's high spades were conserved.

Figure 141 illustrates strategy by the declarer in attempting to knock out the re-entry to the dangerous hand.

North:
♠ KQ743
♡ 84
◇ A106
♣ J63

West:
♠ 108
♡ QJ1093
◇ Q752
♣ A5

East:
♠ J96
♡ 652
◇ K983
♣ K42

South:
♠ A52
♡ AK7
◇ J4
♣ Q10987

Figure 141

We'd better define "dangerous hand." By that I mean the opponent whose hand contains the suit of which he is trying to establish and which we are trying to shut-out.

Let's suppose that declarer has held-up on the opening lead of the heart queen, taken the second round with the king. Counting the available tricks, we can see five spades (if they break), two hearts, one diamond to total eight. We need nine!

To lead the jack of diamonds is virtually hopeless against good defense since West will cover with the queen and after the ace wins, East's king-nine combination ten-aces dummy's 10 spot. All that would do is set-up the defenders' suit for them.

If South makes the routine play of a low club from his hand after winning the heart trick, West will play low and East will win with the king, return his remaining heart, knocking our South's last stopper. Now the moment South leads a second round of clubs, West wins with the ace, cashes two good hearts and down goes McGinty.

The trick is to knock out West's re-entry first!

Accordingly, after winning the heart trick, a low spade is led and taken with dummy's queen. The ace of spades should not be released at once since it's too much of a dead give-away as to where South's strength is located. If South is known to have

♠ A, ♡ AK, and after opening one club, only bid one no trump over a one spade response, he can be presumed not to have too much in the other suits.

So let's conceal the spade ace and lead low towards dummy, winning with the queen. A low club (not the jack) is led from dummy. Not one East out of 100 will go up with the king. South can play any of his equals and the defense is dead! If he takes the ace, there goes the re-entry for his heart suit and if he ducks, trying to retain the ace as a re-entry, the solitary club trick is the ninth declarer needed for the contract.

This, incidentally, is a very common situation and more impossible no trump contracts can be "stolen" by leading toward the defender with the dangerous hand than by leading the other way.

KNOCKING OUT DEFENDERS' CERTAIN RE-ENTRY

As a general rule the declarer, in setting up a suit, will select from two or more suits the suit that will yield the greater or greatest number of tricks.

When, however, the dangerous hand with the long establishable suit may have a sure re-entry and declarer still retains a stopper in the opened suit, the declarer should attempt to knock out the defender's sure re-entry even though the suit so developed may produce fewer tricks than another, longer suit.

	♠ Q 10 7 6 ♡ 9 3 2 ◇ A J 10 9 7 ♣ 2	
♠ A 9 8 ♡ K 10 8 7 6 ◇ 5 4 ♣ J 9 6	N W E S	♠ 5 3 2 ♡ J 5 ◇ K 6 3 ♣ Q 10 8 7 5
	♠ K J 4 ♡ A Q 4 ◇ Q 8 2 ♣ A K 4 3	

Figure 142

In *figure 142,* West opens the fourth-best heart against South's three no trump. Declarer captures the jack with the queen since to hold up would give South only one stopper instead of two.

The only re-entry West might (and does happen) to hold is the ace of spades. The king of diamonds, if with West, is not a positive re-entry since it is in a finessable position and can be captured.

Even though the spade suit can only produce three tricks and the diamond suit four to five tricks (depending on the location of the missing king), the declarer on winning the first heart should bang down the king of spades. If West takes the ace, his hand is immobilized; if West ducks with the ace of spades, South, with one spade trick to his side's credit, can now afford to attempt the diamond finesse.

Note that when East wins with the king of diamonds and returns his remaining heart, South now has the needed nine tricks to fulfill his contract - four diamonds, two hearts, two clubs *and one spade*.

Had declarer attacked diamonds immediately after winning the opening heart lead, he would have been defeated since on taking the king of diamonds, East would return a heart removing South's remaining stopper in the latter suit. Declarer now has eight assured tricks - four diamonds, two hearts and two clubs. The moment South leads a spade to establish his ninth trick, West will grab the ace and cash his three remaining hearts to set the contract.

As an important corollary, let me point out that it is not necessary to completely drive out a positive re-entry in a short suit once the necessary tricks to assure the contract have been achieved. Leading a short suit too often could result in the development of low card tricks, for the defenders, in the led suit. In *figure 142*, only one spade trick was needed. Had dummy's diamond suit been only four cards in length, then two spade leads would have been required in case West refused to win the first spade lead with his ace.

Worry about the defenders' sure re-entries first - then think about possible finesses!

STEALING THE NINTH TRICK

A common stratagem of the declarer who needs one additional trick to fulfill a no trump contract, yet doesn't dare give up the lead to the defenders who can cash setting tricks, is to beguile the defenders into not taking that particular trick.

	♠ Q72 ♡ QJ1074 ◇ 832 ♣ J6	
♠ 1095 ♡ 63 ◇ KJ954 ♣ 854	N W E S	♠ A843 ♡ 982 ◇ Q76 ♣ Q109
	♠ KJ6 ♡ AK5 ◇ A10 ♣ AK732	

Figure 143

West opens his fourth best diamond and since holding up would only reveal South's weakness in the suit, the ace captured the opening lead.

Declarer has eight tricks in sight, five hearts, two clubs and one diamond. Naturally he regretted not being in a four heart contract where 12 tricks can be won by trumping one club and establishing the remaining cards of that suit to permit North, as declarer, to discard both losing diamonds.

Played in a three no trump contract, it's a different matter. Declarer knows that the moment he leads a spade for the needed ninth trick, the defenders will win with the ace of spades to cash their diamond tricks.

So South resorts to a ruse. After taking the ace of diamonds, he first plays the ace and king of hearts, then abandons the heart suit to lead the king of spades.

Now what does this look like to East?

Simply that South doesn't have a small heart with which to enter the dummy. By leading the king of spades, South is attempting to force out the ace of spades in order to make dummy's queen of spades a positive re-entry to that hand for the three apparently marooned heart tricks.

Do you think most Easts are going to take the king of spades with the ace, knowing that the play will give declarer three heart tricks he otherwise would have been unable to reach?

Well, hardly!

So East, cannily applauding his own sagacity, ducks the king of spades and permits that card to win the trick. One moment later he's minus 100 points below the line as the declarer produces a lone, lowly heart to use dummy's three hearts and eventually cash the ace and king of clubs to complete the needed nine tricks.

It should be pointed out that the defenders have signals to indicate the number of cards they hold in suits being led and the play of the six of hearts by West, followed by the three, would have marked that player with an original holding of only two hearts. By adding this figure to the five hearts in the dummy and the three hearts in his own hand, East can account for 10 cards of that suit. The balance, three, must be (and are) with the declarer. East, therefore, should not be taken in by South's ruse.

SETTING UP A SUIT BY DUCKING

	♠ 62 ♡ 1073 ♢ AK7543 ♣ 85	
♠ Q10984 ♡ KJ86 ♢ J9 ♣ K7	N W E S	♠ J53 ♡ 54 ♢ Q106 ♣ QJ643
	♠ AK7 ♡ AQ92 ♢ 82 ♣ A1092	

Figure 144

Where a hand is reentryless, except for the suit to be established and one or more tricks must be lost in the suit (even with the most favorable distribution) the declarer should lose the tricks early, retaining the high cards in the suit for the subsequent dual purpose of capturing the opponents' remaining cards and as re-entries.

In *figure 144*, South receives the 10 of spades opening lead against his three no trump contract. Even if the defenders' five diamonds are divided as evenly as possible, viz., three - two, one diamond trick must be lost. Accordingly, declarer wins the spade lead and leads a low diamond from his hand.

No matter what diamond is played by West, a low diamond is played from the dummy. Declarer can now win five diamond tricks by playing dummy's ace and king to the second and third rounds of the suit. Had declarer played the ace or king on the the first round of the suit, he would have won only two diamond tricks instead of five.

	♠ 84 ♡ 763 ◊ A8765 ♣ J92	
♠ Q10762 ♡ KJ2 ◊ Q10 ♣ Q85	N W E S	♠ 953 ♡ 9854 ◊ KJ9 ♣ 743
	♠ AKJ ♡ AQ10 ◊ 432 ♣ AK106	

Figure 145

In *figure 145*, declarer's problem is to win three diamond tricks with dummy's suit. Played at three no trump, South as declarer receives the six of spades opening lead.

He wins with the jack, now hopes that the five diamonds held by the defenders are split three - two. He leads a low diamond from his hand and plays the five of diamonds from dummy after West's 10-spot. Declarer will win the probable spade lead, lead a second diamond from his hand, and this time play the six of diamonds from dummy after West's queen. South, on regaining the lead, can lead his last diamond and play dummy's ace, capturing the defenders' last high card of that suit. The lead is now in the dummy and that hand's eight and seven of diamonds are winning tricks, ready to be cashed.

There are two important corollaries to ducking plays as in *figures 144 and 145.*

The first is that declarer had sufficient stoppers in the adverse suits to permit him to let the opponents gain the lead when he was deliberately ducking (and losing) tricks.

The second is that the hand containing the suit to be established is short of other re-entries. For instance, if the dummy in *figure 144* had contained the king of hearts and the queen of clubs, there would be little need of ducking since declarer could afford to play the ace and king of diamonds, concede the third round to the opponents and be able to re-enter the dummy with certainty.

SHORT SUIT DEVELOPMENT

One of the few exceptions to the declarer, in no trump, leading the suit in which the greatest number of tricks can be established, is when the declarer needs only one or two tricks to fulfill his contract. In these cases„ the emphasis is placed on the development of the needed tricks in the safest possible manner rather than leading a suit, which while it could produce a greater number of tricks, would jeopardize the contract.

There are usually three identifying clues to this situation..

These are:

First, as previously stated, the declarer needs only one or two tricks to fulfill his contract;

Second, the opening lead has marked the defender for holding only a four card suit originally so that on regaining the lead, the defense can win only the three remaining cards of that suit, in addition to the trick to be conceded.

Third, it will usually be necessary to force out an ace, a card that would have ultimately won a trick for the defenders sooner or later.

West	North / South	East
	♠ K98	
	♡ 854	
	◊ Q8	
	♣ AK432	
♠ Q74	N	♠ A65
♡ KJ72	W E	♡ Q1093
◊ 543		◊ 9762
♣ Q109	S	♣ J7
	♠ J1032	
	♡ A6	
	◊ AKJ10	
	♣ 865	

Figure 146

In *figure 146*, South is the declarer in three no trump. West opens the deuce of hearts. Since West, from the lead, is known to have started with four hearts, East is similarly known to hold four hearts originally. *Reason - declarer sees two hearts in his hand and three more in the dummy. This total of five, plus West's known four cards, add to nine.*

These nine, when subtracted from the 13 cards of the suit, leave the remainder, four, known to be with East. Accordingly, there is no point in a hold-up by South since East, the opening leader's partner, is known to have more hearts than the declarer.

Accordingly, South wins the first trick with the ace. The club suit can be developed with the loss of one trick and would produce four, with a three-two split of the missing five clubs. In the meantime, the defenders will win three hearts, one club and the ace of spades - just enough to beat the contract.

So declarer can't afford to lose one club trick, even though it would establish a total of four tricks in that suit. Of the nine tricks needed to fulfill the contract, seven are immediately available. There is one hope of success.

Do you see it?

If West has the queen of spades, the hand is makeable. Accordingly, after taking the ace of hearts, declarer leads the deuce of spades and over West's four, plays dummy's eight. Since West does have the queen, the best the defenders can do is to win three hearts and one spade.

As you can see, methods of establishing suits and of utiliz- stoppers and re-entries vary with each hand. Knowing when to apply each method comes with experience and practice.

QUIZ EIGHT

1 - What is your opening bid with each of the following hands?

(a)	(b)	(c)
♠ A	♠ K 2	♠ A Q J
♡ K J 8 7	♡ A K Q 7 6	♡ K Q J 8
◊ A Q 10	◊ A 8 4	◊ A 10 6 2
♣ K Q 5 4 3	♣ K 6 3	♣ A Q

(d)	(e)	(f)
♠ A J 8	♠ K 10 3	♠ A K 3
♡ 4 2	♡ A 10 8	♡ K Q J 9
◊ A K Q 7	◊ K Q 9 6	◊ A Q 7
♣ A K 10 5	♣ A J 7	♣ A K 8

2 - Your partner has opened the bidding with one no trump.. The next player passes. What is your response with each of the following hands?

(g)	(h)	(i)	(j)
♠ 4 3	♠ Q J 9 8 7 6 4	♠ K 7	♠ 2
♡ J 6 4	♡ 2	♡ Q J 6 4	♡ A J 10 8 6 3
◊ J 9 8 3 2	◊ J 8 6	◊ 9 6 3	◊ K Q 5
♣ 10 7 5	♣ 5 4	♣ K 8 7 6	♣ Q 10 7

(k)	(l)	(m)	(n)
♠ K 8 3	♠ A J 8	♠ 8 7 6 5 4 2	♠ K 10 8
♡ 10 4	♡ 7 4 3	♡ 10 9	♡ K J 7
◊ K Q 10 8 7	◊ K Q 5 4	◊ J 6	◊ A Q 3
♣ 7 3 2	♣ Q 8 2	♣ 8 5 2	♣ 10 9 8 7

3 - You have opened the bidding with one no trump, holding the hand shown to the left. What is your rebid to each of the following responses?

♠ A J 8 7
♡ K J 3
◊ Q 5 4
♣ A Q 2

(o) Two diamonds
(p) Three no trump
(q) Two no trump
(r) Two spades
(s) Three hearts
(t) Three spades
(u) Two clubs
(v) Four hearts

4 - The bidding has been -

Partner, South	West	You, North	East
One no trump	pass	Two spades	pass
Three spades	pass	?	

What is your rebid with each of the following hands ?

(w)	(x)	(y)
♠ 1087643	♠ AQ9543	♠ K10743
♡ J	♡ 63	♡ 2
◇ 962	◇ 1098	◇ Q9862
♣ 843	♣ 74	♣ 43

ANSWERS TO QUIZ EIGHT

1 - (a) One club; (b) one heart; (c) two no trump; (d) one diamond; (e) one no trump; (f) three no trump.

2 - (g) Pass; (h) four spades; (i) two no trump; (j) three hearts; (k) two no trump; (l) three no trump; (m) pass; (n) three no trump.

3 - (o) Pass; (p) pass; (q) three no trump; (r) three spades; (s) four hearts; (t) four spades; (u) three clubs; (v) pass.

4 - (w) Pass; (x) three no trump - with the king of spades known to be in the opening bidder's hand, the six card spade suit will provide six tricks and opener's 17 or 18 points will certainly provide at least three more. It will be found that the nine tricks needed for game in no trump, when abetted by a long suit, will usually be easier to win than the 10 tricks for the alternative game contract in a suit; (y) four spades.

LESSON EIGHT

HANDS

1.

West	North / South	East
	♠ 86 ♡ K54 ♢ AJ1073 ♣ J32	
♠ KJ754 ♡ 82 ♢ 65 ♣ KQ98	N W E S	♠ Q102 ♡ J973 ♢ Q984 ♣ 76
	♠ A93 ♡ AQ106 ♢ K2 ♣ A1054	

South dealer, N-S vulnerable

South	West	North	East
1 no tr.	pass	2 no tr.	pass
3 no tr.	pass	pass	pass

Opening lead by West, ♠ 5

2.

West	North / South	East
	♠ 954 ♡ K9765 ♢ 953 ♣ K6	
♠ KJ103 ♡ Q42 ♢ AQ6 ♣ AQ10	N W E S	♠ Q62 ♡ AJ83 ♢ J1042 ♣ J5
	♠ A87 ♡ 10 ♢ K87 ♣ 987432	

West dealer, neither side vul.

West	North	East	South
1 no tr.	pass	2 no tr.	pass
3 no tr.	pass	pass	pass

Opening lead by North, ♡ 6

3.

West	North / South	East
	♠ AKQ ♡ Q52 ♢ K65 ♣ A1098	
♠ Q652 ♡ A974 ♢ Q92 ♣ 62	N W E S	♠ 973 ♡ K1063 ♢ J10 ♣ KJ43
	♠ J104 ♡ J8 ♢ A8743 ♣ Q75	

North dealer, E-W vulnerable

North	East	South	West
1 no tr.	pass	2 no tr.	pass
3 no tr.	pass	pass	pass

Opening lead by East, ♡ 3.

4.

West	North / South	East
	♠ AJ5 ♡ QJ965 ♢ 76 ♣ 432	
♠ Q98 ♡ 1042 ♢ KJ108 ♣ A65	N W E S	♠ K3 ♡ AK3 ♢ Q932 ♣ KQ87
	♠ 107642 ♡ 87 ♢ A54 ♣ J109	

East dealer, both vulnerable

East	South	West	North
1 no tr.	pass	3 no tr.	pass
pass	pass		

Opening lead by South, ♠ 4.

SOLUTIONS TO LESSON EIGHT HANDS

1.

South declarer at 3 no trump.

Trick	W	N	E	S
1	♠5	♠6	♠Q	♠3
2	♠4	♠8	♠10	♠9
3	♠7	♣2	♠2	♠A
4	♢5	♢3	♢4	♢K
5	♢6	♢10	♢Q	♢2
6	♣9	♣3	♣7	♣A
7	♡2	♡4	♡3	♡A
8	♡8	♡K	♡7	♡6
9	♣8	♢A	♢8	♣4
10	♠J	♢J	♢9	♣5
11	♣Q	♢7	♣6	♣10
12	♠K	♡5	♡9	♡Q
13	♣K	♣J	♡J	♡10

South wins nine tricks.

2.

West declarer at 3 no trump.

Trick	N	E	S	W
1	♡6	♡3	♡10	♡Q
2	♡5	♡8	♣2	♡2
3	♢3	♢J	♢7	♢6
4	♢5	♢2	♢8	♢Q
5	♢9	♢4	♢K	♢A
6	♠4	♠Q	♠A	♠3
7	♣6	♣5	♣4	♣A
8	♠5	♠2	♠7	♠K
9	♠9	♠6	♠8	♠J
10	♡7	♣J	♣3	♠10
11	♡9	♡J	♣7	♡4
12	♡K	♡A	♣8	♣10
13	♣K	♢10	♣9	♣Q

West makes a small slam.

3.

North declarer at 3 no trump.

Trick	E	S	W	N
1	♡3	♡8	♡A	♡2
2	♡K	♡J	♡4	♡5
3	♡6	♣5	♡9	♡Q
4	♢10	♢3	♢2	♢K
5	♢J	♢4	♢9	♢5
6	♡10	♣7	♡7	♣8
7	♣K	♣Q	♣2	♣A
8	♠3	♠4	♠2	♠A
9	♣4	♢A	♢Q	♢6
10	♣3	♢8	♠5	♣9
11	♠7	♢7	♣6	♣10
12	♠9	♠10	♠6	♠Q
13	♣J	♠J	♠8	♠K

North wins nine tricks.

4.

East declarer at 3 no trump.

Trick	S	W	N	E
1	♠ 4	♠ 8	♠ J	♠ K
2	♢ 4	♢ 10	♢ 6	♢ 2
3	♢ A	♢ 8	♢ 7	♢ Q
4	♠ 2	♠ 9	♠ A	♠ 3
5	♠ 6	♠ Q	♠ 5	♡ 3
6	♣ 9	♣ 5	♣ 2	♣ Q
7	♣ 10	♣ A	♣ 3	♣ 7
8	♣ J	♣ 6	♣ 4	♣ K

East claims the balance, winning 11 tricks. He wins the remaining tricks with the last club, two high hearts and the two unplayed diamonds.

COMMENTS ON LESSON EIGHT HANDS

1-South refuses to win the first and second rounds of spades. This results in East no longer having a card of his partner's suit to return on taking the queen of diamonds.

Plays of this sort, where any player refuses to win an early round of a suit with a winning card, are known as "hold-ups." Note that with the hold-up, West's fourth and fifth spades are as effectively marooned as on a desert island.

2-Utilization of the rule of 11 by West permits him to win four heart tricks. Since the finesse against the king of diamonds is successful, permitting later establishment as a winner of dummy's fourth diamond, the club finesse against the missing king is completely unnecessary, since declarer can discard one of his losing clubs on dummy's fourth diamond, the other on dummy's fourth heart.

3-The hand illustrates that the jack in one hand and the queen in the other, adequately protected, can take a trick in the suit when led by the opponents. Declarer is insured of a heart trick by playing a low heart from dummy's doubleton jack holding when East opens the suit.

Note too that West, on taking the first heart with the ace, returned his fourth best. After cashing the fourth heart, East can safely lead the king of clubs since by bracketing the then lone queen (at that point), East sets up his jack as a potential winner.

Declarer should not be tempted into taking the jack of diamonds with the ace. If he does, there will no longer be an entry into the dummy for the remaining diamonds. This is known as a 'ducking' play.

4-North's play of the jack of spades is the tip-off. Had North the 10 as well as the jack, he would have played the 10. South is therefore marked with the 10. North's play of the jack from the ace-jack is a defensive finesse, intended to avoid making dummy's queen a winner.

Lesson IX

Pre-emptive Bidding

LESSON NINE

PRE-EMPTIVE OR SHUTOUT BIDDING

Early in this text, when we were discussing opening bids, we mentioned that there were certain types of hands which, though short in high cards, would win a lot of tricks if their extremely long suit was trump.

(a)
♠ K Q J 10 8 7 6 5 4
♡ 8
◇ 98
♣ 3

Let's take the hand to the left as an example. Even though it contains six high card points, the hand will probably win eight tricks with spades trumps, none defensively against another trump suit.

You will remember that 13 points are required to open the bidding with a rebiddable suit. This hand totals 11 points. Yet any hand that can take eight tricks should obviously be bid.

No comprehensive bidding system can neglect hands of this type merely because they lack defensive values or 13 points. Accordingly, we do open the bidding with hands of this type, but rather than open with a bid of one of a suit, we would open the bidding with a bid of four spades.

This bid is selected for several reasons.

First, if we had opened the bidding with one spade, our partner would have a perfect right to expect us to have 13 or more points. That we obviously lack.

Second, the prime danger of the hand is, as has been pointed out, that it lacks defensive values. If the opponents get together in any of the other three suits, this hand can't take a trick. For all you can do to prevent it, they might be able to make a grand slam in some other suit or in no trump. Therefore, you must make it difficult, if not impossible, for the opponents to get together and fully show their hand through normal exchange of bidding. The opponents need the early rounds of bidding, the one, two, and three zones, to exchange information as to their holdings and support for each other's suits. That takes time. By opening with four spades, you have cut their communications in the early stages.

Bids of this nature are called "pre-emptive" or "shutout" bids. The terms are used interchangeably. The word "pre-emptive" is derived from the Latin term "prae-emptor" meaning buy first.

With the outstanding high card strength divided between the two opponents, each may not dare enter the bidding at high range, much less get together. You see, an opponent might be willing to risk a bid of two hearts over an opening one spade bid but be extremely reluctant to bid five hearts over four spades. The attendant risk is too great.

Yet the other opponent might have the very cards that would enable the adverse partnership to make five hearts or even six or seven. And should the partner of the opening four spade bidder have the balance of outstanding strength, imagine the size of the penalty you will obtain through his double of an overcall made at the five level.

West	North / South	East
	♠ A92 ♡ 7543 ◇ K105 ♣ 1098	
♠ void ♡ AQ109 ◇ AJ743 ♣ Q752	N W E S	♠ 3 ♡ KJ62 ◇ Q62 ♣ AKJ64
	♠ KQJ1087654 ♡ 8 ◇ 98 ♣ 3	

Figure 147

You can see in *Figure 147* how South's opening four spade bid ties the East-West hands in knots.

East-West can make six hearts, six diamonds or six clubs, but how can they reach any of these contracts after the pre-emptive opening? In fact, it's problematical that they dare enter the auction at all.

Now some of you may be asking, "Why doesn't the West player do something over the four spade bid?"

The reason West doesn't bid is that he can't be sure which of the two remaining players, the opponent to his left, or his partner, holds the missing high cards.

Let's switch the North and East hands of the preceding example so that the cards resemble *figure 148.*

Imagine what would happen to West if he entered the bidding now? He'd be pulverized.

So you see, the opening four spade bid made it possible for South to 'steal' the hand by making it hazardous for the opponents to enter the bidding.

	♠ 3 ♡ KJ62 ◇ Q62 ♣ AKJ64	
♠ void ♡ AQ109 ◇ AJ743 ♣ Q752	N W E S	♠ A92 ♡ 7543 ◇ K105 ♣ 1098
	♠ KQJ1087654 ♡ 8 ◇ 98 ♣ 3	

Figure 148

THE SACRIFICIAL PURPOSE

Certain theorists and writers lay great stress on the fact that these pre-emptive opening bids, if doubled and set, will pay a penalty less than the value of the game or slam the opponents might otherwise have been able to bid and make.

Theoretically, this is true. Actually, there is no guarantee that the opponents would have been able to make anything before the hand is played, and the benefits of what appears a sound sacrifice cannot be weighed with precision, even after the hand is over.

An important psychological factor enters bidding. Just try playing sometime with a partner who keeps taking sacrifices and going down, time after time, and you'll be pretty sick and tired of seeing penalties accrue on the wrong side of the score sheet. It would have been a lot cheaper to let the opponents win the rubber in the first place.

It may be well and good for your partner to say, after going down on each hand, "Well, that's less than they would have made," but the fact remains that you're losing points. Moreover, the fact that the opponents have just held a good hand doesn't mean that your side will get the next good hand. Red or black can come up time after time at a roulette table, and good cards can run one way of the table indefinitely at the bridge table.

Any chronic loser knows that. This reasoning does not apply, however, in duplicate bridge, where each hand is a separate unit to itself and the final contract is selected with an eye to the least loss or maximum gain on that particular hand.

So, if you intend to pre-empt, think in terms of shutting out the opponents, or of making what you bid, or making it difficult for the opponents to find the right contract rather than taking the defeatist attitude of losing points.

HOW TO RECOGNIZE A PRE-EMPTIVE BID

Any pre-emptive opening bid shows a long suit and a weak hand defensively.

1 - The suit is usually seven cards or longer with some solidity.

2 - The hand cannot win more than two tricks defensively.

3 - The hand does not contain *two* rebiddable suits.

4 - The hand does not contain 13 or more points.

Any hand with two and a half or more defensive tricks should NOT be opened with a shutout bid, even with an extremely long suit. The reason is-that with a hand strong in defensive values and high cards, if you open with a shutout bid, your partner will never believe that you had a strong hand; if he has strength, you may miss a slam.

Open strong hands normally.

Pre-empt only with weak hands and long suits!

TYPES OF PRE-EMPTIVE OPENING BIDS

Opening pre-emptive bids are of three kinds.

1 - Three of a suit (major or minor).

2 - Four of a suit (generally a major).

3 - Five of a suit (minor only).

Of these three, the opening bid of four in a suit is the most common, and likewise, the most effective barricade for the opponents to hurdle. We'll discuss it first.

The easiest way to tell whether a hand should be opened with a bid of four is as follows—

1 - It has less than two and a half defensive winners,

2-If vulnerable, the hand contains a minimum of eight winning tricks; not vulnerable, a minimum of seven and a half winners.

Let's look at some typical hands.

(b)	(c)	(d)
♠ A K Q 10 8 7 6 5	♠ void	♠ K Q J 9 8 7 6 5
♡ 7	♡ Q J 10 9 7 6 5 4 3	♡ K 10
◇ J 5	◇ void	◇ 9
♣ 3 2	♣ J 10 9 8	♣ 8 4

(b) Four spades, vulnerable or not. The hand has eight winners with only two defensive tricks.

(c) Four hearts, vulnerable or not. Eight winners, seven in hearts, one in clubs. This is an excellent example of how little high card strength is needed for a pre-emptive opening, as long as the offensive playing strength is present.

(d) If vulnerable, pass. Not vulnerable, bid four spades. The hand contains but seven and a half winners of which seven are in spades, the remaining half in hearts.

IF THE SUIT IS A MINOR

Of course you've noticed that all three of the preceding examples embrace major suits. Let's imagine that they were minor suits instead, and in each case, the long suit was diamonds. Would that affect the opening bids?

Definitely, it would.

It is generally not good policy to pre-empt with four of a minor when holding a solid or virtually solid establishable suit. The reason is that the long suit is even more valuable winning tricks in no trump at 30 points per trick than in diamonds at 20 points per trick. If the opening bid is four diamonds, you can never get back to bid three no trump.

With hand (b), were the eight card suit diamonds, I would pass originally, entering the bidding later. Under no circumstances would I open the bidding with four diamonds.

Hand (c) could possibly be opened with four diamonds, since it is remote that the hand would ever be of much playable value in no trump lacking high cards or re-entries.

Hand (d), were its eight card suit a minor, falls into the bracket of being playable in no trump. For that reason, it should not be opened with a bid of four in a minor. Passing the hand originally and bidding it aggressively later will portray the holding.

FOURTH HAND PRE-EMPTS

Sometimes after three passes, you will hear the fourth player open the bidding with three or four of a suit, as the case may be. His justification was that he wanted to "shut the opponents out of the bidding."

What he overlooked was that the opponents were already out of the bidding. They had previously passed, and if fourth hand didn't honestly feel that he could fulfill his contract, all he had to do was pass, and everybody would have had a new hand.

Don't pre-empt fourth hand unless you have a reasonable expectancy of making your bid. Try to have an additional one half playing trick over the minimum requirements, as eight and a half vulnerable, eight not vulnerable, plus two defensive tricks.

♠ AKJ98765
♡ 32
◇ 8
♣ 95

But let's suppose we don't have eight and a half winners. Let's pretend we have the hand shown to the left and the three previous players have all passed.

Should you bid or pass? If the former, one spade or four?

I would be inclined to open the bidding with one spade, despite the fact that the hand contains a total of only 12 points. The hand has eight probable winners.

If partner can respond freely, you can later rebid with four spades, and have a good expectancy of fulfilling the contract. In the event that partner doesn't have too much in high cards, you can always try to buy the bid at two spades or even three spades, well within your ability to produce. Since with three prior passes, we can feel the missing high card strength pretty well divided, we should be able to make at least a part score.

I do not advocate an opening four spade bid fourth hand with this type of holding since the pre-emptive bid, as has already been pointed out, is intended to shut out the opponents, even at sacrificial cost, and there is no need to sacrifice to shut out opponents who are already out of the bidding.

Under no circumstances should hands of this nature be passed. It is true that opening the bidding with a bid of one permits the opponents to enter the bidding cheaply and you hold little defensive strength. But this is counterbalanced by the suit's great offensive power, plus a fact so generally overlooked—that partner, too, holds 13 cards and that some high ones will generally be included.

Do not open fourth hand pre-emptively without two defensive tricks!

RESPONDING TO FOUR BIDS

Since an opening bid of four in a major automatically places the bidder in a game contract, there is no useful purpose served by additional bids by partner unless he thinks a slam is probable or he is forced to bid higher by the opponents' bidding.

The average player errs in thinking a slam makeable after his partner opens the bidding with four of a suit and he, as responder, holds three taking tricks.

Let's see why.

Usually, the opening four-bidder promises about eight winners if vulnerable, seven and a half not vulnerable. Now, let's say after partner's opening four heart bid, you hold the hand to the left. It contains three primary winners, the ace, king of spades and the ace of diamonds. If the opening bidder has eight winners, that adds to a total of 11. A small slam needs 12. You're one short.

♠ A K 6 5 4
♡ 8 6
◇ A 7 5
♣ Q 6 3

So, for the most part, at least 90 percent of the times when your partner opens with four of a major, you should pass. He's already contracting for two to two and a half tricks more than he himself can win, and your high cards are urgently needed to plug the gap.

If partner's opening was four in a minor, be doubly careful about raising to unmakeable heights, since the bid itself has denied a suit good enough to play three no trump.

Above all, if you have a long suit of your own and just a medium to good hand, don't disturb your partner's pre-emptive opening by showing your suit. There is no reason to expect that your suit is better than partner's. It may not be as good and you may get the bidding too high. Your partner is trying to shut out some suit, and, for all you know it may be the very suit you now contemplate bidding. This is particularly true if your partner has pre-empted in one major and you hold the other.

Of course, if you have an extremely strong hand, then you should take some action that may lead to a slam contract. We'll discuss slam action on the next few pages and in Lesson XIII.

Another reason for not disturbing your partner's pre-emptive opening bid is that since he has extreme length in one suit, he may be extremely short in others. You, as responder, may have taking tricks in suits where declarer does not need them. This is known in bridge as "duplication of values."

WEST	EAST
♠ 76	♠ QJ10
♡ AKJ87654	♡ Q10
◇ void	◇ AKQJ10
♣ 732	♣ KQJ

Take the partnership hands to the left. Uncontestably, West has an opening four heart bid. Many players with the East hand, following partner's four heart bid, would take action of some sort.

They might—

1 - Bid five diamonds.
2 - Bid five hearts.
3 - Bid six hearts.
4 - Bid four no trump.

Yet a Pass is Correct!

Let me show you why by analyzing each of these responses with the probable rebid and result.

First, that of five diamonds. It's really silly to bid a new suit in response to a pre-emptive opening, since the latter bid states that the hand is best playable in that suit. The five diamond bid will evoke only a possible pass by opener (in which case you'll wind up playing the hand at five diamonds) or a possible five heart rebid.

Now for the raise to five hearts. Exactly what does that tell about responder's holding? Absolutely nothing, except a willingness to go higher if opener holds additional values. But the opener has denied additional values or even those needed for an opening one bid by his pre-empt. What else can he do but pass the raise to five hearts?

The six heart "barge" will result in a defeatable contract, since the defenders can grab two black aces and the king of spades.

The four no trump bid will draw the discouraging response (in this case) showing one ace and one king, since with more the pre-empt would have been unnecessary. Following the weak response, the four no trump bidder has no choice but to beat a hasty retreat to five hearts and hope against hope that the hand will not be beaten.

We'll grant that if the opponents open a trump or a diamond the hand can probably make a grand slam. But, if they cash three tricks in two high spades and the ace of clubs, the hand is down one.

But slams are not bid on "ifs" and "buts," but, rather on a better than even chance of producing the contract. Otherwise, why jeopardize a certain game?

Someone might say, "Suppose East held the A K Q J 10 of spades instead of that holding in diamonds? Then the tricks would be where they were needed and the slam makeable."

True, but when responder's high cards are concentrated in one or two suits, he doesn't know whether they're going to be of value to the pre-emptive opener or not. It brings to full realization the all important point that pre-emptive openings not only shut out the opponents but also the partner.

WHAT YOU SHOULD HAVE TO RESPOND TO PRE-EMPTS

Having exhaustively given the 'don't' side of the picture, now let's look at the 10 percent or less of the times when a voluntary response to partner's pre-emptive opening is in order.

The requirements are easy to learn and remember—

1-First round controls of at least two suits, at least second round control of the third. This refers to suits other than the suits bid by partner.

2-Four winners (sure taking tricks), minimum.

WHAT FIRST ROUND CONTROL IS — *

First round control is having the ace or void of a suit. Thus if the suit is led, the trick can be captured either by the ace or by trumping. Naturally, some trumps should be present so that the void can be utilized.

Footnote

* *Controls and slam bidding are discussed in detail in Lesson XIII.*

WHAT SECOND ROUND CONTROL IS –

A king or a singleton is termed second round control. That is because after an adverse ace has been played the king will capture the second round; or the singleton, after being played on the first round of the suit, permits future rounds to be trumped. Naturally, again some trumps must be present in the hand containing the singleton. A singleton king would be second round control just like any other singleton. A singleton ace would provide both first and second round controls.

(e)
♠ A965
♡ Q8
◇ 3
♣ AK9432

For example, your partner has opened with four hearts and you hold either hand (e) or (f).

Hand (e) has first round control of two suits, spades and clubs. It has second round control of diamonds and clubs, has three sure high card winners and a fourth by being able to trump a diamond.

(f)
♠ K5432
♡ J53
◇ void
♣ AKQ96

Hand (f) has two first round controls, the club ace and the diamond void. It has three second round controls in the club king, spade king and diamond void. Further, the club suit is sufficiently solid to permit discarding losers in other suits.

But the spade suit! Some acute observer may remark, "Well, you have the king, all right, but suppose the opponent opens a spade and the ace lies over the king. Now you may have two or more spade losers since the king will be worthless?"

That's quite true if things are just that way.

However, we must admit that's looking at things from the blackest point of view. First, it's a 50-50 chance that the ace is in front of the king. Secondly, there are three other suits that the opponent might open. Why should he choose our Achilles' heel? Third, declarer might have the queen of spades to reinforce the king; and fourth, the declarer, from his pre-empt, is bound to be short in other suits and might have a singleton spade.

So, chances are still pretty well in favor of bidding the slam when the needed second round control of a side suit is the king. Of course, if the suit has been bid in back of the king so that the ace is assumed to be in the bidder's hand, any trick taking value of the king is diminished.

RESPONDING WITH A SINGLETON OR VOID OF PARTNER'S PRE-EMPT

In all of the recommended responses we have thus far illustrated we have been fortunate enough to hold two or three supporting cards of partner's suit.

(g)
♠ KJ97654
♡ 4
◇ A74
♣ J2

This will not always be the case. Sometimes after a four heart bid by partner, our hand may resemble the hand to the left. Should we now respond with four spades?

The answer is an emphatic NO!

Let's see why. Having pre-empted in the heart suit, he is apparently afraid of an adverse spade contract, against which he has no defense. It therefore stands to reason that since he has no high card values against spades, he would similarly have little or no support for that suit if bid by partner.

Every now and then, when your partner pre-empts with one major, you will find yourself holding strength in the other. You see, your partner didn't know who held the other major when he pre-empted. He was afraid it was an opponent. In cases of this sort, your best tactics are to pass and hope an opponent will bid the very suit you considered bidding.

But there are occasions when you have a legitimate right to feel that a slam is within bounds of makeability, even though you may hold a singleton or void of partner's suit.

This is the point I wish to emphasize—with a singleton or void of partner's pre-empt, there is an increasing chance that one or even two tricks might be lost in his suit. His pre-empt by no means guaranteed a solid suit. Even if he has an eight card suit headed by the ace, king and queen, the remaining five cards of the suit may break four-one or five-zero. Therefore, to compensate for a possible trump loser, extra values should be present in responding hand to justify a slam try when holding a singleton or void of partner's pre-empt.

However, should the singleton be a high honor, as the queen, king or ace, the normal requirements for a slam try—four winners, two first round controls and one second round control would still apply. This is because the singleton honor will reinforce the pre-empted suit to the same degree as two or three low cards of the suit.

The following are examples of the reinforcement given a long suit by two or three low cards or a high singleton in the partner's hand.

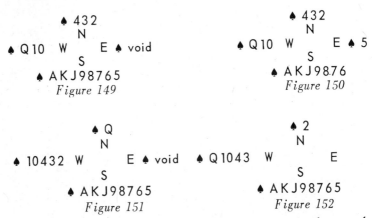

♠ 432
N
♠ Q10 W E ♠ void
S
♠ AKJ98765
Figure 149

♠ 432
N
♠ Q10 W E ♠ 5
S
♠ AKJ9876
Figure 150

♠ Q
N
♠ 10432 W E ♠ void
S
♠ AKJ98765
Figure 151

♠ 2
N
♠ Q1043 W E
S
♠ AKJ98765
Figure 152

Notice how, in *figure 151*, the singleton queen is the equal in reinforcing value of the three small cards in *figures 149* and *150*. In *figure 152*, despite the fact that the partnership holds nine spades between the combined hands, the adverse spade break indicates two spade tricks must be lost. The singleton deuce is not sufficient to bolster even the pre-emptively opened suit in this case.

Accordingly, with a singleton or void of partner's pre-empt, responder should have at least four winners plus first round controls of *all three* remaining suits to justify a slam attempt in view of possible trump losers.

(h)	(i)
♠ void	♠ void
♡ KQ7654	♡ AQ7654
◊ AQJ	◊ AQJ
♣ AK43	♣ AKQ2

Facing an opening four spade bid, I would pass on (h), since first round heart control is missing and the probability of one or two trump losers exists.

On (i), I would reluctantly bid six spades, hoping that partner's spade suit is solid or has no more than one loser. I am not making this response in any spirit of optimism - rather, that my hand is so big that it warrants a slam try.

(j)
♠ 654
♡ KQ7
◇ AQJ
♣ AKQ2

Of course, were (h) changed to resemble (j), I would have no hesitancy making a slam try, since the possibility of trump losers is greatly minimized by by the holding of three spades.

HOW TO MAKE A SLAM TRY AFTER PARTNER'S PRE-EMPT

The danger of jumping immediately to six of partner's suit (from four) with only two aces in your hand is that partner may be ace-less. In fact, he may even be minus the ace and king of of his bid suit.

Some slam convention, agreed between the partnership, as the San Francisco convention, Blackwood or Gerber, should be used to locate aces and kings held by the partnership. These conventions are discussed fully in Lesson XIII.

Remember, if you make a slam try after your partner has opened pre-emptively, the responsibility is entirely yours. His bid warned you that his hand wasn't good enough for an opening one bid.

(k)
♠ K5
♡ A753
◇ AKQ865
♣ A

As to the bid of a grand slam following partner's pre-emptive opening, this is seldom made. The risk of jeopardizing a sure small slam is too great. But in the rare cases, when holding a top honor of partner's suit, three first round controls and five winners, bidding the grand slam is warranted. Hand (k) is an example. Presuming your partner opens with four spades, you should make some ace locating bid. If his response shows the ace of spades in his hand, you should not hesitate bidding seven spades.

PLAYING PRE-EMPTIVELY OPENED HANDS IN NO TRUMP

The experienced duplicate and tournament player will frequently play hands in no trump that normally would be played in suit contracts. This is due to the fact that no trump yields greater trick scores. The difference of these few points in total scoring, transmuted into tournament match points (Lesson XVI) may mean the difference between victory and defeat.

A no trump slam, after an opening pre-emptive bid by partner, should be bid for any one or more of the following reasons.

1 - No trump counts more.

2 - You want the lead coming up to your hand rather than through kings and ace-queens.

3 - There is a danger that a long suit can be trumped.

To bid a slam in no trump opposite a pre-empt, a minimum of two cards of partner's suit is a *must*! Do not bid a slam in no trump with a singleton of partner's suit, even a singleton ace. In all probability, you will find partner's hand devoid of re-entries and you will be unable to use his long suit.

All other requirements as to high cards, winners and controls remain the same as for slams in suit contracts.

WHAT TO DO AFTER AN OVERCALL OF PARTNER'S PRE-EMPT

Following an opening pre-emptive bid of four of a suit by partner, the next player may sometimes make an overcall which will come in either at the four or five level. The overcall will generally be of a suit, infrequently in no trump. Let's consider suit overcalls.

Case A

North, Partner	East, Opponent	You, South	West
Four hearts	Four spades	?	

Case B

Four spades	Five hearts	?	

Cases A and B are the same except in B the overcall has come in one step higher. Before deciding what to do, granting there are high cards present in your hand, your first thought should be, "What can my side make?" The second should be, "What can the opponents make or lose?"

A determining factor will be the vulnerability or lack of it on both sides. If your side is vulnerable and you think you can make five of your suit, you should raise your partner's suit. The vulnerable game and rubber is usually worth more than an inadequate non-vulnerable penalty. On the other hand, if the probable penalty seems greater than anything you can make, you should double for penalty.

The weighing of pros and cons in determining whether to "take the push," and bid, double or pass in these situations requires the most delicate and accurate of judgements. Even experts err in these situations, and the student in the early stages of his development must be expected to make an occasional "wrong guess."

For guidance, let me put it this way: after partner opens with a pre-empt and an opponent overcalls;

1-If you have support for partner's suit, some high card strength and nothing in the opponent's suit, raise your partner;

2-If most or a good share of your "stuff" is in the opponent's suit, double.

3-Prefer a vulnerable game to a penalty of less than 500.

4-Don't let the opponents push you higher than what you feel is your highest makeable contract, unless you wish to bid higher as an inexpensive sacrifice against the opponents' makeable contract.

RESPONDING TO OPENING BIDS OF FOUR IN A MINOR

Thus far, what has been written regarding opening four bids principally concerns major suits. That bid automatically contracts for game. The only reason for responder now bidding is because he thinks a slam possible, or because he has been forced to raise by an adverse bid.

Facing a minor suit pre-empt of four, in most cases, the partner should pass. That is because the opening bid of four in a minor has denied a suit good enough to be used in no trump. At least one and possibly two tricks are missing from the suit itself.

In order to raise to five (game), responder should have:

1-At least one top honor of partner's suit (ace, king or queen).

2-At least three winners distributed between two or more suits.

In order to consider bidding a slam, responder should have:

1-At least two cards of partner's suit, including one of the top three honors.

2-Three first round controls or two first round controls plus second and third round controls of the remaining suit.

3-Four winners, minimum.

It must be borne in mind that an opening bid of four in a minor is not intended to reach game, as opposed to its big brother, the opening bid of four of a major. Therefore, the minor opening bid is apt to be a bit weaker.

In making a penalty double of an opponent's overcall after a four minor opening by partner, the doubler should not count on his partner for even a single defensive trick. He should have all of the required tricks to set the contract within his own hand.

OPENING BIDS OF FIVE

Opening bids of five are confined exclusively to minor suits. Similar to other pre-emptive bids, they show hands weak in defensive strength but long in playing ability. Not vulnerable, the hand should contain eight and a half winners; vulnerable, nine or more.

(1)
♠ 3
♡ 8
◇ K Q 10 9 8 7 6 5 4 3
♣ 2

The hand to the left would be an example of a five diamond opening, vulnerable or not.

RESPONDING TO OPENING FIVE BIDS

The only valid reasons for responding to an opening bid of five in a minor are identical to those for responding to opening bids of four in a major. These are:

1-Slam probabilities;

2-Forced to bid higher through an opponent's overcall.

SLAM REQUIREMENTS TO A FIVE MINOR OPENING

1-Three winners, minimum.

2-Two first round controls and one second round control.

3-A high honor of partner's suit.

For a grand slam, you should have *all* of the following–

1-One top honor of partner's suit and at least two trumps.

2-Three first round controls, other than partner's suit.

3-Four winners, minimum.

PENALTY DOUBLES AFTER A FIVE OPENING BID

To consider a penalty double after your partner opens with a bid of five, you cannot count on him for a single defensive trick. All of the setting tricks *must* be in your hand.

RESPONDER'S TACTICS AFTER AN OVERCALL OF PARTNER'S OPENING BID OF FIVE

After an opening five bid has been overcalled, responder's tactics are identical to those described on pages 320 and 321.

TACTICS AGAINST FOUR OR FIVE NO TRUMP OVERCALLS OF YOUR PARTNER'S PRE-EMPT

When an opponent bids four no trump over your partner's opening bid of four in a suit, the opponent is showing a tremendously powerful hand. This is also true of a five no trump overcall of an opening five bid.

Four and five no trump overcalls of pre-emptive bids show hands so powerful that ordinarily, you should pass, since further bidding by your side may result in a disproportionate sacrifice. Only if not vulnerable against vulnerable opponents should further sacrificial bidding be contemplated, and even then the penalty should not be excessive nor should the opponents be pushed into a grand slam against which there is no defense.

You will learn about these 'powerhouse' overcalls of four and five no trump in Lesson XI on Defensive Bidding.

REBIDS BY OPENER

After having opened with a pre-emptive bid of four or five of a suit, the opening bidder should not ordinarily make a voluntary rebid. That is because he has told his entire story with his first bid.

Should his partner make a forcing bid, as bidding four no trump as a slam try, the opener must rebid. In the event of a penalty double by partner, the opening bidder should pass, relying on his partner's judgement.

TACTICS IN GENERAL

As a whole, pre-emptive tactics by both opener and responder are very similar, whether the opening bid has been four or five, major or minor. Vulnerability or lack of it against the opponents' bidding, naturalness or lack of it in contracts, the apparent makeability of the chosen contract are all determining factors in deciding whether the bidding should continue, stop or the opponents be doubled in their overcalls.

OPENING BIDS OF THREE OF A SUIT

Some readers may have wondered why we first discussed opening bids of four in a suit, then of five, and now we backtracked to opening bids of three of a suit.

Why didn't we take them up in numerical order?

The best advice I can give you, at least in the formative stages of your bridge game, is to completely forget that an opening bid of three of a suit exists and advise you not to use it. Later, with a steady partner who understands the meaning of this bid, it can be used provided the opponents also understand its import. *

The great danger of the three bid is that the average partner, holding one or two taking tricks, will hear you bid 'three,' and say to himself, **"Well, if my partner can bid three all by himself, he ought to be able to make four with my trick or two."**

The trouble is—about four winners in partner's hand, combined with an opening bid of three, are needed to make a game. I'd venture to say that if you gave the same responder's hand to three different players and opened the bidding with three of a suit, you'd get three different responses.

As used by most players, the opening three bid is a weak shutout, showing an extremely long ragged suit or a fair six carder which may have a weak side suit for added distributional values. The hand is extremely weak in high cards, has little if any defensive strength and is intended as a shutout.

The primary purpose of the bid is intended to make it difficult for the opponents to enter the auction. It is not intended to facilitate bidding a game unless opener's partner holds an extremely strong hand.

In recent years, experts have realized that opening three bids can be doubled and penalized too heavily, so they have devised a new tactic—the weak two bid. This is discussed at length in Lesson XVI.

Footnote

* *Any bidding convention whose meaning is only understood by the bidders and not by the opponents is termed a "private convention." It is improper and unethical. The opponents always have a right to know or enquire the meanings of any bids.*

EXAMPLES OF OPENING THREE BIDS

(m)	(n)	(o)	(p)
♠ KJ97643	♠ 8	♠ 7	♠ 92
♡ 5	♡ AJ9654	♡ 85	♡ 62
◇ Q72	◇ J6432	◇ QJ76543	◇ 103
♣ 84	♣ 2	♣ 532	♣ KJ97654

On (n), three hearts, the diamonds are not shown.

These bids are extremely risky.

As I remarked before, I don't recommend them.

RESPONSES TO AN OPENING THREE BID IN A MAJOR

Pass as a general rule.

In order to raise to game, responder should have –

16 points with four or more trumps of partner's suit,

17 points with three cards of partner's suit,

18 points with two cards or a singleton high honor of partner's suit.

Four winners, divided between at least two outside suits.

These are minimums!

If you think you can make a game in some other suit after your partner's opening bid of three in a major, you should bid it then and there. Suppose your partner opened with three hearts and you held the hand to the left. You should bid four spades. There is no point in only bidding three spades, since partner told his entire story with his opening three heart bid and would pass your three spade take out.

(q)
♠ KQJ1098
♡ 4
◇ AQJ8
♣ K7

To a three spade opening bid by partner, raise only to four spades with the hand to the left. Pretend your partner opened three spades holding hand (m) above. Then see how much more accurate a final four spade contract would be than one of six spades. For heaven's sake, don't bid four hearts!

(r)
♠ 102
♡ AQ7643
◇ AJ
♣ AQ3

To contemplate bidding a slam after an opening bid of three in a major suit, responder should have all the following –

(s)

♠ K3 ♡ AQ763 ◇ AKJ ♣ AQ9	1-First round control of all three remaining suits. 2-Either the ace or king of partner's suit and at least two trumps. 3-At least five sure winners.

With the above hand, after an opening bid of three spades, four no trump is the best response.

RESPONSES TO OPENING BIDS OF THREE IN A MINOR

If partner's opening bid was three of a minor, responder should pass in most cases. His excuse for responding will be the probability of game or slam. If game seems certain in another suit, it should be bid directly, as with the first hand on the preceding page. Ordinarily, where game is contemplated after partner's three minor opening, the final contract will be in no trump as the shortest distance between two points. Requirements for responding with three no trump to an opening three minor bid are as follows –

(t)

♠ QJ8 ♡ A7432 ◇ AQ3 ♣ K10	1-Two cards of partner's suit including one high honor. 2-Three sure winners plus positive stoppers in *all* side suits!

Holding the above hand, I would bid three no trump in response to an opening three diamond or three club bid.

To bid a slam following partner's three minor pre-empt requires all of the previously mentioned requirements for slam responses to opening three-bids in a major (shown at the head of this page) and a little more in the way of high card and playing strength. Since this situation will not arise once out of a thousand hands, the student need not be unduly concerned.

RAISES AFTER AN ADVERSE OVERCALL

Responder should not raise his partner's opening three bid after an overcall by an opponent unless he intended to do so had not the overcall been made, or unless the condition of comparative vulnerability indicates the raise or possible sacrifice to be profitable.

(u)

♠ 985	Suppose you held the hand to the left and the bidding was –
♡ 42	
◇ KJ765	Partner, Opener Opponent You Opponent
♣ A108	Three spades pass pass

You naturally passed, since you don't have enough to raise to four spades. Now, let's imagine that an opponent bids four hearts and that bid comes around to you. What should you do now?

That depends on comparative vulnerability. Certainly from the looks of your hand, and the weakness demonstrated by partner's opening three bid, we can expect the opponents to make four hearts. Now the question is – which is cheaper – let them make four hearts or pay a penalty playing four spades, which will probably be doubled.

YOU ARE	OPPONENTS ARE	YOU SHOULD
1-Not vulnerable	Vulnerable	Sacrifice if possible
2-Not vulnerable	Not vulnerable	Tossup
3-Vulnerable	Not vulnerable	Pass in a hurry
4-Vulnerable	Vulnerable	Pass in a hurry

PENALTY DOUBLES AFTER AN OPENING THREE BID

Since the three bid is the weakest of all pre-emptive openings, responder contemplating a penalty double of an opponent's overcall cannot count on opener for any defensive values, whatever. All tricks required to set the contract must come from the doubler's (responder's) hand.

OPENER'S REBIDS

Having shot his bolt with the opening bid, the opener should pass any raise or takeout by partner except, of course, some bid which is forcing. A slam try of four no trump would be typical of the latter. Should responder bid three no trump over the opening three bid, the opening bidder should ordinarily pass if his suit is in any way establishable or has the slightest semblance of some side re-entry. Only if opener's suit is a major and the hand tremendously distributional should a response of three no trump be taken out into four of the major. Penalty doubles by partner should also be passed, since doubler knows from the opening bid the exact defenseless character of opener's hand.

QUIZ NINE

1-You are the dealer. With neither side vulnerable, what do you bid with each of the following hands?

(a)	(b)
♠ AQJ8765	♠ 84
♡ KJ974	♡ 2
◇ 2	◇ AK1098765
♣ void	♣ 54

(c)	(d)
♠ QJ109754 32	♠ J
♡ A	♡ AKJ98765
◇ 74	◇ AQ7
♣ 8	♣ 4

2-Both sides are vulnerable. You are East. The bidding

South	West	North	East
pass	pass	pass	?

What do you do with each of the following hands?

(e)	(f)
♠ A	♠ A8
♡ Q2	♡ KQJ97432
◇ 65	◇ 82
♣ QJ1087654	♣ 10

(g)	(h)
♠ J10	♠ Q10987654
♡ 76	♡ KQ
◇ AKQJ943	◇ 3
♣ A2	♣ 86

3-You are East. North-South are vulnerable, your side is not vulnerable. With the following bidding, what do you do with each of the following hands?

West, Partner, Dealer	North	East, You
Four hearts	Four spades	?

(i)	(j)
♠ KJ86	♠ 7
♡ A2	♡ J62
◇ 2	◇ AKQ2
♣ Q109	♣ AKJ109

(k)	(l)
♠ QJ6	♠ 7
♡ 72	♡ KJ98
◇ A1087	◇ J543
♣ 6543	♣ 10642

4-Neither side is vulnerable. Your partner opens the bidding with four hearts and the next player passes. What do you do with each of the following hands?

(m)	(n)
♠ AQJ87654	♠ AKQ76
♡ J10	♡ 2
◇ 2	◇ 852
♣ K7	♣ KQ109

(o)	(p)
♠ AQ8765	♠ J4
♡ K7	♡ AK
◇ KQJ	◇ Q10876
♣ AQ	♣ AKQ2

ANSWERS TO QUIZ NINE

1-(a) One spade. The hand has 16 points and the strong two suiter demands that both suits, if possible, be shown. (b) pass-the suit can be utilized in no trump and if you open with four diamonds the damage is done. The suit is too strong for three diamonds. Hands of this sort can always be bid after the bidding has been opened elsewhere. (c) four spades. (d) one heart.

2-Since in this question you are fourth hand after three passes, you are not faced with the problem of shutting out the opponents. If you now pass, the hand is over. Accordingly, you bid according to what you think you might make. (e) pass. (f) one heart, not three or four. (g) one diamond. (h) pass.

3-(i) double. (j) I prefer a penalty double, since with vulnerable opponents, you should take sufficient tricks in the minors to beat them for a lucrative penalty despite your lack of cards or tricks in the doubled spade suit. However, a raise to five hearts cannot be too severely criticized, while a slam try is speculative and dangerous, since to successfully take 12 tricks partner must have a solid trump suit. (k) pass. (l) pass. The danger of "saving" at five hearts is that you may "push" the opponents into a makeable slam contract against which you have no defense.

4-(m) pass. (n) pass. (o) four no trump. (p) pass.

LESSON NINE
HANDS

1.

North: ♠ AQJ10 ♡ 4 ◇ J8653 ♣ K43

West: ♠ 7652 ♡ A ◇ K1097 ♣ J1092

East: ♠ K983 ♡ K92 ◇ AQ2 ♣ Q85

South: ♠ 4 ♡ QJ1087653 ◇ 4 ♣ A76

South dealer, neither side vul.

South	West	North	East
4 hts.	pass	pass	pass

Opening lead by West, ♣ J.

2.

North: ♠ A1063 ♡ QJ1082 ◇ J ♣ 432

West: ♠ 82 ♡ 73 ◇ AKQ87654 ♣ 6

East: ♠ KQJ7 ♡ K95 ◇ 102 ♣ AK105

South: ♠ 954 ♡ A64 ◇ 93 ♣ QJ987

West dealer, N-S vulnerable

West	North	East	South
pass	pass	1 cl.	pass
2 dia.	pass	2 sp.	pass
3 dia.	pass	3 no.tr.	pass
pass	pass		

Opening lead by South, ♣ Q.

3.

North: ♠ KQJ1087654 ♡ J ◇ 7 ♣ 42

West: ♠ 2 ♡ Q1094 ◇ Q1092 ♣ Q953

East: ♠ 9 ♡ 32 ◇ 86543 ♣ AKJ86

South: ♠ A3 ♡ AK8765 ◇ AKJ ♣ 107

North dealer, E-W vulnerable

Note – Bid this hand to what you consider the correct final contract before studying the bidding on the next page.

4.

North: ♠ 43 ♡ K43 ◇ 7652 ♣ 8753

West: ♠ J2 ♡ AQ76 ◇ KQ109 ♣ A62

East: ♠ AKQ10875 ♡ 82 ◇ AJ ♣ Q4

South: ♠ 96 ♡ J1095 ◇ 843 ♣ KJ109

East dealer, both sides vul.

Note – Bid this hand to what you consider the correct final contract before studying the bidding on the next page.

RECOMMENDED BIDDING

3.

North	East	South	West
4 sp.	pass	pass	pass

Opening lead by East, ♣ K.

4.

East	South	West	North
1 sp.	pass	2 dia.	pass
4 sp.	pass	4 no.tr.	pass
6 cl.	pass	7 sp.	pass
pass	pass		

Opening lead by South, ♡ J.

BIDDING COMMENTS

1-South's hand, other than the ace of clubs, is completely defenseless. While the hand contains only seven plus taking tricks, the eight card heart suit qualifies it for an opening pre-emptive bid of four hearts. Notice that North takes no action whatever, despite the singleton heart.

2-Many players would be tempted, incorrectly, to open the bidding with the West hand with four or five diamonds. Notice that five diamonds cannot be made, since with the opening of the queen of hearts by North, the defenders must win two hearts and one spade. The key to the bidding is West's pass, then his jump response of two diamonds over East's one club (one more than necessary) to show the near opening nature of his holding. The jump response by a previously passed player is semi-forcing.

3-While South has the required two first round controls for a possible slam try, he lacks the needed second round control of the third suit. If, as South, you plunged the hand into an eventual six spade contract, you had the ignominious pleasure of seeing East take the first two tricks with the ace, king of clubs.

4-East's jump rebid to four spades, lacking any support in the suit from partner, marked East for a virtually solid suit. It is a simple matter for West to count that the combined hands can win all 13 tricks. The six club bid is the San Francisco response to four no trump showing two aces and one king in the responding hand.

SOLUTIONS TO LESSON NINE HANDS

1.

South declarer at four hearts.

Trick	W	N	E	S
1	♣ J	♣ 3	♣ 8	♣ A
2	♠ 2	♠ A	♠ 3	♠ 4
3	♠ 5	♠ Q	♠ K	♡ 3
4	♣ 2	♣ K	♣ 5	♣ 6
5	♠ 6	♠ J	♠ 8	♣ 7
6	♠ 7	♠ 10	♠ 9	◇ 4
7	♡ A	♡ 4	♡ 2	♡ 10
8	♣ 10	♣ 4	♣ Q	♡ 5
9	♣ 9	◇ 3	♡ K	♡ Q

South claims the balance,, winning 11 tricks.

2.

East declarer at three no tr.

Trick	S	W	N	E
1	♣ Q	♣ 6	♣ 2	♣ K
2	♣ 7	♡ 3	♣ 3	♣ A
3	◇ 3	◇ Q	◇ J	◇ 10
4	◇ 9	◇ K	♠ 6	◇ 2

East claims six more diamond tricks from dummy, which with the four tricks already won, complete the contract.

East wins 10 tricks.

3.

North declarer at four spades.

Trick	E	S	W	N
1	♣ K	♣ 7	♣ 5	♣ 2
2	♣ A	♣ 10	♣ 9	♣ 4

North claims the balance, stating that on winning the next trick, he will pull the remaining outstanding trump. North wins 11 tricks.

4.

East declarer at seven spades.

Trick	S	W	N	E
1	♡ J	♡ A	♡ 4	♡ 2
2	♠ 6	♠ J	♠ 3	♠ 5
3	♠ 9	♠ 2	♠ 4	♠ A
4	◇ 3	◇ 9	◇ 2	◇ A
5	◇ 4	◇ Q	◇ 5	◇ J
6	◇ 8	◇ K	◇ 6	♡ 8
7	♣ 9	◇ 10	◇ 7	♣ 4

East claims the balance with solid trumps and the club ace. East wins all 13 tricks.

Comments on next page

COMMENTS ON LESSON NINE HANDS

1-On winning the opening club lead, South is faced with the probability of losing four tricks—two high hearts, one diamond and a club.

The simplest method of attempting to avoid losing a diamond or club trick is for South, after winning the opening club lead, to lead his singleton spade. After West plays a low spade to the trick, a single finesse can be taken against the missing king by playing any of dummy's lower honors. The fault of this line of play is that should the finesse lose (as it will), the defenders will immediately grab their diamond trick, which with two high trumps bound to be lost, automatically beats the hand.

The superior line of play is the trump finesse (figures 58 and 59). If East plays a low spade, South throws the diamond. Beauty of this line of play is that if the finesse loses, in the event of West having the spade king, South has simultaneously gotten rid of a loser. In other words, it's trick for trick. Notice, too, that East is helpless. Had he played low to the second round of spades, South would have thrown a diamond, continued leading spades from the dummy.

2-East does not dare attempt to establish any additional tricks in the spade suit since the heart suit is insecurely stoppered. North could win the first spade, shift to the queen of hearts and trap East's king of hearts. The ace of clubs is cashed before running dummy's diamonds, since East would have no way of returning to his hand to utilize the club ace at a later point.

3-The hand demonstrates the fallacy of bidding six without the required first and second round controls after a pre-emptive opening by partner. The two red kings are worthless duplication.

4-The opening lead presents East with the problem of whether to finesse against the missing king of hearts. East, like any declarer, should count the available tricks. He can see seven spades, four diamonds and two aces. Since these add to 13, the heart finesse would be an unnecessary risk. Note, too, East's overtake of the diamond jack with the queen, since the suit is solid and the play can be made without loss of a trick in the suit. Had dummy not contained the ace of clubs as an entry, this play would have been necessary to use all four diamonds.

Lesson X

PART ONE

Opening Bids of Two in a Suit

PART TWO

Safety Plays

LESSON TEN

PART ONE

OPENING BIDS OF TWO IN A SUIT

Note – The opening bid of 'two in a suit' conventionally signifies an exceedingly strong hand of game or near-game probabilities. It has been used in this fashion almost since the inception of contract bridge. It is safe to say that 99 percent of all bridge players use 'two-bids' in this manner.

Within the past decade, many experts, in the United States and elsewhere, use the opening bid of 'two in a suit' pre-emptively to show a weak hand in a mild attempt to shut out the opponents. This is because they will hold the weak hand far, far more often than the powerhouse type of 'two-bid' which seldom appears.

The reader may wonder how, when the same opening bid can have two separate and distinctly opposite meanings, the partner of the 'two-bidder' knows whether the bid is very strong or very weak. The understanding as to the meaning and use of a bid is resolved by a partnership before starting to bid and play. Thus there should be no future misunderstanding.

However, in the absence of any agreement between partners on this subject, it should be assumed that any opening bid of two of a suit is the conventional strong, forcing-to-game type type to be described in this lesson. The weak type will be discussed in Lesson XVI dealing with Expert Tactics.

Infrequently, you will be fortunate enough to pick up a hand so powerful that you know it will produce a game virtually by itself, with very little or no aid from partner's hand.

In order to tell partner that your hand is so powerful that a game contract must be reached, hands of this sort are opened with bids of "two of a suit." Thereafter, neither partner may pass until a game contract has been reached, or in a minority of cases, an intervening bid by an opponent has been doubled for penalty.

The student may inquire, "Well, if the opener's hand is that strong, why didn't he bid game as his opening bid, as opening with four hearts, or five clubs, or whatever his suit might be?"

There are several reasons why we prefer the two opening to the higher bid.

First, an opening bid of four or five in a suit is pre-emptive and shows a weak hand with a long suit. Here we have a strong hand plus good suits.

Secondly, the opening bidder may wish to show two or more suits in order to find the best fit before the final contract is determined.

Third, the opening bidder may wish to find out if his partner has a playable suit of his own.

Fourth, the opening bidder can ascertain whether the combined hands are strong enough to make a slam.

You will notice that in the opening paragraph I stated that the opening two bid requires little or nothing from partner to make a game.

While in a few cases the opening two bidder may be able to win enough tricks for game single-handedly, in most cases he will be forced to count on his partner for a little help. That 'little something' could be a taking trick in the form of a high card or cards, or perhaps some ruffing value, or perhaps an establishable suit.

To be forcing to game, the two bid must be of a suit and must be the *first* bid at the table by any player. Taking the first qualification, an opening bid of two no trump is *not* forcing to game. It does show an extremely powerful hand of 22 to 24 high card points.

If the opening bid at the table was two of a suit, as two clubs, or two diamonds, or two hearts, or two spades, it would be a forcing two-bid. The bidding must continue to game.

Next, the fact that the bidding opens with two hearts, let us say, does not confine the final contract to that suit. The ultimate contract can be any other suit or no trump, depending upon the future information to be gleaned from the bidding.

On the other hand, if a player opened with one spade and his partner or an opponent bid two hearts, it would not be a forcing two bid, since the two heart bid was not the first bid at the table. It had been preceded by a one spade bid.

The partner of the opening two bidder may have a hand as bleak as the Sahara on a storm swept Sunday afternoon, but he still *must* respond, and keep on rebidding until at least a game contract has been reached. All responder need do is answer correctly, keeping the bidding going until at least game is reached.

CASE A

North, Opener	East	South, You	West
2 hearts	pass	2 no trump *	pass
3 hearts	pass	*You cannot pass!*	

"Now," you may say, **"if my partner felt we could make a game, why didn't he rebid with 'four hearts' instead of making it tough for me. I didn't have anything and he had everything."**

The answer to that is that after your partner opened the bidding with two of a suit, he didn't have to jump again as by bidding four hearts on the next round. He can 'take it easy' by showing his hand's features slowly. But more important, by keeping the bidding at low level, he gives you a chance to do a number of things conveniently.

You may have support for his now rebid suit, or a suit of your own to show, or perhaps prefer no trump. By rebidding three hearts, he gave you a chance to picture your hand while the bidding level remained under game.

The only time responder may pass following an opening two bid by partner is when an opponent overcalls the opening two bid.

CASE B

North, Opener	East	South, You	West
2 hearts	3 clubs	?	

East's three club bid will now come around to your partner so that the bidding will not die, and he will have another chance to bid. It is no longer necessary for you to respond at this point to keep the bidding alive. East has done that for you. If you do bid at this point when it is not necessary, you are making a 'free' response and that, as we already know, shows strength. If you double the three club overcall, you are telling your partner that you can defeat that contract to a greater value than the alternative game your partner promised with his opening two bid.

Footnote

* *A response of two no trump to an opening two bid shows a weak hand.*

REQUIREMENTS FOR OPENING TWO BIDS

1- At least a five card suit, preferably with solidity.

2- The hand should conform to the following point table.

If the suit is a major –

LENGTH OF SUITS	MINIMUM POINTS REQUIRED
Five cards	24
Six cards or longer	23

If the suit is a minor, and is unfit for no trump play, due to unbalanced distribution, voids or worthless singleton –

LENGTH OF SUITS	MINIMUM POINTS REQUIRED
Five cards	27
Six cards or longer	26

If the two bidder's suit is a minor, but all unbid short suits are positively stopped, so that, if partner's hand is trickless, nine or more tricks can be taken in no trump, two bid requirements are identical with major suits at the head of this page.

With 4-4-4-1 distribution, a minimum of 26 points are required.

HOW TO COUNT POINTS FOR A TWO BID

Count points exactly the same as for an opening bid of one in a suit.

Note – When holding a two-suiter and considering opening the bidding with two of a suit, use as your minimum requirements the points required for the longer suit. Thus, if your hand contained two suits, a six card major and a five card minor, you would use the requirements for the six card major, namely, 23 points.

Let's inspect some hands and, by checking their contents, determine whether they qualify as opening two bids.

	HC	DIS	TOTAL	OPENING BID
(a)				
♠ AKJ109	8			
♡ AQJ	7			
◇ KQ	5	1		
♣ A82	4		25	Two spades
(b)				
♠ AKQ108	9			
♡ AKQJ76	10			
◇ 8		2		
♣ 4		2	23	Two hearts
(c)				
♠ AK76	7			
♡ AQ5	6			
◇ KQ4	5			
♣ AK2	7		25	Three no trump
(d)				
♠ AQ	6	1		
♡ A87	4			
◇ AKQJ98	10			
♣ A10	4	1	26	Two diamonds
(e)				
♠ A	4	2		
♡ 63		1		
◇ KQJ1094	6			
♣ AKJ5	8		21	One diamond
(f)				
♠ AKQJ1098765	10			
♡ 3		2		
◇ 2		2		
♣ 7		2	16	Four spades
(g)				
♠ AKJ8	8			
♡ 4		2		
◇ AK63	7			
♣ AK72	7		24	One diamond

BIDDING COMMENTS

(a) A hand containing a five card major suit requires a minimum of 24 points to qualify as an opening two bid.

(b) A distributional two suiter. The longer suit is first bid, the shorter five card spade suit is then bid and rebid. Point requirements for an opening two bid are computed for the longer suit, hearts. The requirement for a six card suit is a minimum of 23 points.

(c) A perfect example of a three no trump opening bid. Two bids are avoided with hands containing only four card suits.

(d) The hand, with its minor suit and 26 points, can produce nine tricks if played in no trump. Point requirements, therefore, are based on the probability of no trump rather than minor suit play.

(e) This hand is far from an opening two bid. Realize that if partner cannot take a trick, how far away from game the hand will be!

(f) A pre-emptive opening.

(g) Only with 26 or more points and 4-4-4-1 distribution can a four card suit be opened with a two bid. Since this hand has but 24 points, it is opened with one diamond.

RESPONSES TO TWO BIDS

So your partner has opened the bidding with two of a suit. What should you do now?

You learned on earlier pages of this lesson that you, as responder, must bid and keep on bidding until a game contract has been reached, or an overcall by the opponents has been doubled.

Now your problem, as responder, is to find the right bid to best describe your hand.

There are two kinds of responses to two bids—positive and negative. A positive response shows strength, a negative response indicates weakness.

There are only two possible negative responses. The first is the response of two no trump where the opponents do not bid; the second is the pass where the opponents overcall and you do not have enough strength for a free bid or penalty double.

Any other bid shows strength!

Where the responder makes a positive response to an opening two-bid, the hand *must* contain at least one king and better still, if possible, an ace. Where the responder's hand contains five or six points in high cards, made up exclusively of queens and jacks, it is better to respond with 'two no trump'. Usually, after opening with a forcing-to-game two-bid, the opener's suit is sufficiently solid to become the final trump suit. Hence, since the bidding is already committed to game, the opener is now concerned with (a), the best final contract; (b), whether slam is makeable. For the latter, he needs 'fast' tricks—high cards that can win tricks immediately as aces and kings. He is not interested in queens and jacks at this point, no matter how useful they may be in subsequent play.

Hence the reason for requiring at least one king when making a positive response to an opening two-bid.

TWO BIDS WITH PART SCORES

When your side has a part score towards game, and your partner opens with a two-bid, you must respond at least once even if you are 'busted' and the two-bid, when completed, would have produced your game when combined with the part score.

Let us suppose your side has a part score of 40 points.

Your partner is the dealer, and the bidding goes—

CASE C

Partner, South	West	North, You	East
2 hearts	pass	2 no trump	pass
3 hearts	pass	*You can pass*	

RULE—The responder, with a weak hand, need respond only once when the two bid, combined with the part score, will produce a game.

You may ask, "**Why should I have to bid at all when I'm broke and the 60 points for making two hearts, plus our part score of 40, would complete our game?**"

There are several reasons for responder bidding at least once. First, the opening bidder may have a two suiter, and the combined hands may play better in the second suit. Give your partner a chance to show his entire hand.

Next, the opening bidder's hand may be big enough to make a slam, and it is necessary for him to locate specific cards in your hand.

Remember these words and remember them well – there is no such thing as an opening two bid to complete a part score – a two bid is a two bid, hot or cold, part score or no part score.

In the following bidding examples, we will presume that your partner opened the bidding with two hearts, your side has no part score and the opponent to your right passed.

It is now your bid.

THE NEGATIVE RESPONSE OF TWO NO TRUMP

The negative response of two no trump in answer to an opening bid of two of a suit is intended to show a weak hand. The hand may vary from a complete bust to one containing six high card points.

When the hand does contain six high card points, and a two no trump response is in order, one of two situations will exist –

1 - Responder lacks trump support for opener's suit.

2 - No biddable suit can be shown at the two level. In other words, in order to show his own suit, responder has to increase the bidding level to the three zone.

The response of two no trump is *artificial!* It is not intended to indicate the slightest desire to play the hand in no trump, only that the hand contains from zero to six high card points.

The following hands are examples of two no trump responses to two heart opening bids.

(h)	(i)	(j)
♠ Q765	♠ A32	♠ Q87654
♡ J85	♡ 65	♡ J
◇ 743	◇ Q743	◇ Q65
♣ 1042	♣ 10632	♣ 1062

(k)	(l)
♠ QJ987654	♠ 2
♡ 2	♡ 104
◇ J8	◇ J87654
♣ 43	♣ 9876

SUIT BIDDABILITY FOR RESPONDER

What is a biddable suit so far as responding to two-bids is concerned?

ANSWER - Equal or better than requirements for opening bids.

A four card suit should contain at least three high card

points as the king or queen-jack combination. This is identical to requirements for opening the bidding. A five card suit, in responding to opening two-bids, should preferably contain at least the queen of the bid suit whereas the opening bidder could open *any* five card suit (Pages 38-39). Any six card or longer suit can be shown by the responder, providing the hand contains the required strength for the bid.

Naturally, there will be hands, particularly those with five card and longer suits, where the hand's high card strength will be elsewhere than in the bid suit. It isn't always possible to have most of one's strength in the bid suit. But when the suit is only four cards in length, then it *must* contain high cards.

The reason is that the opening two-bidder wants to locate partner's strength immediately. He wants to find out how much high card strength is held by the partner, which suits are held, and the location of high card strength. These suits must have quality. The two-bidder is not searching for a four card fit, as is often the case in one over one bidding.

In cases where the responder holds eight points or more with only a four card suit that lacks the required three or more high card points and trump support for opener's suit is also lacking, an immediate response of *three* no trump will describe the hand.

POSITIVE RESPONSES

Positive responses are based on hands which have strength. Hands containing seven points can make positive responses *only* if containing excellent trump support for partner's suit, or holding a suit which can be shown at the two level.

THE SINGLE RAISE

CASE D

Partner	You, Responder	INDICATES
2 hearts	3 hearts	Seven or more points with trump support.

Examples of single raises to opening two bids –

(m)	(n)	(o)
♠ J82	♠ A2	♠ 3
♡ A54	♡ Q876	♡ 8765
◊ 86432	◊ J762	◊ A432
♣ Q9	♣ Q87	♣ 10432

SHOWING A BIDDABLE SUIT AT THE TWO LEVEL

CASE E

Partner	You, Responder	INDICATES
2 hearts	2 spades	Seven or more points.

(p)	(q)	(r)
♠ A 10 8 7 6	♠ K Q 10 5	♠ K Q 4 3 2
♡ Q 5	♡ 9 8 2	♡ 4 3 2
◊ 7 6 2	◊ Q 7 6	◊ 8 7 6 5
♣ 10 9 3	♣ 8 5 4	♣ 2

Had the spade suits in (p), (q) and (r) been clubs or diamonds, the suits could not have been shown at the two level. It would have required a bid of three. Accordingly, a response of two no trump would have been in order with the suits possibly being shown on a later round of bidding.

THE JUMP RAISE TO GAME

Sometimes, after your partner opens with a two bid, you will hold a lot of your partner's trumps, but outside of that, a weak hand. A jump raise from two to four by responder describes the hand perfectly.

CASE F

Partner	You, Responder	INDICATES
2 hearts	4 hearts	Less then seven points, four trumps headed by

the queen or any five trumps, denies holding a king or an ace in the entire hand, also denies having a singleton or void of any suit. In other words, the jump raise shows a 'trump bust.'

(s)	(t)	(u)
♠ 6 5	♠ 7 6 5	♠ 6 5
♡ Q 7 5 4	♡ 9 7 5 4 3	♡ Q 10 6 5 4 3
◊ 7 4 3 2	◊ 8 7 2	◊ J 7 6
♣ 10 8 6	♣ 6 5	♣ 8 7

This bid is excellent in the hands of a trained partnership; with an inexperienced partner it is usually better to first make the negative response of two no trump, later support partner's suit.

The latter sequence of bidding cannot be misunderstood.

WITH EIGHT OR MORE POINTS

With eight or more points, you can not only make all of the previously described responses possible with from zero to seven points but, in addition, you can make responses that may take the bidding to the three level.

Holding eight or more points, a two no trump response or a jump trump raise (from two to four) is absolutely out of the question. You have available a variety of possible strength showing responses. Your task will be to fit the right response to the hand.

SHOWING BIDDABLE SUITS AT THE TWO OR THREE LEVEL

After partner's two bid, it may be necessary for responder to bid three in order to show his suit. For example, if the opening bid was two hearts, responder would be forced to bid three clubs in order to show that suit.

On the other hand, if responder's suit were spades, he could have bid two spades over the opening two heart bid.

With seven points, you are limited to suits that can be shown at the two level, with eight or more points, you can show suits at either the two or three level, so long as they are biddable suits.

What I am trying to impress on you is that with eight or more points, you can show any biddable suit at the three level. *But*—if you can show your biddable suit at the two level, don't bother to bid three. It doesn't show any more strength and only wastes a round of bidding.

CASE G

Partner	You, Responder
2 hearts	3 spades

The bidding to the left is *wrong!* You could (and should) have bid two spades. Responder doesn't have to jump after partner opened with a two bid. Remember that!

	(v)	(w)	(x)	(y)	(z)
♠	KQ32	J2	63	J76	AKJ1087
♡	654	65	Q1096	853	Q72
♢	K108	AQ876	KJ	AK32	Q6
♣	J72	7643	KJ1086	Q43	K5

With the above hands, in response to an opening two heart bid, respond—(v) two spades; (w) three diamonds; (x) three clubs; (y) three diamonds; (z) two spades.

In hand (x), there is a choice of responses. Responder can either show his own suit, clubs, or immediately raise his partner to three hearts. The hand contains 10 high card points, and counting two distributional points in support of partner's heart suit, one for each doubleton, totals 12 points. This total, plus partner's known to 23 to 24 points and the heart fit, make slam a certainty. By first bidding clubs, later supporting hearts vigorously, responder can paint an accurate picture of his hand.

RESPONDING WITH THREE NO TRUMP

All of the preceding suit responses stressed the point that to bid a suit, it must be biddable.

What happens to hands with eight or more points when responder 's suit isn't biddable, and he also lacks trump support for partner's suit?

ANSWER – In these situations, with a balanced or semi-balanced hand containing no singletons or voids and scattered high card strength, the responder bids three no trump.

CASE H

A typical hand would be– (a)	Partner	You, Responder
♠ QJ7	2 hearts	3 no trump
♡ 652		
◊ 10765		
♣ AJ7		

If the suit is anywhere near biddable, I prefer bidding the suit in preference to the three no trump response. Suit showing has several advantages over the three no trump response. For one thing, it makes it easier for opener to locate your suit and strength. For another, it makes opener's rebid easier and cheaper. Try rebidding over a three no trump response and see how awkward it is!

But – do not confuse a three no trump response with a two no trump response. The former shows eight to 10 points; the latter, from zero to seven.

A response of three no trump shows strength; a response of two no trump can show from a complete blank to seven points.

PENALTY DOUBLES AFTER OPENING TWO BIDS

The first thing for you to remember is that after you or your partner have opened the bidding with two of a suit, *any* double by either partner of an adverse bid is for penalty!

CASE I

You, South	West	North, Partner	East
2 hearts	2 spades	double	

CASE J

You, South	West	North, Partner	East
2 hearts	2 spades	pass	pass
double			

Either partner, the responder in Case I or the opening bidder in Case J can double for penalty. In Case I North says he prefers to penalize the opponents to any other result his side might make. In Case J, South says the same thing.

Some of you may now be saying, **"How could North pass in Case J? Didn't he have to keep the bidding open?"**

The moment West entered the bidding, South (the opener) automatically was presented with another chance to bid. Any response by North at this point is voluntary, not forced, and shows strength.

The opponents will seldom bid after an opening two bid. That is because the two bid announces possession of most of the high cards in the deck. There is little left for the other side.

(b)

♠ A K Q 10 8 7
♡ A K Q J 9
◊ 4
♣ 3

When, however, the two bidder's hand is distributional, as shown to the left, it is quite possible that the opponents may enter the bidding. Since you have major suit strength, they may very well have the minors.

REQUIREMENTS FOR FREE RESPONSES

Should your right hand opponent overcall an opening two-bid by your partner, pass with six points or less unless holding one or more trump tricks in the opponent's suit. In which case you should make a penalty double.

A bid of two no trump becomes a free bid, shows a minimum of seven points, plus a stopper in the opponent's suit. A free three no trump response similarly shows a stopper, and a minimum of 10 high card points. In both of these cases, a penalty double will frequently be more lucrative.

Showing a new suit at the two level over the overcall indicates a minimum of six high card points; at the three level, at least nine high card points. It is preferable to have at least a partial fit with opener's suit or that responder's suit be of at least five cards with some solidity.

If showing your suit forces you to the four level as—

CASE K

South, Opener	West	North, You	East
Two spades	Three hearts	Four clubs	

You should have 10 or more points. The moment you enter the four level, your side can no longer play three no trump, which might have been an easier contract. Further, unless you have a good fit with partner's suit, a penalty double may be the better choice.

These point count requirements are approximate, only! What I have tried to convey is that you do not have to bid over an overcall when you're weak; that when you do, you show a little extra; and that with a good supporting fit for partner's suit, you shade these high card requirements a trifle; with a misfit, you should have a little more to make a free response.

TWO BIDS WITH 4-4-4-1 DISTRIBUTION

Good bridge players avoid opening two bids on hands containing no suit longer than four cards. Hands containing 25 to 27 or more points, balanced distribution, and stoppers in all four suits are opened with bids of three or more no trump.

(c)

♠ A K J 8
♡ 2
◇ A K Q 10
♣ A K Q J

The only times that opening two bids are made with four card suits are with 4-4-4-1 patterns. The unbalanced distribution makes the hand unsuited for no trump.

The hand directly above would be opened with a two diamond bid. It contains a total of 29 points. It is just too strong to open with a one bid.

Why do bridge players have this reluctance to open four carders with two bids? Simply that they expect to be forced (by the opponents) to trump the 'off' suit. With only four trumps, the trump suit may not be long enough to stand this forced shortening (which bridge players term the 'dink').

(d)

♠ A K J 8
♡ K 2
◊ A K J 10
♣ A K 3

In the hand to the left, we have 27 points.

Should it be opened with a two bid?

No!

The hand should be opened with a bid of three no trump.

REBIDDING AFTER FIRST RESPONDING 'TWO NO TRUMP'

Let's suppose the bidding has been—

CASE L

Partner, South	West	You, North	East
Two hearts	pass	Two no trump	pass
Three hearts	pass	?	

What do you do now?

Well, one thing you know—you've got to do something! The only excuse for passing is that your side has a part score and game has been reached.

The first thing for you to remember is that with your two no trump response, you've already told your partner that you lacked sufficient strength, or support, or a suit, for a positive response.

So any rebid you now make, even showing a suit of your own, or a rebid of no trump, or perhaps a belated raise of partner's suit, can show primarily one thing—distribution! You've already denied high cards with the two no trump response.

One thing you should be careful about—if your suit is lower ranking than the suit partner opened as a two bid, and that will be the case if partner's suit is a major and your suit is a minor, don't bother to show a suit at the four level unless you'd like to eventually play the hand in that suit. It's probably better to rebid with three no trump.

(e)	(f)	(g)
♠ Q 8 7 6 4	♠ J 2	♠ Q 8
♡ 2	♡ 10 8 7	♡ 6 2
◊ 10 8 6 2	◊ 6 5 4 3	◊ J 9 5 4 2
♣ 5 4 3	♣ 10 7 3 2	♣ 9 8 7 6

(h)	(i)
♠ 2	♠ K
♡ 4	♡ 108765
◇ QJ1098765	◇ J542
♣ J54	♣ 732

With the bidding in Case L on the preceding page, your rebid with each example hand should be: (e) three spades; (f) four hearts; (g) three no trump; (h) four diamonds. If partner bids four hearts, rebid with five diamonds; (i) five hearts, not four. Having first denied high card strength, you should now indicate the powerful support and distribution.

HINTS IN GENERAL

1-Responder, at his first response, should not jump in a new suit, no matter how strong his suit may be. Extra strength or suit solidity can be shown on later rounds of bidding. The early rounds of bidding are conserved for the maximum exchange of information.

2-The responder, in almost all cases, should try to avoid bidding four no trump, or initiating the slam try. These bids, if made, should generally come from the opening two bidder.

3-Holding a two or three suiter in responding to a two bid, suits are shown in the same order as to an opening bid of one of a suit.

4-A response of two no trump does not necessarily show no trump distribution, or a willingness or desire to play the hand in no trump. It is just an artificial bid designed to show a weak hand.

5-The responder who has first bid two no trump, should as his rebid, show a biddable suit of five or more cards if it can be done conveniently.

6-If the two bidder bids two or more suits, the responder should attempt to give a preference exactly as though the bidding had been opened with one of a suit.

PART TWO

SAFETY PLAYS

A suit of 13 cards frequently falls into certain recurring patterns. The manner in which they form is known as *distribution;* the number of times they will combine in various patterns, usually described in percentages (page 109) is termed *probabilities*.

Plays protecting the declarer against uneven distribution of the missing cards of any suit, held by the defenders, are known as 'Safety Plays.' The term is self-explanatory. Safety plays usually are employed to avoid losing one or more tricks to the following combinations of cards, if possible—

1 - Missing singleton honors, particularly queens;
2 - Four cards headed by the jack;
3 - Four cards " " " jack-10.
4 - Four cards " " " queen-10.
5 - Three cards that include the king-10.
6 - Missing king-jack combinations;
7 - Missing queen-jack combinations;
8 - Four trumps held by a defender.

Safety plays fall into two general categories.

Type A - To avoid losing any tricks in a suit, if possible.

Type B - To deliberately lose one trick, perhaps unnecessarily, as insurance against losing more than one trick in that suit.

The simplest safety play revolves about a missing queen. In *figure 153*, the contract is five diamonds which is the 'key' suit in which the safety play is to be made.

West	North / South	East
	♠ A752 ♡ 6 ◊ 1092 ♣ KQ1087	
♠ KQ1096 ♡ J10972 ◊ Q ♣ 93	N W E S	♠ 83 ♡ KQ54 ◊ 7643 ♣ J54
	♠ J4 ♡ A83 ◊ AKJ85 ♣ A62	

Figure 153

West opens the king of spades which is won by dummy's ace. The key card, at this point, is the missing queen of trump (diamonds). Before leading a low diamond from the dummy and finessing, South should lay down either the ace or king of diamonds. The suit might break four - one and that 'one' could be the singleton queen. As a matter of fact, in the preceding hand, it is and can be captured by the simple expedient of first playing a high card before finessing.

	A 10 8 5	
	N	
?	W E	?
	S	
	K J 9 7	

Figure 154

Occasionally, the key suit, with the queen missing, may resemble *figure 154.*

In other words, you can finesse for the queen in either direction. Towards the ace ten or to the king jack. It is a case of button, button, who's got the button. But whichever way you decide, if the queen does not appear on the first card played by an adversary and the bidding has not indicated its location, it is generally best to play a high honor (ace or king) and finesse the next round.

A word of caution: If the opening lead places you in dummy and due to a scarcity of entry cards, you can never return and the ace king of the key suit are in your hand—*the finesse must be taken then and there*!

The next safety play to be studied protects the player against one opponent holding four cards headed by the jack when originally the opponents held five cards in their combined holdings and declarer's side had eight.

	♠ J 8 6 4 ♡ J 7 ◇ Q 5 2 ♣ 10 9 6 3	
♠ K 10 9 ♡ 9 6 5 4 2 ◇ 7 ♣ K J 8 4	N W E S	♠ Q 7 3 2 ♡ Q 10 8 ◇ J 9 8 3 ♣ Q 7
	♠ A 5 ♡ A K 3 ◇ A K 10 6 4 ♣ A 5 2	

Figure 155

South is the declarer at three no trump. West opens the four of hearts, the fourth highest. Dummy 'hops in' with the jack which is covered consecutively by east's queen and declarer's king. The reason for dummy's play of the jack (which has no bearing on this safety play) should be obvious. If West had led away from the heart queen, dummy's jack would have won the opening lead, insuring three heart tricks for north and south.

Returning to safety plays, South maps his plan of play on the hand, counting that he can definitely win one spade trick, two hearts and one club, totalling four. Needing nine to fufill the contract, he requires all five diamond tricks and must guard against the loss of *even one trick in that suit!*

Now South might surmise that East originally held four diamonds headed by the jack, but for South to lead a small diamond to dummy's queen, and on returning a low diamond from dummy, 'stick in' the 10 after East's play of the eight would be the wildest sort of guess. It would be based purely on a hunch that East originally held four diamonds including the jack. Normally, five outstanding cards of a suit will split three – two. How, then, can declarer assure himself that East originally held four diamonds *without guessing?*

THE ANSWER

Why, by first leading the king or ace of diamonds from his hand on which everybody will follow suit. Next, a low diamond is led from the South hand and won with dummy's queen on which *West shows out!* It stands to reason that if West didn't have a second diamond, East is definitely marked with the remaining outstanding cards of that suit so on the third round of diamonds, with the lead coming from dummy, the proven finesse against the jack will be taken.

Should West originally have held four cards including the jack, no method on earth could have prevented him from winning a trick. *So this safety play is efficacious only if the player to the right of the double honor combination* holds the jack four-long. Summarized, the treatment is for the hand containing the double honor (of aces, kings and queens) and in this case, it is the ace king which are together, to lead one of them. Then a low card is led from the hand which just played one of the double honors to the hand holding the single honor *(in figure 155, from South to North)* and if West in this case shows out, the declarer still retains a higher honor over East's guarded jack for the subsequent finesse against the latter card.

	North	
	♠ A94 ♡ J5 ◊ KQ1085 ♣ K72	
West ♠ J762 ♡ AK8 ◊ 964 ♣ 854	N W E S	East ♠ void ♡ 1097432 ◊ A73 ♣ 10963
	♠ KQ10853 ♡ Q6 ◊ J2 ♣ AQJ	

Figure 156

In *figure 156*, the contract is four spades. South can see at a glance that he must lose two hearts and one diamond. To make the contract, he cannot afford the loss of a single trump trick. *The vital difference between this hand and the preceding example is that here there are but four cards missing in the suit as against five in the predecessor.*

Do you see what that means? In *figure 155*, even if the five diamonds held by the opponents were split four–one, each opponent would follow to the first round and the division would only become apparent on the second round, when one opponent would fail to follow suit.

Here, if the suit splits four–zero, the show-out will be apparent at once. The treatment is exceedingly simple. Play a high honor from the hand containing two high honors, so that if one opponent shows out, you still retain a high honor in either hand and can finesse in either direction. In *figure 156*, south would lead the king of spades before releasing dummy's ace.

	North	
	♠ A94 ♡ J5 ◊ KQ1085 ♣ K72	
West ♠ void ♡ 1097432 ◊ A73 ♣ 10963	N W E S	East ♠ J1062 ♡ AK8 ◊ 964 ♣ 854
	♠ KQ8753 ♡ Q6 ◊ J2 ♣ AQJ	

Figure 157

The contract in *figure 157* is four spades by South. Recognize the above hand? Why, it's *figure 156* with the East and West hands transposed. But notice one vital difference. The missing spades include the jack and ten. Try leading a high honor first from the double combination and see if you can avoid losing a trick in the suit. It can't be done. But if you lead low to dummy's ace, West will show out. You will now retain the KQ8 over East's J106 and be able to finesse twice through him. In other words, if it might be necessary to finesse against the J10, it is equally necessary to retain two higher cards in one hand for that eventuality.

So here is a case where we retain the double honor combination if two honors (jack and ten) are missing. Where only the jack is missing with a total of four cards held by the opponents, we would use the method described in *figure 156.*

Be sure before leaving figure 157 that you understand the vital difference between figures 156 and 157. Also if West had held four cards headed by the jack ten, he cannot be prevented from winning a trick!

	♠ 762	
	♡ A963	
	◊ Q954	
	♣ AJ	
♠ AK4	N	♠ Q10983
♡ Q1072	W E	♡ void
◊ J106		◊ 873
♣ Q102	S	♣ 87654
	♠ J5	
	♡ KJ854	
	◊ AK2	
	♣ K93	

Figure 158

In *figure 158,* the contract is four hearts. South has lost the first two spade tricks. In order to make the contract, he can afford to lose one trump trick *but not two.* He must guard against all four missing hearts being in one hand. The solution—when you hold the nine spot in the hand not containing the jack, the hand containing the jack should play its higher honor. (Note, if the eight were opposite the jack and the nine with the jack, it would be equivalent to the nine being opposite the jack, etc.)

In this case, South will lead the king of hearts. East will show out. West can win but one trick with the queen, ten, seven since they are located and dummy retains A96 over those cards. Had West shown out on the first round, a low heart is led to the ace and the third rounded from dummy through the Q10 towards declarer's guarded jack, again holding losers to one. If both defenders follow on the first round, the ace is played to the second and if the suit splits, no tricks will be lost.

	♠ 7632 ♡ A96 ◇ Q954 ♣ AJ	
♠ AK4 ♡ Q1072 ◇ J106 ♣ Q102	N W E S	♠ Q1098 ♡ 3 ◇ 873 ♣ 87654
	♠ J5 ♡ KJ854 ◇ AK2 ♣ K93	

Figure 159

South is the declarer at four hearts in *figure 159*. Again the astute observer will notice that *figure 159* is virtually identical with *figure 158*, with one vital difference. Here there are five hearts missing; in *figure 158*, there were but four. In the latter, all the declarer had to do was to lay down the high heart honor from the hand containing the jack and if all four were in one hand, the division was at once apparent.

Here again the technique of the high honor being led from the hand containing the jack is again followed, but this time if the suit is to split four—one, we will have no news of it the first round. After the high honor is led (the king in this case), a low card is led toward the other hand and if West plays low, dummy will play the nine.

Do you see what this does? Had West originally held four cards with a queen and 10, the nine must win tricks since East has no additional cards of the suit. Thus, dummy's ace is still available to catch one of West's high honors (Q-10). The greatest number of tricks declarer can now lose is one. Secondly, suppose East captures the nine with either the 10 or queen. Eight cards have now been played on the first two rounds of the suit, the opponents hold but one more which must be captured by dummy's ace. Maximum number of tricks that can be lost with a three—two split, one.

In the event that East originally started with four cards headed by the Q-10 when declarer leads low to dummy's ace-nine, West will show out. The ace will win the second round and the nine led through East's Q-10 towards declarer's jack, exactly as in *figure 158*.

Some reader will probably remark at this point that if East had held a doubleton queen, the ordinary play of a low heart to dummy's ace and back to the king-jack would have precluded the loss of any tricks in the suit. True! Granted! But if West had a doubleton queen, you avoid losing a trick when you might have finessed needlessly. And using this play, you will never lose more than one trick in the suit when oft-times, others are losing two and the play is expressly designed to guarantee against the loss of two tricks in the suit on the premise that you can afford to lose one and still make your contract. Obviously, if you cannot afford the loss of even one trick in the suit, you cannot afford this safety play.

The reason for the last statement is that 3-2 division happens 68% of the time as against 28% for 4-1. With the 3-2 split, mathematically the queen will more often be in the hand having three cards. Thus, the finesse should be taken with five cards missing if no safety play is used. This play guards against 4 - 1 splits.

One of the most useful safety plays is illustrated in *figures 160 through 164*. In these and similar cases, the declarer will be missing the king and jack and frequently, the 10 as well, in a suit in which a total of eight cards are held between the declarer's hand and the dummy.

♠ 8652
N
♠ 1097 W   E ♠ KJ
S
♠ AQ43

Figure 160

A typical situation is shown in *figure 160*. The normal line of play, utilizing a single finesse, is to lead the deuce from the north hand. After East's jack, South finesses against the missing king by playing the queen. When the finesse succeeds, the ace is cashed. West's 10 wins the third round.

The important thing for the student to observe is that everything, in *figure 160*, was favorable for the declarer. The missing five spades split three-two and the finesse against the king succeeded. Even so, declarer lost a trick in the suit—to the 10.

Let's utilize a new safety play. In the preceding example, South will first play the ace of spades from his hand, then enter the dummy, North, with a re-entry in some other suit (which is

♠ 865
N
♠ 109 W E ♠ K
S
♠ Q43
Figure 161

not shown). At this point, the remaining cards of the suit are shown in *figure 161*. The five is led from the dummy and East wins with the king as South plays the trey. Later, South's queen catches West's 10. The tricks lost (by declarer) are the same—one—as with *figure 160*, the difference being that in *figure 160*, the 10 won the defender's sole trick; in *161*, it was the king.

Let's go one step further and change the East-West cards to resemble *figure 162*. The normal single finesse of leading the deuce from the north hand and playing the queen over any low card played by East would result in North-South losing one trick to East's guarded king; the safety play of first playing the ace, then entering the north hand to lead a low card through East's king-jack towards South's queen will also find the defenders winning only one trick.

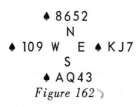

♠ 8652
N
♠ 109 W E ♠ KJ7
S
♠ AQ43
Figure 162

Since in each of these cases, taking the finesse or making the safety play of first releasing the ace, showed that only one trick would be lost either way, the reader may wonder what advantages can be gained by the safety play.

The answer lies in the fact that in *figures 160* through *162*, the finesse against the missing king was *successful*. Now let's see, in *figure 163*, what would have happened had the king been 'wrong.' We're simply going to transpose the East-West hands shown in *figure 160*.

♠ 8652
N
♠ KJ W E ♠ 1097
S
♠ AQ43
Figure 163

The normal line of play, utilizing the single finesse, would be for the declarer to lead the deuce from dummy. After East's low card, South will take the single finesse against the missing king by playing the queen. West wins with the king. Later, South's ace will 'drop' East's nine-spot but South must lose a second trick in the suit to East's 10. Total tricks lost by North-South, two!

But let's suppose that the declarer, in *figure 163,* had first played the ace of spades. Naturally, he saw West drop the jack. Common sense would tell him that if the jack was the lowest card West could play, there were two possibilities. The first is that if West started with two cards and the jack was the lower, the only possible higher card for West to hold is *the king* and that card, when the second round of the suit is led, is alone and will 'drop' without the need of the expenditure of the queen. The latter card can subsequently capture East's 10 and declarer has lost only one trick in the suit instead of two tricks as in *figure 160.*

The second inference that might be drawn from West's play of the jack (in *figure 163)* on South's ace is that the jack was not only West's lowest card but was his only card, in other words, West started with a singleton jack. Even here, the safety play will not lose for the declarer since declarer, after placing the lead in dummy, can lead the second round of the suit from that hand through East's king-10-nine and South's queen will win a second trick.

♠ 8652
N
♠ K W E ♠ J1097
S
♠ AQ43

Figure 164

The superiority of the safety play, as compared with the conventional finesse, is graphically demonstrated in *figure 164.* By taking the finesse and playing the queen from his hand after first leading a low card from the dummy, South will take precisely one trick—the ace, as West's singleton king captures the queen. Use of the safety play, viz., first playing the ace, not only protects the declarer against the possibility of West holding the lone king but after the fact is disclosed as in *figure 164,* affords declarer valuable clues as to the location of the remaining missing cards of the suit.

There are certain possible disadvantages to the use of this safety play, viz., first playing the ace, then leading towards the queen. First, a shrewd defender sitting West (in these cases) could very well drop the jack from a doubleton jack-10 holding to make you believe that he holds the king. Next, once you release the ace of trumps, you lose what is termed "control" of the trump suit. In other words, instead of your side having the highest trump, the ace, and being able to determine which tricks to win or lose when trumps are led, that control passes to the opponents who hold the king.

The principle advantage of the safety play shown in *figures 160* through *164* is that by first playing the ace, the declarer gains some knowledge of the distribution of the missing five cards held by the opponents. The safety play will save the declarer one trick when the king is originally either doubleton or a singleton to the left (in back of) the ace-queen.

The safety play of first playing the ace, then leading towards the queen as protection against singleton and doubleton kings held by the defenders has even greater advantages when the declarer and the dummy hold a total of nine cards of the suit between the partnership.

Let's assume that in *figure 165,* South is the declarer in a six spade contract.

	♠ 843 ♡ KJ108 ♢ A75 ♣ KQ10	
♠ K ♡ 742 ♢ KQ1098 ♣ J643	N W E S	♠ J76 ♡ 963 ♢ J432 ♣ 875
	♠ AQ10952 ♡ AQ5 ♢ 6 ♣ A92	

Figure 165

West opens the king of diamonds, taken by dummy's ace. With the remaining suits 'solid,' declarer's only problem is to avoid losing two trump (spade) tricks. The opponents are known to hold four spades. The conventional line of play would be to lead a low spade from the dummy and after East's six or seven, finesse with the queen. If East has the king and the missing spades divide 2-2, the ace will mop up the remaining cards of that suit and declarer will win all 13 tricks.

But suppose the cards lie as in *figure 165.* The queen will be taken by the lone king. South will trump the subsequent diamond return—then be impaled on the horns of a dilemma as to how the spade suit should be continued. If, as is the case, East holds both remaining spades, a finesse against the jack is required; on the other hand, if the spades were originally 2-2, playing the ace will capture the jack, no matter whether it is with East or West.

Whether South guesses the situation is a matter of conjecture. But there was no need of his jeopardizing the contract by the possibility of guessing 'wrong.' The safety play of first playing the ace of spades would have solved his problems. With the king dropping and obviously singleton, it's a simple matter for declarer to return to the dummy via high heart or club, lead a spade from that hand and take the marked finesse against East's jack. If neither the king or jack appear when the ace is played, declarer enters dummy as before and leads a low spade from dummy towards his hand.

There are three possibilities. First, that East holds both the king and jack of spades. With the lead coming through that holding, East can win only one trick.

Second, West holds both the king and jack, originally held a total of three cards of the suit. With the king, jack and a low card *behind* the ace-queen, the defender could not be prevented from winning two tricks regardless of declarer's line of play.

Third, each defender holds one of the two outstanding honors. In this case, these cards are alone on the second round of spades and will fall together when the suit is led a second time.

Accordingly, the safety play will limit declarer's losers in the suit to one *regardless of how the missing four cards are distributed* with the one exception of the defender sitting behind the ace-queen (West in *figure 165*) having both the king and jack and one or more lower cards where no line of play would curtail declarer's losers.

It should be emphasized that the preceding line of play should be employed *only* when the declarer can afford the loss of one trick to insure a contract. Where the declarer cannot afford the loss of any tricks whatever in the suit, then the safety play *(in figure 165)* cannot be employed since releasing the ace will set up the defenders' king. Let's pretend that in *figure 165*, the contract was seven spades. Having bid the grand slam, declarer can't afford the loss of a single trick. The normal line of play, after winning the opening lead in the dummy, is to lead a low spade from that hand. After East plays a low spade, South will play the queen, hoping that East holds the king.

This line of play will succeed if (a), East has the king and the four missing spades divide 2-2; (b), if East has the king with two low spades with West holding the singleton jack in which case, after the jack falls under the queen, dummy is re-entered via a side suit and a second spade finesse, now marked for success, is taken against East's king.

♠ J874
N
♠ void W E ♠ K102
S
♠ AQ9653

Figure 166

One special but little known safety play is illustrated in *figure 166*. Where 10 cards of a suit are held between declarer's hand and dummy, but the king and 10 are among the three cards held by the defenders, a safety play should be taken to guard against the defender, sitting in front of the ace, holding all three missing cards. Had the suit resembled *figure 167*, and the dummy held two honors, East cannot be prevented from winning a trick. For this safety play to succeed, the declarer and the dummy must hold the ace and the queen and the jack in their combined 10 cards and the hand containing the ace holds *either* the queen or jack but not both. The remaining honor must be in the other partnership hand. Had all three honors, the ace, queen and jack, been in the South hand in *figures 166 and 167*, the correct method of play is to take the necessary number of single finesses against the missing king towards the hand containing the ace, queen and jack.

♠ QJ87
N
♠ void W E ♠ K102
S
♠ A96543

Figure 167

The conventional and incorrect line of play would find the declarer leading the four from the dummy and after East's deuce, playing the queen, hoping that East holds the king and that the missing cards are divided 2-1.

While this line of play will succeed if the missing cards lie as desired, the play provides no protection if all three missing cards are with East as is the case. The reader should see that the moment South has released the queen, East's king-10 insure him a subsequent trick since they sit over dummy's jack.

Correct line of play in *figure 166* is for declarer to lead the jack from the North hand. If East plays a low card, so does South. After the jack wins, the suit is continued with the ace-queen capturing the king-10 without the loss of a trick. Should

East cover the jack with the king, South wins with the ace as West shows out. The marked subsequent finesse against East's 10 follows.

Should East show out when the suit is first led, South will play a low card under dummy's jack and West would win the king. It should be apparent that no play would prevent West from taking a trick with the guarded king behind the ace but that the safety play, as shown, will save the declarer a trick if the defender sitting second-hand has all three missing cards – the king, 10 and a low card.

GUARDING AGAINST FOUR TRUMPS

Probably one of the most fertile fields for safety plays are situations where the declarer must guard against the possibility of one defender holding four trumps. In most of these cases, the declarer can afford to lose one trick but not two. As a general rule, it will be found better to concede that one trick, if necessary, as quickly as possible while both dummy and declarer's hands retain trumps than on a later round when dummy will contain either insufficient trumps or no trumps whatever as protection against an adverse suit.

The following hands are examples of safety plays against bad 'breaks' in the trump suit. Naturally, they are applicable to other suits as well.

	♠ 1052 ♡ AJ5 ◇ 8643 ♣ K103	
♠ J ♡ 8732 ◇ QJ75 ♣ Q852	N W E S	♠ Q976 ♡ 1094 ◇ K109 ♣ J96
	♠ AK843 ♡ KQ6 ◇ A2 ♣ A74	

Figure 168

In *figure 168*, South is the declarer at four spades. The queen of diamonds is opened and taken by the ace. Faced with a certain diamond and club loser, declarer cannot afford to lose more than one spade trick.

South lays down the king of spades, on which West drops the jack. Were the queen-jack doubleton with West, South could now continue with the ace, catching the queen, and avoid the loss of a single spade trick.

But what if the jack were singleton, as is the case? Now the play of the ace would leave East with the queen-nine over dummy's 10 of spades. East would have two sure trump tricks.

But South can take a simple safety measure by, after first playing the king, leading the three of spades towards dummy's 10. East will capture the latter card with the queen but now, South's ace-eight sits over East's nine-seven for the later proved finesse. Only one spade trick will be lost.

While it is true that this safety play will lose a trick had the queen-jack been doubleton with West, the risk of going down were the jack singleton makes it good insurance to give up a possible 30 points in over-tricks to insure the contract.

	♠ 854 ♡ K7 ◊ AQ872 ♣ KJ6	
♠ 7 ♡ Q654 ◊ J653 ♣ 10743	N W E S	♠ QJ63 ♡ J832 ◊ 109 ♣ 952
	♠ AK1092 ♡ A109 ◊ K4 ♣ AQ8	

Figure 169

South, in *figure 169,* is declarer at six spades. Obviously, if the five missing spades divide 3-2, declarer's worries are over.

But let's suppose they divide 4-1 and that the hand with four cards holds both the queen and jack. If West holds these four cards (behind the ace and king), West cannot be prevented from taking two tricks. On the other hand, if East, in front of the ace-king, holds that combination, a safety play will protect the declarer from losing two tricks.

As in most cases where the partnership holds eight cards of a suit minus the queen and jack, the correct line of play is for the declarer to play the ace or king. This protects against a possible singleton queen or jack. After, in this case, each defender plays a low card, dummy can be entered and a low spade led from that hand. East, hoping to conceal his holding, will play his remaining low card. South should play the 10 or nine.

If East started with four spades, the 10 (or nine) must win the trick since West will not have a second spade. On the other hand, if West captures the 10 with the queen or jack, then four of the opponents' five known spades will have been played and it is a simple matter for declarer to capture the defenders' remaining card on regaining the lead.

North:
♠ KJ87
♡ K1083
◇ AJ7
♣ 82

West:
♠ 42
♡ QJ72
◇ 952
♣ Q953

East:
♠ Q10953
♡ void
◇ 1083
♣ J10764

South:
♠ A6
♡ A9654
◇ KQ64
♣ AK

Figure 170

South is in a six heart contract. Frequently, the bidding by the opponents may indicate missing high cards or distribution. Here there is no such clue.

South can afford to lose one trump trick and still make the contract. The correct safety play is to lead a low heart from either hand and if the opponent next to play follows suit, merely cover the card played by the opponent and no more.

Now if the other opponent takes the trick, there will be but two cards outstanding and the ace and king will pick them up. If the other opponent shows out, the card you covered with must win. In *figure 170,* if a low heart is led from South and West plays the seven, North will merely cover with the eight.

North:
♠ 732
♡ J5
◇ 109
♣ AKQ864

West:
♠ QJ1098
♡ K92
◇ KJ86
♣ 3

East:
♠ 64
♡ Q7643
◇ 32
♣ J975

South:
♠ AK5
♡ A108
◇ AQ754
♣ 102

Figure 171

The final contract in *figure 171* is three no trump by South. West makes the normal opening lead of the queen of spades.

Offhand, it would appear that North and South should make at least four no trump if the clubs break. But what if they shouldn't? The best they can count on would be three clubs, two spades, one heart and one diamond, to total seven tricks, two short of the contract.

But five club tricks will still assure the contract. So South will play absolutely safe against the possibility that one opponent had four clubs originally by after winning the opening spade lead, leading a low club and deliberately playing low from the dummy. Now if one opponent originally had four clubs, he has but three remaining and they must fall under the ace, king, queen, insuring five clubs for North-South. Try making the contract if you expect the clubs to divide!

The contract in *figure 172* is six hearts, played by South. West's opening lead of the king of diamonds is trumped in the dummy. The king of hearts is played with East dropping the jack—an ominous indication of the distribution of the adverse trumps. A low trump is led from the dummy and when East discards a club, South *must* play the nine and permit West to win the trick with the 10. Let's see why.

	♠ AKJ876 ♡ K654 ◇ void ♣ AK2	
♠ 2 ♡ 10872 ◇ AKQ987 ♣ 73	N W E S	♠ 10543 ♡ J ◇ 542 ♣ J10986
	♠ Q9 ♡ AQ93 ◇ J1063 ♣ Q54	

Figure 172

If West is permitted to win the second round of trumps with the 10, he's helpless. Should he lead a second round of diamonds, dummy retains a trump, the six-spot, to ruff that lead; any other lead can be won by declarer or dummy with a high card. Either way, West wins one trick—the 10 of hearts.

Let's contrast this play with the alternate (and incorrect) play of the queen or ace of hearts on the second round of that suit. To cash the ace of trumps at this point, then attempt to lead spades would be fatal since dummy would no longer retain a trump, permit West to trump the second round of spades and cash two diamond tricks.

So, realizing his error and seeing the bad trump break, the declarer will abandon leading trumps (after the second round), play the queen of spades, then the nine of spades. A shrewd

West will refuse to trump the second round of spades but instead, discard a club. A third round of spades will be led from dummy. Declarer will feverishly discard a diamond as West throws his remaining club. When the fourth round of spades is led from the dummy, declarer will discard another diamond. This time, West trumps.

I hope you see that South still has one more diamond in his hand since he started with four cards of that suit, trumped the opening lead and discarded two diamonds. Hence, after trumping the fourth round of spades, West will lead a second high diamond. This forces dummy to trump with its last trump, the six-spot. With nothing left but clubs and spades, dummy must lead either suit. Whichever is led, West can trump for the setting trick since declarer was unable to return to his hand to 'pull' West's last trump.

The student should study this hand as an excellent example of defensive play by West since if that player had trumped the second round of spades, instead of discarding both clubs, the contract would have been completed. Try it and see.

A GUESS AVOIDANCE PLAY

A play that is closely allied to safety plays but is primarily a method of avoiding a guess is illustrated in *figure 173*. Where the partnership holds the ace-queen-10-nine between the two hands and wishes to lose no more than one trick in the suit, the usual method of play is to lead the 10 or nine towards the hand *that has the ace*. This is important. Do not lead away from the hand that has the ace, otherwise, you will not be able to capture an adverse king.

```
     Q109
       N
?  W       E  ?
       S
     A32
```

Figure 173

If the opponent playing second-hand plays a low card under the 10, the defender with the ace similarly plays a low card. Obviously, if the second-hand defender holds both king and jack, the 10 will win the trick; if the fourth hand defender holds both king and jack, the declarer will lose two tricks in the suit. Thus far, this play has neither gained or lost.

Let's go one step further. Suppose the fourth hand defender captures the 10 with the jack. In that case, we will re-enter the North hand in *figure 173* via a side re-entry and take a single finesse against the king. However, on the other hand, if West is compelled to play the king to capture the 10, our problems are solved since both the ace and queen are 'high.'

The advantage of this play, when holding from six to eight cards of the suit in question, is that it completely avoids any guessing by declarer as to which defender holds the king or the jack or both cards. Percentage-wise, the play will neither gain or lose.

It should be pointed out that frequently the opponents' bidding will yield definite clues as to the location of missing high cards. An opponent who has bid strongly or has opened the bidding can usually be supposed to hold the majority of the missing high cards; a defender who has not been able to bid on the earlier rounds is usually marked for an absence of high cards but aggressive distribution, as voids and singletons. In these cases, the opponents' bidding will play the determining role in influencing declarer's play. The routine method described in *figure 173* should only be employed in the absence of clues from the opponents' bidding.

QUIZ TEN

1 - What is your opening bid with each of the following hands?

(a)
♠ A K Q 8
♡ J
◇ K Q
♣ A K Q J 7 6

(b)
♠ A Q
♡ K Q J 8
◇ A K Q 7
♣ K Q J

(c)
♠ A K Q J 10 8 7 6 5 4
♡ 2
◇ 3
♣ 4

(d)
♠ A
♡ K Q J 6
◇ A Q 10 7
♣ K J 9 8

(e)
♠ K Q J 10 8 7
♡ A Q J 10 5 4
◇ 3
♣ void

2 - Your partner has opened with two hearts. The next player passed. What is your response with each of the following hands? There is no part score.

(f)
♠ Q J 10 8 7
♡ 8 4
◇ K 7 3
♣ J 5 2

(g)
♠ 7 4
♡ 8 6 5 4 3
◇ J 5 2
♣ 7 6 5

(h)
♠ 8 7 4 3 2
♡ Q 7 6
◇ A 2
♣ J 5 2

(i)
♠ 9 8 4
♡ 6 5
◇ J 7 4 3
♣ 10 6 5 3

(j)
♠ J 10 6 2
♡ 7 5
◇ A J 8
♣ K 5 4 3

(k)
♠ K 9 8
♡ 7 4
◇ Q J 10 9 8
♣ 6 5 4

3 - You have opened the bidding with two hearts, holding hand (1). What is your rebid to each of the following possible responses?

(1)
♠ A 8 3
♡ A K Q J 8 7
◇ A K Q
♣ K

If partner responds	Your rebid is
Two no trump	________
Two spades	________
Three diamonds	________
Three hearts	________
Four hearts	________
Three no trump	________

4-Both sides are vulnerable. The bidding has been –

Partner, South, Dealer	West, Opponent	You, North
Two hearts	Two spades	?

What do you do with each of the following hands?

(m)	(n)	(o)	(p)
♠ J86	♠ Q1097	♠ 873	♠ 8432
♡ Q54	♡ J8	♡ K753	♡ J9765
◊ 7643	◊ K643	◊ A864	◊ 7
♣ 1052	♣ 983	♣ 102	♣ 876

5-The bidding has been –

Partner, Opener	You, Responder
Two hearts	Two no trump
Three clubs	

You hold – ♠ J82
♡ 7643
◊ 10542
♣ K2

What is your rebid?

6 - You are South in each of the following. The lead is in your hand. Designate, on the lines accompanying each diagram, which card you would lead from your hand and the card to be played from the dummy. The opponents did not bid and the contract is immaterial.

	(q)	(r)	(s)
North	♠ K962	♠ K9532	♠ K83
South	♠ AQ1083	♠ AJ84	♠ AQ9764
LEAD	______	______	______
PLAY	______	______	______

ANSWERS TO QUIZ TEN

1-(a) Two clubs; (b) three no trump; (c) four spades; (d) one heart; (e) one spade.

2-(f) Two spades; (g) four hearts; (h) three hearts; (i) two no trump; (j) three no trump; (k) two no trump.

3-Over the first three responses, your correct rebid is three hearts in each case; to a three heart response, some slam try, as four no trump, is in order; you should pass the raise to four hearts, since partner's raise shows in this case at least five worthless trumps, denies as good as a king or a singleton; to a three no trump response, some slam try is again in order.

4-(m) pass; (n) double; (o) three hearts; (p) pass. In the last case, the hand is too weak in high cards for a free raise, despite the excellent trump support. The pass best describes the general weakness of the hand, with a heart raise given later to show the support in that suit.

5 - Four hearts, not three hearts! With four cards of your partner's first suit, hearts, and the king of his second suit, clubs, you have two tremendous supporting 'fits' for his suits. Your first response of two no trump denied seven or more points. The jump preference can only show a tremendous liking for the first suit bid by partner and excellent distribution.

6 - (q) You should lead either the ace or the queen. In the event that one defender shows out, the remaining defender is marked for all of the outstanding cards of that suit. The retention of a high honor in both hands permits the possible finesse against the jack, if necessary, to be taken in either direction.

(r) The ace should be led. This provides protection against either defender holding all four missing cards which include both the queen and 10. If this is the case, the other defender will show out when the ace is led. If West started with all four cards, it is a simple matter to follow with the four-spot and cover any card played by West; if East originally held all four cards, West will show out. This becomes apparent when the ace is led. The four-spot is led to North's king and a low card led from that hand through East's remaining queen-10 towards South's jack. In both (q) and (r), a low card is played from the North hand to the first trick.

With hand (s), the four is led to the first trick and the king is played immediately from the North hand. If all four missing cards (which include the jack and 10) are with West, that player cannot be prevented from taking a trick; conversely, if East holds the missing cards, retention of two higher honors, the ace and queen, permits two finesses against the jack and 10.

LESSON TEN
HANDS

1.

North: ♠ 954 ♡ 73 ◊ 9876 ♣ 10982

West: ♠ Q ♡ Q1098 ◊ J542 ♣ KQ65

East: ♠ J1032 ♡ J5 ◊ Q103 ♣ AJ74

South: ♠ AK876 ♡ AK642 ◊ AK ♣ 3

South dealer, neither side vul.

South	West	North	East
2 sp.	pass	2 no tr.	pass
3 hts.	pass	3 sp.	pass
4 sp.	pass	pass	pass

West opens the king of clubs.

2.

North: ♠ K82 ♡ A10972 ◊ 8642 ♣ 3

West: ♠ AQ7 ♡ KQJ8 ◊ AJ10 ♣ KQJ

East: ♠ J10943 ♡ 654 ◊ K9 ♣ 765

South: ♠ 65 ♡ 3 ◊ Q753 ♣ A109842

West dealer, N-S vulnerable.

Bid this hand, then compare your final contract with that on the following page.

3.

North: ♠ AKJ104 ♡ KJ10 ◊ AK3 ♣ A2

West: ♠ 32 ♡ 765 ◊ Q109 ♣ 108763

East: ♠ 765 ♡ AQ984 ◊ 85 ♣ J94

South: ♠ Q98 ♡ 32 ◊ J7642 ♣ KQ5

North dealer, both sides vul.

North	East	South	West
2 sp.	pass	3 sp.	pass
4 cl.	pass	5 cl.	pass
6 sp.	pass	pass	pass

Opening lead by East, ◊ 8.

4.

North: ♠ KQJ98 ♡ 5 ◊ QJ73 ♣ 865

West: ♠ 7432 ♡ 1098764 ◊ 2 ♣ 73

East: ♠ A ♡ KQJ ◊ AK10965 ♣ AK4

South: ♠ 1065 ♡ A32 ◊ 84 ♣ QJ1092

East dealer, E-W vulnerable

Bid this hand, then compare your final contract with that on the following page.

5.

	♠ 543 ♡ A76 ◇ 42 ♣ AKQ98	
♠ Q ♡ QJ1095 ◇ KJ108 ♣ 763	N W E S	♠ 10987 ♡ K843 ◇ 765 ♣ J2
	♠ AKJ62 ♡ 2 ◇ AQ93 ♣ 1054	

North dealer, neither vul.

North	East	South	West
1 cl.	pass	1 sp.	pass
2 cl.	pass	3 dia.	pass
3 sp.	pass	4 sp.	pass
pass	pass		

Opening lead by West, ♡Q

6.

	♠ AK73 ♡ 8542 ◇ AQ8 ♣ KQ	
♠ Q109 ♡ K ◇ J10764 ♣ 8532	N W E S	♠ 8652 ♡ J96 ◇ 93 ♣ J764
	♠ J4 ♡ AQ1073 ◇ K52 ♣ A109	

South dealer, N-S vulnerable.

South	West	North	East
1 ht.	pass	1 sp.	pass
2 ht.	pass	4 no tr.	pass
5 ht. *	pass	5 no tr.	pass
6 dia.**	pass	6 ht.	pass
pass	pass		

Opening lead by West, ◇J

Hand two bidding.
West dealer, N-S vulnerable.

West	North	East	South
2 n.t.	pass	3 n.t.	pass
pass	pass		

Hand four bidding.
East dealer, E-W vulnerable.

East	South	West	North
2 dia.	pass	2 n.t.	pass
3 dia.	pass	3 hts.	pass
4 hts.	pass	pass	pass

Footnotes

* *The Blackwood slam response to show two aces.*

** *Indicating one king in Blackwood. This and other slam bidding methods will be explained in detail in Lesson XIII.*

SOLUTIONS TO LESSON TEN HANDS

1.

South declarer at four spades.

Trick	W	N	E	S
1	♣ K	♣ 2	♣ 7	♣ 3
2	♣ 5	♣ 8	♣ A	♠ 6
3	♡ 8	♡ 3	♡ 5	♡ A
4	♡ 9	♡ 7	♡ J	♡ K
5	♡ 10	♠ 4	♠ 10	♡ 2
6	♠ Q	♠ 5	♠ 2	♠ K
7	♡ Q	♠ 9	♠ J	♡ 4
8	♣ 6	♣ 9	♣ 4	♠ 7
9	♢ 2	♣ 10	♠ 3	♠ A
10	♣ Q	♢ 6	♣ J	♡ 6
11	♢ 4	♢ 7	♢ 3	♢ A
12	♢ 5	♢ 8	♢ 10	♢ K
13	♢ J	♢ 9	♢ Q	♠ 8

South wins 10 tricks.

2.

West declarer at three no trump.

Trick	N	E	S	W
1	♡ 10	♡ 4	♡ 3	♡ Q
2	♠ 2	♠ 3	♠ 5	♠ A
3	♠ 8	♠ 4	♠ 6	♠ Q
4	♠ K	♠ 9	♣ 8	♠ 7
5	♣ 3	♣ 5	♣ A	♣ J
6	♡ 2	♣ 6	♣ 10	♣ K
7	♡ 7	♡ 5	♣ 2	♡ K
8	♢ 2	♢ K	♢ 3	♢ J
9	♡ 9	♠ J	♣ 4	♡ 8
10	♢ 4	♠ 10	♣ 9	♡ J
11	♢ 6	♢ 9	♢ 5	♢ A
12	♢ 8	♣ 7	♢ 7	♣ Q
13	♡ A	♡ 6	♢ Q	♢ 10

West wins 10 tricks.

3.

North declarer at six spades.

Trick	E	S	W	N
1	♢ 8	♢ J	♢ Q	♢ K
2	♢ 5	♢ 2	♢ 9	♢ A
3	♣ 4	♣ 5	♣ 3	♣ A
4	♣ 9	♣ Q	♣ 6	♣ 2
5	♣ J	♣ K	♣ 7	♢ 3
6	♡ 9	♢ 4	♢ 10	♠ J
7	♠ 5	♠ 8	♠ 2	♠ A
8	♠ 6	♠ 9	♠ 3	♠ K
9	♠ 7	♠ Q	♣ 8	♠ 4
10	♡ 4	♢ 7	♡ 5	♡ 10
11	♡ 8	♢ 6	♣ 10	♡ J
12	♡ A	♡ 2	♡ 6	♡ K
13	♡ Q	♡ 3	♡ 7	♠ 10

North wins 12 tricks.

4.

West declarer at four hearts.

Trick	N	E	S	W
1	♠ K	♠ A	♠ 5	♠ 2
2	♣ 5	♣ A	♣ Q	♣ 3
3	♣ 6	♣ K	♣ 9	♣ 7
4	♣ 8	♣ 4	♣ 10	♡ 4
5	♠ 8	♡ J	♠ 6	♠ 3
6	♢ 7	♢ A	♢ 4	♢ 2
7	♠ 9	♢ K	♢ 8	♠ 4
8	♢ 3	♢ 5	♠ 10	♡ 6
9	♠ J	♡ Q	♡ A	♠ 7
10	♡ 5	♡ K	♡ 2	♡ 7

West claims the last three tricks, winning 12 tricks .

5. South declarer at four spades

Trick	W	N	E	S
1	♡ Q	♡ A	♡ 8	♡ 2
2	♠ Q	♠ 3	♠ 7	♠ K
3	♣ 3	♠ 4	♠ 8	♠ A
4	♣ 6	♣ A	♣ 2	♣ 4
5	♣ 7	♠ 5	♠ 9	♠ J
6	♡ 5	♡ 6	♠ 10	♠ 2
7	♡ 9	♡ 7	♡ K	♠ 6

Declarer claims four additional club tricks and the ace of diamonds, concedes the last trick to the defenders. Declarer wins 11 tricks with five clubs, four spades and two red aces.

6. South declarer at six hearts.

Trick	W	N	E	S
1	◊ J	◊ Q	◊ 3	◊ 2
2	♡ K	♡ 2	♡ 6	♡ A
3	♣ 2	♣ Q	♣ 4	♣ 9
4	♣ 3	♡ 4	♡ 9	♡ 10
5	♣ 5	♡ 5	♡ J	♡ Q

Declarer claims the balance, winning all 13 tricks.

COMMENTS ON LESSON TEN HANDS

1-Success or failure of the contract depends upon declarer's being able to establish his side heart suit. Trump leads must therefore be postponed until the opponents' high hearts have been trumped in the dummy.

East, on over-ruffing the third round of hearts in the dummy, returns a trump in an effort to cut down dummy's ruffing power. Had South taken even one lead of trumps before first leading hearts, he would have been defeated, since East, on over-ruffing, could have led a trump, taking away dummy's last trump.

2-North's opening lead is the 10, top of the intermediate sequence. While West could take the spade finesse against the missing king, the only way he could enter the dummy is via the king of diamonds. Removing the latter card would leave the dummy without an entry, leave the remaining spades marooned.

North's refusal to take the ace of hearts when West led the king may puzzle the student. South's inability to return a heart after taking the club ace, marked West for the remaining hearts. Had North captured the heart king with the ace, West's jack of hearts would have been set up as a trick. By permitting the king of hearts to win, the jack remained a loser. So it was 'trick for trick.' Moreover, had North taken the heart ace, he would have been hard put for a satisfactory next lead.

West's capture of the opening lead with the heart queen, rather than with the jack, is known as a 'falsecard.' The cards are equals, but playing the queen may mislead the opponents as to the location of the jack.

3-The play of this hand is a bit advanced. By first discarding his losing diamond, then trumping the opponent's high diamond, declarer is able to set up dummy's two diamonds for heart discards. The spade queen is retained as a future re-entry.

4 - Notice the following important points. First, West's initial response of two no trump denied seven or more points. Second, East's economical rebid of three diamonds permitting partner to show the heart suit at an under game level. Third, four hearts is makeable; three no trump can be defeated.

5-There are two important points for the student to notice. The first is South's safety play of playing the king of spades when trumps were first led, instead of immediately taking the finesse against the missing queen. The safety play (which cost nothing) protected him against the possibility that the queen was alone, which was the case. Had declarer taken the spade finesse, he would have lost two trump tricks, one to the queen, a second to East's well-guarded 10-spot. Use of the safety play resulted in the loss of only one trump trick, which was unavoidable, to East's 10.

The second point is declarer's lead of the fourth round of spades to 'force out' East's 10. This is one of the rare exceptions to the declarer leading an unnecessary round of trumps in order to permit a defender to win a trick with the 'high' trump since in most cases, it wastes both time for the declarer, and trumps from his hand and sometimes from dummy in addition, and usually accomplishes nothing but rendering unto Caesar what is already Caesar's. But here the lead of the fourth round of trumps has a specific purpose. After East's last trump is gone, South can now play all five of dummy's clubs without fear of East trumping that suit. Had the fourth round of trumps not been led, East would have trumped the third club and exited with a heart. Without an entry, since the ace of hearts was knocked out on the opening lead, dummy's fourth and fifth clubs would be marooned.

Played as shown, declarer will make an overtrick at his four spade contract; if he fails to lead the fourth spade, he will eventually lose all three diamonds and a spade, go down one trick.

6-In the small slam contract, declarer sees that the only possible losing tricks for his side are in the trump suit where the king and jack of trumps are known to be held by the defenders among their four cards of that suit. To complete his contract he can afford to lose one trump trick but not two.

Accordingly, after winning the opening lead of the jack of diamonds in the dummy with the queen, the deuce of hearts is led. After East plays the six, South takes the safety play by putting up the ace. When the singleton king falls, it is a simple matter for the declarer to return to the dummy via a black suit, take the marked finesse against East's jack-nine combination.

The student should notice several points. First, when the declarer wanted to re-enter dummy for the heart finesse against the jack, he led a low club or spade towards dummy, not a diamond. The reason is that diamonds had already been led once and there was a possibility that one defender had started with six cards of the latter suit. (As a matter of fact, West had five). If one defender did have six diamonds, his partner started with a singleton and would trump the second diamond. There was no need, with ample entries in the other suit, to incur this risk.

In general practice, while the defenders still hold trumps, unless a side suit must be led several times for discarding or other purposes, the declarer should lead as few rounds of any one suit as possible to minimize the danger of that suit being trumped. Best practice, where possible, is to first lead one suit, then another, where necessary to get back and forth between the partnership hands rather than lead the same suit twice. I would like to point out that when side suits are led, the declarer should attempt to avoid establishing winning cards for the defenders.

The second point is that the first lead of trumps came from the dummy. The reader may ask, **"Well, as long as you were going to play the ace of trumps as a safety play against the king being singleton, why didn't you win the first diamond in your (South) hand, bang down the heart ace?"**

The answer is that by leading the trump from the dummy, you gave yourself an additional chance to avoid losing any tricks since if East had held a doubleton king-jack originally, you would have been able to play the queen over his jack, not lose any tricks in the suit whatever. Of course, it was possible that East started with a singleton jack and West held the king-nine-six but even there, the play of the queen would hold declarer's heart losers to one.

The safety play of the ace, therefore, is made in case the defender sitting second hand (East in hand six) plays a low card.

Lesson XI

Defensive Bidding

LESSON ELEVEN

DEFENSIVE BIDDING

A defensive bid is any bid made by the side that *did not* open the bidding. Another commonly used term is 'overcall.' They are synonomous.

An overcall is made for one of the following reasons—

1-Because you think you can win the contracted number of tricks with your side's cards.

2-To tell your partner what suit to lead, if the opponents buy the bid.

3-As a possible later sacrifice bid.

4-To push the opponents beyond their ability to complete their contract.

It stands to reason that the overcaller may have more or less strength than the opening bidder. There are overcalls to show both weak and strong hands.

TYPES OF OVERCALLS

1-Immediate minimum overcalls in suits.
2-Delayed overcalls in suits.
3-No trump overcalls.
4-Informatory doubles.
5-Jump overcalls
 (a) Strength showing,
 (b) Pre-emptive.
6-Overcalls in the opponent's bid suit.

BASIC REQUIREMENTS FOR IMMEDIATE OVERCALLS

TO BID AT	IF	MINIMUM POINTS NEEDED
One level	Not vulnerable	10
" "	Vulnerable	12
Two level	Not vulnerable	12
" "	Vulnerable	14

In other words, an overcall when vulnerable shows more strength than a non-vulnerable overcall; and to overcall at the two level requires more strength than one made at the one zone.

COUNTING POINTS FOR THE OVERCALL

Points for overcalls are counted exactly as for an opening bid. If the overcall is made in a suit, high card and distributional points are totaled. For no trump overcalls, high card points only are counted.

PLAYING TRICKS

Playing tricks are estimated probable winners.

If vulnerable, the overcaller should have in playing tricks within his own hand at least all but two of the tricks needed to fulfill the contract; not vulnerable, within three tricks.

Thus, a player overcalling at the two level, requiring eight tricks for fulfillment, should have six winners in his own hand if vulnerable, five winners not vulnerable.

No overcall, even not vulnerable at the one level, should be made on a four card suit! If the hand has only four card suits and isn't strong enough for an informatory double (Lesson XII), pass!

The suit in which the overcall is made should have plenty of what bridge players term 'body.' Another word would be 'solidity'. You are far safer, and less liable to be penalized, overcalling with one spade holding ♠ A K 10 9 8 than ♠ A K 4 3 2.

The reason for having a minimum of 10 to 14 points for the overcall is that after you make the overcall, should the opponents rebid, your partner, with defensive values, may feel that his cards, plus the strength shown by your overcall, can defeat the adverse contract. He has a right to count on you for strength.

Be sure you understand the meaning of an overcall.

It is one thing to open the bidding with a four carder, or to show a four card suit in responding or rebidding, but to overcall with a suit of that length is courting disaster. If the remaining cards of that suit are bunched behind the overcaller, he can be doubled and severely penalized.

Another reason for insistence on five carders or longer in overcalling is that the partner can safely raise with three small cards or a doubleton high honor, normal support for a rebiddable suit, giving the defensive side the ability to 'push' in competitive bidding.

THE IMMEDIATE MINIMUM OVERCALL IN A SUIT

The immediate minimum overcall in a suit consists of the bid of a suit made at the *first* opportunity at the *lowest* (cheapest) level after an opponent opens the bidding.

CASE A

North	East, You
1 heart	1 spade

CASE B

South	West	North	East, You
1 dia.	pass	1 heart	1 spade

When both opponents have bid, as in the second example, greater care by the overcaller is indicated, since they have shown strength, and your partner indicated weakness by passing.

If you overcall on a five card suit, it should preferably be headed by the ace or king or any two or more honors. A six card suit can be headed by any single honor, though naturally, the stronger the suit, the better.

	♠ J52	
	N	
♠ K86 W		E ♠ 109743
	S	
	♠ AQ	

Figure 174

You must always remember that your partner may lead your bid suit, and, if you have no high cards in that suit, his lead may cost a trick. Look at *figure 174*. If, as East, you overcall with spades on that raggedy suit, your partner will very likely lead a spade if South becomes the declarer. And the lead will cost your side a trick, since otherwise, your partner's king would probably have captured the declarer's queen.

Sometimes, in order to make an overcall, one requirement may be waived or stretched in favor of another. Extra length in the bid suit will permit a slight shading of solidity or high card requirements, and vice versa. This is because if the overcall is not made at once, when the price is cheap, it may be too dangerous later on when the opponents' bidding has raised the price too high for you to enter the auction safely.

(a)
♠ 108
♡ KQJ1098
◇ 54
♣ 876

Hand (a) to the left is not a good immediate overcall by any means, despite the solidity of the suit. The hand totals only eight points, with six high card points. But not vulnerable, over an opening one club or one diamond bid by an opponent, you *might* bid one heart. I would never show the suit if it were necessary to bid 'two.' If vulnerable, I would pass immediately under any circumstances, even at the one level, rather than overcall immediately.

You see, while the hand lacks 10 points, it is desirable to tell your partner to lead a heart if he has the opening lead.

Bids of this sort are known as 'lead-directing.' But the trouble is that your partner, after your overcall, may very well make a penalty double of the opponents' final contract, figuring on you to hold some defensive values in the promised 10 or more points. *And you don't have them!*

DELAYED OVERCALLS IN SUITS

A delayed overcall is any overcall not made at the bidder's first opportunity. There are two types.

The first type of delayed overcall is made when the bidder has a long suit, but very little high card strength.

CASE C

North	East, You	South	West
One heart	pass	Two clubs	pass
Two hearts	Two spades		

(b)
♠ KQ10987
♡ 3
♢ 8765
♣ 43

Hand (b) is an example of this type of holding. It has plenty of trump length, but little high card strength. Of course, had the opponents rebid with three hearts or two no trump or some higher bid, the price you'd have to pay to show your suit would be too great for safety. By first passing, overcalling later, you have described your hand perfectly as containing a long suit and lacking 10 points.

(c)
♠ AJ432
♡ 52
♢ K987
♣ 103

The other type of delayed overcall is made when the opponents' weak bidding has marked partner with strength. This is termed 'inferential bidding.' Suppose you hold hand (c) with the following bidding—

CASE D

North	East	South	West, You
One heart	pass	One no trump	pass
Two hearts	pass	pass	Two spades

The fact that the opponents have permitted the bidding to stop at the two level indicated comparative weakness on their parts. Of course, you may say, "Well, why shouldn't I pass the two heart bid rather than take a chance by bidding two spades when I didn't have a solid enough suit to bid one spade?"

The answer to that is—when first it was your turn to bid, your suit wasn't sufficiently solid for an overcall.

However, the opponents' bidding or, rather, their lack of subsequent rebidding, marked your partner for the balance of outstanding strength. So it is actually safer for you to overcall at this later point than earlier in the bidding.

Your next question might be, "Well, if my partner had strength, why didn't he take some action instead of passing?"

The answer to that is—he was in the same position you were after the opening bid. He obviously had some strength, no suits good enough with which to overcall, and not enough for an informatory double. So he, too, had to await developments.

An important reason for bidding rather than passing at this point is the fact that if your side can make a part score, you are foolish to let the opponents play the hand for a partial.

Remember, faint heart ne'er won the bridge game!

It should be emphasized that the two bidding situations just described are not parallel. In the first type of delayed overcall, with hand (b), the two spade bid was made while the bidding was still in progress, and was probably going to continue. With hand (c), a pass by you would have brought the bidding to a close. Therefore, the former type (hand b) shows a long suit and few high cards, the latter (c) some high cards and a suit unsafe for earlier overcalling.

OVERCALLS IN NO TRUMP

An overcall of one no trump over an opening bid of one in a suit shows an extremely powerful hand, which, if anything, is slightly stronger than an opening bid of one no trump.

REQUIREMENTS

Sixteen to 19 high card points. Do not count points for distribution. All four suits should be stopped with a positive stopper in the opponent's bid suit. A double stopper is even better. The hand may not contain any singletons, even a singleton ace.

It stands to reason that the no trump overcall should be exceedingly rich in high card and intermediate strength, since if partner is 'busted,' the bidder should have a reasonably good expectancy of making the contract, or at least coming close.

The no trump overcall is usually predicated on minor suit

strength since with strong major holdings and the equivalent high card strength, an informatory double is usually better.

Bidding one no trump as an overcall when holding a solid minor suit of five cards or more and the requisite stoppers is sometimes excellent strategy, and the playing strength of the long suit permits shading high card requirements to 15 points. However, there is always the possibility that partner may take out your no trump into his long suit for which you lack good support. He may not realize that your no trump is based on a long minor suit. So these deviations from standard practice should be made with care and circumspection.

(d)	(e)
♠ K 7 2	♠ K 2
♡ A J	♡ K 9
◇ K Q 6 4	◇ A K Q 10 6 2
♣ A 10 9 8	♣ Q 7 5

Hands (d) and (e) are examples of one no trump overcalls following an opening bid of one heart or one spade.

THE TWO NO TRUMP OVERCALL

REQUIREMENTS

22 to 24 high card points.

All four suits stopped, and a double stopper in the opponent's suit, unless the hand contains a solid five card or longer suit, in which case a single adverse stopper will suffice. With a solid suit of five or more cards, usually a minor, point requirements may be shaded to an absolute minimum of 21.

THE THREE NO TRUMP OVERCALL

REQUIREMENTS

25 to 27 high card points.

All four suits stopped. Shows the ability to win nine tricks, largely in the minor suits.

NO TRUMP OVERCALLS OF PRE-EMPTIVE BIDS

When an opponent opens the bidding with three or four of a suit, and you overcall with three or four no trump, as the case may require, your overcall takes on an entirely different meaning from a three no trump overcall of an opening one bid.

We know from our lesson on pre-emptive bidding that the reason the opponent opened the bidding with three or four of a suit was to try to shut your side, with superior high cards, out of the bidding.

Now – you don't want to be shut out.

Since you are entering the bidding at either the three or four level with a partner who has not yet shown any strength through bidding, you must have a tremendous hand. Further, any missing strength that you hope your partner might hold could very well be with the remaining opponent. So be careful!

Now – Get This Difference!

1-A three no trump overcall over an opening three bid shows the desire to play the hand in three no trump.

2-A four no trump overcall asks partner to bid his best suit and shows *no* desire to play the hand in no trump.

(f)
♠ K J 10 9
♡ 2
◇ A K Q 7
♣ A K J 10

The four no trump bid is like a giant informatory double – is 100 percent forcing in commanding partner to respond. Hand (f) is an example of a four no trump overcall over an opposing three or four heart opening bid.

"Why don't you double," you may ask?

The reason for not doubling is that you may prefer to make a game, or possibly a slam, particularly if your side is vulnerable and the opponents are not vulnerable.

After your overcall of four no trump, your partner will respond in his best suit. With a strong hand, he will make a strength showing response. Under no circumstances may he pass!

You can see the beauty of this bid. For you to guess which suit your partner can support would be hazardous, whereas the no trump overcall elicits this information immediately. Again it must be emphasized that first, the bid can only be made with hands having game certainty, and that it is completely forcing on partner to respond, even if his best suit is four cards headed by the five spot.

An overcall of four no trump is *not* a request for ace showing.

THE INFORMATORY DOUBLE

The informatory double is the best and most commonly employed strength showing bid at the defensive bidder's command. Whenever the requirements are present, it should be employed.

A full chapter (Lesson XII) is devoted to doubles.

JUMP OVERCALLS

By a jump overcall is meant skipping one or more rounds of bidding in overcalling.* There are two types. First, that of jumping a single round of bidding as –

CASE E		CASE F	
North, Opener	You, East	North, Opener	You, East
One heart	Two spades	One heart	Three clubs

A single jump overcall shows an extremely powerful hand with from 17 to 20 points.

It is *not* forcing. Partner may pass with a weak hand, but if he has any kind of a taking trick, either in high cards or playing strength or ruffing value, he should respond at least once.

(g)
♠ A K J 8 7 6
♡ K 8 2
◊ A 2
♣ K 7

The single jump overcall may be made on either of two types of hands. The first type is a powerful one suited hand; the other, a two suiter. Hand (g) is an example of the one suiter type. The hand should contain at least eight probable winners, in addition to the required point count. The reason for not doubling informatorily with this type of hand is that the double (usually) promises support for the unbid suits, and the only suit you can really support is your own, spades.

(h)
♠ A J
♡ K 2
◊ A K J 10 8 7
♣ Q 6 4

Hand (h) is another example of a single jump overcall over an adverse opening bid. Had the opponent opened with one spade or a heart, you would bid three diamonds. Over a one club opening bid, you need only bid two diamonds.

Footnote

* *Certain experts have recently adopted the use of the single jump overcall as weak or pre-emptive. However, since bidding one more than necessary in a suit, even as an overcall, has denoted an exceedingly strong hand since the early days of bridge, the great preponderance of bridge players use this bid as strong rather than weak.*

This text will conform to majority usage in describing the single jump overcall as strong. Use of this bid as a pre-emptive measure is described in Lesson XVI.

Now there is one little proviso—when the jumped suit is a minor, as hand (h), the jump overcall is highly invitational to partner to bid three no trump if he has a stopper in the adverse suit plus a trick of some kind in his own hand. The jump bidder may lack the stopper—have perhaps a singleton in the opponents' bid suit.

(i)
♠ AK765
♡ 3
♢ AQJ98
♣ K2

The other type of single jump overcall is based on powerful two suiters with at least one suit and preferably both suits of five cards or longer. Hand (i) is an example of a two spade overcall over a one heart or one club opening bid.

Again the reader may ask, "**Why not double informatorily?**" The answer is that it is unwise to double informatorily with a two suiter. First, the likelihood is that partner will respond in the very suit in which you are short. For example, with hand (i), if you double one club, you can expect your partner to bid hearts. Next, if the opponents pre-empt, as by bidding three clubs over your double of one club, you haven't enough bidding space to show both suits safely.

PRE-EMPTIVE JUMP OVERCALLS

Jumping two or more levels of bidding, as one heart by opener, three spades by an opponent, is pre-emptive and is an attempt to shut the other side out of efficient bidding communication. Like all pre-emptive bids, it is made on a long suit, usually seven cards or longer, weak in high cards. The suit has solidity and the hand lacks more than two defensive tricks.

It should be pointed out that part of the effectiveness of the pre-empt (or shutout, if you prefer that term) has been lost, since one of the opponents has been able to open the bidding normally. You are now trying to jam their communications.

A word of warning! Remember vulnerability! When your side is not vulnerable and the opponents are vulnerable, is the golden time for pre-empts. With vulnerability or lack of it equal, be careful. If you are vulnerable, pre-empts are dangerous and should usually be avoided unless your suit is so solid and you have so many taking tricks, as a nine card suit such as AQJ987654, that you can't be hurt if doubled.

THE IMMEDIATE OVERCALL IN THE OPPONENT'S SUIT

That a player can bid the very same suit already bid by an opponent is an idea so fearsome to the average player that it is never dreamed of. Yet the fact that an opponent has opened the bidding, let us say, with a club, does not give him an exclusive license to that suit. There are several ways for the other side to utilize his bid.

With a hand strong enough to make a game unassisted after an opponent opens the bidding, even though partner may not yet have bid, or has already passed, we have a bid which is like a combination of an opening bid of two in a suit (forcing to game) and an informatory double.

That bid is an immediate overcall of the opponent's suit by bidding the minimum number of the very same suit!

CASE G

North, Opener	You, East
One heart	Two hearts!

This in effect says, "**Partner, bid your best suit even if it's only four cards headed by the five-spot. Further, you must keep the bidding alive until we have either reached a game contract or doubled the opponents for penalty. No matter how weak your hand is, mine is strong enough to guarantee we can make a game!**"

Once more the reader may query, "**Well, if your hand is so big that it can make a game, why not bid it at once? Why make a fancy bid, putting pressure on partner to respond with little or nothing?**"

(j)	(k)
♠ A K Q 7	♠ A K Q 10 8 7
♡ 2	♡ void
◇ A K J 10	◇ A Q J 9 8
♣ A Q J 10	♣ K 2

The reason for the cue-bid (bidding the opponent's suit) is that the bidder could have a hand resembling either (j) or (k). After an opening one heart bid by the right hand opponent, you would not know with hand (j) which of your three suits partner can support. Your cue bid of two hearts elicits that information immediately.

With hand (k), your problem is whether to play the hand in spades or diamonds. If the apparent solidity of the spade suit beguiles you, let me state that if partner has three or four diamonds and a singleton spade, it is possible to lay out a hand that can make five or six diamonds, yet go down at four spades.

There are several points I would like to emphasize.

1 - The cue bid is forcing to game.

2 - It is like a super two-bid.

3 - It is *not* necessary to have a void or the ace of the opponent's bid suit to make an immediate overcall of that suit. It is frequently done with a singleton, as in hand (j), and, once in a while, with a worthless doubleton.

THE DELAYED OVERCALL IN THE OPPONENT'S SUIT

In the preceding pages, you learned the meaning of an immediate overcall in the opponent's suit when the latter player opened the bidding.

Suppose, however, the bidding had gone –

CASE H

North, Opener	You, East	South	West
One diamond	Pass	One no tr.	Pass
Pass	Two diamonds		

Is your two diamond bid forcing to game?

Are you showing a powerful hand?

Must your partner respond?

The answer to all of the foregoing questions is a decided *no!* All you are showing is a good, husky diamond suit, and the ability to play the hand in that suit and contract. Your suit is at least five cards in length, probably longer, and fairly solid.

Why, then, didn't you show your diamond suit at once by bidding two diamonds over the opening bid of one diamond?

Because – if you remember what we just finished discussing, the *immediate* overcall of the opponent's suit showed a powerful hand, capable of making a game in some suit other than the opponent's suit. That's just the reverse of this situation.

(1)
♠ J 6
♡ 7 4 3
♢ K Q 10 9 7 6
♣ K 3

Hand (1) is an example of a holding on which you might back in, and bid the opponent's diamond suit. Your partner, even with a singleton of the bid suit, should generally pass since game is highly improbable.

It must be stressed that this delayed overcall in the opponent's suit shows the suit *only* when neither partner has previously bid. A bid of the opponent's suit *after* either partner has bid shows the ace or void of that suit, a bid you will learn in Lesson XIII on Slam Bidding.

Bidding the opponent's suit with the intention of playing the hand in that suit (1) is dangerous and should only be made with a capable partner, and then only when the opponents' bidding is weak. If the opponents' bidding is strong, pass, even though you may have eight cards of one of their suits, rather than get in trouble.

CHOICE OF SUIT WHEN OVERCALLING

The overcaller, with two suits, is faced with a different problem than the opening bidder as to which suit to bid first. For one thing, particularly if one suit is much stronger than the other, and the overcaller intends to bid only once, he will bid the stronger, since that is the suit he wants his partner to lead.

With two suits of five cards or longer each, and 14 points or more, the overcaller will try to show both suits if it can be done with safety. The higher ranking suit is always bid first.

To show two suits, the overcaller should have 14 points or more. Even with six-five, I recommend bidding the higher ranking suit first, regardless of which is the longer. The reason for not bidding the six carder first (if it is lower ranking) and then reversing is that you will not have time or bidding room if the opponents crowd the bidding with bids of their own.

With six-four, bid the six carder first; with seven-five, or seven-four, bid the seven carder first, regardless of rank.

Let's examine some typical hands containing two suits and see what we would bid. In all cases, we will suppose our opponent to the right opened the bidding with one club.

(m)	(n)	(o)
♠ AK654	♠ J10876	♠ J9765
♡ J10876	♡ AK654	♡ AK654
◇ 32	◇ 32	◇ A2
♣ 8	♣ 8	♣ 8

(p)	(q)
♠ AQ765	♠ AJ7654
♡ KJ9764	♡ KQ1063
◇ 3	◇ 3
♣ 2	♣ 2

(m) One spade. You do not intend to show the heart suit unless partner makes a strength showing response.

(n) One heart. You only intend to bid once, and if your side become defenders, you want your partner to lead a heart, not a spade.

(o) One spade. You plan to show the heart suit later if feasible. The hand totals 15 points.

(p) One spade. If the opponents crowd the bidding, you'll be fortunate to show both suits. Don't try to reverse as well. You won't have time!

(q) One spade. The hand's distribution is sufficiently aggressive to warrant showing both suits. The hand totals 14 points.

MISCELLANEOUS OVERCALLS

One of the more common errors made by the newer player is to overcall an opening bid of one or more no trump which has been bid to his immediate right. For example, let's suppose that South opened the bidding with one no trump and you, as the next player (sitting West), bid two of whatever suit you held.

The reason most frequently given for this overcall is that it is intended to show partner what suit to lead for the opening.

But the overcaller has the opening lead! The bid is completely unnecessary.

The bid is bad for two reasons. First, against the no trump's known 16 to 18 points in high cards, there is practically no chance of making a game. But there is a tremendous danger, if your suit is 'stacked' against you, and your partner is 'broke,' that you can be doubled and severely penalized.

For the possible 60 to 90 points you might score, and I use 'might' in the most generous and optimistic of terms, there is the much greater possibility that you can go down 700 points or more.

Why take the chance?

The other reason is that the opponents, despite the opening one no trump bid, may have the bid suit very thinly stopped. In this event, you will probably defeat the no trump contract through the tricks you will win in your suit.

But bidding that suit will warn the opponents of their danger in no trump, and send them scurrying to some much safer suit contract.

Had the bidding gone –

CASE I

South, Opener	West	North	You, East
One no trump	pass	pass	?

Now, as East, a bid by you may be in order. Note that I say 'may.' Here a suit bid would be lead directing, since your partner, not yourself, has the opening lead. A protective informatory double (Lesson XII) could also be considered. But no matter which bid you may select, it is dangerous.

I grant there are a few isolated cases where the overcaller holds highly distributional hands, and where a bid is in order. For example, the opponent to your right opens the bidding with one no trump and you hold–

♠ AJ108765 ♡ 65432 ◇ J ♣ void

a two spade bid is not too bad. It is based on the reasoning that the opponents will probably gallop off nine tricks in the minors to produce three no trump and a spade overcall is relatively safe.

Yet many times I have seen similar holdings defeated with the missing trumps behind the overcaller, and partner holding the minor suit stoppers. The overcall was unnecessary!

When the opponents pre-empt, a player on the other side with a strong hand, and just fair suits, is in the predicament of not being sure whether to bid, double or pass.

The problem of when to bid over pre-empts baffles the greatest experts. Examine *figures 147* and *148* on pages 308 and 309. Pretend you are West.

Do you bid over South's four spade opening bid?

It's a difficult problem. If your partner holds the cards shown in *figure 147*, you're right in overcalling. If his hand resembles that of East in *148*, you're wrong.

Sometimes the bidding goes –

CASE J

South, Opener	West	North	You, East
One heart	pass	Four hearts	?

You hold–♠ AK765 ♡ 2 ◇ AQ87 ♣ Q62.

Of course you want to bid. But do you dare?

You've been 'fixed' by North's pre-empt!

If you have a long, solid suit, then you can back into the bidding with a fair degree of safety, since you can't be doubled and hurt too badly. On the other hand, even with 20 or more points, and scattered strength, it's strictly a guessing contest.

You can either pass, double the opponents for penalty or overcall. If you decide to overcall, be guided by comparative vulnerability. Don't make risky vulnerable overcalls against non-vulnerable opponents.

If you're not sure that you can fulfill your contract, but are fairly certain that you can defeat the opponents' bid, then double for penalty. Nothing beats a sure profit!

RESPONSES AND REBIDS IN DEFENSIVE BIDDING

RESPONSES TO A MINIMUM OVERCALL

After your partner has overcalled, you can do one of the following:

1-Raise partner's suit,

2-Bid a new suit of your own,

3-Bid no trump,

4-Bid the opponents' suit,

5-Double the opponents if they rebid,

6-Pass.

RAISING PARTNER'S SUIT

There are three possible reasons for supporting partner's suit after it was bid as a minimum overcall. These are:

1-You are in a competitive bidding situation (with the opponents) and rather than permit the latter to play the hand, you prefer to bid higher in your partner's suit. In most of these cases, the bidding will usually be at part-score level.

2-Game seems probable.

3-As a pre-emptive measure.

Since partner's immediate overcall in a suit can be made with as little as 10 points if at the one-level and not vulnerable to as high as 16 or 17 points, * the responder (to an overcall) is responsible for showing supporting cards, competing with the

Footnote

* *With 13 to 15 points or more, informatory doubles are preferable to suit overcalls. However, unfavorable distribution of certain hands makes the informatory double unsound in which cases an overcall can be quite strong, particularly when vulnerable and at the two level or higher.*

opponents in order not to sell out too cheaply and reaching game contracts where apparently makeable.

How much strength, in points, do you need to give partner's overcall voluntary raise?

CASE K

East, Opener	South, Partner	West	North, You
One heart	One spade	pass	Two spades

Your raise to two spades is voluntary. Furthermore, it is what bridge players term 'forward-going' or more simply, constructive. It would indicate a minimum of 8 points and a maximum of 12 points and be tantamount to telling partner that he can bid higher if he has additional values over and above the already promised 10 points. Minimum trump support consists of any three small cards, or a doubleton headed by the ace, king, queen or better.

A jump raise to three spades, instead of two, in Case K, would show 13 to 15 points. There are two very important differences between the jump raise of an overcall and the jump raise by responder to an opening bid. The first difference is that a jump, as from one spade to three spades, of an opening bid is forcing to game if the responder has not yet passed. *But*—a single jump in a major of an overcall is *not* forcing—only highly invitational to the overcaller to rebid if he has extra values. The second difference is where the jump response to an opening bid required a minimum of four trumps in the responder's hand (page 63), the jump response to an overcall can be based on a hand containing a minimum of three trumps containing the jack or better. The reason for the lesser requirement in jump raising an overcall is that the latter is known to consist of at least a five card suit with solidity and body whereas an opening bid can be based on a four card suit.

Where partner's overcall has shown 12 or more points, as by overcalling vulnerable or at the two level, these requirements should be lessened proportionately.

The jump to game of an overcall can be made with hands containing 16 or more points or on highly distributional hands with little defensive values.

(r)	(s)
♠ 4	♠ A Q 3 2
♡ K J 8 7 6	♡ Q 10 8 7
◇ A J 7 6 2	◇ K Q 9 8
♣ 4 3	♣ 5

Holding either hand (r) or (s) to the left, if the bidding had proceeded as in Case L, your proper response would be four hearts.

CASE L

East, opener	South, Partner	West	North, You
One club	One heart	pass	Four hearts

With hand (r), your raise is pre-emptive, intended to make it difficult or impossible for the opponents to discover a possible 'fit' in the spade suit; with hand (s), holding 16 points, game is certain after partner's overcall.

NO TRUMP RESPONSES TO PARTNER'S OVERCALL

A response of one or more no trump, after your partner has overcalled in a suit, is *never* made as a denial but rather as an affirmative action to show a desire to bid higher, and to game if possible. Any voluntary response of no trump is a highly constructive, forward-going bid.

REQUIREMENTS FOR NO TRUMP TAKEOUTS

IF OVERCALL WAS AT	YOU HOLD	RESPOND
One level	9 - 12 points	One no trump
One level	13 - 16	Two no trump
One level	17 or more	Three no trump
Two level	12 - 14	Two no trump
Two level	15 or more	Three no trump

At least two cards of partner's bid suit, a positive stopper in the opponent's suit, at least potential stoppers in the remaining unbid suits, no singletons in the hand.

SHOWING A NEW SUIT AFTER PARTNER'S OVERCALL

To show a new suit at the one level,

A minimum of eight points is required to show a new suit at the one level.

If the bidding of a new suit (following partner's overcall) requires showing it at the two zone, a minimum of 10 points should be present.

Now the important thing to remember is this — the minimum overcall didn't require much strength — 10 or more points including those for distribution. So if you, as the overcaller's partner, haven't a good hand, there's little or no chance for game. Then why bid?

There are only three reasons for the overcaller's partner bidding. These are:

1-There is a strong possibility of game,

2-The hand will play better in another contract,

3-In order to buy the bid, you have been forced to bid higher by the opponents' competitive bidding.

After your partner overcalls, don't show a weak suit of your own just because you have a singleton or lack support in partner's suit. There is no guarantee that he'll like yours better!

The biggest penalties in bridge come when two partners have been fighting each other in the bidding, each denying the other's suit on misfit hands by rebidding his own suit until an opponent doubles for penalty. When a hand appears to be a misfit, learn to get out of the bidding as quickly as possible.

There are some hands, it is true, where, after your partner overcalls, you know the combined hands will play better in your suit, regardless of his holding. For example, let's suppose the player to your left opened the bidding with one club. Your partner bid one heart, and the next player passed.

(t)
♠ KQJ1098
♡ 3
◊ Q432
♣ 98

With spades trumps, your hand will win at least five tricks; with hearts trumps, probably none. You would be correct in bidding one spade and, even if partner now bids two hearts, rebidding with two spades.

By that time, we'd hope partner got the general idea that we wanted to play the hand in spades, weren't interested in his heart suit, and passed.

But if your partner is the type of 'hand hog' who insists on playing every hand himself, and the more you bid your suit, the more he'll rebid his, it's better to pass in the first place!

GAME FORCING BIDS AFTER PARTNER'S OVERCALL

The *only* way to force to game after your partner has made a simple overcall is for the overcaller's partner to bid the opponent's suit. For example –

CASE M

South, Opener	West	North	East, You
One heart	One spade	pass	Two hearts

This bid is unconditionally forcing to game. Ordinarily, it shows a tremendous supporting fit for the last suit bid by the partnership, in this case, spades. In some cases, it will mask a solid or semi-solid suit to be shown later.

(u)	(v)	(w)
♠ K J 8 7	♠ Q 10 6 5	♠ J 6
♡ void	♡ 3	♡ A 2
◇ A K J 8 7 4	◇ A K Q 4 3	◇ A 4 3
♣ K Q 9	♣ A K J	♣ K Q J 10 8 7

Holding each of the above hands, and with the bidding in Case M on the preceding page, you would respond with a forcing to game cue-bid of the opponent's heart suit in response to your partner's spade overcall.

The reader will notice that first round heart control is actually lacking in hand (v). Yet the important thing from responder's point of view is to find out how big the overcaller's hand is. The cue-bid of two hearts forces not only another bid from partner, but additional bids until game has been reached.

"Won't the overcaller think the cue-bid shows first round control of the heart suit?" you may ask.

Possibly. But in no other way can you force partner to keep on bidding to game, and that feature outweighs the slight misinformation about your hand.

"Why didn't you respond with either four spades or three diamonds on hands (u) and (v)?" you add.

The answer is simple. Holding either hand (u) or (v), after your partner overcalls with one spade, your problem is not whether the combined hands can make a game (which is a certainty), but rather, can they make a slam?

Had you raised your partner's one spade overcall to four spades, your partner would undoubtedly pass. He can't pass the cue-bid in the opponent's suit, and you will have plenty of bidding time to locate his high cards and decide whether the hand belongs in game, a small slam or possibly even a grand slam.

THE JUMP TAKEOUT IN A NEW SUIT AFTER PARTNER'S OVERCALL

A jump response of one more than necessary in a new suit by the partner of the overcaller is only *semi-forcing*. Suppose, holding hands (u) and (v) with the bidding of Case M on page 402, you had responded 'three diamonds.' That would be a bid of one more than necessary in a new suit.

Had your partner *opened* the bidding, that would be forcing to game.

But your partner didn't open the bidding. He overcalled!

So the single jump in a new suit, facing an overcall, is only semi-forcing and can be passed by a player who has overcalled with a minimum hand.

With 14 points or more, facing a single jump in a new suit, the overcaller should bid again.

The jump of more than one in a new suit by overcaller's partner is pre-emptive, shows a long suit, and little high card strength. It is an attempt to shut out the opponents.

CASE N

South, Opener	West	North	East, You
One club	One dia.	pass	Three spades

Your hand would resemble –

♠ KJ98765 ♡ 2 ◊ J76 ♣ 42

Obviously, partner should pass unless he feels game probable, or, with a fit, he is pushed higher by the opponents' bidding.

EXAMPLES

With the following bidding, you are West. Bid each hand.

CASE O

North, Opener	East, Partner	South	West, You
One heart	One spade	pass	?

What do you do with each of the following hands?

(a)	(b)	(c)	(d)
♠ 7	♠ J106	♠ Q874	♠ Q874
♡ J10643	♡ Q2	♡ 3	♡ 4
◊ K643	◊ AJ97	◊ AJ107	◊ AQJ
♣ Q87	♣ K752	♣ K643	♣ KJ1098
(e)	**(f)**	**(g)**	**(h)**
♠ KJ764	♠ Q2	♠ 74	♠ 74
♡ void	♡ KJ7	♡ 864	♡ 86
◊ AQ108	◊ Q876	◊ KQ543	◊ KQJ975
♣ KJ76	♣ KJ62	♣ K43	♣ 432

(i)	(j)	(k)	(1)
♠ 7	♠ Q 10	♠ J 6 4 3	♠ 2
♡ A Q J 10 7 5 4 3	♡ K Q 10 9 8 7	♡ 7 3	♡ J 8 7 6 5 4
◇ A 2	◇ A Q J 6	◇ A Q J 10 8	◇ A 7 5
♣ J 6	♣ 5	♣ A K	♣ Q 3 2

(a) Pass! A denial bid or rescue of one no trump is unthinkable. Remember that when you disturb partner's minimum overcall, you show a constructive purpose, not lack of support.

(b) Bid two spades. Your partner's overcall guarantees at least a five card spade suit. You have ruffing strength, trump support, and a total of 11 points, after deducting one point for holding only three trumps. If partner has additional values, he will bid again.

(c) Three spades. In support of partner's spade suit, the hand totals 13 points. Not forcing.

(d) Four spades, not two or three clubs. Partner could pass either club bid. In support of spades, the hand totals 16 points.

(e) Two hearts. The cue-bid of the opponent's suit is forcing to game, here shows first round control, and probes the possibility of slam. The hand totals 19 points.

(f) One no trump. 12 high card points.

(g) Pass. If spades and hearts were reversed, you might try two spades.

(h) Two diamonds.

(i) You should either pass or bid four hearts, hoping in the latter case to lose no more than one heart trick to the opponent who bid the suit. A bid of two hearts is wholly incorrect, since partner would assume it to be a cue-bid, showing spade support and heart control. Moreover, the opponent's heart bid may be a complete bluff (psychic).

(j) Four spades. Despite the doubleton trump, you do have normal trump support for a rebiddable suit for which your partner's overcall has marked him. Further, the hand is so powerful in playing strength that you should have an adequate play for game. As in (i), a cue-bid of two hearts would be entirely incorrect, show the opposite of your holding.

(k) Four spades.

(1) Pass.

RAISES OF MINOR SUIT OVERCALLS

In the preceding examples, the overcall happened to be in spades, a major suit. Suppose it was in clubs or diamonds? What I have said previously about point requirements and probable winners applies equally to minors and majors.

A voluntary raise of partner's overcall of a minor suit, particularly if made at the three level of bidding, usually asks the overcaller to do one of three things; first, bid no trump if holding stoppers in the adverse suit; second, lacking the necessary stoppers, show a secondary four card major if present; third, lacking either, and with probability of game, bid five in the minor. To find a second bid, the overcaller should have 14 or more points and game probability.

First, let me show what I mean by a voluntary raise –

CASE P

South, Opener	West, Partner	North	East, You
One heart	Two clubs	pass	Three clubs

But this is a forced raise –

CASE Q

South, Opener	West, Partner	North	East, You
One heart	Two clubs	Two hearts	Three clubs

In other words, in the first example, no one forced you to bid three clubs. Your partner's two club bid was already the highest bid at the table. Your raise merely told him there was a strong possibility of game if he had 14 or more points, plus the required stoppers or secondary major suits.

In the second bidding example, you had to bid three clubs in order to try to buy the bid. The opponent's two heart bid had superseded your partner's overcall. Your action was forced. Thus your three club raise in Case Q does not necessarily show the same willingness to go to game as did Case P; rather, the bidding in Case Q is an attempt to buy the contract as cheaply as possible.

Note that I said "with 14 or more points." It would be suicidal for a player who overcalled with 10 to 13 points to make another bid merely because he received a single raise from partner.

Suppose the bidding had been –

(m)	(n)
♠ K J 8 7	♠ K J
♡ 4	♡ Q 4 3
◇ A K 10 5 4	◇ A K J 7 6 5
♣ J 8 7	♣ K 2

CASE R

North	East, You	South	West
1 club	1 diam.	pass	2 diam.
pass	?		

You are East. Holding hand (m), you should rebid two spades. This is in the hope that partner has four spades, too. If he hasn't, he will bid again, and it will probably be three diamonds, which you can pass.

On (n), the moment your partner raises your diamond suit, it becomes 'solid' for six winners. The king of clubs behind the club bidder gives you a total of seven winners. You should now rebid with two no trump, which your partner, with any extra values, should raise to three no trump. If your hand contained eight or more winners after receiving partner's raise, your rebid should be three no trump.

IF PARTNER MADE A DELAYED OVERCALL

You will remember that on page 388 we described a delayed overcall as an overcall not made at the bidder's first opportunity. Since it showed a weak hand and a long suit, responder should pass in 99 percent of these cases. The only reason for responding voluntarily (without being forced by the opponents' bidding) is a tremendous fit for partner's suit and game probability. Otherwise, pass and hope to buy the bid as cheaply as you can.

Your overcall (of two spades) was based on the reasoning that the missing strength not shown in the bidding is with your partner. Otherwise, the opponents would have bid higher. Since the overcaller is thus counting on high cards from his partner, the latter should take that fact into consideration before taking any action. However, should game seem probable, or the opponents now rebid, the responding hand should certainly raise or take some action. Re-opening the bidding in the fourth position where your side has not yet bid and the opponents bidding is about to die, the low level is known as 'protecting' or 'balancing.'

The practice of 'protecting' or 'balancing' is far more prevalent in duplicate or tournament bridge than in the rubber bridge or party variety. In the latter the matter of the opponents playing a hand at one spade or one no trump is not of serious importance. Whereas in duplicate, permitting the opponents to play the hand in one spade when your side can make, let us say, two hearts, can be the difference between a 'top' or a 'bottom' score.

Re-opening the bidding, when based primarily on inference, requires a great deal of experience and a keen sense of intuition.

IF PARTNER OVERCALLED WITH ONE NO TRUMP

After your partner overcalls with one no trump, you know he has 16 to 19 high card points. The first thing you should ask yourself is, "**Can my side make a game?**" The next question is, "**Will the combined hands play better in no trump or a suit contract?**"

If the answer is yes to the first question, then you should take some affirmative action, as bidding three no trump, or jumping to three or four of your suit, depending on the nature of your hand. In general, 10 or more points in responder's hand, plus those shown by the no trump overcall, will produce a game.

There are several things to remember. First, an overcall in no trump generally denies strong major suit holdings, since with the latter and 16 to 19 points, an informatory double would be preferable.

Next, the overcall in no trump, even of two no trump, is *not* forcing and partner, with little or nothing, should pass.

A takeout to two of a suit is a signoff, shows at least a five card suit and less than five high card points. The no trump overcaller should generally pass his partner's takeout to two of a suit unless he happens to have a very fine fit for that suit, in which case he can give a single raise from two to three of that suit. The raise in a minor is invitational for responder with extra values to bid three no trump; in a major, to rebid with eight or more points.

A jump takeout to three of a suit after partner's overcall of one no trump is forcing to game. This bid is usually made in a major suit with 10 or more points. With the equivalent strength and minor suits, the jump to three no trump is preferable, since nine tricks in no trump will usually be easier to win than 11 in the minor.

With a long suit, and less than 10 points, the jump is made directly to game.

CASE S

North	East	South	West, You
One heart	One no trump	pass	?

(o)	(p)	(q)
♠ 84	♠ QJ8765	♠ J9876543
♡ 76	♡ 2	♡ 6
◇ KJ873	◇ A109	◇ K2
♣ KQJ2	♣ QJ4	♣ 85

(o) Three no trump.

(p) Three spades. Forcing—partner cannot pass.

(q) Four spades.

RESPONDING TO TWO AND THREE NO TRUMP OVERCALLS

Should your partner overcall an opponent's opening bid by bidding two no trump, it is obvious that he needs very little from your hand to make a game. As little as a king will do the trick, or perhaps a secondary stopper in the opponent's suit.

Facing a three no trump overcall, there is no point in the responder contemplating a bid unless he feels his side can make a slam, or that the hand will play better in his long suit than in no trump.

In this latter regard, I would like to point out that two and three no trump overcalls are generally based on long solid minor suits, plus the needed high card strength. The no trump overcaller *wants* to play the hand in no trump; if he wanted you to bid your long suit, he would have doubled informatorily.

So don't bid any kind of a suit after your partner has overcalled with two or three no trump. For example, let's say that your partner overcalled with three no trump over an opening bid of one heart and you hold the following hands—

(r)	(s)	(t)
♠ 9876543	♠ J10876	♠ KJ9876
♡ 2	♡ 64	♡ 10
◇ 54	◇ QJ8	◇ Q543
♣ 1087	♣ J109	♣ K2
Four spades, a signoff.	Pass	Five spades, a mild slam try.

RESPONDING TO JUMP OVERCALLS
SINGLE JUMPS

By a single jump, I mean that your partner bid one more than necessary to overcall. For example, one heart by the opening bidder, two spades by your partner.

Since your partner's single jump overcall has shown an extremely powerful hand, it stands to reason that your side can make a game if you have anything to offer in the realm of trick taking ability.

But the important thing to remember is that the single jump overcall, even though it shows a 'powerhouse,' is *not* forcing! If you are 'busted,' you don't have to respond. However, with the ability to win one trick, whether in high card values, or by trumping some 'off' suit, you should respond at least once. If you have greater strength, you can place the hand in game, or find a second bid.

TABLE OF RESPONSES TO SINGLE JUMP OVERCALLS

HOLDING IN POINTS	BID AS DIRECTED BELOW
0-3	Pass, unless holding five of partner's trumps and a singleton; or four trumps and a void. In these cases, give a single raise.
4-5	Try to find a bid unless holding a singleton or void in partner's suit, in which event you should pass.
6	Find a bid. Any bid suit must be at least five cards or longer; raise partner's suit or bid no trump, depending on your hand.
7 or more	Get to game, or make a forcing to game bid.

Remember—if the hand is apparently a misfit, and you have a singleton or void of partner's suit, it is better to pass than respond with five points or less. Misfit hands require two more points than conventional requirements to produce a game.

Circumstances, of course, alter cases. If you have five points or less and the bulk of it is in the opponent's suit, where it may be worthless to your partner, you should proceed carefully. For example, the king-jack of the opponent's bid suit may not be worth anything if the opponent holds the ace-queen over your combination. On the other hand, if your strength is where it will help partner, either in his suit or in side suits where it can be utilized, you may take slight liberties.

The following are examples of responses to single jump overcalls. There are two sets of bidding for each hand.

CASE T

North	East, Partner	South	West, You
One diamond	Two hearts	pass	?

CASE U

North	East, Partner	South	West, You
One heart	Three clubs	pass	?

Beneath each of the following hands are two bids. Those marked (A) give the indicated response in the first bidding situation, where partner's overcall was two hearts; those marked (B) refer to responses to the three club overcall.

(u)	(v)	(w)	(x)
♠ J10864	♠ J10864	♠ 732	♠ 843
♡ 64	♡ 6432	♡ KJ	♡ 62
◇ Q852	◇ 8753	◇ K643	◇ 987
♣ 107	♣ void	♣ J1087	♣ KJ965
(A) pass	(A) 3 hearts	(A) 3 hearts	(A) pass
(B) pass	(B) pass	(B) 3 no trump	(B) 4 clubs

(y)	(z)	(a)	(b)
♠ KQ542	♠ 6432	♠ 3	♠ K63
♡ 62	♡ Q854	♡ Q108	♡ 85
◇ 987	◇ A	◇ KQ8654	◇ Q1098
♣ 843	♣ K632	♣ J82	♣ KJ107
(A) 2 spades	(A) 3 diamonds	(A) 4 hearts	(A) 3 no tr.
(B) 3 spades	(B) 5 clubs	(B) 3 dia.	(B) 4 clubs

RESPONDING TO PRE-EMPTIVE JUMP OVERCALLS

When your partner overcalls in a suit by jumping more than one level, you must remember that he is showing a long suit and a weak hand. If his overcall places the hand in game, as by bidding four spades over one heart, there is no need for you to respond, unless in very rare cases, you think the combined hands can make a slam.

If his pre-emptive overcall is short of game, the only excuse you have for bidding voluntarily is that you think your hands can produce a game.

PARTNER'S PRE-EMPTIVE OVERCALL WAS	YOU REQUIRE
Three of a minor, as three diamonds over one club.	To bid three no trump, at least a doubleton of partner's suit, and preferably an honor – all unbid suits stopped, and a minimum of 10 high card points. To raise to five of the minor – 19 points, minimum.
Four of a minor.	To raise to five of the minor – 16 points, minimum.
Three of a major.	To raise to four of the major – 16 points, minimum. Preferably, a partial supporting fit.

Slam requirements will be discussed in Lesson XIII.

RESPONDING TO NO TRUMP OVERCALLS OF PRE-EMPTS

There are two possible bidding situations. The first:

CASE V

Opener	Partner	Opponent	You
Three anything	Three no trump	pass	?

You should ordinarily pass unless you think your side can make a slam, or that the hand will play better in your suit than in no trump. Your partner's three no trump bid does not request you to bid, so any bid you make is entirely voluntary. Your partner is perfectly willing to play the hand at three no trump.

CASE W

Opener	Partner	Opponent	You
Four of anything) Three " ")	–Four no trump	pass	?

You must bid! Partner's four no trump is like a giant informatory double.

♠ K J 10 9
♡ 3
◊ A K Q 7
♣ A K J 10

The hand to the left was used on page 391 as (f) to illustrate a four no trump overcall over an opening bid of four hearts. Now, let's pretend you are the partner of the player who overcalled four hearts with four no trump, and see what your response would be with each of the following hands.

(c)	(d)	(e)	(f)
♠ Q643	♠ A76432	♠ AQ74	♠ A5
♡ 1082	♡ 82	♡ A	♡ 743
◇ 10432	◇ J8	◇ J1086	◇ Q109876
♣ 83	♣ 743	♣ Q432	♣ 62
Five spades	Six spades	Five hearts	Six diamonds

Since the four no trump overcall guarantees that any bid you make at the five level can be successfully completed, even if you as responder are completely 'broke,' six to eight points in responder's hand should give you a good play for a small slam, nine points or more for a grand slam. The cue bid in (e) is, of course, showing first round control of the opponents' suit. It does not show the heart suit.

CASE X

North	East, You	South	West, Partner
One heart	pass	4 hearts	4 no trump
pass	*You must bid!*		

The above bidding situation is more complex than its predecessor, since both adversaries have bid and you have previously passed. South's four heart raise is pre-emptive, and West, with a powerhouse, doesn't intend to be shut out. Responses are the same as in the preceding example (Case W) of a direct four no trump overcall of a pre-emptive opening bid.

RESPONDING WHEN PARTNER HAS OVERCALLED BY BIDDING THE OPPONENT'S SUIT

CASE Y

The bidding has been –

North	East
Opener, Opponent	Partner
One of a suit	Two of the same suit

As you know from page 394, this immediate overcall of the opponent's suit by bidding the self same suit shows a tremendous hand, a sort of 'super two bid.' It is forcing to game. Neither partner may pass until game has been reached (or the opponents doubled for penalty). As in responding to overcalls of four no trump, six points in responder's hand facing this immediate cue-bid will generally produce a small slam, nine or more points a grand slam.

RESPONDING AFTER YOUR SUIT HAS BEEN BID EARLIER BY THE OPPONENTS

Once in a rare while, when you are forced to respond, the very suit you might have bid has already been bid by the opponents.

(g)
♠ 1074
♡ J863
◇ 852
♣ 1095

Since you hold no other four card or longer suit, the solution is to make the cheapest bid you can with a three card suit.

Let's suppose you hold hand (g). The bidding has been –

CASE Z

North, Opener	East, Partner	South	You, West
One heart	Two hearts	pass	?

Your response, with hand (g), should be two spades!

That's the cheapest three card suit you can bid.

On the other hand, let's suppose the bidding was –

CASE A

North, Opener	East, Partner	South	You, West
Four hearts	Four no trump	pass	?

Here your takeout should be five clubs, since clubs is the lowest (cheapest) bid you can make over no trump and you do hold three cards of that suit.

Under no circumstances should you pass in these forcing situations, or bid no trump with a bust, purely because your only long suit has already been bid by the opponents. A response of no trump over an immediate cue bid (Case Y) shows a strong hand with eight points or more, a stopper in the opponent's suit and a willingness to play the final contract in no trump. The only reason for not responding three no trump with hand (h) is first, partner won't pass two no trump since it is short of game; and next, if partner has a two suiter, you'd waste one round of bidding, and make it difficult for him to show both of his suits cheaply.

(h)
♠ J98
♡ Q1096
◇ A87
♣ K64

Above all, don't become panic stricken when your hand is weak, and your only four card or longer suit is that bid by the opponents. Remember in these cases, no trump responses show strength, not weakness.

REBIDS BY THE OVERCALLER
WHEN PARTNER HAS PASSED YOUR OVERCALL

In the event that you have made a minimum overcall which your partner passed, the only way you will have another opportunity to bid is for one or both of the opponents to bid.

From this, you should draw the following inference – "**My partner has shown apparent weakness, or lack of support for my suit. The opponents have indicated added strength.**"

You should then ask yourself the question – "**Is it safe for me to rebid?**"

The answer should be "**no**" the vast majority of the times.

The reason is that if the best you could do was make a minimum overcall, there was little chance that your side could make a game, particularly after the opponents showed extra strength through their rebids.

What little hope your side had of making a game vanished when your partner passed your overcall. Now, if you rebid, there is very little you can make your way of the cards, but a good possibility that if your suit lies badly, you can be doubled and penalized. Why chance that for a doubtful part score?

(i)
♠ KQJ987
♡ 3
◇ Q109
♣ K87

Of course, if your suit is extra long and sufficiently solid (as having overcalled one heart with one spade holding hand (i)–) you might rebid with two spades over a raise or rebid of two hearts.

But don't rebid a long suit when you have few or no high cards elsewhere in the hand for defensive values. You may wind up pushing the opponents to a higher (or game) contract which they never would have reached if you hadn't driven them there.

It's far better to let sleeping dogs lie!

IF PARTNER HAS RAISED YOUR OVERCALL

The overcaller, after receiving a raise from his partner, should add the points in his hand to those shown by partner's raise. If the total shows a makeable game or within a point of it, game should be bid at once. Without the probability of game, the overcaller should pass.

Don't try to stretch a two-bagger into a home run. Too many

batters have been thrown out at home plate and the same goes for bridge players who try to stretch partials into games that just aren't there!

IF PARTNER HAS BID A NEW SUIT

As a general rule, if you have overcalled in one suit, and your partner now bids another suit, you should pass. There is a bridge adage that 'both partners don't defend.' This is particularly true if partner took you out from a major suit into a minor, since with any vestige of support for the major, there would be no rhyme or reason for his bidding a suit which forces the contract higher and also yields fewer points per trick.

With a fit for partner's suit and eight to 12 points, give your partner's suit a single raise. Don't rebid your own suit unless it is at least six cards in length with some solidity and you are absolutely certain that the hand will play better in your suit than in partner's. If you have a two-suiter, you may wish to show the second suit with 14 points or more.

But if the hand appears to be a misfit after partner's bid, learn to pass in a hurry. Don't fight your partner or bid no trump as a denial!

IF PARTNER HAS GIVEN YOUR MINOR A VOLUNTARY RAISE

If your overcall was in a minor suit and partner gave you a voluntary raise, try to find a second bid with 14 or more points. If you have a stopper in the opponent's suit, bid no trump; with a biddable four card major suit, show that suit.

As a general rule, game in the minor suit itself (winning 11 tricks) is unlikely against an adverse opening bid.

IF PARTNER BID NO TRUMP OVER YOUR OVERCALL

If your partner voluntarily bid no trump after you made a simple overcall, pass with a minimum hand, unless it has a void or second suit, in which case the latter can be shown.

Rebid any six card or longer suit. Jump the bidding or bid a game if game appears makeable from the combined point count. Raise the no trump with an establishable suit and at least one supplementary stopper in the opponent's suit.

With the following hands, the opponent to your right opened the bidding with one heart. You overcalled with one spade, the next player passed and your partner responded with one no trump.

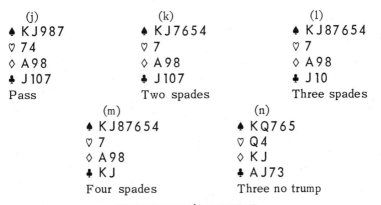

(j)	(k)	(l)
♠ KJ987	♠ KJ7654	♠ KJ87654
♡ 74	♡ 7	♡ 7
◊ A98	◊ A98	◊ A98
♣ J107	♣ J107	♣ J10
Pass	Two spades	Three spades

(m)	(n)
♠ KJ87654	♠ KQ765
♡ 7	♡ Q4
◊ A98	◊ KJ
♣ KJ	♣ AJ73
Four spades	Three no trump

RESPONDER'S REBIDS

If, after your partner has made a minimum overcall, you have shown a new suit and your partner merely rebids the same suit as cheaply as possible, pass unless your suit is six cards or longer and is solid or semi-solid. You are telling your partner that you think the combined hands will play better with your suit as trump than his. With 10 points or more, it is permissable for the responder, though not always desirable, to show a second suit. The latter may be of four cards.

The student should realize that the overcaller usually should have 14 or more points to show a second suit, particularly if his partner has been unable to respond to or raise the first suit.

CASE B

North	East, Partner	South	West, You
One diamond	One heart	Pass	One spade
Pass	Two hearts	Pass	?

(o)	(p)	(q)	(r)
♠ KQ8765	♠ AJ109876	♠ KQ765	♠ KQ765
♡ 86	♡ 3	♡ J	♡ J2
◊ 54	◊ 54	◊ 72	◊ 72
♣ KJ9	♣ K87	♣ K10987	♣ AQ109
Pass	Two spades	Pass	Three clubs

THINGS TO REMEMBER

1-Keep your overcalls sound. Do not immediately overcall with less than 10 points, even if not vulnerable. If your suit is sufficiently long and solid, and the hand lacks 10 points, you should either pass at your first opportunity and overcall later or pre-empt immediately, if the required playing tricks are present.

2-Don't overcall on four card suits!

3-Don't overcall on weak suits!

4-If your partner bids two suits in overcalling, try to express a preference rather than showing a new suit of your own.

5-Don't fight your partner. If you don't like his suit, you have no assurance he'll like yours!

6-The *only* bids that are forcing to game after the opponents have opened the bidding are—(1) A cue bid of the adverse suit—(2)—A bid of four no trump.

7-After your partner overcalls, a jump takeout in a new suit is *not* forcing, only semi-forcing.

8-After your partner overcalls, it is better with support for his suit to raise that suit than show a new suit of your own, particularly if his suit is a major.

9-If you have overcalled with 15 or more points and your partner has given a voluntary raise, try to find another bid if game appears makeable.

10-Voluntary raises of minor suit overcalls are invitational to final three no trump contracts.

QUIZ ELEVEN

1-With neither side vulnerable, your right hand opponent has opened the bidding with one heart. What do you do with each of the following hands?

(a)	(b)	(c)
♠ AKQ7	♠ A4	♠ QJ10987
♡ J84	♡ 753	♡ Q4
◇ K63	◇ KQ542	◇ J63
♣ 1085	♣ 862	♣ 105

(d)	(e)	(f)
♠ KJ432	♠ J10987	♠ KQ987
♡ A109	♡ J4	♡ K2
◇ Q42	◇ AQ7	◇ A104
♣ 86	♣ KJ9	♣ J85

2-With neither side vulnerable, your right hand opponent opened the bidding with one heart. What do you do with each of the following hands?

(g)	(h)	(i)	(j)
♠ A3	♠ KQJ1098	♠ AKJ987654	♠ AKQ108
♡ K98	♡ A	♡ 3	♡ 6
◇ KQ74	◇ KJ5	◇ 62	◇ KQJ107
♣ AJ83	♣ Q103	♣ 3	♣ J8

3-You are East. With neither side vulnerable, the bidding—

South, dealer	West, Partner	North	East, You
One heart	One spade	pass	?

What do you do with each of the following hands?

(k)	(l)	(m)	(n)
♠ 8	♠ 862	♠ A97	♠ 104
♡ J543	♡ 102	♡ 6	♡ Q1087
◇ KQ765	◇ AQ104	◇ KQJ84	◇ A65
♣ 1082	♣ QJ98	♣ KJ93	♣ K1096

4-Your right hand opponent opened with four hearts. Both sides are vulnerable. What do you do with each of the following hands?

(o)	(p)	(q)	(r)
♠ 86	♠ AKJ632	♠ KQJ5	♠ AQ3
♡ Q87	♡ 64	♡ void	♡ KJ9
◇ KQ105	◇ Q52	◇ KQJ98	◇ KQ87
♣ AQ64	♣ 108	♣ AKJ9	♣ AJ10

ANSWERS TO QUIZ ELEVEN

1-(a) Pass. Do not overcall on a four card suit; (b) pass—the diamond suit lacks sufficient solidity and the hand does not have the needed five probable winners; (c) pass—the hand does not have the necessary 10 point minimum; (d) pass—the suit lacks solidity and body; (e) one spade—despite the fact that the spade suit is lacking in top cards, the suit is sufficiently solid and the hand contains too much high card strength to pass; (f) one spade.

2-(g) One no trump; (h) two spades; (i) four spades; (j) two spades.

3-(k) Pass—the fact that you lack support for partner's spade suit does not furnish an excuse to bid two diamonds; (l) two spades; (m) four spades; (n) one no trump.

4-(o) Pass. A penalty double would be highly speculative, since you have three doubtful defensive tricks; (p) Pass—you've been 'fixed' by the opening pre-emptive bid. To bid four spades would be highly dangerous; (q) four no trump; (r) double. This is for penalty, since you should defeat four hearts decisively.

LESSON ELEVEN

HANDS

The student should bid each hand before consulting 'par.'

1-North dealer, neither side vul

North: ♠ 83 ♡ AQJ10 ◇ KJ9 ♣ AQJ7

West: ♠ 76 ♡ 9754 ◇ AQ73 ♣ 643

East: ♠ AQ542 ♡ K863 ◇ 102 ♣ 95

South: ♠ KJ109 ♡ 2 ◇ 8654 ♣ K1082

2-East dealer, N-S vul

North: ♠ K542 ♡ Q543 ◇ 94 ♣ 652

West: ♠ 973 ♡ 62 ◇ AKQ10 ♣ J1097

East: ♠ AQ1086 ♡ KJ108 ◇ 7 ♣ A83

South: ♠ J ♡ A97 ◇ J86532 ♣ KQ4

3-South dealer, both sides vul.

North: ♠ 8 ♡ J107653 ◇ 42 ♣ 7632

West: ♠ AQJ96 ♡ KQ98 ◇ J95 ♣ 8

East: ♠ 10532 ♡ 4 ◇ A103 ♣ KQJ109

South: ♠ K74 ♡ A2 ◇ KQ876 ♣ A54

4-West dealer, E-W vul.

North: ♠ AKJ987 ♡ AJ8 ◇ 2 ♣ A54

West: ♠ 1043 ♡ K42 ◇ AK876 ♣ QJ

East: ♠ 62 ♡ 109763 ◇ 1093 ♣ 1092

South: ♠ Q5 ♡ Q5 ◇ QJ54 ♣ K8763

PAR

1 - North	East	South	West
1 ht.	pass	1 sp.	pass
2 n.t.	pass	3 n.t.	pass
pass	pass		

Opening lead, ♣ 9

2-East	South	West	North
1 sp.	pass	2 dia.	pass
2 hts.	pass	2 sp.	pass
3 sp.	pass	4 sp.	pass
pass	pass		

Opening lead, ♣ K

3-South	West	North	East
1 dia.	1 sp.	pass	3 sp.
pass	4 sp.	pass	pass
pass			

Opening lead, ◇ 4

4-West	North	East	South
1 dia.	2 sp.	pass	2 no tr.
pass	3 sp.	pass	4 sp.
pass	pass	pass	

Opening lead, ◇ 10

SOLUTIONS TO LESSON ELEVEN HANDS

1 -

North declarer at 3 no trump.

Trick	E	S	W	N
1	♣9	♣2	♣3	♣Q
2	♠2	♠9	♠6	♠3
3	♡K	♡2	♡4	♡Q
4	♢10	♢4	♢7	♢J
5	♠A	♠10	♠7	♠8
6	♢2	♢5	♢A	♢9
7	♡3	♢4	♡5	♡A

North claims the balance, winning 10 tricks.

2 -

East declarer at four spades.

Trick	S	W	N	E
1	♣K	♣7	♣2	♣A
2	♢2	♢Q	♢4	♢7
3	♢3	♢K	♢9	♣3
4	♢5	♢A	♠2	♠6
5	♣Q	♣9	♣5	♣8
6	♢J	♢10	♣6	♠8
7	♡A	♡2	♡5	♡K
8	♡9	♡6	♡Q	♡8
9	♡7	♠3	♡3	♡10
10	♠J	♠7	♠4	♠Q
11	♢6	♠9	♡4	♡J
12	♣4	♣J	♠5	♠10
13	♢8	♣10	♠K	♠A

East wins 10 tricks.

3 -

West declarer at four spades.

Trick	N	E	S	W
1	♢4	♢3	♢Q	♢5
2	♠8	♠10	♠4	♠6
3	♡3	♠2	♠7	♠9
4	♣2	♠5	♠K	♠A
5	♣3	♣9	♣A	♣8
6	♡5	♡4	♡A	♡8

West claims the balance, winning 10 tricks.

4 -

North declarer at four spades.

Trick	E	S	W	N
1	♢10	♢J	♢K	♢2
2	♠2	♠Q	♠3	♠7
3	♠6	♠5	♠4	♠J
4	♢9	♢4	♠10	♠A
5	♣2	♣3	♣J	♣A
6	♣9	♣6	♣Q	♣4
7	♡3	♡5	♡2	♡A

North claims the balance, stating that the king of clubs will 'drop' the outstanding club, the 10 spot. The two remaining clubs become winners on which the two hearts can be discarded.

North wins 11 tricks.

Comments on the following page.

COMMENTS ON LESSON ELEVEN HANDS

1 - This is what is known in bridge as a 'lucky' hand, because every card is 'right.' East's opening lead of the nine of clubs requires a bit of explanation. East would normally, without a sequence, lead his fourth best spade from his longer suit.

But spades have been bid by his left hand opponent, making that lead seem unprofitable. Hearts, his alternative lead, were bid by his right hand opponent. Accordingly, East leads a short suit, clubs, hoping to 'hit' his partner's suit. It so happens that the lead neither helped nor hurt.

The hand demonstrates the danger of the unsound overcall - one made on a suit lacking solidity, despite its five card length. If East overcalls with one spade, South should double immediately for penalty. Playing at one spade doubled, East can be defeated three tricks for a lucrative 500 point penalty.

2 - Another hand to demonstrate that you shouldn't overcall with poor suits. If South overcalls with two diamonds, West will double for penalty, defeating the contract four tricks with accurate defense.

East's play of three high diamonds before touching trumps is an attempt to get rid of his losing clubs before the opponents can regain the lead to cash their club trick. The only way East can later enter dummy to take finesses in the trump suit is by trumping his winning hearts. Note how East eventually succeeds in trapping North's well guarded king of trumps.

3 - Had West won the opening diamond lead with the ace, he would have been defeated, since South could then win four tricks — two diamonds and two aces. If North's diamond was originally a singleton, there was nothing West could do about it. South to continue that suit without giving the opponents two diamond tricks. South's choice of a trump lead at trick two is a choice of the least of evils since to cash the ace of clubs would set up as winners dummy's club suit and the lead of the ace of hearts would similarly create winners for the declarer in that suit.

4 - North's single jump overcall shows a powerful hand. The partnership should have no trouble reaching game.

Lesson XII

PART ONE

Doubles

PART TWO

Redoubles

PART THREE

Tactics against Doubles

LESSON TWELVE

PART ONE

DOUBLES

Doubles are of three kinds, informatory, penalty and lead-directing.

The informatory double shows a powerful hand and commands doubler's partner to bid.

The penalty or business double indicates a belief by the doubler that his side can defeat the adverse contract, and wishes to increase the penalty the opponents will pay for non-fulfillment. Lead-directing doubles will be fully discussed in Lesson XVI under 'Expert Bidding Tactics.'

Since the word 'double' is spelled and pronounced the same in both cases, the student should learn to differentiate between each type by the way they are used.

INFORMATORY DOUBLES

While there are five different types of informatory doubles, they have one point in common – partner *must* respond! The only times partner does not have to respond are –

(a) When the opponent to his right bids –

(b) When the responder feels the doubled contract can be defeated more profitably than any other contract.

Now cases (a) and (b) are the exceptions and in 85 percent of the cases when your partner makes an informatory double, he will be expecting you to respond.

Oddly enough, the weaker your hand as responder, the more imperative it is that you bid in answer to your partner's informatory double. This peculiarity stems from the fact that the less you have, the more likely that the opponents will complete their (informatorily) doubled contract. Your loss when they make their doubled contract, plus possible over-tricks, will be as great or greater than any penalty you might normally incur by responding with your best suit, even though that suit may be only four cards headed by the five spot, and your hand doesn't contain even a single face card!

Now it may puzzle you that your partner's informatory double which you (incorrectly) passed with a weak hand became a penalty double netting the opponents over-tricks. But that is the case. When a player says 'double' at the table, he does not add **"I double informatorily,"** or **"I double for penalty."**

He just says 'double,' and if the next three players pass, the double remains in effect and is for penalty. On the other hand, if doubler's partner responds, that takes out (the effect) of the double which becomes informatory.

Informatory doubles, while alike in basic principle, vary according to the situation in which they are used. There are five types of informatory doubles. Type one, the regular informatory double, is the most common, and should first be mastered by the student; the other types should be learned as the student becomes more proficient.

TYPES OF INFORMATORY DOUBLES

1 - Regular,
2 - Secondary,
3 - Repeated,
4 - Distributional,
5 - Protective.

THE REGULAR TYPE

Chief identification of a regular informatory double is that the double is made at the doubler's first opportunity and before partner has bid. In this regard, a previous pass is *not* considered a bid.

CASE A

North, Partner	East	South, You	West
pass	One heart	Double	

Here is a case of a regular informatory double. It has been made at your first opportunity. North, your partner, has not yet bid.

But doubles, to be informatory, have several other distinguishing marks. First, if no trump is doubled, a double of one no trump under these circumstances is informatory; a double of two or more no trump, even if partner hasn't yet bid, is always for penalty.

If the double is of no trump, there are several distinguishing characteristics. Doubles of *opening bids* of one no trump are always for penalty; a double of one no trump made as a response, if one's partner has not yet bid, is informatory; doubles of two or more no trump, are always for penalty.

generally accepted that doubles of three of a minor are informatory; three of a major are optional or co-operative.

By optional or co-operative, I mean that doubler's partner has quite a bit to say in the matter. If, let us say, your partner doubles an opening bid of three spades and you hold hand (a), you might as well pass because you hold high cards in all suits and, with vulnerability being equal, you should reap a substantial penalty.

(a)
♠ K4
♡ A83
◇ QJ76
♣ Q1052

But, let us say, your partner doubles an opening bid of three spades and you hold hand (b), it is apparent that your hand will have little defensive value against the doubled three spade contract, but offensively, with hearts trumps, would have tremendous aggressive values. Thus, you should bid four hearts despite the fact that your partner doubled three spades.

(b)
♠ 4
♡ QJ108765
◇ Q10
♣ K82

As to informatory doubles of opening bids of two in a suit, it depends entirely on how the opening two bid is used. If the two bid is the conventional, game forcing type described in Lesson X, there is no such bid as an informatory double of an opening two bid. There just aren't enough high cards in the deck to provide an opponent with an informatory double.

On the other hand, if the opening two bid is the weak, preemptive type described under Modern Expert Tactics in Lesson XVI, then the best defensive tactics are to use the double as optional, exactly as over an opening bid of three in a major.

The reader should have noticed that I have explicitly stated that any double, to be informatory, must be made before partner has bid. *Any* double, even at the one level, *after* partner has bid, is *always* a penalty double! As a matter of fact, the biggest penalty doubles result from doubles of poor overcalls made at the one and two levels.

Remember also that the double, to be informatory, *must* be made at the doubler's *first* opportunity!

CASE B

North	East, You	South	West
One heart	Double		

CASE C

North	East, You	South	West
One heart	pass	One no tr.	pass
Two hearts	Double		

CASE D

North	East, You	South	West
One club	pass	One heart	pass
One spade	Double		

Above are three doubles. Case B is clearly informatory, since it was made at your first opportunity; cases C and D are for penalty, since in neither case did you double at your first opportunity.

In (C), had East wanted his partner to bid, he would have doubled one heart. In (D), the same reasoning applies, since East did not double one club. His double of one spade says he can defeat that contract.

SECONDARY DOUBLES

In the preceding regular type of informatory double, the double was made after the opponents opened the bidding. In what I term the 'secondary' type, the takeout double is made by the player who opened the bidding and heard his partner pass.

CASE E

North, You	East	South	West
One heart	One spade	pass	pass
Double			

CASE F

One heart	pass	pass	One sp.
Double			

As North, your doubles in cases (E) and (F) are informatory. They have been made at your first opportunity (to double), and your partner's pass is not considered a bid.

But had the bidding gone –

CASE G

North, You	East	South	West
One club	pass	One heart	One sp.
Double			

Case (G) illustrates a penalty double, since it was made after your partner had bid.

CASE H

North, You	East	South	West
One heart	One spade	pass	Two sp.
Double			

Case (H) is a further extension of (E). The double is informatory. It has been made at your first opportunity, it is of less than four of a suit, and your partner has not yet bid. This particular informatory double would show an extra powerful hand, since you are forcing your partner to bid at the three level, contracting for nine tricks with a partner who was unable to bid voluntarily.

At this point I can hear someone asking, "**Suppose I open the bidding, and an opponent bids my other suit, and my partner passes. Now I want to double for penalty.**"

Sad to relate, you can't! If you double in this position, the double would be informatory and your partner will respond, the very thing you least desire. In that case, it is frequently better to let the opponents play the hand in (what is for them) the wrong suit and go down 50 or 100 points per trick rather than attempt to play the hand yourself.

CASE I

North, You	East	South	West
One spade	Two dia.	pass	pass

(c)
♠ AK64
♡ AJ6
◇ KQJ8
♣ 109

With the bidding in case (I), you hold hand (c). Both sides are vulnerable.

It should be readily apparent that it is practically impossible for the opponents to make two diamonds against your hand. Since your partner is unable to make any 'free' response, any North-South game is exceedingly remote. Thus, any possible penalty paid by East-West would be better than any contract played by North-South. In actual play, East-West went down two tricks for a score of minus 200 points.

Further, were you to double two diamonds, thus commanding your partner to bid in case (I), your double would promise excellent support for the unbid suits, and you can see that while you have fair support for the heart suit, you have no club support whatever.

REPEATED INFORMATORY DOUBLES

If a double is informatory the first time it is made, it logically follows that a second double by the same player will similarly be informatory if partner has not yet bid, and the doubled contract is less than two no trump, three or less in a minor or of less than four in a major.

CASE J

North	East, You	South	West
One heart	Double	One no trump	pass
Two hearts	Double		

CASE K

One heart	Double	Two hearts	pass
pass	Double		

Both cases (J) and (K) are informatory doubles. Again it should be pointed out, as in case (H), that the doubler's hand should have extra values, either in high cards, suit solidity, playing strength or a combination of these qualities, for a repeated informatory double.

This is only logical, since if partner is too weak to bid voluntarily, the doubler must have compensating strength to win the required tricks to complete the eventual contract.

CASE L

North	East, You	South	West
pass	One heart	One spade	pass
pass	Double	Two spades	pass
pass	Double		

I would like to stress that South's second bid of two spades in case (L) is intended to block out, or make difficult, West's response.

You see, if West now responds over the intervening two spade bid, he is making a 'free' response. He (West) is bidding when he doesn't have to bid. This voluntary action shows some strength, because without it West should pass. Thus South, in a mildly pre-emptive sort of way, is attempting to prevent the opponents from getting together, and to prevent West from showing his suit.

The same reasoning applies to South's bid of one no trump in case (J) and South's bid of two hearts in case (K). Both are intended to make it difficult for West to respond.

I would also like to emphasize that when an opponent takes out partner's double, as in cases J, K and L, any obligation or compulsion on doubler's partner to bid is removed. Any response at this point by doubler's partner is entirely voluntary and shows some strength.

DISTRIBUTIONAL DOUBLES

The distributional double is one of the greatest, yet most overlooked, weapons in defensive bidding. It enables the defenders to back into the bidding with a hand under opening bid strength, yet one that possesses great offensive potentialities.

CASE M

North, You	East	South	West
pass	pass	pass	One ht.
Double			

(d)
♠ A J 7 6
♡ 3
♢ K 10 8 2
♣ Q 10 9 7

Your hand would resemble (d).

Now, what inferences can your partner draw? First, from the fact that you couldn't open the bidding, you lack 13 points with a rebiddable or two biddable suits, or 14 points and a biddable suit.

So he knows you didn't have enough for an opening bid.

Next, he knows it's an informatory double, since you doubled at your first opportunity and the quantity doubled places it in the informatory bracket.

"**Well, why didn't you overcall instead of doubling?**" you may ask. The answer is that your suits may be of four cards (as they are in hand d), or your five card suits are too shaded to bid.

But—if you can 'hit' your partner's suit, and find a fit, your side may be able to play the hand for a partial, or push the opponents to unmakeable heights.

The distributional double should not be made with less than 10 points, and then only when holding a singleton of the opponent's suit. When holding a doubleton of the adverse suit, the doubler should have a minimum of 11 points.

It must be stressed that in making these 'back-in' doubles you should have excellent support for any unbid suit your partner may bid, or a rugged five card or longer suit of your own.

PROTECTIVE DOUBLES

Protective doubles, the fifth and last type of informatory doubles, are dangerous in inexperienced hands and should be strictly left alone until the student has mastered the basic types.

Actually, a protective double is an informatory double which re-opens the bidding when the opponents are permitting their bidding to die at low level, and neither the prospective doubler or his partner have yet bid.

CASE N

North	East	South	West, You
One heart	pass	pass	Double

CASE O

pass	pass	One heart	pass
Two hearts	pass	pass	Double

The protective double is based on the logic (or inference, if you prefer that term) that from the opponents' inability to bid higher, the partner of the protective doubler is marked with the unaccounted for high card strength. The double, therefore, protects his hand so that his cards aren't wasted in permitting the opponents to play a low contract when your side can make some part score your way of the cards.

Both cases (N) and (O) are ticklish situations. Both doubles by West are protective. With inexperienced partners, particularly in rubber bridge, it is far better for West to pass and sell out cheaply, perhaps too cheaply, than to take the risk of losing hundreds of points.

However, in tournament and duplicate play, and in rubber bridge between good players, virtually every West would take action with 10 or more points rather than give up too cheaply.

In case (O), technically we have a penalty double, since the double of the heart suit was not made at the player's first opportunity. Yet good common sense will tell the student that the double couldn't possibly be for penalty. If one opponent had an opening heart bid, and the other a heart raise, that's their best contract.

Why would you possibly double the opponents' best contract except to get your partner to bid? It certainly couldn't be that you expected to defeat two hearts!

As to the student's inquiring why East, in case (N) took no action, despite the fact he is presumed to have some high cards,

East's hand might have resembled hand (e).

(e)
♠ A 4
♡ K J 10 8 7
◇ Q J 10 7
♣ J 4

Well, East, your partner, didn't want you to bid some suit for which he lacked support. Had he doubled, he would have asked you to bid. His double would have been informatory. And that's just what he didn't want. But if you double protectively, he can pass and let the opponents play the hand at one heart, doubled.

(f)
♠ K J 8
♡ 3
◇ A J 4 3 2
♣ Q 4 3 2

In case O, your partner's hand might resemble hand (f) to the left. Obviously, he had neither a safe overcall or double.

But when you double, he can now safely enter the bidding. He will respond with two diamonds and you're back in the bidding picture.

For safety, when using protective doubles, the minimum requirements should be similar to 'Distributional Doubles.' In other words, a minimum of 10 points.

If your double forces your partner to respond at the three level, your hand should be somewhat stronger with a minimum of 11 points and good distribution.

But don't make protective doubles if most of your strength, or most of your length, is in the opponents' suit. You've got them where you want them!

REQUIREMENTS FOR INFORMATORY DOUBLES

HOLDING	POINTS NEEDED minimum
3 worthless cards of the opponent's suit	15
2 worthless cards of the opponent's suit	14
1 worthless card of the opponent's suit	13
void	15

It may strike the reader as strange that in the above table, the first three cases indicate that the fewer losers in the opponent's suit, the correspondingly less high card strength is required for an informatory double. Then along comes a void with no losers that upsets the trend.

The reason for this contradiction is that when the doubler is void of the opponent's suit there is a good possibility that partner will have extreme length in the doubled suit. If partner decides to pass (see following pages on business passes), he will be shocked and aggrieved to find you shading high card requirements in favor of distribution. Thus, when he needs you to help take tricks defensively, all you can offer is offensive distribution. Accordingly, when you feel that your partner may leave your double 'in,' have a little extra in high card values.

There are several important points I would like to stress. First, in the case of the repeated informatory double (page 432), additional high card strength is required for each successive double. Add four points for each additional double.

Thus, if your distribution, according to the table on the preceding page, required 15 points for the first informatory double, a second double would require 19 points, and a third double, if informatory, 23 points. This will be true with all types of informatory doubles.

That's only common sense!

Both the distributional and protective types of informatory doubles require less minimum high card strength than that shown in the foregoing table. The distributional double is made after previously being unable to open the bidding; had you the strength shown in the table, you would have opened the bidding. The protective double is based as much on the high cards you think your partner holds as those you hold, and is more a refusal to sell out cheaply than an indication of high card strength. You should have a minimum of 10 points in both cases.

Next, do not make an informatory double with a two-suited hand, even if the hand meets the necessary high card requirements. It is far better to merely make a simple overcall, or if the hand is sufficiently powerful, make a strength showing single jump overcall. For example, the opponent to your right opens the bidding with one heart and you hold the hands shown to the left.

(g)	(h)
♠ K Q J 9 6	♠ K Q J 9 6
♡ 8	♡ 8
◇ K 10	◇ A 10
♣ A J 10 7 6	♣ A K 10 9 8

With hand (g) I would merely bid one spade; with (h), two spades. The reader may say, "Why not double with either hand? Both have more than the required 13 point requirement with a singleton in the opponent's suit."

There are two reasons why the overcall is better than the double with two-suiters. The first is the natural expectancy that partner will have length in the very suit in which you are short.

Had you (incorrectly), with hands (g) and (h), doubled one heart informatorily, you could expect a two diamond response from your partner. At this point, to show your spade suit, it is now necessary to bid 'two spades.' Later, if you do get to show the clubs at all, it will be at at least the three-zone or possibly even higher.

The other (and even more important) reason for not doubling with two suiters is that the opponents may interpose a bid making it difficult, if not impossible, to show both suits.

For example, let's say you hold hand (i) with the following bidding.

(i)

♠ AQ864
♡ J
♢ K2
♣ AJ542

CASE P

East, dealer	You, South	West	North
One heart	Double	Three hts	pass
pass			

Well, it would take a very brave South to enter the bidding with three spades. Moreover, the hand might play far better in clubs, and it's a little late to find out which suit your partner would prefer.

West's pre-emptive raise has 'fixed' you. In fact, that's the purpose of West's raise—to try to shut out your side, or to make it dangerous for your side to enter the bidding. Had West thought he could profitably defeat any suit you might bid, he would have redoubled to show his strength. You will learn more about these tactics against informatory doubles on following pages of this lesson.

Incidentally, if your hand (after an opponent opens) offers a choice between an overcall on a ragged suit, or a weak informatory double, the latter is *far* preferable. The reason is that the double immediately locates partner's best suit; the overcall can get you into trouble if the missing cards of your suit are 'stacked' badly.

(j)

♠ A742
♡ 4
♢ K5432
♣ A108

Holding hand (j), after an opening heart bid by the right hand opponent, a double is far superior to any other alternative. To overcall either two diamonds with that ragged five carder or one spade with a weak four carder would be a bridge felony.

To make an informatory double, the doubler *must* have one or both of the following—good support for any of the unbid suits partner may bid or an excellent five card or longer suit of his own. For example, you sit South, holding hand (k).

(k)

♠ AKJ98
♡ K73
♢ J2
♣ A109

CASE Q

East, dealer	You, South	West	North
One heart	Double	pass	Two dia.
pass	Two spades		

So we have a new rule—to show a suit after first making an informatory double, the doubler guarantees a rebiddable five card or longer suit.

Most American experts feel that a double of one major guarantees excellent support for the other; that a double of a minor promises good support for both majors.

THE BUSINESS OR PENALTY PASS

On succeeding pages, you will learn what to do when your partner has doubled informatorily. In 99-44/100 percent of these cases, you will be forced to respond when the opening bidder's partner (your right hand opponent) does not bid.

Mind you, I stress 'opener's partner *did not bid.*' For example,

CASE R

East, Dealer	South, Partner	West	North, You
One heart	Double	Pass	?

Now it is up to you to bid. In fact, you have been ordered to bid. *But*—had West stuck in any kind of a bid over your partner's informatory double, such as a bid of a spade, or of two hearts, or one no trump, or anything at all, you no longer would have had to bid, since West's bid 'took out' your partner's informatory double and relieved you of the necessity of bidding. Had you bid over any bid made by West, your response would have been termed a 'free response,' since it was made voluntarily over an opposing bid. It would show a certain amount of strength.

There are two separate occasions when you may pass your partner's informatory double. I have just described the first case immediately above, where you have a weak hand and the opponent to your right bids after your partner has doubled.

The other time you may pass is when your partner has doubled informatorily the very suit you wanted to double for penalty.

(1)
♠ 8
♡ Q J 10 8 7
◇ A J 7 6
♣ J 5 2

Suppose your partner made an informatory double of one heart and you held the hand to the left. You should be able to defeat one heart decisively, yielding far more points than you would have received by bidding and playing two diamonds.

A pass by you at this point would say, **"Partner, even though you asked me to bid, I feel that it would be more profitable for us to let the opponents play the hand at one heart, doubled, than to play the hand ourselves."**

What you have done by passing is to convert partner's informatory double into a penalty double. When you pass your partner's informatory double, you are showing, *not weakness*, but sufficient strength to beat the doubled contract.

A pass showing the ability to beat the doubled contract is known as a penalty or, if you prefer, a business pass.

REQUIREMENTS FOR A PENALTY PASS

1 - At least five cards of the doubled suit with good solidity.

2 - A minimum of five high card points.

Do not pass with five worthless trumps of the opponent's suit and little or no strength because you don't know what to do. You must find some kind of a bid!

DOUBLER'S TACTICS FOLLOWING PARTNER'S PENALTY PASS

	♠ 4 2 ♡ 7 3 ◇ 10 8 6 2 ♣ A 7 5 3 2	
♠ 5 ♡ K J 10 8 ◇ A 9 7 3 ♣ K Q J 8	N W E S	♠ Q J 10 9 8 ♡ Q 5 4 ◇ K 5 ♣ 9 6 4
	♠ A K 7 6 3 ♡ A 9 6 2 ◇ Q J 4 ♣ 10	

Figure 175

Following a penalty pass of an informatory double, the opening lead by the doubler should be a trump.

The reason behind the trump lead is that partner's pass showed control of the trump suit. Therefore, the defenders should 'pull' the declarer's trumps, and not permit him to take tricks by trumping losers with small trumps.

In *figure 175,* with South dealer, the bidding has been –

CASE S

South	West	North	East
One spade	Double	pass	pass!

West should open the singleton trump. This is one of the few cases where the lead of a singleton trump is recommended for the opening lead.

If West makes the normal opening of the king of clubs, South will make the contract. The play will go as follows – Dummy's ace wins, and South trumps a low club. The ace of hearts is cashed, and a heart trick is lost. The defenders will now switch to a trump. South wins. A heart is trumped in dummy, another club trumped by South. This gives South a total of seven tricks as follows – two clubs trumped in the South hand, one heart trumped in the dummy, the ace of clubs, the ace of hearts, and the ace, king of spades.

Yet the opening lead of the singleton trump will defeat the contract two tricks. With this line of play, East's eight forces South's king. The ace of clubs is cashed, and a low club ruffed by South. The ace of hearts is played, and a low heart follows. East wins the second heart with the queen, leads the queen of spades. South can now win only the ace and king of spades, the ace of clubs, the ace of hearts, and one trumped club for five tricks instead of the previous seven.

A SECOND DOUBLE AFTER PARTNER HAS MADE A PENALTY PASS OF YOUR INFORMATORY DOUBLE

Let us say the bidding has proceeded –

CASE T

North, Dealer	You, East	South	West, Partner
One heart	Double	pass	pass
One spade	Double		

Your first double is obviously informatory, since it was made at your first opportunity, and partner has not yet bid. What kind of double is your second double? Is it informatory or penalty? Would you call it a repeated double, where you are still asking your partner to bid?

Case T is a specialized situation, where the second double has become a penalty double, even though your partner has not bid. You see, in a way, your partner really did bid. He passed your informatory double of one heart. This penalty pass showed strength, and the ability to beat one heart. Thus his pass was really a strength showing bid.

(m)
♠ AQ108
♡ 3
♢ KJ109
♣ KQ73

You hold hand (m) in case T. Why did North bid one spade on the second round of bidding,

The answer is that your partner's pass of one heart told him that the opponents felt that he was going to be beaten at one heart; that the cards of that suit were 'stacked.'

Now he's bid one spade in an attempt to extricate himself, and escape. His hand would resemble that shown as (n). The moment your partner tells you by the penalty pass that one heart can be defeated, you know that one spade can also be defeated. Therefore, your second double is for penalty.

(n)
♠ KJ74
♡ A7654
♢ A2
♣ A4

PENALTY OR BUSINESS DOUBLES

Penalty or business doubles have been discussed under previous headings. They are doubles made for the purpose of increasing the penalty the opponents will pay for failure to fulfill their contract. Thus the doubler shows his belief that his side can defeat the opponents' bid.

A penalty double can be identified in one or more of the following ways –

1-It is a double made after partner has bid.

2-It is made after doubler's first opportunity.

3-It is a double of two or more no trump, or of four or more of a suit.

Any one or combination of the above factors is sufficient to class the double as penalty.

Remember that a double of three in a major (before partner has bid) is considered optional, which means that partner may either pass or bid according to his hand.

REGULAR BUSINESS DOUBLES

The best rule I can give you about when to double is –

"Whenever you think you can beat 'em, double first; worry about it later."

Naturally, I do not expect you to take this as advice to double an adverse two heart bid for a 100 point penalty when your side can make a vulnerable game in some other denomination, but on the whole a quick penalty doubler gets far richer than the player who permits himself to be 'pushed' to unmakeable heights by the opponents' bidding.

The most ridiculous statement ever made is a person glibly remarking, **"When I double 'em, they stay doubled, and I always set them."**

Anyone who talks like that isn't doubling often enough, because due to bad breaks, unfortunate opening leads, partner's not having the values promised by his bid or freak distribution, some penalty doubles are bound to be made by the opponents.

On the other hand, if you see a player whose penalty doubles are frequently made, you may conclude that he is doubling too lightly. As a generality, you should expect the opponents to complete about 15 percent of your business doubles. What you will make from the other 85 percent will more than repay you for your losses on the 15 percent they make!

The subject of optional or co-operative doubles is one where the student's judgement and good common sense will have as much to do with the final decision as to whether the double is informatory or for penalty as any words I might write.

We first touched on co-operative doubles on page 429. Exploring the subject further, let's suppose the bidding was –

CASE U

West, Dealer	North, Partner	East	South, You
Three hearts	Double	pass	?

(o)	(p)	(q)
♠ J876	♠ 1087643	♠ KJ98765
♡ J42	♡ 2	♡ 2
◇ A96	◇ KQ76	◇ A109
♣ K105	♣ 43	♣ Q4

With (o), I would pass, since your high cards should be of material assistance in defeating the three heart contract, and you have no suit that would give you a reasonable expectancy of game elsewhere.

Hand (p) offers little defensive merit, save for the diamond strength. The six card spade suit, the distributional two suiter and lack of strength in the doubled heart suit makes it appear that the hand will yield far more in spades than against a doubled heart contract. My preference would be a takeout to three spades, though some players might even advocate a jump to four spades.

Holding hand (q), game in spades is certain, and slam is entirely possible. Either of these contracts should prove far more lucrative than setting the opponents at a three heart doubled contract. My preference would be a takeout to five spades as a slam try.

The question of whether you leave in, or take out, partner's co-operative double is guided by whether you think you can make more setting the opponents at their doubled contract or playing the hand your way of the table.

But co-operative doubles occur far more frequently at low range than over pre-emptive openings.

Read this paragraph carefully! It is when a player makes a penalty double at low range (the one or two level) that his partner must realize that he, too, shares the responsibility for the success or failure of the double.

You see, the old days of doubling for penalty and later saying to partner, "**Always leave my doubles in. When I double, I've got them beaten in my own hand,**" are gone forever. If all of the setting tricks have to be in the doubler's hand, you're not going to get to double very often.

On the other hand, if you can double for penalty after your partner has bid, knowing that you can count on him for the high card values promised by his previous bid, then you can double far more frequently.

The success or failure of all low range co-operative doubles depends a great deal on one's partner. If his high card values are shaded in favor of distribution, or if his hand contains an extremely long suit or suits promising few defensive winners, then he should take out the co-operative double by rebidding his suit, or perhaps showing a second suit. Otherwise, he should pass and leave the double 'in.'

Let us say the bidding has been –

CASE V

North, Dealer	East	South, You	West
One heart	pass	One spade	Two clubs
Double	pass	?	

(r)	
♠ J	
♡ K Q 10 9 8	
◇ A 10 9 8	
♣ A Q 7	

North holds hand (r).

Let's see what you should do with either of the following hands.

With hand (s), you should be very happy to let the opponents play two clubs, doubled. They should be slaughtered.

(s)	(t)
♠ A K 10 8	♠ K Q 10 9 6 5 4
♡ 5 2	♡ 5 2
◇ K 6 5	◇ K 6 5
♣ 9 4 3 2	♣ 2

On hand (t), it's a different story. Your hand will take few tricks defensively against two clubs. Offensively, in spades, it would probably produce a game. So you would take out the double, probably by bidding three spades.

The student may ask, "How can I tell when my partner's penalty double is co-operative?" The answer is that *all* low range penalty doubles (at the one and two level) are co-operative.

The question of when to leave in, or take out, partner's low range penalty double is a very ticklish matter. Even the finest players make the wrong decision occasionally. The quick low range penalty double does infer that the hand is a misfit, since, with good support for partner's suit, a possible game might prove more lucrative than the alternative penalty.

After opening the bidding, the doubler's partner should not leave in (pass) the co-operative double with a hand containing some of the following attributes:

1-An extremely long suit (six cards or more) with a minimum 13 point hand.

2-Lack of high cards promised by an earlier bid.

3-A void or singleton in the doubled suit, and a minimum 13 or so point hand.

4-An aggressive two-suiter.

Do not make low range penalty doubles without tricks in the doubled suit. To remark, after an unsuccessful penalty double, "I had everything else but trumps, so I couldn't see how they'd make their bid," is ridiculous. It's very easy to complete a seven or eight trick contract by trumping losers in each hand (cross-ruffing). Also, do not make a low range penalty double without taking tricks or length in the opponent's suit on the basis that if you don't have them, your partner must. That's wishful thinking!

RESPONSES TO DOUBLES

Your partner has doubled an opponent's bid. Your right hand opponent has passed. What do you do?

The first thing is to ask yourself whether the double was informatory or penalty. If the latter, your partner has stated his ability to defeat profitably the opponent's bid. You should therefore pass.[1]

But let us say that your partner has made an informatory double. In this case, you *must* respond unless the intervening opponent interjects a bid taking out the double or you feel that you can defeat the doubled contract.[2]

It is now up to you to tell your partner whether you have a strong or weak hand, and which suit you hold.

WITH A WEAK HAND

You *must* bid!!!

This is the hardest thing for a beginner to learn and believe. Let me show you why. The weaker your hand, the more likely it is the opponents will make their contract; in fact, they may even win a few over-tricks.

"But I'd rather let them make their bid with an overtrick than bid that awful hand of mine and go down," you may reply.

Admitting that the situation may present a choice of evils, that is not the case. Responding is correct—passing with a 'bust' is 100 percent wrong.

Let us pretend you sit West with the following bidding –

CASE W

North	East, Partner	South	West, You
One heart	Double	pass	?

You hold the following hands –

(u)	(v)	(w)
♠ 7643	♠ 843	♠ 87
♡ 73	♡ J102	♡ QJ76
◇ QJ87	◇ K105	◇ 10654
♣ 1092	♣ 9765	♣ 842

FOOTNOTES

1 - See co-operative doubles on pages 429, 442, 443 and 444.
2 - See business (penalty) passes on pages 438, 439 and 440.

On hand (u), your response would be one spade. The reason for not bidding two diamonds is that the double usually invites a major suit response and that one spade keeps the bidding lower than the bid of two diamonds.

With hand (v), respond two clubs.

Hand (w) calls for a two diamond response. As you will learn on later pages, a response of one no trump shows a strong hand. The heart suit is both too weak and too short, and the hand too weak, for a penalty pass.

Now all of the above hands are pretty weak. Not one has five high card points, or even a five card suit.

But your partner's double has commanded you to bid your best suit, and you have done exactly that. Perhaps you will go down, and fail to make your contract. That's not your responsibility. Your partner commanded you to bid, and you did. Whatever happens after that is his affair.

Do you remember the old time song, "**You made me do it, I didn't wanna do it,**"

Well, that summarizes the situation perfectly.

Do not bid one no trump as a response to partner's informatory double with a weak hand, just because you hold a stopper in the opponent's suit. It is far better to bid any other suit of four or more cards rather than to bid no trump. For instance, your partner has doubled one heart informatorily. You hold –

(x)	(y)
♠ 8743	♠ J 10
♡ KJ65	♡ Q962
♢ 86	♢ 543
♣ 1043	♣ J876
Bid one spade	Bid two clubs

A response of one or more no trump (to informatory doubles) is reserved for strong hands as will be shown later.

WHAT TO DO WHEN YOUR ONLY SUIT OF FOUR OR MORE CARDS IS THAT BID BY THE OPPONENTS, AND DOUBLED BY YOUR PARTNER

In examples (x) and (y), you were fortunate enough to hold a second four card suit in addition to four cards of the opponent's suit.

We already know that with five cards or more with solidity of the opponent's suit, and at least five high card points, you can leave partner's informatory double 'in,' and make a penalty pass.

Frequently, however, your partner may double informatorily, and your only suit of four or more cards will be in the opponent's suit. To make matters worse, you will have a weak hand.

What do you do?

It is obvious that you have no hope of winning enough tricks in your own hand for a penalty pass, and you have no other suit to bid.

The answer is—you bid your cheapest (nearest in rank) three card suit. For example, your partner doubled one heart informatorily. You hold—

(z)	(a)
♠ J86	♠ 87
♡ Q743	♡ J10643
◇ J92	◇ J109
♣ 1043	♣ 876
Bid one spade	Bid two clubs

Anything is better than passing, or bidding one no trump.

WITH A CHOICE OF TWO SUITS

TWO SUITS OF EQUAL LENGTH

(b)	(c)
♠ Q1087	♠ 6
♡ Q1087	♡ Q10876
◇ 1082	◇ 42
♣ J9	♣ Q10876

With two suits of equal length, and about the same high card strength, bid the higher ranking first in responding to an informatory double. This will permit showing the second suit conveniently, if desirable.

With the above hands, we will presume our partner to have doubled one diamond informatorily. With (b), the correct response is one spade; with (c), one heart.

BETWEEN A MAJOR AND A MINOR OF EQUAL LENGTH

In responding to an informatory double, the major suit should always be shown before a minor suit of equal length, even if the minor suit is considerably stronger.

(d)	(e)
♠ 10643	♠ J
♡ J72	♡ 108765
◇ AJ76	◇ KJ987
♣ 102	♣ 102

Presuming that partner has doubled one club informatorily, and you hold either hand to the left, your response on (d) should be one spade; on (e), one heart.

(f)
♠ J 8
♡ J 9 7 6 5
◇ A 10 4 3 2
♣ 2

Over an informatory double of one spade, doubler's partner should respond two hearts with hand (f).

The reason for the choice of a major suit over a minor is that the informatory double usually promises good major suit support and invites a major suit response.

RESPONDING WITH A FIVE AND A FOUR CARD SUIT

1 - If both suits are majors, bid the longer first.

2 - If both are minors, bid the longer first.

3 - If the longer is a major, bid it first.

4 - If the longer is a minor, bid the *major* first!

(g)
♠ 8 7 6 5 4
♡ A J 9 8
◇ 10 4
♣ J 2

Illustration of Situation One

Holding hand (g), your partner has doubled one club. The correct response is one spade. This follows the rule of bidding the longer of the two majors.

(h)
♠ J 6
♡ K 2
◇ Q J 7 6
♣ 10 5 4 3 2

Illustration of Situation Two

Your partner has doubled one spade informatorily. Your response with (h) should be two clubs. The longer of two minors is bid first.

(i)
♠ 6 5 4 3 2
♡ 8 2
◇ A J 10 9
♣ 10 2

Illustration of Situation Three

Respond one spade over an informatory double of one club. The longer major suit is preferred to the shorter minor, even though the latter may be stronger in high cards.

(j)
♠ J 7
♡ 10 6 4 3
◇ J 9
♣ K Q 5 4 3

Illustration of Situation Four

First, let's suppose your partner has doubled one diamond informatorily and you hold hand (j). Your response should be one heart, not two clubs. Had your partner doubled one spade, your correct response would be two hearts, not two clubs.

By now the reader can see that in responding to an informatory double, the major suit is given preference over the minor because the double inferentially promises major suit support.

Sometimes, however, the responder to an informatory double may feel or sense that his side will ultimately become defenders.

In cases of this sort, when holding two or more suits, the responder may bid the suit he wishes his partner to lead defensively rather than the suit in which the hand might best be played. For example, he might bid two clubs with hand (j) for lead directing purposes.

This is the exception, however. As a rule, the major is given preference over the minor in responding to informatory doubles, even when the minor is stronger, longer, or both.

RESPONDING WITH A SIX AND A FOUR CARD SUIT

1-If both suits are majors, or both are minors, bid the six card suit first.

2-If the six carder is a major, and the four carder a minor, bid the former first.

3-If the six carder is a minor, and the four carder a major, the latter is shown first if it is possible to bid it at the one level; if it is necessary to enter the two level to show either suit, the six card minor is bid first.

(k)
♠ K642
♡ 987654
◊ J
♣ 86

Illustration of Situation One

Your partner has doubled one club. Your response with hand (k) should be one heart.

(l)
♠ J9
♡ 3
◊ KJ87
♣ 1075432

Had your partner doubled one heart or one spade informatorily, your response with (l) should be two clubs. This follows the rule that when both suits are minors, or majors, the longer is bid first.

(m)
♠ 765432
♡ 96
◊ KJ108
♣ 4

Illustration of Situation Two

Your partner doubled one club. Your response is one spade.

(n)
♠ J876
♡ 32
◊ J87654
♣ 2

Illustration of Situation Three

Your partner has doubled one club. With hand (n), your correct response is one spade.

(o)	
♠ J8	
♡ J876	
◊ 4	
♣ J87654	

On hand (o), in response to an informatory double of one diamond, you would respond one heart; had partner doubled one spade informatorily, the correct response with the same hand would be two clubs.

WITH SIX AND FIVE CARD SUITS

1-Bid the major before the minor, regardless of which is the longer.

2-If both suits are minors, or both are majors, bid the higher ranking suit first.

STRENGTH SHOWING RESPONSES TO INFORMATORY DOUBLES

Responding to informatory doubles is exactly like any other bidding situation: with strength you make a response that shows power; with a weak hand, you indicate that fact by your response.

Weak responses consist of responder bidding his suit at the cheapest possible level. Thus, if our suit were spades and our partner doubled one heart or one club, the cheapest we could bid our spade suit would be at the one level. So we would say 'one spade.' If our partner doubled diamonds, hearts or spades, and our suit was clubs, the cheapest level at which we could show our suit would be at the two level. Correspondingly, we would bid two clubs.

It stands to reason that if bidding a suit as cheaply as possible (in response to partner's informatory double) doesn't show a strong hand or suit, a response *not made* at the cheapest level would show strength.

This is true!

Let's pretend we had the following bidding –

CASE X

North, Opener	East, Partner	South	West, You
One heart	Double	Pass	?

Here are some possible responses –

You, West, May respond	Indicates
One spade	Weak, made at minimum level
Two spades	Strong, a jump response
Two clubs or diamonds	Weak, made at minimum level
Three " " "	Strong, a jump response

The student now may ask, "When is a hand good enough to be classed as strong, and warrant a jump response?"

The following rules will be of help.

1-A single jump response shows a hand almost good enough for an overcall. If stronger, so much the better.

2-If made at the two level on a four card suit, the hand contains 10 or more points; at the three level, 12 or more points.

3-A single jump response with a five card or longer suit can be made with eight or more points at the two level; 10 or more points at the three level.

4-Jump responses to informatory doubles are *not* forcing to game. A player who has doubled informatorily with a 'minnie' may pass. Accordingly, if you are sure of being able to make a game after partner's double, bid it at once, or cue bid the opponent's suit with the right types of hands.

5-Hands just under 'jump response' requirements are bid at minimum levels, later rebid once if advisable, and if the opportunity presents itself. For example,

(p)

♠ KQ765
♡ 84
◇ J53
♣ 876

CASE Y

North, Opener	East, Partner	South	West, You
One heart	Double	Pass	One spade
Two hearts	Pass	Pass	Two spades

CASE Z

One heart	Double	Pass	One spade
Pass	Two spades	Pass	Three spades

6-Be sure you understand the difference between an overcall on a four card suit and a response to an informatory double with a four carder. The former is unsound, because you don't know where the remaining cards of the suit may be; the response, even a jump response, on a four carder is proper, since the double promises either support or a good five card suit elsewhere.

CASE A

North, Opener	East, Partner	South	West, You
One heart	Double	Pass	?

(q)	(r)	(s)
♠ KJ98765	♠ KQ109876	♠ AJ74
♡ 2	♡ 63	♡ 2
◇ AJ10	◇ A2	◇ KQ73
♣ 43	♣ J5	♣ K1098
Bid four spades	Bid four spades	Bid two hearts

As a rule, hands capable of making a game after partner's informatory double should be bid to game immediately, or a game forcing bid made. Do not take a chance of partner passing even a jump response, which is only semi-forcing.

The cue bid of the opponent's heart suit with hand (s) in case A will puzzle the student momentarily. Stop and think. The bid can't show a powerful heart suit, or you would have made a penalty pass of your partner's informatory double. The hand is sufficiently strong, together with partner's informatory double, to absolutely guarantee a makeable game.

Yet the doubler might easily pass a jump response of two spades. The suit isn't good enough for a jump to four spades, and responder isn't sure which is the best partnership suit. The cue bid 'passes the buck' back to the doubler, says in effect, **"Partner, what is your best suit? I can support whatever suit you bid and, moreover, my hand is so strong that we must continue bidding until game is reached."**

It should be stressed at this point that a void or the ace of the opponent's suit is *not* necessary for this bid. All you are making is a forcing to game bid.

NO TRUMP RESPONSES

It again cannot be too emphatically emphasized that a response of one no trump to partner's informatory double is a *strong* bid and does not, contrary to most beginners' beliefs, merely show a 'bust' or a stopper in the opponent's suit.

Minimum requirements for a one no trump response to an informatory double are –

1 - At least eight high card points.

2 - Good intermediate cards.

3 - No singletons in the entire hand.

4 - At least three suits stopped, including one good stopper in the opponent's bid suit.

5 - A willingness to play the hand in no trump.

In connection with number five, I often have heard players say, **"I bid no trump, partner, because you forced me to bid. I never thought you'd leave me there!"**

What a ridiculous thought!

A two no trump response would show a minimum of 12 high card points, two stoppers in the opponent's suit, and game probability. In lieu of a double stopper, a single stopper plus a good, ready to run minor suit of five cards or longer is a satisfactory equivalent. With a similar holding in a major suit, the jump response in the suit is preferable to bidding no trump.

A three no trump response would show 15 or more high card points, stoppers in the opponent's suit and game certainty.

NO TRUMP RESPONSES TO DISTRIBUTIONAL DOUBLES

Don't!

A distributional double is a double made by a player who couldn't even open the bidding. So his double is based on distribution and the ability to trump the opponent's suit. Your partner is asking you for your best suit. He isn't interested in no trump.

Even with eight or more high card points and stoppers in the opponent's suit, bid your best suit of four or more cards; if you haven't a four carder, bid your cheapest three carder.

NO TRUMP RESPONSES TO PROTECTIVE DOUBLES

A 'protective' double has been described as a double which re-opens the bidding at low range to avoid selling out too cheaply to the opponents, who have stopped, or are about to stop bidding.

Since your partner, in making the protective double, has presumed you to have high cards, you must realize that he has already taken your (supposed) cards into consideration. Accordingly, you should tread on eggs and tend to underbid slightly, rather than bid the full value of your cards.

No trump should only be bid in responding to protective doubles when you really want to play the hand in no trump, have no suit of your own, and have extra values over the requirements for no trump responses given on this and the preceding page.

You must realize that your partner's double and your response may push the opponents higher. That's what your partner is trying to do—buy the bid cheaply, or push the opponents too high to complete their contract.

Now if you bid no trump, the opponents will know which player on your side holds the missing cards in their suit, and finesse accordingly. This may result in their winning additional tricks. On the other hand, if you make a suit response to the protective double, the opponents (if they play the hand) still won't know where their missing cards may be located.

FREE RESPONSES

It may seem strange that I have deliberately left one of the most important parts of this lesson on Doubles towards the end, but I have. You see, the factor of 'free' responses could affect every responding situation.

First, what is a 'free' response? The answer is that it is any response made over any intervening bid by an opponent. In other words, it is a response made when the responder does not have to bid.

Let's take some typical responding situations –

North, Opener	East, Partner	South	You, West
	CASE B		
One heart	Double	Pass	One spade
	CASE C		
One heart	Double	Two hearts	Two spades
	CASE D		
One heart	Double	One spade	Two clubs
	CASE E		
One heart	Double	One spade	Double
	CASE F		
One heart	Double	Redouble	One spade

Of the five bidding situations listed, case B is the only situation where the response is *not* free. Here your partner has doubled informatorily, forcing you to bid.

In case C, you didn't have to bid two spades. Any compulsion on your part was removed when your right hand opponent bid two hearts. This 'took out' or literally obliterated the effect of the informatory double. So if you do bid at this point, you are bidding when you don't have to. In order to do that you need strength.

Well, the next question is – **"How much strength did you as West need to make a free response, as in cases C and D?"**

The answer is - About the same or a shade less than required for a jump response as shown on pages 450, 451 and 452.

This brings us to the question, **"Why did South bid two hearts in case C?"** This question would also hold true had South interfered with a three heart bid, or bid a spade in cases D and E. The answer is that South 'stuck in' his nuisance bid to try to keep you, West, from responding.

Sharp opponents, as in case E, when their partners have been doubled informatorily, will bid the very suit they expect their opponents to bid. They will bid that suit with few or no cards in that suit in the effort to bluff the opponents from bidding that suit. This is known as a 'psychic' bid.

(t)
♠ J 9
♡ 10743
◇ K976
♣ 742

Suppose South's hand, in case E, was as shown to the left. His partner has opened with one heart. The next player doubles.

What suit do you think he expects the opponents to bid? Spades, of course. It's his weakest suit, and the informatory double of one heart invites a spade response. So South, by bidding one spade, tries to throw a monkey wrench into the opponents' bidding.

You should suspect the opponent of 'psyching' whenever he bids the same suit you intended to bid as a response to your partner's informatory double. In these cases, you will probably have four or more cards of that suit, a suit for which supporting cards have been inferentially promised by partner's informatory double.

If your hand contains the above qualities, plus at least five high card points, you should double for penalty, as in case E. This double is for penalty, since partner has already bid (by doubling), and not only exposes the 'psych,' but makes it easy for either your partner or yourself to bid the suit later.

You see, the fact that an opponent has bid a suit you know to be 'phony' certainly shouldn't dissuade you from later making your normal response.

For heaven's sake, don't go bidding two spades over the bid of one spade in case E. That would show everything but spades.

Case F illustrates something new, a redouble after an informatory double. Redoubles are a subject by themselves and will be treated separately in the next part of this lesson.

Suffice it to say that a player may redouble after an opponent has made either an informatory or penalty double. Where an informatory double has been redoubled, as in case F, the redouble shows possession of a very strong hand.

What is more important, after a redouble, the partner of the doubler is not compelled to bid. Modern bidding technique requires the doubler's partner to bid with strength, pass with a weak hand after a redouble.

PART TWO

THE REDOUBLE

There are three kinds of redoubles.

1 - After an opponent's informatory double.
2 - After a penalty double.
3 - For rescue (S.O.S.).

Let's discuss the first type. Your partner has made a bid, and your right hand opponent doubles informatorily.

CASE A

North, Partner	East	You, South	West
One heart	Double	Redouble	

By redoubling, you indicate that you hold the balance of power in the remaining high cards of the deal. Let's imagine you hold hand (a) to the left. Your hand contains 12 high card points. Since there are 40 high card points in the deck, we can draw some pretty accurate inferences as to their whereabouts.

(a)
♠ KJ107
♡ J4
♢ K76
♣ A1074

Your partner needed a total of 13 or more points to open the bidding. Of these 13 points, he would ordinarily have a minimum of 12 high card points with the balance in distribution.

The doubler needed points for his informatory double. Let's do some adding.

BIDDER	HIGH CARD POINTS SHOWN
Opener	12 (approximate)
Doubler	12 (approximate)
You	12
	36

Since there are only 40 high card points in the deck, and from the bidding we have accounted for 36 of those points in the first three hands. According to our addition, if the others have minimums for their bids, the doubler's partner will be lucky to hold four points!

Thus the doubler's hand is trapped between two equally powerful opponents, and can be badly battered when it bids. How do you show that fact to your partner?

By redoubling!

The redouble announces to partner that the redoubler has the balance of outstanding high card strength, holds a hand equal or almost equal in strength to those shown by the opening bidder and doubler. The redouble will convey one of two separate, distinct messages.

1-That good support for partner's bid suit is present, together with high card strength; and that a biddable, makeable game is a definite probability.

2-That enough high card strength is present, perhaps without any support for partner's suit, so that any suit either opponent may bid can be doubled for a lucrative penalty.

Were the redouble able to talk, this is what it would say, **"Partner, I have a powerful hand. I guarantee that we can either make a game or set the opponents at any suit they may bid."**

The redoubler's bid on the next round discloses which of the two types of hands he holds. Naturally, if he raises partner's suit, his hand is of the former type; if he doubles the opponents, it is of the latter group.

High card requirements for the redouble vary in proportion to the support held for partner's suit. The more trump support you have for his suit, the less high card strength will be required to redouble, and vice-versa.

REDOUBLE REQUIREMENTS *

PARTNER'S TRUMPS HELD	MINIMUM POINTS NEEDED
Four headed by the jack or better.	10
Three headed by the queen plus some ruffing strength.	11
Neutral support, as a doubleton honor, or three small cards.	12
Singleton or void.	13

Footnote

* *If the redoubler has previously passed, he may shade his high card requirements by one or two points, particularly where 11 or more points are ordinarily required, but in no case, even after having previously passed, should a player redouble with less than eight points in high cards.*

I fully realize that it takes a great deal of intestinal fortitude, particularly for a newer player, to redouble when holding a singleton or void of partner's suit, even with the recommended 13 points, or more.

Yet it is correct. Let me show you why.

Should either opponent bid following your redouble, you will be in position to obtain a huge penalty by saying 'double.' Your partner in these situations will ordinarily pass any bid by an opponent around to you for action on your part.

On the other hand, should everyone now pass (following your redouble), your partner will play the hand at one of his suit, redoubled. This doesn't happen very often. But if it does, remember that if his bid was originally one heart, or one spade, completing that contract redoubled is worth 120 points.

In other words, making your one bid is going to give you a game! Further, any over-tricks your side can win are worth 200 or 400 points each, depending on vulnerability.

Despite your trump shortage, you have nothing to worry about, since your high cards, plus those promised by partner's opening bid, should complete a one bid 99 times out of a 100.

DOUBLER'S PARTNER'S TACTICS AFTER A REDOUBLE

Modern technique, after your partner has doubled informatorily and the next player has redoubled, is to pass with weak hands, bid only with strength or strong suits.

CASE B

North	East, You	South	West
One heart	Double	Redouble	

Your hand (b)	Partner's hand (c)
♠ AQ1084	♠ 765
♡ 95	♡ J102
◊ AQ42	◊ 1053
♣ K4	♣ J872

Let's imagine that your partner, in a frenzied effort to escape from the redouble, incorrectly bids two clubs. North promptly doubles for penalty.

Now, to show your spade suit, you must bid 'two spades.' Had your partner passed, you could have bid one spade. The opponents are more apt to double a bid of two spades than that of one spade, particularly after they have already doubled one bid, that of two clubs, for penalty.

The point about passing with weak hands is that it isn't necessary for doubler's partner to bid after a redouble since the redouble gives the doubler another chance to bid. That's the key to the situation.

Now there are two times when doubler's partner *can* bid with a weak hand after a redouble. The first time is when he has a good five card or longer suit with some degree of solidity.

(d)
♠ J 2
♡ 8 6 4
◇ J 10
♣ Q 10 9 8 7 6

Pretend West holds hand (d) in bidding sequence B. A two club takeout would be in order. The suit is sufficiently long and solid to be playable, even with little in supporting cards from doubler.

The other situation where a response (over the redouble) is justified may be a bit more difficult for the student to grasp. Remember what is meant by suit rank. In other words, diamonds rank above clubs, hearts above diamonds, and spades above hearts.

(e)
♠ J 9 7 6
♡ 7 6 2
◇ J 5 3
♣ 7 5 2

Again let's return to the bidding in Case B. West, your partner, holds hand (e). You have doubled one heart, and it has been promptly redoubled.

West should now bid 'one spade,' even with his weak hand, and weaker suit. The reason he can bid is because his suit is the next ranking over the doubled suit. If he finds you with support, fine; if you can't support that suit, he hasn't increased by a single step the amount you will have to bid to show your suit. You can still bid two clubs or two diamonds, whichever your suit may be, over the one spade takeout, exactly as you would have done over one heart redoubled.

This reasoning applies had West bid one diamond over one club redoubled, one heart over a redoubled diamond bid, or two clubs over a redouble of one spade. This last is a bit more risky since it forces the bidding into the two level and may convey to doubler that the suit is better than it actually is.

(f)
♠ J 5 3
♡ 8 7 6
◇ J 10 5 3
♣ 6 5 2

Holding hand (f), had your partner doubled one club, and the next player redoubled, you should bid one diamond, since it is the ranking suit. Had your partner doubled any other suit, and a redouble followed, you should pass.

Similarly, with hand (e), the only time you should bid one spade is over a redouble of a one heart bid. Had your partner doubled any other suit, and the next player redoubled, you would have no excuse for entering the bidding.

Let your partner bail himself out as cheaply as possible!

RESPONDING WITH A STRONG HAND AFTER A REDOUBLE

	North	
	♠ J 8 ♡ Q 10 9 8 ◇ K 9 5 3 ♣ A 7 6	
West ♠ K 7 6 5 ♡ 3 2 ◇ A Q J 10 ♣ K J 4	N W E S	**East** ♠ A Q 10 9 4 2 ♡ 4 ◇ 8 7 6 3 ♣ 9 8
	♠ 3 ♡ A K J 7 6 5 ◇ 2 ♣ Q 10 5 3 2	

Figure 176

When you have a strong hand, and your partner's informatory double has been redoubled, make a jump response if the requirements (shown on page 451) are present, just as though the redouble had not occurred.

It is possible that the opening bidder may have opened the bidding largely with distributional values, and that the redouble is partially based on a supporting 'fit.'

CASE C

South	West, Partner	North	East, You
One heart	Double	Redouble	Two spades!

You must get the idea over to your partner, who otherwise would be impressed by North's redouble, that you have high cards, strength and a good suit.

OPENER'S TACTICS AFTER A REDOUBLE BY PARTNER

After your partner has redoubled your left hand opponent's double of your bid, one of two things will happen –

1-Your right hand opponent will pass.

2-Your right hand opponent will bid.

In the first situation, you should pass. What better contract could you want? As I've already remarked, a redoubled contract of one of a major suit when made produces a game.

You see, there's always the possibility that the doubler and his partner may get their signals crossed, and leave the redouble 'in.' Over-tricks are worth 200 or 400 points each, depending on vulnerability. And if the doubler rescues himself from the redouble, you should ordinarily pass if you can't double it yourself, and see what your partner plans to do. If you can't double the opposing bid, perhaps your partner can!

In the second situation, where the doubler's partner responds over your partner's redouble, you should again pass, in most cases when it is again your turn to bid and you are unable to make a penalty double. The idea is to see what your partner wants to do.

However, if you can double for penalty, you should take vulnerability into consideration before bidding. If your side is vulnerable, and the opponents not vulnerable, be sure that the expected non-vulnerable penalty is at least the equivalent of a probable vulnerable game. With equal vulnerability or lack of it, a sure profit from a penalty double is far superior to a doubtful game.

After you have bid, and your partner redoubles the opponent's informatory double, I have stated that ordinarily you should pass any bid made by doubler's partner in order to see what your partner plans to do.

There are three possible reasons for your not passing. These are –

1- You can make a penalty double. Comparative vulnerability plays the determining role.

2- Your hand is so powerful distributionally, with an extremely long suit, and has so little defensive value, that you prefer to play for a sure game rather than a penalty. But be certain the game is sure!

3- You hold a powerful two-suiter, lacking defensive values. It is sometimes better to bid the second suit at once, giving a picture of your hand. But remember, if you have two suits, there is no reason why your partner can't hold the other two suits, and can 'whack' the opponents in whatever remaining suit they elect to bid.

With vulnerable opponents, it's usually better to pass any takeout by doubler's partner unless your hand (as opening bidder) is so tremendously distributional that you want to show that fact. Even here it is usually better to give your partner who redoubled an opportunity for action.

After all, his redouble guaranteed high cards. He's not going to pass. If he does make a penalty double, and your hand can't support it because you're distributional, you can always take out his double, since all low range penalty doubles are more or less co-operative.

But at least give your partner who redoubled a chance!

THINGS TO REMEMBER

1-The redoubling side should ordinarily either get to game or double the opponents.

2-A redouble does not necessarily show support for partner's bid suit.

3-The opponents, after your side has redoubled, cannot ordinarily play an undoubled contract. Your side should either double them, or play the hand.

REDOUBLES AFTER BOTH PARTNERS HAVE BID

A player may redouble after both he and his partner have bid, as in case D.

CASE D

North, You	East	South, Partner	West
One club	Pass	One heart	Double
Redouble			

Your redouble has the same meaning as on the preceding pages. It shows an extra powerful hand (20 or more points) and the desire to either double for penalty, or to reach a game.

If you have opened with a minimum or near minimum hand, do not redouble. Pass and see what happens. The opponents may have more strength than your side. When you redouble, you show extra values.

REDOUBLES FOLLOWING PENALTY DOUBLES

Up till now, all of our discussions of what to do after a redouble have dealt exclusively with redoubles after informatory doubles. Now let's see what to do about redoubling after an opponent has made a penalty double.

Let's suppose the bidding was –

CASE E

North, Partner	East	South, You	West
One heart	Pass	One spade	Pass
Two hearts	Pass	Three hearts	Pass
Four hearts	Double	?	

(g)
♠ KQ86
♡ Q75
◇ K2
♣ 6542

Your hand is shown as (g). Every bid you made is solid and warranted by your values. Should you redouble?

Emphatically not!

Well, why not?

There are several valid reasons against redoubling.

1-Someone at the table is in error. Your partner thought he could make four hearts when he bid it. East doesn't think so. One of them is mistaken.

2-Making the doubled contract should be sufficient reward.

3-The possibility of opponent escape.

Let's analyze the reasons, one by one. Perhaps the missing trumps are badly bunched. When your partner bid four hearts, he didn't know that. The opponent who doubled, does. Or the cards may lie wrong. Aces can be behind kings, and key finesses can be 'off.'

Then too, there is always the possibility that your partner, in his anxiety to bid a game, may have stretched his hand in order to make his last bid.

Now for the opponents' side. Every now and then, you will encounter the sort of person who, with three sure defensive tricks in his hand, will double adverse major suit game bids with the remark (to himself), "Well, it's a free double."

By a 'free double' is meant that the double will not, by itself, give the other side a game not already contracted; that its only effect will be to double the trick score, yield bonuses for completion and over-tricks; and to increase possible penalties.

That's the superficial appearance. Actually, so called free doubles can be very expensive in doubled trick score below the line, over-tricks, and what's more important, the double locates cards and bad trump 'breaks,' giving declarer additional information which may help him make an otherwise unmakeable contract.

As to one side or the other being mistaken, a player in a recent championship holding hand (h) overcalled. His partner, holding a side ace and a king, later doubled the opponents' final contract of six clubs. He was the mistaken party.

(h)
♠ Q J 10 9 8 7 6
♡ 5 4 3
◇ J 10 3
♣ void

But the opponents aren't always mistaken. Never underestimate the opponents. They have just as many brains as you and your partner.

The second factor is that making the double should be sufficient reward. If, in home rubber bridge, you are doubled and make the contract, that should be good enough. If you make an over-trick, so much the better.

In duplicate play, this principle of not redoubling promiscously applies to an even greater extent. Remember this – if you are in a normal contract and are doubled and go down one, remember that it will happen to others. So you'll get an average result. Redouble and you'll get an abnormal result, and probably a zero.

The only time you should redouble an opponent's penalty double is when you are certain of two things: first, that you can make the contract; second, if the opponents run out (escape) to their suit, you can defeat their contract an equal or greater amount than you would have made playing a doubled contract.

Let's suppose you're not vulnerable and bid four hearts. An opponent doubles. If you make the bid, you'll receive 240 points in trick score, 50 points for fulfilling the doubled contract and 300 points for game. *

That totals 590 points. Now, if you redouble and the opponents bid four spades, or something else, and you double, make sure you'll get at least 590 points. Otherwise, you'll be shortchanged.

OPPONENT ESCAPE

The previous paragraphs touched lightly on the fact that the opponents, warned by your redouble that you expect to make the doubled contract, may escape the redouble's consequences by bidding an additional amount of their suit. This is a very important reason against redoubling penalty doubles.

Footnote

* *In duplicate scoring, the 300 points for bidding and making a non-vulnerable game are added directly to the trick score; in rubber bridge play, the 300 points represents an intangible, yet present, value towards winning the rubber.*

Suppose the bidding went –

CASE F

North, Partner	East	South, You	West
One heart	One spade	Two hearts	Two spades
Three hearts	Three sp.	Four hearts	Double
Pass	Pass	Redouble	Four spades?

In the above sequence, South proclaims to the world and sundry his conviction that four hearts will be made. Now, perhaps West's double was a bit on the thin side, a bit hopeful. Do you expect East-West to sit still and let your side play four hearts, redoubled? Well, hardly. They escaped to four spades.

North-South now have the alternative of bidding five hearts or doubling four spades. The former is decidedly risky in view of the fact that West thought he could beat four hearts when he doubled. Granting that you'll beat four spades when you double, do you think with both opponents bidding spades that you're going to beat it as much as you would have made making four hearts, doubled?

THE BLUFF REDOUBLE

In the early days of bridge, the poker or bluff factor entered into bidding far more often than at present. There were many cases where bluff redoubles swindled gullible opponents.

For instance, when doubled in a hopeless contract, a player might redouble in the hope of scaring either opponent into returning to their suit, even though the redoubler knew he didn't have the chance of the proverbial snowball of completing the redoubled contract. The redouble, then, was pure bluff; if the opponents didn't run, the penalty was sometimes catastrophic.

As opponents grew older and wiser, a player learned to trust his partner's doubles rather than the opponents' redoubles.

A WORD ON COURAGE

In the event that you do double for penalty and hear an opponent redouble, think before you run. Perhaps the redouble is intended to scare you – to try to make you run.

Remember this – don't be frightened into making a bid, because of an adverse double or redouble, that you would not have otherwise made. There are exceptions, it's true, but if your bidding and that of your partner is sound, once you thought you had enough tricks to beat the opponents and doubled them, their redouble shouldn't change your mind.

To borrow a poker term – *stand pat!*

MATHEMATICAL ODDS ON REDOUBLES

Redoubling will sometimes increase the trick score a far greater amount than the corresponding penalty. In these cases, where the possible loss is light and the yield great, a redouble may be in order.

There are three factors controlling these odds. They are: first, whether the suit is major or minor; second, the amount of the bid; third, vulnerability or lack of it.

Let's examine the following table, realizing that making four hearts or four spades undoubled will yield 120 points, and producing five of a minor 100 points.

	First Trick PENALTIES		Trick Score	
	Not vul.	Vul.	Major	Minor
Not doubled	50	100	120	100
Doubled	100	200	240	200
Redoubled	200	400	480	400

By checking the above figures, it at once becomes apparent that if you are doubled while vulnerable in a minor suit game contract, you can lose 200 points for failing by one trick. On the other hand, you will receive 200 points below the line for completion. By redoubling, both scores are increased to 400 points.

So in the minor at game level when vulnerable, it's a dead even affair. And remember this – we are presupposing only a possible one trick set. Suppose we go down two or more tricks. Then the additional penalty tricks cost 600 points each, while over-tricks are only worth 400 points each.

But let's examine the one really bright spot – the major suit bid of game or more when not vulnerable. Here, by redoubling, you change the below trick score from 240 to 480, whereas the possible under-trick loss is but 100 points, from 100 to 200. Thus you stand to gain 240 points as against losing an additional 100, pretty good odds. If the opponents have no cheap escape, a redouble when you are confident of making the bid is in order.

SLAM REDOUBLES

Major suit slams, when not vulnerable, can be redoubled profitably when success seems probable and the opponents do not have a ready escape. This is particularly true when the opponents are vulnerable.

When your major suit slam is doubled, the trick score would be 360 points. Redoubled, it amounts to 720 points. The penalty (redoubled) only goes from 100 doubled to 200 points redoubled. That's a possible loss of an additional 100 points as against a gain of 360 points.

It is for this and other reasons that doubles of slams, particularly non-vulnerable slams, are termed 'sucker doubles.'

The ideal condition, then, for a redouble, is when the redoubling side is not vulnerable, is in a major suit game or higher and the opponents cannot escape to a cheap 'save.' These conditions are in effect only a small minority of the times you will be doubled.

As a general rule, redoubles of penalty doubles don't pay!

THE SOS REDOUBLE

The SOS redouble is exactly what its name implies, a redouble asking for rescue by redoubler's partner. Many years ago this bid was in frequent use by players who made bad bids and then asked to be rescued after being doubled. As bridge progressed, players discovered that it was better to make sound bids and good overcalls, not requiring rescue. As a result, the old style SOS redouble went out of style. This would be an example of the obsolete form.

CASE G

North	East	South	West
One heart	One spade	Double	Pass
Pass	Redouble (help)		

What it really amounts to is that East, in case G, has made a bad overcall and wants his partner to extricate him from the mess. East's redouble in this situation resembles an informatory double, asking his partner to bid his best suit.

The redouble could not possibly be considered as showing the ability to make the doubled contract, because why would any player, confident of making a doubled contract, warn the opponents of that fact, and prod them into further bidding?

East would be far better off keeping still, making his doubled contract with a possible over-trick. His tactics would follow the previously described course of not telling the opponents to escape.

There is one place, however, where the SOS redouble has a legitimate function, and the writer has used it with great success and thoroughly recommends it. This situation is following a penalty pass of an informatory double.

CASE H

You, North	East	South	West
One heart	Double	Pass	Pass *
Redouble **			

Used as above, the redouble has the identical meaning of the informatory double.

When a player who has opened the bidding redoubles immediately after an opponent's informatory double, the opening bidder is showing a hand that contains additional values over those required to open the bidding. The redoubler will usually have about 20 points or more. His redouble does not request a rescue; rather, it promises that he is capable of bidding again or of doubling any bid by the opponents.

CASE I

North, You	East	South	West
One heart	Pass	Pass	Double
Redouble			

In order to distinguish a redouble showing power from its SOS cousin, remember –

1- A redouble following a penalty pass is SOS.

2- A redouble immediately following an informatory double shows power.

Holding a two-suiter after partner has passed your opening bid and your right hand opponent has doubled informatorily, it is better to show your other suit at once (strength permitting) than

Footnote

* *A penalty or business pass, showing the ability to defeat the doubled contract.*

** *Asking to be rescued in partner's best suit.*

to redouble with a strong hand. If you pass, and the opponents start bidding, the bidding level may be too high for you to show your second suit safely.

Any jump rebid by the opening bidder, after an opponent has doubled informatorily and partner has previously passed, is *not* forcing.

CASE J

You, North	East	South	West
One heart	Pass	Pass	Double
Three hearts			

CASE K

You, North	East	South	West
One heart	Pass	Pass	Double
Three clubs			

Neither bid is forcing on partner, South, to bid even once. They both do show extra powerful hands, and, if partner has any slight values, he should try to find some kind of a response.

PART THREE

TACTICS AGAINST INFORMATORY DOUBLES

These tactics against informatory doubles are, of course, by the side which has been doubled.

In the main, the partner of the doubled bidder will carry most of the responsibility. If you will bear in mind a picture of a football player running interference for the ball carrier, you will have an excellent idea of the partner's task. He, too, is a blocker, only he attempts, with weak hands, to prevent or block the doubler and his partner from getting together.

At present we will pretend in all of the following situations that your partner has opened the bidding with one heart and the next player doubled informatorily. We'll analyze each possible type of response you can make.

First, a simple basic principle—any bid except a redouble denies enough strength to redouble. Thus, a bid or pass made over an opponent's informatory double shows a hand not strong enough to redouble.

THE SINGLE RAISE

CASE A

Partner, North	East	South, You	West
One heart	Double	Two hearts	

A single raise of partner's suit over an informatory double shows an extremely weak hand. With four trumps of partner's suit, any distribution will do, even 4-3-3-3. With three trumps, some ruffing value should preferably be present. The hand will contain a total of four to nine points.

(a)	(b)	(c)
♠ 87	♠ 3	♠ K82
♡ J1087	♡ QJ76	♡ Q765
◇ K765	◇ 8762	◇ 654
♣ 832	♣ 10543	♣ 973

(d)	(e)
♠ 108765	♠ 654
♡ Q109	♡ A82
◇ Q876	◇ 987432
♣ 3	♣ 7

The sole purpose of the single raise is a mild attempt to keep the doubler's partner from responding. For him to bid over the raise would require a 'free response' necessitating some strength. The mild interference bid makes it far more difficult for the opponents to get together.

CASE B

Partner, North	East	You, South	West
One club	Pass	One heart	Double
Two hearts			

(f)
♠ 87
♡ AJ9
♢ 642
♣ AQJ98

The two heart raise in case B again shows a weak hand, not much in excess of the opening bid except that it contains heart support. It would be made with hand (f).

Again, the only purpose of the two heart raise is the mild attempt to keep doubler's partner from responding. There will be no danger of your getting into trouble if you merely bear in mind that with a strong opening a redouble would be in order.

THE DOUBLE RAISE

CASE C

Partner, North	East	You, South	West
One heart	Double	Three hearts	

Over the double, you've bid three hearts. This bid must indicate a minimum holding of four trumps. The hand will range from 10 to 12 combined points.

You are slightly stretching your values, since the double raise without the intervening informatory double would normally show from 13 to 16 points. Your partner must not take this double raise as showing a powerful hand. Had you from 13 or more points, you would have redoubled.

The double raise over an informatory double is *not* forcing! Partner, with a minimum opening, may pass.

(g)	(h)
♠ Q7	♠ 3
♡ J1086	♡ A10875
♢ AJ74	♢ J876
♣ J82	♣ Q109

Hands (g) and (h) would call for a double raise over the double, following an opening heart bid by partner.

CASE D

North, Partner	East	South, You	West
One club	Pass	One heart	Double
Three hearts			

(i)	(j)
♠ 862	♠ 8
♡ AQJ7	♡ K754
◇ 86	◇ Q92
♣ AQJ9	♣ AQ1086

The same sort of message is conveyed by opener's double raise in case D. The opener slightly stretches his hand to make it difficult for the doubler's partner to respond. Again, the double raise requires a minimum of four trumps and is not forcing.

THE TRIPLE RAISE

CASE E

North, Partner	East	South, You	West
One heart	Double	Four hearts	

(k)	(l)
♠ 8	♠ A
♡ AJ74	♡ KJ432
◇ 65	◇ 8765
♣ K98742	♣ 1087

Since in bidding over the opposing double you are permitted to slightly shade the requirements for raises, the triple raise to game can be made with from nine to 12 points.

THE ONE-OVER-ONE RESPONSE

The one-over-one response is the most frequent bid over an informatory double. Let's change partner's opening bid to one club, have the bidding proceed –

CASE F

North, Partner	East	South, You	West
		(One diamond	
One club	Double	(One heart	
		(One spade	

A one-over-one response would be a bid of any suit in response to partner's opening bid of one of a suit. Of course, had your partner opened with a heart, it would have been impossible for you to show your diamond suit at the one level.

In order to be specific, we'll pretend that our suit for responding purposes is spades, and we will analyze what a response of one spade, over an informatory double, would show.

The bid of one spade would indicate –

1-At least a five card suit. (To bid a four card suit over a double is a bridge atrocity). Always remember that it is the opponent who has been commanded to bid, not you!

2-A suit of some solidity and body. It should contain plenty of reinforcing intermediates, as sevens, eights, nines and tens.

3-The hand will range in combined high card and distributional point count strength from about four to eight. In fact, the stronger your hand (lacking the requirements for a redouble) the less necessary it is for you to bid at this point. This will not seem strange if you remember that a bid over a double does not show a strong hand.

The following hands would be good examples of one spade bids over an informatory double of partner's opening bid.

(m)	(n)	(o)	(p)
♠ QJ987	♠ AJ987	♠ Q109876	♠ AQ1076
♡ 62	♡ 3	♡ 92	♡ 765
◇ 874	◇ J876	◇ J4	◇ 92
♣ 1062	♣ 942	♣ 753	♣ 876

There are two important points to remember in making a one-over-one response over the opponent's double.

First, a one-over-one response in this situation is *not* forcing, even if the bidder has not previously passed. The opening bidder is at full liberty to pass the response, and frequently should. For that matter, no response except a redouble is forcing when bid over the double, not even a jump raise, or jump bid in a new suit. Unless the opening bidder feels some hope of game, he can pass your response.

(q)	(r)
♠ AK76	♠ A5432
♡ Q106	♡ J865
◇ KJ7	◇ 109
♣ Q109	♣ Q3

Nothing would be sillier than to bid one spade holding either hand (q) or (r) had partner opened with a one bid of a lower ranking suit and the next player doubled. With (q), you should redouble. With hand (r), you should pass and await developments. Your only good excuse for bidding would be if partner had opened with one heart or one spade. In either case, you would raise to three of that suit for pre-emptive purposes.

Second, there is always the strong possibility that the opponent about to respond to his partner's informatory double will bid the same suit you were going to bid! How often have you considered overcalling with some suit, but passed instead, only to find that the opponent bids that suit, and you sigh with grateful relief for having passed.

The identical situation, that the opponent will bid the same suit you contemplated bidding, will occur about 20 percent of the time. Since the doubler's partner must respond, and you do not, it is far better to pass doubtful hands and hope the opponents get in trouble, rather than plunge in, knee deep, yourself.

Remember that your only reason for bidding over the opponent's double is to keep them from further bidding. If you want them to bid, redouble or keep still!

A NON-JUMP TWO-OVER-ONE RESPONSE

By a non-jump two-over-one response, I refer to any bid of two of a suit when it is the cheapest response you can make when you bid your suit. For example,

CASE G

North, Partner	East	South, You	West
One heart	Double	Two clubs	

To bid over the opponent's intervening double, your suit must be of at least five cards with some solidity. The hand should contain from four to eight points in high cards. With a six card or longer suit, the high card requirements can be slightly lessened.

A JUMP BID IN A NEW SUIT

CASE H

North, Partner	East	South, You	West
One club	Double	Two spades	

CASE I

North, Partner	East	South, You	West
One heart	Double	Three clubs	

Despite the fact that the two spade bid in case H, and the three club response in case I are bids of one more than necessary, the opening bidder need not respond. If he does, any action on his part is strictly voluntary.

In this regard, I would like to state that Goren gives this situation of bidding one more than necessary over the double, as a 'one round force.' In other words, the opening bidder must bid at least once more, though not necessarily continue bidding until game is reached.

(s)	(t)
♠ AJ108765	♠ 10
♡ 8	♡ J6
◇ J76	◇ 876
♣ 109	♣ KQJ9876

I prefer to regard the bid as semi-pre-emptive, showing a suit of about seven cards or longer, with some solidity and a hand containing no more than eight points in high cards. Hand (s) would be an example of the two spade bid in case H; hand (t), of the three club response in case I.

A RESPONSE OF ONE NO TRUMP

Let's suppose the bidding resembles that of case J.

CASE J

North, Partner	East	You, South	West
One club	Double	One no trump	

This bid is generally used after partner has opened with one of a minor suit and has been doubled informatorily. Its main purpose is to shut out, or make difficult, a response by doubler's partner, meantime masking excellent support for partner's minor suit, permitting that suit to be 'run' in no trump.

(u)	(v)
♠ Q8	♠ AJ76
♡ J109	♡ 10875
◇ K654	◇ K92
♣ KJ62	♣ 64

Some smattering of high card strength in the unbid suits should be present, to furnish stoppers or potential stoppers. Holding hand (u) with the bidding as in case J, a bid of one no trump would be good strategy, since you wish to block out a possible spade or heart response by West. On the other hand, with hand (v), a pass would be correct, since you hold excellent defensive values against either major suit and, lacking a club fit, should let the opponents' bidding progress to see 'which way the cat will jump.'

THE PASS

It has frequently been remarked that the pass is the best, yet most neglected, bid in bridge. To a great extent, this holds true after one's partner has been doubled informatorily.

Having read the previous pages on when to bid or redouble after an opponent doubles, the obvious inference is that when requirements for a bid or redouble are lacking, one should pass.

This is completely correct!

Let's suppose, with the bidding in case K, you hold any of the hands marked (w) to (z), inclusive.

CASE K

North, Partner	East	You, South	West
One heart	Double	Pass	One spade
Pass	Pass	?	

Your pass can mask a variety of holdings.

(w)

♠ J86
♡ 1065
◇ J765
♣ 532

A complete blank. You would continue passing.

(x)

♠ Q109
♡ 1073
◇ KJ7
♣ Q1086

A fair hand without a strong suit, lacking support for partner's bid suit. With hand (x), you would probably bid one no trump on the second round of bidding.

(y)

♠ KJ108
♡ Q7
◇ QJ6
♣ 10842

A good hand, lacking just enough high card strength to redouble. On the first round, you passed to see what was going to happen. You should now make a penalty double of one spade. If your partner can't support the double, and takes it out by rebidding, respect his wishes. See co-operative doubles on pages 429, 430, 442 and 443.

(z)

♠ 76
♡ 84
◇ AK1086
♣ K1097

Again you have a good hand, but this time it includes a rebiddable five card suit. You passed on the first round because you hoped the opponents might bid clubs or diamonds, which you could double. But since the opponents bid spades, instead, you now bid two diamonds.

Thus, by first passing, later bidding, you have effectively diagrammed your hand. It is as though you said, **"Partner, I didn't want to bid on the first round without appearing too weak. I have strength, though not enough to redouble."**

The opening bidder's tactics, following a second round response by partner, who passed after an opponent's informatory double, can only be determined by the nature of his hand. If he (the opening bidder) holds 16 or more points, plus either a staunchly rebiddable suit or a good fit with partner's suit, promising some likelihood of game, he should rebid. Otherwise, he should pass responder's second round response.

Since responder's first round pass (over the intervening informatory double) can conceal such a variety of hands, only future rounds of bidding can reveal the hidden secrets. You'll be surprised how much you'll learn by passing!

PSYCHIC BIDS

The most frequent and effective use of psychic bidding surrounding informatory doubles is the fake one-over-one response over an informatory double to shut out a feared bid by the remaining opponent of that particular suit.

CASE L

North, Partner	East	South, You	West
One heart	Double	One spade	

(a)
♠ 8
♡ J 10 6 5
◇ Q 10 8 7
♣ Q 9 7 6

Hand (a) would be a typical illustration of a psychic one spade bid in case L.

This bid is very common among better players. It is particularly effective against less experienced players, who are reluctant to make quick penalty doubles. With hand (a), South will escape, if doubled, by bidding two hearts.

This type of psychic bid is generally made in a major when holding no more than two cards of the suit. It is sometimes made with a singleton, and even with a void. Naturally, the bid is fraught with peril for the bidder, since the fewer cards of the suit he holds, the more partner may hold, and the latter may take the response seriously by giving a substantial raise. After all, he doesn't know at that moment that the bid's psychic.

But, the more experienced the partner, the less the danger of getting in trouble, since he first should realize that if he holds great strength in a suit for which doubler promised support, it is scarcely likely that you, too, would have strength there.

Sometimes, however, you'll hear everybody pass after you've made a psychic response with a doubleton or so in your hand. I've seen it happen. In that event, keep your chin up. Don't let your face reflect your feelings. Go about playing the hand as though everything were entirely normal and you might be able to use one of your spades for ruffing purposes before your bid is exposed. The opponents will find out soon enough. Don't let your face give you away.

DEFENSE TO PSYCHIC RESPONSES

As mentioned in the foregoing paragraphs, a player, after his partner has been doubled, may bid the very suit he expects his opponent to bid.

I touched lightly on this subject on page 455. If, after your partner's informatory double, you hold five or more points in high cards, plus at least four cards of the bid suit, you should expose the 'psych' by doubling for penalty.

With the following bidding, you hold hands (b) and (c).

CASE M

North	East, Partner	South	West, You
One club	Double	One spade	Double

(b)	(c)
♠ KJ65	♠ A10865
♡ Q108	♡ J74
◇ J964	◇ Q1098
♣ Q2	♣ 3

Holding either hand (b) or (c), you should double South's one spade bid at once!

"But suppose I follow your advice and double one spade," you ask, **"and South, in case M, now bids two clubs. What do I do now?"**

The answer is simple. When next it is your turn to bid, you bid the suit you previously doubled for penalty. What could be clearer in import to your partner?

In other words, the bidding would now resemble that shown in case N.

CASE N

North	East, Partner	South	West, You
One club	Double	One spade	Double
Pass	Pass	Two clubs	Two spades

The opponent's psychic response has not prevented you from finding the spade suit, and if your partner, who doubled, sees any hope of game, he can raise your suit.

THE PSYCHIC REDOUBLE

A psychic redouble can sometimes be used to bluff the opponents from reaching game, and, at the same time, mask a weak hand containing little but support for partner's bid suit.

CASE O

North, Partner	East	South, You	West
One heart	Double	Redouble	

(d)
♠ 85
♡ Q1098
◇ J52
♣ Q7432

Your hand could be that shown as (d). The normal action of bidding two hearts over the double wouldn't scare anybody. Moreover, that bid would disclose the fact that you had heart support and a very weak hand.

But by redoubling, you may bluff the opponents into believing that your hand is far stronger than it actually is. You may keep the opponents from bidding a makeable game and may even be able to play the hand your way of the table cheaply and undoubled.

Of course, you can waive the requirement about reaching game. You know you have lied about your holding. Pass partner's next bid as quickly as possible, and, should he double any low range adverse bid for penalty after your redouble, yank out the double by bidding the cheapest number of his suit, in this case, hearts. Your partner will quickly be aware that something is amiss.

QUIZ TWELVE

1-In each of the following, is the double informatory or penalty?

	South, You	West	North, Partner	East
(a)	One heart	One spade	Double	
(b)	One club	One spade	Pass	Two spades
	Double			
(c)	One no trump	Two hearts	Pass	Pass
	Double			

2-Identify each double in the following as informatory or penalty. The question refers to the second double in d, e and f.

	West	North, Partner	East	You, South
(d)	One heart	Double	Pass	Pass
	One spade	Double		
(e)	One heart	Double	Pass	One spade
	Two hearts	Double		
(f)	One heart	Double	Two hearts	Pass
	Pass	Double		
(g)	Four spades	Double		

3-With both sides vulnerable, your right hand opponent has opened the bidding with one heart. What do you do with each of the following hands?

(h)	(i)	(j)	(k)
♠ A	♠ K 10 7 4	♠ A K Q 8 6 3	♠ 8 4
♡ 7 6 3 2	♡ J	♡ 5	♡ K J 9 8
◇ A J 10 7	◇ A Q 9 7	◇ A Q J 9 8	◇ A Q 7
♣ K J 9 8	♣ K Q 7 3	♣ K	♣ K Q 9 5

4-Your partner has doubled one heart informatorily, and the next player passes. What do you do with each of the following hands?

(l)	(m)	(n)
♠ A J 8 4 3	♠ 8 6	♠ Q 10
♡ 6	♡ 10 7 5 4 3	♡ Q 10 3 2
◇ K Q 5	◇ J 6 3	◇ K 10 6
♣ 8 6 4 3	♣ 9 5 2	♣ K 4 3 2

(o)	(p)
♠ J 8 4 3	♠ 6
♡ 10 7 4 3	♡ Q 10 9 8 7
◇ 9 8 6	◇ A Q 10
♣ 4 2	♣ Q 9 8 7

5-Both sides are vulnerable. The bidding has been –

North, Opener	East, Partner	South	West, You
One heart	Double	Redouble	?

What do you do with each of the following hands?

(q)	(r)	(s)	(t)
♠ 864	♠ 10982	♠ 864	♠ J8
♡ 103	♡ 65	♡ 53	♡ 64
◊ J643	◊ 1087	◊ QJ1084	◊ 1083
♣ J643	♣ 9652	♣ 762	♣ AKQ1087

ANSWERS TO QUIZ TWELVE

1-(a) Penalty. The double is after partner has bid.
(b) Informatory. You have doubled at your first opportunity before partner has bid.
(c) Penalty. Any double after an opening bid of one no trump is always for penalty.

2-(d) Penalty. Partner's penalty pass showed strength.
(e) Penalty. Partner has already bid.
(f) Informatory. You have doubled at your first opportunity, and partner has not bid. North's two heart bid is intended to shut your side out of the bidding.
(g) Penalty. A double of four or more is always penalty.

3-(h) Pass. A double is unthinkable since you are unable to support the expected spade response.
(i) Double.
(j) Two spades.
(k) Pass. Hope the opponents overbid, so that you can later make a penalty double.

4-(l) Two spades; (m) two clubs – the cheapest three card suit; (n) one no trump; (o) one spade; (p) pass.

5-(q) Pass; (r) one spade – it is the next ranking suit; (s) two diamonds; (t) three clubs.

LESSON TWELVE
HANDS

Each hand should be bid by the student before checking 'par.'

1 - North dealer, neither vul.

	♠ KJ987 ♡ Q10 ♢ A43 ♣ A108	
♠ 32 ♡ K6543 ♢ KJ ♣ 7652	N W E S	♠ AQ654 ♡ A2 ♢ Q87 ♣ KJ9
	♠ 10 ♡ J987 ♢ 109652 ♣ Q43	

2 - East dealer, N-S vul.

	♠ J6 ♡ 84 ♢ AQJ865 ♣ Q83	
♠ 743 ♡ Q9532 ♢ 432 ♣ 54	N W E S	♠ AQ10985 ♡ A10 ♢ 7 ♣ K1097
	♠ K2 ♡ KJ76 ♢ K109 ♣ AJ62	

3 - West dealer, both vul.

	♠ 10962 ♡ QJ43 ♢ J10 ♣ 1094	
♠ QJ3 ♡ 1098 ♢ 9532 ♣ A75	N W E S	♠ K8 ♡ AK765 ♢ A74 ♣ Q86
	♠ A754 ♡ 2 ♢ KQ86 ♣ KJ32	

4 - West dealer, E-W vul.

	♠ 5 ♡ KJ108 ♢ A972 ♣ KQJ8	
♠ AK763 ♡ A962 ♢ QJ4 ♣ 10	N W E S	♠ 42 ♡ 73 ♢ 10863 ♣ A7532
	♠ QJ1098 ♡ Q54 ♢ K5 ♣ 964	

PAR

1 -

North	East	South	West
1 sp.	pass	pass	pass

Opening lead by East, ♢ 7

2 -

East	South	West	North
1 sp.	dbl.	pass	3 dia.
pass	3 n.t.	pass	pass
pass			

Opening lead by West, ♠ 3

3 -

West	North	East	South
pass	pass	1 ht.	dbl.
pass	1 sp.	dbl.	2 sp.
pass	pass	pass	

Opening lead by East, ♡ K

4 -

West	North	East	South
1 sp.	dbl.	pass	pass
pass			

Opening lead by North, ♠ 5

SOLUTIONS TO LESSON TWELVE HANDS

1-

North declarer at one spade.

Trick	E	S	W	N
1	♢ 7	♢ 9	♢ K	♢ A
2	♠ A	♠ 10	♠ 2	♠ K
3	♢ Q	♢ 2	♢ J	♢ 3
4	♢ 8	♢ 10	♠ 3	♢ 4
5	♡ A	♡ 7	♡ 4	♡ Q
6	♡ 2	♡ 8	♡ K	♡ 10
7	♠ 4	♡ 9	♡ 3	♣ 8
8	♠ 6	♢ 5	♣ 2	♠ 7
9	♠ Q	♢ 6	♡ 5	♠ 9
10	♠ 5	♣ 3	♡ 6	♠ 8
11	♣ K	♣ 4	♣ 5	♣ 10
12	♣ J	♣ Q	♣ 6	♣ A
13	♣ 9	♡ J	♣ 7	♠ J

North wins five tricks, going down two tricks.

2-

South declarer at three no tr.

Trick	W	N	E	S
1	♠ 3	♠ 6	♠ 8	♠ K
2	♢ 2	♢ 5	♢ 7	♢ K
3	♢ 3	♢ 6	♡ 10	♢ 10
4	♢ 4	♢ J	♣ 7	♢ 9
5	♡ 5	♢ A	♠ 5	♠ 2
6	♠ 4	♢ Q	♠ 9	♡ 6
7	♣ 4	♢ 8	♠ 10	♡ 7
8	♣ 5	♣ 3	♣ 9	♣ J
9	♡ 2	♣ 8	♣ 10	♣ A
10	♡ 3	♣ Q	♣ K	♣ 2
11	♠ 7	♠ J	♠ A	♣ 6
12	♡ 9	♡ 4	♠ Q	♡ J
13	♡ Q	♡ 8	♡ A	♡ K

South wins nine tricks.

3-

North declarer at two spades.

Trick	E	S	W	N
1	♡ K	♡ 2	♡ 8	♡ 3
2	♡ 6	♣ 2	♡ 9	♡ Q
3	♢ A	♢ 6	♢ 2	♢ J
4	♢ 7	♢ 8	♢ 3	♢ 10
5	♣ Q	♣ K	♣ A	♣ 10
6	♢ 4	♢ Q	♢ 5	♡ 4
7	♠ 8	♠ A	♠ 3	♠ 2
8	♠ K	♠ 4	♠ J	♠ 6
9	♣ 6	♣ 3	♣ 7	♣ 9

North concedes one more trick to the adverse high trump, the queen of spades.

North wins eight tricks, losing one heart, one diamond, one club, and two spades.

4-

West declarer at one sp., dlbd.

Trick	N	E	S	W
1	♠ 5	♠ 2	♠ 8	♠ K
2	♣ J	♣ A	♣ 4	♣ 10
3	♣ 8	♣ 2	♣ 6	♠ 3
4	♡ 8	♡ 3	♡ 4	♡ A
5	♡ 10	♡ 7	♡ Q	♡ 2
6	♢ 2	♠ 4	♠ Q	♠ A
7	♢ 7	♢ 3	♢ K	♢ Q
8	♢ 9	♣ 5	♠ J	♠ 6
9	♡ J	♣ 7	♠ 10	♠ 7

North-South win the balance defeating the doubled one spade contract two tricks.

COMMENTS ON LESSON TWELVE HANDS

1 - With most of his strength in the opponent's spade suit, East should pass. South is far too weak to respond, and West lacks a sound overcall.

After winning the opening lead with the ace of diamonds, North's play of the king of spades is based on the only possible combination that could prevent losing an unnecessary trump trick, viz., that one opponent holds six spades headed by the ace, and his partner has the singleton queen.

Not knowing the location of the missing high clubs, North prefers to discard a possible losing club on the third round of hearts rather than trump. Had North trumped, East should refuse to over-ruff, discarding a club instead. While this gives North a ruffing trick, he will later win but one club trick in its place.

2 - East's play of the eight, rather than playing the ace and a second round of spades, is designed to permit partner to retain a spade for a future lead of that suit should partner regain the lead and originally hold a doubleton spade.

After winning with the spade king, South can count eight certain tricks, viz., six diamonds, the king of spades and the ace of clubs. Since for his opening bid East is marked for the outstanding high clubs, the ace of hearts and probably the king of clubs as well, for declarer to lead a heart from dummy towards his king to develop the ninth trick would be fatal since East, on winning with the heart ace, could cash his remaining spades. The club finesse offers a 50 percent chance of success. Note that the finesse is delayed until after first cashing six diamond tricks in order to force East to discard as many spades as possible since East must also protect his king of clubs and retain the ace of hearts.

3 - The hand furnishes an example of competitive part score bidding. After South's informatory double, North correctly bids his spade suit rather than bid no trump with a weak hand.

4 - This is our old friend, *figure 175*, from page 439. It demonstrates the efficacy of an opening trump lead after partner has made a penalty pass. Note South's overtake with the queen of hearts of his partner's 10 in order to lead a second round of trumps.

Lesson XIII

Slam Bidding

LESSON THIRTEEN

SLAM BIDDING

Slam bidding is the exchange of information, usually in the later bidding stages, to determine whether sufficient values are present to enable the partnership to win 12 tricks for a small slam or 13 tricks for a grand slam.

Slam bonuses are as follows –

	NOT VULNERABLE	VULNERABLE
SMALL SLAM	500	750
GRAND "	1000	1500

While doubling or redoubling a slam contract will increase the trick score below the line, slam bonuses are not increased by doubling or redoubling. These slam bonuses are the same for all suits and for no trump.

Naturally, no credit is given for a slam bid but not made. Similarly, no bonus is awarded for a slam made but not bid. To receive a slam bonus requires both bidding and fulfilling the contract. Bidding a small slam and winning all 13 tricks still yields only the small slam bonus; bidding a grand slam and falling short, taking only 12 tricks, finds the bidder not receiving a small slam bonus, but paying a one trick penalty instead.

Either partnership may contract for a slam, whether they opened the bidding or entered secondarily. Generally, it is a safe assumption that when one side has a sound opening bid, the other cannot win 12 tricks, much less 13. There are rare exceptions due to freak distributions where voids and singletons will neutralize adverse aces and kings; but in the main, this will hold true.

THE IMPORTANCE OF BIDDING SLAMS

Due to the tremendous bonuses for successful slam completions, accurate slam bidding will frequently be the difference between profit and loss. The missing of the two biddable slams during the course of an evening will result in the loss of over a thousand points, a tremendous factor in the final net result.

On the other hand, stretching a sure game into bidding an unmakeable slam bears the same relationship as a ball player foolishly attempting to stretch a three base hit into a home run and being thrown out at the plate. The former wasted a game worth hundreds of points, the latter a three-bagger!

Thus a slam, to be bid, should be within bounds of makeability. I would put the required chances of success as follows—to bid a small slam, the bidder should have at least a 60% chance of success; a grand slam should be almost 100% certain.

What do I mean by a 60% chance of success? Well, let's say that we're considering bidding a small slam, and know we have one certain losing trick. Our chance of winning the remaining 12 hinges on a finesse which normally has a 50% chance of succeeding.

Should we bid the slam?

Ordinarily, yes, since plus the 50% chance, we can add the possibility of a squeeze or end-play which might raise our 50% chance a bit higher. If the slam depends upon a trump split, where the mathematical odds are in your favor, it should be bid.

Another example of a recommended small slam is the type of hand where two finesses need be taken. If both succeed, the hand will make seven; if one works, the hand makes six. This type of small slam should be bid since there is a 50-50 chance that one finesse will succeed, and the play of the hand may even obviate the need of one of the finesses.

CONTROLS AND TAKING TRICKS

Slam bidding is the most precise of all bidding situations. To complete a game in no trump requires winning nine of the possible 13 tricks, or 69 percent of the total. Thus, in a no trump game, 31 percent of the possible tricks can be lost, and the contract still can be made. In a major suit game, the declarer can afford to lose 23 percent of the 13 tricks, and still make his game.

But in a slam contract it's a different story. In a small slam, the declarer can afford to lose only one trick, and that's a mere 7.7 percent; in a grand slam, no tricks whatever.

Naturally, slam bidding requires greater accuracy.

To successfully complete slam contracts, two abilities must be present; first, the obvious requisite of being able to win the required 12 or 13 tricks; second, the ability to prevent the opponents from taking tricks in any suit.

Cards which perform this preventative task are known as 'controls.' These controls will be present in the suits other than trump, the suits in which we do not plan to win many tricks.

Naturally, it would be extremely foolish to bid a slam merely because we can win all 13 tricks in certain suits if, before we can obtain the lead, the opponents can win two or more tricks in other suits. We lacked controls in the latter suits.

Control of the side suits is fully as important as the ability to win the requisite number of tricks. One cannot succeed without the other.

HOW TO RECOGNIZE THE SLAM BIDDING PERIOD

Controls are shown during the slam bidding period. This period can be readily identified. It is when a player:

1-Voluntarily makes a bid of more than game;

2-Uses a recognized slam convention;

3-Overcalls the opponent's suit; *

4-Shows a new suit after an earlier suit has already been given a strength showing jump raise.

This is what I mean by a voluntary bid of more than game.

CASE A

North	East	South	West
One spade	Pass	Three spades	Pass
Five spades			

The bid of five spades, one more than needed for game, was entirely voluntary for North. He could have bid four spades. But in Case B –

CASE B

North	East	South	West
One spade	Two hearts	Four spades	Five hearts
Five spades			

In case B, North's five spade bid is not a slam try. In order to try to buy the bid he has been forced to bid five spades over West's bid of five hearts.

Case A is a slam try, case B is not.

Footnote

* *The cue-bid of the opponent's bid suit has many meanings, depending on the surrounding bidding. See pages 87, 394, 395, 396, 413 and Lesson XVI.*

CONTROLS

Controls are of three grades or abilities.

1-Controls that can win or control the first round of a suit.

2-Controls that can win or control the second round of a suit.

3-Controls that can win or control the third round of a suit.

They are correspondingly known as first, second or third round controls.

FIRST ROUND CONTROLS

♠ void
♡ KJ87
◇ KQ1098
♣ AJ65
N
W E
S
♠ 432
♡ AQ1096
◇ AJ5
♣ Q2

Figure 177

An ace is first round control. Obviously, the moment that suit is led, the hand containing the ace can win the first trick. Nothing could be simpler.

A void is similarly rated as first round control providing trumps are present, since the lead may be trumped.

In figure 177, with hearts trumps, North has two first round controls. They are the spade void and the club ace. As a matter of fact, as long as dummy retains trumps, the spade void gives the North hand not only first round control, but control of subsequent rounds as well.

SECOND ROUND CONTROLS

♠ K87
♡ Q1096
◇ KQ864
♣ A
N
W E
S
♠ 42
♡ AKJ87
◇ AJ
♣ KQJ7

Figure 178

The king is considered second round control That is because once the ace has been played, the king is the remaining highest card of that suit.

The reader, who by this time should be highly critical of any unproven statements, should now say, "Suppose in Figure 178 the West player opened a spade and the East held the ace behind the king? Now the king isn't second round control, and the defense can win two spade tricks."

Let's take another type of case where the king might not be second round control. In *figure 179*, North has second round spade control, yet if West lays down the ace of spades for the opening lead East can trump the next round, with North's second round control vanishing in smoke.

```
            ♠ K875
            ♡ Q1096
            ◇ KQJ9
            ♣ A
               N
♠ A109643   W     E   ♠ Q
               S
            ♠ J2
            ♡ AKJ87
            ◇ A10
            ♣ KQJ6
```

Figure 179

Well, then you may say, "**Since the king may or may not be positive second round control, should you bid a small slam whose success may hinge on the undisclosed location of an adverse ace, or the remote possibility that the second round can be trumped?**"

Yes!

You will remember that a small slam should be bid with a 60 percent or greater chance of success. First, there is a 50 percent possibility that the ace will be 'right,' in other words, in front of the king. Next, even if the ace is 'wrong,' there is a good probability that the suit may not be opened. After all, there are four possible suits for an opponent to lead, and that they will unerringly strike your Achilles' heel is only one chance out of four.

THE SINGLETON AS SECOND ROUND CONTROL

```
♠ Q43
♡ 2
◇ KJ743
♣ AK82
   N
W     E
   S
♠ AKJ962
♡ 1043
◇ A2
♣ QJ
```

Figure 180

A singleton, providing trumps are present, is also considered second round control. In *figure 180*, South is the declarer in a six spade contract. Note that East-West have all of the high hearts between them, yet are unable to win more than one trick in that suit.

North's singleton heart is the answer. Once that card has been played, North's trumps bestride the heart suit like a Colossus, ready to ruff the second and subsequent heart rounds.

THIRD ROUND CONTROLS

By now, the reasoning behind the assignation of values to controls should be apparent. If the ace or a void is first round control, and the king or singleton is second round control, what would you say would be third round control?

Why, the protected queen, or any doubleton, of course.

You may wonder why, since we can't afford to lose two tricks in a small slam contract, we are worrying over winning or losing the third round of some suit.

♠ Q 10 9 8
♡ 6 3 2
◊ A J 6
♣ K 8 4
N
W E
S
♠ A K J 7 4
♡ A K 9 5 4
◊ K
♣ Q J

Figure 181

In figure 181, South may bid a small slam in spades which, despite his imposing array of high cards, cannot be made, since third round control of the heart suit is lacking. This loser, plus the ace of clubs, defeats the contract.

Yet put the queen of hearts in the North hand, or change the North hand's heart holding to a doubleton, and third round control will be present, with the hand being makeable. Third round controls cannot be overlooked in slam bidding. Many slams are bid and not made through lack of them. An ability to locate these controls, or their absence, is indispensable to precision slam bidding.

DISTRIBUTIONAL VERSUS HIGH CARD CONTROLS

♠ void
♡ Q 8 7 6
◊ K Q 7 4 2
♣ K J 9 2
N
W E
S
♠ 10 5 3
♡ A K J 5 4
◊ J 10
♣ A 8 6

Figure 182

Which is better, the reader may ask, the high card type of control, as aces, kings and queens, or the distributional type?

For defensive purposes, the high card type, of course. For play offensively in suit contracts, the distributional type is better. This is because the distributional type affords not only control of the designated round, but of subsequent rounds, in addition.

Let's study a void with its first round control. In *figure 182*, the void spade suit in the North hand, in support of partner's heart suit, not only provides first round control of spades, but control of the second and third rounds as well.

In other words, South need not worry about losing a spade trick even were the suit led three times. And this is of great importance where the declarer has to relinquish the lead at some point. In *figure 182*, South must knock out the ace of diamonds. But even with an opening spade lead South is entirely safe from losing a spade trick as long as the dummy retains a trump.

The relative superiority of the distributional control over its high card brother is emphasized to even a greater extent in considering the singleton as second round control. With trumps present, the singleton cannot help being positive second round control. A king, for reasons previously explained, might not, under adverse circumstances, be able to win the second round of the suit. Moreover, the singleton furnishes third round control, where the king does not.

♠ A43
N
W E
S
♠ K52

Figure 183

Even though South has second round spade control in figure 183, and North has first round control, third round control is lacking.

In figure 184, North's singleton provides both second and third round controls, assuming, of course, that trumps are present.

♠ 4
N
W E
S
♠ A52

Figure 184

The doubleton affords positive third round control of side suits through the ability to trump the third round, whereas the queen may or may not be third round control, depending on the location of the missing, adversely held honors, just as the location of the opponents' ace affected the trick taking ability of a king.

Let's pretend that the declarer's side suit is spades in both figures 185 and 186. Any other suit can be trump.

♠ 32
N
W E
S
♠ A7654

Figure 185

In figure 185, the ace can win the first round. The second must be lost, but the third round can be trumped.

	♠ Q32		
	N		
♠ J8	W E	♠ K109	
	S		
	♠ A7654		

Figure 186

In figure 186, the queen's theoretical third round control is neutralized by the adverse location of East's king. Two spade tricks must be lost, despite the fact that both first and third round controls are present.

This must not be construed to mean that the king or queen do not possess their nominally rated values. Generally, they do because of additional reinforcing lower cards held by the partnership. But once in a while kings and queens are smothered by aces and kings held by the opponents. For this reason, plus the fact that distributional controls can win not only the designated round, but lower rounds as well, the distributional control is a bit more valuable in the play of trump contracts.

In no trump, there is no question of choice between high card and distributional controls. The former is the *only* consideration in no trump, since ruffing value has merit only in trump contracts. Distributional values, therefore, are not counted in bidding no trump slams.

COMBINATION CONTROLS

We have discussed separately the two types of controls—high card and distributional. Sometimes we have a combination of both.

When a high card control, as the ace, king or queen is either singleton or doubleton, we have a combination control. To obtain its value — *to the high card value, add the distributional control value.*

♠ A
♡ KJ86
◇ AQ1095
♣ Q53
N
W E
S
♠ 432
♡ AQ1095
◇ 32
♣ AKJ

Figure 187

For example, let's take a singleton ace. Its high card value yields first round control. The distributional value of a singleton is second and third round control. Therefore, the combined value of a singleton ace is first, second and third round controls. Nothing difficult about that.

In figure 187, you have an example of how the singleton ace of spades in the North hand affords these values.

A doubleton ace, you may ask? Well, the ace is first round control. A doubleton furnishes third round control. The combination gives both first and third round controls. In *figure 187*, had North the ace and one small spade, he would have first and third round controls.

A doubleton king furnishes second and third round controls as follows—the king is second round control, the doubleton is third round.

A singleton king? That's easy, too. The king is second round control. The singleton is both second and third round control. The combination yields second and third round controls.

As to queens, the distributional value will sometimes be greater than their high card control value. Take a singleton queen, for example. The queen controls the third round, the singleton offers second and third round controls. The combination, then, is second and third round control. A doubleton queen is third round control.

A doubleton ace king, as ♠ A K, furnishes first, second and third round controls. The ace is first round, the king is second and the doubleton third round control.

TABLE OF CONTROLS

HOLDING	CONTROL YIELDED		
	First	Second	Third
Void	Yes	Yes	Yes
Singleton		Yes	Yes
Doubleton			Yes
Ace (with two or more low cards)	Yes		
King (with two or more low cards)		Yes	
Queen (with two or more low cards)			Yes
Ace (singleton)	Yes	Yes	Yes
King (singleton)		Yes	Yes
Queen (singleton)		Yes	Yes
Ace (doubleton)	Yes		Yes
King (doubleton)		Yes	Yes
Queen (doubleton)			Yes
Ace king (with other cards)	Yes	Yes	
Ace king (alone)	Yes	Yes	Yes

POSITIONAL FACTORS AFFECTING CONTROL VALUES

As has been stated previously, the capturing powers of certain cards, particularly kings and ace-queen combinations, can be greatly affected by the location of the missing remaining high cards of that suit. Where the location of the missing high cards is fairly well known, usually through the opponents' bidding, it will frequently be found that the hand will play more advantageously from one side of the table than the other.

This permits leads, and essentially opening leads, coming up to rather than through the cards with which one's side hopes to win tricks. It can be accomplished by a player holding the king or ace-queen of the opponents' suit, maneuvering the bidding so that he, rather than his partner, becomes the declarer, which insures that the opening lead come from the defender to the left of the card in question.

	♠ K 5 ♡ Q 7 4 ◇ K Q 6 4 3 ♣ A J 7	
♠ 8 6 ♡ 9 6 3 ◇ 10 7 5 2 ♣ 6 4 3 2	N W E S	♠ A Q J 10 9 7 3 ♡ 5 2 ◇ 9 8 ♣ 8 5
	♠ 4 2 ♡ A K J 10 8 ◇ A J ♣ K Q 10 9	

Figure 188

Let's take *figure 188*. South has opened the bidding with a heart, and East has overcalled with spades. Further bidding has shown that all of the needed controls and winners are present, and now North is considering bidding a small slam.

Yet if South plays the hand, even with the solid heart suit, the small slam will be defeated, since West's opening spade lead through North's king will permit the defenders to win two spade tricks before South can pull trumps and discard his two losing spades on dummy's diamonds.

Yet a small slam can be made, simply by permitting North to play the hand, either in a six no trump contract or the slightly less favorable contract of six diamonds. Now, because the lead is coming up to North's king, rather than through it, the king retains its second round control value.

♠ A J
♡ 10
◇ K Q J 10 8 7 6
♣ A Q 8

N
W E
S

♠ K Q 10 6
♡ A K Q J 7
◇ 5 4
♣ 9 2

Figure 189

An ace-queen combination can be changed from first and third controls to first and second by the simple expedient of making the holder of that combination the declarer so that the opening lead, if in that suit, will come up to, not through, the combination.

Figure 189 is a hand from a recent tournament where East held the guarded king of clubs. Note that any slam contract played by South is doomed with a club opening, since positive second round club control is lacking, and a trick must be lost to the diamond ace.

Yet make North the declarer, either at six diamonds or six no trump, and, should East open a club, North has both first and second round club controls.

It should be pointed out that an ace-queen becomes first and second round controls only as long as the lead is coming up to the hand containing that combination. When the left hand defender, or declarer, leads the suit, an ace-queen reverts to its normal first and third round control values.

THE REQUIRED NUMBER OF CONTROLS

A grand slam requires possession of all four first round controls. Once the opening lead has been won, the solid trump suit plus the side suits should provide the great bulk of the tricks with a second, or even a third round control, plugging up gaps in the side suits.

Control requirements for a small slam will vary according to the solidity of the trump suit. If the latter has no losers, the partnership must have first round controls in two suits, but can be satisfied with second round control of the third. If the trump suit has a loser, first round controls of all three remaining suits must be present, since you cannot afford to lose a first round trick elsewhere.

Of course, the more controls you have, the better off you are, and it is not possible to have too many. Whether in addition to the required first round controls, certain second round controls are needed depends on whether the opponents will be able to regain the lead.

POINT COUNT REQUIREMENTS FOR SLAMS

Ordinarily, a total of 33 points in the combined hands should produce a small slam; 37 points or more, a grand slam. These are minimums. Infrequently, slams will be bid and made with fewer points, but in these cases, freak distributions, with voids and singletons, will be present.

For suit slam bidding, all types of points are counted; in no trump slam bidding, no points are counted for distribution.

TRUMP SUIT REQUIREMENTS

The partnership should have at least seven trumps of the final trump suit between the partnership, and preferably more. With seven or eight cards held in the trump suit, it should contain (between the partnership) at least three of the top four trump honors; with nine or more trumps between the combined hands, two of the top honors will usually suffice.

It is a comparatively simple matter to tell when the partnership holds a total of nine or more cards in the trump suit. Some typical examples are –

You hold

(a)	1-Where your rebiddable suit has received a double raise.			
♠ A Q 8 6 5				
♡ A Q 5	North, You	East	South	West
◇ K J 6	One spade	Pass	Three spades	Pass
♣ A 2				

You hold

(b)	2-Where you hold normal trump support for a suit partner has already jump rebid.			
♠ Q 8 2				
♡ K J 10 6 4	North, Partner	East	South, You	West
◇ A J	One spade	Pass	Two hearts	Pass
♣ K 10 9	Three spades			

This situation would also apply had partner raised your two heart response to four hearts, thus showing the four or more trumps required for the double raise.

You hold

(c)

♠ Q84
♡ AJ965
♢ AKJ2
♣ 3

3-Where a suit has been twice rebid without support having been given, and responder holds normal support that has not yet been disclosed.

North, Partner	East	South, You	West
One spade	Pass	Two hearts	Pass
Two spades	Pass	Three dia.	Pass
Three spades)			
Four spades)‾			

You hold

(d)

♠ QJ84
♡ AQ1096
♢ 7
♣ KJ2

4-Where responder holds sufficient trumps for an immediate double raise, and partner has been able to rebid his suit before the raise was given.

5-Holding two or more trumps after a pre-emptive opening.

6-After a triple raise as one spade – four spades.

In all of the six above cases, it may be assumed that there are nine or more trumps between the partnership, and that the trump suit, under normal conditions of suit division, does not have more than one loser, if that.

METHODS OF SHOWING CONTROLS

The slam bidding period is the showing or locating of controls after the preliminary stages of bidding have revealed powerful hands between the partnership with strength in excess of game requirements.

Some players do not even bother to show or locate controls. Whenever they think a slam makeable, they plunge directly into slam without further ado as –

North's hand

(e)

♠ AKJ876
♡ 3
♢ AQJ
♣ KQ4

CASE C

North	South
One spade	Three spades
Six spades	

(f)	(g)
♠ Q1095	♠ Q1095
♡ A842	♡ KQJ
♢ 2	♢ K10987
♣ AJ96	♣ 2

In case C, South could have responded with three spades holding either hand shown to the left. Had he hand (f), in partnership with hand (e), a grand slam is a laydown; with hand

(g) as dummy, six spades can be beaten by the defenders cashing two aces.

Jumping directly to six or seven has been termed the 'direct method,' though a better term for it would be 'barging.' It is inaccurate. However, it has one advantage. Since no other suits or controls are shown, the opponents have had no information as to the location of side strength or weakness, are at a far greater guess than when defending against more informative methods, and are apt to guess wrong on the opening lead.

Some control showing methods, for that is all slam bidding conventions are, are capable of locating only aces. Others can show aces and kings. One specialized method takes in every type of control, from first to third, both high card and distributional.

My advice to you, in learning slam bidding conventions, is to learn the simpler ones first. Some of them can be mastered in five minutes. After you have learned the simpler ones, then you may go after the more complete methods which will permit you greater latitude in demonstrating control of the side suits.

Standard slam conventions include –

1 - The Culbertson Four-Five No Trump Convention.
2 - Blackwood.
3 - San Francisco.
4 - The Culbertson Five No Trump Bid.
5 - A free bid of five in a major.
6 - Gerber.
7 - Cue-bidding.

ON SLAM CONVENTIONS IN GENERAL

Until Ely Culbertson and his staff announced the (then) revolutionary four-five no trump convention, slam bidding had either been a matter of guesswork or the individual showing of controls, which, because of complexity, was used only by a handful of experts.

The four-five no trump convention was the first attempt, in its inventor's words, to 'show aces in bunches.' Virtually every successor, as the Blackwood, San Francisco, Gerber, etc., do the same thing – show aces in bunches.

But there are some important differences.

The Culbertson four-five no trump convention *requires* that a player hold specific cards to bid four no trump and his partner's responses are similarly rigid. In Blackwood and other conventions, four no trump may be bid, in some cases, without a single ace in the bidder's hand.

What, then, is the advantage of one method over the other?

The principle (and not to be underestimated) advantage of the Culbertson four-five no trump is that the partner of the four no trump bidder *knows* what high cards his partner holds. The partner can take an active role in determining the final contract by combining his cards with those shown by partner's four no trump. Here, either partner has equal voice in determining the final contract.

In Blackwood and other similar slam conventions, the four no trump bid simply 'asks' for information on aces and possibly later, kings. While minimum requirements in aces are recommended for minor suit slam tries, there are no requirements in high cards to bid four no trump when the agreed suit is a major except the probability of slam. Thus the partner, in a Blackwood or San Francisco or Gerber sequence of slam bidding, becomes simply an 'answerer' or if you prefer, a 'stooge.' The responder can play no role in determining the final contract since he cannot possibly know his partner's cards. The four no trump bid shows nothing; it merely asks.

Having given the disadvantages of the latter methods, what are the advantages. Well, there are many. First, the very lack of requirements to bid four no trump permits the bid to be made and aces ascertained on many hands where, using a more rigid system, the bid could never have been made. But even more than that is the virtue of simplicity. The Blackwood convention literally swept the Culbertson method into the corner because of Blackwood's ease and understandibility.

But the disadvantage of any 'ace-showing in bunches' convention is that where several aces may be missing from the bidder's hand, the response may show *how many aces but not which aces are held!* For example, let's suppose a Blackwood bidder holding two aces, bids four no trump. He's therefore missing two aces. His partner shows one ace. How can the four no trump bidder tell which of the two missing aces is present and which is absent?

He can't!

Further, all of the slam conventions mentioned locate aces and, if desired, kings. Not one of them can pinpoint a void suit or a singleton, yet these distributional features, had they been discovered during the bidding, would have been equal or superior to high cards. True, the Blackwood convention does have a void-showing convention which is included in the pages to follow but not one player out of a hundred has even heard of it.

During the past two decades, Culbertson attempted to popularize what he termed 'asking bids.' This was a slam bidding method which enabled the partnership to locate, not only aces and kings, but singletons and voids. It was extremely accurate. It was also highly complex. The result was that the first debut of 'asking bids' had a momentary vogue, then died; the second (and even more complex) version foundered shortly before its originator's untimely death.

Having given you the 'do's and don'ts' of the various conventions, my recommendation to you, at this point, is first to master basic Blackwood. Learn how to ask for and show aces and later, kings. As you gain experience, study the other corollary Blackwood features.

Each system listed has some advantages over another. Don't attempt to learn them all at once. It's not necessary. With Blackwood, your slam bidding will be comprehensible to your partner, whether you play in New York, Seattle, San Francisco, Miami or Indianapolis. As you play more bridge, then investigate the advantages of other methods. You'll find each listed in the text to follow and further recommendations at the conclusion of this lesson.

THE CULBERTSON FOUR-FIVE NO TRUMP CONVENTION

In the Culbertson four-five no trump convention, a bid of four no trump shows a specific holding in the bidder's hand, that he holds *either* any three or more aces, or two aces and a king of any suit bid by the partnership. Since these requirements are rigid, the convention has lost in popularity to Blackwood, San Francisco and Gerber, whose requirements for bidding four no trump are more flexible.

Full credit for the invention of the use of the four no trump bid as a slam convention belongs to Ely Culbertson and his staff. For fuller details on this convention, the reader is referred to texts by that author.

THE BLACKWOOD CONVENTION

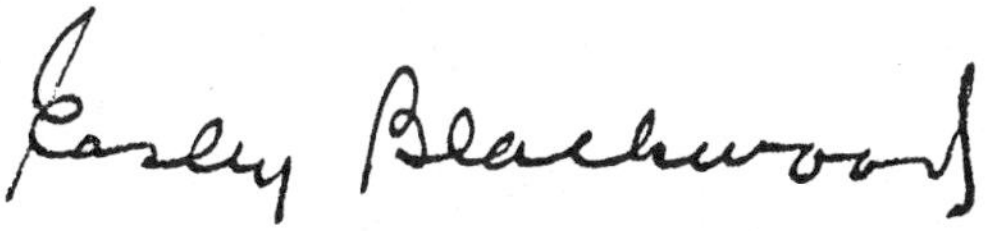

The Blackwood Slam Convention, now universally used, is a simple method of locating the number of aces and kings held by a partnership in slam bidding. A bid of four no trump requests partner to show the number of aces held. After the ace-showing response, a rebid of five no trump (by the four no trump bidder) then asks for kings. Any other rebid than five no trump is a signoff.

BLACKWOOD RESPONSES TO FOUR NO TRUMP

HOLDING	RESPOND
No aces or four aces	Five clubs
One ace	Five diamonds
Two aces	Five hearts
Three aces	Five spades

AFTER FIVE NO TRUMP

HOLDING	RESPOND
No kings or four kings	Six clubs
One king	Six diamonds
Two kings	Six hearts
Three kings	Six spades

EXAMPLES

♠ J842
♡ J5
◇ KQJ9
♣ A108

N
W E
S

♠ KQ1076
♡ A10
◇ A2
♣ KQJ3

Figure 190

CASE D

You, South	Partner, North
One spade	Three spades
Four no trump	Five diamonds
Six spades	

South knows that a grand slam is unmakeable, since the bidding has indicated that the opponents hold an ace. Therefore, there is no point in probing for kings, since South has no intention of bidding seven. As a matter of fact, if the opponents open a heart, it will be necessary for South, after winning the opening lead with the ace, to quickly lead three rounds of diamonds, discard the 10 of hearts on the third round and hope that the trick is not trumped by an opponent. Otherwise, if trumps are led immediately, the opponents, on taking the ace of spades, will grab their heart trick. Of course, with any other lead than a heart, South has easy sailing, having plenty of time to knock out the ace of trumps, pull trumps, discard his losing heart on dummy's diamonds.

It should be apparent that any player at the table may initiate the slam try, no matter whether he opened the bidding, responded, overcalled, or supported his partner's overcall.

CASE E

♠ A K 7 6 5
♡ Q J 5 2
◇ A J
♣ A 4

N
W E
S

♠ 2
♡ A K 10 8 6 4
◇ Q 4
♣ K Q 3 2

Figure 191

North, Opener	South, You
One spade	Two hearts
Four hearts	Four no trump
Five spades *	Five no trump
Six diamonds **	Seven hearts

* *Showing three aces.*
** *Showing one king.*

Had North shown only two aces, South would have signed off at six hearts. On learning that the partnership holds all four aces, South's problem is whether to bid six or seven hearts. By locating any king in the North hand, South knows that seven is a lay-down. If North's king is the king of spades (as is the case), South can discard his losing diamond on the spade king; if the king is the king of diamonds, there is even less of a problem. Had North shown two kings (by responding 'six hearts' over five no trump), South could even bid seven no trump in safety, since 13 tricks are assured.

I would like to point out three very important, yet generally overlooked, things in slam bidding.

First, in responding to four no trump, whether you're using Blackwood, San Francisco, Gerber or Culbertson, you *cannot* count a void as an ace in computing your ace-showing response. Neither can you count a singleton as a king in showing kings!

Second, if you have all four aces and want to find out how many kings your partner has, you *must* bid four no trump first.

Now this may strike you as silly, because you know your partner will respond with five clubs to show no aces. He can't have any, because you've got them all. But after he bids five clubs you now bid five no trump, asking for kings, and you'll get the information you're seeking.

CASE F

♠ J864
♡ K2
♢ KJ7
♣ K432

N
W E
S

♠ AKQ9
♡ A108764
♢ A
♣ A2

Figure 192

South, Opener	North, Partner
One heart	One spade
Four no trump *	Five clubs **
Five no trump ***	Six spades x
Seven spades	

* *Asking for aces.*
** *No aces.*
*** *Asking for kings.*
x *Three kings.*

It is sometimes possible that even though the partnership may not hold all four aces between them, a slam is makeable if enough kings are present. In these cases, after a bid of four no trump, and the subsequent response, five no trump is bid.

But – and this is a big 'but,' don't bid four no trump unless you're fully equipped to play five of whatever contract you've already selected; don't bid five no trump unless you're sure you can make at least six. You see, the moment you bid five no trump, even if your partner doesn't have the necessary kings, the response forces you automatically to the six level!

The reader may ask, "Well, if you've got all four aces in your hand and all you want to do is find out about kings, why bother with bidding four no trump? Why not bid five no trump at once?"

The answer to that is that a bid of five no trump, not preceded by four no trump, has an entirely different meaning as you will see on pages 514 and 704.

The third and last point I want to make is that in Blackwood you may want to initiate the slam try of four no trump, yet you don't hold an ace. You may hold all the kings, or almost all of them, and want to find out how many aces your partner has. Ordinarily, his response is simple and automatic. If he holds an ace, he bids five diamonds; with two, five hearts; with three five spades.

After a response of five clubs in Blackwood, the four no trump bidder will not have any difficulty in determining whether responder has no aces or all four aces. The first clue, of course, is that if the four no trump bidder has one or more aces, obviously his partner cannot have four aces.

♠ A 10 9 5
♡ A
◇ A 2
♣ A Q J 7 6 5

N
W E
S

♠ K Q J 8 7 6
♡ K 2
◇ K Q 5
♣ 4 2

Figure 193

Let's suppose you're South in *figure 193* and hear your partner open the bidding with one club. You naturally respond with one spade. Your partner raises to four spades.

Well, there's one thing we know. He must have some aces. Why? Well, he opened the bidding, and you have most of the kings. Next, he gave you a tremendous raise, so he had to have still extra strength. Now examine the bidding in case G.

CASE G

North, Opener	You, South
One club	One spade
Four spades	Four no tr.
Five clubs	

What does the five club bid by North show? Why, all four aces, to be sure.

The point I want to make is that a response of five clubs to a bid of four no trump can show *either* no aces or all four aces. In 95 percent of the cases the five club response will show no aces. Only in the rare cases where a player has already shown tremendous strength, and the four no trump bidder has no aces, does the five club response show all four aces.

The next point I would like to make, in discussing Blackwood, is that infrequently there are times where the aceless hand (having bid four no trump and located all four aces to be with partner) will now wish to ascertain the number of kings held by the partnership.

Let's return to *figure 193*. By bidding four no trump, we have already discovered that our partner holds four aces by his five club response. To find out about kings, the four no trump bidder now rebids with five no trump, exactly as in all Blackwood situations. The complete bidding structure with *figure 193* would then resemble case H.

CASE H

North, Opener	South, You
One club	One spade
Four spades	Four no trump
Five clubs	Five no trump
Six clubs	Six spades
Pass	

Well, why didn't South bid seven spades? The answer is that he knows his partner doesn't have the king of clubs and that the partnership has a possible losing club trick, making seven a risky contract. Had North one king, he would have responded six diamonds over the five no trump bid, and South could have safely contracted for the grand slam in spades.

Again, let me emphasize as strongly as possible that the only time a five club response (to four no trump) shows all four aces in Blackwood is when the five club bidder has already shown tremendous strength, something he couldn't have done with an aceless hand. In all other cases, five club responses show no aces, and believe me, the latter situation is in the vast preponderance!

SIGNING OFF WITH FIVE NO TRUMP IN BLACKWOOD

The danger, of course, with Blackwood or any other slam convention is 'getting too high' when the bidding indicates two or more aces missing after the slam try. This can be avoided, in Blackwood, by requiring two aces to bid four no trump when the agreed suit is clubs; a minimum of one ace if the suit is diamonds. Where the agreed suit is either hearts or spades, four no trump may safely be bid without an ace in the bidder's hand, providing there is a strong probability of slam from the earlier rounds of bidding.

Nevertheless, there will be rare times where a player bids four no trump and discovers only too late, and to his dismay, that he is too high and between Scylla and Charybdis.

This will happen when a player, hoping to play the hand in a minor suit slam, has bid four no trump without the recommended number of aces for that bid. Let's say that his suit is diamonds and he's made the error of bidding four no trump on an aceless hand. His partner's response is five hearts, showing two aces.

The player now wishes he were somewhere else than at this

particular table since he wants to get back to his suit, diamonds, and this necessitates a bid of six, obviously unmakeable since the opponents are known to hold two aces. Further, he cannot leave the contract at five hearts since that response was completely artificial and was intended to show possession of two aces, not the heart suit.

To avoid either catastrophe, there is an escape hatch in Blackwood permitting the partnership to play the hand at five no trump in this situation. It is accomplished by the four no trump bidder, after his partner's response, bidding 'five' of any previously unbid suit. The partner must automatically respond 'five no trump' which becomes the final contract.

The reader will notice that no trump may not be the ideal contract but it's a case of any port in a storm – anything's better than playing it in the wrong suit (shown as an ace-showing response) or deliberately getting too high in order to return to the right suit.

The reader should further notice that the four no trump bidder couldn't bid the five no trump since his partner would correctly assume it to be a king-showing request and respond accordingly. The five no trump bid had to come from the partner so that it could be passed.

The situation is illustrated in *figure 194* and bidding cases I and J.

♠ J 10
♡ Q 9 6
◇ K J 4
♣ A Q 10 8 7

N
W E
S

♠ K Q 8
♡ K J 10
◇ A Q 10
♣ K J 9 6

Figure 194

CASE I

South	West	North	East
1 club	pass	3 clubs	pass
4 no trump	pass	5 diamonds	pass
?			

If South now bids five no trump, he is asking his partner how many kings he holds; and that's just what South doesn't want to know. South is aware that the opponents hold two aces, and that slam is impossible.

In other words, the complete bidding with *figure 194* would resemble case J.

CASE J

South	West	North	East
1 club	pass	3 clubs	pass
4 no trump	pass	5 diamonds	pass
5 hearts	pass	5 no trump	pass
pass			

Under no circumstances, using Blackwood, should South's belated five heart bid be considered a cue-bid, or showing a secondary suit. It goes without saying that this convention is extremely dangerous in the hands of an untrained partnership. When the agreed suit is clubs, at least two aces should be present in the four no trump bidder's hand; with diamonds the agreed suit, at least one ace should be present.

SHOWING VOIDS

Distributional controls, particularly in slam bidding, are most difficult to show. The presence of voids, singletons and doubletions, usually become known only after the dummy has been faced.

A void in the opponent's bid suit, *after partner has bid*, can best be shown by cue-bidding the opponent's bid suit. But when the void is in an unbid suit, the problem is more difficult.

I have already stated that a void suit cannot be counted as an ace in responding to Blackwood nor can a singleton be counted as a king in further control-showing. This principle holds true in every ace and king system of responses.

But using Blackwood, a void can be shown through the simple expedient of bidding 'six' of the suit in which the response would normally have been made at the five level.

♠ K8765
♡ A432
◇ void
♣ A976

Let's assume you hold the hand to the left as North and your partner, South, opens the bidding:

South	West	North	East
One spade	pass	Three spades	pass
Four no trump	pass	Six hearts!	

Since with two aces, your normal response to four no trump would have been a bid of five hearts, responding one step higher, at the six level, can only show one thing—two aces plus a void.

Again we come to that key disadvantage of showing controls in bunches—while you show a void, you have not indicated the suit in which the void is held.

Another disadvantage to this method is that since it requires a jump to the six level, the entire bidding level of 'five' has been lost to the partnership and the four no trump bidder is no longer able to ask for kings by bidding 'five no trump.'

As I mentioned earlier, these void-showing responses to Blackwood aren't understood by one out of 100 players and I suggest you not use them until you've mastered the more conventional methods.

WHEN THE OPPONENTS BID

The question frequently asked is **"What do I do after my partner has bid four no trump and the opponent 'sticks in' a bid before I have a chance to respond?"**

The interference bid, by the opponent, is usually made for one of three possible reasons. These are:

1 - To make your response awkward or impossible;
2 - As a possible sacrifice;
3 - For lead-directing purposes.

The third reason can be largely discounted since most lead-directing overcalls are made at far lower bidding levels where possible penalties, if doubled, would be far less than at the five zone. The primary reason will usually be to impede your normal response to partner's slam try.

WHAT YOU SHOULD DO

Any double by you, of the opponent's bid, would be for penalty. In this event you should be reasonably certain that any penalty your side will receive will be equal or greater to the score your side would have made had you or your partner played the hand. Comparative vulnerability will play a major determining role in making the decision.

If, however, you are uncertain whether to double or not, you should pass without any hesitation and leave the decision as to double or continue bidding up to your partner. This is known as a 'forcing pass' and says to partner – **"I've left the decision up to you."** Partner *must* do something – either double or bid!

In this connection, if your hand contains the high cards or length in the opponent's suit that warrants doubling, you should not leave the decision up to your partner since without these cards, he can't possibly double. Further, you should not hesitate for any noticeable period, then pass, and thus convey to partner through your hesitation that you hold certain values meriting further bidding but that you weren't sure exactly what to do. This is highly unethical. Try to make your bids, passes and doubles, at the same rate of speed and in the same tone of voice.

Should you feel a slam to be makeable (and more profitable) than doubling the opponent's interference bid for penalty, it is still possible, in Blackwood, to show the number of aces held. This is accomplished by bidding the next ranking suit (over the interference bid) to show one ace, the suit two steps higher to show two aces, etc. Let me give you an example.

North, Partner	East	South, You	West
One spade	Two diamonds	Three spades	Four diamonds
Four no trump	Five diamonds		

If you held one ace in the above sequence, you *could* respond by bidding five hearts; with two aces your response would be five spades; three aces, five no trump, etc.

BLACKWOOD AFTER NO TRUMP

I have previously stated that where the *last* bid, preceding four no trump, was made in no trump, the four no trump bid *is not* Blackwood asking for aces but rather, a mild slam invitation asking partner to go on to slam with maximum or slightly extra values.

North	East	South	West
One heart	Pass	One spade	Pass
Three no trump	Pass	Four no trump	

The four no trump bid is invitational only—shows approximately nine to 10 points.

Where a suit has been agreed on, either by a direct raise or inferentially through a jump takeout in a new suit, a four no trump bid is Blackwood and does ask for aces.

North	East	South	West
One heart	Pass	Three hearts	Pass
Three no trump	Pass	Four no trump	

or

One heart	Pass	Two spades	Pass
Two no trump	Pass	Four no trump	

In both of the above cases, the four no trump bid is conventional Blackwood.

A little known, albeit highly useful convention devised by the system's originator, permits a player to ask for aces as in conventional Blackwood where the bidding has been predominantly in no trump where ordinarily the four no trump bid would be only invitational. This is accomplished by a player bidding 'four' of the cheapest *unbid* suit following the last bid in no trump.

North	East	South	West
One heart	Pass	One spade	Pass
Three no trump	Pass	Four clubs!	

or

One heart	Pass	Two clubs	Pass
Two no trump	Pass	Four diamonds!	

I must caution the reader that while these conventions are extremely useful in the hands of a skilled partnership, they are not known by one of a 100 players and before their use, it should be ascertained that partner is familiar with them.

As a further word of caution, don't attempt to teach new, complicated conventions to a strange partner just prior to playing. You'll only confuse him. Racing cars aren't meant for family driving!

Where the cheapest unbid suit has been used as a Blackwood request for aces, responses are as follows –

HOLDING	BIDS
No aces	Next ranking suit
One ace	One suit higher
Two aces	Two suits higher

Thus if partner's ask was 'four clubs,' you'd respond four diamonds with no aces, four hearts with one ace, four spades with two, etc.

After the response, the cheapest suit-bidder, if interested in locating kings, can bid five no trump and the responses are the same as in conventional Blackwood.

SAN FRANCISCO RESPONSES

What are known as San Francisco responses to four no trump are very popular in northern California, and further north on the West Coast.

HOLDING	RESPOND
No aces, no kings	5 clubs
No aces, one or two kings	5 clubs
1 ace, no kings)	5 diamonds
No aces, three kings)	
1 ace, 1 king	5 hearts
1 ace, 2 kings	5 spades
1 ace, 3 kings)	5 no trump
2 aces, no kings)	
2 aces, one king	6 clubs
2 aces, two kings	6 diamonds
2 aces, three kings	6 hearts
2 aces, four kings	6 spades

The difference between San Francisco and Blackwood is that San Francisco shows aces and kings in one bid, Blackwood requires two bids, the first to show aces, the second to show kings.

While in San Francisco responses there are two bids, those of five diamonds and of five no trump, which have some ambiguity, the four no trump bidder can pretty well tell his partner's holdings from his own hand.

In San Francisco, the four no trump bidder is required to hold at least two aces to bid four no trump; in Blackwood, there are no requirements to make this bid.

EXAMPLES

Using San Francisco, your partner has bid four no trump. The correct response is shown beneath each hand.

(h)	(i)	(j)
♠ KJ87	♠ A	♠ AQ753
♡ 2	♡ KJ9	♡ J42
◇ KQ43	◇ J954	◇ 76
♣ K1092	♣ KQ543	♣ Q109
5 dia.	5 spades	5 dia.

(k)	(l)
♠ KQ42	♠ AK432
♡ KJ1098	♡ AJ76
◇ J2	◇ J5
♣ Q2	♣ Q10
5 clubs	6 clubs

THE CULBERTSON FIVE NO TRUMP BID

The Culbertson free bid of five no trump, when not preceded by four no trump, is one of the finest slam conventions invented. Basically, it requests the partner to bid seven of the agreed trump suit if holding any two of the top three honors (ace, king or queen) of that suit. For example –

CASE K

♠ AQ43
♡ KQ543
◇ J2
♣ 65

N
W E
S

♠ KJ652
♡ AJ
◇ A
♣ AKQ87

Figure 195

South	North
One spade	Two hearts
Three clubs	Four spades *
Five no trump **	Seven spades ***

* *A jump preference, showing a decided preference for the first bid suit.*

** *Do you have two of the top three honors?*

*** *I do!*

Lacking any two of the three top honors in the agreed trump suit, responder signs off by bidding six of the agreed suit. With two of the three top honors, as previously described, he bids seven of that suit.

A VOLUNTARY BID OF FIVE IN A MAJOR

The voluntary bid of five in a major is the simplest of all slam conventions. When either partner bids five of a major without being 'pushed' to five by the opponents, he is asking his partner to bid six of the agreed trump suit if the partner holds any two aces, and to bid seven of that suit if holding three aces.

A free bid of five in a minor does not carry any slam significance whatever, since the bid is simply one of game.

The bid of five in a major as a slam try is primarily used in conjunction with the San Francisco convention, where the bidder has only one ace, yet wishes to make a slam try that will not get the hand past the five level if the responding hand has only one ace.

Let's turn back to bidding case A on page 489. Here you have an example of a voluntary bid of five in a major. This is a slam try. On the other hand, the bidding in case B is not a slam try, since in order to purchase the contract at spades North was forced to bid five spades over the opponent's bid of five hearts.

"What's the point of this bid," you may ask. "Why don't you just bid four no trump to find out how many aces your partner has?"

The answer is that if you're using San Francisco, a player wishing to make a slam try may hold only one ace, and he needs two in order to bid four no trump in San Francisco. Using this convention, he can bid five of the agreed major suit. If his partner has two aces, the suit is raised to six; with three aces, to seven; with one or no aces, responder simply passes.

♠ Q6
♡ J876
◇ AJ6
♣ KQ32
N
W E
S
♠ K109
♡ AKQ1094
◇ KQJ
♣ 4

Figure 196

For example, take the bidding in case L.

CASE L

South	North
One heart	Two clubs
Three hearts	Five hearts
Pass!	

I would like to point out, that used in conjunction with the San Francisco convention, a free bid of five in a major absolutely *denies* two or more aces in the 'five-bidder's' hand, since with that holding a bid of four no trump (which shows two or more aces in San Francisco) should have been employed.

THE GERBER FOUR CLUB CONVENTION

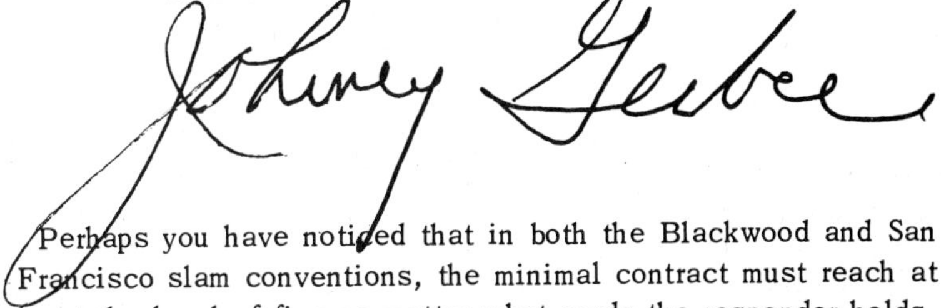

Perhaps you have noticed that in both the Blackwood and San Francisco slam conventions, the minimal contract must reach at least the level of five no matter what cards the responder holds. That is because the slam try starts with a bid of four no trump and the cheapest possible response is that of five clubs.

To make it possible for the bidding to stop at four in situations where there are insufficient aces to make a slam, the Gerber convention inaugurates the slam inquiry with a bid of four clubs rather than that of four no trump. Partner's responses can then be made at the level of four, as four diamonds, four hearts, etc. rather than at the five level as over four no trump. Here's how the Gerber convention works.

TO A BID OF	HOLDING	RESPOND
Four clubs	No aces or all four aces	Four diamonds
	One ace	Four hearts
	Two aces	Four spades
	Three aces	Four no trump

After hearing the number of his partner's aces, if the four club bidder is now interested in ascertaining how many kings partner holds, he now bids the cheapest (lowest ranking) suit over whatever ace-showing response partner may have made. This now asks for kings as in the following table.

IF PARTNER'S RESPONSE WAS	FOUR CLUB BIDDER NOW BIDS
Four diamonds	Four hearts
Four hearts	Four spades
Four spades	Four no trump
Four no trump	Five clubs
Five clubs	Five diamonds

Kings are shown by the responder in the same manner as aces. For example, suppose you hold the North hand in *figure 197.*

♠ K54
♡ AJ765
◇ K
♣ K764

N
W E
S

♠ A2
♡ KQ109
◇ AQ876
♣ A2

Figure 197

CASE M

South, Partner	North, You
One diamond	One heart
Four clubs *	Four hearts **
Four spades ***	Five hearts x

* *How many aces?*

** *One. With no aces, the response would have been four diamonds.*

*** *How many kings?*

x *Three.*

The minimum (cheapest) king-showing response can show either no kings or all four kings exactly as with aces.

"Well," you may say, "bidding that slam didn't require Gerber. We could have used Blackwood or San Francisco to achieve the same contract."

True, on this hand, but let's change the cards around a bit so that they resemble those diagrammed in *figure 198.*

♠ Q 5 4
♡ J 6 5 4 3
◇ K
♣ K 7 6 4

N
W E
S

♠ K 2
♡ K Q 10 9
◇ A Q J 10 9
♣ Q J

Figure 198

Here the bidding would resemble case N.

CASE N

South, Partner	North, You
One diamond	One heart
Four clubs	Four diamonds*
Four hearts	Pass

* *No aces.*

Now, have you noticed an apparent discrepancy? On page 516, in the third paragraph, I stated that after hearing about partner's aces, or lack of them, a rebid of the next ranking suit by the four club bidder requested partner to show the number of kings held. Yet in case N, when South bid the next ranking suit, hearts, over the four diamond response, North passed.

The Gerber solution is quite simple. When the four club bidder's rebid in the next ranking suit happens to be the agreed trump suit, that is a signoff. If, on the other hand, the four club bidder is still interested in finding out about kings, he would skip one suit (the agreed trump suit) in rebidding. In other words, were South, in *figure 198,* interested in kings, he would have bid four spades, not four hearts, as his rebid over partner's four diamond response.

Of course, you should realize that I am constructing these bidding situations. Obviously, with three aces 'off' the hand, South should not make any further slam try over his partner's four diamond response.

Any bid other than the next ranking suit, after a response to four clubs, is an *absolute* signoff, and the responder *must* pass.

CASE O

♠ 76
♡ KQ765
◊ KQJ2
♣ 43

N
W E
S

♠ AKQJ954
♡ A2
◊ 4
♣ KQ8

Figure 199

South, Opener	North, Responder
One spade	Two hearts
Four clubs	Four diamonds*
Four spades**	

* *No aces.*

** *The signoff. If South were interested in kings, he would have bid four hearts, the next ranking suit.*

So there are two ways for the four club bidder to sign off in Gerber. The first we described was bidding the minimum number of the *agreed* trump suit when it was the next ranking suit over the ace showing response; the other method was to make any jump bid after the ace-showing response.

At this point, you should be asking, "**What is the agreed trump suit? The final heart suit was never supported in figures 197 and 198, nor was the spade suit ever rebid in figure 199.**"

The agreed trump suit is the suit which has been previously bid and supported by the partnership, or any suit bid by the four club bidder as a jump after the response to a four club slam try.

CASE P

♠ 3
♡ AKQJ1087
◊ KQ
♣ AQ5

N
W E
S

♠ AKJ87
♡ 2
◊ 643
♣ K762

Figure 200

South, Opener	North, Responder
One spade	Four clubs
Four hearts	Six hearts*
Pass	

**Knowing the opponents to hold an ace, North stops at six.*

The weakness of the Gerber convention is that some players are apt to confuse a four club bid as showing a club suit, rather than as a slam try. In fact, when the bidding gets high, it is sometimes difficult to show a club suit at the four level when using Gerber.

(m)

♠ AQ1087
♡ 2
◊ K9
♣ AKJ109

Suppose you hold hand (m) to the left, with the bidding in case Q.

CASE Q

South, You	West	North	East
1 spade	2 hearts	3 dia.	pass
4 clubs			

Certainly your four club bid is intended to show a club suit, and is not a slam try. The slam try can come later. First, you'd like to find out if your partner can give you a spade preference, which might indicate that he held the king of spades.

For the reason that use of the Gerber convention sometimes makes it difficult to show or rebid a club suit at the four level without having it mistaken as a slam try, many American experts use Gerber only after a suit has been raised earlier, or when there has been a jump to four clubs from a bid of one or two in a suit, or after opening bids in no trump. Used in these ways, there can be no misunderstandings between the partnership.

CUE-BIDDING

Cue-bidding is the locating of controls, one at a time. It is the most accurate of methods, since it locates specific controls. Since inference plays a large part of each bid, this method is more complex, and more difficult of mastery than the 'bulk' ace-locating methods previously described. As a result, cue-bidding is used primarily by the more expert player.

Let me give you some examples of cue-bidding.

CASE R

♠ Q 10 8 7
♡ 3 2
◊ A J 2
♣ K 5 4 3

N
W E
S

♠ A K J 6 5 4
♡ A 4
◊ K Q 7
♣ A Q

Figure 201

South, Opener	North, Responder
One spade	Three spades
Four clubs *	Four diamonds **
Four hearts ***	Five clubs ****
Seven spades	

* *The ace of clubs.*
** *The ace of diamonds.*
*** *The ace of hearts.*
**** *The king of clubs.*

Since spades is the agreed suit, there is no possibility that either partner will pass the other's bid until there is a return to the spade suit. Had South, the original cue-bidder, bid any number of spades as his rebid, instead of making further cue-bids, that would have been a signoff, and indicated his choice of final contract. In other words, had South bid four spades, or six spades, instead of four hearts, the four spade, or six spade contract would have been where South wanted to play the hand.

Had the responder, North, bid the minimum number of the agreed suit, spades, instead of showing further controls, the bid of the minimum number of spades would deny further controls, say, **"Partner, I have nothing else to show. The rest is up to you."**

Thus, a four spade bid by North, instead of five clubs, would deny holding the king of diamonds. The original cue-bidder would then either make another cue-bid or plant the hand in the final contract.

The great advantage of cue-bidding is that it locates specific cards rather than the number of aces and kings held. In *figure 201*, South can safely bid the grand slam, since he knows he can deposit the losing heart on dummy's king of clubs. Had North shown the heart king, and not the king of clubs, the queen of clubs is still a possible loser.

Another great advantage of cue-bidding is in showing duplication – whether the responder has the right or wrong controls.

CASE S

♠ Q 10 8 7	South, Opener	North, Responder
♡ 4 3	One spade	Three spades
◇ A K 5 4	Four clubs	Four diamonds *
♣ J 10 9	Five clubs	Five diamonds **
N	Five spades	Pass
W E	* *The ace of diamonds.*	
S	** *The king of diamonds.*	

♠ A K J 6 5
♡ Q J 10 9 8
◇ void
♣ A K Q

Figure 202

Do you see how South found out that North held the ace and king of diamonds, worthless cards, since they duplicated his void, and that North held nothing in hearts, where South needed controls the most?

SUMMARIZED

1-Any slam convention, whether four no trump, or five no trump, or cue-bidding, or asking bids, or Gerber, is *absolutely forcing!*

The partner *must* respond, unless an opponent sticks in an intervening bid!

2-Where no trump has been the only denomination bid by the partnership, a bid of four no trump is *not* forcing; it only shows extra values in excess of three no trump as a mild slam invitation.

3-After the bidding on a hand has been in progress, even though perhaps only one bid or pass at the table has been made, you cannot remind or tell your partner what slam convention you are using, or are about to use. Bidding conventions must be decided before bidding, not during! Similarly, the opponents should be informed as to your conventions beforehand.

4-In most slam bidding conventions, as Blackwood, San Francisco, Gerber and asking bids, the player making the slam try is the *complete boss!* He asks the questions. All the responder does is tell how many aces and kings he has. The final decision as to the ultimate contract is completely that of the slam bidder; the responder has nothing to say in the matter.

5-No aces are required to bid four no trump in Blackwood or four clubs in Gerber; San Francisco requires two aces. However, using Blackwood, two aces should be present to bid four no trump if the agreed suit is clubs; one ace if the suit is diamonds.

6-Don't lie in your response. Many players who have opened the bidding with minimum or sub-minimum hands attempt to 'brake down' the bidding by withholding an ace or king in their responses.

Don't! Tell the truth. Once you lie to your partner, he'll never believe you again.

QUIZ THIRTEEN

1 - Your side is vulnerable, the opponents are not vulnerable.

North, Partner	East	South, You	West
One heart	One spade	Three hearts	Pass
Four hearts	Pass	Pass	Four spades
Five hearts	Pass	?	

Is your partner's five heart bid a slam try?

2 - Which of the following provides second round control? (a) doubleton; (b) singleton; (c) guarded king; (d) singleton king?

3 - Rate the doubleton ace-king (AK) in terms of controls furnished.

4 - Using Blackwood, South is the dealer in the four bidding examples immediately following. The opponents do not enter the bidding. Bid each pair of hands, from opening bid to what you consider the correct final contract.

	(e)	(f)	(g)	(h)
North	♠ KJ87	♠ K9	♠ J2	♠ Q2
	♡ A6	♡ 103	♡ A73	♡ A743
	◊ KQ10987	◊ 76	◊ 1098	◊ AKQ863
	♣ 2	♣ AKQJ765	♣ KQJ84	♣ 2
South	♠ AQ96	♠ AJ87	♠ AQ1087	♠ AKJ987
	♡ K72	♡ AK42	♡ KQ954	♡ K2
	◊ A6	◊ K3	◊ J6	◊ 74
	♣ KJ94	♣ 1042	♣ A	♣ AQ6

5 - You hold hand (i) to the left. With neither side vulnerable, the bidding has been –

(i)
♠ J2
♡ AKQ108
◊ AK95
♣ A

You, South	West	North, Partner	East
Two hearts	Pass	Three clubs	Pass
Three dia.	Pass	Three hearts	Pass
?			

What do you bid?

6 - You have opened the bidding with three no trump and your partner raises to four no trump. Is his bid a request for you to show aces and kings?

7-As South in the accompanying bidding sequence, you hold hand (j). What is your rebid, if any, after North's five heart bid?

(j)
♠ KQJ86
♡ KQ1052
◇ A3
♣ 2

You, South	West	North, Partner	East
One spade	Pass	Two clubs	Pass
Two hearts	Pass	Five hearts	Pass
?			

8-Can you count a void as an ace in responding to four no trump bids in San Francisco and Blackwood?

ANSWERS TO QUIZ THIRTEEN

1-No. His first heart bid was forced by the opponent's four spade bid.

2-(b), (c) and (d).

3-First, second and third round controls.

4-

(e) South	(e) North	(f) South	(f) North
1 club	1 diamond	1 spade	2 clubs
1 spade	4 spades	2 hearts	4 clubs
4 no trump	5 diamonds	4 no trump	5 diamonds
6 spades		6 no trump	

(g) South	(g) North	(h) South	(h) North
1 spade	2 clubs	1 spade	2 diamonds
2 hearts	3 hearts	3 spades	4 no trump
4 hearts	pass	5 hearts	7 spades

5-Four hearts. Your opening two bid showed your hand's strength. That you can use your partner's club suit is doubtful—all your partner did was express a simple preferance—not give you a raise—and you have two immediate spade losers.

6-No. There has been no suit agreed on.

7-Pass. The free bid of five in a major asks you to bid six if you hold two aces. You don't, so the pass is in order.

8-No! A void can never be counted as an ace in responding to four no trump. However, a void may be cue-bid as a control.

LESSON THIRTEEN

HANDS

Each hand should be bid by the student before checking 'par.'

1-North dealer, neither vul.

West		North / South		East
		♠ AK8764 ♡ KJ95 ◊ void ♣ A86		
♠ Q2 ♡ Q102 ◊ AKQJ98 ♣ Q3		N S		♠ J1093 ♡ 3 ◊ 76 ♣ 1097542
		♠ 5 ♡ A8764 ◊ 105432 ♣ KJ		

2-East dealer, N-S vul.

West	North / South	East
	♠ K53 ♡ KQJ1064 ◊ 953 ♣ 10	
♠ AJ10976 ♡ 8 ◊ 8762 ♣ K3	N W E S	♠ Q ♡ A7 ◊ AKJ104 ♣ AJ762
	♠ 842 ♡ 9532 ◊ Q ♣ Q9854	

3-South dealer, E-W vul.

West	North / South	East
	♠ KQ109 ♡ A8543 ◊ A2 ♣ J9	
♠ 32 ♡ J96 ◊ J1097 ♣ Q765	N S	♠ 654 ♡ KQ107 ◊ 86543 ♣ 2
	♠ AJ87 ♡ 2 ◊ KQ ♣ AK10843	

4-West dealer, both vul.

West	North / South	East
	♠ 2 ♡ KQJ1086 ◊ J72 ♣ KQ4	
♠ J8643 ♡ 952 ◊ A3 ♣ J92	N W E S	♠ AKQ95 ♡ A4 ◊ KQ1098 ♣ A
	♠ 107 ♡ 73 ◊ 654 ♣ 1087653	

Blackwood is used in the following sequences –

1-North	East	South	West
1 spade	pass	2 hts.	3 dia.
4 dia.	pass	4 hts.	pass
4 no tr.	pass	5 dia.	pass
6 hearts	pass	pass	pass

West leads the diamond king.

2-East	South	West	North
1 dia.	pass	1 sp.	2 hts.
3 clubs	pass	4 dia.	pass
4 hts.	pass	4 sp.	pass
4 no tr.	pass	5 dia.	pass
6 dia.	pass	pass	pass

South leads the two of hearts.

3-South	West	North	East
1 club	pass	1 ht.	pass
1 spade	pass	4 sp.	pass
4 no tr.	pass	5 hts.	pass
7 spades	pass	pass	pass

West leads the diamond jack.

4-West	North	East	South
pass	1 ht.	2 hts.	pass
2 sp.	pass	4 sp.	pass
5 dia.	pass	7 sp.	pass
pass	pass		

North leads the king of hearts.

SOLUTIONS TO LESSON THIRTEEN HANDS

1-

South declarer at six hearts.

Trick	W	N	E	S
1	♢ K	♡ 5	♢ 7	♢ 2
2	♠ 2	♠ A	♠ 3	♠ 5
3	♠ Q	♠ 4	♠ 9	♡ 4
4	♡ 2	♡ 9	♡ 3	♡ A
5	♡ 10	♡ K	♣ 2	♡ 6
6	♢ 8	♠ K	♠ 10	♢ 3
7	♢ 9	♠ 6	♠ J	♡ 7
8	♣ 3	♣ A	♣ 4	♣ J
9	♡ Q	♠ 8	♣ 5	♢ 4
10	♣ Q	♣ 6	♣ 7	♣ K
11	♢ J	♡ J	♢ 6	♢ 5
12	♢ Q	♠ 7	♣ 9	♢ 10
13	♢ A	♣ 8	♣ 10	♡ 8

North-South win 12 tricks.

2-

East declarer at six diamonds.

Trick	S	W	N	E
1	♡ 2	♡ 8	♡ 10	♡ A
2	♢ Q	♢ 2	♢ 3	♢ A
3	♡ 3	♢ 6	♢ 5	♢ K
4	♡ 5	♢ 7	♢ 9	♢ J
5	♠ 2	♠ A	♠ 3	♠ Q
6	♠ 4	♠ J	♠ 5	♣ 2
7	♠ 8	♠ 10	♠ K	♢ 4

East now claims the balance. Do you see how?

Dummy is re-entered either by trumping the losing heart, or via the king of clubs. East's losing clubs are discarded on dummy's good spades.

East-West win all 13 tricks.

3-

South declarer at six spades.

Trick	W	N	E	S
1	♢ J	♢ 2	♢ 3	♢ Q
2	♠ 2	♠ 9	♠ 4	♠ 7
3	♠ 3	♠ 10	♠ 5	♠ J
4	♢ 7	♠ Q	♠ 6	♠ 8
5	♣ 5	♣ J	♣ 2	♣ K
6	♣ 6	♣ 9	♢ 4	♣ A

South now claims the balance, stating that he is trump-finessing against West's marked queen of clubs.

North-South win all 13 tricks.

4-

West declarer at seven spades.

Trick	N	E	S	W
1	♡ K	♡ A	♡ 7	♡ 2
2	♠ 2	♠ A	♠ 7	♠ 3
3	♡ 6	♠ K	♠ 10	♠ 4
4	♢ 2	♢ 8	♢ 4	♢ A
5	♢ 7	♢ Q	♢ 5	♢ 3
6	♢ J	♢ K	♢ 6	♡ 5

West now claims the balance, stating that the remaining heart in his hand will be discarded on dummy's diamond suit.

East-West win all 13 tricks.

COMMENTS ON LESSON THIRTEEN HANDS

1-South realizes he cannot possibly trump all of his losing diamonds in the dummy. Accordingly, he must set up dummy's spade suit to provide diamond discards, and the trump suit provides the needed entries for establishment of the spade suit.

Even though South couldn't be expected to guess the location of the queen of hearts, notice that after two high trumps have been played, declarer entered dummy with the ace of clubs. As long as a trump remained in dummy, West could not take a diamond trick.

The reason for West not over-trumping an early round of spades was because he hoped declarer would make the error of trumping a second round of diamonds in the dummy, using the dummy's last trump.

2-Hand two demonstrates a simple safety play of first playing a high card (the ace of diamonds) rather than taking an immediate finesse against the missing queen of trumps. After 'pulling' the remaining trumps held by the defenders, the spade suit is 'trump-finessed.'

3-Hand three furnishes another example of the 'trump-finesse,' this time in the club suit. After pulling trumps, the ace and king of clubs are cashed. When East shows out on the second round of clubs, West is marked for the queen. It is a simple matter now to lead the 10 or eight of clubs. If West 'puts up' the queen, dummy trumps, and South's remaining clubs are winners; if West plays low on the third round of clubs, dummy merely discards a worthless heart.

4-East's immediate cue-bid of two hearts over the opponent's one heart opening bid shows a tremendous hand, and the bid is forcing to game for the East-West partnership. It stands to reason that if the East-West hands can make a game even if West's hand is completely worthless, the presence of the ace of diamonds should mean the possibility of slam. West cue-bids that ace, after receiving the raise to four spades. With all necessary key-cards accounted for, East bids the grand slam which is an absolute laydown.

Lesson XIV

Three Card Minors

PART ONE

Opening Bids

PART TWO

Responding

PART THREE

Rebidding

LESSON FOURTEEN

THE BIDDING OF THREE CARD MINOR SUITS

It may seem strange to the student that after being told in previous lessons that no suit of less than four cards should be bid, now to learn that there are times and places where opening bids based on three card minor suits are not only permissable, but recommended. Nevertheless, this is the case.

There are three points I wish to emphasize.

First, the three card suit, when bid, must be in a minor.

Second, the bid is a makeshift (though a necessary one) that is used only when a better bid is not available.

Third, if you have opened the bidding with a weak hand on a three card minor, as by bidding 'one club,' and your partner now raises to two clubs, you should not be afraid to play the hand in that contract even though you have only three trumps. Under no circumstances should you become panicky and try to escape from the two club (or diamond contract, as the case may be) by bidding no trump or some four card suit. Any voluntary rebid on your part shows extra high card values; if you have them, fine; if you don't, be happy to play the hand cheaply, knowing that your partner has the additional trumps needed to bolster your three card holding.

The three card minor bid is very frequently used. It enables you to bid safely on a lot of hands on which you might otherwise find your rebid awkward or your partner's response difficult.

THREE CARD MINOR OPENING BIDS

There are three situations where the bidding should be opened with a three card minor suit instead of the normal choice of suits.

1-The hand does not contain a biddable suit but does have 14 or more points.

2 - The player, with 13 to 16 points, would find rebidding awkward had the normal choice of suits been bid first.

3 - When the opening bidder holds 17 or more points, his partner's response (with a weak hand) is made much easier.

(a)
♠ J843
♡ J972
◊ AJ
♣ AQ7

Let's examine the first situation, where the suit or suits are not biddable, yet the hand contains opening bid strength. In hand (a) you have a total of 14 points, including one point for the doubleton diamond.

By opening the bidding with a club, you make the entire bidding structure easier for both you and your partner. If your partner responds with one diamond, you can now bid one heart; if he bids one heart or one spade, you would simply give a single raise to two of that suit.

Now, let's imagine that you had bid the higher ranking of touching suits first—in this case, spades. If your partner bids one no trump, you can never investigate the possibility that he has four cards of some lower ranking suit. He might have four hearts and the fit will not be discovered until too late.

♠ Q2
♡ A1084
◊ 1096
♣ J976

N
W E
S

♠ A1074
♡ KJ96
◊ J4
♣ AQ3

Figure 203

Figure 203 is an example of the second situation. South is the dealer, and from what you were previously told, one spade would be the correct opening bid, since it is the higher ranking of touching suits of equal length.

Very well, let's suppose that South does open the bidding with one spade. North's response would be one no trump. South, with a total of only 16 points, realizes that his partner has from seven to 10 points, lacks spade support, and that game is improbable. He should therefore pass. Yet the hand belongs in hearts, and had South opened the bidding with one club it would have been a simple matter for North to have responded with one heart.

The student should realize that where the opening bidder's hand is strong, it is more than likely his partner's hand will be weak, and it is much easier for a weak responder to bid over an opening bid of one club or one diamond than over an opening bid of one heart or one spade.

	♠ Q2
	♡ J7654
	◇ KJ3
	♣ 1098
	N
W		E
	S
	♠ AK86
	♡ AQ82
	◇ 72
	♣ K76

Figure 204

Figure 204 is an illustration of this situation. Had South opened with one spade, North's response would be one no trump, whereas had South opened with one club, it would have been a simple matter for North to respond with one heart.

Someone may point out that had South opened with one spade, he could still have bid two hearts over North's one no trump response, so the heart fit would have been found anyway.

But let's suppose that North's suit had been diamonds instead of hearts. In other words, we've transposed the diamond and heart holdings. Now the bidding may get too high.

It should be pointed out that the three card minor opening has its maximum usefulness with medium or weak hands containing shaded major suits of four cards or less. It *should not* be used with powerful hands that could be opened with bids of one or more no trump, or hands containing suits of *five* cards or more. With five card suits elsewhere in the hand, once you incorrectly open with a three card minor, the moment you show your five card suit you paint an incorrect picture of your distribution.

So there's your first rule—when the bidding is opened with a three card minor, the hand contains no suit of five or more cards.

"All very well," you may say, **"but suppose I open the bidding with a three card minor, say by bidding one club, and my partner now raises me to two clubs, or even three? What do I do now?"**

You do exactly as though your suit were of four or more cards! If you have opened a minimum hand, and your partner can only bid two clubs, you should pass. In all probability, partner lacks four or more diamonds, hearts or spades, or he would have made a one over one response over one club. Accordingly, he must have four or more clubs. With seven trumps between the partnership, there is no reason to dread that contract. As a matter of fact, if your hand as opener is weak, and your partner's hand is so weak that the best he can do is give you a single raise, you'll have a bargain if you can get to play the hand in two clubs. The opponents have more strength than your side and are obviously missing something their way of the table.

If your partner gives you a double raise in your suit by bidding three clubs, again you should act exactly as though your club suit were a genuine one of four or more cards. With a 'minnie' you should pass; with 16 or more points and stoppers in *all* side suits, you should bid three no trump; if you feel the partnership holds 29 points or more, you should bid five clubs, though the three no trump contract will generally be superior to the minor suit game contract.

There is an additional advantage to using three card minor openings in that when the hand is played later in some other contract, the defenders may be dissuaded from leading the suit in which the three card minor was originally bid. And that suit may be only thinly protected.

The following characteristics indicate when the three card minor opening should be used.

1 - The hand does not contain a biddable four card suit of the other minor. If it does, the four card minor suit should be bid since there is no need of a three card minor opening.

2-The hand does not contain a five card or longer suit.

3-The hand contains no singleton. When there is, a better choice of opening bids (other than the three card minor) will be available, since either the hand will contain three four card suits or at least one five carder. If you don't believe me, lay out the cards and see!

4-To be biddable, the three card minor *must* be headed by at least the ace, king or queen, or any combination of these honors.

5-With two three card minors present, both meeting the above requirements, unless one suit is predominantly stronger than the other, open with a club rather than a diamond. That permits a one diamond response to one club, whereas, if you open with one diamond holding a minimum hand, and your partner bids 'two clubs,' you'll be stuck for an easy rebid. However, were your clubs ♣ Q62 and the diamonds ◊ AKJ, the latter suit would be preferable for the opening bid.

6-Generally, when the hand is opened with a three card minor, good major suit support is present. This may be four cards of one major, or four cards of both majors, but never five cards, as already stressed.

(b)	(c)	(d)	(e)
♠ A Q 4	♠ J 5 3 2	♠ Q 8 5 4	♠ K 7 4 3
♡ K Q 4 2	♡ A 10 8 5	♡ K J 6 5	♡ A 9 6
◊ J 4 2	◊ A 9	◊ A Q 8	◊ A Q 10
♣ K 9 3	♣ A 10 2	♣ K 2	♣ Q 7 4
One club	One club	One diamond	One dia.

The reason that a three card minor should not be used as the opening bid when the hand also contains a five card suit is that later bidding and rebidding a higher ranking five card suit would be a reverse, indicate the three card minor to be still longer, which, of course, is not true.

(f)
♠ K 10 9
♡ K J 10 9 8
◊ 8 4
♣ A Q 5

Holding hand (f), the bidding in case A would be completely wrong, paint an erroneous picture of the distribution.

CASE A

You, Opener	Partner
One club	One diamond
One heart	Two diamonds
Two hearts?	

Since by rebidding the hearts you show them to be at least five cards in length, the first lower ranking bid suit, clubs, must be longer, since you reversed the bidding. This is obviously not true.

The reason for insisting that the three card minor be headed by one or more of the three top honors in the suit is that, after opening the bidding in that suit with a weak hand, no assurance exists that your side will play the hand. In the event you become a defender, and your partner leads your suit, the lead should be beneficial to your side, winning or promoting tricks. This is just as true with three card minors as their longer brothers discussed in Lesson Two on pages 38 and 39.

Some inexperienced players, enchanted with the ease and flexibility of the bid, will sometimes open on almost any kind of a three card minor, as 1075 or J92. This is wholly incorrect.

Similarly, opening a two card minor, even the AK alone, is equally wrong, because if your partner, with only four cards of that suit, raises your bid to the two level, you will have only six trumps in the combined hands against the opponents' seven.

RESPONDING TO THREE CARD MINOR OPENINGS

If your partner opens with a club or a diamond, you haven't any definite knowledge whether he has opened on a three-carder or whether he holds four or more cards of the bid suit.

You *must* treat any minor suit opening as genuine, indicating four or more cards in the bidder's hand. Ninety percent of the time this will be true. However, if responder finds five or six clubs in his hand after hearing his partner open the bidding with one club, it's a pretty safe guess that the opening bid was on a three card suit.

REBIDS BY THE THREE CARD MINOR OPENER

When Partner Has Already Passed

The opening bidder's rebids here and elsewhere will be a lot easier if the student will remember that responses normally forcing, had partner not previously passed, are no longer forcing, even for one round. In other words, if you open with one club, and your partner responds one heart, you can pass if he'd passed earlier and couldn't open the bidding.

(g)

CASE B

	North, Partner	East	South, You	West
♠ Q J 8 2				
♡ A J 6				
◇ K 10 5	Pass	Pass	One club	Pass
♣ K 10 2	One heart	Pass	Pass	

Of course, it doesn't always follow that, as the opening bidder, you should always pass the response of a partner who couldn't open the bidding. Partner may have a good hand which with yours can make a game, and still he didn't have enough for an opening bid. The opener should *try to rebid* if additional values are present. Change the five of diamonds in hand (g) to the five of hearts and a raise to two hearts would be in order.

Further, particularly in duplicate play, or against sharp rubber bridge opponents, if you pass one heart as in the preceding bidding sequence, the opponents will take it as an admission of weakness, and probably enter the bidding. So, if you can find a safe rebid, it will force the opponents to enter the bidding at a higher range, something they may be unwilling or unable to do. Your rebid would have a mildly pre-emptive effect.

(h)
♠ QJ82
♡ AQ65
◇ KJ3
♣ 86

Now, let's suppose you lack support for your partner's response as:

CASE C

North, Partner	East	South, You	West
Pass	Pass	One dia.	Pass
Two clubs	Pass	?	

Of all suits to bid, your partner has selected the one you like the least! Should you now rebid 'two hearts' or 'two spades?' Heavens, no! That would be a reverse. Should you now bid two no trump? That would show a strong hand, with game probability, and you have a weak one. You certainly don't have club support for a raise.

So that leaves only one thing to do, pass! Admitting that you lack club support, the probability when partner enters the two level to show a minor is that he has at least a five card suit. I would rather let my partner play a reasonably makeable contract than through unwarranted rebids get myself too high in an alternative contract.

Remember, you don't have to rebid! Your partner previously passed!

However, every now and then, your partner, who couldn't open the bidding earlier, makes a jump bid (normally forcing) after you have opened the bidding with a three card minor. The jump may take one of three forms.

1-He may jump in your suit, as one club – three clubs. *Note* – The jump in the originally bid minor is only semi-forcing.

2-He may jump in a new suit, as one club by you – two hearts by partner.

3-He may bid two no trump.

Again, let me remind you that while the second and third situations are absolutely forcing to game, and the first semi-forcing, had not partner previously passed, they are no longer forcing, since partner *did* pass! The best we can say for them is that they are now semi-forcing. If you have opened a 'minnie,' game is improbable, and you should pass. On the other hand, if the bidding indicates a possibility of game, you should try to find at least one more bid.

Situation One - Your partner, who had previously passed, now raises your one diamond opening bid to three diamonds.

YOU HOLD

(i)	(j)
♠ K Q 8	♠ K 9 6 2
♡ K 10 9 6	♡ A 8 4 2
◇ A J 6	◇ K J 6
♣ Q 10 9	♣ K 5

On (i), I would now bid three no trump. The opening bid contains 15 points in high cards, with good stoppers in all three other suits. Under no circumstances should you now bid three hearts. Partner, to all intents and purposes, denied hold- four or more hearts by his failure to bid that suit.

On (j) you should pass three diamonds. You have a 'minnie,' and partner couldn't open the bidding. Be happy you've found the right spot.

Situation Two – Your partner, who previously passed, bids two hearts or two spades over your one diamond opening.

(k)
♠ A J 10 7 5
♡ Q 5 3
◇ 10 9 8
♣ A 2

I would raise to three of his suit with both hands (i) and (j). His hand could resemble (k). Had partner's response been three clubs, I would bid three no trump with (i), pass with (j).

Situation Three – If partner, who has previously passed, now responds with two no trump.

I would raise to three no trump with (i), pass with (j).

The one thing I again want to caution you about is the habit many inexperienced players have of rushing into two no trump, or some new four card suit, the moment their three card minor has been raised from the one to the two level. These second bids on weak hands after a three card minor opening are not based on values held by the bidder, but rather on fright, a dread of playing a three card trump suit.

Don't run out of a three card minor into some other suit or contract when you lack the high card values for a second bid. Sit still and have confidence in partner's raise. This holds true whether partner has previously passed or not.

OPENER'S REBIDS

When Partner Has Not Previously Passed

After opening the bidding with a three card minor when partner has not previously had a chance to bid, rebid normally over his response, just as though your minor suit were of four cards.

Continue one-over-one bidding as far as warranted. A jump in a minor, as one club – three clubs is semi-forcing. An immediate single jump in a new suit, or in no trump, is forcing to game.

If you open with a three card diamond suit, and your partner 'sticks you' with a two club response, a two no trump rebid, even with a minimum hand, is better than showing a four card major at the two level. The latter would be a reverse, would paint an incorrect picture both of distribution and high card strength, whereas the two no trump rebid may involve only a slight stretch of high card values.

The point I am making is that once you open the bidding, and your partner forces you to bid again, you must find the best possible rebid even if it involves 'fudging' a little. It isn't always possible to have the perfect bid or rebid for every situation.

Some nervous soul, reading this text, may inquire, **"Golly, what if the opponents double one club and I'm left to play it there? I'm in awful shape with only three trumps."**

In other words, the bidding has gone as in case D.

CASE D

(1)	North, You	East	South, Partner	West
♠ K J 8 6	One club	double	Pass	Pass
♡ A 10 9 2	*Climb! Get out of there!*			
◊ 7 4				
♣ A Q 5				

In the above bidding sequence, holding hand (1), you know from West's penalty pass that the clubs are badly stacked against you. West's pass showed the ability to defeat one club. (See pages 438 and 439). Accordingly, you must try to escape to some better contract.

If you and your partner understand that a redouble by you at this point is SOS for rescue purposes, (pages 467,468) it's the perfect bid to extricate you from this hot-spot. If there's any chance of the redouble being misconstrued by partner and left in, bid your cheapest four card suit (in this case, hearts) and hope you 'hit' your partner with three or four cards of that suit. If that suit gets by without a double, fine; if it does get doubled, then you might test one spade.

But don't worry. This last situation doesn't happen once in a blue moon. On the other hand, the three card minor opening is an invaluable tool, adding great flexibility to the bidder's repertoire.

PART TWO

RESPONDING WITH THREE CARD MINORS

I am going to show you an extremely useful bid, that of the three card minor in responding.

There are many hands which your partner will open with one heart or one spade and you hold 10 to 12 points. You don't have enough to raise to three of his suit, yet you are near the maximum for a single raise. Were there such a bid as two and a half hearts or spades, it would fit your hand perfectly, but, unfortunately, no such bid exists. Thus we have to find a bid to fit the occasion. The three card minor, if present, does this admirably.

(m)
♠ K J 6
♡ J 4 3 2
◊ 9 5 3
♣ A J 2

Suppose your partner opened the bidding with one heart and you held hand (m) to the left. What would you respond? The hand has 10 points, after subtracting a point for 4-3-3-3 distribution. It is near maximum for a single raise.

The ideal bid on your part is two clubs. That advice may raise a feeling of dismay within you. **"Suppose my partner passes and leaves me there,"** you ask.

Well, he can't. If you previously haven't had a chance to bid, and have responded with two clubs at your first opportunity, your takeout into a new suit is absolutely forcing for one round, and your partner *must* rebid!

Now, let's further suppose he rebids with two hearts, merely rebidding his own suit. Here you can raise him to three hearts, which is tantamount to saying, **"Partner, I didn't have enough strength originally to raise you from one heart to three, but I do have enough for a single raise from two hearts to three. You also realize, partner, that I didn't have enough to take you from two hearts to four, or I would have bid the game."**

If partner, the opening bidder, has additional values, he can now bid four hearts. If he hasn't, he can pass three. You'll admit that's an easy, simple way of bidding 'in between' hands.

Some reader may ask, **"Well, as long as you're making a temporizing bid** (which is the name of this type of bid), **why not bid one spade over one heart? That would keep the bidding still lower, also be forcing for one round?"**

The danger of bidding an artificial suit of three cards, higher in rank than the suit you intend to support later, is that partner may raise your suit. Since your suit of three cards is higher in rank than his suit, you can't return to his suit without increasing the contract.

For example –

CASE E

Partner, Opener	You, Responder
One heart	One spade
Three spades	Four hearts
Four spades	Five hearts? ?

But if the suit in which you have responded artificially is lower in rank than partner's, you can always return to his suit without increasing the contract.

CASE F

Partner, Opener	You, Responder
One heart	Two clubs
Three clubs	Three hearts
Four clubs	Four hearts

For this excellent reason, responding with three card suits is confined to minors, when the temporizing three carder is lower ranking than the previously bid suit. Thus, bidding one diamond over one club would be dangerous, whereas bidding two clubs over one spade or one heart would be safe.

Of course, if you have a normal one over one response with a four card suit, or can give a normal double raise, the three card minor need not, and should not, be employed. The three card minor, as a response, is an *emergency bid*, designed for those in-between hands between a single and a double raise, when no other bid appropriately fits the responding hand.

The responding hand, when using a three card minor, may contain a five card or longer suit providing it is in partner's suit; the three card minor should not be employed if the five card suit is elsewhere than in partner's suit.

THREE CARD MINOR RESPONSES AFTER HAVING PASSED

Don't!

Should you have passed originally, you should *never* respond to partner's opening bid with a three card minor, even though you may hold a hand bordering between a single and double raise of his suit. The reason is that, since you've already passed, your response is no longer forcing. Your partner, with a minimum hand, may pass, leaving you to play the contract in your three card minor, whereas the best place to play the hand is in his suit (for which you hold support). It is better to support partner's suit at once, requirements being present.

PREFERENCE BIDS AFTER THREE CARD MINOR RESPONSE

Suppose, with hand (m) on page 538, you have responded with two clubs to your partner's opening bid of one heart. Your partner now rebids with two diamonds. Some players would be inclined to give a jump preference (page 242) which, so far as holdings in both of partner's suits are concerned, is justified.

However, an additional factor must be considered. You have already strained your high card values to the hilt in order to find the two club response. The only reason you could make this 'stretch' was the heart 'fit.' A three heart jump preference would show still additional values which you do not possess. Thus your correct preference is two hearts (over partner's two diamonds).

FREE THREE CARD MINOR RESPONSES OVER AN OVERCALL

On hands containing 10 to 12 points, where an opponent 'sticks in' an overcall over your partner's opening bid, the three card minor response is not only unnecessary, but actually undesirable. That is because the free single raise of partner's suit shows the equivalent amount of strength.

(n)

♠ 863
♡ J762
◇ KJ4
♣ AJ8

CASE G

Partner, North	East	You, South	West
One heart	One spade	Two hearts	Pass

Without the intervening spade bid, your best response would have been two clubs. This bid, plus a later single raise in hearts, would show a hand too good for a single raise, not enough for a double raise to three hearts.

But the free raise to two hearts! That shows more than the single raise over a pass. So now we don't need the three card minor.

Remember, the three card minor is intended for use only when there is no better bid. Here there is!

PART THREE

THE THREE CARD MINOR AS AN ARTIFICIAL REBID

There are many times when both the opening bidder and the responder wish to make some rebid that will force partner to bid again. The use of the short minor suit, when used in forcing situations, is ideal for this purpose.

CASE H

North	East	South	West
1 spade	Pass	2 hearts	Pass
3 diamonds			

West	North / South	East
	♠ A8643 ♡ AK7 ◊ AK10 ♣ 85	
♠ Q5 ♡ J96 ◊ J8642 ♣ J92	N W E S	♠ KJ107 ♡ 104 ◊ Q973 ♣ Q76
	♠ 92 ♡ Q8532 ◊ 5 ♣ AK1043	

Figure 205

Figure 205 furnishes an excellent example of the three card minor as an artificial rebid by the opening bidder.

In case H, after opening the bidding with one spade, North is hard pressed to find a good rebid. To give a jump raise to four hearts should ordinarily show at least four cards of partner's suit. The spade suit is not rebiddable; a rebid of no trump would be unsound due to the lack of a club stopper (in the North hand).

The use of a three card minor, as long as it is lower in rank than the agreed suit, is ideal for creating forcing rebids. The bid offers great flexibility in rebidding, both for the opening bidder and the responder.

In the above hand, South would probably rebid four clubs over North's three diamond bid, and the partnership should have little difficulty reaching a final contract of six hearts.

CASE I

South	West	North	East
1 heart	Pass	1 spade	Pass
3 clubs			

North:
♠ K 10 6 4 2
♡ 6
♢ J 5 3 2
♣ A 10 8

West:
♠ J 3
♡ K 9 8
♢ A 10 9 8 7
♣ 6 4 2

East:
♠ 7 5
♡ J 7 4 3
♢ K Q 6
♣ 9 7 5 3

South:
♠ A Q 9 8
♡ A Q 10 5 2
♢ 4
♣ K Q J

Figure 206

Figure 206 is another example of the use of the three card minor as an artificial rebid by the opening bidder.

Note that South's rebid was three clubs, not two clubs. The reason should be apparent. A simple rebid of two clubs would not be forcing, and North would probably pass. But the jump bid in a new suit is absolutely forcing to game. North must rebid.

North's probable rebid would be four clubs, giving South a choice of rebids. South might now simply bid four spades, which North would pass in a hurry; or South might bid four no trump, which could lead to an eventual six spade contract.

CASE J

South	West	North	East
1 heart	Pass	1 spade	Pass
2 spades	Pass	3 dia.	Pass
4 dia.	Pass		

North:
♠ K Q 8 7
♡ K J 9 6 5
♢ K 9 7
♣ 3

West:
♠ 10 9 6 5 4
♡ 7
♢ J 8
♣ Q J 9 8 7

East:
♠ 2
♡ Q 10
♢ 6 5 4 3 2
♣ A K 6 5 4

South:
♠ A J 3
♡ A 8 4 3 2
♢ A Q 10
♣ 10 2

Figure 207

Having located the 'right' cards in partner's hand with the above bidding, North (using Blackwood) will probably bid four no trump. Six hearts will be an easy final contract for the partnership to fulfill.

Had North simply bid three hearts over South's opening bid of one heart, the latter's rebid would be four hearts, and the lay-down slam would be missed. Correspondingly, a four heart rebid (instead of three diamonds) in case J would be passed by South.

Use of the three card minor permitted the partnership to explore the hand further, without any danger of the bidding being dropped short of game.

There are several things I'd like to point out in connection with the use of short minor suit bids.

1 - For opening bid purposes, the minor suit must have at least three cards, and they must contain the queen or higher cards in the bid suit. The hand cannot contain any five card or longer suit, nor a singleton or void.

2 - For responding and rebidding, the short minor can be any length – from a singleton to three cards, as long as it is lower ranking than the suit in which you eventually plan to play the hand. Further, the hand may have any distribution, as singletons, voids, long suits and the like.

3 - Where the short minor is used as a rebid or response, it must be forcing. It would be silly to have tremendous spade support, hear partner bid one spade, then make a temporizing response of two clubs if you've previously passed. Your partner *could* pass. For still another example, see *figure 206*, page 542.

4 - When used as a response or rebid, the hand bidding a short minor should have support for partner's suit, or a solid or semi-solid suit of his own. To make a forcing rebid without the slightest idea of which suit you intend to play the hand in, would be just as silly as the captain of an ocean liner ordering full speed ahead, not knowing his destination.

TO THE READER

After reading these pages on short minor bids, you may feel them hazardous, "all right for experts, but not for me."

Don't feel that way!

These bids are *indispensable* in the tight spots of bidding. They are standard practice by the best players. Try using them. After they've solved knotty bidding problems, you won't be without them.

Some players may ask, "How do I know, after my partner bids a club or a diamond, whether he has a real suit, or he's bidding a three-carder?"

You don't know, then and there. But you will on the next round. Treat every minor bid as legitimate. Ninety percent of them are. If you do open a three card minor, and your partner gives you a single raise as from one club to two clubs, don't be afraid to play it there, particularly if you have a weak hand. What better place could you want? And above all, don't try escaping to other suits or no trump (with a weak hand) when your partner has supported your three card minor.

QUIZ FOURTEEN

1 - What is your opening bid with each of the following?

(a)	(b)	(c)
♠ K9643	♠ A862	♠ AJ87
♡ A865	♡ K543	♡ K98
◇ 2	◇ AQ7	◇ KJ7
♣ AQ7	♣ J2	♣ AQ2

(d)	(e)
♠ KQ105	♠ J964
♡ AQJ	♡ AQ108
◇ 1093	◇ AKJ
♣ Q98	♣ 74

2 - You hold hand (f) and open the bidding with one club. Your partner has not yet had an opportunity to bid, and the opponents do not enter the bidding. What is your rebid to each of the following responses by partner?

(f)
♠ K764
♡ A952
◇ A3
♣ K64

PARTNER'S RESPONSE		YOUR REBID
One heart	(a)	________
One diamond	(b)	________
Two clubs	(c)	________
Three clubs	(d)	________
Two hearts	(e)	________
Two diamonds	(f)	________

3 - The bidding has been —

Partner, North	East	South, You	West
Pass	Pass	1 diamond	Pass

You hold hand (g). What is your rebid to each response listed below?

(g)
♠ QJ4
♡ A876
◇ AJ5
♣ Q109

PARTNER'S RESPONSE		YOUR REBID
Two clubs	(a)	________
Three diamonds	(b)	________
Two spades	(c)	________
One heart	(d)	________

4 - Your partner is the dealer. You hold hand (h). What is your response if he opens with (a) one heart; (b) one spade?

(h)
♠ AJ82
♡ J943
◇ 62
♣ K86

5-Suppose you are the dealer, and pass, holding hand (h). What is your response if your partner opens with (a) one heart; (b) one spade?

6-You are the dealer and open the bidding with one spade on each of the following hands. Your partner responds with two hearts. The opponents do not bid. What is your rebid in each case?

(i)	(j)	(k)
♠ A K 4 3 2	♠ A Q 10 8 7	♠ A Q 10 9
♡ K J 9	♡ K Q 5 4	♡ 10 6 3
◇ 4 3	◇ 2	◇ A J 10
♣ A K Q	♣ Q 3 2	♣ A Q J

ANSWERS TO QUIZ FOURTEEN

1-(a) One spade; (b) one diamond; (c) one no trump; (d) one club; (e) one diamond.

2-(a) Two hearts; (b) one heart; (c) pass; (d) three no trump; (e) three hearts; (f) two no trump.

3-(a) Pass; (b) pass; (c) three spades; (d) pass. Don't forget you are not compelled to rebid since your partner originally passed.

4-(a) One spade; (b) two clubs. Since with situation (a), a one over one response of one spade is available, there is no need of a temporizing minor suit response.

5-(a) Two hearts; (b) two spades. Since you have support for partner's suit, it is better to show it at once, rather than bid a new suit which partner may pass. Your response is no longer forcing, since you have previously passed.

6-(i) Three clubs; (j) three hearts—after all, your hand, other than the excellent heart support, is little better than a minimum opening. If partner cannot bid over three hearts, game is unlikely. Under no circumstances should you have rebid three clubs to force partner to rebid. (k) three no trump.

LESSON FOURTEEN

HANDS

Each hand should be bid by the student before checking 'par.'

1-North dealer, neither vul.

North: ♠ A874 ♡ 10643 ◊ 42 ♣ AKQ

West: ♠ 1095 ♡ KJ ◊ Q975 ♣ 7652

East: ♠ QJ6 ♡ AQ5 ◊ J108 ♣ J1098

South: ♠ K32 ♡ 9872 ◊ AK63 ♣ 43

2-East dealer, N-S vul.

North: ♠ 1083 ♡ A7 ◊ K102 ♣ A10875

West: ♠ 76 ♡ K92 ◊ J7643 ♣ Q92

East: ♠ KQ52 ♡ J1086 ◊ AQ8 ♣ K6

South: ♠ AJ94 ♡ Q543 ◊ 95 ♣ J43

3-South dealer, both vul.

North: ♠ A2 ♡ J64 ◊ J84 ♣ K7432

West: ♠ J1075 ♡ 1083 ◊ A52 ♣ J109

East: ♠ K86 ♡ Q97 ◊ 109763 ♣ Q8

South: ♠ Q943 ♡ AK52 ◊ KQ ♣ A65

4-West dealer, E-W vul.

North: ♠ A6 ♡ K865 ◊ 87532 ♣ 106

West: ♠ KJ98 ♡ Q1097 ◊ AQ ♣ Q53

East: ♠ 1043 ♡ J2 ◊ J96 ♣ AKJ87

South: ♠ Q752 ♡ A43 ◊ K104 ♣ 942

1-North	East	South	West
1 club	pass	1 dia.	pass
1 heart	pass	3 hts.	pass
4 hearts	pass	pass	pass

East leads the spade queen.

2-East	South	West	North
1 dia.	pass	2 dia.	pass
pass	pass		

South leads the heart trey.

3-South	West	North	East
1 club	pass	2 clubs	pass
2 no tr.	pass	3 no tr.	pass
pass	pass		

West leads the five of spades.

4-West	North	East	South
1 club	pass	3 clubs	pass
3 no tr.	pass	pass	pass

North leads the diamond trey.

SOLUTIONS TO LESSON FOURTEEN HANDS

1-

North declarer at four hearts.

Trick	E	S	W	N
1	♠ Q	♠ K	♠ 5	♠ 4
2	♣ 8	♣ 3	♣ 2	♣ A
3	♣ 9	♣ 4	♣ 5	♣ K
4	♣ 10	♠ 2	♣ 6	♣ Q
5	♠ 6	♠ 3	♠ 9	♠ A
6	♠ J	♡ 2	♠ 10	♠ 7
7	♡ 5	♡ 7	♡ J	♡ 3
8	◇ 8	◇ K	◇ 5	◇ 2
9	♡ A	♡ 8	♡ K	♡ 4
10	♡ Q	♡ 9	♣ 7	♡ 6
11	♣ J	◇ 3	◇ 7	♡ 10
12	◇ 10	◇ 6	◇ 9	♠ 8
13	◇ J	◇ A	◇ Q	◇ 4

North-South win 10 tricks.

2-

East declarer at two diamonds.

Trick	S	W	N	E
1	♡ 3	♡ 2	♡ A	♡ 6
2	♡ 4	♡ 9	♡ 7	♡ 8
3	◇ 5	◇ 3	◇ 2	◇ Q
4	♣ 3	♣ 2	♣ 8	♣ K
5	♣ 4	♣ Q	♣ A	♣ 6
6	♠ A	♠ 6	♠ 3	♠ Q
7	♡ 5	♡ K	◇ 10	♡ 10
8	♠ 9	♠ 7	♠ 8	♠ K
9	◇ 9	◇ 4	◇ K	◇ A

East claims the balance.

East-West win nine tricks.

3-

South declarer at three no tr.

Trick	W	N	E	S
1	♠ 5	♠ 2	♠ K	♠ 3
2	♠ 7	♠ A	♠ 8	♠ 4
3	◇ A	◇ 4	◇ 6	◇ K
4	♠ J	♡ 4	♠ 6	♠ Q
5	♣ 9	♣ 2	♣ 8	♣ A
6	◇ 2	◇ 8	◇ 3	◇ Q
7	♣ 10	♣ 3	♣ Q	♣ 5
8	♡ 3	♡ 6	♡ 7	♡ K

South now claims the balance, since by playing the king of clubs, the remaining clubs will be winners. The jack of diamonds and the ace of hearts win the last two tricks.

North-South win 10 tricks.

4-

West declarer at three no tr.

Trick	N	E	S	W
1	◇ 3	◇ 6	◇ 10	◇ Q
2	♣ 6	♣ J	♣ 2	♣ 3
3	♠ A	♠ 3	♠ 2	♠ J
4	◇ 2	◇ 9	◇ 4	◇ A
5	♣ 10	♣ 7	♣ 4	♣ Q
6	♡ 8	♣ A	♣ 9	♣ 5
7	♡ 5	♣ K	♡ 4	♡ 7
8	♠ 6	♣ 8	♡ 3	♡ 9
9	◇ 5	♠ 10	♠ 5	♠ 8
10	◇ 7	♠ 4	♠ 7	♠ 9
11	◇ 8	◇ J	♠ Q	♠ K

West concedes the last two tricks.

East-West win 10 tricks.

COMMENTS ON LESSON FOURTEEN HANDS

Hand one clearly shows the advantages of one-over-one bid-even with highly shaded suits, as against the old fashioned style of rebidding with one no trump.

In playing the hand, declarer first discards dummy's losing spade on his high club, trumps a spade, then leads trumps. East's overtake of his partner's king of hearts with the ace at trick nine costs the defense nothing, since they are 'equals,' permits East to lead a third round of trumps, 'pull' two adverse trumps for one.

On hand two, North's heart return at trick two is in the hope of trumping a later round of that suit. South naturally refuses to put up (play) the queen on this trick, since it would gain nothing for the defenders, as East (from North's lead) is marked with both the jack and 10 of hearts.

East's play of the king of clubs, before leading an additional round of trumps, is to permit him to trump the third round of clubs, if necessary, before the defenders can draw his (East's) last trump.

Hand three illustrates several points. First, the declarer, by driving out the diamond ace, knocks out the defenders' sure re-entry; next, by ducking the second round of clubs, South leaves himself with a club entry to an otherwise re-entryless hand.

On hand four, West realizes that he hasn't time to drive out both adverse high hearts in order to establish two heart tricks for his side. Success of the contract hinges on South holding the queen of spades.

Note South's play of the 10 of diamonds on the opening lead. This is known as a 'defensive finesse,' permits South to retain the king of diamonds over dummy's jack, hold declarer to two diamond tricks, whereas playing the king would (in this case) give the declarer three tricks in the suit. South's later play of the four of diamonds at trick four is based on the reasoning that West's ace must now be alone, since North has shown five diamonds by originally leading fourth-best, later a lower card.

Lesson XV

PART ONE

Part Score Bidding

PART TWO

Psychic Bidding

PART THREE

Competitive Bidding

LESSON FIFTEEN

PART ONE

PART SCORE BIDDING

In rubber bridge, either side or both may have part scores toward game. Naturally, since they need fewer points to complete their game, they will not need to contract for so many tricks. Without a part score, a pair considering bidding a game in spades, let us say, would have to bid and make four of that suit. With a part score of 60, a bid of two spades would accomplish the same purpose. And the same hand that, without the part score, might have been bid to four spades has, with a part score of 60, been bid to only two spades.

In other words, there was no need to bid four spades as long as your side had a part score of 60. Two spades was game. Similarly, a bid of one no trump or two clubs with the 60 part score would also have completed your game.

"Is there any advantage to bidding four spades," you ask, **"when your side may need only 30 or 60 points to complete a game?"**

There is no advantage to bidding a game, as four spades, or five clubs, or three no trump, if with a part score you can complete your game with a bid of fewer tricks *provided* – the opponents don't push you higher, or you don't intend bidding towards slam.

Now, the latter is most important! I venture to say that more makeable slams are not bid because the bidding side has a part score than for any other reason. In other words, there is a tendency to underbid with a part score so that there is not a complete exchange of information during the available bidding period.

♠ Q1087
♡ A43
♢ Q2
♣ KJ106

N
W E
S

♠ AKJ65
♡ 5
♢ A543
♣ AQ3

Figure 208

With the North-South hands in *figure 208*, and no part score, the bidding would probably be that shown in case A.

CASE A

South	West	North	East
One spade	Pass	Three spades	Pass
Four clubs	Pass	Four hearts*	Pass
Four no tr.	Pass	Five dia. **	Pass
Six spades	Pass	Pass	Pass

* *Showing controls (cue-bidding).*

** *Blackwood, showing one ace.*

Now, let's suppose that North-South have a part score of 60. Poor players would probably bid as in case B.

CASE B

South	West	North	East
One spade	Pass	Two spades	Pass
Pass	Pass		

Both South and North would be saying to themselves, "**Why should I bid more? Two spades puts us out.**"

Now there are lots of other considerations when either side or both have a partial. They will not apply to duplicate (tournament) bridge, since there are no part scores in that game.

1-SHOULD YOU HAVE MORE OR LESS STRENGTH TO OPEN THE BIDDING WHEN THE OPPONENTS HAVE A PARTIAL?

More!

Let's suppose you are South in *Figure 209*, the opponents have 60 towards game and your side has nothing. With North the dealer, the bidding has been –

CASE C

North	East	South	West
Pass	Pass	?	

♠ J32
♡ J86
◇ K752
♣ K72

♠ K9876	N	♠ AQ4
♡ K943	W E	♡ 2
◇ Q10	S	◇ A9864
♣ QJ		♣ 10965

♠ 105
♡ AQ1075
◇ J3
♣ A843

Figure 209

Do you want to open the bidding with one heart?

There's no question that, as South, you have 13 points with a rebiddable suit and a secondary biddable suit. *But*—if you open the bidding, and the opponents now start to bid, are you going to be able to outbid them so they can't complete their game?

If you do open the bidding with one heart, West will probably overcall with one spade. Your partner, North, will pass. East will raise to two spades. The opponents (with their part score of 60) have now contracted for game.

You're in the soup!

If you attempt to outbid the opponents by bidding three hearts or three clubs, both highly dangerous with a passing partner, you'll be doubled and slaughtered. What should be clear is that the hand might have been passed out if you hadn't opened the bidding.

On the other hand, let's look at *Figure 210.* With East-West 60 towards game, and North dealer, the probable bidding would be

♠ 532
♡ J86
◇ QJ107
♣ K72

♠ K9876	N	♠ J104
♡ K93	W E	♡ 2
◇ K83	S	◇ A9642
♣ QJ		♣ 6543

♠ AQ
♡ AQ10754
◇ 5
♣ A1098

Figure 210

CASE D

North	East	South	West
Pass	Pass	1 heart	1 sp.
Pass	2 sp.	3 hearts	?

If West bids three spades, you can defeat it one trick, or your side is capable of making four hearts. But the point I am trying to make is that in *figure 210*, you are capable of rebidding, even with a passing partner. In other words, once you opened the bidding in the face of an adverse part score, you didn't have to surrender the moment the opponents started bidding.

So remember this — When you open against an adverse part score, be sure you can bid again, even though your partner may be weak, and the opponents enter the bidding.

2-WHEN YOUR SIDE HAS THE PARTIAL

You can (and should) open with minimum hands, and even slightly shaded minimums, when your side has a part score, and the opponents lack any partial. By the time you have opened the bidding, and your partner has responded, it may be too late or too dangerous for the opponents to enter the bidding. By completing your part score contract, plus your previous partial, you have been able to 'get away' with an easy, makeable game.

CASE E

	North	
	♠ K32 ♡ 87 ◇ Q6543 ♣ K98	
West ♠ J9 ♡ AJ654 ◇ K7 ♣ 5432	N W E S	**East** ♠ Q10 ♡ 1092 ◇ A1098 ♣ AQJ6
	♠ A87654 ♡ KQ3 ◇ J2 ♣ 107	

Figure 211

South	West	North	East
1 sp.	pass	2 sp.	pass
pass	pass		

You can see how dangerous it would be for either East or West to enter the bidding. West certainly can't overcall safely with two hearts, and East is taking his life in his hands to contemplate a shaky informatory double which would require a response (from a passing partner) at the three level. Yet East-West can make four hearts, and North-South have stolen the hand for two spades!

WHEN BOTH SIDES HAVE A PART SCORE

The best advice I can give you is to open the bidding with any hand, even minimums, that contain several safe rebids, and pass hands that do not permit safe rebids. Since both sides may be chary of opening the bidding, due to the opposing part scores, border-line hands may be passed out.

If you do pass a minimum hand in these situations, and the bidding is opened by an opponent, you should attempt, if you can do it safely, to enter the bidding. If available, the distributional double (page 433) is your most effective weapon.

THE PRE-EMPTIVE VALUE OF THE SPADE SUIT

The spade suit is the best suit in the deck! That is because once a player bids a spade it is necessary for the other side to enter the two range to overcall with a suit. Thus, possession of the spade suit is a decided asset, and particularly in part score bidding, where you want to make it difficult for the opponents to enter the bidding.

PART SCORE RESPONDING AND REBIDDING

"Do I have to respond with a weak hand when my partner opens the bidding and we have a part score?" is a frequently asked question.

ANSWER – With a partial of 40 points or more, any opening bid of one is *virtually* forcing if it does not complete the game. Responder should find some kind of bid with three to five points, and with six or more points should make the response he would have made had the part score not been present.

(a)
♠ J86
♡ 42
◇ Q5432
♣ 1076

For example, your partner opens the bidding with one spade and you hold hand (a) to the left. Your side has a 60 partial. You should bid two spades.

Now, I know a lot of readers will exclaim, **"Why, you've only a total of four points and the single raise requires a minimum of six. Further, you even lack normal trump support** (three cards headed by the queen or better) "

True, but with 60 part score, your side needs only a total of eight tricks to produce a game and, for that reason, you are permitted to shade requirements a trifle.

"Suppose my partner had opened the bidding with one heart and I held hand (a) with a 60 part score," you inquire.

Well, I would still try to find a bid, and with this hand the best possible bid would be one no trump. I grant it is not a good bid, and a far cry from the six points ordinarily needed. But the part score changes the situation.

Further, once both partners have bid in a part score situation, the bidding cannot be dropped short of game. For instance, when holding a weak hand, the responder cannot merely bid once, then pass his partner's next bid short of game, saying, **"I stretched my hand once to find a bid and I'm not going to do it again."** Game must be reached. Each bid is forcing to game.

"Suppose our part score, plus my partner's opening one bid, will total the 100 points needed for game. Do I have to bid then?"

ANSWER – When the one bid, plus the partial, completes the game, ordinarily the responder should not bid without the needed normal requirements of six or more points. There is one exception, and that is when the opponents also have a part score. In these cases, to pass with hands of three to five points would be a clear admission of weakness, would only be an invitation to the opponents to enter the bidding and perhaps complete their own game. By feigning a slight degree of strength that you do not possess, you will probably keep the opponents out of the bidding. In other words, your bid has a pre-emptive effect.

But you should respond with six points or more, even though your partner's one bid, plus your partial, 'puts you out.' There are several important reasons for this action.

First, if the opener's hand is weak, your response makes it difficult for the opponents to enter the bidding. *Figure 211* furnishes an excellent example. Suppose you held the North hand, and your side has a part score of 70. Since your partner's one spade bid completes your game, you may feel there is no need of your bidding, since game has been reached. Yet if you pass, East will certainly back into the bidding with an informatory double, and the fat's in the fire. A two spade raise by you keeps the opponents out of the auction.

The other (and equally important) reason for responding with six or more points is that your partner, as opener, might have a 'big' hand, but, if you pass, a biddable and makeable slam could readily be missed. As a matter of fact, a lot of slams are not bid because, due to the part score, partnerships did not feel it necessary to fully show their values.

What I have said in regard to the responder making his normal response even though the opening bid, plus the part score, completes his game applies equally to the opening bidder's first rebid.

The opening bidder should, in most cases, make the same rebid he would have made without the part score being present. The same reasons apply as for the responder's rebids; first, it has a pre-emptive effect; next, it explores the possibility of slam.

	♠ K8532 ♡ AK ◇ Q87 ♣ QJ7	
♠ J9764 ♡ 1092 ◇ J1094 ♣ 10	N W E S	♠ Q10 ♡ Q8765 ◇ A653 ♣ 94
	♠ A ♡ J43 ◇ K2 ♣ AK86532	

Figure 212

Figure 212 illustrates the North-South partnership to reach a lay-down slam because of a 60 part score, and North's failure to make a normal rebid.

North dealer, both vulnerable, N-S with 60 part score.

CASE F

North	East	South	West
1 sp.	pass	2 cl.	pass
pass	pass		

North explained his failure to rebid by stating that "we needed only 40." What he failed to take into account was that had not his side been blessed with that 60 partial, he certainly would have rebid with three clubs. Even with the part score, a raise was justified and fully safe.

However, if the opener's hand is a bed-rock minimum, or if a 'fit' is lacking, he can pass partner's response if it completes the game when combined with the partial. This is particularly true if the responder has previously passed.

(b)
♠ AJ876
♡ Q2
◇ J109
♣ AQ10

Holding hand (b) you have a part score of 60. Your partner has previously passed. He now responds with two hearts. You might as well pass. Two hearts seems as good a place as any to play the hand.

But – if you have opened the bidding with a full opening bid and your partner, who has not passed, makes a response that would normally be forcing on you to rebid, you should rebid at least once.

BIDDING OVER SCORE

"If I raise or bid over game with a part score," you ask, **"won't my partner think I'm making a slam try?"**

ANSWER—It depends entirely on the nature and amount of the response or rebid. A single raise or response of one no trump shows exactly the same holdings as though the part score weren't present—and leaves further action up to the opening bidder. On the other hand, let's suppose your side has a 60 part score and your partner bids three spades after you've opened with one spade. That can be construed as a mild slam try, since he could have bid only two spades to complete the game. Similarly, with the 60 part score, a two no trump response would be a mild slam try, since one no trump would have been enough for game. Pre-emptive responses, as a jump from one to four, or one to five of a suit, are exactly the same as without part scores—show weak hands, long trump holdings, and are attempts to shut the opponents out, not slam tries.

In all of the following bidding situations, North-South have a part score of 70, and South is the dealer.

CASE G

South	West	North	East
1 heart	pass	1 spade	pass
2 hearts	pass	3 hearts	

North's raise to three hearts is a mild slam try.

CASE H

South	West	North	East
1 heart	pass	1 spade	pass
3 spades			

Since one spade would have completed the North-South game, South's three spade raise is strongly slam invitational.

CASE I

South	West	North	East
1 heart	pass	1 spade	pass
2 spades			

South's two spade raise shows slightly better than an opening bid, and is mildly pre-emptive.

CASE J

South	West	North	East
1 heart	pass	1 spade	pass
2 clubs			

With his second bid of two clubs, South is merely showing a two-suiter, and is by no means inviting a slam.

CASE K

South	West	North	East
1 heart	1 spade	2 hearts	

North's raise to two hearts has been partially forced by West's one spade overcall. While the free raise of two hearts shows slightly greater values than had West not overcalled, the two heart raise is by no means a slam try.

CASE L

South	West	North	East
1 heart	pass	2 no trump	

North's two no trump response is definitely a mild slam invitation, since with the 70 part score, either South's one heart bid or a response of one no trump would have been sufficient to complete the game. The two no trump response shows 14 to 16 high card points.

CASE M

South	West	North	East
1 heart	pass	1 spade	pass
2 no trump			

The two no trump rebid shows 18 to 20 high card points, is a mild slam try in case responder, North, also has extra values.

The reader may have noticed that, in an effort to permit the slam invitation being made within the bounds of safety, the requirements for the two no trump response in Case L (with a part score) of 14 to 16 points have been slightly broadened from the 14 or 15 points needed without a part score (page 83). Similarly, South's rebid of two no trump in Case M would show, with a part score, 18 to 20 points, whereas without the part score it would indicate either 18 or 19 high card points (page 195).

Where mild slam invitations are made, as in cases G, H, L and M, they merely show extra values in excess of minimum requirements for that particular bid and are *not* forcing in the slightest degree. The partner, with a minimum hand or lack of slam probability, can and should pass!

PRE-EMPTIVE OPENING BIDS WITH PART SCORES

Pre-emptive opening bids of three, four and five of a suit when possessing a part score are exactly the same as though the part score didn't exist. In other words, if your partner opens the bidding with four spades, even though your side has a 60 partial, he has a weak hand and a long suit; he's trying to shut out the opponents, just as though the part score didn't exist.

OPENING BIDS OF TWO IN A SUIT WITH A PART SCORE

I have stated in Lesson 10 on page 343 that there is no such thing as opening the bidding with a 'two bid' merely to complete a part score into a game.

In other words, let's suppose your side has a part score of 40 points. You wouldn't open the bidding with a bid of two hearts or two spades just because you thought you could make two. A two bid is a two bid, hot or cold, part score or no!

TRAPPING

There are many hands on which, after your side has opened the bidding, you feel a slam to be improbable, but can easily make a game with the aid of your part score. But if the nature of your hand also has great defensive character, it may be more profitable for your side to double the opponents if they bid.

The trick is to entice them to enter the bidding by feigning weakness. Suppose, with your side having a 60 partial, the bidding had been as in Case N.

(c)
♠ J2
♡ AQ96
◊ Q1087
♣ K95

CASE N

You, North	East	South	West
Pass	pass	1 spade	pass
1 no trump			

Actually, holding hand (c), you have far, far more than a one no trump response. You could respond with either two no trump, two diamonds or two hearts. But by pretending weakness you may entice one of the opponents to enter the bidding. If he does, wham! You'll double any bid made for a terrific penalty.

Trapping, or 'playing possum' can also be done by the opening bidder, as in Case O.

(d) CASE O

	You, South	West	North	East
♠ Q 6				
♡ A K J 8	1 heart	pass	1 spade	pass
◇ A Q 10 7	1 no trump			
♣ K J 10				

Obviously, with 20 high card points, you would be fully justified in rebidding two no trump. Why have you only bid one no trump?

The answer, of course, is to tempt an opponent into bidding in order to defend against your part score.

For these tactics to be effective, there are two important provisos: the first is that even though the response (or rebid) is an underbid, a game contract has already been reached; the second, that the vulnerability is at least equal, or that the opponents are vulnerable against your being not vulnerable, so that the probable penalty, should they enter the bidding and be doubled, be in excess of the game you otherwise would have made.

These tactics are highly successful against aggressive opponents who 'just hate to sell out cheaply.' The danger, of course, is that your partner may have a big hand capable of making a slam but, since he was fooled by your weak response or rebid, takes no further bidding action.

That is the risk you take!

PART TWO

PSYCHIC BIDDING

In Lesson 12 on Doubles, I briefly mentioned psychic bids (pages 477-479). But psychic bids can be used in other places—in opening bids, in responses and in rebidding.

To redefine a psychic bid, it is a bid intended to mislead the opponents. It corresponds exactly to a bluff bet in poker. It can lie as to the amount of strength held by the bidder, or as to the location of that strength. It has one great disadvantage—if it fools the opponents, it may also fool the partner.

HISTORY OF PSYCHIC BIDDING

No discussion of psychic bidding could possibly be complete without a brief history of the subject. Psychic bidding was pioneered by Dorothy Rice Sims. Mrs. Sims, in addition to being one of the first woman 'greats' in bridge, is the widow of P. Hal Sims, one of the outstanding figures in bridge, and is the daughter of Isaac Rice, a patron of chess.

With this background, Mrs. Sims in the late 30's startled and baffled contemporary players by bidding them 'where they ain't.' When she bid a spade, she might have hearts or any other suit, or possibly 13 low cards without the semblance of opening bid requirements.

In recent years, Roth-Stone and Kaplan-Sheinwold players (Lesson 16) include psychic opening bids as part of their system. Other than that, psychic opening bids appear only infrequently. However, you should learn how to recognize psychic bids and be able to defend against them. Properly used, and infrequently, they have advantages.

THE WEAK OPENING

The 'phony' opening bid is made on an extremely weak hand lacking the normal requirements of 13 or more points. The purpose of the bid would be to fool the opponents into thinking that an opening bid was present. As a result, the opponents might be dissuaded from bidding a normal game or slam contract.

When a player makes a psychic opening bid, he should remember two things —

1-He should bid his long suit;

2-After opening a psychic, he should pass thereafter. He should even pass a game force, as a jump bid in a new suit. In other words, nothing should drag another bid out of him.

(e)
♠ J8765
♡ 32
◇ 863
♣ 1054

A typical psychic opening one spade bid is shown to the left as hand (e).

PSYCHIC RESPONSES TO AN OPENING BID

After your partner has opened the bidding, there is no need for you, as responder, to bid without the normal high card requirements. To do so would only court disaster.

But when you are fairly certain your side will play the hand, bidding some weak suit or holding may influence the opponents into not leading that suit, permit your side to gain valuable time in developing tricks.

(f)
♠ AJ9
♡ 754
◇ KJ10
♣ Q1087

CASE P

Partner, North	East	South	West
1 club	pass	1 heart	

In this particular case, you hope to eventually play the hand in three no trump. By bidding one heart, you may discourage the opponent from opening that suit, a suit which might be only thinly stopped in your partner's hand. Of course, you should realize that it is possible your partner has excellent heart support, and if he bids three or four hearts over your one heart bid, you will find it next to impossible to play the hand in no trump. That is the risk you take.

This camouflage of bidding a weak holding to avert that opening lead is sometimes used in suit bidding, particularly where you hope to reach a slam where the opponents might be able to win two or more tricks in the suit you plan to bid.

	♠ A ♡ K J 8 ♢ A K Q J 9 7 ♣ 5 3 2	
♠ 10 9 8 7 ♡ 3 2 ♢ 6 5 4 ♣ K J 9 7	N W E S	♠ 6 5 4 3 2 ♡ 5 4 ♢ 10 8 ♣ A Q 10 6
	♠ K Q J ♡ A Q 10 9 7 6 ♢ 3 2 ♣ 8 4	

Figure 213

CASE Q

South	West	North	East
1 ht.	pass	2 cls.	pass
2 hts.	pass	4 no tr.	pass
5 dia.*	pass	6 hts.	pass
pass			

* *Blackwood, showing one ace.*

You can see that with any other opening lead than a club, the North-South hands can make a grand slam in hearts. The two club response, of course, is to steer the opening lead into another channel. With a club opening lead and continuation, the slam contract would be defeated.

PSYCHIC REBIDS

For the opening bidder or the responder to make a psychic rebid is for the same reason as *Figure 213* – to bid a short suit in order to fool the opponents into not leading that suit.

After either partner has opened the bidding or responded, there is no excuse for bidding with worthless hands.

PSYCHIC BIDS OVER INFORMATORY DOUBLES

This subject is discussed at length on pages 477 to 479.

DEFENSE TO PSYCHICS

(g)
♠ A K Q J 10 8
♡ J 2
♢ A Q 6
♣ K 4

Suppose you held hand (g) and heard the opponent to your right open the bidding with one spade. Do you think he had a spade bid? Well, hardly.

Of course, the opening bidder could have had five or six small spades in his hand. More likely, he had only two or three small spades, and bid the suit in an effort to keep you or your partner from ever bidding spades. If the outstanding spade suit had been divided between you and your partner, the psychic opening spade bid might have accomplished its purpose.

HOW TO EXPOSE A PSYCH

When an opponent has bid a suit which you hold, and you feel his bid to be 'phony,' correct technique is first to double informatorily, then bid the doubled suit at the first opportunity.

(h)
♠ KQJ1087
♡ AJ10
♢ 7
♣ A52

With hand (h), you hear the opponent to your right open the bidding with one spade, and you suspect the bid to be psychic. The bidding would resemble that of Case R.

CASE R

East	You, South	West	North
One spade	double	pass	Two hearts
pass	Two spades *		

* *Showing a real spade suit!*

Under no circumstances should you attempt to expose what you feel to be an opponent's psychic bid of your own suit by immediately bidding the same suit directly after the opponent has bid it. For example, the following would be incorrect—

CASE S

East, Opponent	You, South	West	North
One spade	Two spades		

The bidding illustrated in case S would show everything *except* the spade suit! Bids of this type are analyzed on pages 394, 395 and 396.

The previous examples have illustrated exposing possible psychs by the right hand opponent. Sometimes both opponents have bid by the time it is your turn to bid, and then exposing a possible psychic bid by the left hand opponent (who bid first) requires slightly different measures.

RULE –

1- Bidding the suit shown by the left hand opponent indicates you hold that suit, and wish to play the hand in that suit.

2- An immediate overcall of the right hand opponent's suit by bidding that suit is game-forcing, denies possession of that suit.

(i)
♠ KJ109876
♡ AQ
♢ 4
♣ 543

CASE T

West	North	East	You, South
1 spade	pass	2 hearts	2 spades!

The bidding in case T illustrates showing possession of a playable suit that has already have been bid by the left hand opponent. The bid is *not forcing*, though the partner should bid with any probability of game, and should not rescue into some other suit merely because he has one or no cards of the bid suit.

It is entirely possible that West's opening spade bid was genuine, containing four or five spades headed by the ace-queen. On the other hand, it could be completely fictitious.

(j)

♠ 42
♡ A
◇ A K J 10 9
♣ A K Q 6 4

CASE U

West	North	East	You, South
1 spade	pass	2 hearts	3 hearts

You hold hand (j) with the bidding in Case U. Your three heart bid is a game-force, and your partner must continue the bidding until at least game is reached. For all you know, with the tremendous high card strength in your hand, West's opening bid may have been completely psychic. Then again, he might have a legitimate opening bid. The cue-bid of the right hand opponent's suit uncovers the possible psych, locates which of the two remaining suits partner can support better, and probes the possibility of slam, something an immediate jump to five clubs or five diamonds could never do.

THE NON-FORCING TWO CLUB OVERCALL OF ONE CLUB

Up to this point, you have been told that an immediate overcall by you in the same suit that has been bid by the opponent to your right (before your partner has bid) is forcing to game, shows a tremendously powerful hand, and absolutely denies holding the suit in which you are making the cue-bid.

This subject is discussed at length on pages 394, 395, 396 and also on pages 567 and 568.

There is one possible exception — the club suit.

The reason for the club suit being excepted is that many players prefer to open hands that might present rebidding problems with the 'short club,' or, as we've termed it, the three card minor.

Accordingly, there will be far more times you will hold a legitimate club bid after the opponent has opened the bidding with a club than any other suit. You may logically think he's psyching. Actually, he's bidding a three card minor!

From a defensive point of view, should your partner have the opening lead, the one suit you'd like him to lead is clubs. If you first double the suit, later bid it in the conventional manner of exposing a psych, as shown in Case R, by the time your partner has responded to your informatory double and you have gotten around to bidding your club suit, you'll be at the three or four level, and that may be too high for safety.

In order to keep the overcalling at low level, still permit the defense to show real club suits after what is suspected to be a three card minor opening, many players use the bid of an immediate overcall of two clubs over an adverse one club opening as *non-forcing*, merely showing the club suit.

	♠ AJ762 ♡ 852 ♢ Q5 ♣ 987	
♠ K10 ♡ 3 ♢ K864 ♣ KQJ652	N W E S	♠ Q98 ♡ KJ964 ♢ 10732 ♣ 4
	♠ 543 ♡ AQ107 ♢ AJ9 ♣ A103	

Figure 214

Let's suppose you are West in *Figure 214* and hear South open the bidding with one club.

Using the conventional method of first doubling, then bidding the suit to expose what you consider a psych, you would run into trouble by getting too high.

The bidding would probably resemble that of Case V.

CASE V

South	West	North	East
One club	Double	One spade	Two hearts*
Double	Three clubs	Pass	Pass
Double	Pass	Pass	Pass

* *East, with an excellent five card major suit, can hardly be criticized for making a free response of 'two hearts' after his partner's informatory double. After all, East had every right, particularly after North's spade bid, to expect heart support from his partner.*

Now once South has tasted blood by doubling two hearts for penalty, it's only natural that he would double three clubs for the same reason. This, in bridge, is known as the 'rhythm of doubling.' Against perfect defense, which would require North to 'duck' the king of spades when led by West, the latter player would eventually lose three diamond tricks and one trick in each of the remaining suits to go down one trick at two clubs; two tricks at three clubs. The trouble is – three clubs will probably be doubled whereas two clubs will not be.

Let's suppose that West, in *figure 214*, is employing the non-forcing overcall of two clubs over one club as merely showing a playable club suit. The bidding would resemble that shown in Case W.

CASE W

South	West	North	East
One club	Two clubs	Pass	Pass
Pass			

Notice that West has been able to show his club holding safely; that North has been blocked out of his spade response since he lacks the necessary values for a 'free' response at the two-level; and East has been warned that his partner's hand is primarily clubs and that heart support cannot be promised.

Be sure, if you use the two club overcall over one club as non-forcing, all three other players at the table are aware of that fact. To use it as non-forcing with a partner who might give the bid its conventional forcing-to-game meaning would certainly lead to disaster, while for the opponents not to be aware of the meaning of your bids would be unethical, since you and your partner would in effect be using a private convention.

Remember, the *only* suit in which the immediate overcall of that suit is non-forcing is the *club* suit, and then, only by agreement. In all other suits, to show holding that suit after it has been bid by the opponent, you must immediately double that suit, later bid it at your first opportunity!

PRE-EMPTIVE JUMPS IN THE OPPONENT'S BID SUIT

Infrequently, a player may pre-empt in the very suit that has been opened by an opponent. In these cases, the suit is a minor, the opening is based on a three card or shaded holding, and, of course, the pre-emptive bidder is attempting to shut out the major suits and is completely capable of playing the hand in the bid suit, despite the fact that the opponent has originally bid it. Naturally, the pre-emptive overcall is *not* forcing!

	♠ K J 9 8 ♡ Q 10 7 6 ♢ Q 4 3 2 ♣ 6	
♠ 4 ♡ 3 ♢ J 10 8 ♣ A Q J 10 9 7 5 4	N W E S	♠ 7 5 3 2 ♡ K 9 5 4 ♢ A 9 7 6 ♣ 3
	♠ A Q 10 6 ♡ A J 8 2 ♢ K 5 ♣ K 8 2	

Figure 215

In *Figure 215*, South is the dealer. With North-South vulnerable, the bidding could be that of Case X.

CASE X

South	West	North	East
1 cl.	4 cls.	?	

Obviously, North has been fixed by West's pre-empt. The combined North-South hands can make either five spades or four hearts (East must make a heart trick on the over-ruff of the second round of clubs when played in hearts). Whether they would be able to reach either contract is questionable, and, if they decide to double the four club bid for penalty, the best they can do is collect 100 points for a one trick, non-vulnerable penalty.

EXPOSING PSYCHIC RESPONSES AND REBIDS

When you have previously passed, any double you will ordinarily make at some later point in the bidding will be for penalty. This affords you opportunities to double suit bids made by the opponents on weak or fictitious holdings, bids made for the purpose of discouraging an opening lead of that suit, and pretending strength that is not present. Doubles of this sort are known as 'lead-directing.'

(k)

♠ 10 8 7
♡ J 6 4
♢ A Q J 9 7
♣ 6 2

CASE Y

East	South, You	West	North
1 heart	pass	1 spade	pass
2 dia.	double!		

Now it may very well be that East had a real diamond suit, but it is more likely that he is bidding a short holding in order to avert a diamond opening lead in some later contract. By doubling two diamonds, you expose a possible psych. If the diamond bid is genuine, and both opponents pass, you can probably defeat that contract. Under no circumstances can your partner construe your double to be informatory, since you passed and didn't double at your first opportunity.

NOTES ON PSYCHIC BIDDING

1-To be completely ethical, your partner should not know (any more than the opponents) that any bid you have made is psychic. For your partner to know, and the opponents to be in the dark would be a private convention, which is the equivalent of dishonest practice.

2-Psychics do not pay, as a general rule. That is why they have pretty well gone out of style. For every time you get away with something, you may get caught for a whopping penalty on two others. Psychics should not be used with inexperienced or strange partners. You'll only get in trouble.

3-If you bid a short suit in responding or rebidding in order to avert a lead, try to keep these bids in a suit lower ranking than the suit in which you eventually intend to play the hand. In other words, it isn't too bad to bid clubs, diamonds or hearts over a spade bid if you eventually intend to go back to spades, anyhow, but to psych a spade over a club, diamond or heart is dangerous, since if your partner raises spades you can never get back to the right suit without increasing the contract.

4-If you do open with far less than 15 points, remember two things: first, open in your long suit; second, pass any response by your partner.

5-If, from the looks of your hand, you have reason to believe someone at the table is psyching, believe your partner's bidding!

PART THREE

COMPETITIVE BIDDING

In most bidding situations, both sides will enter the auction and will vie for the final contract. Where the bidding is keenly competitive, then strategy as well as high cards play deciding roles.

No text, particularly within the confines of a chapter, could possibly treat with every possible competitive situation. But the advice contained on this and succeeding pages should cover many of these contested situations.

1-Don't push the opponents, through your rebidding, into a contract you can't defeat, or a game or slam contract they otherwise wouldn't have reached. This is only good common sense. It's silly, if the opponents are through bidding at two spades, for you to now bid three hearts, hear them bid three spades, then four spades, and be able to do nothing about it. Unless you are equipped to double the contract into which you push them, leave well enough alone.

2-If an opponent has been bidding two suits, let's say spades and hearts, and winds up at four hearts, don't double that suit for penalty (even though you know you can beat it) unless you can also double the alternative contract, or feel certain your partner can double it. There are many famous hands in bridge where the player on lead against six no trump doubled holding the ace and king of a suit insuring a certain set, only to have the other opponent take out to seven of a suit and make it, since the doubler's partner didn't know what suit to lead.

3-Slam doubles were termed 'sucker doubles' by Hal Sims. They are losing propositions, since the odds are in favor of the doubled pair, and the double may locate key cards, permitting the slam to be made. Unless the slam was bid for sacrificial reasons, or the double is of the lead directing variety, don't double slams for penalty!

4-There is no such thing as a 'free double.' By that is meant doubling the opponents for penalty after they've already reached a game contract, so that the double can cost nothing but the doubled trick score. Actually, it can be very expensive if the opponents redouble and make the bid, and if they make overtricks, then it's really expensive. Further, the double may locate the card or cards the declarer needs to find in order to make the contract.

5-When the opponent to your right has bid no trump, and you will be on lead and hold a solid suit as ♢ AKQJ87, don't bother to bid your suit. Just pass! If you bid two diamonds, you'll warn the opponents of their danger, and they'll run out to some safer suit contract. You've got them where you want them – in no trump, the one contract you can handle.

6-Don't under-rate the opponents. They're smart, too!

7-Holding an extremely long suit and little defensive value, as hand (1) to the left, after the opponents have opened the bidding, it is sometimes better strategy to bid the suit as cheaply as possible, then rebid it one step at a time. By the time you've bid two spades, then three spades, and possibly four spades, the opponents may elect to double, never guessing that you hold a nine card suit.

(1)
♠ AKJ1087654
♡ 3
♢ J
♣ 72

8-Be guided by comparative vulnerability. As a general rule, don't sacrifice if vulnerable against non-vulnerable opponents. It just doesn't pay. With vulnerability equal, remember that the value of a vulnerable game is considered to be 500 points, a non-vulnerable game 300 points.

9-One of the greatest weaknesses of new players is in 'taking the push' in competitive bidding situations. By that I mean they bid higher than they wish to because of interference bidding by the opponents. For example –

CASE Z

South	West	North	East
1 heart	1 spade	3 hearts	pass
4 hearts	pass	pass	4 spades
5 hearts!			

Now, South only bid five hearts because he was pushed to that contract by East's four spade bid. Sad to relate, many players like South just hate to give up a good hand, permit the opponents to push them one step higher. This is called 'taking the push.'

The best advice I can give is to only take the push when absolutely certain of making the higher contract, and that the game or slam bonus will be in excess of the points you would have received by doubling the opponents. If you have the slightest doubt as to your ability to complete the higher contract, you should pass, and leave the decision up to your partner. Passes of this sort are known as 'forcing passes.'

10-When both partners have shown strength in the bidding, a pass by either player over an intervening bid leaves the decision up to his partner as to whether to double for penalty or go on with the bidding. A pass of this nature, which actually forces the partner to 'do something,' is an application of the forcing pass described in the previous paragraph.

Take a look at the bidding in Case Z. Suppose South, instead of bidding five hearts, had passed. That wouldn't mean that he wanted his partner to pass, too. What it did mean is that South was leaving the decision to bid or double up to his partner.

11-If you have opened a 'minnie,' and your right hand opponent sticks in a bid, any obligation you have to rebid has been removed. Pass! It is the most eloquent expression of weakness yet invented. If your partner can't bid again, you're better off out of the auction; if he does bid, you can still re-enter the bidding. You'll never go down 800 passing!

12-Don't overcall on four carders! If you do, you'll go broke. It is far better to make distributional informatory doubles after you've previously passed than to back into the bidding with shaded or ragged suits, even if five cards long.

13-Unless you have a good five card suit of your own, remember than an informatory double of a minor suit shows good major suit support, a double of one major indicates good supporting cards for the other.

14-When most of your strength or length is in the opponent's bid suit, pass. Hands of this sort are defensive in character, not offensive. Let the opponents get in trouble. Don't place any obstacle in the way of their getting too high.

15-In part score situations, learn to 'trap.' Many an aggressive opponent can be tempted into bidding if he thinks the other side is stealing something.

16-With some opponents, a pre-emptive opening bid acts on them as a red flag on a bull. They just hate to be shut out. With this type of opponent, mix up your signals, and pre-empt with hands a little stronger than usual. When the opponent enters the bidding, double for penalty, if possible.

QUIZ FIFTEEN

1-You are the dealer, playing rubber bridge. Both sides are vulnerable and the opponents have a part score of 40 points. What do you do with each of the following hands?

(a)	(b)	(c)	(d)
♠ 8	♠ KJ10987	♠ 2	♠ QJ109
♡ 10432	♡ AQ109	♡ KQJ98765	♡ K1098
♢ AQ106	♢ 2	♢ KJ9	♢ J3
♣ AQJ9	♣ Q8	♣ 4	♣ AKQ

2-The situation is the same as in the preceding question except that this time your side has the part score of 40, and the opponents have nothing. What is your opening bid, if any, with each hand shown above?

3-The bidding, with both sides vulnerable, and your side having a part score of 30 is –

(e)	East, dealer	You, South	West	North, Partner
♠ KJ10				
♡ AK74	pass	1 heart	pass	2 clubs
♢ KQ52	2 spades	?		
♣ Q8				

You hold hand (e). What do you do?

4-With neither side vulnerable, and your side having a 60 part score, your partner deals and opens the bidding with one spade. The next player passes. What is your response with each of the following hands?

(f)	(g)	(h)
♠ J87	♠ Q106	♠ 86
♡ 2	♡ KJ8	♡ J542
♢ 108654	♢ A107	♢ Q432
♣ J632	♣ KJ32	♣ J97

(i)	(j)
♠ 2	♠ J843
♡ J64	♡ A
♢ QJ10876	♢ KJ64
♣ 953	♣ Q1073

5-Both sides are vulnerable, and both have part scores of 60. The bidding has been –

(k)	North, dealer	East, Partner	South	West, You
♠ 54				
♡ 32	pass	1 heart	pass	2 clubs
♢ 108	2 spades	double	pass	?
♣ AJ109765				

You hold hand (k). What do you do?

6-Neither side is vulnerable. The bidding has been –

(l)	North	East, Partner	South	West, You
♠ KJ98	1 heart	double	1 spade	?

♡ 7 — You hold hand (l). What do you do?
◇ QJ1098
♣ J103

7-Both sides are vulnerable. The opponent to your right opens the bidding with one spade. What do you do with hand (m)?

(m)
♠ KJ986
♡ 2
◇ AQ8
♣ A432

8-Your side is vulnerable, and the opponents are not. The bidding has been –

(n)	West	North	East	South, You
♠ KQJ1086				
♡ 2	pass	pass	1 spade	?

◇ A32 — You hold hand (n). What do you do?
♣ KQ4

9-You are North in the following bidding sequence. Neither side is vulnerable. The bidding has been –

(o)	South	West	North	East
♠ J				
♡ A8732	4 hearts	pass	pass	4 spades
◇ 652	pass	pass	?	

♣ 8763 — You hold hand (o). What do you do?

10-You hold hand (p), sit West in the following bidding sequence. Both sides are vulnerable.

(p)	South	West	North	East
♠ 9432				
♡ J1097	1 heart	pass	3 dia.	pass
◇ A63	3 no tr.	pass	4 clubs	pass
♣ J7	4 dia.	pass	6 hearts	pass
	pass	?		

What do you do?

11-With both sides vulnerable, the opponent to your right opens the bidding with one no trump. What do you do with hand (q)?

(q)
♠ AJ7
♡ 10
◇ 954
♣ KQJ1086

ANSWERS TO QUIZ FIFTEEN

1-(a) Pass. After opening with one diamond, the hand would contain no safe rebid should the opponents enter the bidding. (b) One spade; (c) three hearts; (d) one spade. I prefer bidding a spade rather than the three card minor opening because of the former's pre-emptive value.

2-(a) One diamond; (b) one spade; (c) three hearts; (d) one club.

3-Double. East couldn't open the bidding. With your powerhouse, and if partner has the strength promised by his two club response, the overcall should be slaughtered for 800 to 1100 points.

4-(f) Two spades; (g) two no trump; (h) one no trump; (i) two diamonds – if partner rebids two clubs or two hearts, pass – if his rebid is two spades or two no trump, you should now rebid three diamonds; (j) three spades.

5-Three clubs. Your extreme length in clubs and absence of supporting trumps unfits the hand for the penalty double.

6-Double. Your partner's informatory double of one heart promised spade support. You hold spades. South's spade bid is psychic, intended to keep you from bidding that suit. When doubled, he intends to escape back to hearts. At that point you or your partner should bid spades.

7-Pass. The spade bid could very well be legitimate.

8-Double, then later bid spades.

9-Pass in a hurry! Your partner's four heart bid indicated a near defenseless hand. What are you going to do if you push the opponents to six spades, or even seven?

10-Pass. A double is unthinkable, even though you hold an ace and sure trump trick. Where the player holding this hand doubled, the opponents ran out to six no trump which made.

11-Pass. If the opponents stay in no trump, you hold a readily establishable suit and a sure re-entry. Why warn them of their danger by bidding two clubs?

LESSON FIFTEEN
HANDS

1. North dealer, neither vul.

North: ♠ A 10 4 3 ♡ 6 ◊ Q 10 7 ♣ K J 6 3 2

West: ♠ K 8 7 ♡ A K 5 3 2 ◊ A 6 5 ♣ 7 4

East: ♠ 9 6 5 2 ♡ Q J 4 ◊ K 3 ♣ Q 10 9 8

South: ♠ Q J ♡ 10 9 8 7 ◊ J 9 8 4 2 ♣ A 5

North	East	South	West
pass	pass	pass	1 heart
double	2 hts.	3 dia.	3 hearts
pass	pass	pass	

Opening lead by North, ◊ Q.

2. East dealer, N-S vul.
E-W with a part score of 60.

North: ♠ 10 8 6 5 3 ♡ 9 7 6 ◊ 10 2 ♣ A 4 3

West: ♠ A 2 ♡ K 5 4 ◊ Q J 9 8 ♣ J 10 7 2

East: ♠ K Q 7 4 ♡ A J 10 8 ◊ 7 6 ♣ K 9 5

South: ♠ J 9 ♡ Q 3 2 ◊ A K 5 4 3 ♣ Q 8 6

East	South	West	North
1 sp.	pass	1 no tr.	pass
pass	dbl.	rdbl.	pass
pass	2 dia.	dbl.	pass
pass	pass		

Opening lead by West, ♠ A

3. South dealer, both vul.

North: ♠ A 8 ♡ 7 6 ◊ K Q 8 6 4 ♣ 5 4 3 2

West: ♠ Q J 10 5 3 ♡ A 3 2 ◊ J ♣ Q 9 7 6

East: ♠ K 7 2 ♡ K Q 9 5 4 ◊ 10 2 ♣ A J 10

South: ♠ 9 6 4 ♡ J 10 8 ◊ A 9 7 5 3 ♣ K 8

South	West	North	East
pass	pass	1 dia.	dbl.
1 no tr.	dbl.	pass	pass
2 dia.	3 sp.	pass	4 sp.
pass	pass	pass	

Opening lead by North, ◊ K.

4. West dealer, E-W vul.

North: ♠ 2 ♡ A Q 10 ◊ K Q 10 8 7 4 ♣ 9 5 4

West: ♠ A Q 10 8 4 ♡ K 7 6 3 ◊ 5 ♣ K Q 3

East: ♠ K J 9 7 ♡ 4 ◊ A 6 3 2 ♣ A J 10 8

South: ♠ 6 5 3 ♡ J 9 8 5 2 ◊ J 9 ♣ 7 6 2

West	North	East	South
1 sp.	dbl.	rdbl.	pass
pass	1 no tr.	dbl.	pass
pass	2 dia.	pass	pass
2 sp.	pass	3 dia.	pass
3 hts.	pass	4 cl.	pass
5 cl.	pass	6 sp.	pass
pass	pass		

Opening lead by North, ◊ K.

SOLUTIONS TO LESSON FIFTEEN HANDS

1. West declarer at 3 hearts.

Trick	N	E	S	W
1	◇ 7	◇ 3	◇ J	◇ A
2	♣ 6	♣ 8	♣ A	♣ 4
3	♠ 4	♠ 2	♠ Q	♠ 7
4	♠ A	♠ 5	♠ J	♠ K
5	◇ 10	◇ K	◇ 2	◇ 5
6	♠ 10	♠ 6	♣ 5	♠ 8
7	♣ K	♣ 9	◇ 4	♣ 7
8	◇ Q	♡ 4	◇ 8	◇ 6
9	♡ 6	♡ Q	♡ 7	♡ 2
10	♣ 2	♡ J	♡ 8	♡ 3
11	♣ 3	♣ 10	♡ 9	♡ K
12	♠ 3	♠ 9	♡ 10	♡ A
13	♣ J	♣ Q	◇ 9	♡ 5

East-West win eight tricks, are down one.

2. South declarer at 2 dia., dbld.

Trick	W	N	E	S
1	♠ A	♠ 3	♠ 7	♠ J
2	◇ Q	◇ 2	◇ 6	◇ 3
3	◇ J	◇ 10	◇ 7	◇ K
4	◇ 8	♡ 6	♠ 4	◇ A
5	♣ 7	♣ A	♣ 5	♣ 6
6	♣ 2	♣ 3	♣ K	♣ 8
7	♠ 2	♠ 5	♠ K	♠ 9
8	◇ 9	♠ 6	♠ Q	◇ 4
9	♣ J	♣ 4	♣ 9	♣ Q
10	♡ 4	♡ 9	♡ 10	♡ 2
11	♡ 5	♡ 7	♡ J	♡ 3
12	♡ K	♠ 8	♡ A	♡ Q
13	♣ 10	♠ 10	♡ 8	◇ 5

North-South are down three for a 800 point penalty.

3. West declarer at 4 spades.

Trick	N	E	S	W
1	◇ K	◇ 2	◇ 3	◇ J
2	♣ 2	♣ 10	♣ K	♣ 6
3	♣ 3	♣ J	♣ 8	♣ 7
4	♠ A	♠ 2	♠ 6	♠ 10
5	♣ 4	♣ A	♠ 4	♣ 9
6	◇ 4	◇ 10	◇ A	♠ 3
7				

West claims the balance, staing that he will first "pull" the outstanding trumps. West wins nine tricks, is down one.

4. West declarer at six spades.

Trick	N	E	S	W
1	◇ K	◇ A	◇ J	◇ 5
2	◇ 4	◇ 2	◇ 9	♠ 10
3	♠ 2	♠ 7	♠ 3	♠ 4
4	◇ 7	◇ 3	♣ 2	♠ Q
5	◇ 8	♠ 9	♠ 5	♠ 8
6	◇ 10	◇ 6	♣ 6	♠ A
7	♣ 4	♣ 10	♣ 7	♣ 3
8	♣ 5	♠ K	♠ 6	♡ 3
9	♣ 9	♣ 8	♡ 2	♣ K
10	◇ Q	♣ A	♡ 5	♣ Q
11	♡ 10	♣ J	♡ 8	♡ 6
12	♡ A	♡ 4	♡ 9	♡ K
13	♡ Q	♠ J	♡ J	♡ 7

East-West win 12 tricks.

Lesson XVI

Duplicate Bidding, Scoring, Play Modern Expert Tactics

LESSON SIXTEEN

PART ONE

DUPLICATE BIDDING, PLAY AND SCORING

Duplicate bridge (which is also called tournament bridge) is a means of playing bridge in which a direct comparison of results can be achieved. For example, let's say that on a particular hand we bid four spades and make five. Another pair, playing the identical hand, bids four spades and makes only four. Naturally, we've done better than they have.

The real difference between rubber bridge and duplicate bridge is that in the former, when a hand has been played, it is finished; in duplicate, the hand, while being played, is kept intact so that after each player has finished playing his 13 cards, the hands are re-assembled for the next contestants to play. Thus each hand can be replayed in its original form, sometimes as often as 25 times.

"How is this done?" you may ask.

The answer lies in a rectangular tray with four pockets, known as a duplicate board, and shown below. It is oblong in shape, and has an arrow pointing the long way of the board. One end of the room in which the tournament is being held is designated as 'North,' and all of the arrows on the boards will point toward that position. The bridge player at each table sitting nearest the point of the arrow is designated as the 'North' player, his partner as 'South', and the remaining players, the opponents, 'East' and 'West', exactly as on a compass.

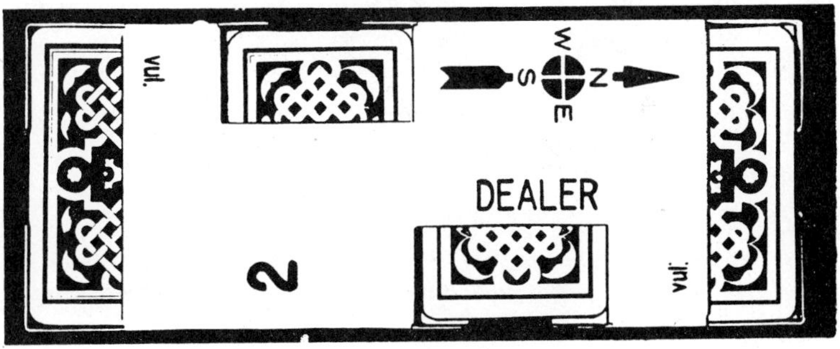

Figure 216

One of the pockets will be marked 'dealer,' and that player will deal all 52 cards after they have first been shuffled. The cards are only dealt at the very start of the duplicate, never a second time during any one session, even should there be no bidding (the hand being passed out) on that particular deal.

Red paint or ink on any pocket indicates that that side is vulnerable. Vulnerability will change from board to board, so that on certain hands, one pair or both or no one may be vulnerable. Similarly, the dealing position changes from one board to the next.

Once the cards have been dealt, the bidding starts with the dealer, exactly as in rubber bridge. At the conclusion of the bidding, the player to the left of the declarer makes the opening lead, exactly the same as in rubber bridge.

Now comes the big difference!

In rubber bridge, each player contributes a card to the current trick, placing it in the center of the table. One defender keeps all of the tricks won by his side, and the declarer keeps his side's tricks. Each trick naturally contains four cards, one card from each player.

In duplicate, to prevent mixing up these cards so that each player keeps his hand intact for succeeding players, the method of playing to a trick is as follows. Each defender and declarer, when playing to a trick, merely puts his card on the table directly in front of himself. Players do *not* put cards in the center of the table, nor does any card from one hand ever join a card from another hand.

The declarer calls the card he desires played from the dummy. It is placed, by dummy, face up in front of that player.

When all four players have played to a trick, each player takes his own card, turns it over (face down), puts it along the edge of the table nearest him, pointing the long way of the card toward the side winning that trick.

After the hand has been played out, each player will have his original 13 cards face down in front of him, along the edge of the table. By counting the number of cards pointing towards his side, and those pointing towards the opponents, it is a simple matter to determine the number of tricks won by either side.

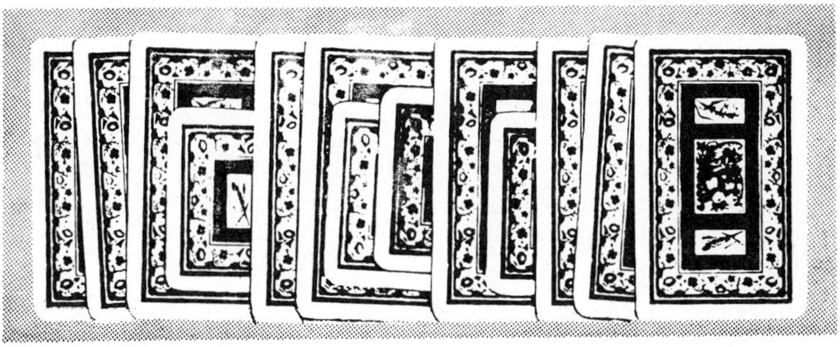

Figure 217

The above illustration shows how cards are 'turned' to indicate which side won each trick. This player's side won nine tricks, lost four.

With both sides in agreement as to the number of tricks won and lost, each hand of 13 cards is returned to the pocket from which it was originally withdrawn. In cases where the hand is dealt and played for the first time, each player places his 13 cards in the pocket nearest him after playing the hand.

DUPLICATE SCORING

The most common form of scoring duplicate (tournament) bridge is by means of what we term 'match points.' This is in contrast to the method used in rubber and party bridge called 'gross point' scoring. Let me show you the difference, and how match points are computed.

Gross scoring is the totaling of every point won, including honors. Further, in gross scoring, the partners continue playing against the same opponents until one pair or the other have won the rubber, that is, the first two games. A rubber bonus is then awarded the winners.

In duplicate with match point scoring, honors do not count. Next, there is no rubber bonus, since each hand is a separate unit to itself. A bonus of 300 points is given for bidding and making a non-vulnerable game, 500 points for a vulnerable game. A bonus of 50 points is awarded for bidding and making any part score, regardless of vulnerability.

You see, if total (gross) score were used in duplicate, a pair who were recipients of a gift, let us say, of 1400 points because some opponents decided to go on a bidding binge, could win enough points on that hand (through no merit of their own) to win a tournament, even though they played bad bridge through the remainder of the hands.

Match points limit the number of points that can be won on any one hand. It doesn't matter whether a pair is plus 1400 points or plus 50; they can't get more than a given number of match points on any one hand.

Here's how they're computed. Let's say that there are 10 tables of players in the tournament. That means that each hand will be played 10 times, and each time it is played there will be one pair sitting in the North-South direction (of the duplicate board) and one pair sitting East-West.

Mr. Jones and Mrs. Smith, sitting North-South, have the best score of all the pairs sitting in that direction. Just to take an arbitrary figure, we'll say they're plus 980 points for bidding and making six spades, not vulnerable. This figure was reached by totaling the trick score for six tricks at 30 points per trick, 300 points bonus for a not vulnerable game and the 500 point not vulnerable small slam bonus. Since it is a 10 table tournament, and they have the best score (in their direction), they receive nine match points. In other words, they receive one point for every team whose score they beat. Since Jones and Smith defeated nine pairs sitting North-South, they received nine points on this particular hand. If there had been a total of eight pairs sitting their way (including themselves), they'd have beaten the scores of seven pairs, and received – that's right – seven points. Each remaining pair of contestants similarly receives one point for each pair that they outscore.

When two or more pairs have the identical score in total points, they receive one-half a match point for each pair they tie, one point for each pair they excel. Thus, if three pairs tie each other, beat four pairs (the figures are taken at random), they would receive five points each. This is computed as follows – two ties at one-half point each, plus four points for beating four pairs. The total is five points. This method is followed both ways of the table so that there is a best score (top is the tournament term) North-South and a best score East-West.

What may seem strange to you is that a team can be minus and still get a top score in match points. Suppose you sat North-South and were only minus 230 points. The other pairs sitting in your direction are minus greater amounts, ranging from 450 points to minus 980 points. You would have the best score, since you lost fewer points than any other pair sitting in your direction.

The score sheet shown below is known as a 'travelling score,' since it accompanies that particular board. The score sheet shows the scoring and match points on board number one, where neither side is vulnerable. Scores represent a nine table duplicate. The score sheet is folded and not inspected by any player until the result is about to be entered. It is then re-folded and inserted in one of the board's pockets.

In explanation, each North-South pair enters its result on the same line as its pair number. Thus North-South pair one would record its score opposite the printed number one in the very first column, and other North-South pairs would similarly enter their scores against their respective numbers.

The North player at each table enters the entire score, except the match points, which naturally cannot be computed until the hand has been played by all of the contestants.

In the second column, the North player enters the pair number of his East-West opponents; the third column indicates the contract; the fourth column designates which player was the declarer; the fifth and sixth columns the number of tricks made, or by which the contract failed; the seventh and eighth columns, 'North-South plus,' or 'North-South minus,' indicate the total score made by the North-South pair, or lost by them. It might be simpler to describe the 'North-South minus' column as the East-West plus column, because that's what it actually amounts to. In fact, some travelling scores are printed that way.

Now to explain each score. Against pair one North-South, the East-West opponents, pair one, sacrificed by bidding five hearts, and this was doubled as indicated by the little 'd' under contract. North-South collected 300 points.

Pair two North-South failed to bid a game, reaching a three spade contract, making five. This netted North-South 200 points computed as follows – 150 points for five spade tricks at 30 points a trick, plus a 50 point bonus for completing a part score.

Board No.________

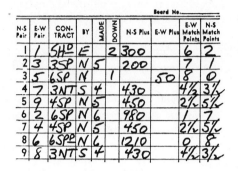

N-S Pair	E-W Pair	CON-TRACT	BY	MADE	DOWN	N-S Plus	E-W Plus	E-W Match Points	N-S Match Points
1	1	5H D	E		2	300		6	2
2	3	3SP	N	5		200		7	1
3	5	6SP	N		1		50	8	0
4	7	3NT	S	4		430		4½	3½
5	9	4SP	N	5		450		2½	5½
6	2	6SP	N	6		980		1	7
7	4	4SP	N	5		450		2½	5½
8	6	6SP D	N	6		1210		0	8
9	8	3NT	S	4		430		4½	3½

Figure 218

Pair three went down one trick at six spades, lost 50 points.

Pair four North-South bid three no trump with South the declarer. Four no trump was made. The trick score is 130 points plus a non-vulnerable game bonus of 300 points.

On the fifth line we find North-South pair number five playing against East-West pair nine. North is the declarer at four spades, makes five. The trick score of 450 is derived from totaling five spade tricks at 30 points per trick, plus the 300 point bonus for the non-vulnerable game.

Pair six North-South bid and made a small slam in spades. Six tricks in spades at 30 points per trick, plus 300 points for game, and 500 for the small slam, yield the 980 points shown.

North-South pair seven's score is the same as that of pair five.

Pair eight bid six spades, were doubled, and made it. This gave them a total score of 1210 points as follows—360 points for six tricks in spades, doubled; 300 for game; 500 points for slam; and 50 points for fulfilling a doubled contract.

North-South pair eight's score duplicates that of pair four.

Now for the match-pointing. Which pair North-South has the best score? Why, pair eight, since they're plus 1210 points. They had a better score than the remaining eight pairs, so they receive eight match points. The next best score is that of pair six with 980 points, beating seven pairs, and getting seven points. After that we have a tie between pairs five and seven with 450 points each. Since these pairs beat five pairs, tie each other, they receive five and one half points each. This scoring is continued until we reach North-South pair three who are minus 50 points. This pair has the poorest score of those sitting in the same direction (North-South). Since they beat no one, they get nothing, or as bridge players put it, a 'zero.'

How about scoring the pairs sitting East-West?

These scores are computed exactly the same as those sitting North-South. The best East-West score is that of East-West pair five (third line) who are plus 50 points. Since that beats the score of the other eight East-West pairs, it receives the maximum for a nine table duplicate, eight points.

The second best score East-West is that of pair three on the second line who are only minus 200 points whereas all of the other East-West pairs are minus from 300 to 1210 points. Pair three is better than seven East-West pairs, and receive seven match points as a result. This method of scoring is continued until reaching pair six East-West who are minus 1210 points. Since they (like pair three North-South) beat no one in their direction, they also receive a zero.

RECIPROCALS

The astute reader may have noticed that the East-West match point score is always the North-South score subtracted from maximum. For example, with our nine table tournament, we have a maximum (or top) of eight points. Now let's look at the first line of our travelling score. Pair one North-South received two points. To quickly obtain the East-West score, subtract two from the maximum eight, and that leaves six, the actual East-West score. This method saves time in computing scores, since the East-West scores need not be computed separately. There are still other short cuts in scoring that you will learn with experience.

After all of the travelling scores have been computed, each pair's scores are totaled, and the pair with the greatest number of match points is adjudged the winner, the pair with the second greatest number of points second, etc.

THE PRIVATE SCORE

Figures 219 and 220 illustrate, respectively, the front and back sides of what is known as a private score card. The card serves two functions: first, to keep a record, for the partnership, of the result achieved on each played hand; second, to apprise the opponents of conventions used by each partnership.

It is extremely important that at least one member of each partnership originally fill out as required the convention side of the card. You will notice that this side is apparently printed upside-down. This is deliberate so that when the inside pages on which the scores are entered *(figure 220)* face towards you and are folded, after making the entry, the convention side is pointed away from you towards the opponents so that they may read the card. The reason for keeping the entry side folded is to prevent, even inadvertently, opponents from seeing on your card results from hands they have yet to play.

COMPETITIVE

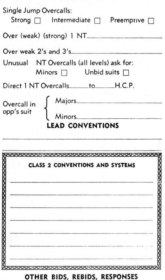

Single Jump Overcalls:
Strong ☐ Intermediate ☐ Preemptive ☐

Over (weak) (strong) 1 NT________

Over weak 2's and 3's________

Unusual NT Overcalls (all levels) ask for:
Minors ☐ Unbid suits ☐

Direct 1 NT Overcalls____to____H.C.P.

Overcall in opp's suit { Majors________ Minors________

LEAD CONVENTIONS

____

CLASS 2 CONVENTIONS AND SYSTEMS

____

OTHER BIDS, REBIDS, RESPONSES

____

San Francisco Chronicle
THE VOICE OF THE WEST

OFFICIAL CONVENTION CARD

Pair Number________

NAMES________

GENERAL APPROACH: Standard American ☐

Other________

Opening 1 NT____to____H.C.P.

Resp: Stayman; Forcing ☐ Non-Forcing ☐

Gerber ☐ Other________

Weak 2 bids____to____H.C.P.
(Min. 6 - Max. 12)

Forcing Resp. and Rebids { ________

Opening 2 Club forcing to:
Game ☐ 2 NT ☐ 3 of Major ☐

Do Not Open 4-Card Majors
1st/2nd Pos ☐ 3rd/4th Pos ☐

1 NT Resp. to Major forcing 1 round ☐

1 NT Resp. to (1♣); (Minors)____to____H.C.P.

1 NT rebid by opener____to____H.C.P.

Psychics: Frequent ☐ Occasional ☐

Description and Controls { ________

Figure 219

There are several reasons for recommending that you keep a private score while playing duplicate bridge. First, it is mandatory that the opponents be made aware of any non-standard conventions and/or variations you may emply. Certainly they are entitled to know if you're using weak two-bids, for example. As to the need of keeping track of your results, this is not only for your protection but greatly multiplies the pleasure you will receive from duplicate bridge. After a tournament, nothing can be more fun than enjoying with friends comparisons of results achieved on identical hands. And since even the best of scorers make errors, a private score will protect you if a score is entered incorrectly. By all means keep a private score.

The thing to remember, in keeping a private score, is that the entry for each hand played is made on the line corresponding to the number of the board (hand) just played. In other words, after playing board number one, the entry is made on line one; if you've just finished playing board six, you'd enter the result on line six, etc.

DO NOT COMPARE SCORES DURING THE SESSION—IT IS UNETHICAL

Vul.	Bd. No.	vs.	Contract & Declarer	Plus	Minus	Pts. Est.	Pts.	Vul.	Bd. No.	vs.	Contract & Declarer	Plus	Minus	Pts. Est.	Pts.
None	1							E-W	19						
N-S	2							Both	20						
E-W	3							N-S	21						
Both	4							E-W	22						
N-S	5							Both	23						
E-W	6							None	24						
Both	7							E-W	25						
None	8							Both	26						
E-W	9							None	27						
Both	10							N-S	28						
None	11							Both	29						
N-S	12							None	30						
Both	13							N-S	31						
None	14							E-W	32						
N-S	15							None	33						
E-W	16							N-S	34						
None	17							E-W	35						
N-S	18							Both	36						

YOUR SCORES MUST BE CONCEALED AT ALL TIMES DURING THE SESSION

Figure 220

Each vertical column on the scoring side has a useful function. Let's look at *figure 220*. The first column, headed by the abbreviation 'Vul' refers to the vulnerability (or lack of it) on the respective board. Thus on board one, neither side is vulnerable; on board two, north-south are vulnerable; on number three, east-west are vulnerable and on number four, both sides are vulnerable. Where only one side is indicated as vulnerable, the other side is not vulnerable.

The second column headed 'Bd. No.' for board number, is simply the number of each board. These numbers determine where you will enter the result since, after playing board 11, you'd enter the result against number 11.

A word of caution! This is the big difference between scoring on the travelling score (see preceding pages) and scoring on the private score.

PRIVATE SCORE - Score on the line corresponding to the board number.

TRAVELLING SCORE - North (only) scores on the line corresponding to the North-South pair number.

To make certain you understand the difference, let me give a specific example. Let's pretend we're partners and we are pair number seven sitting north-south at table number seven. We are playing board number 10. The board and the private score indicate both sides to be vulnerable. We bid and make four hearts for a gross score of 620 points.

On the private score, we enter the score of plus 620 on line number 10, together with other pertinent information as to the contract, opponent's number, etc. On the travelling score, the entry of plus 620 is made on line number seven, which is the north-south pair number.

To repeat, entries on private scores are made on the line corresponding to the board number; on the travelling score, the result is entered by the north player on the line of his pair number.

The column headed 'Contract and Declarer' is self-explanatory. Since space in each column is limited, this entry is made in abbreviated form as four hearts by North being written '4H-N'. Where a contract is doubled or redoubled, the fact should be indicated as a small, elevated 'd' or 'rd' following the final contract. Four hearts doubled would be written '$4H^{d}$' and redoubled would be '$4H^{rd}$.'

The columns headed 'plus and minus' indicate whether your side has won or lost points. If your side scored points, no matter how - whether by bidding and completing your contract - or from penalties or bonuses - the entry should be in the plus column; on the other hand, if the opponents scored points, the entry will indicate you to be minus. The same, of course, will apply to your opponents - if you're plus, they're minus and vice-versa.

The two final columns headed 'Pts. Est.' and 'Pts.' stand for, respectively, 'Points Estimated' and 'Points.' These are the match points referred to a few pages earlier. Since many players enjoy estimating, after each hand, the number of points they will receive from it, the first column is provided for that purpose. The second column permits the entry of the points actually received at the conclusion of the session.

In entering the initial of the declarer, as 'N' for North or 'E' for East, as the case may be, use only the initial of the person who actually played the hand. Do not write, for declarer, NS, for North-South. Both partners did not play the hand. Only one was declarer and it is that initial that should be used.

THE RECAP SHEET

Event ______________________________

Session ______________________________

AMERICAN C

		Rank	Total	1	2	3	4	5	6	7	8
Pair No.	NORTH-SOUTH NAMES		Points	O	N-S	E-W	B	N-S	E-W	B	O
1											
2											
3											
4											
5											
6											
7											
8											
9											
10											

Figure 221

The recap sheet (recap is the bridge-player's term for 're-capitulation') is the summary sheet on which the match points from all of the travelling scores are posted, as on a ledger, then added. The names of each pair are listed to the left and the total points won by each pair, derived from adding the match points scored on each hand played, indicate the winners.

Recap sheets, as are most ledger sheets, are rather bulky affairs, varying from approximately 20 inches in length to about a yard for those used in championship matches. A portion of a typical recap sheet is shown as *figure 221* on the previous page.

The player has nothing to do with the recap sheet since the posting of the match points from the travelling scores and their subsequent addition is entirely the function of the scoring staff.

In some matches and particularly those of championship calibre where they are used exclusively, 'pickup slips' are employed in place of travelling scores. Pickup slips are small cardboard squares that permit the entry of only one result as compared with a travelling score where all results on one hand are listed on one sheet. The reason for use of the pickup slip is that it makes impossible, after playing a hand, to know what has previously happened on the hand when played at other tables whereas on a travelling score, previous results are listed and known after playing the hand. Pickup slips are collected at the completion of each round of play by 'score caddies,' usually local teen-agers, who bring them to the scorers for recording on the recap sheet. A typical pickup slip is shown as *figure 222*. East-West pair one are shown as having bid four hearts and making five, not vulnerable, on board five against North-South pair two.

FORM 102 **TURN THIS FACE DOWN**
Printed in U.S.A. **MARK "X" ON BACK**
Do Not Discuss Previous Scores

No Erasures Make Out a New Score	North-South Contract	Made	Down	East-West Contract
		5		4H
		TRICK SCORES		120
OK		EXTRA TRICKS		30
By E-W		Part Score, Game and Doubled Bonus		300
		SLAM BONUS		
		Premium For Defeating Contract		

Board No.	N-S Plus	N-S No.	E-W No.	E-W Plus
5		2	1	450

Figure 222

MOVEMENTS

Readers who have played some party bridge are familiar with 'progressions,' where the winning pairs, after a given number of hands, move onward to other tables; and the losers stay behind. This method gives a slight amount of progression, but does not guarantee that most or all of the players meet each other competitively.

In duplicate bridge these progressions are known as 'movements.' There are many types of movements. We have movements for pairs of two players, known as 'pair movements;' individual movements, where each player in a duplicate plays both with and against the other contestants; team of four movements designed for teams of four players and others.

For the player who intends to conduct duplicate bridge tournaments either among his friends or for some social organization, I cannot recommend too strongly that he purchase "Duplicate Bridge Direction" written by George W. Beynon. This is not only a textbook for tournament directors, but also contains various types of movements for different size groups.

Before starting a tournament, the tables are usually arranged in rows, with sufficient space between each table to permit easy access for each player, yet far enough apart so that players at one table cannot hear the bidding at the next table. The long way of the room is usually designated as North and South, and the rows of tables follow the conformation of the room.

The easiest movement to direct, and most common for pair contests is known as the 'Mitchell movement.' In a 'Mitchell,' the North-South players at each table remain seated throughout the match; each pair of East-West players, after playing their respective opponents with the boards on hand, then move to the next higher numbered table, while the boards are moved to the next lower number table. In a 'Mitchell,' both the North-South and East-West pairs derive their pair numbers from their original starting table, so that the pairs beginning play at table number four, for instance, would be pair four North-South and pair four East-West.

In practice, the tournament director will 'call the move,' so that all East-West pairs, and the boards, will move simultaneously. This is necessary, since otherwise players might progress before the boards were passed to the next table.

With an odd number of tables (1-3-5-7-9, etc.) by the time the lowest numbered East-West pair has met the highest numbered North-South opponents, every North-South pair will have met all the East-West pairs and all of the boards will have been played the same number of times as there are tables in play, providing the movement is carried to completion. With an even number of tables, the simplest way to prevent pairs from playing the same hand twice is, after half the boards have been played, to request all East-West pairs to skip one table in the progression.

The reader may have noticed that in the Mitchell movement the East-West players play only against the North-South pairs, and vice-versa. This means that the North-South players never meet other North-South pairs, and similarly for those sitting East-West. To remedy this defect, other progressions have been developed, known as Howell, McKenney-Baldwin, Ach-Kennedy, and others which permit more pairs to meet. These progressions have been worked out and are printed on cards. They are known as 'guide' cards, can be purchased inexpensively from any bridge supply house. In these movements, each pair takes its pair number from the guide card at its starting table. The scoring is the same, however, in all pair movements.

Individual duplicate tournaments, where partnerships change after each round, similarly use guide cards or slips to insure proper progression of players. Team of four movements vary according to the number of tables and the type of scoring.

In general, 26 boards (hands) will make up a full session's play. This amount may vary slightly up or down according to the number of tables in play and the hour at which it is desired to terminate the tournament.

To summarize duplicate scoring, for successfully completing a contract,

1- A bid of less than game, add 50 points to *all* tricks won;

2- Bidding and making a non-vulnerable game, add 300 points to *all* tricks won;

3- Bidding and making a vulnerable game, add 500 points to *all* tricks won.

4- Honors do not count and are not scored in duplicate;

5- All other bonuses and penalties are identical to rubber bridge scoring.

PART TWO

MODERN EXPERT BIDDING METHODS

No one person, whether it be Goren, Culbertson or the early pioneers of bridge as Whitehead, Work and others, can be said to have a monopoly of ideas. Modern methods are the result of the contributions of many persons.

In the pages to follow are included many advanced techniques, authored in many cases by their inventors. Of these, the most important by far is what is known as the 'Stayman Convention', or simply, 'Stayman'. Employed by 95 percent of better bridge players world-wide, it is to old-fashioned methods of no trump bidding as the machine gun is to the bow and arrow.

I strongly recommend that you master and employ Stayman. Through the latter's generosity, this text is privileged to include the latest features of Stayman bidding, authored by the originator, Mr. Samuel M. Stayman. In his highly recommended book, DO YOU PLAY STAYMAN? published by Odyssey Press, Inc., of New York City, the reader will find a far more complete description of these highly successful methods used almost universally.

Whether you decide to master other conventions is a matter for your personal preference. Each is intended to serve a specific function. No players, even top experts, employ all conventions. In the formative stages of your bridge career, I suggest you 'keep it simple'. With the exception of Stayman, which is a 'must', use as few artificial conventions as possible.

I would like to express my gratitude to the various bridge players and authors whose ideas and articles are included in this book. Many of them, as Belladonna, Blackwood, Fishbein, Gerber, Jacoby, Le Dentu, Reese, Rosler, Roth, Sheinwold, Stayman have written books of their own to which the reader, desiring a fuller discussion of these methods than this work will permit, are referred.

RESPONSES TO NO TRUMP

THE STAYMAN CONVENTION

What is now known as the 'Stayman Convention' was originated in the mid '40's as World War II was ending. Tens of thousands of bridge hands, played over a period of many years, had demonstrated that hands which had been opened with bids of one or more no trump and eventually played in no trump, would very often have produced more favorable results if played in a major suit. This was true when both partnership hands held four cards each of the *same* major suit, a fact discovered only after the bidding was over and the dummy faced on the table.

Since with ordinary methods, a takeout to two or three of a suit by the responder to a no trump indicated a suit of at least five cards, the problem was to devise a bidding method which, after a bid of one or more no trump, could accurately locate a four-four major suit fit or the lack of such a fit. The Stayman Convention of today does that, and more.

Through the years, experience and additions to the convention now make it possible to find out whether a hand opened in no trump is likely to play better in no trump or in a minor suit contract.

The methods to be described are known as 'forcing' Stayman. By that is meant that after a bid of one no trump, (either as an opening bid or as an overcall) and a response of two clubs in Stayman, the no trump bidder *may not stop bidding* below the level of two no trump. Naturally, with adequate strength, the final contract may go still higher as to game or even slam. Forcing Stayman is best employed with the 'strong' no trump, i.e., 16 to 18 high card points.

Non-forcing Stayman permits, after an opening bid or overcall of one no trump, the bidding to be dropped at low levels. This version has its maximum usefulness where weak (12 to 14 high card points) no trumps are employed. It will be described on later pages.

It is suggested that the new player use the strong no trump coupled with forcing Stayman. As his or her experience increases, the non-forcing type may also be employed, if desired.

Complete descriptions of both will be found in the most recent text by Samuel M. Stayman, published by Golden Press.

THE FORCING STAYMAN CONVENTION

REQUIREMENTS FOR OPENING BIDS OF ONE NO TRUMP

16 to 18 high card points.

Distribution, either 4-3-3-3 or 4-4-3-2 or 5-3-3-2, if the five card suit is a minor. Strength in at least three suits. A worthless doubleton may be included, but not unless all other suits are stopped.

REQUIREMENTS FOR OVERCALLS OF ONE NO TRUMP

17 or 18 high card points, never a minimum 16 points.

Distribution the same as for opening bids of one no trump but including at least one positive stopper and possibly two stoppers in the opponent's bid suit. Generally the overcall will have strong minor suit overtones since with great major suit strength, an informatory double would be preferred.

THE STAYMAN TWO CLUB RESPONSE

The Stayman Convention is basically identified by the response of 'two clubs' to an opening bid or overcall of one no trump.

It should be impressed at this time that in Stayman a response of two clubs to a bid of one no trump *does not show clubs! Instead, it artifically asks two questions.*

1 - Does the no trump bidder's hand contain a four card major suit?

2 - If so, which major?

The two club response is absolutely forcing on the no trump bidder to rebid. He *must* answer the above questions by his rebid.

REQUIREMENTS

To respond with two clubs, the responder must hold both a minimum of eight points and at least four cards of a major suit. Both high card and distributional points may be counted for the two club response. While the two club response forces the no trump bidder to rebid, it is not forcing to game. *Do not* bid two clubs without a four card or longer major suit.

"Well, on what sort of hands would I bid two clubs,?" you ask.

(a)	(b)	(c)
♠ KJ96	♠ Q743	♠ AQ7432
♡ A2	♡ J965	♡ KJ98
◇ Q1074	◇ AJ72	◇ 3
♣ 1087	♣ 3	♣ K4

(d)	(e)	(f)
♠ J8	♠ A7432	♠ 10
♡ Q754	♡ K8543	♡ QJ1086
◇ KJ7	◇ Q109	◇ KQ87
♣ Q1096	♣ void	♣ J96

After an opening bid of one no trump by partner, you would bid two clubs as a response with each of the above hands. Let's see why.

With (a), your entire problem is whether to play the hand at game in spades or in no trump. To play the hand in spades, your partner should also hold four spades. You'll quickly find out by bidding two clubs.

The rebid by the no trump bidder will describe his hand perfectly, as you will see.

On hand (b), the question is - does the no trump bidder have four hearts or does he have four spades? You don't have to guess - you simply bid two clubs.

With your 16 points in (c) counting distribution, opposite your partner's known 16 to 18 points, you expect that the combined hands will produce a slam. But if your partner holds four hearts the hand will probably play better there than in the spade suit. So you bid two clubs to explore that possibility.

On (d), the purpose of the two club bid is to ascertain whether or not opener has four hearts.

On (e), the question again is - does partner have four hearts or four spades. Even if he doesn't, you will later insist on a game contract in a major suit.

With hand (f), you would first bid two clubs, later go on to a game in hearts or no trump.

RESPONSES OF TWO HEARTS OR TWO SPADES

A response of two hearts or two spades to an opening bid or overcall of one no trump indicates -

(a) A total of seven points or less;

(b) A suit of five cards at least with distributional advantage or a six card or longer suit.

(c) Lack of game probability.

Since this bid, viz., a takeout from no trump to two of a major, shows a weak hand, it should be pointed out that *there are no minimum high card requirements for this bid.* It can be made with extremely weak hands if the unbalanced pattern gives promise of a better play in a suit contract (under game) than in partner's no trump.

(g)	(h)	(i)
♠ J 10 9 6 5	♠ void	♠ K J 8 7 6 2
♡ 2	♡ 9 7 6 5 4 3	♡ 3 2
◇ Q 4 3 2	◇ 8 7 5	◇ 8 7 6
♣ 5 3 2	♣ 9 4 3 2	♣ 10 5
Two spades	Two hearts	Two spades

THE TWO DIAMOND RESPONSE

The response of two diamonds to one no trump is a recent (1962) addition to the Stayman Convention, its purpose being to probe, from the responder's point of view, whether the combined partnership hands would eventually play better in a minor suit contract or in no trump. In other words, the two diamond bid serves responder to indicate minor suit hands somewhat as the two club bid probes for majors.

Naturally, for a responder to be interested in possibly playing the hand in a minor rather than no trump, there must be valid reason.

REQUIREMENTS -

(a) Responder's hand must contain a minimum of 10 points in high cards.

(b) Responder's hand contains one minor suit at least six cards in length, or two minors distributed 5 - 4 (or longer), with at least one void or a singleton.

Note - with balanced distribution, as 6-3-2-2, even with worthless doubletons, a minor suit and 10 or more points, no trump will usually be the preferable contract.

Aside from the already pointed out fact that the two club response shows major suit holdings and the two diamond response minors, there are two important differences. These are:

(a) The two diamond response is forcing to game; the two club response is not.

(b) The two club response requests the no trump bidder to show a major suit if he holds one; the two diamond response, as you will see, asks the no trump bidder not to show a minor suit if held, but rather, to show if strength is concentrated or if all suits appear to be stopped.

EXAMPLES OF RESPONSES OF TWO DIAMONDS (STAYMAN)

(j)	(k)	(l)
♠ 2	♠ A J 9	♠ 4 3 2
♡ K 4	♡ void	♡ A
◇ Q 10 8	◇ Q J 10 8 7	◇ K Q 7 4
♣ A J 10 9 7 6 5	♣ K J 9 4 2	♣ Q J 10 9 4

THE THREE CLUB OR THREE DIAMOND RESPONSE

The meaning of the immediate responses of either three clubs or three diamonds to one no trump are likewise modifications of earlier Stayman methods.

Since both a response of two clubs (majors) and two diamonds (minors) are artificial and compel the no trumper to rebid, it is logical that there should be some way for the responder to show that he holds a genuine club or diamond suit and desires to play the hand below game. A responder to an opening no trump too weak to seek game bids three clubs or three diamonds to describe such a hand.

The requirements for this bid are exactly the same as for a response of two hearts or two spades (page 601) with the difference that the suit is a minor rather than a major.

The important thing for the reader to realize is that the responder's hand is unbalanced, and that the minor suit is far from solid. With balanced hands or with solid or semi-solid suits, responder will prefer a no trump contract.

EXAMPLES OF THREE CLUB AND DIAMOND RESPONSES

(m)	(n)	(o)
♠ void	♠ Q 8	♠ 4
♡ J 7 6	♡ 3 2	♡ 9 8 4 3
◇ K 3 2	◇ Q J 10 7 6 2	◇ 10 6
♣ 10 8 7 6 5 4 2	♣ 8 6 2	♣ A 9 8 7 6 5

OTHER RESPONSES
THE IMMEDIATE JUMP TO GAME

When holding a long suit with sufficient total strength in high cards and distribution to indicate that a game contract (but not a slam) may be successful, the responder can jump to game immediately. This bid, of course, is a signoff, since the opener's one no trump bid has already described that player's range of strength.

The jump to game is almost always in a major suit, rarely in a minor.

EXAMPLES

(p)	(q)	(r)
♠ J 8 7 6 5 4 3 2	♠ K 2	♠ 4
♡ 2	♡ A 10 8 7 6 5 4	♡ J
◇ Q 10 9	◇ void	◇ Q J 10 9 8 7 6 5 4
♣ 5	♣ 6 4 3 2	♣ K 9
Four spades	Four hearts	Five diamonds

THE JUMP TO THREE OF A MAJOR

A response of three hearts or three spades to a bid of one no trump is -

(a) Forcing-to-game;

(b) Shows 10 or more points;

(c) A good suit, usually six cards or longer, sometimes five.

Unlike a two club response which asks opener to show a four card major suit (if present), the three heart or three spade bid shows a suit that does not require four supporting cards in partner's hand.

The fact that responder has bid three hearts or three spades does not irretrievably commit the partnership to a final contract in that suit; the hand may still, if determined preferable, play in no trump for strategic reasons such as the advantage of having the opening lead come up to, not through, the no trump bidder's high card holdings.

EXAMPLES

(s)	(t)	(u)
♠ AQ10976	♠ J9	♠ Q108
♡ 4	♡ KQ1097	♡ AQ5432
◇ KQ	◇ AJ1062	◇ K6
♣ QJ98	♣ K	♣ J4
Respond three spades	Respond three hearts	Three hearts

THE RAISE TO TWO NO TRUMP

A raise of opener's one no trump to two no trump shows eight or nine high card points and balanced or semi-balanced distribution. In the event that the hand contains a readily establishable five card or longer suit, usually a minor, the high card requirements may be shaded one point.

EXAMPLES

(v)	(w)	(x)
♠ K43	♠ Q10	♠ A86
♡ Q107	♡ J98	♡ 1073
◇ KJ43	◇ KJ1074	◇ J6
♣ 862	♣ J107	♣ K10872

THE RAISE TO THREE NO TRUMP

Holding 10 to 13 high card points and a balanced or semi-balanced hand (no voids or singletons), the responder should immediately raise to three no trump.

EXAMPLES

(a)	(b)	(c)
♠ KJ7	♠ Q8	♠ A109
♡ Q6	♡ 873	♡ KQ6
◇ AJ96	◇ QJ10	◇ J8764
♣ J432	♣ AJ1087	♣ J92

Holding 10 or more points and a balanced or semi-balanced hand, the responder should immediately raise to three no trump.

Responder should also raise directly to three no trump holding eight or nine high card points and a six card or longer good minor suit. The hand may be unbalanced.

EXAMPLES

(d)	(e)	(f)
♠ 3	♠ J 8 4	♠ 4 2
♡ K 10 6	♡ 3 2	♡ 10 3
◊ A Q 8 4 3 2	◊ 4	◊ K Q 10 7 4 3
♣ 6 5 3	♣ A Q J 8 4 3 2	♣ K 7 2

RESPONDING WHEN AN OPPONENT OVERCALLS PARTNER'S NO TRUMP

Infrequently, after your partner has opened the bidding with one no trump, your right hand opponent will stick in some kind of an overcall.

What do you do, using Stayman?

Since the opponent had to bid at least two of his suit to overcall, you are no longer able to respond with a bid of two clubs.

The first thought that should enter your mind is the possibility of a penalty double of the opponent's overcall. Your partner, by his opening bid of one no trump, has indicated possession of 16 to 18 high card points. In addition to the cards that you may hold, the determining factor on whether to double, to bid or to pass, is what is known as 'comparative vulnerability.'

YOU ARE	OPPONENTS	COURSE OF ACTION
Not vul.	Not vul.	If game is makeable, you should bid; otherwise, double.
Not vul.	Vul.	Penalty double
Vul.	Vul.	Double if game is not certain; double if penalty appears greater than two tricks; bid probable game if penalty appears two tricks or less.
Vul.	Not vul.	The vulnerable game is usually preferable to a non-vulnerable penalty; if game is not probable, a penalty double should be made.

The question of whether to double for penalties or to bid is a vexatious one, even to the expert and the table contains only general recommendations on courses of action - certainly not rigid rules of procedure.

The decision between choosing to double the opponents or to bid, is to take that course of action which is expected to yield the greater number of points. If, by doubling and penalizing the opponents, you can score more points than by bidding a game or part-score your way of the table, obviously the double is correct. On the other hand, if you are virtually certain that your side can make a game, to settle for a penalty that would be of lesser value would be incorrect.

This is not to infer, that after partner's opening bid of one or more no trump, and an overcall by the right hand opponent, that you as responder must either bid or double. To choose either course requires certain values - in high cards or long suit or values in the opponent's suit, depending on the course of action chosen.

Without the necessary values to bid or double, the responder should pass his right hand opponent's overcall, even though one's partner has opened with a bid of one or even two no trump. Opening bids of one or two no trump *are not forcing on partner to bid.*

The value of a non-vulnerable game is estimated at 300 points and that of a vulnerable game at 500 points, in addition to the trick score. These figures are used in duplicate bridge and are also the *intangible* value of games in rubber bridge. Assuming as a fair average that game can be made by bidding and making four hearts for a trick score of 120 points, we would have as a total score, if not vulnerable, 420 points; if vulnerable, 620 points.

Hence it follows that if your side can score 420 points, the smallest penalty that will exceed that figure is 500 points, which you will receive by doubling and setting a vulnerable opponent two tricks or a non-vulnerable opponent three tricks.

If you're vulnerable and can score a game worth a total of 620 points, the alternative penalty double must yield a greater number of points. This, in the case of non-vulnerable opponents, must require a doubled penalty of four tricks to yield 700 points; however, if the opponents are vulnerable, a doubled penalty of only three tricks would yield 800 points, far more than the value of even a vulnerable game.

When game is far from certain and there is assurance, from your cards and those promised by partner's opening no trump, that the opponent's overcall can be defeated, the penalty double is usually preferable to any part score that your side can make. This is particularly true if the opponents are vulnerable since even a one trick penalty, if doubled, will yield 200 points, more than the total value of most part scores.

In general, it is safe to say that when the opponents are vulnerable and your side is not, the odds are in favor of the penalty double; with equal vulnerability or lack of it, the deciding factor is the cards themselves; when your side is vulnerable and the opponents are not, great care should be taken to insure that any possible penalty equal the value of a probable game.

A FREE RESPONSE AT THE TWO LEVEL

Let us assume the bidding has been -

CASE A

PARTNER,OPENER	WEST	YOU,NORTH	EAST
1 N.T.	2 dia.	2 hts. or 2 sp.	

A free response at the two level in this situation shows a good five card or longer suit and a somewhat unbalanced hand containing four to seven points. *It is not forcing.* The opener may pass. It is simply an attempt to compete, in a part score situation, rather than sell out to the opponents.

(g)
♠ K Q 7 5 4
♡ 8 7
◊ 5 3
♣ 10 8 4 3

(h)
♠ J 7 4 3 2
♡ 5 4 3
◊ 7
♣ Q 4 3 2

For example, you would bid two spades with (g) but pass with (h) in the above auction. The important thing for you to realize is that had West passed, (rather than bid two diamonds), a two spade response on (h) would have been in order. The reason for bidding, on (h), is that the hand, if played in spades, would take tricks otherwise impossible if played in no trump and by bidding two spades, you select a contract of two spades in preference to the no trump contract.

However, after the opponent overcalls with two diamonds, there is no need for you to bid two spades with (h) to get out of no trump. The opponent's two diamond bid has done that for you. Hence, a free two spade bid by you, although not forcing, would show more strength than you actually hold. The danger of a free, competitive bid with (h) is that your partner would have every right to expect more playing strength. He might, with a maximum, compete with three spades or double a higher bid by the opponents for penalties, expecting you to have more high card strength or a longer suit that you can rebid, taking out the double. Either course could be disastrous if you, with (h), act freely.

The best action in these situations, when you're completely 'broke' and an opponent overcalls, is to pass! Always remember that in bridge, whenever a person bids voluntarily, a promise of a certain range of strength is indicated.

A FREE RESPONSE AT THE THREE LEVEL

Free responses at the level of three vary. If in a minor suit, they are competitive and opener will pass unless he holds a maximum and a fine fit; if bid in a major, they are forcing to game.

CASE B

SOUTH, OPENER	WEST	YOU,NORTH	EAST
One no trump	Two spades	Three hearts	

CASE C

SOUTH, OPENER	WEST	YOU,NORTH	EAST
One no trump	Two hearts	Three spades	

In case (b), you were forced to bid 'three' in order to overbid the opponent's two spade overcall; in case (c), the three spade response was a single jump takeout since a response of only two spades would simply have been competitive and not forcing. Since both bids, that of three hearts in case (b) and that of three spades in case (c) are made at the level of three, the bidding must reach at least a game contract.

WITH FOUR CARDS OF A MAJOR

Probing for a four-four major fit with a two club response is no longer possible after an opponent overcalls with a bid of two of his suit. The reason is obvious - since the overcaller either bid two clubs, two diamonds, two hearts or two spades- it is no longer possible for responder to bid two clubs.

♠ ♡ ◇ ♣

REBIDS BY THE OPENING NO TRUMP BIDDER

As in all bidding situations, whether opened with one or more of a suit, or in no trump, any rebid or future action by the opening bidder is entirely dependent upon possible bids both by partner and the opponents. For the most part when the bidding is opened with one no trump, the opponents will not bid. That is because the opening bidder holds a substantial share of the high cards and an overcall is dangerous, presenting the possibility of being doubled and severely punished.

WHEN RESPONDER HAS BID TWO CLUBS

The two club response by partner specifically asks the opening no trump bidder whether he holds a four card major.

(i)	(j)	(k)	(l)
♠ AJ98	♠ KQ	♠ KJ92	♠ AQ9
♡ Q107	♡ AJ83	♡ A1083	♡ KJ8
◇ KQ96	◇ KJ10	◇ K2	◇ K106
♣ A10	♣ KJ76	♣ KQJ	♣ A1098

CASE D

SOUTH	WEST	NORTH	EAST
One no trump	Pass	Two clubs	Pass
?			

You are South, having opened the bidding with each of the above hands. Holding (i), your rebid would be two spades; with (j), two hearts; with (k), two spades, and with (l), two diamonds.

Hand (k) brings us to a new facet of Stayman - when holding four cards of both major suits, after a two club response to an opening no trump, the opener's rebid is two spades - the higher ranking suit. In other words, a rebid of two spades allows the possibility that opener also holds four hearts but a rebid of two hearts would deny possession of four spades.

Lacking either four hearts or four spades, the opener's rebid is the automatic one of 'two diamonds.' The last bid simply says that the opening bidder does not have four cards of either major - *it does not say anything about opener's strength* (as in earlier Stayman) nor does it show a diamond suit. It is an *artificial bid that says "no" to partner's question about major suit length.*

AFTER A RESPONSE OF TWO DIAMONDS

The response of two diamonds to an opening bid of one no trump as indicating that responder holds an unbalanced hand with length only in the minors is new. A response of two diamonds, as described on pages 601 and 602, requests the opening bidder, if high card strength is *concentrated* in one major suit and the other major suit is weak in high cards, to bid the major suit in which the high card strength is held.

The strength-locating major suit bid will frequently be a suit of less than four cards. If the greatest major strength happens to be held in a four card suit, this is merely coincidental.

With both major suits stopped, the opening no trump bidder's rebid (after a two diamond response) would be two no trump. Remember that a response of two diamonds to an opening bid of one no trump *is forcing to at least a game contract and that neither partner may stop bidding below game.*

CASE E

SOUTH, YOU, OPENER	WEST	NORTH	EAST
One no trump	Pass	Two diamonds	Pass
?			

You hold -

(m)	(n)	(o)
♠ AKQ	♠ A2	♠ J4
♡ J108	♡ KJ109	♡ AQJ
◇ QJ87	◇ K876	◇ AQ92
♣ KJ6	♣ AQJ	♣ QJ108

With (m) your rebid would be two spades; with (n) two no trump; and with (o) two hearts.

As stated earlier, the opener's rebid is designed to pinpoint the major suit in which he holds a concentration of high card strength. It is *not* intended to locate the suit in which the opening no trump bidder may have the greatest length nor is it intended to check either minor suits or major suits in the opener's hand.

In rebidding to a response of two diamonds, the opening no trump bidder simply embarks on the partnership inquiry of the strength held by opener in the suit in which responder (who guarantees a singleton or void) is weak. This course will determine whether no trump or the minor suit (game or slam) should be the final destination.

AFTER A RESPONSE OF THREE CLUBS OR THREE DIAMONDS

Let's suppose the bidding has proceeded:

CASE F

SOUTH, YOU, OPENER	WEST	NORTH	EAST
One no trump	Pass	Three clubs or Three diamonds	Pass
?			

You should usually pass. Your partner's three club or three diamond bid is intended to show a weak hand with a long club or diamond suit. Examples of this response are shown on page 603. If you hold a super-fit in the minor suit and a maximum, you may rebid with three no trump.

REBIDDING AFTER A JUMP TO THREE HEARTS OR THREE SPADES

When you have opened the bidding with one no trump and your partner has responded with a bid of either three hearts or three spades, his response *is forcing to at least a game contract.* Hence you are compelled to rebid.

Your partner has shown 10 or more points and at least five cards of the suit shown. With four cards in the major, he would have employed the Stayman 'two club' response. Since game is obviously makable, your partner's decision to bid three hearts or spades rather than contracting for the makable game at once can be based on one or more of the following reasons.

1 - He is not certain whether the hand will play better in his suit or in no trump. He will make that decision after hearing your rebid which will describe your hand.
2 - He may have a second suit to show and request a preference.
3 - He may wish to make a subsequent slam try after hearing your response.

Let's suppose the bidding has been -

CASE G

SOUTH, YOU, OPENER	WEST	NORTH, PARTNER	EAST
One no trump	Pass	Three hearts	Pass
?			

(p)	(q)	(r)
♠ AJ97	♠ K4	♠ AQ6
♡ K2	♡ KJ8	♡ KQ2
◊ AQ96	◊ AJ108	◊ A94
♣ K1072	♣ KJ93	♣ Q875

(p) Your rebid would be three no trump. You certainly lack good supporting cards for your partner's suit - in fact, hearts is the poorest holding in your hand.

(q) Here the immediate raise to four hearts is indicated. You not only hold excellent support for partner's suit in the form of three trumps which include the king and jack but in addition, the doubleton spade may permit partner to ruff his losing spades in your dummy hand.

(r) Again a raise to four hearts is in order. It would be a mistake to conceal from partner your excellent heart support. While the hand suffers slightly from having 4-3-3-3 distribution, thus not affording any possible ruffing value for partner's losers, to make anything but a constructive, forward-going rebid would be an error.

REBIDDING AFTER A JUMP TO GAME BY PARTNER

Let's presume, after you have opened the bidding with one no trump, your partner jumps to game in a suit as by bidding four hearts or four spades or possibly five clubs or five diamonds. *You must pass!*

Your partner's response indicates the probability of game (page 603) and denies any desire to continue further, as to slam. Since the bid is a signoff, any further bid by you would be to disregard the message conveyed by partner's bid. Always remember that you have pretty well described your hand with your opening bid of one no trump.

REBIDDING AFTER A RAISE TO TWO NO TRUMP

When there has been no intervening bid by the opponent and your partner has raised your opening bid of one no trump to 'two,' he is simply asking you whether your no trump is a minimum 16 points or whether it has 17 or 18 points.

If you have only 16 points, you should pass; holding 17 or 18 points, bid three no trump.

Should your partner's raise to two no trump be made over an overcall by your left hand opponent, a rebid to three no trump should contain, in addition to the required 17 or 18 points, at least one stopper in the opponent's suit.

REBIDDING AFTER A RAISE TO THREE NO TRUMP

After opening with one no trump and receiving a raise to three no trump, the opening bidder *must pass!* You have described your holding with your first bid and it hasn't changed just because of partner's response. To make any form of slam try at this point would be heinous. Opener would be rebidding the same values again, and will injure partnership confidence if he does anything but pass.

FURTHER ACTION AFTER A PENALTY DOUBLE OF PARTNER'S RESPONSE

Since partner's possible response of two clubs or two diamonds is artificial and is intended to show strong major suit holdings in the case of a two club response and strong minors with the two diamond bid, it is highly possible that the opponent sitting behind your partner may have strong holdings in whichever of these two suits partner may bid. An alert opponent may double the response as a means of indicating to his partner that he should lead that suit.

CASE H

SOUTH, YOU, OPENER	WEST	NORTH, PARTNER	EAST
One no trump	Pass	Two clubs	Double

(s)
♠ J 9
♡ 10 5 3
◇ 8 7 6
♣ K Q 10 8 2

(t)
♠ K 10 8
♡ K 2
◇ A Q J 4
♣ A J 9 7

East's hand is shown to the left as (s). His double is obviously for the purpose of requesting a club opening lead, should partner be the opening leader.

There is one possibility, generally overlooked by the new player, of playing the hand in the doubled contract, in this case, clubs. Let's suppose your opening no trump resembled hand (t) to the left. Certainly no contract, if your partner has three or more clubs, could please you better than that of two clubs, redoubled. East's clubs aren't going to take the tricks that player anticipated, due to the strong holding and strategic location of your clubs.

In these cases, holding a minimum of four good cards in the doubled suit, the no trump bidder *should redouble*. This, in effect, tells partner to 'stay put' in the redoubled contract if partner holds any three or more cards of the redoubled suit. The advantages are obvious - two clubs, redoubled, if made will produce a game by winning only eight tricks. Secondly, each over-trick will yield you 200 points if not vulnerable and 400 points, vulnerable. Add a couple of over-tricks to the score and see how many points can be won.

But the important thing is that the opponents, after the redouble, will usually have no place to go. East, in doubling two clubs, expected your side 'to run.' He was jolted by the news that you were not only willing but highly desirous of playing a redoubled contract. Should either the doubler or his partner try to rescue themselves by bidding some suit at the two level, they can often be doubled and severely punished.

Realize, however, that in these situations, the opening no trump bidder must redouble - he cannot pass! There are two reasons. The first is that without the redouble, partner will have no knowledge of your desire to play for game bonus in the club contract and will run from what he knows is an artificial contract. Another reason for redoubling is that if your side can make a game, highly probable after your partner's response indicating at least eight points facing your 16 to 18 points, you must receive at least the equivalent of game if you decide to remain in clubs. A doubled two club contract yields only 80 points towards game, short of the 100 required and over-tricks are worth 100 and 200 points each, not vulnerable and vulnerable, respectively. Thus you would not score as many points playing a two club doubled contract, even with a few over-tricks, as you would have made in a game contract elsewhere.

Without four or more cards in the doubled suit, the no trump bidder should make his normal rebid over the opponent's double of the two club or two diamond response.

CASE H

YOU, OPENER	WEST	NORTH, PARTNER	EAST
One no trump	Pass	Two clubs	Double
?			

(u)	(v)	(w)
♠ AJ97	♠ KQ	♠ KJ10
♡ KJ6	♡ QJ75	♡ AJ9
◇ A87	◇ A1097	◇ KQ86
♣ A32	♣ KQ4	♣ K32

(u) Rebid two spades.
(v) Two hearts.
(w) Two diamonds. You lack four cards of a major. The fact that you hold four diamonds is coincidental. You can also pass if you choose.

REBIDS BY THE RESPONDER

There will be only four situations where the responder will bid twice or more. These are :

1 - Responder has first bid two clubs;
2 - Responder has first bid two diamonds;
3 - Responder has bid two of a major which opener has raised to three (of that suit);
4 - Responder has bid three of a major as his initial response.

AFTER A FIRST RESPONSE OF TWO CLUBS

Obviously, after first responding two clubs to partner's opening one no trump, responder's rebid will be based, to a large extent, on partner's rebid. It can be succinctly stated as a simple question - *does the opening bidder hold four cards of the same major suit in which responder holds four cards?* If the answer is yes, continue in that suit; if the answer is no, then responder returns to no trump, bidding either two or three no trump, depending upon the strength of his hand.

But there is an important new proviso - only if the responder holds *five or more cards* of a major suit can he show that suit if partner's rebid denied holding four cards of the major suit.

CASE I

PARTNER,OPENER SOUTH	WEST	YOU NORTH	EAST
One no trump	Pass	Two clubs	Pass
Two diamonds	Pass	?	

Let's suppose you hold each of the following hands.

(x)	(y)	(z)
♠ Q 10 9 8	♠ 8 7 3 2	♠ K J 8 7
♡ J 2	♡ A J 10 8 6	♡ K 2
◇ A J 6 4	◇ K 3 2	◇ Q J 7
♣ 8 3 2	♣ 4	♣ J 9 5 3

(x) Your rebid is two no trump. This is a sign-off, showing inability to bid game. Partner should pass with 16 points, bid three no trump with more.

(y) Two hearts. When you bid two clubs, you were hoping that partner could show a possible four card heart or spade holding in which case you would have raised his suit. But though he lacks four hearts, the suit is still highly playable. Your bid of two hearts, after partner denied a heart suit, shows at least a five card suit and leaves the decision whether to play the hand in hearts or no trump up to the opening no trump bidder.

(z) Three no trump is correct. With 11 high card points facing 16 to 18, game is probable. A two spade bid at this point would be incorrect since it would promise five spades after partner's two diamond bid denied a holding of four spades.

AFTER A FIRST RESPONSE OF TWO DIAMONDS

The first response of two diamonds to a one no trump opening was based on minor suit length containing at least one five card minor with an accompanying singleton or a six card or longer minor suit.

The opening bidder's rebid simply stated "I have concentrated strength in this (bid) suit and no stopper in the other major." If over your response of two diamonds, partner's rebid was two no trump, he affirms that he has both major suits stopped.

Armed with the knowledge of where partner's strength is located and where he is weak, it becomes a simple matter to determine whether the combined hands will best play in responder's minor suit or in no trump.

CASE J

PARTNER, OPENER		YOU	
SOUTH	WEST	NORTH	EAST
One no trump	Pass	Two diamonds	Pass
Two hearts	Pass	?	

(a)
♠ 4
♡ Q J 8
◇ K 3 2
♣ A Q 10 9 8 7

Holding hand (a), the danger of a possible no trump contract is apparent after partner has shown that a great portion of his high card strength is in hearts and not in spades, where responder is missing strength as well. Played in five or six clubs, the heart strength is exactly where it will be needed to bolster responder's queen-jack holding; in no trump, the Achilles' heel of the spade suit has become evident.

(b)
♠ Q J 10
♡ void
◇ K J 8 7 6 4
♣ K 4 3 2

With hand (b), responder's problem as to whether the hand will best play in diamonds or no trump has been speedily resolved by the opener's rebid of two hearts. The opener is now known to be weak in spades and strong in the heart suit. Hence the heart suit is securely stopped despite responder's void and there is nothing to be feared from that suit in an eventual no trump contract.

AFTER BEING RAISED FROM TWO OF A MAJOR TO THREE

Let us presume the bidding has gone as in Case K.

CASE K

SOUTH, PARTNER	WEST	YOU, NORTH	EAST
One no trump	Pass	Two hearts	Pass
Three hearts	Pass	?	

There are three possible courses of action open to you. These are:

1 - Pass;

2 - Bid four hearts;

3 - Bid three no trump.

Your partner, by his raise to three hearts, has shown a maximum 17 - 18 points plus a good supporting fit for your heart suit. This may even include a doubleton in some side suit affording another point for ruffing value, bringing his total point count still higher. You could have bid two hearts with any of the following hands –

(c)	(d)	(e)
♠ 4	♠ 2	♠ 43
♡ 876542	♡ K10942	♡ KQ9876
◇ J109	◇ 732	◇ 876
♣ 832	♣ Q1096	♣ 109

(c) You would pass. Even with your partner's encouraging response, there is no hope for game. Be happy you've found the right suit.

(d) Counting distribution, the hand is worth seven points. Partner has shown a maximum no trump, plus excellent heart support. While not at all secure, the chance of making a game is sufficient to warrant bidding four hearts.

(e) Three no trump. Coupled with partner's known heart support, the heart suit should produce six tricks in no trump. It is presumed that partner can win three tricks in the remaining suits, particularly with the advantage of the opening lead coming up to, rather than through, the no trump. While the game contract is not a sure thing, one thing is certain - it's going to be a lot easier winning nine tricks at no trump than 10 tricks with hearts as trumps.

AFTER FIRST RESPONDING WITH THREE OF A MAJOR

As in every rebidding situation, the responder's rebids, after first responding with three of a major to partner's opening bid of one no trump, depend upon his hand and the nature of his partner's rebid. It will be rare that the opponents will interpolate a bid in these situations since the fact that the opening no trump bidder promised 16 to 18 high card points and responder has shown a minimum of 10 points leaves little for the opponents. Therefore in considering rebids, it will be presumed that the opponents have not entered the bidding.

After your response of three of a major, your partner, the opening bidder, has made either of the following rebids.

1 - He raised your suit to four.

2 - He bid three no trump.

Since as a rule of thumb, 33 points will be required to produce a small slam and 37 points a grand slam, the following table will be of value in this rebidding situation.

After having responded with three of a major to partner's opening no trump which partner raised to four of the major, you should:

RESPONDER HOLDS IN POINTS	COURSE OF ACTION
10 to 13	Pass
14 to 16	Investigate, through the agreed slam convention, the possibility of slam.
17 to 19	Small slam seems certain.
20 or more	Grand slam seems certain. Necessary controls in aces, kings and fit should be checked.

Where the responder has initially bid three of his suit and the opening no trump bidder has rebid with three no trump, the responder may elect to rebid or to pass. Assuming the bidding has been as in Case L.

CASE L

SOUTH, PARTNER	WEST	YOU, NORTH	EAST
One no trump	Pass	Three spades	Pass
Three no trump	Pass	?	

You hold each of the following hands.

(f)	(g)	(h)
♠ A J 8 6 4	♠ K Q 10 9 8 7	♠ K J 9 8 6 4 2
♡ K J 7 6 5	♡ A 7 6	♡ 6 5
◇ Q 3 2	◇ 4 2	◇ A
♣ void	♣ 3 2	♣ J 3 2

(f) You should rebid four hearts, asking partner to choose between your two major suits. It is a safe axiom that most two-suiters, if played in the suit with the better fit, will generally win one more trick than if played in no trump.

(g) Pass. The spade suit will produce just as many tricks in no trump as if played in spades. Partner has not shown any particular desire to support spades.

(h) Four spades.

SUBSEQUENT REBIDS BY THE OPENING NO TRUMP BIDDER

There will be times where the opening bidder will rebid twice or more. These will usually be where -

1 - Responder after first bidding two clubs bids a major suit of which the opening bidder has denied holding four cards.

2 - The no trump bidder holds four cards of *both* major suits.

3 - The responder shows a second suit, thus asking for a preference.

4 - The opening bidder, after a response of two clubs, has bid two of a major which responder raises to three.

5 - Partner makes a slam try.

Let's take the first case. A typical bidding situation would be:

CASE M

YOU, SOUTH	WEST	NORTH, PARTNER	EAST
One no trump	Pass	Two clubs	Pass
Two hearts	Pass	Two spades	Pass
?			

Your two heart bid denied a four card spade suit. When North now bids two spades, he shows a five card or longer spade suit. Your rebid will be determined by (a) the length and quality of your spades; (b) the total point count and whether the hand is evenly balanced or might afford some ruffing value, if played in a spade contract.

(i)	(j)	(k)	(l)
♠ A 10	♠ K J 2	♠ K 2	♠ A J 4
♡ K J 8 6	♡ A Q 3 2	♡ K Q 8 7	♡ K 8 6 3
◇ A J 9	◇ Q J 10	◇ A J 10 9	◇ A K 9 2
♣ K 10 8 6	♣ K 10 9	♣ K Q 7	♣ K 7

(i) Two no trump. The hand is not only minimum but lacks good spade support.

(j) Three spades. Even with 4-3-3-3 distribution and a hand offering no ruffing value, you must raise your partner holding good supporting cards for his suit. He can still bid three no trump if he is 5-3-3-2 and you will play it there.

(k) Three no trump. With only two cards in spades you can not raise. But holding full 18 points, you must advise your partner that you hold a maximum by making the descriptive bid of *three*, not two, no trump.

(l) Four spades. Holding excellent three cards, support the spades. Since you have a maximum of 18 points and a doubleton in clubs, a single raise is not adequate to describe your hand. Certain post-graduate players would bid three diamonds. In this sequence, a new suit by opener is used to mean precisely that opener holds a maximum, a fine fit and the suit bid is a cue-bid to show where opener is strong. This usage permits slam investigation at low levels. I approve.

CASE N

SOUTH, OPENER	WEST	NORTH, PARTNER	EAST
One no trump	Pass	Two clubs	Pass
Two spades	Pass	Two no trump	Pass
Three hearts			

(m)
♠ K J 8 7
♡ A 9 6 5
◇ K J
♣ A 10 7

This hand is a good example calling for the above bidding. Your partner, by his two club club response, promised four or more cards of a major suit. Obviously from his two no trump rebid, he wasn't interested in your spade suit. Hence, it must be hearts and holding four cards in each major suit, spades are shown first, hearts later. If your holding were a maximum you would bid four, not three, in this sequence. Partner has already shown a minimum. He is allowed to pass three hearts, if you bid only three.

CASE O

SOUTH, OPENER	WEST	NORTH, PARTNER	EAST
One no trump	Pass	Three hearts	Pass
Three no trump	Pass	Four diamonds	Pass
?			

The opening bidder is asked for either a (preference) bid of four hearts or a raise to five diamonds, according to his holding.

CASE P

SOUTH, OPENER	WEST	NORTH, PARTNER	EAST
One no trump	Pass	Two clubs	Pass
Two hearts	Pass	Three hearts	Pass
?			

Partner's raise is *not* forcing to game. It simply requests the opening bidder to go to game holding a 17 or 18 point no trump or to pass with a minimum 16 points. I might add that if the opening bidder does find reason to go on, it will usually be by bidding four of the major. However, if three no trump seems easier, possibly because opener has 4-3-3-3 distribution, this rebid may be selected. Partner will still have the final choice of passing or bidding four hearts.

CASE Q

SOUTH, OPENER	WEST	NORTH, PARTNER	EAST
One no trump	Pass	Two clubs	Pass
Two spades	Pass	Four clubs	Pass
?			

North's bidding indicates a tremendous spade fit plus a hand of slam probability. His four club rebid, in response to two spades, is conventional Gerber asking partner to tell him how many aces he holds. If you do not play Gerber, another bid would be used to deliver the same message.

I would again like to emphasize that had North's first response been four no trump (rather than two clubs), it would not have been Blackwood.

STAYMAN AND OPENING BIDS OF TWO NO TRUMP

One of the great advantages of the Stayman Convention is that it permits exploration of the possibility of a four card major suit fit below game after a hand has been opened with two no trump.

This is done in the same way as responding to an opening bid of one no trump, except that instead of bidding two clubs over one no trump, the bidding starts one level higher with responder bidding three clubs over two no trump.

After receiving a response of three clubs Stayman to his opening bid of two no trump, opener rebids as follows -

1 - Three spades, if he holds four cards in spades. (He may also have a four card heart suit).

2 - Three hearts, if he holds four hearts but not four spades.

3 - Three diamonds, if he has no four card major suit.

Obviously, responder's strength requirements for the bid of three clubs (over two no trump) are considerably lower than those needed to bid two clubs over one no trump. He is facing a much stronger hand and he needs much less than the partner of a player whose holding is 16 to 18 points.

In addition to holding four or more cards of a major suit, responder's hand needs only four high card points or even less with exceptional distribution. The reason for this should be easy to understand. The opening two no trump promised about

21 to 24 high card points. Ordinarily, to make a game in no trump or a major, 26 points are needed. But when a larger part is concentrated in one hand and transportation (between the hands) is difficult, it may take 27 or even 28 points to have a satisfactory play. It is not always possible to refine this position other than to seek a total which here will be 25 to 28 points, when responder bids with four.

The second difference between responding to one no trump and to two no trump is that, after a two no trump opening bid, *any response is forcing to game,* while a two club response to one no trump is forcing only to two no trump or three of a major. Thus when responder bids after an opening bid of two no trump, neither partner is expected to stop bidding until game, at least, is reached.

For the responder to take out two no trump into three diamonds, hearts or spades, the suit should be at least five cards in length with an unbalanced hand. The bid may be made with as little as four points. Six card or longer major suits should always be shown and may be very weak in high card point count.

A jump to four of a major, or to five of a minor, after partner has opened with two no trump shows a long suit, game possibility and denies interest in or enough strength for slam.

A responder holding nine or more points with distributional advantages should investigate slam probabilities after partner has opened two no trump.

REBIDDING AFTER A TWO NO TRUMP OPENING

We have already discussed opener's rebids to a three club response, in that four card major suits are shown if held and lacking four cards of a major, the rebid by opener should be three diamonds.

Let's assume the bidding has been as in Case R.

CASE R

SOUTH, YOU	WEST	NORTH, PARTNER	EAST
Two no trump	Pass	Three clubs	Pass
Three diamonds	Pass --	(Three hearts (Three spades	Pass
?			

Since your partner, by bidding a major suit in which you have denied holding four cards, has shown at least five, the only question is whether you should raise his suit to four or bid three no trump. This obviously depends upon your hand. If you do elect to rebid with three no trump and your partner persists in his suit by bidding four hearts or spades as the case may be, you should then pass.

In the event that your partner's immediate response was three of a major, you know that he has five or more cards in his suit. Again your rebid will either be to raise partner to four of his suit or to bid three no trump, depending upon your hand. If, over your three no trump rebid, partner goes on to 'four' of his suit, you should pass. Your partner's bidding has shown a complete distaste for no trump and a desire to play the hand at game in his suit.

Lastly, if your partner's first response was to raise your opening two no trump to three no trump, you should pass - rapidly!

STAYMAN AFTER PARTNER'S OVERCALL OF ONE NO TRUMP

Let's suppose the bidding has proceeded as in Case S.

CASE S

NORTH, DEALER	EAST, PARTNER	SOUTH	WEST, YOU
One diamond	One no trump	Pass	?

One of the tremendous advantages of the Stayman Convention is that it permits exploration of a possible four-four major suit fit after an opponent opens the bidding and partner overcalls with one no trump.

The one no trump overcall shows 17 or 18 high card points (page 599) and occasionally 19 points without fillers.

The responses to a one no trump overcall in Stayman are exactly the same as to an opening no trump bid. In other words, a takeout of two clubs to one no trump is artificial and forcing for one round; any takeout to two hearts or two spades shows a five card suit, a weak hand and a desire to play the hand below game in that suit.

If one club was the opponent's opening bid, a two club bid by you after partner's overcall of one no trump should be treated as conventional Stayman asking partner to show a four card major. The later bidding may show it was a really strong hand and intended as a cue-bid of the suit already bid by the enemy.

Where partner's overcall of one no trump is made over an opening bid of one diamond, use of a two diamond bid by you to show a hand strong in minor suit holdings is not advisable. The reasons are these. First, play in a final diamond contract (by your side) is unlikely since the opponent apparently has strength there. This leaves only clubs as a possible minor suit contract and your partner is inferentially marked for club strength since with strong major holdings, he probably would have chosen an informatory double in preference to the no trump overcall.

In cases where partner's no trump overcall is made over an opening bid of one heart or one spade, a response of two diamonds has the conventional meaning of showing minor suit length in the responder's hand and asks the no trump bidder to clarify his holding as described on pages 610 and 611.

♠ ♡ ◇ ♣

NON - FORCING STAYMAN

Previous pages have discussed what is known as *forcing* Stayman in which a response of two clubs to an opening bid or overcall of one no trump promises eight or more points in the responder's (two club) bidder's hand and guarantees that the partnership bidding will continue until *at least* a contract of two no trump or three of a suit has been reached.

A widely used variation of the Stayman Convention is termed *non-forcing*. In the latter, the response of two clubs can be made with far less than eight points. While the no trump bidder is compelled to rebid once after partner's two club response, there is no further obligation on either partner to bid again.

The main advantage of non-forcing Stayman, as compared with the forcing variety, is that it permits responder with a weak hand to help find the best part-score spot, and, if he is really weak, to escape with minimum damage. Its chief drawback is on hands where responder has about eight or nine points facing a strong notrump; since the two club Stayman bid does not promise any strength, it is more difficult for responder to invite game.

Non-forcing Stayman (or Two Way Stayman – see page 627) is used by pairs playing weak no trumps (11-14 points), who need more often to find an escape route. In addition, it is used a great deal by duplicate bridge players, for at duplicate, it can be as important to get to the part score contract that scores highest as to reach a sound but close game.

Let's assume you are South in the following bidding sequence and hold hands (a) and (b).

CASE A

NORTH	EAST	SOUTH, YOU	WEST
One no trump	Pass	Two clubs	

(a)	(b)
♠ Q 8 6	♠ J 8 6 5 4
♡ 10 7 4 3	♡ J 7 4 2
◇ 9 7 6 4 3	◇ 3
♣ 5	♣ 8 7 3

Your partner will make one of the following rebids -

Two diamonds
Two hearts
Two spades

Holding hand (a), if partner's rebid is two diamonds, you will pass with alacrity. Of course, partner's two diamond bid *did not* show possession of a real diamond suit - far from it! He might have four or five diamonds in his hand, since he obviously lacks either four hearts or four spades, but he might have only three diamonds or perhaps, only a doubleton. But that's relatively unimportant, since you have enough diamonds in your hand to bolster whatever holding he has and any suit contract, from your point of view, is better than one no trump.

Of course were your partner's rebid to hand (a) either two hearts or two spades, you'd pass with equal rapidity.

With hand (b), the purpose of the two club response is to ascertain whether partner has four hearts or four spades. If he bids either suit, you will happily pass. If his rebid is two diamonds, you will then bid your five card suit, spades, and your partner should pass.

Using non-forcing Stayman, other responses than two clubs have the same meanings as with the forcing variety. A takeout to two diamonds, two hearts or two spades shows a weak, distributional hand with absence of game probability. The artificial two diamond bid (pages 601-602) is not used with non-forcing Stayman - hence, a response of two diamonds shows a weak hand with a five card or longer diamond suit and little else.

A jump to three of a major, as by bidding three hearts or three spades, in response to one no trump is forcing to game, the point count varying from 13 opposite a weak no trump to a minimum of 10 facing a strong 16 to 18 point no trump. In each case the suit should be of at least five cards.

A jump to game in a suit, as by bidding four hearts or five clubs, shows a distributional hand with probability of game. The bid is seldom made in the minor since no trump contracts, coupled with the minor suit, require fewer tricks for game and are more lucrative in scoring.

After bidding two clubs, using non-forcing Stayman, if responder bids a new suit at the three level, it is forcing. For this purpose, clubs are considered a "new suit," so if responder holds a weak hand with a long club suit, he should jump to three clubs over one no trump, just as in forcing Stayman. In the bidding sequence

CASE B

NORTH	EAST	SOUTH	WEST
One no trump	Pass	Two clubs	Pass
Two hearts	Pass	Three diamonds	

South has a very good hand and is looking for a slam in diamonds (or, if he later supports the suit, in hearts).

If the bidding goes

CASE C

NORTH	EAST	SOUTH	WEST
One no trump	Pass	Two clubs	Pass
Two diamonds	Pass	Three hearts	

South has enough for game, probably with five hearts and four spades, and is asking North to select the best game contract – four hearts or three no trump.

Using non-forcing Stayman, if the opening no trump bidder

holds two four card majors, he should bid two hearts over two clubs (rather than spades, as in forcing Stayman). This will help the partnership reach the right part score when responder is weak.

VARIATIONS AND MODIFICATIONS

All of us are acquainted with the neighborhood youngster who, on getting his first automobile, modifies it by either changing the exterior, the engine, or both.

The same is true in bridge. There is scarcely a convention that some player hasn't changed, modified or otherwise improved. Whether the change or modification is an improvement over the original is a matter of debate. By and large, the originators themselves of the conventions, as Samuel Stayman and Harry Fishbein, feel that these attachments and modifications detract rather than add to the efficacy of their brain-childs. The inventor of the modification, however, naturally feels it to be an improvement over the original version.

This text has been designed to be the most inclusive, the most complete, available. Accordingly, it would not be complete without these variations. However, their inclusion does not indicate either approval or lack of same.

VARIATIONS TO STAYMAN

TWO WAY STAYMAN

A method that has gained popularity recently is Two Way Stayman, originated by David Carter of St. Louis and also known as CARTER, in which either a two club or a two diamond response to one no trump asks the no trump bidder to bid a major suit if he has one. The difference between the two responses is that two clubs may be made on a very weak hand or an invitational hand (as in non-forcing Stayman), while a bid of two diamonds over one no trump commits the hand to game. Two Way Stayman is especially popular with players who use weak no trumps, and our example hands are based on responding to a 12 to 14 high card point no trump. However, the convention can be used with any range no trump opening.

The two club response is treated just like non-forcing Stayman, with one important exception. Since responder could have bid two diamonds rather than two clubs if he wanted to force the hand to game, all responder's rebids at the three level (other than three no trump, of course) are invitational, not forcing. You are South, the responder, with the following hands:

CASE A

NORTH	EAST	SOUTH	WEST
One no trump	Pass	Two clubs	Pass
Two diamonds	Pass	?	

(a)	(b)
♠K 1064	♠Q65
♡AJ1083	♡AQJ95
♢7	♢Q7
♣954	♣1095

Remember that you are playing that an opening bid of one no trump shows only 12 to 14 high card points, so that responder needs 11 or 12 points to invite a game and 13 or more to insist on game. With hand (a), South simply signs off in two hearts. North must pass.

With hand (b), South rebids three hearts, asking partner to bid four hearts or three no trump if he has a maximum one no trump opening, or to pass if he has a minimum. Note that if North-South were not playing Two Way Stayman, South would have an awkward problem over one no trump. He could bid two hearts, and perhaps miss a good game. He could overbid by jumping to three hearts immediately, forcing to game, and get his side overboard. Or he could invite game by responding two no trump, but the hearts will then be shut out – and hearts may be the best place to play the hand.

As in regular non-forcing Stayman, if the no trump bidder has both majors, he should bid hearts first.

With 13 or more points facing a weak no trump (10 points opposite a strong no trump), responder knows that he wants to be in game somewhere, but he may not always know what will be the best contract. Two diamonds sets off a chain of investigation. Once responder bids two diamonds, both partners must keep bidding until some game contract is reached. This method is very helpful on potential slam hands, as the bidding can be kept at a low level without fear of partner passing.

CASE B

NORTH	EAST	SOUTH	WEST
One no trump	Pass	Two diamonds	Pass
Two no trump	Pass	Three hearts	Pass
Three spades	Pass	Four diamonds	Pass
Four hearts	Pass	?	

In the above bidding sequence, South asks about North's majors with his two diamond bid. North rebids two no trump to deny a four card major or a five card minor suit (he would rebid three clubs or three diamonds with a five card suit). South shows five or more hearts – he already has indicated a good hand – and North shows that he has a concentration of cards in spades. With the other suits stopped and no fit for hearts, North would simply rebid three no trump. South indicates his second suit with four diamonds, and North shows that his spade bid was based on a fit for hearts. Now if South has 17 points or less, he will simply pass, and North-South will have reached their best game. But suppose he was interested in a slam, with either of these holdings:

(a)	(b)
♠8	♠Q 103
♡AQJ87	♡AQJ87
◊AKQ3	◊AKJ4
♣J65	♣7

With hand (a), South with pass four hearts, for his spade singleton will be of little use opposite partner's high cards there. With (b), South checks on aces via a Blackwood four no trump bid, and goes on to slam unless there are two aces missing. His queen of spades will be a very valuable card.

SUMMARY

Using Two Way Stayman, a jump to three clubs or three diamonds directly over the one no trump bid is a sign off, indicating a weak hand with a long minor suit. If responder has a fair six card minor and about 11 points, he first bids two clubs and then three of his minor to ask opener to bid three no trump with a maximum and a fit. Immediate jumps to three hearts or three spades by responder are, as in other Stayman varieties, forcing to game: the jumps show good hands with good suits. Jumps to game in a suit – four spades or five diamonds – are also sign-offs, and indicate distributional hands that should provide a good play for the contract.

When responder bids two diamonds over one no trump, opener rebids a four card major if he has one (spades first if he holds both – he will be able to show his hearts on the next round) or a five card minor; otherwise he bids two no trump. Any bid short of game that responder now makes is forcing; if opener rebids two hearts or two spades and responder does not have a fit for opener, or a long suit of his own, he should rebid two no trump to let opener show a second suit if he has one.

REBID TO SHOW BOTH MAJORS

In cases where the opening no trump bidder holds four cards of both major suits, Stayman advises first bidding 'two spades' and later, if responder lacks four spades, for the opening no trump bidder to show the heart suit. The (Stayman) recommended method, then, might be as in the following bidding sequences -

CASE A

NORTH	EAST	SOUTH	WEST
One no trump	Pass	Two clubs	Pass
Two spades	Pass	Two no trump	Pass
Three hearts			

CASE B

NORTH	EAST	SOUTH	WEST
One no trump	Pass	Two clubs	Pass
Two spades	Pass	Three no trump	Pass
Four hearts			

In both cases, North can safely assume that his partner, South, holds four hearts from the fact that the latter has indicated an interest in a possible major suit contract, yet has shown no interest in the spade contract. Hence, if he doesn't have spades, he must have hearts. It's as simple as A-B-C.

However, there are players who find this method of showing the opening no trumper's major suits "one at a time" cumbersome and awkward, and they have devised a simple variation to Stayman to cure this – if opener rebids three clubs over the two club Stayman inquiry, he says, "Partner, I have four cards in both major suits – take your pick of which one interests you." Responder thus finds out about a four-four suit fit below game level, and a contract of three no trump is not ruled out. The no trumper's hand could well be something like hand (a) at the left. In two bids, he has told partner that he holds 16-18 points, four cards each in hearts and spades, and two cards in one minor suit and three in the other one. Advocates of the three club rebid to show both majors think this is pretty efficient, and it is hard to quarrel with them.

(a)
♠ K J 8 6
♡ A Q 4 3
◊ K 6
♣ A 7 5

Of course, this method of rebidding can be used only with forcing Stayman, where the two club bidder promises at least eight points, enough to invite a game, for it is no longer possible to stop at the two level. Over three clubs, responder invites game by bidding three of the major suit in which he is interested; opener can go on to four of the major or, if he has much of his strength concentrated in the minor suits, he can bid three no trump with a maximum. If responder wants to be in a game contract opposite a minimum opening no trump, he can jump to four of his major directly over three clubs.

OTHER OPENING BIDS OF ONE NO TRUMP

In the early days of contract bridge, the opening bid of one no trump became stabilized as a strong balanced hand, usually with four or more honor tricks. Translated into modern terms, this is 16-18 points – the 'strong no trump' almost universally used.

Almost – but not quite. In recent years, there has been an increasing use of weak no trump opening bids. They are basic structural beams in the Kaplan-Sheinwold (page 745) and Precision Systems (page 752), and non-vulnerable weak no trumps have long been a part of the Acol System (page 758). In addition, some expert players who use the 'strong' no trump have watered down the requirements from 16-18 high-card points to a range of 15-17. One of New England's leading women players, Mrs. Ethel Keohane, once referred to her 15-17 no trump range as 'decent, but not moral.'

THE WEAK NO TRUMP

The weak no trump is usually played to show a high-card-point range of 12 to 14 points, although in a few systems (notably Precision), the range is increased to 13 to 15 points. Like the strong no trump, this opening bid shows a balanced hand; because it is correspondingly weaker, the opening bidder often has one unstopped suit, possibly a small doubleton, and sometimes even two unguarded suits. The distributional patterns for a weak no trump opening are 4-3-3-3, 4-4-3-2 and 5-3-3-2 when the five card suit is a minor.

Although most of the players who use weak no trumps are probably adherents of the Kaplan-Sheinwold System, the bid can be used with Standard American methods. Playing the weak no trump, a minor-suit opening followed by a rebid of one no trump over responder's one-level bid shows a strong hand, 16-18 points.

The following are examples of weak no trump opening bids:

(a)	(b)	(c)
♠AK5	♠87	♠10962
♡643	♡AQ9	♡K3
◇QJ2	◇KQ743	◇AQ85
♣KJ106	♣Q104	♣K109

Most "weak no trumpers" use either non-forcing Stayman or Two-Way Stayman to locate a 4-4 major suit fit. Forcing Stayman is not practical politics with the weak no trump, as responder often wants to locate a playable part-score at the two level.

The responder to a weak no trump bids very much as the responder to a strong no trump – except that he needs about the equivalent of an additional ace to invite a game or drive to a game. Thus, opposite a 12-14 no trump, responder needs 12 points (11 with a good five or six card suit) to invite game; 13 or more points to force to game or to jump to three no trump or four of a major suit.

Proponents of the weak no trump claim these advantages for the method:

(1) An opening bid of one no trump is pre-emptive, since opponents, if they bid, have to come in at the two level. And, of course, it is much more likely that the opponents will want to bid when opener has a weak hand than a strong one.

(2) The weak no trump solves awkward rebidding problems on balanced minimum opening hands, since opener announces his strength within very narrow limits. This is especially true when the partnership also uses five card major suit opening bids.

(3) The method makes an opening one no trump a more useful tool, since minimum balanced hands are dealt much more frequently than strong ones. Since all no trump opening bids, whether strong or weak, are narrowly defined, constructive bidding is more accurate when it starts with a no trump opening.

THE WOODSON TWO-WAY NO TRUMP

William B. Woodson of Greensboro, North Carolina, an outstanding American player and theorist, uses the opening bid of one no trump to show *two* types of hands – one containing from 10 to 12 points; the other possessing from 16 to 18 points. As in other no trump bidding methods, Woodson gives no value to distributional values in counting points for opening bids of no trump.

This method has one great advantage – it is difficult, if not impossible, for the opponents to determine whether the opening no trump is strong (16 to 18 points) or weak (10 to 12 points) until it is too late or too dangerous for them to enter the bidding. Since the opponent, to overcall the one no trump opening, must enter the bidding at the two level, the opening no trump bidder actually can be making a mild pre-emptive opening bid with hands containing only 10 to 12 points, hands that might not qualify for opening bids of one of a suit.

Here are typical Woodson opening bids of one no trump:

(a)	(b)	(c)	(d)
♠ A86	♠ AQ7	♠ K543	♠ AK87
♡ K42	♡ K952	♡ Q72	♡ A10
◇ Q73	◇ KJ9	◇ A53	◇ KJ43
♣ Q952	♣ A76	♣ K42	♣ Q108

The responder then bids as follows:

RESPONSE	INDICATES
Pass	0 to 7 points and no five card suit.
Two clubs	8 or more high card points or seven points with a five card or longer suit. Opener *must* rebid.
Two diamonds Two hearts Two spades	Less than seven high card points and a five card or longer suit.
Two no trump	14 or 15 high card points with balanced distribution or 13 high card points with a five card establishable minor suit.

The rebids over a response of two clubs are:

Two diamonds or two hearts	10-12 points
Two spades or two no trump	16 points
Three clubs	17-18 points

Responder can use a bid of three diamonds on the second round to check for four-card major suits.

If one no trump is doubled, the one no trump bidder redoubles to show the weak no trump range of 10-12 and demand a rescue.

Responder can sign off with two spades, two hearts or two diamonds if he has no prospects of game opposite a strong no trump; and may head directly for game if he wishes to be in game opposite the weak variety.

Until the contrary is proved, the defenders should bid on the assumption that the no trump bid is weak. A double is in order with a full opening bid or better.

TRANSFER BIDS

That many hands would win additional tricks if the opening lead came from one side rather than the other, is apparent.

♠KJ1087 ♡KJ96 ◇K2 ♣K2	W
	S ♠AQ ♡AQ ◇AQJ10987 ♣AQ

Figure 224

Suppose, in *figure 224*, that South is the declarer at three no trump. The contract is iron-clad since West must make the opening lead. With the (probable) opening lead of a spade by West, South must win two spade tricks. After winning the first trick, the ace and queen of diamonds are led. On winning the king of diamonds, West will lead a second spade. South will win, cash his remaining diamonds and, with accurate play, be able to end-play West to make five no trump.

But suppose the same hand is played in the same contract but with a different cast. This time North will be the declarer and East will make the opening lead. And East, being blessed with four spades, also opens that suit.

The lead comes through, not up to, the ace-queen of spades. The spade queen is played, but the finesse loses to the king and a spade return knocks out the ace. West must regain the lead with the king of diamonds after which he will cash his remaining spades to defeat the contract one trick.

Result with South declarer and West on lead, 11 tricks for North-South.

Result with North declarer and East on lead, 8 tricks for North-South.

Three tricks and the contract pivoted on who played the hand and who led!

This situation will be present where one hand of the partnership is predominantly stronger than the other so that the opening lead should, from the declarer's point of view, come up to the strong hand. Obviously, where both partnership hands are of equal or near-equal strength, it generally will not matter from which side the opening lead is made.

More strength on one side than the other situation will be prevalent when a player bids one or more no trump. Since the strong one no trump bidder promises 16 to 18 high card points, it will be rare that his partner has anywhere near that amount of strength; make the opening bid two no trump with 22 to 24 points and the disparity between the partnership hands becomes greater.

Now let's go one step further. Suppose you have an extremely long heart suit and very little else. Your partner opens the bidding with one no trump. The best chance, perhaps the only chance, for game lies in playing the hand at four hearts. But to accomplish this, you'll have to bid hearts and your partner's hand – the strong hand that bid no trump – will become the dummy and the opening lead will be made through it, rather than up to it. Moreover, once placed on the table, the opponents are looking at the bulk of the high card strength of the partnership and can quickly determine any Achilles' heels – weak points open to attack – strong suits to be avoided.

The problem, then, when holding a long major suit opposite a no trump, is to compel one's partner to bid the very suit you normally would have bid, such as spades in *figure 225*.

	North	
	♠ QJ98643	
	♡ 43	
	◇ 62	
	♣ K8	
♠ A52	N	♠ 7
♡ K652	W E	♡ J1098
◇ AJ9		◇ 10753
♣ 762	S	♣ A1054
	♠ K10	
	♡ AQ7	
	◇ KQ84	
	♣ QJ93	

Figure 225

In *figure 225*, the bidding, with South dealer and vulnerability immaterial, would *ordinarily* be –

CASE A

S	W	N	E
1 NT	p	4♠	p
p	p		

East has a very normal opening of the jack of hearts. After taking the losing finesse to West's king, North cannot avoid the loss of four tricks - one in each suit - to go down one.

Three no trump played by South can be defeated by an even greater margin. Despite the fact that the opening lead of the fourth-best heart by West (against three no trump) will give the declarer two heart tricks, the defense simply refuses to win the first round of spades. The end result will be that declarer can win only six tricks – one spade, two hearts, one diamond and two clubs.

The only makable game contract is four spades *if played by South*. And that's where the transfer bid enters. The trick is to make the opening no trump bidder (South in *figure 225*) the declarer with his partner's long suit, spades, as trump. This, of course, requires South to know that his partner wants him to bid four spades or whatever the suit may be.

This is accomplished by what have become known as 'transfer', bids. The first of these to achieve popularity were (and are still) known as 'Texas' or the Texas Convention.

TEXAS

The Texas Convention is quite simple. In response to an *opening* bid of one or two no trump, a jump by partner to four diamonds *commands* the no trump bidder to rebid with the minimum number of the next ranking suit, viz., four hearts; a similar response of four hearts likewise commands a rebid of the next ranking suit, hence, four spades.

Let's examine *figure 225* again and instead of the bidding in Case A, substitute the bidding in Case B, using the Texas Convention.

CASE B

SOUTH	WEST	NORTH	EAST
One no trump	Pass	Four hearts	Pass
Four spades	Pass	Pass	Pass

The reader can see that a four spade contract if played by South is unbeatable since declarer, South, will be able to develop a club trick for the discard of a losing heart from the North hand before the defenders can drive a heart through the ace-queen.

SOUTH AFRICAN

The transfer variation bearing this esoteric name was designed to eliminate a major flaw in the Texas Convention, namely, human frailty - the average bridge-player's forgetfulness.

Too many times a player who has agreed to use Texas transfer bids has forgotten that he is using it. Since an ordinary response of four hearts to an opening bid of one no trump shows a desire to play the hand at four hearts, it is not unexpected that every now and then, a player being a creature of habit, will forget that he is using Texas and that he was supposed to bid 'four spades' over partner's response of four hearts. The end-result being, of course, that instead of making a game at four spades, the stunned and shocked responder finds himself playing a four heart contract with one or two little hearts or perhaps no hearts whatever in his hand for trump, rather than in the desired spade contract.

Since, in response to an opening bid of one or two no trump, bids of four clubs or four diamonds are virtually impossible, the South African transfer bid employs them as demanding major suit rebids. First, let's see why the responses of four clubs and four diamonds are not logical to opening no trump bids.

When after partner's opening bid of one or two no trump, the responder has an extremely long minor suit with probability of game, there are two logical final game contracts. These are, first, three no trump; secondly, five clubs or five diamonds. Of the two, the former is far preferable since the same number of tricks won in no trump will produce the greater trick score, of vital importance in tournament play. The alternative minor suit game in response to no trump would only be considered where the responder's hand is completely distributional with voids or singletons and an extremely long suit, usually eight cards or longer, not solid and lacking any high cards making it almost impossible of establishment or later usage. In other words, it's good for clubs or diamonds and nothing else. In these cases the responder would bid five clubs or five diamonds, never four!

Having demonstrated that a response of four clubs or four diamonds just 'can't be,' (except for those players who use four clubs as Gerber after a one or two no trump opening bid) it stands to reason that the response, when made, must carry some significant message. And it does. Using South African, it commands the no trump bidder to rebid with the suit two ranks higher.

SOUTH AFRICAN SUMMARIZED

TO OPENING BIDS OF ONE OR TWO NO TRUMP

A RESPONSE OF	COMMANDS OPENER TO BID
Four clubs	Four hearts
Four diamonds	Four spades

JACOBY TRANSFER BIDS

Oswald Jacoby of Dallas, Texas, one of America's outstanding players and analysts, not merely at bridge but at virtually all games, put his inventiveness to work and reasoned that if transfer bids were effective at the four level they would be just as effective at the level of two. The 'declarer advantage' of the strong no trump opening would be as useful in a contract of two spades as in four spades.

In addition, Jacoby thought, transfers would make it easier to bid both balanced hands and two-suited hands after partner's no trump. He was right. The 'declarer advantage' of the transfer principle turned out to be only a small – but important – fraction of the merits of Jacoby transfers.

Using Jacoby transfers, responder requests the one no trump opener to bid as follows:

RESPONSE	REQUESTS OPENER TO BID
Two clubs	A four card major (the Stayman convention)
Two diamonds	Two hearts
Two hearts	Two spades
Two spades	Three clubs
Two no trump	Three no trump with a maximum, pass with a minimum
Three clubs	Three diamonds

Note that the transfer takes place in the *suit* immediately below responder's real suit – the two no trump response retains its usual meaning of a game invitation in no trump.

How can opener tell whether responder is strong or weak? He can't – not yet. But all he has to do is follow instructions and complete the transfer, and partner will clarify his hand on the next round.

Using Jacoby transfers, responder would bid two hearts over one no trump on all of these hands:

(a)	(b)	(c)
♠Q109764	♠K109764	♠AQ853
♡3	♡3	♡Q4
◇J842	◇KJ42	◇1093
♣75	♣75	♣876

(d)	(e)	(f)
♠AQ853	♠KQ10876	♠AQ1072
♡Q4	♡2	♡2
◇K103	◇QJ32	◇AJ95
♣876	♣Q4	♣KJ3

With hand (a), responder just wants to reach the safest part-score contract – two spades. He bids two hearts, the Jacoby transfer, opener dutifully bids two spades, and responder passes. Now the strong no trumper's honors are protected against being led through.

With hand (b), responder wants to invite a game in spades. He transfers via two hearts, then raises partner to three spades, asking him to go to game with a maximum and a good spade fit.

Responder also wants to invite game with hand (c), but he doesn't know whether the deal is better played in spades or no trump. He transfers to two spades, then rebids two no trump, showing a balanced hand with eight to nine high card points. Opener can pass, sign off at three spades, or carry on to three no trump or four spades.

With hand (d), responder knows that the combined hands have enough high cards to be in game, but again there is a choice between spades and no trump. He transfers to spades via a two heart response, guaranteeing at least a five card suit, then jumps to three no trump at his next turn. Opener will pass with a doubleton spade or go on to four spades with three card or better trump support.

Once partner bids one no trump opposite hand (e), responder knows exactly where he wants to play the hand. Using Jacoby, he responds two hearts to make partner the declarer in spades, then jumps directly to four spades. The same lead advantage gained through Texas transfers has thus been achieved.

With hand (f), responder can tell that the partnership's assets put them in the slam zone – but how good the play for slam will be depends on fit. He describes his hand by transferring to spades and then bidding his diamond suit. A new suit bid by responder after transferring creates a game force, and, if one of the suits is a minor, frequently indicates slam interest. Opener will know whether to encourage or sign off based on his fit for responder's suits.

If responder holds a five card minor suit and a four card major suit, he can transfer to the minor suit and then bid his major if he is interested in a slam. Otherwise he attempts to locate a 4-4 major suit fit via an initial response of two clubs – the Stayman convention – then signs off in the appropriate game. Transfers to the minors are used mostly on two different types of hands: weak hands with long suits, where responder intends to pass the transfer; and hands with slam interest.

If the opponents interfere with an overcall or a double, all transfer signals are off, and bids revert to their natural meanings.

JACOBY OVER TWO NO TRUMP

The Jacoby Transfer is also used over an opening bid of two no trump, both to make the stronger hand declarer and to help in bidding two suited hands. Again, three clubs is Stayman, three diamonds transfers to three hearts, and three hearts transfers to three spades.

A Jacoby transfer response of three spades over two no trump shows a hand with slam interest in one or both minor suits. Opener signs off in three no trump with a bad hand for slam, or bids his better minor if he is interested, too.

THE FLINT CONVENTION

The Flint Convention, named after its originator Jeremy Flint of London, is another transfer convention. Purpose of the convention is to permit the partnership to stop in a part score contract after one member of the partnership has opened the bidding with two no trump.

Since an opening bid of two no trump promises 22 to 24 high card points (page 277) and 26 points will normally produce a game in no trump or a major suit, it would appear that the convention has its maximum application when the responder to an opening two no trump has less than two to four points plus a long suit for trumps. This combination is rare - possibly once of each several thousand hands - but nevertheless, a convention has been devised to cope with the miniscule number of hands on which the situation may arise and what is even more amazing (to this author) is that it has achieved a fair degree of popularity, particularly among those persons who enjoy listing each and every new convention as they appear.

Basically, the Flint convention, in order to sign off in a part score after partner's opening two no trump bid, requires responder to bid three diamonds. The opening bidder is automatically required to bid three hearts, regardless of the nature of his hand. In other words, the three heart rebid is artificial and *does not indicate presence of a heart suit.*

If the responder's suit is hearts, he can pass his partner's bid of three hearts; if responder's suit is either spades or clubs or diamonds, he will bid (over three hearts) either three spades or four clubs or four diamonds, respectively, any of which his partner must pass.

Additional variations permit the opening bidder after partner's Flint response of three diamonds to rebid three spades when holding an excellent heart suit and good high card controls to insure reaching game if partner's suit is hearts. Obviously, if partner's suit is spades, the latter will simply pass.

A response of three diamonds and a later bid of three no trump by the responder shows a real diamond suit, and is mildly slam invitational.

TRANSFERS SUMMARIZED

Of the transfer conventions, the Jacoby transfer bids have by far the widest usefulness and are highly recommended.

There are two points I would like to emphasize. The first is in relation to the use of the Gerber slam convention. This convention has its greatest usefulness after one's partner has opened with one no trump. Since a response of four clubs when using Gerber requests partner for aces, it cannot simultaneously be used as a command for opener to bid four hearts as in South African transfer bids. It must be one or the other!

Second, don't use or attempt to invent some form of transfer bid of your own, in an attempt to baffle unsuspecting opponents, such as with opening suit bids. Don't have a bidding system where an opening bid of one club shows a diamond suit, bids of one diamond show hearts, heart bids show spades, etc. These have all been tried and found wanting. They're illegal for tournament play, and they won't add to your popularity in your rubber bridge circle either.

DEFENSE AGAINST OPPONENT'S ONE NO TRUMP OPENING

LANDY

The Landy Convention, named after its inventor, the late Alvin Landy, former Executive Secretary of the American Contract Bridge League, was originally designed as defense against weak no trumps. Nowadays, however, many players use the convention over strong no trumps as well. It has the widest popularity of conventions of this type.

In the second position (immediately following the opening no trump bid) there are three basic calls in Landy. These are:

1 - Two clubs;

2 - Double;

3 - Two diamonds, hearts or spades.

The overcall of two clubs requests a major suit takeout by partner, if necessary, on a suit of only three cards. The two club bid promises at least four cards in each major and a strong hand, usually 13 to 15 points.

2 - Doubles are always for penalty, never informatory, and indicate the expectation of defeating one no trump. Hands can vary from those containing readily establishable suits and positive re-entries to those with 15 or more scattered high card points.

3 - Any suit bid such as an overcall of two diamonds, two hearts or two spades, is simply competitive - it shows the ability and desire to play the hand in that denomination and not sufficient strength or suit solidity for the alternative penalty double.

RESPONSES

Responses to the convention are usually natural and simple although a minority of players have devised responses with special meanings. *These responses apply only after the Landy bid of two clubs.*

1 - Three clubs (over partner's two clubs). Requests the Landy bidder to describe his hand by bidding the longer or stronger major suit. This bid is forcing.

2 - Three hearts or three spades. Strongly invitational but not absolutely forcing. May even be made with a three card suit since partner is known to have four or more cards of that suit.

3 - Two diamonds indicates a weak hand and a diamond suit, preferably of five or more cards.

4 - Two no trump and three diamonds are natural, strength-showing but not completely forcing.

5 - Pass. Indicates a weak hand with a long club suit.

NOTE - The Landy convention is not customarily used by the player in the fourth (re-opening) position.

CASE A

NORTH	EAST	SOUTH	WEST
One no trump	Pass	Pass	Two clubs*

*Indicating a club suit, primarily for lead-directing purposes.

DEFENSE TO LANDY

A double of two clubs by the opening bidder's partner shows strength and is similar in meaning to a redouble after right hand opponent's informatory double.

MODIFIED LANDY

A modification of the Landy convention that is popular in some areas of the country is a two diamond overcall of the opponent's one no trump as the takeout bid showing both major suits with about 13 to 15 points. The two club overcall, using this modification, shows a similar hand with both minor suits. With a weak hand and a preference for clubs, partner can simply pass the two club takeout bid.

ASTRO OVER NO TRUMP

by paul Allinger
roger STern
lawrence ROsler

Astro makes it possible to compete against a one no trump opening, holding 5 - 4 or longer in two suits. Suppose one no trump is opened on your right and you, not vulnerable, hold hand (a).

(a)
♠ x
♡ K 10 x x
◊ A J 10 x x
♣ A x x

Your hand is too good to pass, but if you bid diamonds you may miss the hearts. For a hand like this we use the Astro takeout of *two clubs*. This shows four or five *hearts* and length in a minor. Partner can show four card or longer support for your guaranteed major - the 'anchor suit' - at any level. He may show support at the two-level even with only three cards.

Lacking support for the anchor suit or a strong suit of his own to bid, partner does not try to guess your second suit. He simply makes the cheapest bid - in this case, two diamonds. This 'neutral response' asks you to clarify your hand; it does not promise more than two cards in that suit. With the above hand you would pass, for the neutral response has hit your long suit. if you had five hearts instead of the four you have already promised you could bid two hearts, and if your long suit were clubs you could bid three clubs.

(b)
♠ K J x x
♡ x x
◇ x
♣ A K J x x x

Here is another example: For hand (b) we use the Astro takeout of *two diamonds*. This shows four or five *spades* and length in a second suit (may be hearts). Over two diamonds the neutral response is two hearts.

Before using Astro you must plan your rebid over the neutral response. With the hand above you would bid three clubs; with five hearts you could pass; with five spades you could bid two spades.

Of course, using Astro you give up the natural overcalls of two of a minor, but this is little cost compared with the gain. With a long minor you can jump to three, making it difficult for the opponents to compete. With a two-suiter including a major you use Astro, and with both minors you can use the 'unusual' two no trump overcall.

Here is an Astro hand from a pair tournament:

(c) WEST	(d) EAST
♠ Q 3	♠ J 10 8 5 2
♡ A J 9 6 2	♡ 4
◇ A Q 10 5	◇ K 9 8
♣ 8 4	♣ J 9 6 3

CASE A

S	W	N	E
1 NT	2 ♣	Pass	2 ◇
Pass	2 ♡	Pass	2 ♠
Pass	Pass	Pass	

2 ♣: Astro, showing four or five hearts and a minor.

2 ◇: The neutral response. The spades are too weak to show at this point.

2 ♡: The planned rebid, showing five hearts.

2 ♠: East may not pass with a singleton heart - if this were adequate support West would simply have overcalled two

hearts rather than use Astro. East could now have bid two no trump (forcing) to demand West's second suit. Instead he bid two spades, hoping for a surprise fit but otherwise ready to play in West's minor.

Two spades was made for a top. At most other tables West passed one no trump, which South made. At some tables West overcalled two hearts, and went down when East passed. Not playing Astro, East could not tell that West had only five hearts.

AN ASTRO QUIZ

CASE B

OPPONENT	PARTNER	OPPONENT	YOU
One no trump	Two diamonds	Pass	?

(e)
♠ K x x
♡ J x x
◊ x x x
♣ K x x x

Answer - Bid two hearts, the neutral response, with (e). You have a bad hand and should try to get out cheaply. Partner may readily have four spades and five hearts; if he does not have five hearts, he will not pass.

(f)
♠ K x x
♡ x
◊ x x x
♣ K x x x x x

Answer - Bid two spades holding hand (f). You may not bid two hearts with a singleton and you should not bid three clubs holding adequate support for partner's spades.

(g)
♠ A Q x x
♡ A x x
◊ x x x x
♣ x x

Answer - Bid three spades with (g), inviting game. You have a proven eight or nine card fit.

(h)
♠ A Q x
♡ A x x
◊ x x x x x
♣ x x

Answer - Bid two no trump (a forcing 'cue bid') with (h). Holding three key cards you should invite game, but may not jump to three spades without four cards in the suit. Partner can bid up to four spades relying on you for *three card* support. With only a four card suit, he can bid his long suit at the three or four level.

CASE C

OPPONENT	YOU	OPPONENT	PARTNER
One no trump	Two clubs	Pass	Two diamonds

(i)
♠ x x
♡ A Q x x
◇ A K J x x x
♣ x

Answer - Bid three diamonds on (i). Game is possible, perhaps in no trump. If partner had responded 'two hearts', the correct bid would again be 'three diamonds'. It would be wrong to raise hearts, for partner knows *you* have four, and he might have only three. After bidding Astro you should not voluntarily bid or raise the anchor suit without five card length.

(j)
♠ K x x
♡ A J x x
◇
♣ A J 10 x x x

Answer - With (j), bid two spades. If you had four or five spades you would have used the two *diamond* takeout. As you can therefore have at most three spades, why not show them en route to bidding your minor? If partner does not fit spades he can bid two no trump, over which you will specify your minor.

SUMMARY: ASTRO OVER NO TRUMP

Over an opening one no trump bid (strong or weak), either directly or in the reopening position, two *clubs* shows four or five *hearts* and length in a minor; two *diamonds* shows four or five *spades* and length in a second suit (may be hearts). A response in the next suit is neutral.

RIPSTRA

J.G. Ripstra of Wichita, Kansas, devised the following methods to show a three-suited hand after an adverse no trump bid, particularly weak, by the opponent to the immediate right.

Basically, bidding one minor indicates extreme shortage in the other plus length in the bid minor and both majors.

(a)	(b)
♠ K Q 9 6	♠ A Q 4 3
♡ A J 8 6	♡ K 10 9 7
◇ 4	◇ K Q 10 6
♣ K J 9 8	♣ 4

With hand (a) to the left, the Ripstra bid over one no trump would be two clubs, thus denying diamonds; the two diamond bid with (b) denies clubs. The Ripstra bid promises at least four cards in both majors, but the bid minor suit may be only three cards in length.

BROZEL

Lucille Brown and Bernard Zeller invented this method of competing against an opponent's one no trump opening. A double, either immediately or in fourth seat, shows a one-suited hand. If the doubler's partner is strong, he passes; if he is weak and does not wish to defend against one no trump doubled, he bids two clubs. The doubler then bids his real suit, and partner passes.

All overcalls of one no trump show two suits, as follows:

Two clubs	–	clubs and hearts
Two diamonds	–	diamonds and hearts
Two hearts	–	hearts and spades
Two spades	–	spades and a minor
Two no trump	–	both minors

The Brozel convention is also used after opening bidder's partner has made a weak response to one no trump. A double again shows a one-suited hand; if doubler's partner does not wish to defend, he bids the next higher-ranking suit and passes doubler's bid. Simple overcalls of the weak response show two suits: diamonds = diamonds and hearts; hearts = hearts and spades; spades = spades and a minor. An overcall of two no trump is a weak three-suited takeout bid, and a cue-bid is a strong take-out, inviting game.

TWO BIDS

THE WEAK TWO BID

Unless you are the seventh son of a seventh son, you have, no doubt, discovered that the strong two bid, 24 points or more, occurs about as often as a solar eclipse. Yet, if you are like 95% of the bridge players, you use these bids, which means that you must reserve one entire zone of bidding – that of two of a suit – for hands that you rarely hold – not even once a session!

On the other hand, how often have you been dealt a good six-card suit but were too weak to open the bidding. Wouldn't it be splendid if you could show this type of hand with one bid?

Howard Schenken, one of the original Four Horsemen, the world's first great bridge team, and an outstanding American player, thought that an opening bid of two of a suit could be put to better use. Since the weak hand with a good suit came up far more often than the strong two-bid, he proposed that an opening bid of two diamonds, two hearts, or two spades should show this type of hand, while a two club opening bid could be reserved to describe a strong two bid *in any of the four suits*, or a strong balanced hand that could not be shown with a one or two no trump opening.

The strong two club bid will be discussed shortly. For the moment though, there are three things I'd like to point out about the weak two bid.

First, if you use weak twos, be sure that both your partner and your opponents know about it before the bidding begins on that particular hand, even before you look at your hand.

Second, a weak two bid shows a hand that is too weak for an opening bid of one. Since it is a pre-emptive bid, designed to make it difficult for the opponents (whose strength may be divided) to enter the bidding, this two bid is not forcing.

Third, you may open with a weak two only in diamonds, hearts and spades. Two clubs is a strong bid and is forcing.

With these facts in mind, let's see what you should have to open the bidding with a weak two.

REQUIREMENTS

There are three essential ingredients of a weak two bid – a good suit, the right distribution, and the right high-card strength.

Preferably, you should have a six-card suit that should be capable of producing at least four tricks, assuming normal distribution of the outstanding cards. For example, Q J 10 5 4 2 would be minimum. You expect to lose tricks to the ace and king, but that should be all. Five-card suits are not long enough to guarantee safety against adverse distribution, and with a seven-card or longer suit, you are probably worth a pre-emptive three or four bid.

The hand should not contain a good four-card (or longer) side suit, nor any four cards in an unbid major. In addition, you should never be void in a side suit. The reasons for these restrictions are obvious. With four-card support for some other suit, your partner could easily hold that suit, in which case the hand will almost certainly play better in that suit, rather than in your long suit. Similarly, with a void, your hand is far too potent offensively because partner might have a fit for either of your side suits, and thus he will be able to ruff his losers in your void suit in your hand. Ideally, your distribution should be 6-3-2-2 or 6-3-3-1, but 6-4-2-1 is permitted if your four-card suit is a weak minor.

Most players who employ weak two bids restrict the strength of the hand to six to 12 high-card points with most of the strength concentrated in the six-card suit. The hand should not contain two aces because a pre-emptive bid, which is what the two-bid is, is rarely this strong defensively. One of the advantages of weak two bids is that they permit you and your partner to find a sacrifice against the opponents' game contract; if you hold two aces, however, there is a good likelihood that the opponents may not be able to make a game, but your partner won't know this.

In my personal experience, the spread between six and 12 high card points, even with an experienced partnership, is too great for accurate bidding. I have seen expert players open the bidding with two hearts holding both of the following hands:

(a)	(b)
♠9	♠9
♡KJ10987	♡AKQ1086
◇Q432	◇J109
♣108	♣432

Both qualify as weak two bids. Hand (a) has six high card points; hand (b) has 10. But what a difference! Hand (b) contains two possible defensive tricks, hand (a) none. Hand (b) has a good chance of game if partner has the 'right' cards, while partner needs a powerhouse to produce game opposite hand (a).

Yet if both are opened with two hearts, partner must be clairvoyant to tell one from the other.

The most successful practitioners of weak two-bids voluntarily limit the range of their bids to a much closer margin, such as six to nine high card points or eight to 11 high card points, or six to 10 points not vulnerable and nine to 12 points vulnerable. Some add the additional qualification that their weak two-bids contain one or one and a half defensive tricks so that partner contemplating a penalty double of a possible opposing bid can be fairly certain that the opening bidder will take some tricks. These are matters of personal preference. What I would recommend though, is that players just beginning to use the weak two should apply the 'Rule of Two and Three' in deciding whether or not to open the bidding. That is, you should be within three tricks of your contract if you are not vulnerable, two tricks if you are vulnerable.

Now that you are familiar with the requirements for a weak two bid, what would you open in each of the following hands? If you do not open with a weak two, why?

(a)	(b)	(c)
♠KQJ965	♠108	♠J2
♡43	♡A	♡KJ10876
◇K82	◇QJ10987	◇KJ2
♣53	♣543	♣A6
(d)	(e)	(f)
♠J87432	♠KJ63	♠J43
♡A104	♡85	♡A3
◇K54	◇KQJ432	◇98
♣2	♣10	♣KQ10962

(a) Two spades. This is a classic two bid. you have a fine suit, the right distribution and less than opening bid strength.
(b) Two diamonds. True, you have a side four-card suit, but this does not necessarily bar you from making a weak two bid. Your hand is ideal in all other respects, and if you don't show your diamond suit now, you may never get another chance.
(c) Two hearts. You are close to the strength for a one bid. Yet your hand is so weak defensively it is better to make a 'heavy' weak two bid than risk a possible disaster after a one bid. (Partner might overbid or double the opponents into game.)
(d) Pass. The spade suit is simply not good enough for a weak two bid.
(e) Pass. Never open a weak two with a good four-card major on the side. If you do open two diamonds and your partner has something like five spades to the ace, it is very unlikely that you will ever locate your spade fit.

(f) Pass. This hand qualifies in all respects for a weak two bid in clubs, except for one thing. You can't make a weak two bid in clubs! Two clubs is always a strong bid.

RESPONSES TO WEAK TWO BIDS

After a weak opening two bid, the responder knows that his partner has fewer than 13 points. Otherwise, he'd have opened with a bid of one of a suit. Accordingly, if the responder lacks the equivalent of a sound opening bid, there will rarely be a play for the game.

A single raise by responder of partner's opening weak two bid, such as raising an opening two spade bid to three spades, is fully as pre-emptive in nature as the opening bid. With a strong hand and game probability after partner's opening weak two bid, the responder must jump to game at once. The direct jump to game may also be made on a weak hand with excellent support for partner's suit, such as hand (g) that follows. Pity the poor opponents who must now guess which hand responder has.

It goes without saying that whatever method of raising is selected by the reader, both partners should understand it. My personal preference is towards the all or nothing method, reserving the single raise as pre-emptive.

There are two schools of thought among players using weak opening two-bids as to which responses are forcing and which are not. When weak two-bids were first developed, any response short of game other than supporting opener's suit was forcing for one round. Thus if the opening bid (weak) was two hearts, a response of two spades, two no trump or three of a minor compelled the opening bidder to rebid at least once.

This permitted shenanigans by a sharp responder, who might attempt to steal a suit or contract from opponents he felt held that suit.

(g)
♠J864
♡3
♢A9654
♣1076

For example, let's say our sharp operator holds hand (g) to the left, hears his partner open the bidding with two spades. The next player passes. Since our responder knows the opening bidder hasn't four or more hearts, the opponents must have the heart suit. The probability is that the opponent to his left is about to bid hearts. Accordingly our sharp operator, over his partner's two spade bid, may very likely bid three hearts.

In recent years, some players have decided to use two no trump as the only forcing response over a weak two bid and treat suit responses as natural and non-forcing. Regardless of which method you adopt, you and your partner will have to decide what the weak two bidder is supposed to do when his partner responds two no trump. Among exponents of the weak two, the three most popular ideas of bidding over the two no trump response are the following:

FEATURES

By far the simplest and most widely accepted method is the use of a two no trump response to a weak two bid to request the weak two bidder to show some additional feature in his hand – an ace, king, or queen-jack. Opener simply rebids in the suit where the feature is located. Thus, in the sequence: opener, two hearts – responder, two no trump – opener, three diamonds, the opening bidder promises values in diamonds. If opener does not have a side feature, he rebids three of his suit, or three no trump if his suit is solid (A K Q 4 3 2 would be the minimum for a solid suit).

OGUST

Because 'features' rebids are not particularly accurate – responder never knows whether the weak two bidder is minimum or maximum for his bid regardless of whether he shows a feature or not – Harold Ogust of New York City, long time associate of Charles Goren and a great player in his own right, developed a structure of rebids over the two no trump response by which opener could show simultaneously a good or bad hand with a strong or weak suit. Opener rebids on the three level according to the following table:

OGUST REBIDS AFTER TWO NO TRUMP

Three clubs – poor hand, weak suit
Three diamonds – poor hand, strong suit
Three hearts – good hand, weak suit
Three spades – good hand, strong suit
Three no trump – solid suit

A good hand would be one at the top of the strength for a weak two, while a suit headed by three honors, including two of the top three (e.g., K Q 10 7 4 2), could be considered a strong suit. Note that opener's rebids have nothing to do with the suit he is bidding. They are merely a conventional means of telling partner the quality of the weak two bidder's hand and suit.

THE McCABE ADJUNCT

The McCabe adjunct, named after its originator, Joseph McCabe of Columbia, S.C., is a simple and useful convention designed to permit the partner of the weak two-bidder to set the final contract.

In other words, let's suppose, after an opening bid of two diamonds, the responder wants to play the hand at three clubs, or three hearts or three no trump or four spades or any contract whatever.

This can be accomplished by using the McCabe adjunct (to the weak two-bid). In order to set the final contract, the responder bids two no trump. The opener, regardless of the nature of his hand, is compelled to bid 'three clubs.' Whatever rebid is made by the responder is to be the final contract. Let's take a few examples.

OPENER		RESPONDER
Two diamonds		Two no trump
		(Pass
		(Three diamonds
Three clubs	----------------	(Three hearts or spades
		(Three no trump
		(Four hearts or spades, etc.

Opposite the opener's three club (forced) rebid are various possible responses. Each is intended to be the final contract. The opening bidder may not like it but, in the words of Tennyson,

"*Theirs not to reason why,*
Theirs but to do or die."

By using the McCabe adjunct, the responder exercises his prerogative of determining the final contract.

THE TWO CLUB OPENING BID

Back at the beginning of the section on weak two bids (page 652) I mentioned that the two club bid is used as a substitute strong two bid in any of the four suits, or to show a balanced hand that does not fall within the point range for a one or two no trump opening bid. Before discussing how to handle the two club opening, there are two differences between the two club bid and normal strong two bids that I'd like to point out.

First, two clubs is an *artificial* bid. It says nothing about the club suit, although opener might, coincidentally, have a real club suit. In essence, two clubs simply says, "Partner, I have a good hand. Bid something and then I will describe what I really have " The responder must bid over the two club opening, just as he must bid over a regular strong two-bid.

Secondly and equally important, the weakness response to the standard strong two bid is 'two no trump'; to the two club opening, the weakness response is 'two diamonds'. With a strong

TWO CLUBS TO SHOW A BALANCED HAND

The reader may have noticed that there are certain gaps in the no trump bidding structure.

OPENING BID REQUIREMENTS

One no trump	16 to 18 high card points
Two no trump	22 to 24 high card points
Three no trump	25 to 27 high card points

The gap occurs between 19 to 21 high card points. There is no bid to show hands in this bracket. Thus, if you open with a bid of one of suit and partner has four or five points, he may well pass and you could easily miss a game.

The two club bid allows you to show this in-between hand easily. You open two clubs, then over partner's response of two diamonds, rebid two no trump. Partner will then know that you have 19 to 21 high card points and a balanced hand and he may pass if he lacks sufficient values for game.

This structure of using a forcing two club opening bid to show balanced hands is so efficient, in fact, that many duplicate players have revised the no trump opening bid scale according to the following table:

One no trump	16 to 18 high card points
Two no trump	21 to 22 high card points
Three no trump	25 to 26 high card points
Two clubs, two no trump rebid	23 to 24 high card points
Two clubs, three no trump rebid	27 to 28 high card points

Hands of 19 or 20 points will probably not produce a game unless responder can respond to an opening bid of one of a suit, so these hands can be shown by a one bid, followed by a jump to two no trump.

TWO CLUBS TO SHOW A STRONG TWO BID

(a)
♠AKQ1087
♡4
◇AKQ2
♣A3

Obviously if you hold hand (a), you cannot open two spades since this would be a weak two bid. Therefore, you open two clubs, then rebid two spades over whatever response partner makes. Don't worry. Partner cannot pass your two spade rebid, just as he cannot pass if you opened two spades using strong two bids.

For the majority of players, a sequence such as, opener, two clubs – responder, two diamonds – opener, two spades, is forcing to game. That is to say, two clubs followed by a suit rebid is the exact equivalent to opening with a strong two bid in that suit. Even if partner has a 'bust', he must keep the bidding open until game is reached.

There is alternative method, however, that permits the partnership to stop below the game level after a two club opening bid, which I heartily recommend. This method is to play that responder must keep the bidding open until opener rebids his 'real' suit. For example, look at hand (b). You open two clubs and let's say that partner responds two diamonds (the negative response). You then bid two hearts and regardless of what partner rebids, your rebid is three hearts. This three heart bid is non-forcing; partner may pass if he is completely 'broke', but he should raise you to game with any values whatsoever. If you can make game in your own hand, you simply jump to game after you have shown your suit. This

(b)
♠A3
♡AKQ10953
◇KJ10
♣6

treatment can be extended to the minor suits as well. Thus in Case A

CASE A

SOUTH, YOU, OPENER	NORTH, PARTNER
Two clubs	Two diamonds
Three clubs	

North must bid again over three clubs, but if you subsequently rebid four clubs, he does not.

Using this method, a two club opening bid is forcing to two no trump, three of opener's major suit, or four of opener's minor suit. If you do not use this method, then a two club opening bid is forcing to two no trump, or to game.

Here are two typical examples of two club opening bids:

(c)	(d)
♠AQ10	♠5
♡K98	♡KQJ
◇A1096	◇AKQ1052
♣AK10	♣AKQ

Hand (c) is a balanced hand containing 20 high card points. Hand (d) is an unbalanced hand worth 26 points, 24 points in high cards and two points for distribution.

What would be your rebid if partner responds two diamonds, negative? Is your rebid forcing?

On hand (c), you would rebid two no trump, announcing a balanced hand of between 19 and 21 points. This bid is not forcing.

On hand (d), you would rebid three diamonds, which is forcing. If partner has an ace and some support for diamonds, you should be able to make a slam.

RESPONSES

You are using the artificial two-club opening bid as forcing to at least a contract of two no trump. Your partner has opened the bidding with two clubs and your right hand opponent passes. Let's see what your response would be with each of the following:

(e)	(f)	(g)	(h)
♠ Q87654	♠ Q8	♠ K2	♠ J
♡ 6	♡ A107	♡ A98765	♡ J109
◇ Q62	◇ Q1097	◇ 4	◇ AQJ987
♣ 1062	♣ 10743	♣ Q1087	♣ 432

(e) Two diamonds. You not only lack the seven points required to make a positive, strength-showing response exactly as to a strong two bid *(page 345)* but also lack the minimum of one king or one ace required for a positive response *(page 343)*. Over your partner's possible rebid of two hearts, expected from the fact that you have a singleton heart, or of two no trump, you should then show the spade suit.

(f) Two no trump. This response to the two club opening is strength-showing, indicating at least eight high card points, balanced or semi-balanced distribution and is the equivalent of a three no trump response to a strong opening two-bid, (*page 348*). Be sure you understand these differences.

A response of two no trump to a strong two bid is weak.

A response of two no trump to a two club opening shows strength.

A response of two diamonds to two clubs is weak and the equivalent of a two no trump response to the strong two bid.

(g) A response of two hearts is obvious. The suit is rebiddable and the hand, counting distribution, totals 12 points. If a fit can be found, slam is probable.

(h) Three diamonds, not two! With a *real* diamond suit and sufficient strength to make the positive response, you must jump the bidding one level. The minimum response of only two diamonds would be the negative response denying seven points and not indicating any suit in particular, much less diamonds.

RESPONDER'S REBIDS

In general, once opener has clarified what type of hand he has, responder will simply make a descriptive rebid of his own. For example, if the bidding has gone as in Case B

CASE B

SOUTH, OPENER	NORTH, RESPONDER
Two clubs	Two diamonds
Two hearts	

responder may raise hearts, bid a decent suit of his own, or rebid two no trump.

Similarly, if opener's rebid is two no trump, responder bids as he would over a two no trump opening bid, keeping in mind that opener's point range is 19 to 21 points, not 22 to 24. If the partnership is using the Stayman Convention (see page 598), three clubs would be Stayman, but only if responder's first bid was two diamonds, while three diamonds, three hearts and three spades would all be natural bids, offering opener a choice of games.

SPECIAL RESPONSES TO STRONG TWO BIDS

Standard methods of responding to strong forcing-to-game opening two-bids, are given on *pages* 599 through 609. Briefly, there are two possible standard responses to show weak hands, these are, first, a response of two no trump; secondly, an immediate jump to game in opener's suit as bidding four hearts in response to an opening bid of two hearts.

There are two other types of responses to strong two bids. These are, first, what are known as *ace-showing* responses; the other is termed *ranking suit.*

Let me make clear that if you elect to use one set of responses to strong two bids, you cannot simultaneously use another method.

ACE-SHOWING RESPONSES

The purpose of the ace-showing response to strong two bids is to inform the opening bidder immediately which, if any aces, are held by the responder. If two or more aces are held by the responder, the cheaper ace is shown first; the higher-ranking ace or aces later.

You hold hand (a) and sit North with the following bidding.

CASE A

(a)	SOUTH	WEST	NORTH	EAST
♠ A 4				
♡ 6 3 2	Two hearts	Pass	Two spades	Pass
◊ J 10 8 7	Three clubs	Pass	Three no trump	
♣ 10 5 4 2				

You are North, holding hand (b) in Case B.

CASE B

(b)	SOUTH	WEST	NORTH	EAST
♠ J 10 8 6 4				
♡ A 10	Two dia.	Pass	Two hearts	Pass
◊ 5 4	Two spades	Pass	Three clubs	Pass
♣ A 4 3 2	Three dia.	Pass	Three no tr.	Pass

Holding hand (c) with the bidding in Case C.

(c) CASE C

Hand	SOUTH	WEST	NORTH	EAST
♠ Q974				
♡ J8	Two hearts	Pass	Two no trump	
◇ 10863				
♣ Q43				

When the responder runs out of aces as in Cases A and B, his rebid is the minimum number of no trump. With an aceless hand as (c), the response to a strong two bid is two no trump.

If you are using two clubs as your only strong bid, ace-showing responses can be employed in exactly the same manner as over a natural strong two bid.

RANKING SUIT

Designed to permit the strong hand to be the declarer (and remain concealed) in the event that the responder is weak, some players employ what is known as ranking suit, also known as the Herbert (next suit) negative. The idea behind the method is similar to the reason for employing transfer bid *(pages 638-644)*.

When the responder has less than a positive response, viz., six points or less, instead of conventionally responding with the 'bust' response of two no trump, the response is in the next higher ranking suit.

(d) CASE D

Hand	SOUTH	WEST	NORTH	EAST
♠ J9				
♡ 108	Two hearts	Pass	Two spades	
◇ Q7643				
♣ J542				

Your response of two spades *does not* indicate presence of a biddable spade suit. Since it is the next suit higher in rank than partner's opening heart bid, it (the minimum spade response) simply denies holding the seven or more points required for any positive response.

(e) CASE E

Hand	SOUTH	WEST	NORTH	EAST
♠ AQ1097				
♡ J9	Two hearts	Pass	Three spades !	
◇ Q543				
♣ 85				

To make a positive (strength-showing) response as with hand (e) when the suit held happens to be the next higher ranking suit, the correct response is a single jump in the suit as in Case E.

Using ranking suit, the responder should not bid two no trump when lacking seven or more points. Thus when partner's opening bid happens to be two spades, the next ranking suit would be clubs. Hence, the 'bust' response in this event would be a bid of three clubs as in Case F.

CASE F

SOUTH	WEST	NORTH	EAST
Two spades	Pass	Three clubs	

The ranking suit principle can also be extended to auctions that start with an artificial, strong opening bid of two clubs, with two important differences. First, since responder can show weakness by bidding two diamonds, if you use the ranking suit idea, known as a *second negative*, it applies to responder's *second* bid and then it shows a completely worthless hand. Secondly, a rebid of two spades as in Case G

CASE G

SOUTH, OPENER	NORTH, RESPONDER
Two clubs	Two diamonds
Two hearts	Two spades

is not a second negative. It shows a real suit with some values. The ranking suit in this instance would be three clubs, which would also be the second negative had opener rebid two spades instead of two hearts.

To give you a better picture of the use of the second negative, suppose you picked up hand (f). Your partner opens two clubs and you, quite properly, bid two diamonds. However, your two diamond response hardly does justice to your hand! You are so weak you must warn partner not to bid a game or slam unless he can be sure of making it in his own hand. So your second bid, depending on what your partner bids, would be the next ranking suit as in Cases H, I, and J.

(f)
♠853
♡10742
♢J43
♣952

CASE H

SOUTH, OPENER	NORTH, YOU, RESPONDER
Two clubs	Two diamonds
Two spades	Three clubs

CASE I

SOUTH, OPENER	NORTH, YOU, RESPONDER
Two clubs	Two diamonds
Three clubs	Three diamonds

CASE J

SOUTH, OPENER	NORTH, YOU, RESPONDER
Two clubs	Two diamonds
Three diamonds	Three hearts

In all of these Cases, your rebid says nothing about the suit. It is a second negative saying, "Partner, you know I have a bad hand because I responded two diamonds to two clubs. But I'm warning you. I have a *really* bad hand." So warned, opener should end the auction with his next bid.

STEP RESPONSES TO STRONG, ARTIFICIAL TWO CLUB OPENING BIDS

This idea was borrowed from the Italians, and is used only over an artificial two club bid, never over a normal strong two bid. It's purpose is to determine immediately whether or not the partnership has sufficient aces and kings for slam, and to accomplish this goal, responder's bids are based not on points but on the number of 'controls' he has, counting a king as one control and an ace as two controls, according to the following scale:

OPENER	RESPONDER
Two clubs	Two diamonds—zero or one control (at most one king)
	Two hearts—two controls (one ace or two kings
	Two spades—three controls (an ace and a king)
	Two no trump—three controls (three kings)
	Three clubs—four controls
	Three diamonds—five or more controls

After the responder has made a control-showing bid, the auction proceeds just as it would using any other methods.

Admittedly, 'step' responses may put a strain on the memory of the average player, but there is no denying their accuracy.

(b)
♠AQ6
♡AQ9
◇AKQJ53
♣7

Suppose you open hand (b) two diamonds and your partner makes a 'step' response to two no trump, announcing three kings. You now know that you cannot make a grand slam, being off the ace of clubs, but you will almost certainly make a small slam in either diamonds or no trump since partner is known to hold the king of spades, king of hearts, and king of clubs. If you were not playing step responses and partner responder two no trump over two clubs, you wouldn't know whether you could make slam at all!

SPECIAL OPENING BIDS OF TWO DIAMONDS

THE FLANNERY TWO DIAMOND OPENING

William L. Flannery of Pittsburgh, Pennsylvania, recently devised an artificial bidding method of showing, by a two diamond opening bid, weak to medium hands (not strong enough to reverse) containing five hearts and four spades. Overall hand strength will contain 11-15 high card points. However, with 11 points, the hand must contain at least two and a half defensive tricks; a bad 16 points is considered as 15 points.

In responding to a two diamond opening, responder counts points for distribution as follows—with three cards of the trump (major suit) to be supported, distribution is counted normally—three points for a void, two for a singleton, one for a doubleton. When holding four trumps, the scale is increased to five, three and one, respectively.

With a weak hand and an equal number of hearts and spades, responder will bid 'two hearts' since he knows partner has more (five) hearts than spades. With more spades than hearts and a similarly weak hand, responder bids two spades. Both bids, either of two hearts or two spades, are signoffs although opener can bid a four card minor if holding a maximum hand with 5-4-4-0.

(a)	(b)
♠ 865	♠ 962
♡ 742	♡ 86
◇ K763	◇ J964
♣ Q43	♣ A876

After a two diamond opening, responder would bid 'two hearts' with (a); bid 'two spades' with (b).

A response of three hearts or three spades to the two diamond opening are limit raises in the bid suit showing 10-12 points including distribution, and invite opener to go on to game.

An immediate response of either three clubs or three diamonds asks the opening bidder to bid three no trump if he has ace or king doubleton, or queen third in that suit.

Responses of four clubs and four diamonds are South African transfer bids (page 641) indicating a desire to have the opening bidder as declarer in the major suit indicated.

A response of two no trump is forcing and requests the opening two diamond bid to describe his hand which he does in the following manner:

(a) A rebid of three hearts shows 4 - 5 - 2 - 2 and 11 - 13 points;

(b) A rebid of three no trump shows 4 - 5 - 2 - 2 with 14 - 15 points;

(c) Three clubs shows 4-5-1-3 and three diamonds 4-5-3-1. A rebid by responder of three hearts or three spades indicates 10 - 12 points and only three trumps. Opener may pass with a minimum.

(d) Four clubs shows 4-5-0-4 and four diamonds 4-5-4-0.

All responses over doubles are the same as though there had not been a double.

Reverses, viz, opening one heart and later rebidding two spades promise 17 - 18 points. Opening with one heart, later rebidding three spades promises 19 - 20 points.

Some of today's experts, who use a two diamond opening bid for other purposes, have adopted two hearts to show the Flannery-type hand. The responses and rebids over two hearts are exactly the same as over two diamonds.

THE ROMAN TWO DIAMOND BID

At the conclusion of the 1959 international matches won by Italy over teams representing the United States and Argentina, players throughout the world were amazed to see that on hand 94 of the match, the Italian (Roman) bidding methods included a bid that permitted the opening bidder to simultaneously disclose both his distribution and strength and subsequently reach a game contract, while their American counterparts, holding the same cards at the other table, made a normal opening bid and consequently missed the game.

The bid that made this possible is known as the Roman two diamond bid. Summarized, an opening bid of two diamonds shows a three-suited hand with either 5-4-4-0 or 4-4-4-1 distribution and 17 points or more. It is forcing on responder for at least one round.

RESPONSES

Two no trump is a game try with seven to nine or more points.

Any suit response, as two hearts or two spades or three clubs is a signoff and shows less than seven points. In responding with a weak hand, the responder will bid his cheaper or cheapest suit of four or more cards, perhaps only three cards, even though it may be shorter than a longer suit which would require being shown at a higher level.

REBIDS BY OPENER

After a two no trump response, the opener now bids his void or singleton! His partner now knows that there are at least four cards present in each of the remaining three suits.

Should responder bid a suit, thus showing a weak hand, the opener with a minimum and four cards of partner's suit may pass; with a maximum, raise partner's suit. Lacking support for partner's suit, opener will then bid the suit immediately higher in rank than partner's response and the next bid by partner places the final contract.

To show how efficiently the two diamond bid works, here's hand 94 from the 1959 matches. East dealer, neither side vulnerable.

When the Italian pair held the North-South cards, the bidding was:

EAST	SOUTH	WEST	NORTH
Pass	Pass	Pass	Two diamonds
Pass	Two spades	Pass	Four spades
Pass	Pass	Pass	

WEST		EAST
	♠ A J 10 8 ♡ K 8 7 6 2 ◊ A K Q 5 ♣ void	
♠ K Q 7 ♡ A 10 9 4 ◊ 9 4 2 ♣ 10 7 3	N W E S	♠ 6 3 ♡ Q J 5 3 ◊ J 10 6 ♣ A K 9 4
	♠ 9 5 4 2 ♡ void ◊ 8 7 3 ♣ Q J 8 6 5 2	

Figure 226

West opened the diamond deuce, dummy winning. Declarer trumped four hearts in his hand and three clubs in the dummy. That made eight tricks. Dummy's two remaining high diamonds made tricks nine and 10 with the ace of spades being trick 11.

When the United States held the North South cards, North made the normal opening bid of one heart. Everybody passed and South went down one. With an apparently misfit hand, South could scarcely be blamed for passing his partner's opening bid of one heart.

The difference between success and failure was the Roman two diamond bid.

RAISES OF PARTNER'S SUIT

LIMIT RAISES

While in standard bidding a double raise in opener's major suit, viz., as opener, one spade - responder - three spades, is forcing to game and promises 13 - 16 total points in the responder's hand (page 63) certain players prefer to use the bid as invitational and non-forcing, promising 10 to 12 points in the responder's hand. A typical hand for responder is shown as (a). The accurate description of responder's hand accomplishes a treble purpose, to wit, it gives the bidder maximum pre-emptive value against the opponents; secondly, it permits the opening bidder to pass and not contract for an unmakable game when the total point count between the combined hands indicates less than the 26 points ordinarily needed to produce a games; and lastly, it serves to describe those in-between hands, hands just a little too good for a single raise of partner's suit and not quite strong enough for the forcing method of the double raise promising 13 to 16 points. In other words, were there such a bid, the limit raise describes hands worth a raise to two and a half hearts, or spades, or whatever suit partner may have opened.

(a)
♠4
♡K1086
◇Q1096
♣K932

CASE A

North	South
One heart	Three hearts

Limit raises are best employed on hands where responder, with four or more trumps for partner, has no good side suit of his own. If responder has 10 to 12 points concentrated in a side suit plus partner's suit, he will do better to bid his own suit first and then support partner.

ARTIFICIAL FORCING RAISES

When limit jump raises are agreed upon, many players also agree to play one or more substitutes for the normal forcing raise, showing 13 to 16 points in support. The most popular artificial raises are the jump to three no trump, the Swiss Convention, the Jacoby Two No Trump Convention, and splinter bids.

THREE NO TRUMP AS A FORCING RAISE

The majority of American players who play that a jump raise of opener's suit is invitational, rather than forcing to game, use an immediate jump to three no trump over a major suit opening to show four card trump support and 13 to 16 points. (With an even better hand, responder will jump shift.) Opener signs off with a minimum hand by bidding four of his major – he should not worry about rebidding a four card suit, since responder guarantees at least four trumps. Opener may not pass, since the major suit has definitely been agreed upon. If opener bids anything other than four of the trump suit, he is indicating a better-than-minimum opening bid (16 points or more) and an interest in slam.

The jump to three no trump over a minor suit opening retains its standard meaning, 16-17 points and a balanced hand. If limit jump raises in the minor suits are played, responder indicates that he has a forcing raise by first bidding a side suit and then jumping in opener's minor.

If the opponents overcall, the jump to three no trump also retains its standard meaning – 16 to 17 points, with the enemy suit stopped at least twice. Responder could indicate a game forcing raise of opener's suit by cue-bidding the opponent's suit first, then supporting partner.

JACOBY TWO NO TRUMP RESPONSE

Oswald Jacoby, the inventive Texan, developed a substitute game forcing major-suit raise that permits opener to show his pattern and strength below the game level. An immediate jump to two no trump by responder shows a four-card or better trump holding and at least 13 points (there is no upper limit on responder's strength). Opener rebids as follows:

HOLDING A	OPENER'S REBIDS
singleton	– three of the singleton suit
void	– four of the void suit (if opener has a spade void and a dead minimum hand, he may choose to bid only three spades to stay below the game level)
minimum balanced hand	– jump to four of agreed suit
balanced hand with extra values (14-15 points)	– three no trump
good hand with no singleton	– three of agreed suit

Responder, if he too has extra values, takes it from there.

THE SWISS CONVENTION

A recently introduced adjunct to limit raises is known as the Swiss Convention. In this method, a jump from one to three of partner's suit after partner has opened with a major promises 10 to 12 points in responder's hand, excellent trump support and is invitational but non-forcing.

Rather than employ an artificial response of three no trump to indicate the conventional forcing-to-game double raise with 13 to 16 points, the Swiss Convention employs artificial responses of either four clubs or four diamonds to promise 13 to 15 high card points and good trump support for partner's suit. The four club or four diamond (Swiss) response promises a relatively balanced hand, usually 4-3-3-3 or 4-4-3-2 or possibly 5-3-3-2 since with a side suit of five or more cards and 13 to 15 high card points, it would be preferable to first bid the side suit, then support partner's suit on a later round.

Basically, the Swiss Convention is as follows. To partner's opening bid of a major:

(1) A response of four diamonds promises three aces or two aces and the trump king in responder's hand along with good trump support.

(2) A response of four clubs shows 13 to 15 points in high cards, in addition to good supporting trumps (four or more) for partner's suit, but fewer than three aces, or two aces and the trump king.

There are alternative interpretations of the Swiss four clubs and four diamond bids. For example, some Swiss practitioners use four clubs to show good controls, while four diamonds shows good trumps. This is a matter of individual preference.

SPLINTER BIDS

Like the Swiss Convention, a 'splinter bid' is a double jump (two more than a minimum call) over the opening bid to show four-card trump support and a hand worth a raise to game. The resemblance ands right there. Swiss is always used to show a balanced hand; a splinter bid *guarantees* a singleton or void. In Swiss, the four club and four diamond bids show nothing at all about the suit – they are strictly artificial – while a splinter bid shows shortness in the bid suit. Obviously, one cannot play Swiss and 'splinter' at the same time.

Using splinter bids, opener bids one spade. What should responder bid holding (a) and (b)?

(a)	(b)
♠KQ54	♠KQ54
♡AJ9	♡Q83
♢4	♢5
♣K10543	♣K10543
Four diamonds	Two clubs

Hand (a) qualifies as a splinter bid of four diamonds. Responder is strong enough to force to game, and he will be very happy to get to slam if opener has a better-than-minimum hand that fits well, i.e., contains no wasted values in diamonds.

Hand (b) contains some of the ingredients for a splinter bid – excellent trump support and a singleton. However, (b) is nowhere near strong enough in top cards to make a splinter bid, even though there will probably be a good play for four spades if partner fits reasonably well. Responder should bid two clubs, showing his suit, then raise spades over opener's rebid. This is more descriptive than an immediate limit jump raise to three spades, even if the partnership is using limit raises.

Most partnerships who have adopted splinter bids use them directly only over major suit opening bids, but they can be used in response to minor suits as well. The partnership need not employ limit raises to also use splinter bids. If forcing jump raises are retained, then: opener – one heart, responder – three hearts, can be used to show a balanced hand with 13 to 16 points and heart support; the splinter bid raise would be used with unbalanced hands.

SPLINTER BIDS LATER IN THE AUCTION

Double jumps to show a singleton or a void need not be restricted to responder's first bid. They can be used later in the auction, by either opener or responder, to indicate good trump support for the last bid suit and a singleton in the suit jumped in.

In the following auctions, the last bid is a splinter bid (if the partners have agreed to use them).

CASE A

Opener	Responder	
One diamond	One heart	
Three spades		Heart support, singleton spade, strong hand

CASE B

Opener	Responder	
One spade	Two clubs	
Four diamonds		Club support, singleton diamond, strong hand

CASE C

Opener	Responder	
One spade	Two clubs	
Two hearts	Four diamonds	Heart support, singleton diamond, strong hand

FRAGMENT BIDS

Splinter bids are a recent outgrowth of a device to show hand patterns that was invented some years ago by Monroe Ingberman of New Paltz, N. Y., formerly of Chicago. The Ingberman method is called the fragment bid. Whereas the splinter bid shows a singleton or void in the double jump suit, the fragment bid shows a singleton or void in the unbid suit. Splinter bids are often used by responder at his first turn to bid; the fragment bid, by its very nature, cannot be employed until the second round of the auction.

Both of these devices are most useful in reaching slams with minimum high cards, often because one partner holds worthless cards in some suit opposite his partner's singleton. Of late, splinter bids, no doubt because of their relative simplicity, have overtaken fragment bids in the popularity stakes, but either treatment is sound.

Using fragment bids, a *double* jump in a new suit on the *second* round of bidding shows:

(a) An excellent supporting fit for the *last* suit bid by partner;

(b) Two or three cards (maximum) in the fragment suit (inwhich the double jump is made).

(c) A void or singleton in the fourth suit.

First, let's review the difference between a single jump and a double jump.

CASE A

NORTH	EAST	SOUTH	WEST
One diamond	Pass	One heart	Pass
One spade	Pass	Four clubs	

Your four club bid is a double jump since a bid of three clubs would have been a single jump, viz., one more than necessary. A rebid of two clubs would have been a minimum rebid.

Let's illustrate this again, assuming the opponents do not enter the bidding.

CASE B

PARTNER, SOUTH	YOU, NORTH
One club	One diamond
One heart	One spade* Two spades** Three spades***

*The rebid of one spade is normal one over one bidding, showing four or more spades and compelling opener to rebid at least once more if you, North, have not previously passed.

**A two spade rebid by you is forcing to game. The partnership must continue bidding until at least a game contract is reached. There are no inferences relative to distribution.

***The fragment bid since it is a double jump, viz., from one heart to *three* spades. A heart fit is indicated with two or three spades (maximum) and a singleton or void in clubs.

Typical bidding sequences would be:

CASE C		CASE D		CASE E	
NORTH	SOUTH	NORTH	SOUTH	NORTH	SOUTH
1 dia.	1 ht.	1 cl.	1 ht.	1 cl.	1 ht.
3 sp.		4 dia.		1 sp.	4 cl.

Case C-North has shown a maximum of three spades, a void or singleton club and good heart support.

Case D-The four diamond bid sets hearts as trumps, promises a maximum of three diamonds plus a singleton or void spade suit.

Case E-The four club bid indicates a doubleton or tripleton club holding and a void or singleton diamond.

The reader will have noticed that in all cases listed the fragment bid set the last suit bid by the partnership as the agreed trump suit. This is the usual practice.

However, there is a possible variation permitting the fragment bid to set as the agreed trump suit the *first* suit bid by the partner when the agreed (first) suit bid was a major and the second suit a minor.

CASE F

NORTH	SOUTH
One heart	One spade
Two clubs	Four diamonds

This latter variation is not standard and should not be employed until complete familiarity has been achieved in conventional use of the fragment bid, viz., that a double jump on the second round of bidding sets the last suit as trump with the standard meanings of doubleton or tripleton in the bid suit and a void or singleton in the fourth suit.

THE TRUSCOTT CONVENTION

Originated by Alan F. Truscott, internationally known player and author, formerly of England and now of New York City where he is the bridge-editor of *The New York Times*, this convention is designed to enable a partnership to differentiate between two types of hands when bidding over an opponent's takeout double.

CASE A

NORTH	EAST	SOUTH	WEST
One heart	Double	Three hearts	

(a)
♠ 4
♡ KJ86
◊ Q963
♣ Q1098

(b)
♠ 2
♡ KJ86
◊ AQ976
♣ J42

Conventially, any raise of partner's suit over an opponent's takeout double is intended to be pre-emptive and make it difficult or impossible for the doubler's partner to enter the bidding.Further examples are contained on pages 470 to 472 of this text.

However, there will be situations where, after one's partner has opened the bidding and the right hand opponent has doubled for takeout, that a player has the requirements for a legitimate double raise, viz., 13-16 points and four or more trumps including at least the jack. Since a jump to three or four hearts with hand (b) would be pre-emptive, responder jumps to two no trump to show a legitimate double raise. In other words, holding hand (b) and using Truscott, the bidding would resemble that of Case B.

CASE B

NORTH	EAST	SOUTH	WEST
One heart	Double	Two no trump	

The opening bidder *must* then rebid. A new suit bid is a cue bid, trying for slam, while a repeat of opener's suit is a signoff. Under almost no circumstances should he raise the no trump since the latter is purely artificial.

Advantage of the Truscott method over the conventional redouble with 10 points or more is that the latter permits the opponents to enter the bidding cheaply and find a possible cheap 'save'. When the responder has a strong, legitimate double raise lacking defensive values against a possible adverse major suit contract, the Truscott convention serves the double purpose of describing the hand and making it difficult for the opponents to enter the bidding. Using Truscott, the jump raise of partner's suit over the double retains its pre-emptive meaning.

TWO NO TRUMP TO SHOW LIMIT RAISE

When Alan Truscott made the trans-Atlantic journey from London to New York, he introduced the Truscott convention here. It caught on, especially in the East, but became somewhat Americanized. As generally used today, the jump to two no trump over the opponent's takeout double indicates not a game forcing raise of 13 to 16 points, but a limit raise of partner's suit – that is, about 10 to 12 points and good trump support.

CASE C

NORTH	EAST	SOUTH	WEST
One heart	Double	Two no trump	

(c)
♠ 102
♡ AQ94
◇ KJ76
♣ 982

South, holding hand (c) has enough to warrant an invitation to game in hearts, although he is not strong enough to force to game opposite a minimum opening bid. Since a jump to three hearts would be pre-emptive, he cannot make this jump. Rather than redouble and let West enter the bidding at a low level, South shows his strength and heart support with a jump to two no trump. North then rebids three hearts with a minimum hand, on which he must decline the invitation, and four hearts with anything extra. He must not pass two no trump – South could be very unbalanced, and a firm trump holding in hearts is assured.

INVERTED MINOR SUIT RAISES

Minor suits are the step-children of contract bridge. Since a minor suit game requires that declarer take 11 tricks, compared to only 10 in a major suit and a mere nine in no trump, clubs and diamonds are often shunted aside in the bidding. To allow for more thorough exploration of hands where opener starts the proceedings with one club or one diamond, a few modern players (mostly disciples of the Kaplan-Sheinwold school) use their minor suit raises 'backwards' or 'inverted.' That is, a simple raise of one club to two clubs, or one diamond to two diamonds, is strong and forcing; a jump raise to three is pre-emptive, made on a weak hand with little hope of game.

CASE A

Opener	Responder
One diamond	Two diamonds

(a)
♠A2
♡A103
◇KQ1086
♣842

Responder, with hand (a) has a very powerful hand opposite his partner's one diamond opening bid. Yet, using ordinary methods, there is no really satisfactory bid on the hand. With clubs unstopped, a jump to two no trump is ill-advised. A jump to three diamonds (forcing) takes care of the problems on this round, but should responder bid again if opener rebids three no trump? If he passes, a diamond slam may be missed; if he bids again, the partnership may get too high.

The inverted strong raise to two diamonds, guaranteeing at least 10 points, keeps the bidding low and allows for exploration of the best contract.

CASE B

Opener	Responder
One diamond	Three diamonds

(b)
♠9
♡Q43
◇K109852
♣J86

With hand (b), responder's first desire is to keep the opponents out of the bidding, hoping that the enemy will not find their spade fit. It is not unlikely that the opponents can even make a game. In order to make it as difficult as possible for them to bid, responder makes the pre-emptive raise to three diamonds. Now left-hand opponent may not be strong enough to enter the bidding at the three level.

GAME TRIES

When opener's one heart or one spade bid is raised to two hearts or two spades by responder, opener, with 16 to 19 points, knows that his side has a good chance for game if partner has near the top of his six to 10 point range. Sometimes the play for four hearts or four spades (or possibly three no trump) will depend on how well the two hands fit, rather than solely on their combined high card count.

Accordingly, after the single raise of a major, opener will often rebid to invite game.

POWER RAISES

CASE A		CASE B	
Opener	Responder	Opener	Responder
One spade	Two spades	One spade	Two spades
Three spades		Two no trump	

(a)
♠KQ9743
♡A4
◇AQ3
♣Q10

With hand (a), opener wants to know whether partner has made a weak raise with only six or seven points, or whether his two spade bid was based on more substantial values. To find out, he rebids three spades. Partner will pass with a minimum, carry on to four spades with a little extra.

(b)
♠AQ1032
♡K94
◇KJ
♣KQ4

With hand (b), opener is also interested in game if responder is maximum for his two spade raise. However, since opener has a balanced hand with stoppers in all suits, nine tricks may be easier than 10. Opener's rebid of two no trump asks responder to evaluate his hand, and give responder a choice of four actions:

(1) With a minimum and a balanced hand – only three spades and no ruffing values – he passes two no trump.

(2) With a minimum and a distributional hand – four trumps and a short suit that can be ruffed in dummy – he signs off at three spades.

(3) With a maximum balanced hand (8-10 points) he raises to three no trump.

(4) With a maximum distributional hand, he jumps to four spades.

LONG SUIT GAME TRIES

Often opener has a better-than-minimum opening bid with a weakish holding in a side suit. After partner's single raise of his major suit opening, he can tell that game will be a good bet if partner has values or shortness in his side suit but not otherwise, even if responder is at the top of his single raise. He asks partner's opinion about game prospects by bidding a new suit at the minimum level.

CASE C

(c)		
♠AQJ107	Opener	Responder
♡9	One spade	Two spades
◇Q983	Three diamonds	
♣AQ5		

Three diamonds asks responder to evaluate his hand in terms of his diamond holding. Now let's look at some possible hands for responder:

(d)	(e)	(f)
♠K843	♠K843	♠K843
♡AJ7	♡8765	♡A876
◇752	◇KJ7	◇7
♣J84	♣J8	♣J842

With hand (d), responder would automatically have bid four spades had opener tried for game with three spades or two no trump. However, once opener indicates that he needs help in diamonds, responder's holding of three small cards in that suit becomes a liability. He signs off by bidding three spades, warning opener that he does not like his diamond holding at all.

Diamonds are the best thing about responder's holding in hand (e). Even though he is slightly weaker in high cards than in hand (d), responder jumps cheerfully to four spades, knowing that his king-jack of diamonds are pure gold.

Had opener bid one diamond to start the auction on hand (f), responder would have had terrible support for partner. But the opening bid was one spade, and that will be trump. Opener will be able to ruff his diamonds in dummy, so responder accepts the game invitation by jumping to four spades.

Remember that after a major suit opening bid has been raised, any new suit bid by opener is forcing. Responder may not pass.

SHORT SUIT GAME TRIES

Long suit game tries are standard operating procedure for most expert American bidders. But there are some who have carried further the principle of looking for fitting games after the single raise of the major suit opening bid, with 'short suit' game tries. In this method, opener's rebid of a new suit over partner's single major suit raise shows shortness, a singleton or void in the bid suit. The principle was first presented as part of the Kaplan-Sheinwold System, but it can be adopted by standard bidders who use five card major openings.

Here is how short suit game tries work. If opener has a balanced hand with 17 to 19 points, he invites partner to go on to game by rebidding three spades or two no trump. These game tries are just the same as in standard methods. But if opener is very distributional, with a hand including a singleton or void, and he is strong enough to rebid, he asks responder's opinion by bidding that short suit.

(g)
♠AQ1083
♡KJ4
◇AJ87
♣6

CASE D

Opener	Responder
One spade	Two spades
Three clubs	

Three clubs is a short suit game try. Let's give responder two very similar hands.

(h)	(i)
♠KJ7	♠KJ7
♡10932	♡10932
◇6432	◇KQ
♣KQ	♣6432

Hand (h) started out as a near-maximum raise of one spade to two spades. But its market value falls sharply when partner announces that he has a singleton or void in clubs. Instead of having nine points in support, it is now down to only four working points. Responder signs off at three spades, hoping that the partnership is not overboard. Look at the difference with hand (i). Responder had never figured that his four small clubs were worth anything—and now he knows that they are facing a singleton. His king-queen of diamonds must be useful to partner, so he jumps to four spades.

Proponents of short suit game tries present in their behalf that when opener has a singleton, responder's values in either side suit are probably valuable. Long suit tries remain greatly more popular, however, probably for two reasons (1) short-suit tries distort the bidding when opener has a real two suiter; (2) the short suit try may enable the opponents to find a profitable save against the game.

TWO WAY GAME TRIES

Robert Ewen of New York City, the author of an excellent book, "Opening Leads," has invented a method that permits the use of both long suit and short suit game tries simultaneously, after a major suit opening bid and single raise. General strength game tries are made by bidding one spade – two spades – three spades, or one heart – two hearts – three hearts.

When hearts are the agreed trump suit, opener makes a short suit game try by rebidding: two no trump (spade shortness), three clubs (club shortness) or three diamonds (diamond shortness). A rebid of two spades by opener forces responder to bid two no trump. Then responder makes a long suit game try in clubs or diamonds by bidding three of his suit, or a long suit try in spades by bidding three hearts.

When spades have been agreed as trump, opener's rebids of three clubs, three diamonds or three hearts are short suit tries in the respective suits. To make a long suit game try, opener rebids two no trump, which forces responder to bid three clubs. Opener then rebids three diamonds (long suit try in diamonds), three hearts (long suit try in hearts), or three spades (long suit try in clubs).

Responder then evaluates his hand as described above under long suit and short suit tries, and acts accordingly.

This method of trying for game is very accurate, but it is also very complicated, and is recommended only for the most experienced partnerships.

DRURY CONVENTION

There is a modern tendency to open 'light' in third and even fourth seat, especially when playing duplicate bridge. Couple this trend with the fact that bids by a passed hand are not forcing on opener, so that it is hard for a responder to make exploratory bids once he has passed, and you see the reason for the popularity of the Drury Convention, invented by the late Douglas A. Drury of Canada, later of San Francisco.

Using Drury, a response of two clubs by a passed hand to partner's major suit opening asks, 'Partner, do you have the full values for an opening bid, since I have a pretty good hand and would like to know whether or not to explore for game? Or have you a sub-minimum opening bid, in which case we should find our best part score at the lowest possible level?' Opener rebids two diamonds to show a sub-minimum opening bid (he cannot pass two clubs); any other bid promises a full opening bid and is natural.

The two club bidder – who promises to bid again after partner's two diamond response – should have at least 10 points, but he need not have any fit for opener. If responder has a real club suit, he first bids two clubs and then three clubs over whatever opener rebids. If he bids a new suit on the two level after the two diamond response, it may be only four cards long.

SLAM CONVENTIONS

Blackwood – four no trump asking for aces – is the simplest of all slam conventions, and the most popular. Blackwood, and its offspring, Gerber, have given rise to several modifications. The San Francisco variation of Blackwood is given in the text (see page 513), for it is widely used on the West Coast; others are outlined here, as well as a modernized version of the Grand Slam Force (see Culbertson Five No Trump convention, page 514).

ROMAN BLACKWOOD

One Italian method that caught on quickly after it was introduced in the United States is Roman Blackwood. This is a modification of the Blackwood convention that usually permits the four no trump bidder to determine which aces the partnership holds, as well as the total number of aces. Roman Blackwood is used whenever Blackwood would be employed. The one disadvantage of the method is that when hearts are the agreed trump suit, the partnership may find itself overboard when two aces are missing.

RESPONDING TO FOUR NO TRUMP (ROMAN BLACKWOOD)

RESPONSE	
Five clubs	– No aces or three aces
Five diamonds	– One ace or four aces
Five hearts	– Two aces of the same color or two major aces or two minor aces
Five spades	– Two aces of different colors – this will always work out to one major and one minor ace – specifically, clubs and hearts or spades and diamonds.

To ask for kings, a player first bids four no trump and after his partner's response, rebids with five no trump. The king-showing responses are identical to those listed above with the difference that the responses are made at the six level.

KEY CARD BLACKWOOD

In this Blackwood variation, the king of the agreed trump suit is counted as an ace – thus there are 'five aces' in the deck.

RESPONDING TO FOUR NO TRUMP (KEY CARD BLACKWOOD)

RESPONSE	SHOWS
Five clubs	No aces or four aces
Five diamonds	One ace or five aces
Five hearts	Two aces
Five spades	Three aces

To ask for kings, the Blackwooder bids five no trump in the usual manner. Responses are the same as in regular Blackwood, except that responder does not show the king of trumps.

This is a useful convention in many auctions in which the agreed trump suit is absolutely clear to both partners – one would not want to be in slam off an ace and the king of trumps. However, there are many slam sequences in which the agreed trump suit is not 100 per cent obvious, in which case there may be a misunderstanding when using Key Card Blackwood. Unfortunately, it's not possible to stop in the middle of bidding a hand and say, "Partner, let's play regular Blackwood on this deal." You have to make up your mind beforehand.

BLACKWOOD OVER INTERFERENCE: DOPI AND DEPO

The standard method of responding to four no trump when right hand opponent puts in a nuisance bid is to double for penalties and make a forcing pass when in doubt as to whether your side has a slam; if the partner of the four no trump bidder feels that slam is very likely and will be more profitable than doubling the opponents, he can show his aces by bidding the next higher suit to show one ace, skipping one suit to show two aces, etc. (pages 510-511).

With increased competitive bidding the latest fashion, two different methods of showing aces when the opponents bid over four no trump have been devised. The first of these is DOPI, an acronym for Double = zero (o) Pass = One (1). Responder doubles with no ace, passes (a forcing pass, of course) with one ace, bids the cheapest possible suit with two aces , and bids the next highest-ranking denomination to show two aces.

CASE A

NORTH, PARTNER	EAST	SOUTH, YOU	WEST
One spade	Two hearts	Three spades	Four hearts
Four no trump	Five hearts	?	

A bid of five spades by you would show two aces, five no trump would show three aces, and six clubs all four aces.

The alternate convention is DEPO (Double = Even, Pass = Odd). Over the opponent's interference after the four no trump bid, a double shows an even number of aces (zero, two or four) and a pass shows one or three aces. The Blackwood bidder can almost always figure out which it is and act accordingly.

A few very experienced partnerships use DOPI when the response would be at the five level, DEPO at the six level.

MODIFIED GERBER

The Gerber convention, as intended by its originator, John Gerber, is described on *pages 515 through 519*. One of its tremendous advantages, over Blackwood, is the fact that the request for kings can come without waste of bidding space if sufficient aces have been located to warrant a further slam try. Gerber, as originated, employs the bid of the next ranking suit to 'ask' for kings. Should the next ranking suit be the agreed trump suit, then the 'ask' for kings is made in the next higher-ranking suit.

CASE A

NORTH	EAST	SOUTH	WEST
One diamond	Pass	One heart	Pass
Four clubs*	Pass	Four hearts	Pass
Four spades**			

*Since a bid of three clubs would be a single jump and forcing, the jump to four clubs, when using Gerber, is a slam try, asking for aces.

**Partner's four heart response indicated one ace. The four spade bid, being the next higher-ranking suit, now asks for kings in the same manner.

Since there is some possibility, in less experienced hands, of the suit rebid by the four club bidder (the four spade rebid in Case A) being misunderstood as showing a secondary suit, some players have modified or simplified the Gerber Convention so that

1 – A bid of four clubs asks for aces;

2 – A bid of five clubs, preceded by four clubs and after partner's response, then asks for kings. Responses to the latter would be as follows:

(a) Five diamonds	No kings or four kings
(b) Five hearts	One king
(c) Five spades	Two kings
(d) Five no trump	Three kings

ROMAN GERBER

Some American players have adapted Roman methods in Blackwood (pages 684-685) to Gerber. This offers the advantage of locating specific aces in the majority of cases.

RESPONDING TO FOUR CLUBS (ROMAN GERBER)

RESPONSE	SHOWS
Four diamonds	No aces or three aces
Four hearts	One ace or four aces
Four spades	Two aces of the same color or two major aces or two minor aces
Four no trump	Two aces of different colors, one a major, the other a minor

Roman Gerber may also be employed to locate kings by the four club bidder rebidding the cheapest suit (other than the agreed trump suit). Kings are then shown in the same manner.

MODIFIED GRAND SLAM FORCE

The jump to five no trump, skipping over four no trump, is a request to partner to bid seven of the agreed trump suit holding two of the top three trump honors, ace, king or queen. It is described in the text under its original title, the Culbertson Five No Trump Bid, on page 514. Today, the convention is more usually known as the Grand Slam Force.

This is such a useful device that many players have expanded it, so that the Grand Slam Force can be used in conjunction with Blackwood, except when clubs are the agreed trump suit. When any other suit is trumps, the Blackwood bidder bids six clubs over the ace-showing response to announce all four aces and to invite partner to bid seven holding two of the top three trump honors.

In another variation of the Grand Slam Force, responder is able to describe his trump holding more accurately over the jump to five no trump. He responds as follows:

RESPONSE	
Six clubs	– None of the top three honors in the agreed trump suit.
Six in the agreed trump suit	– One of the top three trump suit honors.
Seven in the agreed trump suit	– Two of the top three trump suit honors.

THE BARON GRAND SLAM TRY

Leo Baron, a former Englishman now residing in Southern Rhodesia, is, in addition to being a player of championship caliber, a many time author and originator of distinctive bidding methods.

What is known as the Baron Grand Slam try is an inquiry, after a suit has been supported or agreed on, asking partner whether he holds good trumps! This is accomplished by bidding the suit directly in rank beneath the agreed trump suit.

CASE A	
NORTH	SOUTH
One spade	Three spades
Five hearts	

In the bidding sequence shown as Case A, spades are the agreed trump suit and hearts, naturally, is the suit beneath spades in rank.

The five heart bid asks partner South, to bid six of the agreed trump suit if holding excellent trump support; to sign off at five with minimum trump holdings. Correspondingly, a jump of six in Baron as a rebid of six hearts in Case A by North would ask partner to bid the grand slam with excellent trump support, stop at six without it.

The degree of trump support required to go to slam is largely dependent upon the previous bidding and the amount of support already shown.

BARON TWO NO TRUMP RESPONSE

Although the Baron Two No Trump Response is not, strictly speaking, a slam convention, it is included in this section because it was designed to make slam bidding easier. The convention is very simple – it simply reverses standard practice in regard to responder's no trump jumps after partner has opened the bidding with one of a suit.

Using Baron, a jump to three no trump over opener's one-of-a-suit shows a balanced hand with 13-15 points. Opener then selects the final contract or probes further. With a balanced hand of 16-18 points, the sort of hand on which standard bidders jump to three no trump, responder bids only two no trump. This leaves plenty of room for slam exploration below the game level. It is a sound treatment, providing, of course, that both partners remember it, for balanced powerhouses opposite an opening suit bid often present the most difficult bidding problems in reaching or avoiding slams.

DOUBLES

Doubles were originally introduced into bridge to increase the value of penalties and thus to add more excitement to the game. But the double as a bidding tool has now gone far beyond the role of punishing the opponents when they step out of line. The takeout, or informatory, double of an opponent's opening bid is probably the most widely used convention in the entire bridge universe. The modern expert also keeps a few other non-penalty doubles in his bidding arsenal.

One of the most popularly acclaimed 'modern' doubles is the negative double, which made its first appearance as part of the Roth-Stone system. It is a pleasure to be able to have Al Roth himself introduce you to the negative double. All one need say about Alvin Roth is that many of his fellow experts consider him the greatest bridge player in the world.

THE NEGATIVE (SPUTNIK) DOUBLE

by

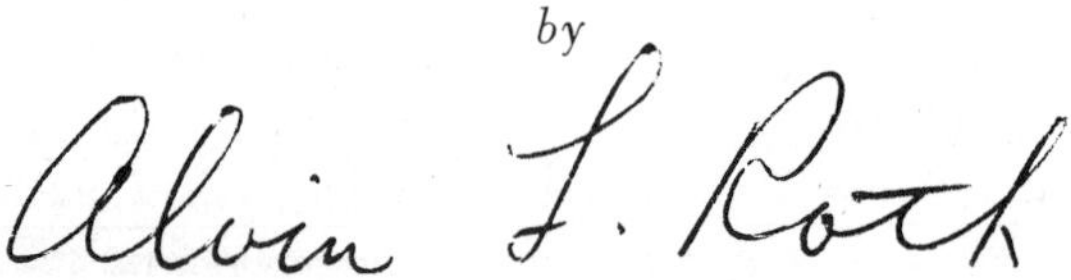

The negative double, devised by Alvin Roth and Tobias Stone, made its appearance at the bridge table simultaneously with the launching of Russia's first successful satellite. Since the latter was given the now famous name of 'Sputnik,' the title attached itself to this bidding convention so that players refer to use of the negative or sputnik double as synonomous.

The negative double is designed to permit its users to compete in the auction with hands that under conventional methods would be passed because they lack the necessary values for a free response.

Basically, a negative double is a double after one's partner has opened the bidding and the right hand opponent has overcalled.

CASE A

NORTH, PARTNER	EAST	SOUTH, YOU	WEST
One diamond	One spade	Double !	

Using the convention, your double is negative.

The reader may rightfully say, "Why, any double after one's partner has bid is for penalty, even at the one level" *(page 441)* and be completely correct. But this is playing standard methods and sputnik is anything but standard. It is a special convention designed to meet a specific situation.

Your negative double, in this case, asks your partner who opened the bidding with one diamond, to show any other suit of four or more cards he may hold. If you have doubled spades, as is the case, your double promises good heart support of four or five cards; conversely, a sputnik double of one heart would promise similar four or five card spade support and a sputnik double of a minor would indicate good supporting cards in both majors in the hope that your partner, who opened the bidding, has a secondary suit.

To the question, "Why don't you, in Case A with a good heart suit, bid 'two hearts' over the one spade bid instead of using sputnik?" there are two likely reasons. The first is that a free response of two hearts, being free, would show at least 12 points (*page 86*) and be virtually forcing to game. The sputnik double can be made with seven or more points and the right type of hand. The second reason for employing sputnik rather than bidding two hearts is that the latter bid would also indicate an excellent heart suit and your heart suit, while of four or five cards, may be anything but robust.

(a)
♠ J 4
♡ Q 10 8 6 5
◊ Q 6
♣ K J 7 2

Holding hand (a), the player using conventional methods with the bidding in Case A, would be compelled to pass as South. With sputnik, he can compete. The double asks partner if he holds four or more cards of either unbid suit, in this case, clubs and hearts. Lacking either, the opener may rebid a rebiddable suit or bid no trump, depending upon his holding.

The opening bidder responds to the double in accordance with his assessment of game prospects. A cue-bid would be the only absolute force. With strength in the opponent's suit he can make a penalty pass.

The negative double treatment can be extended to the following situations:

(a) High-level overcalls, whether strong or pre-emptive, up to and including four spades. The higher the overcall the more likely it is that the opener will decide to pass for penalties, so a shaded raise often should be given in preference to the double.

(b) A natural overcall at the two or three level in a minor suit after a no trump opening bid. The double would then show support for one or both major suits, but would not be forcing to game.

DEFENSE

When the right-hand opponent has made a negative double, the situation is similar to a bid over an opposing take-out double. A redouble shows high-card strength, and may expose an opening psychic bid. A jump raise of the overcaller's suit would be pre-emptive.

DISADVANTAGES

1 – You can no longer make first round penalty double of opponent's overcalls.

ADVANTAGES

1 – A secondary suit fit, if present, can be ascertained on hands where otherwise it would not be discovered until the bidding was concluded or the opener had sufficient strength to reverse or make a takeout double;

2 – The responder may enter the bidding competitively on hands that ordinarily would be passed.

THE RESPONSIVE DOUBLE

In the February, 1953 issue, *The Bridge World* contained an article by Dr. F. Fielding-Reid on what he termed, "The Responsive Double." A second supplementary article appeared in the June issue of that magazine.

This excellent convention, which I whole-heartedly recommend, eliminates a loop-hole in takeout and penalty doubles.

Under existing methods, any double after one's partner has bid (or doubled) is for penalty.

Now let's take a case covered by the responsive double.

CASE A

NORTH, OPENER	EAST, PARTNER	SOUTH	WEST, YOU
One diamond	Double	Two diamonds?	

(a)
♠ J876
♡ K1054
◊ 3
♣ K965

You hold hand (a). You no longer have to bid, since South's two diamond bid "took out" your partner's takeout double. Yet you've enough cards to warrant a bid, but you don't know which suit to bid. Should you bid spades, or hearts or clubs?

Dr. Fielding-Reid's theory is that "the double of the preemptive raise of a suit originally doubled for takeout by partner should also be a takeout double."

In other words, if, instead of guessing which suit to show with hand (a), you simply double South's two diamond bid, you are now asking your partner to bid his best suit. This eliminates guessing, and prevents your side from being jammed by preemptive raises after takeout doubles.

A double by West in case A, asking partner to bid, is the responsive double. After a responsive double, any other double by the partnership is for penalty, as in case B.

CASE B

NORTH, OPENER	EAST	SOUTH	WEST
One diamond	Double	Two diamonds	Double*
Three diamonds	Double**		

* The responsive double.

** A penalty double, since it follows a responsive double.

The responsive double can be applied to double raises over a takeout double, as well as single raises, as in cases C and D.

CASE C

NORTH, OPENER	EAST	SOUTH	WEST
One heart	Double	Three hearts	Double*

CASE D

NORTH, OPENER	EAST	SOUTH	WEST
One diamond	Double	Three diamonds	Double*

* Responsive doubles, asking partner to bid.

There is one disadvantage to the responsive double, at least in my eyes, and that is that there are times when the takeout doubler's partner wants to double for penalty, and he can't, because, using the responsive double, he's asking his partner to bid.

	(b)	
	♠Q5 ♡4 ◇Q97543 ♣Q1086	
♠A1064 ♡AQ765 ◇KJ10 ♣2	N W E S	♠K32 ♡832 ◇86 ♣KJ973
	♠J987 ♡KJ109 ◇A2 ♣A54	

Let's pretend, with hand (b), that we have the bidding in case E.

CASE E

SOUTH	WEST	NORTH	EAST
1 club	dbl.	3 clubs	?

Here East would like nothing better than to double for penalty, but if he's using the responsive double he is asking partner to bid. That's what he doesn't want!

In other words, you can't have your cake and eat it, too! Either a double, after partner's takeout double, of a pre-emptive raise is for penalty or it is responsive. It cannot be both!

The question is—which method gives the greater advantage? The inventor, Dr. Fielding Reid, advocates use of the responsive double over all pre-emptive single and double raises, after partner has made an informatory double.

My personal feeling is that it can be used profitable in all pre-emptive single and double raise situations after partner has doubled, except the double raise in clubs, that is, with bidding as in Case E. There is logic behind my reasoning. When the bidding goes one club, double, three clubs, very often the opening bidder may have a three card club suit, the partner of the club bidder four clubs. If the doubler has only a singleton club, then his partner would have five clubs, and might want to double for penalty.

This situation will exist far more often when the suit concerned is clubs than with all three remaining suits combined. That is because more three card minors are bid in the club suit than in diamonds.

Further, I feel that any double of a pre-emptive raise at the four level, after partner has doubled for takeout, is for penalty, and is not responsive. Case F illustrates this point.

CASE F

NORTH, OPENER	EAST	SOUTH	WEST
One heart	Double	Four hearts	Double*

* A penalty double.

Whether you use the responsive double, and how you use it, is purely a matter of personal preference. But, in any event, as in other unorthodox conventions, be sure that both your partner and the opponents are aware that you are using it.

RESPONSIVE DOUBLES AFTER OVERCALLS

A few players have extended the principle of the responsive doubles to auctions in which an opponent opens the bidding, partner overcalls, and third hand raises opener's suit.

CASE G

NORTH	EAST	SOUTH	WEST, YOU
One heart	One spade	Two hearts	Double

Playing standard methods, your double would be a penalty double. If you and your partner, East, have agreed to play responsive doubles after overcalls, however, the double is now for takeout, just as it would be if partner had doubled one heart. The double shows the two unbid suits, at least four in each. In Case G, West should hold clubs and diamonds. East will then bid whichever suit he has length in.

LEAD DIRECTING DOUBLES

There are many times, as a defender, you would like to be able to tell your partner which suit to open. Unfortunately, you will not have sufficient strength on most of these occasions to enter the bidding, or the suit you would like partner to lead has already been bid by an opponent.

Perhaps you remember the anecdote of the player who asked for a review of the bidding, and on reaching the second suit bid by the dummy, raised her voice to such a pitch that there could be no doubt in the partner's mind as to the desired lead.

The practice of conveying information by vocal inflection or intonation being regarded as reprehensible and unethical, a legitmate means of informing partner which of bid suits to lead can be found in the lead directing double.

Lead directing doubles are of four kinds.

1 – Against suit contracts.

2 – Against no trump.

3 – Against slams.

4 – Following any artificial response, as to slam conventions, Stayman, etc.

AGAINST SUIT CONTRACTS

A lead directing double of a suit contract can be identified in this fashion:

1 – It is a business or penalty double made in the middle of the auction.
2 – The doubler ordinarily expects the opponents to return to another suit and does not expect to be on the opening lead.
3 – Leading the doubled suit will be good for the defenders and will not enable declarer to unload losing tricks of another suit.

Pretend you sit East and the bidding has proceeded:

CASE A

SOUTH	WEST	NORTH	EAST
One spade	Pass	Two hearts	Pass
Two spades	Pass	Three clubs	Double

(a)
♠J5
♡A104
♢J109
♣KJ1086

East's hand will probably resemble hand (a) to the left. Note that it is a business double, since, to be for takeout, it would have had to be made at East's first opportunity, which East passed (over two hearts). Secondly, East feels that he can win four club tricks and a heart if the double is left in, and third, a club lead by partner through North's suit will not lose any tricks for the defenders. But to double three clubs on the preceding bidding holding hand (b) would be suicidal since dummy, the club bidder, will probably have a club suit headed by the ace-king or even the ace-king-queen. Declarer, who must be short in the suit, will obtain valued discards at once. As a general rule, do not double an opponent's bid at low range unless you want partner to lead the doubled suit, should the opponents escape to another.

(b)
♠J
♡A105
♢J10
♣J1098765

AGAINST NO TRUMP

Lead directing doubles find their greatest and most successful use against no trump contracts. How many times have you yearned to have your partner lead a suit bid by the dummy. Dummy may have a very shaded suit and you hold the remaining cards. In any event, you had no accurate way to inform your partner what to lead, so he led his own suit. Alas, you held no supporting cards and declarer made the contract.

Doubles of no trump fall into six categories:

1 – When neither defender has bid and dummy has bid one suit.
2 – When neither defender has bid and dummy has bid two suits.
3 – When leader has bid and partner doubles.
4 – When doubler has bid.
5 – When both defenders bid.
6 – When a suit bid by dummy has been doubled.

In all of the above situations, the hand *not on lead* doubles. Obviously for the leader to double would not call for the lead of any specific suit – he just expects to defeat the contract, and he knows what he wants to attack.

You, the reader, will sit West in all of the following bidding situations.

Situation A – Neither you nor your partner have bid – partner doubles an adverse no trump contract for penalty . . . Example:

CASE B

SOUTH	WEST	NORTH	EAST
One heart	Pass	One spade	Pass
Two clubs	Pass	Two hearts	Pass
Two no trump	Pass	Three no trump	Double
Pass	Pass	Pass	

RULE – Lead your highest card of suit bid by dummy (spades) with three or less cards in suit. With four, lead fourth best unless from a sequence, in which case lead the top card of the sequence.

Situation B – Dummy has bid two suits, let us say, spades and hearts, and the final contract is in no trump, doubled by your partner.

RULE – Of the two suits bid by dummy, open the suit in which you are the *weaker*, because, conversely, partner will be the stronger. If you hold hand (c), and dummy has bid both majors, certainly partner's double is not commanding a spade lead when you have the king jack four long. Open with the eight of hearts.

(c)
♠ K J75
♡ 83
◇ J64
♣ 10864

If your holdings are equal in both suits, open the suit which has not been rebid by dummy or in which declarer's support appears weaker.

Situation C – You have made a bid, either originally or overcalling, and partner doubles the adverse no trump.

RULE – Lead your bid suit. Make the normal opening, whether fourth highest or top of a sequence, as the hand dictates. Forget the suit or suits bid by dummy in this case. Your partner holds supporting cards in your suit and is telling you to lead it.

Situation D – Your partner has bid a suit. Whether he bid it originally or as an overcall is immaterial. He now doubles the no trump for penalty.

RULE – Lead his suit! The following recommendations should be followed. With a singleton of partner's suit, it's a matter of Hobson's choice. The singleton is led. Holding any doubleton, the higher card is first led. With three cards, lead bottom unless you can lead the top of a sequence. With four or more cards of partner's suit, unlikely in view of the eventual enemy no trump contract, the fourth-best is led except from a sequence. Even when the tripleton or longer holding of partner's suit is headed by the ace, the bottom card from three or the fourth-best from four or more is led, *not the ace!*

After partner who has bid and is not on lead doubles an adverse no trump, it is only the rare exception that permits the opening leader to open his own suit and disregard the doubled command to lead partner's suit. In these cases, the opening leader will have a solid or virtually solid sequence of his own, at least a five card suit plus a positive re-entry.

Not to open partner's bid suit, particularly after partner's double has requested that the suit be led, is a major felony, particularly where the opener is leading from either a worthless holding of a suit, such as 97643 or one headed by a tenace, such as KJ1086. To open the suit would result in the loss of time in the case of the former and probably result in the loss of a trick in the case of the latter, should declarer have the ace-queen.

Situation E – Both you and your partner have participated in the bidding. The opponents reach a final no trump contract and your partner doubles, obviously for penalty. You are on lead.

RULE – As a general measure, it is preferable to lead your partner's suit unless your own is solid and leading it cannot cost you a trick. It is better with broken holdings, such as suits headed by king jack, ace queen, or ace jack to wait and have your partner lead that suit through declarer up to you. Thus the recommendation of partner's suit. Of course, if your suit resembles KQJ87 and you hold a definite re-entry, attack at once.

Situation F – You have bid, but your partner has doubled a suit bid by dummy during the auction. You sit west.

CASE C

SOUTH	WEST	NORTH	EAST
One heart	One spade	Two clubs	Double
Two no trump	Pass	Pass	Pass or double

Your partner's double of two clubs shows a strong club holding over dummy's bid suit and indicates a safe opening lead. Unless your spade suit is virtually solid, open a club.

AGAINST RESPONSES TO FOUR NO TRUMP

Various slam conventions as Blackwood and Gerber employ artificial responses to indicate the number of high cards held by the responder. They have a definite point in common, viz., that the suit bid in response as five diamonds or five spades, whatever the case may be does not promise a suit holding but rather a definite number of high cards.

Thus if you sit behind the player responding to four no trump, hear that individual bid a suit which you would like your partner to lead, *double!* Thus you can indicate a safe, sound opening lead to your partner without ever directly entering the bidding. Be sure, however, that your holding in the suit is headed by cards capable of taking tricks, such as aces, kings and queens. Do not double with a long worthless holding merely to frighten the opponents – you might well talk partner out of his normal lead, which might have beaten the final contract.

DIRECTED LEADS AGAINST DOUBLED SLAMS

Some years ago, Theodore Lightner of New York, one of America's outstanding experts, devised what is now known as the Lightner Slam Double Convention. It may be summarized as follows:

1 – When your partner doubles a slam contract, he commands you to make your most abnormal opening lead.

2 – If he has bid a suit, you are not to lead it.

3 – If dummy has bid a suit, lead it.

4 – If declarer has bid two suits, you should open the second suit bid by declarer. This is because many shrewd players, after establishing an agreed trump suit between the partnership, may bid a short suit secondarily in the expectation of averting a lead in that suit, later discarding those losers in dummy.

5 – Holding some extremely long holding in a suit, whether bid or not by opponents, lead that suit since partner is in all probability void and can ruff the first round.

NOTE – The Lightner Slam Double Convention requesting an abnormal opening lead is only applicable where the opponents have voluntarily and freely reached a slam contract in the full expectation of fulfilling it. Where an adverse slam contract has been reached with no apparent hope of fulfillment – possibly as a sacrifice – the convention is not relevant – and any double calls for the normal opening lead.

	North	
	♠J2	
	♡Q432	
	♢AKJ9	
	♣753	
West		**East**
♠74		♠65
♡97		♡AKJ1086
♢1086432		♢void
♣K64		♣QJ1098
	South	
	♠AKQ10983	
	♡5	
	♢Q75	
	♣A2	

The diamond opening defeats the contract.

CASE D

S	W	N	E
1♠	Pass	2♢	3♡
4♠	Pass	5♠	6♣
6♠	Pass	Pass	Dble.

PRE-EMPTIVE BIDDING

With emphasis more and more on pre-emption, the tendency among many top players is to use many bids, customerily considered as strength-showing ever since contract bridge began, as weak or pre-emptive. The weak no trump *(page 629)* is an example. Still others are the weak jump overcalls, weak, pre-emptive re-raises, and gambling three no trump.

WEAK JUMP OVERCALLS

To explain this as simply as possible, bidding one more than necessary, whether as an overcall or as a response, has always indicated an extremely powerful hand. Let's take an easy example.

(a)
♠AKJ87
♡A
♢42
♣KQJ016

CASE A

NORTH	EAST	SOUTH	WEST
Pass	One diamond	Two spades	

The two spade bid is semi-forcing, conventionally, and shows 17 to 20 points *(page 329)*. It indicates a powerful one-suiter or a strong two-suiter as hand (a). The reason for not doubling for takeout is that the hand is not prepared for the expected heart response.

(b)
♠KQ10987
♡4
♢32
♣Q1096

Since the weaker type of hand as (b) occurs far more frequently, many players now use the overcall of one more than necessary as pre-emptive and showing a good suit usually of six cards, and a weak hand. This is contrary to the established playing habits of a large portion of the players, although espoused by Goren in his recent texts.

WEAK JUMP RESPONSES

Pre-emption is carried even one degree further in responding to partner's opening bid as in Case B.

CASE B

NORTH	EAST	SOUTH	WEST
One heart	Pass	Two spades!	

In all standard methods, bidding one more than necessary in a new suit, by a player who has not previously passed, promises *(page 75):*

1 - 19 points or more;

2 - A good 'fit' for partner's suit, or
A solid or semi-solid suit of one's own, or
A combination of both.

But the advocate of 'everything weak' would bid two spades, facing partner's opening heart (or any other) bid, holding the aforementioned hand (b). In one bid, the partner has been advised to pass, since the bid is now non-forcing and of the lack of game probability. Similarly, bidding for the opponents has been made more difficult.

It should be stressed that a jump of two or more levels, in suit bidding, is always pre-emptive. The foregoing relates only to single jumps.

If the reader is puzzled and may wonder how a bid may show strength one time and weakness the next, the answer is that they can't exist at the same time, any more than the fabled irresistible cannon ball and immovable wall. If a player uses strong single jump overcalls and strong, forcing to game single jump responses (which is my recommendation), he cannot simultaneously use the weak variety. It must be one or the other.

ONE, TWO, THREE

Still another conversion, by a group of avante garde players, of a bid long considered to be strength-showing and highly invitational to game, to one pre-emptive in nature and indicating a hand weak in high cards, is the free rebid by the opening bidder of his suit to the three level after responder has given a single raise.

CASE C

NORTH, DEALER	EAST	SOUTH, PARTNER	WEST
One heart	Pass	Two hearts	Pass
Three hearts!			

On *page 203*, a three heart bid is described as promising 17 to 19 points in the opening bidder's hand. Purpose of the bid is to request partner, if holding a maximum for the single raise, to go to game. If responder has less, he can pass the bid of three hearts.

Since normally the voluntary rebid of three hearts by the opening bidder would indicate at least 17 points and a jump to game at least 20 points, it is equally reasonable that failure to rebid at this point would deny 17 or more points. Thus by passing, the opening bidder has described his hand to the opponents as weak, ranging between 13 and 16 points.

Now let's let our thinking go one step further. The partner of the opening bidder could only give a single raise – from one heart to two hearts. This would indicate six to 10 points in almost all cases.

So any failure by opener to rebid, after receiving a single raise from partner, would indicate a minimum 13 to 16 point opening bid to the opponents. Should North pass (instead of bidding three hearts) in the above bidding sequence, East still has another chance to bid. He has become aware from the opponents' weak bidding that his side has some strenght – not enough strength, perhaps, to make a game but certainly enough to compete in the auction, particularly at low level and either buy the contract or push the opponents to unmakable heights.

So for North to pass is an open invitation for east to bid. Any bid or double by East at this point is known as 'protective' or 'balancing' *(pages 428, 434, 435)*.

To make it difficult or virtually impossible for the opponents to enter the bidding when a minimum (13 to 16 point) hand has received a single raise, a new convention uses the voluntary rebid to the three level by opener, as in Case C, as *completely pre-emptive*. The responder, even with a maximum, *must pass*.

If the opener has additional values, as a hand with 17 to 19 points, to invite a game he must make some other bid that is forcing, such as a new suit at the three level. With game a certainty, he should either jump directly to game or make some bid that is equally forcing to game.

THE GAMBLING THREE NO TRUMP

First used by Acol (English) bidders and later incorporated by Stayman in his first work published in 1946, an opening bid of three no trump, rather than indicating the conventional 25-27 high card points and a balanced hand *(page 278)*, is used to in-

(a)
♠4
♡ 863
◇ AKQJ742
♣Q85

dicate a solid minor suit usually of seven cards, possibly eight, and little if any side suit strength.

Hand (a) to the left is typical. Side-suit strength will never exceed one king, usually one queen will be maximum. Advantage of the bid is its highly pre-emptive effect. If doubled, the bidder, if desired, can always escape to the suit held.

OPENING BIDS OF FOUR CLUBS AND FOUR DIAMONDS AS STRONG MAJOR SUIT PRE-EMPTS

(a)
♠6
♡KQ1096543
◇K87
♣8

(b)
♠6
♡AKQ98732
◇KJ5
♣8

Using standard methods, either hand (a) or hand (b) would be opened, non-vulnerable, with a bid of four hearts – it's important to put the bidding at as high a level as one safely can before the opponents can get together in spades. But suppose it is partner who holds the balance of high cards – especially if he has a hand with a couple of aces. If the opening pre-empter has hand (a) and he bids on, the value of the game may be lost forever. If he passes over hand (b), a sure slam could be missed.

A few expert players today resolve these problems by using opening bids of four clubs and four diamonds to show strong opening pre-emptive hands in hearts and spades, respectively. Hand (b) would be opened four clubs; Reverse the major suit holdings and the opening bid would be four diamonds. With hand (a), opener would pre-empt with four hearts.

If responder is weak, he simply bids four of the 'transfer' suit. If responder has values that might be useful in a slam, he can bid the intervening suit as a slam try. For example, if after opener bid four clubs on hand (b) partner bid four diamonds, opener has a simple route to slam. He rebids four no trump, Blackwood. If responder holds one ace, he signs off at five hearts; opposite two aces he bids six hearts, and if partner, bless him, has three aces, opener can gamble on seven no trump, knowing that it will be no worse than on a diamond finesse.

Of course, using this treatment, one can no longer bid four clubs or four diamonds on a hand with a very long suit and very little outside strength. This gap is filled by the pre-empter opening either three of his minor or five of his minor as the strength of his holding and the vulnerability dictate.

DEFENSES TO PRE-EMPTIVE BIDS

THE FISHBEIN CONVENTION

by

What is now termed the Fishbein Convention was originated by me some years ago as a means of letting my partner know, without guessing on his part, when I wanted to double opposing opening three bids for penalty and when, after such a bid, I wanted my partner to bid.

Prior to the introduction of the Fishbein Convention, most players used (and many still do) what is known as the Optional Double. This, in effect, says, after a double of an opening bid of three spades, for example, "Partner, if your strength is scattered, I think we can defeat the contract. But if you have an extremely long suit and think we can make something our way, then take out my double by bidding your suit."

There were two great flaws. The first was that the doubler didn't think he could defeat the adverse contract - he knew he could. In fact, he could have taken his hand to the bank and borrowed money on it.

Let's suppose you are East. North is the dealer, neither side vulnerable and with the bidding in Case A, you hold hand (a).

(a)
♠ A Q 10 8
♡ K 6
◊ A J 9 4
♣ K Q J

CASE A

NORTH	EAST	SOUTH	WEST
Three spades	?		

Of course you want to double - for penalty. You can murder three spades and there's no 'think' about it. So you want to convey the idea to your partner that this double is for penalty and you don't want him taking it out.

(b)
♠ KJ97642
♡ 5
◇ J532
♣ 8

Should the reader ask, "What kind of a three bid could the opener have to permit this possible holocaust,?" the actual hand is shown as hand (b). Card for card, it was played in the final rounds of the 1958 national championships. The hand was bid 52 times and 47 times, the opening bid was three spades!

I would like to emphasize at this point that the fact that a suit is opened pre-emptively with a bid of three - or even four - does not indicate that suit to be solid or even semi-solid. In the 1930's, the formative years of contract bridge, Culbertson and other authorities gave as examples of pre-emptive opening bids long and virtually solid suits as ♠ KQJ8765. But the value of pre-emption was so great and means of combatting pre-emption so vague, that suits became more and more raggedy. As long as the suit was long, the hand weak and vulnerability (or lack of it) favorable, pre-emptive opening bids were made more and more frequently in order to harass the opponents.

In self-defense, therefore, I devised what is now known as the Fishbein Convention so that my partner would know when my doubles were for penalty. Here it is - in all its simplicity.

After an opening bid of three of a suit (major or minor), any double by the player in the next position is always for penalty; a double by the player in the last position is optional (co-operative).

CASE B

NORTH	EAST	SOUTH	WEST
Three hearts	Double*		

*Penalty

CASE C

NORTH	EAST	SOUTH	WEST
Three hearts	Pass	Pass	Double**

**Co-operative

FOR TAKEOUT

Since doubles in the second position as in Case B are always for penalty, it stands to reason that there must be some method of compelling partner to respond. Let's suppose you hold hand (c) to the left and sit East. Your side is vulnerable with North the dealer in Case D.

(c)	CASE D			
♠ AKJ10	NORTH	EAST	SOUTH	WEST
♡ 2	Three hearts	Three spades***		
◇ AQ108				
♣ KQJ7				

***The Fishbein Convention, bidding the next-ranking suit for takeout.

The Fishbein Convention is that when your right hand opponent opens the bidding with three of a suit, any bid by you in the next ranking suit at the lowest possible level is the equivalent of a takeout double and compels your partner to respond.

EXAMPLES

OPENER'S BID	FOR TAKEOUT, OVERCALL WITH
Three clubs	Three diamonds
Three diamonds	Three hearts
Three hearts	Three spades
Three spades	Four clubs

Note that in the above, over an opening bid of three spades, I have omitted the cheapest possible bid of three no trump but instead, overcalled with four clubs. That is because to be for takeout, the overcall must be in the cheapest *suit.* When the overcall is of three no trump, it shows a desire and ability to play the hand in that contract.

So far we have explained two phases of the Fishbein Convention, first, how to double for penalty; the second, compelling partner to bid. There is still a third and equally important situation, viz., competing in the auction with a suit of one's own.

Rule - The bid of any suit, except the next ranking suit, by the player to the left of the opening three-bidder, shows possession of that suit and naturally, a good hand, since you're entering the bidding at the three level or even higher.

CASE E

NORTH	EAST, YOU	SOUTH	WEST
Three clubs	Three hearts) Three spades) —		

Either the three heart bid or the three spade bid promises the suit and is competitive - had you bid three diamonds, it would have been the next-ranking suit and compelled partner to bid.

CASE F

NORTH	EAST	SOUTH	WEST, YOU
Three clubs	Pass	Pass	Three diamonds Three hearts Three spades

Not one of the three possible bids accredited to you in Case F is forcing—not even the three diamond bid, although it is the next ranking suit. The reason is—it is only Fishbein (for takeout) when made by the player immediately following the opening pre-emptive bid—in other words, in sequence F, it is simply competitive and not forcing. The partner will bid if warranted by his holding and subsequent possible bidding, otherwise he should pass.

Obviously, there will be times, using the Fishbein Convention, that the next ranking suit (after an opening pre-empt of three) will be *your* suit. In other words, over a three heart opening, you really hold a good spade suit.

CASE G

NORTH	EAST, YOU	SOUTH	WEST
Three hearts (d)	Three spades	Pass	?

♠ AQJ98
♡ 2
◇ KQJ7
♣ A109

There is no question that you have been partially 'fixed' by the opposing pre-emptive bid. What future course of action you take depends entirely on your partner's response. If you're fortunate enough to hear your partner bid four spades (thus showing spades), you'd pass; if partner makes a minimum response of four clubs or four diamonds - the question of whether you should bid four spades or, in the case of the diamond response, raise to five, is debatable.

But to show possession of a suit when it is the next ranking suit, the suit is simply rebid as in Case H.

CASE H

NORTH	EAST, YOU	SOUTH	WEST
Three diamonds	Three hearts	Pass	Three spades
Pass	Four hearts*		

*The suit.

REQUIREMENTS

When the Fishbein Convention is used as the equivalent of an informatory double, the recommendation is a minimum of 15 points. (I would prefer 17. EWR).

RESPONDING TO FISHBEIN

Using Fishbein after one's left hand opponent has opened with three of a suit, a player's course of action depends upon the bid made by partner.

A - If partner has made a penalty double, in 99 44/100% of cases, the player should pass. Only the greatest of freaks and absolute certainty of slam or vulnerable game should influence the player into taking out the double.

B - If partner, by bidding the next-ranking suit, has ordered you to bid, the response should be normal, precisely as though responding to a takeout double (pages 445-459). With a weak hand, bid your best suit as cheaply as possible; with seven points or more, make a jump response. Remember that a response of no trump shows good stoppers in the opponent's suit, a good hand and a desire to play the hand in no trump.

C - Partner competes in the auction, either by bidding in the second seat a suit other than the next ranking or no trump, or by any bid in the fourth position. If partner's bid is less than game and you feel game to be makable, you should bid it at once. Similarly with a strong hand, slam may be possible and should be explored. One of the best means, if holding the ace (or void) of the opponent's suit, is to cue-bid that suit.

MODIFIED FISHBEIN

As with virtually all conventions, bridge-players have found ways to change, modify and adapt the Fishbein Convention to still further purposes. It should be emphasized that, as with the Stayman Convention, these modifications have not been approved by the original inventor, Mr. Fishbein.

CHEAPER MINOR

One disadvantage, to some players, is the inability to compete in Fishbein after a pre-emptive opening bid when actually holding the next ranking suit. For example, your right hand opponent opens with three diamonds and you bid three hearts. Since it's the next ranking suit, partner is going to bid with the probability that he'll bid three spades and possibly, four. In the case of the latter, you'd pass but over a three spade response, since you're not equipped to support that suit, you'd be virtually compelled to bid four hearts.

(e)
♠ J8
♡ KQ10987
◇ K2
♣ A32

There is no way, in straight Fishbein when holding the next ranking suit, to bid it (as three hearts in the above) and be able to play it there if partner is 'broke'.

In order to devise a method permitting players to compete in the next ranking suit without compelling partners to respond, two similar means were devised.

The first of these is known as "Cheaper minor for takeout." In other words, after an opening bid of three, an immediate overcall in the cheaper minor is the equivalent, in straight Fishbein, of bidding the next ranking suit for takeout.

CASE I

NORTH	EAST	SOUTH	WEST
Three clubs	Three diamonds		

CASE J

NORTH	EAST	SOUTH	WEST
Three hearts	Four clubs		

CASE K

NORTH	EAST	SOUTH	WEST
Three diamonds	Four clubs		

Notice that either clubs or diamonds can be for takeout, depending upon which is the cheaper. The advantage, if any, of the method is demonstrated in Case J where it is possible for East to bid three spades without compelling his partner (if weak) to bid and in Case K where East might again wish to compete with a heart suit yet lacking any certainty of being able to make four.

THE CLUB TAKEOUT

Another modification of the Fishbein Convention employs, after an opening pre-emptive bid, a bid of the fewest number of clubs for takeout rather than the cheaper minor. In other words, over an opening bid of three clubs, diamonds, hearts or spades, an immediate overcall of four clubs requests takeout by partner.

In my opinion, this is inferior to the cheaper minor method. Again, it is a matter of style and personal preference.

THE FOURTH SEAT

All of the preceding has been based on the assumption that to use the Fishbein Convention, either straight or modified, the convention can only be employed by the player in the second seat, viz., immediately following the pre-empt and that all bids in the fourth seat are natural.

Some players prefer to use Fishbein, straight or modified, in both second and fourth positions. There are both advantages and disadvantages and the decision as to which method should be employed is a matter of personal preference. Fishbein strongly recommends that the convention be used only in the second position, viz., immediately following the pre-empt.

AGAINST WEAK TWO BIDS

The increase in the use of the weak, pre-emptive two bid has led to the use of the Fishbein Convention, straight or modified, against this type of pre-empt. This, too, is a matter of preference although Fishbein recommends use of the convention only against three bids and not against weak two bids. However, it has been my personal experience that the Fishbein Convention is equally effective against pre-empts both at the two and three level.

The Fishbein Convention is not applicable against opening bids of four of a suit. In these cases, any suit bids show possession of the suit and all doubles are for penalty and not, in any way, co-operative, except in the most extreme of cases in the responder's hand.

THE WEISS CONVENTION

Although, when not playing Fishbein, a double of the opponent's pre-empt is termed 'cooperative', in expert hands the double is more and more takeout oriented. Larry Weiss of Los Angeles, a talented photographer as well as a noted bridge player and theorist, decided that the most frequently held hands with which to punish a pre-emptive opening bid were not those with a trump stack – in which case you'd like to be using Fishbein – but those on which one opponent has a strong balanced hand. Accordingly, in the Weiss methods, a double of an opening pre-empt, in either seat, shows a balanced hand with 16 or more points and no particular strong suit. Partner then converts the double to a penalty double by passing or bids a suit of his own. For takeout, with an unbalanced hand, the cheaper minor is bid, just as in the Fishbein variation. Any other suit overcall over a pre-empt is natural.

OVERCALLS

Perhaps the most significant way in which bridge bidding today differs from that of 30 years ago is in the area of competitive bidding. Much of this section on Modern Expert Bidding Methods is devoted either to defensive bidding – competing after the opponents have opened the bidding – or to countering defensive bidding.

Many of today's experts use what are called 'wide-range' overcalls – that is, a simple overcall may be made on a very strong hand. Partner responds to this overcall much as he would to an opening bid; with 10 points or so, responder should envision a possible game and should not pass partner out. When using wide-range overcalls, takeout doubles are reserved for hands with support for all unbid suits. Players tend to combine 'wide-range' simple overcalls with Weak Jump Overcalls (see page 701).

Some of the modern weapons for defensive bidding are described below; others are contained in the sections on Pre-emptive Bidding, Cue Bids, and No Trump Bidding.

PRE-EMPTIVE JUMP RAISES OF OVERCALLS

When partner overcalls and you have good support for his suit and a weak unbalanced hand, it behooves you to get in the opponents' path. With you have four or more trumps and a side singleton in support, your cards are much more valuable on offense than on defense.

In standard methods, a jump raise of partner's overcall shows a strong hand, 13 to 15 points, and invites partner to go on to game if he has better than a minimum. This jump raise makes it difficult for the opponents to bid more—but you are so powerful that they are probably better off passing anyway.

The hands on which you want to impede the opponents' orderly exchange of information are those on which *they* hold the preponderance of high cards.

CASE A

NORTH	EAST, PARTNER	SOUTH	WEST, YOU
One diamond	One spade	Pass	Three spades

(a)
K1095
7
954
QJ1085

Using pre-emptive jump raises of overcalls, your jump to three spades in Case A, not vulnerable, indicates a hand like (a). Your trump support and distributional values will keep you out of serious trouble even if you are doubled; and if North-South wish to compete, they will have to find a fit at the four level. Vulnerable, partner would expect you to hold about a king more in high cards.

With the 13 to 15 point hand in support of partner's overcall, responder would first cue bid two diamonds and then jump in spades over East's rebid (See Invitational Cue Bids, page 732).

INTERMEDIATE SINGLE JUMP OVERCALLS

The standard meaning of a single jump overcall – one more than necessary to bid the suit – is an extremely powerful hand with an excellent suit (usually six cards or longer) or a two-suiter, either worth 17 to 20 points. The next most popular use of the single jump overcall is to indicate a weak hand and pre-empt the opponents (page 701).

Recently some players have devised and are employing a bid which contains the best features of each of the foregoing, a bid which shows some additional strength over and above the conventional overcall, yet at the same time has pre-emptive value. This is known as the intermediate jump overcall.

(e)
♠ K Q J 8 7 6
♡ 2
◇ A J 9
♣ Q 4 3

Hand (e) to the left is typical of the intermediate type of single jump overcall. A bid of two spades, for example, over an opening bid to one's right, promises a suit of six cards or longer with some solidity and a hand containing 13 to 16 points. The bid is in no way forcing but partner should respond with an hand promising hope of game or with need of further pre-emptive action.

Needless to say, a jump of two or more levels, as overcalling with a bid of three spades over an opposing opening bid to one's right is 100 percent pre-emptive, regardless of whether strong, weak or intermediate single jump overcalls are employed.

THE UNUSUAL NO TRUMP

Another convention devised by Roth and Stone that has gained popularity is what has become known as the "unusual no trump."

The reader will remember that takeout doubles are intended to show hands strong in the major suits *(page 438)*. The unusual no trump was designed to show minor two-suited hands.

CASE A

NORTH	EAST	SOUTH	WEST, YOU
One spade	Pass	Two spades	Two no trump

(a)
♠ 4
♡ K2
◇ QJ1087
♣ AJ1086

Your hand is shown as (a) to the left. Could your partner possibly believe that you wanted to play the hand in no trump?

Well, hardly!

One opponent has bid spades; the other supported the same suit. They have a very fine spade fit, perhaps, the entire spade suit. To remain in no trump would be suicidal since the opponents would quickly run their spade suit. The no trump, then, has an unusual meaning and that's where the convention derives its name.

If the reader, looking at hand (a) above, wonders why you as West didn't make a takeout double (instead of bidding no trump), the answer is that when a player makes a takeout double of one major, he promises good supporting cards for the other. In Case A, a double of two spades would virtually guarantee heart support. This is anything but true.

To overcall with either three clubs or three diamonds would be extremely hazardous since bidding either is pure guess-work.

By bidding two no trump when obviously unable to play the hand in no trump, a player can compel his partner to choose between the two minor suits. To be unusual, the no trump must have one or more of the following characteristics:

1 – The bid of no trump occurs after:
  (a) One opponent has bid a suit and it has been supported by the other opponent;
  (b) The no trump bidder has previously passed and later bids no trump over a bid by an opponent or opponents;
  (c) The no trump bidder jumps to two no trump over an opening bid of one in a suit by an opponent;

2 – Partner has not yet bid. Note – a pass is not considered a bid. An example of (a) is the bidding in Case A.

CASE B

NORTH, YOU	EAST	SOUTH	WEST
Pass	Pass	Pass	One heart
One no trump			

(b)
♠ J
♡ 3
◇ K98765
♣ A10984

Your bid of one no trump in Case B is again unusual. Having failed to open the bidding, you can scarcely have the conventional 16 to 18 high card points. Hence, to bid one no trump over an opening bid by an opponent, particularly with a partner similarly unable to open the bidding, must convey a special message.

CASE C

NORTH	EAST	SOUTH	WEST, YOU
One spade	Pass	Two hearts	Two no trump

(c)
♠ void
♡ 7
◇ Q109864
♣ KJ10732

Again your two no trump must be unusual. North's opening spade bid indicated a minimum of 13 points; his partner's response showed at least 10 points. It is hardly possible for you to have 22 to 24 high card points after this bidding. There just aren't enough points in the deck. By bidding two no trump in Case C, you would have a hand resembling (c).

CASE D

NORTH	EAST	SOUTH	WEST, YOU
Pass	Pass	One spade	Two no trump

The bidding in Case D is illustrative of the third condition, 1(c) where you have jumped to two no trump after an opening bid of one of a suit. Most players agree to play the jump to two no trump after an opening one-bid by the opponent as unusual, since to show the conventionally powerful 22 to 24 high card point two no trump, a takeout double followed by a rebid of two no trump could be employed. In other words, holding 22 to 24 high card points and a stopper in the opponent's spade suit, the hand would be shown as in bidding sequence Case E.

CASE E

NORTH	EAST	SOUTH	WEST
Pass	Pass	One spade	Double
	Two clubs)		
Pass	Two diamonds)–––	Pass	Two no trump
	Two hearts)		

Where both opponents have bid, each a different major suit, and a player who could have overcalled one no trump instead bids two no trump, the no trump must be clearly unusual since again, as with the bidding in Case D, there just aren't enough points in the deck. Case F is illustrative.

CASE F

NORTH	EAST	SOUTH	WEST, YOU
One heart	Pass	One spade	Two no trump

It should be emphasized that since some players use a jump to two no trump as strength-showing and not unusual and others prefer first doubling, later bidding no trump (Case E), the method chosen is a matter of personal preference or as bridge-players say, of 'style' (see *page 409*).

REQUIREMENTS

Having described rather fully how to recognize the unusual no trump, it's time to describe what you should have to make the bid.

First, your hand is predominantly minor suit in character. It must contain at least a total of nine minor suit cards between the two minor suits and better still, 10 cards or even more. Obviously, the bid does not infer a stopper in the opponent's suit – in fact, it denies strength in that major.

Second, and this is extremely important, the vulnerability factor *must* be favorable. This is explained at length on *page* 606. You must remember that if you are using the unusual no trump at the one-level, you're compelling your partner to bid at the level of two; if your unusual no trump is at the two-level, your partner must bid three as a minimum response. Since your partner has not bid, he cannot be counted on for any strength whatever – in fact, he may not have a four card or longer minor suit – most of his length may be in the majors where you need it least.

Accordingly, when employing the unusual no trump, you must be extremely careful that any possible penalty, taken sacrificially, would be less than the possible score that the opponents might have made had they played the hand. The ideal situation for employing the unusual no trump is when your side is not vulnerable and the opponents are vulnerable. When your side is vulnerable and the opponents are not vulnerable, the unusual no trump should not be employed unless the hand is strong, not only in distribution but also in high cards.

With equal vulnerability, viz., both sides are vulnerable or both sides are not vulnerable, again caution must be employed. In these situations, the hand should preferably have at least 10 cards in the minor suits.

Point count requirements for employment of the unusual no trump vary with vulnerability and whether the partner will be compelled to respond at the two level, three level or even at the four level. When bid at the one level, not vulnerable against vulnerable opponents, the unusual no trump can be employed with very few high card points, especially when holding 10 or 11 minor suit cards. Hand (d) is illustrative. When it is necessary to bid the unusual no trump at the two level, more high card strength should be present, with a minimum total point count of eight points not vulnerable and 10 vulnerable. In these cases, 10 or more minor suit cards are presumed to be present. With nine, the high card requirements should be increased. The unusual no trump *should not be employed if holding only eight cards or fewer in the minors.*

(d)
♠3
♡2
◊J109876
♣J10987

RESPONDING

When your partner has bid an unusual no trump, he is requesting you to bid your longer minor suit. In fact, 'request' is too mild a word – 'command' would be better. There are several possibilities. These are:

1 – You have a minor suit of four or more cards with a weak hand;

2 – You have a minor suit of four or more cards with a strong (7 or more points) hand.

3 – You have four or more cards in both minor suits;

4 – You lack four cards of either minor.

Let's take the first situation together with the bidding in Case A on *(page* 714*)*. You hold hand (e) to the left. Your response would be three diamonds. Again with the bidding in Case A, you hold hand (f). Your partner has guaranteed at

(e)
♠J97
♡Q876
◊6543
♣42

(f)
♠1082
♡Q542
◇AK93
♣K2

least four diamonds and probably more. Your club king must fit his holding in that suit. A bid of four diamonds would be correct if your partner's unusual no trump was made when not vulnerable. If his hand resembles that shown as (a), he will bid five; if, on the other hand, it is similar to (d), he can pass. Should your partner's unusual no trump be made when you are vulnerable so that you can count on him for some high card strength, a jump to five diamonds is in order.

When holding four or more cards in both minors after an unusual no trump by partner, be guided by the following:

(a) If both minors are of equal length, bid the weaker in high cards. The stronger suit will prove more useful as the side suit.

(b) If the minor suits are of different length, bid the longer.

The main problem you will encounter is when holding three or fewer cards of a minor suit after an unusual no trump by partner.

(g)
♠J97
♡108643
◇953
♣62

For example, you hold hand (g) with the bidding in Case A. The last thing your partner wants to hear about is your heart suit. He's interested in only one thing – whether you have more diamonds or more clubs. The answer is diamonds, of course. So you'll bid three diamonds over partner's unusual two no trump bid and rely on partner's promised length in that suit. Had your partner's unusual no trump been made at the one level, as in Case B, you simply would have responded with two diamonds.

VARIATION TO THE UNUSUAL NO TRUMP

As just described, use of the unusual no trump specifically requests partner to bid either of the minor suits. Frequently, however, the situation has arisen where before the unusual no trump has been bid, the opponents have already bid one of the minors together with one of the majors. In other words, the bidding will resemble Case G.

CASE G

NORTH	EAST	SOUTH	WEST, YOU
One club	Pass	One heart	?

(h)
♠K7654
♡void
◊QJ8765
♣42

Holding hand (h) with favorable vulnerability, you would be very much interested in ascertaining whether partner had any length in either of your two suits, spades or diamonds. To overcall with either would indicate both a better hand and better suit than actually present; to make a takeout double would promise still greater strength plus the possibility that partner, if 'loaded' with hearts and five or more high card points, could leave in the double *(pages 438-439).*

To meet this situation, many players have adopted the unusual no trump so that where it is bid as before and the opponents have bid two suits, one of which is a minor, the unusual no trump requests partner to choose between either of the unbid suits, regardless of minor or major.

Use of the unusual no trump in this guise is described, on convention cards, as requesting a takeout in an unbid suit. In other words, if both of the opponents' suits have been majors, the unusual no trump requests a minor suit response; if one of the opponents' suits has been a minor and the other a major, the request is for a choice between the remaining two suits.

Requirements for the bid and responses are similar to those previously described for exclusive minor suit takeouts.

COMIC NO TRUMP OVERCALL

Originated by Nicol Gardener, one of London's top players and theorists, an overcall of one no trump of an opponent's bid can show either of two types of hand, standard with 16-18 high card points *or* a weak hand containing a long suit. Hence it is known as a 'two way' bid.

After an overcall of one no trump, the partner usually responds with two clubs (artificial) to permit the no trump bidder to define his hand. Holding the strong hand, opener rebids 'two no trump'; if weak, he bids his suit.

Advantage of this method is that it permits entering the bidding with a degree of pre-emption when holding a weak hand containing a long suit, something which would not be possible when strong single jump overcalls are being employed.

CUE BIDS

To the average player, the bidding of a suit previously bid by an opponent has one meaning, viz., to indicate possession of first round control of the adverse suit. The control can either be the ace or a void.

But as mentioned in a footnote on *page 489*, the cue bid of an opponent's bid suit has many possible meanings and in order to clarify each, I am grouping the various types, many of which have not been previously mentioned, in this section of the text.

Before proceeding, I wish to make two points. The first is that we are discussing only cue bids of a suit or suits already bid by an opponent. We are not discussing cue bids (showing controls for slam tries) of suits *not bid* by the other side. The latter are described on *pages 519* and *520* of this text.

The second point, in discussing cue bids of the opponents' bid suit, is that many bids in bridge, spelled and pronounced alike, have different meanings depending on how and where they are employed. The best illustration I can give of this is to ask you to pronounce the word 'pear.' Would your auditor know whether you meant pear or pair or pare? Of course not! The word would take on its meaning from those surrounding it — the context. And the same is true with cue bids.

THE CUE BID BEFORE PARTNER HAS BID

A cue bid of the opponent's suit before one's partner has bid is the equivalent of an opening strong two-bid and an informatory double. It is forcing to game. There are other usages of the immediate cue bid which will be discussed later in this section.

(a)

♠ K Q J 9		CASE A		
♡ 4	EAST	SOUTH	WEST	NORTH
◇ A K Q 10	One heart	Two hearts	!	
♣ A K J 10	Bids of this type are discussed on *page 394*.			

DELAYED CUE BIDS BEFORE PARTNER HAS BID

(b)
♠ J 9
♡ K J 10 9 7 6
◇ A 4 3
♣ 8 6

CASE B

EAST	SOUTH	WEST	NORTH
One heart	Pass	One no trump	Pass
Pass	Two hearts		

Bidding the opponent's suit at a later opportunity as in Case B when unable to take any action whatever at an earlier opportunity shows length and fair solidity in the suit, the ability and desire to play the hand with that suit as trump. It *does not* show a strong hand. It does not compel partner to bid! If you had a strong hand with probability of game, you would not have passed earlier!

TWO CLUBS OVER ONE CLUB, NON-FORCING

General usage of the three card minor as a convenient means of opening the bidding *(pages 529-533)* frequently find players holding five card or longer playable minor suits after their right hand opponents have opened the bidding, presumably with three cards of that suit. Note that I said 'presumably.' Even though you may hold five or six clubs or diamonds after an opening bid of one club or one diamond respectively, there is still a possibility that the opponent could have five or six cards of that suit.

(c)
♠ 8
♡ 10 8 6
◇ A 4 3
♣ K Q 10 9 8 7

Let's suppose you hold hand (c) to the left and your right hand opponent opens the bidding with one club.

Your club length makes it likely that your right hand opponent has but three clubs. The important things, of course, are that you must convey to your partner that you, not the opponent, are the real possessor of the club suit; that you are equipped to play the contract in that denomination; in the event that the opponents buy the contract and that your partner has the opening lead, a club lead will be safe and desirable defensively.

But since a bid of two clubs over one club would be forcing to game, as in Case A, and indicate *everything but clubs*, just the reverse of the situation, a special usage has been devised to show the minor suit as a non-forcing bid.

When agreed by the partnership and made known to the opponents, the immediate cue bid of two clubs over one club shows clubs with the normal strength for an overcall and is non-forcing, as in Case C.

CASE C

EAST	SOUTH, YOU	WEST	NORTH
One club	Two clubs		

Also by agreement, some partnerships extend the convention to the diamond suit so that the cue bid of two diamonds over one diamond is similarly non-forcing, showing a playable diamond suit.

PRO AND CON

One bid cannot simultaneously have two meanings and the reader must appreciate that if an immediate overcall of two clubs over one club and/or two diamonds over one diamond shows the suit and is non-forcing, it cannot also, at the same time, indicate to partner the type of hand illustrated as (a) in the foregoing as forcing to game.

In other words, something has to give. You can have one or the other but not both at once. The question of relative frequency is the determining factor. The number of times you will hold a real club suit after a short (three card) club bid to your right will far outweigh, perhaps 100 to one, the number of times you will hold a hand capable of making a game in a suit other than clubs after your right hand opponent has opened with that suit.

My recommendation, therefore, is to use the immediate overcall in the club suit as described in the previous paragraphs—as showing the suit and completely non-forcing. Since almost all three card minor opening bids are in the club suit and rarely in diamonds, the convention (as non-forcing) has little application in the higher-ranking suit minor. In the majors, the immediate overcall of the opponent's bid suit is never used to show the suit. This subject is also discussed in detail on *pages 568 through 570*. Where the immediate cue bid of the opponent's suit is confined to the club suit in order to show possession of that suit, there is little chance of partnership misunderstanding.

THE CUE BID AFTER PARTNER HAS BID

The cue bid of an opponent's bid suit after one's partner has bid takes on an entirely different significance than cue-bidding before a bid of partner. Conventionally, the cue bid after partner has bid indicates–

1 – Sets the last suit bid by the partnership as the agreed trump suit;

2 – Promises an excellent supporting fit for that (the last bid) suit;

3 – Promises first round control in the adverse suit, viz., ace or void;

4 – Is forcing to game with inference of slam probability.

(d)

	CASE D			
♠ K J 9 6				
♡ A Q J 9 7	SOUTH, YOU	WEST	NORTH	EAST
◇ K 4 3	One heart	Pass	One spade	Two clubs
♣ A	Three clubs			

Your hand, as (d), is shown for the bidding in Case D. Rather than immediately jump to four spades, which your partner might very well pass, your highly descriptive cue bid conveys all four messages listed above.

Since this type of cue bid is the most common, let's have another example as with hand (e) and case E.

(e)

	CASE E			
♠ K Q 3				
♡ Q 10 8 7 6	NORTH	EAST	SOUTH, YOU	WEST
◇ void	One heart	Two diamonds	Three diamonds	
♣ A K J 9 2				

Again your cue bid of three diamonds promises first round control of the opponent's diamond suit, sets the last bid suit, hearts (in this case, the only suit bid by the partnership) as trump, promises good supporting cards for the suit and is forcing to game with slam probability.

THE CUE BID TO REQUEST NO TRUMP

In more recent years, cue-bidding the opponent's suit after partner has bid has been extended to have still another message, to wit, to ask partner (who has previously bid) to bid no trump if holding a stopper in the opponent's bid suit. When the cue bid of the opponent's bid suit requests partner to bid no trump with a stopper in the adverse suit rather than rebid the previously bid suit or show another suit, there will be the following characteristics.

1 – Your agreed partnership suit will often be a minor which, in many cases, will have been supported.

2 – The cue bidder does not himself possess a stopper. The reason for this should be obvious. It will be rare that both partners will each hold a stopper in the opponent's suit. A player holding a stopper, hence capable of biddingno trump on his own, should not ask partner who probably doesn't have a stopper, to make a bid he is capable of making.

3 – The opponentshave not supported the adverse suit. Should this be the case, requesting partner to bid no trump with a probable stopper as Qxx could find the queen sandwiched between the ace on one side and the king on the and being no stopper whatever.

Let's look at a typical hand and use of the cue bid to evoke a no trump response from partner.

CASE F

EAST, DEALER	SOUTH, PARTNER	WEST	NORTH, YOU
One heart	One spade	Pass	Two clubs
Pass	Three clubs	Pass	Three hearts

If your partner, South, has a heart stopper, you have requested him to bid no trump (in this case, three no trump), regardless of his stoppers or holdings in the other suits.

	♠ K 2 ♡ J 4 ◇ Q 9 7 ♣ K Q J 9 7 6	
♠ 10 9 8 6 ♡ 5 3 2 ◇ K 5 3 2 ♣ 5 2	N W E S	♠ J 7 ♡ A K 10 9 6 ◇ A 10 8 6 ♣ 4 3
	♠ A Q 5 4 3 ♡ Q 8 7 ◇ J 4 ♣ A 10 8	

Figure 227

You can see by examining *figure 227* that North-South are lay-down for three no trump. After North hears his partner's three club raise, North knows his partner probably has the club ace, insuring that his side will take six club tricks. With the king of spades solidifying South's spade suit, nine tricks seem assured.

But North can't bid three no trump, in view of the lack of a heart stopper, and his problem is to get his partner, if possible, to make that bid.

In normal usage, an overcall of the opponent's bid suit carries a specific message, according to the surrounding circumstances.

1 – If the player overcalls the opponent's suit *BEFORE* his partner has bid, he is commanding his partner to bid, and has created a game force.

2 – If a player bids the opponent's suit *AFTER* his partner has bid, he is cue-bidding. His bid ordinarily shows first round control of the opponent's suit, as the ace or a void, and is also forcing to game, and is mildly slam invitational. Usually the cue-bid of the opponent's suit sets the last suit bid by the partnership as the agreed trump suit and inferentially shows excellent support for that suit. On rare occasions, the bidder may have a solid suit of his own which will become the final trump suit.

♠Q2
♡Q107
♢AQ10976
♣QJ

♠J1093	N	♠85
♡5432	W E	♡AKJ986
♢84	S	♢void
♣875		♣K10963

♠AK764
♡ void
♢KJ532
♣A42

Figure 228

Figure 228 illustrates the second type of overcall of the opponent's suit. East dealer, neither side vulnerable.

CASE G

EAST	SOUTH	WEST	NORTH
1 ht.	1 sp.	pass	2 dia.
2 hts.	3 hts.	pass	3 no tr.
pass	4 dia.	pass	4 sp.
pass	7 dia.		

The bidding requires a word of explanation. South's three heart bid, over East's rebid, shows one of two things—either first round control of the adverse suit (as is the case), or it is a request for a heart stopper to no trump.

How is partner to know which meaning the bid has? The answer is simple.

Should North, in *figure 228*, show a heart stopper by bidding no trump—

1—If the player who originally cue-bid the opponent's suit (South in *figure 228*) raises the no trump, or leaves the contract in no trump, then he has used the cue bid as a means of getting the partner to bid no trump.

2—If the player who cue-bid the opponent's suit takes out his partner's no trump bid (made after the cue bid) into a suit, he is showing first round control of the adverse suit. This is the case in *figure 228*.

Now there are a few other points I'd like to touch on, while we're on the subject of cue-bidding the opponent's suit. First, a lot of players erroneously feel that, after a fit has been found, to show the ace of the opponent's suit as first round control, the ace must be alone, or in other words, singleton.

That is not correct. For example, had East bid clubs in *figure 228*, after South found the diamond fit, it would have been quite correct for him to have cue-bid the club ace, despite the fact that in addition to the ace, the hand contained two low clubs.

The next thing I want to point out is that this type of cue bid can be used by either partner, after an opponent or both opponents have bid.

CUE-BIDS IN RESPONSE TO TAKEOUT

That a player should cue bid the opponent's suit in response to partner's takeout double will seem strange to the reader, yet it has become standard expert practice. Suppose, holding hand (f) as South, the opponent to your left opens the bidding with one diamond and the bidding proceeds as in case H.

(f)
♠K1098
♡A976
◇4
♣KJ73

CASE H

WEST	NORTH	EAST	SOUTH
One diamond	Double	Pass	?

You are faced with several problems.

1 – Which suit, spades or hearts, is your partner better equipped to support?

2 – To respond with 'two' of either suit would be to show a far better suit than actually present; to bid only one would show a much weaker hand than you have.

Rather than guess, between two or more suits, which to bid in response to partner's double, you have a simple way of 'passing the buck' to your partner, who doubled. You simply cue bid the opponent's suit which in case H above would be a bid of two diamonds on your part.

"**Wouldn't that show a diamond suit,?**" you ask.

Well, hardly. Let's suppose, after a takeout double of one diamond by your partner, you held hand (g). Nothing would make you happier than to have the opponent playing the contract at one diamond, doubled. So if your partner doubled, you'd simply pass.*

(g)
♠A2
♡8
◇KJ9765
♣Q432

Accordingly, a cue bid to partner's informatory double merely says, "**Partner, I have a good hand but I'm not sure which suit to choose. Please bid your best suit so that I don't have to guess.**"

As used by most players, the cue bid response to a takeout double *is not* forcing to game but is highly invitational. The doubler is requested to show a major suit if he holds one; if doubler has both majors, he should bid the longer, or stronger if both are the same length.

---

*See penalty pass, *pages 438-439.*

CUE BIDS AFTER THE OPPONENTS HAVE BID TWO SUITS

When the opponents have bid two suits and your partner has bid, a cue bid of the first suit bid by the opponent to your left has an entirely different meaning than a cue bid of the second suit bid by the opponent to your right. Let's pretend that in Cases I and J you sit South and West is the dealer.

CASE I

WEST	NORTH	EAST	SOUTH, YOU
One club	One heart	One spade	Two clubs

CASE J

WEST	NORTH	EAST	SOUTH, YOU
One club	One heart	One spade	Two spades

In Case I, your two club bid shows a playable club suit, the ability to play the hand with clubs as trumps and is *not forcing*. This is actually a situation akin to the use of 'two clubs over one club, non-forcing.' *(Pages* 722-723).

RULE - When the cue bid is *not* of the last suit bid by the opponent, it shows the suit, not the control, and is not forcing.

It should be pointed out that this situation is not at all uncommon. Your hand could very well resemble that shown as (h) to the left. The very last thing you want to hear from your partner is a heart rebid and you certainly can handle a possible two club contract with little fear of penalty. Further, you have indicated a safe opening lead to partner, one that he ordinarily would not have made in the light of the suit having been bid by the opponent to his right.

(h)
♠Q7
♡3
♢QJ9
♣KQ109876

Let me give a corollary case, one in which your partner did not bid.

CASE K

WEST	NORTH	EAST	SOUTH, YOU
One diamond	Pass	One spade	Two diamonds

Since you did not cue-bid spades, the latter suit bid by the opponents, your bid of two diamonds can mean only one thing—that you have a playable diamond suit and a fair hand.

Now, in Cases L and M, let's examine situations where the opponents have bid two suits and your cue bid is of the latter suit. The intent of the cue bid will depend entirely upon whether one's partner has yet bid.

CASE L

WEST	NORTH	EAST	SOUTH, YOU
One diamond	One heart	One spade	Two spades*

*A cue bid of the opponent's last bid suit, *after* one's partner has bid, shows a good supporting fit for the last suit bid by the partnership, sets that suit as the agreed trump and guarantees first round control (ace or void) of the opponent's suit. (*page* 315).

(i)
♠void
♡KQ985
♢43
♣AQJ872

Hand (i) would be typical of your holding in bidding sequence L. By inference, you have marked yourself for heavy club strength (since the opponents have bid spades and diamonds and your partner hearts). You probably have a void, furnishing first round control of the adverse spade suit and a tremendous fit for partner's heart suit. (See also Invitational Cue Bid, page 732).

CASE M

WEST	NORTH	EAST	SOUTH, YOU
One club	Pass	One diamond	Two diamonds**

**When the opponents have bid two suits and one's partner has not yet bid, a cue bid of the opponent's second suit is *unconditionally* forcing upon partner to respond and that the final contract must be of at least game. The cue bid *does not* show first round control, rather a powerful two-suiter as hand (j).

(j)
♠AK10876
♡AQJ986
♢4
♣void

Your problem, after the opponents' bidding, is to be able to show both suits and compel partner to give a preference. Since the cue bid forces your partner to continue bidding until at least game is reached, you will have the desired opportunity to show both suits. Further, if a decided preference for one suit over the other can be obtained, there is a strong probability of slam.

The reader can see that holding hand (j), if the player simply flips a coin for heads or tails in order to determine whether to bid four spades or four hearts, there are three end results.

First, the partner will think the four heart or four spade bid, as the case may be, is pre-emptive, showing a long one-suiter and a weak hand *(page 393)*, just the reverse of the situation. Second, there is a 50-50 chance of landing in the wrong suit. Third, a makable slam could readily be missed.

DEFENSIVE CUE BIDS

When the bidding is highly competitive between both sides, it is highly possible that the opponents will, in all probability, outbid you. This can be for a variety of reasons:

1. – As a possible sacrifice;
2. – Because they have more and better cards;
3. – Since they hold the higher-ranking suit.

This situation will usually prevail when both sides have each agreed on a trump suit and the opponents have bid a second suit.

CASE N

NORTH	EAST	SOUTH	WEST, YOU
One club	One diamond	One heart	Two diamonds
Two spades	Pass	Four spades	?

(k)
♠874
♡Q9654
♢K9654
♣void

For you to bid five diamonds is not only futile but highly dangerous since first, you have no high card defense to either a five spade or six spade contract. Then, too, your partner may even double a five spade contract, the last thing you'd like to hear unless your partner could be induced to open a club.

But a cue bid of five clubs at this point brings the opponents' house of cards tumbling down. Certainly it can't be game-forcing, since the best you could do previously was to give your partner's diamond bid a single raise to only the two level and moreover, your partner didn't have enough strength to bid even a second time.

Watch what happens after a five club cue bid. The opponents are now faced squarely with the problem of whether to bid five spades or to double five clubs. If they elect to bid five spades, your partner has been alerted to open a club, rather than make his normal diamond lead. You will trump immediately with the expectation of putting your partner back in the lead with a diamond return or whatever suit he may indicate with the Lagron Echo (page 174). On winning the return, he leads another club which you trump. Your side has won the first three tricks and the hand will have been beaten.

If the opponents choose to double five clubs as the lesser of the evils, you or your partner can bid five diamonds as the planned escape. The penalty the opponents will receive should be far less than they would have scored making four or five spades. Naturally, if your five club bid is not doubled, your partner *must* bid five diamonds. It should be emphasized that the defensive cue bid should only be employed with favorable vulnerability, described on *page 606*.

INVITATIONAL CUE BIDS

By partnership agreement, some players have changed the normal meaning of a cue bid in the opponents' suit or suits after partner has overcalled. They use a cue bid (either of the only enemy suit or the last-named one) as the only strong response to an overcall. It is forcing on the overcaller to bid again, and invites game, but it does not promise first round control in the suit nor does it guarantee a fit for partner. It merely invites game, rather than create a game force. The overcaller bids another suit, if he has one; bids no trump with the opponents' suit(s) well stopped; jumps with a very strong suit and extra values. Otherwise he simply rebids his own suit at the minimum level. The cue bidder may pass a simple suit rebid; otherwise he too describes his hand.

Using invitational cue bids, the meanings of other responses to overcalls are changed. The bid of a new suit by overcaller's partner is encouraging but not forcing; and a raise or a jump raise is pre-emptive, showing a fit and distributional values rather than high card strength.

JUMP CUE BIDS

Jump cue-bidding, viz., bidding more than the minimum number required to overcall, in a suit previously bid by the opponents shows a long (seven or more card) suit, ability and willingness to play the hand with that suit as trump and is *completely not forcing.*

(1)
♠QJ9
♡42
◇7
♣KQJ10876

CASE O

WEST	NORTH	EAST	SOUTH, YOU
One club	Pass	One diamond	Three clubs

You bid three clubs, as in Case O, holding hand (1). The bid is entirely pre-emptive. Its primary purpose is to make it difficult, for the opponents to ascertain a possible spade or heart fit. Had you wanted to make a forcing bid, you would have bid two diamonds, a cue bid of the last suit bid by the opponents. The fact that you jumped doesn't make it forcing—only pre-emptive.

CUE BIDS TO SHOW TWO SUITS

After the opponents have opened the bidding against you, it is a rare and glorious occasion indeed when you hold a hand so strong that you want to force partner to game no matter what his holding. The immediate cue bid of the opponents suit to show a very powerful hand is, therefore, one of the more idle weapons in the bridge player's arsenal, and many experts now use this call to describe a purely competitive hand, usually limited in strength, and usually showing a two-suited pattern.

Michaels and Astro (see below) are the most commonly used two-suit takeouts. Others include Colorful Cue Bids (shows two suits of the opposite color to the opponent's suit—clubs and spades after a diamond cue bid, etc.); Top-and-Bottom Cue Bids (shows highest—and lowest-ranking unbid suits—spades and clubs after a heart cue bid); Upper Two Suit Cue Bid (shows both majors after a minor suit cue bid, hearts and diamonds after a spade cue bid). All of these two-suited cue bids show about the same strength as a Michaels Cue Bid.

ASTRO CUE BIDS

Like the Astro convention used as a defense to the opponents' one no trump opening (page 648), Astro Cue Bids were developed by Paul Allinger, Roger Stern, and Larry Rosler. Over a minor suit opening, an immediate cue bid shows six cards (occasionally five) in the other minor plus four (sometimes five) hearts. Over a major suit, the cue bid shows four cards in the unbid major and six clubs. These particular suit patterns are, according to the convention's inventors, the most difficult to describe using natural overcalls and takeout doubles.

This is an example of a vulnerable Astro cue bid of one spade.

(a)
♠87
♡AKJ6
◇4
♣AJ10942

Using normal methods, this is a difficult hand to describe. A club overcall risks losing the heart suit; a heart overcall would promise a five card or longer suit; a double (reasonable) if the clubs and diamonds were interchanged) leaves you unprepared for a diamond response, since a three club bid after doubling would show a much stronger hand. The Astro cue bid, two spades, shows a good hand when vulnerable, with the two specific suits.

(b)
♠6
♡K10765
◇8
♣K109753

Not vulnerable, the Astro cue bid may be made on a much weaker hand, such as (b). Over a one diamond opening bid, the cue bid of two diamonds shows both suits at once, and will permit the partnership to compete if there is a club or heart fit.

The strength held for any Astro bid should be concentrated in the two long suits. This is the safety factor in all Astro auctions, for it allows partner to evaluate his defensive potential accurately.

After the cue bid, the bidding follows a natural course. Partner knows the cue-bidder's approximate distribution, and can bid either promised suit or the fourth suit at whatever level seems best. A jump in either of the promised suits is a tactical move, never a game try. Responder can invite game by raising the cue bid, or by bidding two no trump.

SUMMARY: ASTRO CUE BIDS

1♠-2♠: 6♣, 4 or 5♡.
1♡-2♡: 6♣, 4 (or 5) ♠.
1◇-2◇: 6♣, 4 or 5♡.
1♣-2♣: 5 or 6◇, 4 or 5♡.

The playing strength required depends on the vulnerability.

THE MICHAELS CUE BID

The late Mike Michaels was one of the outstanding players and theorists of bridge. In both Washington, D.C., and Miami, where he later moved, he was associated with Charles Goren's bridge activities.

An immediate cue bid in the opponent's suit used as a take-out double. The bid is made with a two-suited rather than a three-suited hand:

(c)	(d)
♠J10943	♠KQ64
♡AJ1062	♡J10764
◇6	◇A4
♣87	♣87

If an opponent opens with a minor suit the cue bid is recommended with either of these hands unless the vulnerability is unfavorable. Over a minor suit the emphasis is on the major suits; there should be at least nine cards in the major suits and 6-11 points.

Over a major suit the cue bid shows the unbid major suit and an unspecified minor suit:

(e)	(f)
♠7	♠void
♡QJ1095	♡109874
◇75	◇AKJ62
♣AJ1062	♣Q64

On each of these hands two spades would be bid over one spade. If partner does not fit the unbid major he can bid no trump as a request to the cue bidder to show his minor suit.

The major suit cue bid is unlimited in point-count: the cue bidder may have a strong hand and plan to take further action.

Over either type of cue bid partner will usually bid the full value of his hand if there is a known fit; and in some circumstances he may put pressure on the opponents by making an advance sacrifice. He can also make use of a second cue bid to ask for further definition of the cue bidder's hand.

At unfavorable vulnerability freakish distribution is needed to make the cue bid.

DEFENSE

The opening bidder's partner should double the cue bid with a hand which would redouble a take-out double and is interested primarily in defense. A raise in opener's suit should be made with a hand worth a traditional free single raise after an over-call: this has some pre-emptive value.

SPECIAL OPENING LEADS

RUSINOW LEADS

What are now known as 'Rusinow Leads' in the United States and as 'Roman Leads' in Europe were originated in the mid-30's by the late Sidney Rusinow, then of New York and later of Beverly Hills, California together with Walter Malowan of New York City, both top-ranking American players.

Conventionally, the lead of a king can be made from a sequence headed by the king as KQ or KQJ or KQx; it similarly can be made from any sequence headed by the ace, king and any one or more additional cards as AKx, AKQx, AKJx, etc. If the leader's partner sees the queen or the ace in his hand or the dummy, the leader is known to have the other honor. Thus leading the king with the queen in dummy or partner's hand would indicate partner to have the ace and one or more additional cards; conversely, with the ace held by leader's partner or in the dummy, the lead is known to have the queen (page 158).

When the king is led and neither the ace or queen is visible to leader's partner, the latter cannot tell at the first trick which combination is held by the leader. The Rusinow sequence is designed to prevent this ambiguity.

Instead of the conventional leading of the top of the sequence except for leading the king from a holding of ace, king and one or more cards, the Rusinow sequence leads the next to the top card of the sequence.

TABLE OF RUSINOW LEADS

HOLDING	LEAD
AKx	King
KQx	Queen
QJx	Jack
J10x	10
10 9x	Nine

Thus there can be no mistaking the leader's holding. When the king is led, partner is known to have the ace and additional cards; the lead of the queen would promise the king and additional cards, etc.

Let me emphasize three points. When holding a doubleton (two-card) sequence, the higher is led first. Thus with KQ alone, the king would be led; with QJ, the queen, etc. The next to the top is led only with three or more cards of the led suit.

Second, this convention applies *only* to leading suits *not* bid by partner. In leading partner's suit, conventional means are employed (pages 163-166).

Third, with three or more honors in sequence, after first leading next-to-top, the leader's second lead is the card directly below that led originally. For example:–

HOLDING	FIRST LEAD	SECOND LEAD
AKQ	King	Queen
KQJ10	Queen	Jack
J10987	10	Nine

In the Roman Club system, the second-best is also led from an interior sequence as

HOLDING	LEAD
KJ109	10
Q1098	Nine

The Rusinow method is recommended, by its advocates, primarily for use against trump (suit) contracts where it is necessary leader's partner know exactly leader's high cards in the led suit. It has not been recommended for use against no trump since in the latter, the emphasis is on determining whether the best suit has been opened rather than locating specific cards.

Advocates of Rusinow leads point, with great emphasis, to the hand illustrated in *figure 229*, in which players using this method were able to defeat South's contract of four hearts and employment of conventional leads permitted the contract's fulfillment.

	♠ 963 ♡ KJ4 ♢ AKJ87 ♣ Q7	
♠ KQ ♡ A3 ♢ 964 ♣ K65432	N W E S	♠ A872 ♡ 52 ♢ 1053 ♣ J1098
	♠ J1054 ♡ Q109876 ♢ Q2 ♣ A	

Figure 229

With East-West vulnerable and North the dealer, the bidding had been:

NORTH	EAST	SOUTH	WEST
1 dia.	Pass	1 ht.	Pass
2 hts.	Pass	4 hts.	Pass
Pass	Pass		

Where conventional opening leads were used, declarer had no difficulty making the contract. The king of spades was opened and East signaled encouragingly with the eight. The queen of spades followed and East, seeing no reason to overtake his partner's trick, completed the echo by dropping the deuce. That proved to be the end of the spade suit for the defenders. West, lacking a third spade, was compelled to lead another suit. On winning, South drew trumps, after conceding a trick to the ace, and ultimately discarded both remaining spades on dummy's diamonds. Playing Rusinow leads, however, when East saw first the king and then the queen led, he knew partner had only a doubleton spades, so he won the queen of spades with the ace and gave partner a spade ruff. The ace of hearts was the setting trick.

There is, however, one serious flaw in the method which has been completely overlooked by adherents of Rusinow leads. This is illustrated in *figure 230*. Assuming North to be dealer and with vulnerability immaterial, we have:

NORTH	EAST	SOUTH	WEST
1 ht.	Pass	1 sp.	Pass
2 sp.	Pass	4 sp.	Pass
Pass	Pass		

```
            ♠ K J 7
            ♡ A Q J 8 6
            ◇ K
            ♣ 5 4 3 2
♠ 6 3 2                   ♠ 5 4
♡ 9 7 3          N        ♡ 10 5 4
◇ 10 6 5 4 3 2  W   E     ◇ A 9 8 7
♣ Q              S        ♣ A J 10 9
            ♠ A Q 10 9 8
            ♡ K 2
            ◇ Q J
            ♣ K 8 7 6
```

Figure 230

East-West were employing the Rusinow sequence. West opened the singleton queen of clubs. Since the lead of this card would promise possession of the king, East saw no reason to play the ace but simply played an encouraging card. Hopes of defeating the hand now went a-glimmering. On winning with the king, declarer immediately drew trumps, ran five rounds of hearts, discarding all three remaining low clubs. The defense wound up winning one trick - the diamond ace.

Using conventional leads, the lead of the queen would deny holding the king. Hence, the latter card would be marked with declarer and East would have no reason for not playing the ace. With the latter card winning the first trick and the return of the jack of clubs, West would trump off South's king and the defense would ultimately win three club tricks, a club ruff (of the king) and the ace of diamonds to defeat the contract two tricks.

The difference then, was a matter of four tricks - ducking the queen of clubs permitted declarer to win a total of 12 tricks; playing the ace and returning the suit held the declarer to eight. Whether the system's advantages outweigh the difficulty of reading the lead of a singleton honor is a matter of opinion and for the player himself to determine.

ACE FROM ACE-KING

Some players have chosen to clear up the ambiguity of the lead of the king by choosing always to lead the *highest* of touching honors – just the opposite of Rusinow leads. The only difference from standard practice this entails is that from a holding of ace, king and one or more low cards, the ace is led. The only drawback to this method is that one often wants to lead an unsupported ace against a high level contract; and partner, not knowing whether or not opening leader has the king, will be unsure if he should encourage or discourage when an ace is led.

JOURNALIST LEADS

This entire system of leads was presented by 'Journalist' (Larry Rosler, of Murray Hill, New Jersey, and Jeff Rubens, of New York City) in The *Bridge Journal*. Leads against both suit and no trump contracts are covered, but the leads apply to trick one only.

AGAINST NO TRUMP CONTRACTS

LEAD	SHOWS OR ASKS
Ace	Asks partner for count by playing a high card from an even number and a low card from an odd number, or to unblock if necessary.
King	Asks partner to indicate whether he'd like the suit continued.
Queen	Asks partner to unblock the jack, if he holds it. The lead could either be from a sequence such as K Q 10 9 x x or form Q J 10 x x.
Jack	Denies a higher honor; shows jack-ten to length.
Ten	Shows a high honor – ace, king or queen. Could be led from A 10 9 x x, K 10 9 x x, Q 10 9 x, or A J 10 x x or K J 10 x x. (The suit could be any length,

	but the lead is normally from a four card or longer holding.)
Nine	Shows the ten and no higher honor.
High spot card	Second highest card held in the suit. Shows length, usually, but asks partner to use his judgment about continuing the suit or shifting when he obtains the lead.
Low spot card	Shows interest in the suit led – partner is asked to continue the suit unless he clearly has a constructive shift to make. The lowest card is led from any length, not fourth best as in standard practice.

AGAINST SUIT CONTRACTS

Honor leads	The lower of touching honors is led, except in a suit partner has bid.
Spot card leads	From an odd number of cards in the suit (three, five, seven), the lowest card is led. From four or six, the third highest card is led. From three or four small cards, the highest card below the nine (which would show the ten) may be led to indicate the suit is weak in top cards if the opening leader thinks it is more valuable to show this than to give the count in the suit. The higher card, whether a spot card, an unsupported honor, or honors in sequence, is led from a doubleton.

TWO FIVE CARD BLACK SUITS

The customary practice, holding any two suits each of five cards, is to open the bidding with the higher-ranking suit *(pages 121 - 123)*. The reason is that it permits, if partner is weak, a preference that will not increase the contract.

When the two suits are black, viz., clubs and spades, opening the bidding with one spade will necessitate a rebid of *three* clubs by opener if partner's response was either two diamonds or two hearts. If the opener's hand was weak or if either or both of his suits are weak, the end result would be getting too high.

Accordingly, with two five card black suits, the practice has grown up to treat them, when the hand is weak or the spade suit is weak, identically as opening the bidding with two four card black suits *(page 147)*.

The following recommendations will be of service.

With 16 points or less and five clubs and five spades:

1 - Holding a rebiddable club suit and a poor spade suit, open with one club; later, if possible, show the spade suit.

2 - With a rebiddable spade suit and a poor club suit, open and rebid spades. Do not show the club suit if it will require bidding 'three'.

3 - With rebiddable suits in both clubs and spades, open with one club, later bid and rebid spades.

With 17 points or more and five spades and five clubs:

1 - With a rebiddable club suit and a poor or fair five card spade suit, open with a club, later bid and rebid the spade suit if warranted by future bidding. This will sometimes involve rebidding a spade suit technically not quite rebiddable as K9764 but the important thing is to inform partner that there are five spades present.

2 - With a rebiddable spade suit and poor clubs, open with one spade. Whether the spades are rebid or clubs next shown depends upon the pattern of subsequent bidding.

3 - With both good spades and clubs, open with a spade, later bid and rebid clubs to show five cards of each suit.

What it boils down to is this - holding a weak hand when one five card black suit is weak and the other strong, open with the strong suit; with strong hands and two strong suits they should be shown in normal order, viz., higher-ranking of two five card suits first.

BIDDING SYSTEMS

ROTH-STONE

The Roth-Stone System, developed in the early 1950's by Alvin Roth and Tobias Stone, both of New York City, was the first successful attempt to break away from traditional bidding methods used by most American players. At that time many of the system's ideas were considered to be revolutionary, even radical, but virtually all of today's experts employ some Roth-Stone methods, such as Negative Doubles (see page 690) and Unusual No Trump (see page 714), and even average players have adopted features such as five-card majors.

At the heart of the system is a unique method of evaluation (counting points). To open the bidding, points are counted in the normal way – ace-4 points, king-3, queen-2, jack-1, void-3, singleton-2, doubleton-1 – with one important addition. With a six- or seven-card major, or a *good* six- or seven-card minor, one and two points are added, respectively. For the response and subsequent bidding though, points for voids, singletons and doubletons are adjusted, either up or down, depending on whether a good trump fit is found. To illustrate, look at hand (a). If the opening bid is one club, responder may count two points for his singleton diamond because he has adequate support for clubs. However, he may not count any points for the singleton over a one diamond opening bid since he has no support for diamonds. A doubleton, also, would be considered no support. Similarly, if the opening bid is one heart, the excellent heart support allows responder to increase the value of the singleton to three points, and over one spade, its value soars to four points. A similar re-evaluation is made by opener depending on the response, and both hands are constantly readjusted as the auction progresses.

(a)
♠AJ832
♡KJ75
◇2
♣Q106

Opening bids show 14 or more points, at least 10 in high cards. Thus, hand (b), which would be opened by many players, does not qualify for a Roth-Stone opening bid, while hand (c) does. The latter evaluates to 14 points – 10 high-card points, three short-suit points, and one point for the six-card spade suit.

(b)	(c)
♠A1043	♠AQ9863
♡K75	♡A1042
◇KJ9	◇98
♣Q86	♣7

The main structural features of Roth-Stone are five-card major suit opening bids in first and second seat, strong no trumps, a forcing-to-game opening bid of two clubs, weak two bids, (*see page* 652) and a three no trump opening to show a strong preempt in *any* of the four suits.

Responses are mostly non-standard. Single raises of opening bids of one heart or one spade are very strong, 10 to 12 points, and are never passed by a first- or second-seat opener. Two-over-one responses are similarly strong, normally forcing to game (unless responder rebids his suit at his next turn) and guarantee at least 11 points and that responder will bid again. With a hand that does not qualify for a major suit raise, responder can make a forcing bid of one no trump. Strong major suit raises are shown by an artificial jump to three clubs, which shows a minimum of four trumps and 13 points. Other jump shift responses, however, are weak, except by passed hands. A jump to two no trump normally describes a balanced hand of 13 or more points, while a jump to three no trump is Blackwood!

Roth-Stone also employs unusual responses to no trump opening bids. Over one no trump, two clubs is forcing Stayman and two diamonds is Stayman but with slam interest. These two Stayman bids are reversed over a two no trump opening bid.

In general, the guiding principle of Roth-Stone bidding is that all initial bids are based on solid values. Contrast this with the Kaplan-Sheinwold System where the approach is light initial action – weak no trump, light opening bids, etc.

FIVE CARD MAJORS

One of the major contributions to bridge of Roth and Stone, which deserves special examination here; has become known as 'the five card major.' First introduced to the American playing public in their wide-selling book. "The Roth-Stone System" published in 1953, the practice of five card or longer major suit opening bids has gained, rather than lost popularity, since its advent.

In the first or second position, the bidding *is never opened with a four card major suit.* If the hand warrants an opening bid but the major suit is of four cards, it must be opened with a minor suit – of four or more cards, if present – or, if necessary, a three card minor. The three card minor should, if possible, be headed by an honor but this is secondary to the principle of not opening four card major suits as dealer or second hand.

RESPONDING

As in all modern systems, the responder must show *any* suit of four or more cards that can be bid at the one level rather than bid one no trump. Similarly, the opening bidder must show any higher-ranking suit that can be bid at the one-level. It should be stressed that whereas the first or second seat player must have five cards of a major for an opening bid of that suit, subsequent bids by either partner do not have that qualification – the poorest of four card suits can be shown.

ONE NO TRUMP RESPONSE FORCING

Unlike so-called standard systems, where a response of one no trump indicates six to 10 high card points in the responder's hand and denies support for opener's suit, *and is completely non-forcing*, a response of one no trump, when made as a response to a first or second-seat opening bid of a major suit, shows:

1 – 6 to 11 points;

2 – Less than a two-over-one response, which guarantees another bid by responder;

3 – Less than a single raise (10 to 12 points) and at least three trumps;

4 – *ANY* distribution – may even include four or five cards of partner's suit. *But most important of all, it is forcing for one round!*

(a)
♠x
♡QJxx
◊QJxxx
♣10xx

Hand (a) to the left is an example of a one no trump response in Roth-Stone to an opening one heart bid. The heart support can be shown later.

REBIDS BY OPENER

Exceedingly clear inferences can be drawn by the partner of a Roth-Stone opening bidder. For example, in the bidding as Case A.

CASE A

NORTH, PARTNER	EAST	SOUTH, YOU	WEST
One spade	Pass	One no trump	Pass
Two spades			

Your partner, North, has marked himself as holding at least six spades. The logic should be clear. As dealer he wouldn't have opened the bidding with less than five spades. So he didn't have to rebid the suit to tell you what you already knew, viz:, that he'd started with a five card suit. Hence, his rebid was intended to serve only one purpose, to wit, to tell you that he had six.

And that's another cardinal point of Roth-Stone bidding. The rebid of a non-supported major suit by the first or second-hand indicates a six card or longer suit.

When the opening bidder has bid a five card major to which partner has responded one no trump, his possible rebids may be:

1 – Only a six card or longer major may be rebid;

2 – *Any* secondary suit *must* be bid. This can be a four card major or minor.

3 – With 5-3-3-2 distribution, rebid two clubs or two diamonds, whichever suit contains three cards. If you have 5-2-3-3 with three cards in both minors, prefer clubs to diamonds as a rebid.

THIRD HAND BIDS

The Roth-Stone system employs light third and fourth hand opening bids, where indicated. Four card major suits, in these positions, are permitted. Sound opening bids can be shown by opening with one club, guaranteeing a rebid over a possible response of one diamond. An opening bid of one heart or one spade in third or fourth seat *guarantees a rebid only if partner makes a jump shift in a new suit.*

For complete details on these and other features of the Roth-Stone system, the reader is referred to Bridge Is A Partnership Game and other texts by these authors.

KAPLAN-SHEINWOLD HIGHLIGHTS

WEAK NO TRUMP, FIVE CARD MAJORS, WEAK TWO BIDS, INVERTED MINOR RAISES

by

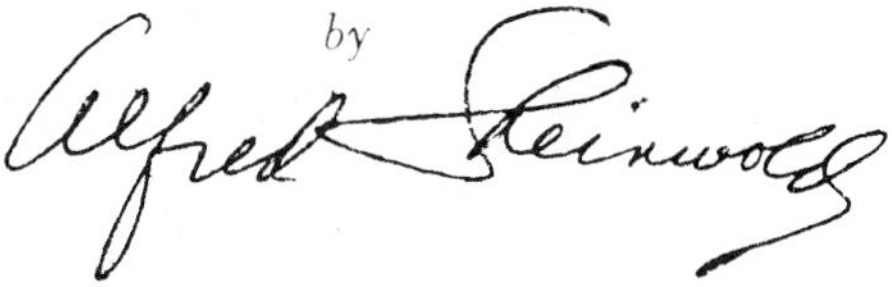

The weak no trump, 11 to 14 points with balanced distribution, not vulnerable, is the cornerstone of the Kaplan-Sheinwold System. An opening bid of one in a suit must show a hand not suitable for an opening bid of one no trump; therefore it must contain more than 14 points or unbalanced distribution.

(a)	(b)
♠ KJ53	♠ KJ532
♡ AQ95	♡ AQ95
◇ 74	◇ 74
♣ K84	♣ K8
Bid one no trump	Bid one spade

Five card majors: the opening bid of one spade or one heart promises a five card or longer suit. If the hand is worth an opening bid of one in a suit but does not contain a biddable (five card) major, a three card or longer minor suit should be bid. *With three cards in each minor, open with one club.*

(c)	(d)	(e)	(f)
♠ J9754	♠ AK75	♠ AK75	♠ AK75
♡ AK5	♡ J85	♡ KQ74	♡ KQ74
◇ KQ74	◇ KQ74	◇ J85	◇ J85
♣ 8	♣ A2	♣ 82	♣ K2
One spade	One diamond	One no trump	One diamond

Weak two bids: The opening bid of two spades, two hearts or two diamonds promises a strong six card suit in a hand that is not quite worth an opening bid of one. In third position the weak two bid may be made on a five card suit if the hand calls for a slightly sub-standard opening bid.

(g)	(h)	(i)
♠ AQJ874	♠ QJ9874	♠ QJ9874
♡ 52	♡ A2	♡ A2
◇ 963	◇ 963	◇ 963
♣ 85	♣ 85	♣ A5
Two spades	Pass	One spade

RESPONSES

To weak no trump: pass balanced hands with 11 or fewer points. Try for game with 12 points (or 11 points and a five card minor suit); make sure of getting to game with 13 to 18 points. Look for a slam with 19 or more points. Use the Stayman Convention with 12 or more points.

To one of a major: raise to two (of the major) with three or more trumps and six to 10 points (including distributional points). Raise to three with four or more trumps and 10 to 12 points. Bid one no trump and make a jump raise at next turn with three and 10 to 12 points. Bid three no trump (artificial and forcing) with Qxxx or better in trumps and 13 or more points (see page 671).

Respond one no trump with only one or two trumps and 10 or fewer points. A response of two in a lower ranking suit shows roughly the values of an opening bid and virtually commits the partnership to game.

To one of a minor: originated by Kaplan and Sheinwold are what are now known as 'inverted' minor raises (see page 678). In so-called standard systems, the single raise from one to two promises six to 10 points, rarely 11 or 12 (*page 63*) and the single jump from one to three 13 to 16 points. Kaplan-Sheinwold stresses, as do other systems, the showing of *any* four card or longer major suit if possible but reverses (hence the term 'invert') procedure in minor raises. Since common sense dictates that the need of pre-emption is greater with weak hands than with strong ones, a raise of partner's minor from one to three is pre-emptive, promises at least five trumps and less than nine points in high cards; a single raise of partner's minor, as from one club to two clubs, promises trump support and at least nine high card points and is forward-going and constructive.

OTHER FEATURES

Treatment of strong hands is much the same as in other systems in which weak two-bids are used. Treatment of the five card major is much the same as in the Roth-Stone System, from which also the negative double has been borrowed.

ONE CLUB FORCING

Since the swaddling clothes days of bridge, experts have used, in one form or another, the opening bid of one club to show a hand of better than minimum opening bid strength. This method was popular in the 'thirties—then was rarely used for nearly three decades. Today, there has been renewed interest in 'Big Club' systems, thanks to the success of the World Champion Italian Blue Team and, on the national scene, the young Precision team that won three major national team championships in less than two years.

The first of the one club forcing systems was devised by Harold Vanderbilt, who also invented contract bridge and modernized scoring. In the Vanderbilt methods, an opening bid of one club showed a better than minimum hand that was not good enough to open with a forcing two-bid—what today would be valued at 16 to 20 points. In most of the modern 'Big Club' systems, the one club opening has no upper limit. It's forcing for one round only, but opener can make a forcing rebid byjumping, even if responder shows a bust.

Almost all one club systems have the following in common: The one club bid is forcing, and bears no relation to the club suit. A response of one diamond is also artificial, and shows a very weak hand. Responder need not bid again unless opener shows additional strength—as by jumping. Having limited his strength by his first one diamond response, however, responder is then free to show slender values by raising partner's real suit or by introducing a suit of his own.

The above comments apply to the major one club systems now in use: Schenken, Precision, Blue Team, which are described on the following pages. (The Roman Club, which also appears herein, is not a true 'Big Club' system.) However, in addition to these well-codified methods, some players, most of whom learned their bidding in the 'thirties, employ a 'homemade' club system. These players generally open one club on almost any hand that does not contain a five card spade, heart or diamond suit, and which is unsuitable for a one no trump opening. The club bid does not necessarily promise any great strength, but it is forcing, since opener may be very short in clubs. Again, the one diamond response (usually) shows a weak hand; the rest of the bidding tends to be natural. Of course, any interference directly over the one club opening relieves responder of any obligation to bid, since opener will have another chance to describe his hand.

The one club forcing method seems ideal in theory. Both the opening bidder and the responder first show the amount of strength held and thereafter, show suits. Unfortunately, while ideal in some bidding Utopia, it is far from true. The opponents, with their 26 combined cards, certainly have a good say in the matter and one well-placed pre-empt, such as a bid of three spades over the one club bid, could wreck bidding communications completely.

Actually, the one club forcing method has still another disadvantage. If, after the opening bid of one club, the opponents take over the bidding and the club bidder never rebids, the opening leader (whose partner bid the strong club) will not have the slightest clue as to what is the best defensive lead.

In rebuttal to these drawbacks, Howard Schenken, architect of his own big club system, argues, **"In my opinion, the great weakness in all popular American systems lies in the opening suit bid of one. It is almost unlimited. For example, an opening bid of one diamond might be made on:**

(a)	(b)
♠xx	♠xx
♡Axx	♡AKQ
◊AJ10xx	◊AKxxx
♣Kxx	♣AKJ

Hand (a) has 12 high card points, hand (b) twice that number; yet according to most authorities one diamond is the correct bid with both.

I do not believe it is possible to bid with accuracy when there can be such a spread between minimum and maximum opening suit bids."*

Although the big club systems seem to be gaining popularity almost daily, and their adherents claim that the advantages far outweigh such drawbacks as have been indicated here, natural bidding still seems to be the most sensible approach for all but, perhaps, the most experienced player. Nevertheless, if you are going to play in expert company, especially if you plan to enter the duplicate fray, you would be welll advised to learn at least the basics of Schenken, Precision and Blue Team, for some of your opponents will be using these systems.

THE SCHENKEN BIG CLUB

Although many experts have recognized the efficiency of a strong, artificial, forcing opening bid of one club, it was not until Howard Schenken of New York City, one of the world's greatest players, devised his Big Club System that America had a modern, forcing club system of its own. Schenken hoped that his system would be instrumental in breaking the streak of

---

*The above quote appeared in the July issue of the American Contract Bridge League's *Bulletin*.

Italian successes in World Championship play, and while his hopes were not realized, his system did introduce the forcing club idea to American players, many of whom have since adopted either his system or one based on similar principles. For a more complete description of his methods, Schenken's book, "Big Club," published by Simon and Schuster.

The Schenken system revolves around an opening bid of one club, which shows 17 points or more, although strong distributional hands with as few as 14 points may also qualify as a one club opening. One diamond is the conventional negative response, zero to six points, and two clubs is an artificial semi-positive response, showing seven or eight points with at least one king or an ace. Other responses are natural and forcing to game. If an opponent overcalls the one club bid, double by responder is for takeout and shows nine or more points.

After a one diamond response, simple suit rebids are non-forcing, but jump rebids are forcing for one round. One and two no trump rebids show respectively 19 to 20 and 21 to 22 points.

Other opening suit bids of one are natural, but limited to a maximum of 16 points, so responder usually does not bid with fewer than eight points. Responses are also natural and standard, except that jump raises are limited and non-forcing, as is a jump to two no trump. A one no trump opening is strong, 16 to 18 points.

Since a minimum hand with a club suit cannot be opened with one club, a two club opening bid is used to show this hand. Two diamonds by responder asks opener to bid a four-card major if he has one.

Besides one club, there is another strong forcing opening bid in the system, namely two diamonds, which usually describes a powerful, unbalanced hand that needs only one or two key cards in the other hand to make a slam. Responses are ace-showing. With no aces, responder bids two hearts. With one ace, responder bids the suit in which the ace is held (two no trump with the ace of hearts). With two aces, responder jumps in the higher-ranking ace if the aces are in touching suits, jumps to three no trump with non-touching aces, or jumps to four clubs with the black aces. Opener may then make a minimum rebid to ask for kings and queens to be shown in the same manner. Opener may have a balanced hand when he opens two diamonds, in which case he will rebid two no trump with 23 to 25 points, or three no trump with 26 to 27 points.

Opening bids of two hearts and two spades are weak two bids (see page 652). Two no trump is a specialized opening bid in the system, showing at least five cards in both minor suits with 10 to 12 points for a non-vulnerable opening bid, but 13 to 16 points if vulnerable.

Three-level opening bids are pre-emptive with the exception of three clubs, which shows a solid six- or seven-card club suit with 10 to 15 points. Finally, a three no trump opening is based on a solid minor suit with stoppers in all the side suits (queen doubleton or better).

Just as Culbertson was "the" new system of the 'thirties, Goren, of the 'forties, Roth-Stone of the 'fifties, and Kaplan-Sheinwold of the 'sixties, indications are that the system of the 'seventies will be the Precision Club. The system is the brain-child of C.C. Wei, a Chinese shipping magnate who resides in New York City. The bridge community first became aware of Precision when it carried on unheralded Chinese team into the runner-up spot in the 1969 and 1970 Bermuda Bowl World Championships. Then a young team of players from the New York City area used Precision to take three of the top U.S. National Team Championships (the Spingold twice and the Vanderbilt) in the short space of 19 months – and the reputation of Precision was assured.

The Precision System is the first one club forcing method to gain widespread endorsement by both expert and average bridge players. It has been adopted by the Italian Blue Team, many time World Champions, and by countless duplicate players. I am pleased that this summary of Precision has been written especially for the latest edition of "Contract Bridge Complete" by Thomas M. Smith of Greenwich, Connecticut, a member of the Precision Team that won the 1970 and 1971 Spingold and the 1972 Vanderbilt. Until recently, Tom Smith was Business Manager of the American Contract Bridge League Bulletin, and he is the author of numerous articles on bridge bidding and play.

For a complete presentation of the Precision System, the reader is referred to "Precision Bidding in Bridge" by C.C. Wei

(Barclay, Port Chester, New York, $3.00).

Ernest W. Rovere

THE PRECISION CLUB

by

Thomas M. Smith

Construction of bidding systems has long been the private domain of renowned, accomplished bridge players, but C. C. Wei is the exception. He readily admits that he is not in the expert class and that his main interest lies in the *theory* of bidding—why a pair failed to bid a laydown game or slam, or hopelessly overbid to some terrible contract. After studying the underpinnings of bidding, Mr. Wei borrowed a few features from other systems, added some new ideas of his own, mixed well, and produced an astonishingly simple, successful system that within four years after its introduction captured the imagination of players of all degrees of ability, from the famed "Blue Team" on down, throughout the world.

Since several features of the Precision System have already been discussed in this section of the text, I will merely refer the reader to these treatments, then concentrate on the unique ingredients of Precision: five-card major suit opening bids in all seats with one no trump as a forcing response (see page 743); weak two bids in the majors (see page 652); gambling three no trump (see page 703); and opening bids of four clubs and four diamonds as strong major suit pre-empts, with the added restriction that opener normally has a solid suit with at most one side king or ace.

With the exception of a 22 to 24 point two no trump opening, one club is the only strong opening bid in the system, but it is slightly weaker than other strong, artificial one club bids. It shows a minimum of 16 points with any distribution, perhaps a bit less if opener has exceptional distribution.

With zero to seven points, responder makes the conventional negative response of one diamond. Responses of one heart, one spade, two clubs and two diamonds are 'positive' and guarantee at least a five-card suit and eight or more points. If he has a balanced positive hand, responder bids one no trump with eight to 10 points, two no trump with 11 to 13 points (or 16 points plus), or three no trump with 14 to 15 points. Jump responses are pre-emptive, usually four to seven points, and the higher the jump, the longer the suit. To illustrate, opener, one club—responder, two spades, shows a six-card spade suit, while a jump to three spades would be based on a seven-card suit.

The astute reader may have noticed that there is one hand pattern that is not covered by this structure of responses, to wit, a positive 4–4–4–1. Responder cannot bid a five-card suit because he doesn't have one, nor can he bid no trump because his hand is unbalanced. So he wheels out the 'impossible negative.' His first response is one diamond, then, depending on opener's rebid, he either jumps in no trump if opener rebids in his short suit, or jumps in his singleton. Hand (a) illustrates this method.

(a)
♠ KJ73
♡ 2
◇ A1084
♣ Q975

Over an opening bid of one club, responder bids one diamond. If opener's rebid is one or two hearts, responder jumps to either two or three no trump, while if opener's rebid is anything else, responder jumps in hearts.

In principle, positive responses are forcing to game. However, if both hands are dead minimum for their bids, the auction could stop in two no trump, or three of either opener's or responder's major suit.

After a negative diamond response, opener's rebids follow the usual pattern of all strong, forcing club systems. Simple suit rebids are non-forcing, while jump suit rebids are forcing for a round. One, two, and three no trump rebids show respectively 16 to 18, 19 to 21, and 25 to 26 points.

Over positive responses, the auction tends to develop naturally, except that after no trump responses, a minimum rebid in clubs by opener is the Stayman Convention (see page 598). If responder has made a positive response in a suit, however, opener may avail himself of an exciting, though optional, feature of the system—trump suit asking bids—and all he has to do is to raise responder's suit one level, as in Case A.

CASE A

SOUTH, OPENER	NORTH, RESPONDER
One club	One heart
Two hearts	

Responder shows the quality of his suit by a series of artificial step rebids as follows: first step—suit headed by none of the three honors (ace, king, or queen); second step—five-card suit headed by one honor; third step—five-card suit to two honors; fourth step—six-card suit to one honor; fifth step—six-card suit to two honors; sixth step—suit headed by all three honors.

After responder has made his artificial rebid, a new suit by opener is then a 'control asking bid.' Again responder rebids artificially by steps, but this time to show controls in the asked suit as follows: first step—no control; second step—second-round control (the king or a singleton); third step—first-round control (ace or void); fourth step—first- and second-round control (singleton ace, ace-king, or ace-queen). These asking bids are not essential to the system but do add a high degree of accuracy to slam bidding.

If the one club opening bid is overcalled, responder may show a five to eight point hand by making a negative double (see page 690), a simple response in a five-card or longer suit, or by bidding the cheapest amount of no trump with a stopper in the opponent's suit. A direct cue-bid of the opponent's suit is used to show a positive hand. Jump responses in a suit are pre-emptive, although some players prefer that these show positive hands containing a broken six-card or longer suit.

Opening bids of one diamond, one heart and one spade are natural and limited to a maximum of 15 points. Only the diamond suit may be less than five cards in length, and while it is normally a four-card or longer suit, one diamond may be opened on a three-card suit if the hand does not fit conveniently into any of the system's other opening bids, as with hand (b).

(b)
♠ 3
♡ A K 10 5
♢ A J 7
♣ J 9 6 5 3

Responses to limited opening bids are standard with several important exceptions. First, since opener is known to have fewer than 16 points, responder is under no obligation to keep the bidding open with a minimum hand of, let's say, six or seven points. Second, a jump response of two no trump shows a balanced hand of 16 points or more (see Baron Two No Trump, page 688). Third, a raise of one diamond to two diamonds is strong and forcing for a round (see Inverted Minor Suit Raises, page 678). Finally, over opening bids of one heart and one spade, responder makes a limit jump raise with four or more trumps and 11 to 13 points (non-forcing), jumps to three no trump with a balanced strong raise, four or more trumps (forcing to four of opener's suit), or makes a Splinter Bid (see page 673) with an unbalanced strong raise (also forcing to four of opener's suit).

One of the great advantages of a forcing club system is that when the opening bid is not one club, opener's hand is limited to the 11 to 15 point range. Thus opener may bid aggressively at his next turn, such as making a jump shift or a reverse, or jumping to two no trump, when he has the 14 to 15 point hand and the right values. To illustrate, suppose that opener held hand (c) and that responder had hand (d). A Precision auction might proceed as diagrammed in Case B.

(c)	(d)
♠4	♠Q63
♡82	♡A954
♢AKJ87	♢42
♣AK543	♣Q1086

CASE B

SOUTH, OPENER	NORTH, RESPONDER
One diamond	One heart
Three clubs	Four clubs
Five clubs	

Three clubs showed a top-drawer non-one club opening bid, and four clubs announced that game was possible. With all controls opener could not resist the temptation to try for game, and thus the excellent contract of five clubs was reached.

The Precision one no trump opening bid has often been described as the 'in-between notrump' because it is neither weak nor strong. It shows 13 to 15 points and a balanced hand that might possibly contain a five-card minor, but certainly not a five-card major.

In response, two clubs is non-forcing Stayman and two diamonds is game-forcing Stayman. Two clubs, however, does not necessarily show a weak responding hand. Responder often has enough values to invite game, or to insist on game but simply wants to find out whether the game should be played in a four-four major suit fit or in three no trump.

Two diamonds, on the other hand, always guarantees enough high card strength for game and often has slam implications. Over two diamonds, opener shows a four-card major, a five-card minor, or rebids two no trump.

Responses of two hearts, two spades, three clubs, and three diamonds to one no trump are signoffs, while jumps to three hearts and three spades are natural and game-forcing. Texas transfers (see page 640)

An opening bid of two clubs is similar to the Neapolitan System. Opener usually promises 11 to 15 points with a six-card or longer club suit, possibly with a side four- or five-card suit, or a good five-card club suit with a side four-card major. (With five clubs and four diamonds, the opening bid will usually be one diamond.) A two diamond response asks opener if he has a secondary suit. If he does not, opener rebids two no trump with two side suits stopped, or three clubs with one side suit stopped. Responder can then find out which suits opener has guarded by a series of artificial rebids.

All bidding systems that have gained any degree of respectibility have the machinery to describe, within broad limits, all possible distributional hands worth an opening bid. In Precision, the two diamond opening bid covers the one hand that cannot be shown by any other opening bid – an 11 to 15 point hand that contains four cards in each major suit with four or five clubs. If opener has such a hand with five clubs, obviously a two club opening bid might result in the partnership missing a major-suit fit, while any other suit opening bid would lie about the length of the bid suit. Thus the specialized two diamond opening bid.

Responder may sign off by bidding two hearts, two spades, or three clubs (opener's known suits), or by passing with a long diamond suit. Jump responses in hearts, spades and clubs invite game, and a two no trump response asks opener to rebid artificially to describe within precise limits his distribution and high card strength, and whether or not he has a singleton diamond honor (ace, king, or queen). Alternatively, a three diamond response can be used for this purpose.

Minor suit pre-emptive opening bids at the three level usually guarantee a semi-solid suit with a side stopper, or a solid suit, so that responder can accurately estimate the chances for three no trump.

These, then, are the chief features of the Precision System. Perhaps the greatest strengths of the system are the highly descriptive nature of all opening bids and that it is a completely natural system. Balanced hands are either opened one or two no trump, or one club followed by a no trump rebid. Similarly, unbalanced hands are opened in a suit or one club followed by a suit rebid. And all opening bids fall within carefully defined point ranges. With such a foundation to build an auction on, it's no wonder that Precision bidding is so accurate.

FOREIGN BIDDING SYSTEMS

Terence Reese, born at Epsom and residing in London, England, has often been called "The greatest bridge player in the world." His championship wins are innumerable and include many world and European titles. In addition to his ability at the card table, he has authored many outstanding books on bridge. Among them, all highly recommended, are Bridge For Bright Beginners; Reese on Play; Play Bridge With Reese; Develop Your Bidding Judgment; and many others.

One of the originators of Acol bidding, a system that is widely used in Great Britain and elsewhere and which is presented under his authorship on the following pages, Reese also devised the Little Major, a highly artificial system that enjoyed spectacular, although brief success in the early 1960's. Recently he has been experimenting with an English version of the Precision System.

Ernest W. Rovere

THE ACOL SYSTEM

by

Terence Reese

Acol, played by the great majority of British tournament players, derives its name from first being played in a North London street of that name. It was originated by a group of players including S. J. Simon, M. Harrison-Gray, I. MacLeod, J. C. H. Marx and myself.

Although it contains an artificial two club opening bid and strong intermediate two-bids, it is basically an approach-forcing system. The general style of bidding is more natural than in Standard American. Many more bidding sequences are non-forcing than in American methods.

OPENING BIDS OF ONE IN A SUIT

Playing tricks, rather than honors or points, are the standard.

(a)
♠ 10 4
♡ K 7 3
◇ J 2
♣ K Q J 10 5 2

Hand (a) to the left is considered a fair tactical opening except perhaps, when vulnerable against non-vulnerable opponents. Opening bids with such moderate strength in high cards can be made freely since the system contains many firm sign-off bids. For example,

CASE A

OPENER	RESPONDER
One club	Two no trump
Three clubs	

is a sign-off at Acol.

(b)
♠ A K 7
♡ 9 5
◇ A K 8 3
♣ A Q 7 4

Hand (b) contains five and a half honor tricks by the old Culbertson standards, but it would still be opened with a bid of one diamond. It is not suitable either for an opening bid of two clubs or any other suit.

OPENING BIDS OF ONE NO TRUMP AND RESPONSES

A variable no trump is generally played, about 12 - 14 points when not vulnerable and 15 - 17 points when vulnerable. Simple (minimum) responses in a suit are weak, and non-forcing Stayman (pages 627 - 629) is used.

RESPONDING TO BIDS OF ONE IN A SUIT

A response of one no trump suggests about six to nine points as in standard American bidding. A response of two no trump indicates 11 - 13 points and *is not forcing*. In the same way, a jump raise to three of a suit is a limit bid. A raise in partner's suit to four is pre-emptive. Most Acol players use the Swiss Convention (page 672) to distinguish between the different types of raises.

THE ACOL TWO-BID

Opening bids of two diamonds, two hearts and two spades are made with what can be described as hands of 'power and quality'.

(c)	(d)	(e)
♠ AKQJ73	♠ KQ98	♠ A
♡ A94	♡ AKJ10763	♡ K64
◇ KQ7	◇ K2	◇ AJ10985432
♣ 10	♣ void	♣ void

These hands belong to a class which is difficult to describe when two bids are of one of two extreme types - either forcing to game as in standard American methods or weak and pre-emptive.

Opening bids of two of a suit are *forcing for one round*. The weakness response is two no trump. Most players follow the principle that a single raise of opener's suit should promise at least one ace. A double raise indicates good support but no ace. An ace is not required for a positive response in another suit.

OPENING BIDS OF TWO CLUBS

An opening bid of two clubs is *forcing to game*, except that a rebid of two no trump by opener over his partner's response, promising 23 points, may be passed.

(f)
♠ AKJ1086
♡ AQ7432
◇ void
♣ J

The bid is made on hands containing game-going strength and containing at least five honor tricks, rarely a minimum of four and a half honor tricks.

Hand (f) is obviously of game-going strength but it lacks the five honor tricks needed for the

(g)
♠ AKQ1096
♡ A102
◇ AK3
♣ 4

opening two club bid. Hence it is opened with two spades and not two clubs. Hand (g) should be opened with two clubs.

The weakness response to two clubs is a bid of two diamonds. There are no exact standards for a positive response. At the range of two, a fair suit such as KQ864 and a side queen, is sufficient. A response of two no trump suggests a minimum of about eight points including two kings, and a response of three no trump would indicate the equivalent of three kings and a jack.

OPENING BIDS OF TWO NO TRUMP AND THREE NO TRUMP

An opening bid of two no trump suggests 20 - 22 points. A response of three clubs is Stayman. Holding 23 - 24 points, the opener bids two clubs and rebids with two no trump; with 25 points, after opening with two clubs, he rebids three no trump.

Acol players have used the 'gambling three no trump' (page 703) for many years before this bid made its appearance in America. The bid shows a long and solid minor suit with no more than a queen in the remainder of the hand. If the responder does not with the hand to play in three no trump, he takes out into four clubs (or more), allowing the opening bidder to name his suit.

SLAM CONVENTIONS

The Culbertson 4 - 5 no trump convention (page 502) is traditional for Acol players, but many prefer the simpler Blackwood (page 503). Many leading players use Roman Blackwood with the full schedule of responses - that is to say,

RESPONSE	SHOWS*
Five hearts	Two aces of the same color.
Five spades	Two aces of the same rank (both major or both minor).
Five no trump	Two dis-similar aces, viz, one red and the other black and not touching. This works out to spades and diamonds or hearts and clubs.

Footnote

* *This differs from the Table on page* 503. *Using the English method, the player wishing to ask for kings may use the next ranking unbid suit as a rebid.* (ewr)

DEFENSIVE BIDDING

Jump overcalls are strong but not forcing. They suggest the equivalent of an opening bid containing a good suit.

Theoretically, a two club response to partner's informatory double is a weakness response but a four card major, after partner's informatory double, should be shown even with weak hands.

Against pre-emptive three-bids, most players use the Reese Defense, also known as x - 3 - x. Over a pre-emptive opening bid of three hearts or three spades, a double would be for penalty and a bid of three no trump a request for takeout. Against opening three-bids in the minors, the double is for takeout and three no trump natural and shows a willingness to play the hand in that contract. In the protective (fourth seat) position, doubles are always optional although primarily for takeout.

ADDITIONAL CONVENTIONS

The following conventions are standard for tournament players using Acol.

1 - The unusual no trump (page 714).

2 - Responsive double up to three diamonds (page 692).

3 - Kock-Werner redouble (page 821).

4 - Swiss Convention (page 672).

5 - Truscott Convention (page 676).

6 - South African transfer bids (page 641). Many players employ this convention for opening bid purposes, four diamonds asking for four spades and four clubs for four hearts. These bids denote stronger hands than an immediate opening bid of either four hearts or four spades.

7 - Flint Convention (page 645).

8 - Baron Grand slam try (page 688).

9 - Fourth suit forcing. In most cases, a bid of the fourth suit in an unopposed auction *does not* guarantee either length or strength in the named suit: it is simply a means of keeping the bidding alive. North's bid of two hearts *may* be a genuine suit but he may also hold nothing of value in the heart suit. South is asked to make further descriptive bid. He will not bid no trump unless holding a heart stopper.

SOUTH	NORTH
One spade	Two clubs
Two diamonds	Two hearts!

ITALIAN BIDDING SYSTEMS

From 1956 until their retirement after the 1969 World Championship, the Italian "Blue Team", captained for most of this period by Carl Alberto Perroux of Modena, Italy, enjoyed a string of successes in international play that is unlikely ever to be matched: ten World Championship Bermuda Bowls and two World Olympiad Team titles.

(Ed. note: Italy is likely to win the 1972 Olympiad this June, in which case add the following note in parentheses after the above revision: (The Blue Team emerged from their retirement in 1972 and, using the Precision System, captured their third Olympiad title.)

Much of the team's success derives from excellent and long standing partnerships; some from sheer excellence in play of the cards; but a great deal stems from two highly complicated and, in many instances, artificial bidding systems. There are basically two principal Italian systems generally known as The Roman System and the Neapolitan System.

It is a tremendous privilege to include, in this book, an authoritative article on the Roman Club System by Giorgio Belladonna, co-inventor of the system with Dr. Walter Avarelli, both of whom reside in Rome.

Belladonna has been a stalwart member of the Blue Team that has won twelve World Championships and innumerable European titles. Under the rankings compiled for the first time in 1972 by the World Bridge Federation, Giorgio Belladonna was listed as the premier bridge player of the entire world.

(Ed. note: Change twelve to thirteen if Italy wins the 1972 Olympiad.)

Ernest W. Rovere

THE ROMAN CLUB

by

In the 1950 Italian championship, the Roman team which included Avarelli, Bianchi, G. C. Manca, G. Manca, Iozia, Mondolfo and myself, played a new bidding system which, afterwards, became famous as "The Roman Club."

The principle idea behind the system was to indicate, on the very first bid, the distribution of the opening bidder's hand. Therefore the system was revolutionary since it placed the emphasis on distribution rather than, in conventional means, on strength.

The first step in that direction was that opening bids of one club or of one no trump would show balanced hands, either 4-3-3-3 or 4-4-3-2. After this decision we looked for the way of treating opening bids of three-suiters (4-4-4-1 and 5-4-4-0) and also unbalanced hands. The latter, if the long suit were clubs, could not be opened with 'one club' since that bid would promise a balanced holding.

Hence, to show three-suiters we decided on two possible bids. An opening bid of two clubs promised a three-suiter with 12 - 16 points; an opening bid of two diamonds also indicated a three-suiter, but a stronger hand, containing 17 - 20 points.

Holding one-suiter unbalanced hands, the opening bid was made in whatever suit was held unless it were clubs in which case the opening bid was made in a three card suit.

With a two-suiter and an unbalanced hand, and when the suits are unequal in length, the shorter suit is bid first similar to Canape; when the suits are of equal length, the lower ranking suit is bid first with the exception of a two-suiter of equal length with clubs as one of the suits. A two-suiter of spades and clubs, or hearts and clubs, with equal length in both, hold-

12 - 16 points, would be opened with a bid of 'two spades' or 'two hearts', respectively.

The decision to bid the longer suit on the second round seemed the better for us; in fact, the inconvenience we found in traditional methods* of opening with the longer suit resulted in sometimes having the shorter, second suit shut out, and outweighed the risk of opening with the shorter suit and bidding the longer on the second round. Besides, we have tried to lessen that risk by incorporating that other indispensable principle of the system, viz., using a response of the next-ranking denomination as a negative response as responding 'one diamond' to an opening bid of one club or bidding 'one spade' to an opening bid of one heart or responding with 'one no trump' to partner's opening bid of one spade.

BIDS TO SHOW BALANCED DISTRIBUTION

ONE CLUB, 12 - 16 POINTS

RESPONSES

One diamond - Negative, with zero to seven points.

Responses of one heart, one spade, two clubs or two diamonds positive and forcing for one round. When holding two suits as responder, the shorter suit is bid first.

The following responses are forcing to game:

Any reverse bidding	
Any jump bidding	
One no trump	12 - 16 points with balanced distribution.
Two no trump	17 or more points with balanced distribution.
Two hearts, two spades	At least 12 points with a suit of five or more cards containing at least two major honors.
Three clubs, three diamonds	A K Q or A K J and three or four more lower cards in the suit without additional side suit strength.

FOOTNOTE

* *Referred to as Standard (American) in Le Dentu's article on Canape.*

OPENING BIDS OF ONE NO TRUMP

Opening bids of one no trump promise balanced hands containing 17 - 20 points.

RESPONSES

Two clubs	Negative, zero to five points, unbalanced distribution. Opener must rebid 'two diamonds', leaving to the responder the conclusion of the bidding.
Two diamonds	Conventional, with six or more points *and* a major suit of *four* cards. Opener must show a major suit, if held, and strength.
Two hearts, two spades	At least six points and a five card or longer suit.
Two no trump	Six or seven points, lacking a four card or longer major suit.
Three clubs, three diamonds	At least 11 points and a five card or longer suit.
Three no trump	Balanced distribution, eight - 12 points, lacking a major suit of four or more cards.

OPENING BIDS OF ONE CLUB

A second type of hand that may be shown with an opening bid of one club is one with balanced distribution and 21 - 22 points. A rebid by opener by a jump in no trump is descriptive.

OPENING BIDS OF TWO NO TRUMP

Opening bids of two no trump promise 23 - 24 points and balanced distribution.

RESPONSES

A response of three clubs is conventionally negative. Opener must rebid with three diamonds.

A response of three diamonds is conventional with responder holding a four card or longer major.

A response of three no trump denies four cards of a major suit and is a signoff.

Responses of either three hearts, three spades, four clubs or four diamonds are positive and promise the suit to be five cards or longer.

BIDS TO SHOW UNBALANCED DISTRIBUTION

OPENING BIDS OF ONE CLUB

The reader will have noticed that this is the third way in which an opening bid of one club may be employed. In this situation, an opening bid of one club will show a very strong hand, possibly a two-suiter, with three losers or less.

To distinguish it from its predecessors, the opener makes a jump rebid in a suit at his next turn, which asks responder to rebid artificially by steps to describe his support for that suit.

There is yet another type of unbalanced hand that may be shown by an opening bid of one club – a two-suiter of 17-20 points with a four-card or longer club suit and a five-card side suit. This type of hand was difficult to describe in the original Roman System, so in 1967 we suggested that a one club opening, followed by a club rebid by opener should describe this specific two-suiter. Thus, there are four distinct possible interpretations of a one club opening bid.

OPENING BIDS OF ONE DIAMOND, ONE HEART AND ONE SPADE

Opening bids of one of a suit (other than clubs) promise at least 12 points with the hand having four or more losing cards. With a one-suiter, the suit will be at least five cards in length. Holding a two-suiter, the opening bid will be in the shorter (with suits of unequal length) or the lower-ranking, if the same number of cards are held in both.

RESPONSES

The conventional negative, viz., the cheapest bid, is employed with hands of less than eight to nine points.

THE NEAPOLITAN CLUB
(BLUE TEAM CLUB)

The Neapolitan system was developed by Eugenio Chiardia, one of the original members of the famed Blue Team. After Chiardia left the team in 1964, Benito Garozzo, many times World Champion and one of the leading Italian bidding theorists, gradually revised the system and renamed it the "Blue Team Club." It is this version of the system that has achieved a considerable following among many of the leading American players, including four members of the two-time World Champion Aces.

OPENING BIDS OF ONE CLUB

Opening bids of one club are forcing, generally promise 17 points or more.

Responses are artificial and indicate either points or "controls," counting a king as one control and an ace as two controls. Hence, the cheapest response of one diamond shows zero to five points; one heart indicates six or more points, but fewer than three controls; responses of one spade through two diamonds describe three, four, five, or six controls respectively; and two no trump shows seven or more controls. Jump responses to two of a major or three of a minor promise long decent suits with fewer than six points.

If the opening bid of one club is overcalled, a pass is normally the equivalent of a one diamond response and a negative double replaces the one heart response. Other responses show controls as in the preceding paragraph. This method of combating interference varies depending on the level that the overcall is made at.

After a one club opening and a one diamond response, the auction will usually continue until a final contract of at least one no trump is reached. It must proceed to at least two no trump over a one heart response, and if responder has made a control-showing response, such as one spade, the bidding cannot die below the game level.

Jump rebids in a suit by opener are forcing to game. Over a rebid of no trump by opener, responder may employ Stayman.

OPENING BIDS OF ONE DIAMOND, ONE HEART AND ONE SPADE

Opening bids of one diamond, one heart and one spade are natural, showing possession of the bid suit and hands from 12-16 points in most cases. Any suit is regarded as biddable. Holding two suits of equal length, the higher ranking is bid first. With a two-suiter of unequal length, the shorter is bid first (Canape) unless the longer suit is higher-ranking and the hand is weak.

Responses are usually normal. Jump raises and a response of two no trump are limited. The two no trump response promises 4-3-3-3 distribution and 11-12 points. Jump takeouts to new suits are made with 13 points or more and solid or near-solid suits. With a two-suiter, Canape is used to indicate the second suit to be longer. With a one-suiter (shown on a second round of bidding), the first suit may be artificial and temporizing.

Any response at the two level is forcing for a round on both players, or until two no trump is reached, and opener must rebid a five-card suit if he has one. After a one heart or one spade opening bid and a two level response, responder can jump to four clubs or four diamonds at his next turn to show a strong hand with a minimum of four-card support for opener's major.

With a strong opening bid, 14-16 points, opener can make a jump rebid or reverse, depending upon his holding.

OPENING BIDS OF ONE NO TRUMP

Opening bids of one no trump show either of two types of balanced hands: 13-15 points with three cards in each major suit and four or five clubs, or 16-17 points with any balanced distribution. A two club response shows 8-11 points and asks opener to make a descriptive rebid. With the stronger hand, opener rebids two spades, after which responder may inquire about a 4-4 major-suit fit by rebidding two no trump (Stayman convention).

With 12 points or more, responder bids two diamonds. Opener then rebids two hearts or two spades with four cards in the bid suit and 16-17 points, three clubs with 16-17 points and no four-card major, or two no trump with the 13-15 point no trump.

Jump responsee at the three level show six-card suits headed by two of the top three honors and 6-7 points. Responses of four clubs and four diamonds are transfers to four hearts and four spades respectively.

OPENING BIDS OF TWO CLUBS

Opening bids of two clubs are natural and promise a good club suit with 12-16 points. Normally opener will have a one-suiter with six or more clubs, but he may have a four- or five-card side suit if his strength is 15-16 points. (With a weaker hand, opener would open with a one bid in his shorter, higher-ranking suit.)

If responder bids two diamonds, opener shows his second suit if he has one. Otherwise he rebids two no trump with stoppers in two suits other than clubs, or three clubs with one side suit stopped.

Other two level responses are natural and non-forcing. Jump responses to the three level are forcing to game and guarantee solid or semi-solid suits. If responder has a game-going hand with a broken suit, he first bids two diamonds, then bids his suit at his next turn.

OPENING BIDS OF TWO DIAMONDS

Strong 4-4-4-1 hands are difficult to handle in all strong one club forcing systems because of the inability of opener to describe his hand accurately on the subsequent rounds of bidding. In 1967, Garozzo suggested that two diamond opening bids be used to describe precisely this type of hand—4-4-4-1 pattern with 17-24 points.

The responses and subsequent bidding tend to be highly artificial. Two hearts by responder asks opener to clarify the strength of his hand and to pinpoint his singleton, which he does generally by rebidding in the suit below his singleton. Rebids of two spades through three clubs show 17-20 points, three diamonds through three no trump show 21-24 points. Responder may then bid opener's known singleton to further narrow down his point range and to discover how many controls opener has.

A two spade response is a weak bid, 0-4 points, that promises at least three spades. With a minimum and support for spades, opener passes; without support, he removes to two no trump. With a maximum, with or without support for spades, opener rebids in the suit below his singleton at the three level.

A response of two no trump shows a good six-card suit, which responder will bid at his next turn, headed by two of the two three honors or any three honors, but little strength on the side. Responses at the three-level are natural and describe weaker six-card suits with more outside strength.

OPENING BIDS OF TWO HEARTS AND TWO SPADES

Opening bids of two hearts and two spades are similar to the American weak two bid, except that the strength is 8-11 points. The only forcing response is two no trump.

OPENING BIDS OF THREE CLUBS

Opening bids of three clubs are specialized, natural pre-empts, describing a solid or semi-solid club suit with a side trick.

DEFENSIVE BIDDING

Overcalls are normal but are made freely on weak hands. Jump overcalls are intermediate. In responding to a takeout double, the Herbert Convention (page 664) is employed.

Canape has become one of the world's standard methods of bidding. Employed mainly in Europe and particularly in France, many of its features are included in other systems as Acol and Italian.

The author of the definitive article to follow is José Le Dentu, a prominent Paris attorney. An outstanding champion in his own right, winner of innumerable European titles, competitor in world championships, he has authored many books on bridge, is a columnist and an editor of the Revue Francaise de Bridge.

No one is better qualified to write on Canape than Monsieur Le Dentu.

Ernest W. Rovere

CANAPE

by

Canape is not exactly a system but a convenient and technical way of bidding two-suiters. Generally known as the 'shorter suit first', its scientific name could be 'the five card reverse'.

HISTORIC BIRTH OF CANAPE

Canape style seems to have been studied and discussed for the first time in a great championship more than 30 years ago. The hand was dealt in a famous match that occurred in Paris in July, 1933 between a French team on which Pierre Albarran was playing and an American team that included Ely Culbertson.

The match was scored not at 'contract' but at 'plafond' in which slams had not to be bid. It was stopped at the 102nd deal (after this board had been incorrectly reversed) and the referees agreed to a draw. Perhaps board number 96 gave Pierre Albarran the idea to create the Canape.

	♠ Q962 ♡ AK1073 ◇ A10 ♣ QJ	
♠ AJ743 ♡ 2 ◇ KQJ8 ♣ AK8	N W E S	♠ K ♡ Q9854 ◇ 752 ♣ 10762
	♠ 1085 ♡ J6 ◇ 9643 ♣ 9543	

First table

SOUTH	WEST	NORTH	EAST
Josephine Culbertson	Aron	M. Gottlieb	Albarran
Pass	1 diamond	Double	Pass
2 clubs	2 spades	Pass	3 diamonds
Pass	Pass	Pass	

Result - East-West made three diamonds for a score of 110 points.

Second table

SOUTH	WEST	NORTH	EAST
Venizelos	Ely Culbertson	Bellanger	Lightner
Pass	1 spade	2 hearts	Double
Pass	Pass	Pass	

Result - North down three tricks, doubled, for minus 500 points.

"Very lucky board for the Americans," wrote the French commentator. "It's due to the opening bid. The French West opened 'one diamond', but at the other table Culbertson chose 'one spade'. Who was right? The French players discussed it. Albarran likes one diamond better....."

Today some players are still discussing such choices as if the problem has not been solved since the birth of the game!

Bridge is ruled by 'physics' that do not vary from one deal to another. There are only *two scientific ways to bid two-suiters.* You begin either with *the longer* suit or with *the shorter.* You must choose, with partner, one of those two systems and, after this choice, you have only to follow their theoretical principles which are quite logical.

Culbertson in the Blue Book established methodically the laws of the 'longer suit' which became the 'Standard System', or, if you like it better, the 'natural' way (to bid two-suiters).

The other way is the Canape, the rules of which were published in 1947 by Pierre Albarran in a book of more than 200 pages about 'the easiest and most precise method of bidding two and three-suiters'. Two years later we simplified the chief features of Canape and began regularly to include it in every edition of our standard French books on bidding.

SHORTER SUIT AND FIVE CARD REVERSE PRINCIPLE

Let's have a short review of these rules which are the very opposite of standard methods.

First of all, *Canape style is applicable only to opening bids of one in a suit and to their non-jump responses.* It is not Canape when the opening bid is two in a suit or when making a jump shift response.

The basic principle is that when holding two biddable suits, you must begin by bidding the shorter.

(a)

♠ Axx
♡ KQJxx
◇ xx
♣ AQxx

CASE A

SOUTH	NORTH
One club	One spade
Two hearts	

The opening bid should be 'one club'. On the next round, you bid your hearts.

The corollary is fundamental: *a reverse bid necessarily shows the second suit of at least five cards.* Hence in Case A, South can't have less than five hearts.

For players first using Canape, the following will be of assistance: when you intend to declare two suits, bid your major suit on the first round if of four cards; bid it on the second round if of five cards.

However, a modern system of bidding must combine both the principle of length and that of strength. For instance, you can't make a reverse bid as in Case B with minimum opening values. Your hand should not be too weak to make a reverse. But, as the second suit is the better, it's not necessary that the hand be as strong as the requirements of the standard system (page 132). In Canape, 15 high card points or three and a half honor tricks are sufficient.

CASE B

SOUTH	NORTH
One diamond	One spade
Two hearts	

As you will have at least two points for distribution, *you can reverse with any hand of 16 points or more, including points for distribution.*

One of the chief advantages of Canape is the more frequent use of reverse bids at the two-level, which are too rarely employed in Standard Systems.

In Canape, the one-over-one is no longer an ambiguous bid.

With the bidding in Case C, South's bid of one spade guarantees at least five spades and a minimum of 14 high card points.

CASE C

SOUTH	NORTH
One club	One diamond
One spade	

The bid is not forcing. The club suit could be of only three cards if you think your hand too good to open with one spade and rebid two spades.

An opening bid of one club followed by bidding spades on the second round is a very convenient method of announcing hands of 15-16 points with a five card major suit.

(b)
♠ AKJxx
♡ xxx
◇ xx
♣ AKx

When you are not strong enough to make a reverse, you begin by bidding the longer suit and subsequently rebidding it. Holding hand (c), the opening bid would be one spade. But substitute the king of diamonds for the jack, the opening bid would be one diamond with spades as a rebid.

(c)
♠ AKxxx
♡ xx
◇ AJxx
♣ xx

Here are the applications of the Canape Rule.

1 - FOUR CARD SUITS (4 - 4)

Bid the higher ranking suit first.

(d)
♠ KQJx
♡ xx
◇ AQxx
♣ Q10x

With hand (d), bid one spade. If partner responds two clubs, you can rebid two no trump which does not announce more than 14 - 15 points.

2 - SUITS OF UNEQUAL LENGTH (4 - 5 and 4 - 6).

Bid the shorter suit first (opposite ot the Standard rule).

(e)
♠ xx
♡ AQxx
◇ AQxxxx
♣ x

Open hand (e) with one heart. Exception—with a hand of weak opening strength, open the bidding and rebid with the higher-ranking, longer five or six card suit as your hand is not strong enough for a reverse.

(f)
♠ AQxxxx
♡ x
◇ 10x
♣ AJxx

Hand (f) should be opened with one spade and the suit rebid. However, were the king of diamonds substituted for the 10, the correct opening bid would have been one club.

3 - LONG SUITS OF EQUAL LENGTH (5 - 5)

Bid first the lower ranking suit except with a minimum opening. In the Standard System you normally open with the high ranking suit. In Canape style, it's just the contrary because you would reverse on the next round in order to show a five card, higher-ranking suit (generally a major).

CASE D

SOUTH	NORTH
One diamond	One heart
One spade	One no trump
Two diamonds	

South's bid of one spade in Case D, made on the second round of bidding, indicates the suit to be of at least five cards. His rebid of the diamond suit promises five diamonds and a hand with about 15 high card points.

4 - THREE-SUITERS (5 - 4 - 4 and 4 - 4 - 4 - 1)

(g)
♠ KQxxx
♡ AJxx
◇ void
♣ KQxx

Methods for showing three-suiters are similar to two-suiters. For example, holding hand (g) to the left, open the bidding with one heart and on the next round, bid the spade suit to show it to be five cards in length. If necessary, clubs may be bid on the third round to give an exact picture of the distribution.

EFFECTS OF CANAPE RULES

In the 'five card major' system invented by Mott-Smith , which is a special adaptation of the Standard System, the idea is that any opening bid in a major promises at least five cards of that suit. In the Canape the idea is quite different: one must reverse or rebid a major suit to show five cards and *a four card major suit is bid at the first opportunity* in order to ascertain a possible major suit contract and to shut out the opponents.

The effects are of various kinds - take, for instance, the famous principle of preparedness.

Its purpose has been changed a little. Everybody knows that this principle in the Standard System consists of facilitating the exchange of bids between the partnership (frequent short club openings). In the Canape, preparedness consists above all making it difficult for the opponents to interfere (frequent one spade pre-empts). There are *four* bridge players around a table, not two!

What are the consequences of the Canape opening on the other bids?

Footnotes

Geoffrey Mott-Smith (1902-1960) of New York City, war-time cryptographer, player, writer and theorist, for many years constructed the hands used in the Intercollegiate Championships. His advocacy of opening bids of five card majors was adopted by Roth-Stone, Kaplan-Sheinwold and other systems (page 741) with the corollary that to rebid a major suit would promise six or more cards since the original bid promised five.

SUPPORT

The general principle is that you must have *four* small cards, at least, to support partner's first bid suit. But after receiving this support in a major, the opener will generally conceal his longer, second suit. Games have frequently been stolen by this camouflage.

RESPONSES

Responder must avoid passing the partner's opening bid holding only one or two cards of the bid suit. If no one-over-one response is available, *one no trump should be bid holding from five to 10 points.*

When responder holds a two-suiter, he bids his suits in the same Canape style as the opening bidder. For instance, North's reverse in Case E indicates at least 10 points and that the spade suit is at least five cards long. All other bidding situations follow logical application of the Canape rule.

CASE E

SOUTH	NORTH
One diamond	One heart
Two diamonds	Two spades

A GENERAL VIEW ON CANAPE

Canape might be included in any complete system either with the strong or the weak no trump, either with the 'strong, forcing-to-game two-bid' or 'two clubs forcing', etc. . . . . .

The Albarran system with Canape uses for instance the classic no trump (together with Stayman), opening bids of two clubs forcing with ace-showing responses, opening bids of two diamonds, two hearts and two spades as intermediate two-bids promising 20 to 23 points including both high cards and distribution.

The famous French pair Jais and Trezel play a special Canape called the 'Tendance Canape' with opening bids in three card majors. Reversing at the one level does not always promise a five card suit.

South's rebid of one heart in Case F could indicate a heart suit of only four cards.

CASE F

SOUTH	NORTH
One club	One diamond
One heart	

CASE G

SOUTH	NORTH
One club	One spade
Two hearts	

But South's Canape reverse to the two-level in Case G does promise at least a five card suit. The reverse, since it shows 15 - 17 points, is not forcing.

When vulnerable, Jais and Trezel use the classic strong no trump, but when not vulnerable, their no trump opening is very weak: nine to 12 points! *

A very aggressive system.

Canape has many qualities.

It is *easy to play, precise and aggressive.* After many years of experiment I have found that the chief criticism lies in the fact that you must always have four trumps to support the opening suit, and that you must sometimes avoid passing partner's opening bid with only two cards of his suit.

Footnote

* *A weak no trump opening bid in the United States is usually 11 - 14 points.*

LAWS OF CONTRACT BRIDGE

♠♡♢♣

PRELIMINARIES TO THE RUBBER

1. THE PLAYERS—THE PACK

Contract Bridge is played by four players with a pack of 52 cards of identical back design and color, consisting of 13 cards in each of four suits. Two packs should be used, of which only one is in play at any time; and each pack should be clearly distinguishable from the other in back design or color.

2. RANK OF CARDS

The cards of each suit rank in descending order: Ace, King, Queen, Jack, 10, 9, 8, 7, 6, 5, 4, 3, 2.

3. THE DRAW

Before every rubber, each player draws a card from a pack shuffled and spread face down on the table. A card should not be exposed until all players have drawn.

The two players who draw the highest cards play as partners against the two other players. When cards of the same rank are drawn, the rank of suits determines which is higher—spades (highest), hearts, diamonds, clubs.

The player with the highest card deals first and has the right to choose his seat and the pack with which he will deal. He may consult his partner but, having announced his decision, must abide by it. His partner sits opposite him. The opponents then occupy the two remaining seats as they wish and, having made their selection, must abide by it.

A player must draw again if he draws one of the four cards at either end of the pack, or a card adjoining one drawn by another player, or a card from the other pack; or if, in drawing, he exposes more than one card.

THE DEAL

4. THE SHUFFLE

Before the cards are dealt they must be shuffled thoroughly, without exposure of the face of any card. The shuffle must be performed in full view of the players and to their satisfaction.

The pack to be used in each deal is prepared by the left-hand opponent of the player who will deal it. Preparation of the pack includes collecting the cards, shuffling them, and placing the shuffled pack face down at the left of the next dealer.

A pack properly prepared should not be disturbed until the dealer picks it up for his deal, at which time he is entitled to the final shuffle.

No player other than the dealer and the player designated to prepare the pack may shuffle.

5. THE CUT

The pack must always be cut immediately before it is dealt. The dealer presents the pack to his righthand opponent, who lifts off a portion and places it on the table toward the dealer. Each portion must contain at least four cards. The dealer completes the cut by placing what was originally the bottom portion upon the other portion.

No player other than the dealer's right-hand opponent may cut the pack.

6. NEW CUT–NEW SHUFFLE

There must be a new cut if any player demands one before the first card is dealt. In this case the dealer's right-hand opponent cuts again.

There must be a new shuffle, followed by a cut:

(a) If any player demands one before the dealer has picked up the pack for his deal. In this case the player designated to prepare the pack shuffles again.

(b) If any player demands one after the dealer has picked up the pack but before the first card is dealt. In this case only the dealer shuffles.

(c) If a card is turned face up in shuffling. In this case the player who was shuffling shuffles again.

(d) If a card is turned face up in cutting. In this case only the dealer shuffles.

(e) If there is a redeal (see Law 10).

7. CHANGE OF PACK

The two packs are used alternately, unless there is a redeal.

A pack containing a card so damaged or marked that it may be identified from its back must be replaced if attention is drawn to the imperfection before the first card of the current deal is dealt.

A pack originally belonging to a side must be restored on demand of any player before the last card of the current deal has been dealt.

8. THE DEAL

The dealer distributes the cards face down, one at a time in rotation into four separate hands of thirteen cards each, the first card to the player on his left and the last card to himself. If he deals two cards simultaneously or consecutively to the same player, or fails to deal a card to a player, he may rectify the error, provided he does so immediately and to the satisfaction of the other players.

The dealer must not allow the face of any card to be seen while he is dealing. Until the deal is completed, no player but the dealer may touch any card except to correct or prevent an irregularity.

9. ROTATION OF THE TURN TO DEAL

The turn to deal passes in rotation, unless there is a redeal. If a player deals out of turn, and attention is not drawn to the error before the last card has been dealt, the deal stands as though it had been in turn, the player who dealt the cards is the dealer, and the player who has missed his turn to deal has no redress; and the rotation continues as though the deal had been in turn, unless a redeal is required under Law 10.

10. REDEAL

When there is a redeal, the current deal is canceled; the same dealer deals again, unless he was dealing out of turn; the same pack is used, unless it has been replaced as provided in Law 7; and the cards are shuffled and cut anew as provided in Laws 4 and 5.

There must be a redeal:

(a) If, before the last card has been dealt, it is discovered that

(i) a card has been turned face up in dealing or is face up in the pack or elsewhere;

(ii) the cards have not been dealt correctly;

(iii) a player is dealing out of turn or is dealing with a pack that was not shuffled or not cut, provided any player demands a redeal.

(b) If, before the first call has been made, it is discovered that a player has picked up another player's hand and has seen a card in it.

(c) If, before play has been completed, it is discovered that

(i) the pack did not conform in every respect to the requirements of Law 1, including any case in which a missing card cannot be found after due search;

(ii) one player has picked up too many cards, another too few;
(iii) two or more players on opposing sides have allowed any cards from their hands to be mixed together, following a claim that a redeal is in order.

11. MISSING CARD

When a player has too few cards and a redeal is not required by Law 10 (c), the deal stands as correct, and:

(a) If he has played more than one card to a previous trick, Law 68 applies;

(b) If a missing card is found elsewhere than in a previous trick, that card is deemed to have belonged continuously to the deficient hand and must be restored to that hand; it may become a penalty card, as provided in Law 23 or 49, and failure to have played it may constitute a revoke.

12. SURPLUS CARD

When a player has too many cards and a redeal is not required by Law 10 (c), the deal stands as correct, and:

(a) If the offender has omitted to play to a trick, Law 68 applies.

(b) If the offender has picked up a surplus card from a previous trick, or from dummy's hand, or from the other pack, or elsewhere, such surplus card must be restored to its proper place; and

(i) If the surplus card is in the offender's hand when it is discovered, there is no penalty.
(ii) If the surplus card has been led or played, the offender must substitute for it a card from his hand that he can legally play to the trick and if possible a card of the same suit as the surplus card, and the offense is subject to the rectification and penalty provisions of Laws 62 to 65.

GENERAL LAWS GOVERNING IRREGULARITIES

13. PROCEDURE FOLLOWING AN IRREGULARITY

When an irregularity has been committed, any player—except dummy as restricted by Law 43—may draw attention to it and give or obtain information as to the law applicable to it. The fact that a player draws attention to an irregularity committed by his side does not affect the rights of the opponents.

After attention has been drawn to an irregularity, no player should call or play until all questions in regard to rectification and to the assessment of a penalty have been determined. Premature correction of an irregularity on the part of the offender may subject him to a further penalty (see Law 26).

14. ASSESSMENT OF A PENALTY

A penalty may not be imposed until the nature of the irregularity to be penalized has been determined and the applicable penalty has been clearly stated; but a penalty once paid, or any decision agreed and acted upon by the players, stands, even though at some later time it be adjudged incorrect.

With the exception of dummy, either member of the nonoffending side may impose a penalty, but without consulting his partner.

15. WAIVER OR FORFEITURE OF PENALTY

The right to penalize an offense is forfeited if a member of the nonoffending side

(a) waives the penalty;

(b) consults with his partner as to the imposition of a penalty before a penalty has been imposed;

(c) calls (Law 34) or plays (Law 60) after an irregularity committed by the opponent at his right.

Rectification or validation proceeds as provided in the law applicable to the specific irregularity.

16. UNAUTHORIZED INFORMATION

Any player except declarer may be subject to penalty if he conveys information to his partner other than by a legal call or play.

Information conveyed by an illegal call, play or exposure of a card is subject to the applicable law in Part V or VI.

If any player except declarer conveys information to his partner by means of a remark or an unmistakable gesture or mannerism that suggests a call,* lead, play, or plan of play; and if attention is drawn to the offense and the penalty is assessed forthwith, as provided in Laws 13 and 14:

(a) If the offense occurs before the auction closes, (penalty) either member of the nonoffending side may require both members of the offender's side to pass during the remainder of the auction; and if the offender becomes a defender, then when first it is the turn of the offender's partner to lead, including the opening lead, declarer may either

---

*After a deal has been completed, a player should not draw attention to the score, except to correct an error in recording. See Proprieties II (g).

(i) require the offender's partner from leading a specified suit, or

(ii) prohibit the offender's partner from leading a specified suit; this prohibition continues for as long as the offender's partner retains the lead.

(b) If the offense occurs after the auction closes, (penalty) declarer or either defender, as the case may be, may prohibit the offender's partner from making:

(i) a lead improperly suggested; this prohibition applies to any one lead, including the opening lead, and continues for as long as the offender's partner retains the lead; or

(ii) a play improperly suggested; this prohibition may be applied to only one play.

The rights of the nonoffending side are not affected by an intervening call or play by the offending side. If the offender's partner has called after the offense, but before a member of the nonoffending side has subsequently called, his call may be canceled. If the offender's partner has led or played after the offense, and before a member of the nonoffending side has subsequently played, he may be required to withdraw his card and to substitute a card that does not conform to the improper suggestion, and a defender's card so withdrawn becomes a penalty card.

THE AUCTION

Correct Procedure

17. DURATION OF THE AUCTION

The auction begins when the last card of a correct deal has been placed on the table. The dealer makes the first call, and thereafter each player calls in rotation. When three passes in rotation have followed any call, the auction is closed.

18. BIDS

Each bid must name a number of odd tricks, from one to seven, and a denomination. A bid supersedes the previous bid if it names either a greater number of odd tricks, or the same number of odd tricks in a higher denomination. A bid that fulfills these requirements is sufficient; one that does not, is insufficient. The denominations rank in descending order: no trump, spades, hearts, diamonds, clubs.

19. DOUBLES AND REDOUBLES

A player may double only the last preceding bid, and then only if it was made by an opponent and no call other than a pass has intervened.

A player may redouble only the last preceding double, and then only if it was made by an opponent and no call other than a pass has intervened.

A player should not, in doubling or redoubling, state the number of tricks or the denomination; but, if he states either or both incorrectly, he is deemed to have doubled or redoubled the bid as it was made.

All doubles and redoubles are superseded by a subsequent legal bid. If there is no subsequent bid, scoring values are increased as provided in Law 84.

20. REVIEW OF THE AUCTION

A player who does not hear a call distinctly may forthwith require that it be repeated.

Before the auction closes, a player is entitled to have all previous calls restated when it is his turn to call, unless he is required by law to pass.

After the auction closes declarer or either defender may require previous calls to be restated. A defender's right to such a review terminates when a member of his side has led or played to the first trick; declarer's right terminates when he has played to the first trick or dummy has spread any part of his hand.

A request to have calls restated should be responded to only by an opponent. Dummy or a player required by law to pass may review the auction at an opponent's request and should correct errors in restatement.

21. CALL BASED ON MISINFORMATION

A player has no recourse if he has made a call on the basis of his own misunderstanding.

A player may, without penalty, change any call he may have made as a result of misinformation given him by an opponent, provided his partner has not subsequently called. If he elects to correct his call, his left-hand opponent may then, in turn and without penalty, change any subsequent call he may have made.

22. PROCEDURE AFTER THE AUCTION IS CLOSED

After the auction is closed:

(a) If no player has bid, the hands are abandoned and the turn to deal passes in rotation.

(b) If any player has bid, the final bid becomes the contract and play begins.

Irregularities

23. CARD EXPOSED OR LED DURING THE AUCTION

Whenever, during the auction, a player faces a card on the table or holds a card so that his partner is able to see its face, every such card must be left face up on the table until the auction closes; and

(a) If it is a single card below the rank of an honor and not prematurely led, there is no penalty, and when the auction closes the card may be picked up.

(b) If it is a single card of honor rank, or any card prematurely led, or if more than one card is so exposed, (penalty) the offender's partner must pass when next it is his turn to call; and if the offender subsequently becomes a defender, declarer may treat every such card as a penalty card (Law 50).

24. IMMEDIATE CORRECTION OF A CALL

A player may substitute his intended call for an inadvertent call, but only if he does so without pause. If legal, his last call stands without penalty; if illegal, it is subject to the applicable law.

25. CHANGE OF CALL

A call substituted for a call made previously at the same turn, when it is too late for correction as provided in Law 24, is canceled; and

(a) If the first call was illegal, the offender is subject to the applicable law.

(b) If the first call was a legal one, the offender must either

(i) allow his first call to stand and (penalty) his partner must pass when next it is his turn to call; or

(ii) make any legal call and (penalty) his partner must pass whenever it is his turn to call.

The offender's partner may also be subject to a lead penalty as provided in Law 26.

26. UNAUTHORIZED INFORMATION GIVEN BY CHANGE OF CALL

When a player names a denomination not selected as his final call at that turn (as in changing a call* or in making or correcting an illegal call), then if he becomes a defender:

*Except as permitted under Law 24.

(a) If such denomination was a suit, (penalty) declarer may prohibit the offender's partner from leading that suit the first time the offender's partner has the lead, including the opening lead, and for as long as he retains the lead.

(b) If such denomination was no trump, and if the offender's partner is to make the opening lead, (penalty) declarer may require the offender's partner to make the opening lead in a specified suit.

When a player has substituted another call for a double or redouble, the penalties provided in Law 27 (c) apply.

27. INSUFFICIENT BID

An insufficient bid made in rotation must be corrected, if either opponent draws attention to it, by substituting either a sufficient bid or a pass.* A double or redouble may not be substituted. If the call substituted is

(a) the lowest sufficient bid in the same denomination, the auction proceeds as though the irregularity had not occurred.

(b) any other sufficient bid, (penalty) the offender's partner must pass whenever it is his turn to call.

(c) a pass, (penalty) the offender's partner must pass whenever it is his turn to call; and if the offender's partner is to make the opening lead, declarer may either

(i) require the offender's partner to lead a specified suit, or
(ii) prohibit the offender's partner from leading a specified suit; this prohibition continues for as long as the offender's partner retains the lead.

If the offender attempts to substitute a double or redouble, it is canceled; he must pass and is subject to the penalty provided in subsection (c) above.

If a player makes an insufficient bid out of rotation, Law 31 applies.

Call Out of Rotation

28. CALLS CONSIDERED TO BE IN ROTATION

A call is considered to be in rotation

(a) when it is made without waiting for the right-hand opponent to pass, if that opponent is required by law to pass.

(b) when it is made by the player whose turn it was to call, before a penalty has been imposed for a call out of rotation by an opponent; it waives any penalty for the call out of rotation and the auction proceeds as though that opponent had not called at that turn.

*The offender is entitled to select his final call at that turn after the applicable penalties have been stated, and any call he has previously attempted to substitute is canceled, but Law 26 may apply.

29. PROCEDURE AFTER A CALL OUT OF ROTATION

A call out of rotation is canceled if either opponent draws attention to it. The auction reverts to the player whose turn it was to call. The offender may make any legal call in proper turn but may be subject to penalty under Law 30, 31 or 32.

30. PASS OUT OF ROTATION

When a player has passed out of rotation

(a) before any player has bid, or when it was the turn of the opponent on his right to call, (penalty) the offender must pass when next it is his turn to call.

(b) after any player has bid and when it was the turn of the offender's partner to call, (penalty) the offender must pass whenever it is his turn to call; the offender's partner may make a sufficient bid or may pass, but may not double or redouble at that turn; and if the offender's partner passes and subsequently is to make the opening lead, declarer may either

(i) require the offender's partner to lead a specified suit, or

(ii) prohibit the offender's partner from leading a specified suit; this prohibition continues for as long as the offender's partner retains the lead.

31. BID OUT OF ROTATION

When a player has bid out of rotation

(a) before any player has called, (penalty) his partner must pass whenever it is his turn to call.

(b) after any player has called and when it was the turn of the offender's partner to call, (penalty) the offender's partner must pass whenever it is his turn to call; and if the offender's partner is to make the opening lead, declarer may either

(i) require the offender's partner to lead a specified suit, or

(ii) prohibit the offender's partner from leading a specified suit; this prohibition continues for as long as the offender's partner retains the lead.

(c) after any player has called and when it was the turn of the opponent on the offender's right* to call:

(i) If that opponent passes, the bid out of rotation, if sufficient, must be repeated and there is no penalty. If the bid out of rotation was insufficient it must be corrected as provided in Law 27.

(ii) If that opponent makes a legal bid, double, or redouble,** the offender may in turn make any legal call and (penalty) the offender's partner must pass when next it is his turn to call.

---

*A call made after a player has called and when it is the turn of the opponent on the offender's left to call is treated as a change of calls and Law 25 applies.

**An illegal call by that opponent may be penalized in the usual way, after which this subsection (c) (ii) applies.

32. DOUBLE OR REDOUBLE OUT OF ROTATION

When a player has doubled or redoubled out of rotation, and Law 36 or 37 does not apply:

(a) If it was the offender's partner's turn to call, (penalty) the offender's partner must pass whenever it is his turn to call; the offender may not thereafter, in turn, double or redouble the same bid he doubled or redoubled out of turn; and if the offender's partner is to make the opening lead, declarer may either

(i) require the offender's partner to lead a specified suit, or

(ii) prohibit the offender's partner from leading a specified suit; this prohibition continues for as long as the offender's partner retains the lead.

(b) If it was the turn of the opponent on the offender's right to call:

(i) If the opponent on the offender's right passes, the double or redouble out of rotation must be repeated and there is no penalty.

(ii) If the opponent on the offender's right bids, the offender may in turn make any legal call, and (penalty) the offender's partner must pass when next it is his turn to call.

33. SIMULTANEOUS CALLS

A call made simultaneously with one made by the player whose turn it was to call is deemed to be a subsequent call.

34. CALL IN ROTATION AFTER AN ILLEGAL CALL

A call by a member of the nonoffending side after an illegal call by the opponent on his right, and before a penalty has been imposed, forfeits the right to penalize that offense. The illegal call is treated as though it were legal, except that an inadmissible double or redouble or a bid of more than seven is treated as a pass; and Law 35 or 37 may apply.

35. RETENTION OF THE RIGHT TO CALL

A player may not be deprived of any turn to call by one or more passes following a pass out of rotation, when there has been no subsequent bid. All such passes are canceled, the bidding reverts to the player who has missed his turn, and the auction continues as though there had been no irregularity.

Inadmissible Calls

36. INADMISSIBLE DOUBLE OR REDOUBLE

Any double or redouble not permitted by Law 19 is canceled; and:

(a) If the offender has doubled or redoubled a bid that his side has already doubled or redoubled:

(i) The offender may substitute a legal bid, and (penalty) his partner must pass whenever it is his turn to call, and if the offender's partner is to make the opening lead declarer may prohibit the lead of the suit illegally doubled or redoubled, for as long as the offender's partner retains the lead; or

(ii) The offender may substitute a pass, and (penalty) his partner must pass whenever it is his turn to call, either member of the nonoffending side may cancel all previous doubles or redoubles, and if the offender's partner is to make the opening lead, declarer may require the offender's partner to lead a specified suit, or prohibit the offender's partner from leading a specified suit; this prohibition continues for as long as the offender's partner retains the lead.

(b) If the offender has doubled a bid made by his side, redoubled an undoubled bid, or doubled or redoubled when there has been no bid, the offender in turn must make any legal call, and (penalty) his partner must pass when next it is his turn to call.

If the right of the nonoffending side to penalize is waived or forfeited, as provided in Law 15, the offender is deemed to have passed and the auction proceeds as though there had been no irregularity.

37. BID, DOUBLE OR REDOUBLE IN VIOLATION OF THE OBLIGATION TO PASS

A bid, double or redouble by a player who is required by law to pass is canceled, and (penalty) both members of the offending side must pass during the remainder of the auction, and if the offender's partner is to make the opening lead, declarer may either

(a) require the offender's partner to lead a specified suit, or

(b) prohibit the offender's partner from leading a specified suit; this prohibition continues for as long as the offender's partner retains the lead.

If the right of the nonoffending side to penalize is waived or forfeited, as provided in Law 15, the offender's bid, double or redouble, if otherwise legal, stands at that turn; but if the offender was required to pass for the remainder of the auction he must still pass at subsequent turns.

38. BID OF MORE THAN SEVEN

A bid of more than seven by any player is canceled, and (penalty) both members of the offending side must pass during the remainder of the auction, and if the offender's partner is to make the opening lead, declarer may either

(a) require the offender's partner to lead a specified suit, or

(b) prohibit the offender's partner from leading a specified suit; this prohibition continues for as long as the offender's partner retains the lead.

If the right of the nonoffending side to penalize is waived or forfeited as provided in Law 15, the offender must substitute a pass; any call that may have been made subsequently is canceled; and the auction proceeds as though there had been no irregularity. No play or score at a contract of more than seven is ever permissible.

39. CALL AFTER THE AUCTION IS CLOSED

A call after the auction is closed is canceled, and

(a) If it is a pass by a defender or any call by declarer or dummy, there is no penalty.

(b) If it is a bid, double or redouble by a defender, (penalty) declarer may either

- (i) require the offender's partner, when first it is his turn to lead, to lead a specified suit; or
- (ii) prohibit the offender's partner, when first it is his turn to lead, from leading a specified suit; this prohibition continues for as long as the offender's partner retains the lead.

THE PLAY

Correct Procedure

40. COMMENCEMENT OF PLAY

After the auction closes, the defender on declarer's left makes the opening lead. After the opening lead dummy spreads his hand in front of him on the table, face up and grouped in suits with the trumps on his right. Declarer plays both his hand and that of dummy.

41. INFORMATION AS TO CONTRACT

After it is too late to have previous calls restated, as provided in Law 20, declarer or either defender is entitled to be informed what the contract is and whether, but not by whom, it was doubled or redoubled.

42. DUMMY'S RIGHTS AND LIMITATIONS

Dummy is entitled to give or obtain information as to fact or law; and provided he has not forfeited his rights (see Law 43) he may also:

(a) question players regarding revokes as provided in Law 61;

(b) draw attention to an irregularity, or try to prevent one.*

Except as provided in this law, dummy may not on his own initiative participate in the play, or make any comment on the bidding or play of the current deal, or draw attention to the score, and if he does so, Law 16 may apply. If dummy consults with declarer as to the imposition of a penalty, the right to penalize is forfeited as provided in Law 15.

43. FORFEITURE OF DUMMY'S RIGHTS

Dummy forfeits the rights provided in 42 (a) and (b) if he exchanges hands with declarer, leaves his seat to watch declarer play, or, on his own initiative, looks at the face of a card in either defender's hand; and if, thereafter,

(a) He is the first to draw attention to a defender's irregularity, declarer may not enforce any penalty for the offense.

(b) He warns declarer not to lead from the wrong hand, (penalty) either defender may choose the hand from which declarer shall lead.

(c) He is the first to ask declarer if a play from declarer's hand constitutes a revoke or failure to comply with a penalty, declarer must substitute a correct card if his play was illegal, and the penalty provisions of Law 64 apply.

44. SEQUENCE AND PROCEDURE OF PLAY

The player who leads to a trick may play any card in his hand.** After the lead, each other player in turn plays a card and the four cards so played constitute a trick.

In playing to a trick, each player must if possible follow suit. This obligation takes precedence over all other requirements of these Laws. If unable to follow suit, a player may play any card.**

A trick containing a trump is won by the player who has contributed to it the highest trump. A trick that does not contain a trump is won by the player who has contributed to it the highest card of the suit led. The player who has won the trick leads to the next trick.

---

*He may, for example, warn declarer against leading from the wrong hand.

**Unless he is subject to restriction after an irregularity committed by his side.

45. CARD PLAYED

Each player except dummy plays a card by detaching it from his hand and facing it near the middle of the table. Declarer plays a card from dummy's hand by moving the card toward the center of the table. If instructed by declarer to do so, dummy may play from his hand a card named or designated by declarer. In addition, a card must be played:

(a) If it is a defender's card held so that it is possible for his partner to see its face.

(b) If it is a card from declarer's hand that declarer holds face up in front of him and that is touching or near the table.

(c) If it is a card in dummy touched by declarer except for the purpose of arranging dummy's cards or of reaching a card above or below the card or cards touched.

(d) If the player who holds the card names or otherwise designates it as the card he proposes to play. A player may without penalty change an inadvertent designation if he does so without pause; but if an opponent has, in turn, played a card that was legal before the change of designation, that opponent may without penalty withdraw any card so played and substitute another.

(e) If it is a penalty card, subject to Law 50.

(f) If it is a card in dummy's hand that dummy has illegally suggested as a play, unless either defender forbids the play of such card, or an equal of it, or a card of the same suit, as provided in Law 16.

A card played may not be withdrawn except as provided in Law 47.

46. PARTIAL DESIGNATION OF A CARD TO BE PLAYED FROM DUMMY'S HAND

When declarer instructs dummy to play a card from dummy's hand, as permitted by Law 45, but names only a suit or only the rank of a card, or the equivalent, without fully specifying the card to be played, declarer must complete his partial designation. Dummy must not play a card before declarer has completed his partial designation, and if dummy prematurely plays a card, Law 16 applies on that trick only, unless a defender has subsequently played.

47. RETRACTION OF A CARD PLAYED

A card once played may be withdrawn only:

(a) to comply with a penalty, or to correct an illegal play;

(b) after a change of designation as permitted by Law 45 (d);

(c) after an opponent's change of play, to substitute a card for one played.

Penalty Card

48. EXPOSURE OF DECLARER'S CARDS

Declarer is not subject to penalty for exposing a card, and no card of declarer's or dummy's ever becomes a penalty card. Declarer is not required to play any card dropped accidentally.

When declarer faces his cards after an opening lead out of turn, Law 54 applies.* When declarer faces his cards at any other time, he is deemed to have made a claim or concession of tricks and Law 71 applies.

49. EXPOSURE OF A DEFENDER'S CARDS

Whenever a defender faces a card on the table, holds a card so that it is possible for his partner to see its face, or names a card as being in his hand, before he is entitled to do so in the normal course of play or application of the law, (penalty) each such card becomes a penalty card (Law 50).

50. DISPOSITION OF A PENALTY CARD

A penalty card must be left face up on the table until it is played or is permitted to be picked up. When a penalty card is permitted to be picked up, it ceases to be a penalty card.

A penalty card must be played at the first legal opportunity, whether in leading, following suit, discarding, or trumping. If a defender has two or more penalty cards that can legally be played, declarer may designate which is to be played. The obligation to follow suit, or to comply with a lead or play penalty, takes precedence over the obligation to play a penalty card, but the penalty card must still be left face up on the table and played at the next legal opportunity.

When a defender has or first obtains the lead while his partner has a penalty card, declarer may require him to lead the suit of the penalty card or prohibit him from leading that suit for as long as he retains the lead. If declarer exercises this option, the penalty card may be picked up. If declarer does not exercise this option, the defender may lead any card; but the penalty card remains a penalty card. The defender may not lead until declarer has indicated his choice.

If a defender has two or more penalty cards in one suit, and declarer requires the defender's partner to lead that suit, the defender may pick up every penalty card in that suit and may make any legal play to the trick.

---

*Declarer should, as a matter of propriety, refrain from spreading his hand.

If a defender has penalty cards in more than one suit, declarer may prohibit the defender's partner from leading every such suit; but the defender may then pick up every penalty card in every suit prohibited by declarer and may make any legal play to the trick.

51. PENALTY CARD ILLEGALLY PICKED UP

When a defender attempts illegally to restore a penalty card to his unfaced hand, such card must be replaced face up on the table on demand of declarer; but if in the meantime that defender has played another card and declarer has thereafter played from either his hand or dummy, the card illegally picked up ceases to be a penalty card and need not be replaced on the table.

52. FAILURE TO LEAD OR PLAY A PENALTY CARD

When a defender fails to lead or play a penalty card as required by Law 50, he may not, on his own initiative, withdraw any other card he may have played.

If a defender leads or plays another card when he could legally have led or played a penalty card,

(a) declarer may accept the defender's lead or play, and declarer must accept such lead or play if he has thereafter played from his or dummy's hand, but the unplayed penalty card remains a penalty card; or

(b) declarer may require the defender to substitute the penalty card for the card illegally led or played. Every card illegally led or played by the defender in the course of committing the irregularity becomes a penalty card.

Lead Out of Turn

53. LEAD OUT OF TURN ACCEPTED

Any lead out of turn may be treated as a correct lead. It becomes a correct lead if declarer or either defender, as the case may be, accepts it or plays a card before attention is drawn to the irregularity. A card so played by declarer from either hand may not be withdrawn unless its play constituted a revoke. Law 57 applies if such card is played by the defender at the right of the player from whose hand the lead out of turn was made.

54. OPENING LEAD OUT OF TURN

When a defender makes the opening lead out of turn:

(a) If declarer accepts the lead as provided in Law 53, dummy's hand is spread in accordance with Law 40 and the second card to the trick is played from declarer's hand; but if declarer first plays to the trick from dummy's hand, dummy's card may not be withdrawn except to correct a revoke.

(b) If declarer may have seen any of dummy's cards (except cards that dummy may have exposed during the auction and that were subject to Law 23) he must accept the lead.

(c) If declarer begins to spread his hand as though he were dummy,* and in so doing exposes one or more cards, and if subsection(b) above does not apply, the lead must be accepted, declarer must spread his entire hand, and dummy becomes declarer.

When declarer requires the defender to retract his opening lead out of turn, Law 56 applies.

55. DECLARER'S LEAD OUT OF TURN

When declarer leads out of turn from his or dummy's hand and either defender requires him to retract such lead:

(a) If it was a defender's turn to lead, declarer restores the card led in error to his or dummy's hand without penalty.

(b) If declarer has led from the wrong hand when it was his turn to lead from his or dummy's hand, he withdraws the card led in error; he must lead from the correct hand, and, (penalty) if able to do so, a card of the same suit. Failure to observe this obligation in playing from his own hand may subject him to penalty under Law 65.

Either defender's drawing attention to declarer's lead out of turn is equivalent to requiring its retraction. Dummy's drawing attention to declarer's lead from the wrong hand does not affect the rights of the opponents.

56. DEFENDER'S LEAD OUT OF TURN

When declarer requires a defender to retract his lead out of turn:

(a) Declarer may treat the card illegally led as a penalty card and apply the provisions of Law 50; or

(b) Declarer may allow the card illegally led to be picked up; and if the offense occurred

- (i) on the opening lead, or on a subsequent lead when it was the other defender's turn to lead, (penalty) declarer may require the offender's partner to lead the suit of the card led out of turn, or prohibit him from leading that suit for as long as he retains the lead.

---

*Declarer should, as a matter of propriety, refrain from spreading his hand.

(ii) when it was declarer's or dummy's turn to lead, declarer leads from the correct hand and (penalty) when first it is the turn of the offender's partner to lead, declarer may require him to lead the suit of the card led out of turn, or prohibit him from from leading that suit for as long as he retains the lead.

57. PREMATURE LEAD OR PLAY BY A DEFENDER

When a defender leads to the next trick before his partner has played to the current trick, or plays out of turn before his partner has played, (penalty) declarer may require the offender's partner to play:

(a) his highest card of the suit led; or
(b) his lowest card of the suit led; or
(c) a card of another suit, specified by declarer.

Declarer must select one of these options and if the offender's partner cannot comply with the penalty selected he may play any card, as provided in Law 59.

When, as a result of the application of the penalty, the offender's partner wins the current trick, he leads to the next trick; and any card led or played out of turn by the other defender becomes a penalty card (Law 50).

A defender is not subject to penalty for playing before his partner if declarer has played from both hands; but a singleton or one of two or more equal cards in dummy is not considered automatically played unless dummy has played the card or has illegally suggested its play as provided in Law 45 (f).

58. SIMULTANEOUS LEADS OR PLAYS

A lead or play made simultaneously with another player's legal lead or play is deemed to be subsequent to it.

If a defender leads or plays two or more cards simultaneously, and if only one such card is visible, he must play that card; if more than one card is exposed he must designate the card he proposes to play and each other exposed card becomes a penalty card (Law 50).

If declarer leads or plays two or more cards simultaneously from either hand, he must designate the card he proposes to play and must restore any other card to the correct hand. A defender who has played to the only visible card played by declarer may, without penalty, withdraw the card played and substitute another.

If the error remains undiscovered until both sides have played to the next trick, Law 68 applies.

59. INABILITY TO LEAD OR PLAY AS REQUIRED

A player may play any correct card if he is unable to lead or play as required to comply with a penalty, either because he has no card of the required suit, or because he has only cards of a suit he is prohibited from leading, or because of his obligation to follow suit. The penalty is deemed to have been paid, except that the obligation to play a penalty card at the first legal opportunity continues.

60. PLAY AFTER AN ILLEGAL PLAY

A play by a member of the nonoffending side after the opponent on his right has led or played out of turn or prematurely, and before a penalty has been imposed, forfeits the right to penalize that offense. The illegal play is treated as though it were legal, unless it constitutes a revoke. If the offending side had a previous obligation to play a penalty card or to comply with a lead or play penalty, the obligation remains at future turns (see Laws 52 and 65).

When a defender plays after declarer has been required to retract his lead out of turn from either hand, but before declarer has led from the correct hand, the defender's card becomes a penalty card (Law 50).

A play by a member of the offending side before a penalty has been imposed does not affect the rights of the opponents and may itself be subject to penalty.

The Revoke

61. FAILURE TO FOLLOW SUIT – INQUIRIES CONCERNING A REVOKE

Failure to follow suit in accordance with Law 44 constitutes a revoke. Any player, including dummy,* may ask a player who has failed to follow suit whether he has a card of the suit led, and may demand that an opponent correct his revoke.

62. CORRECTION OF A REVOKE

A player must correct his revoke if he becomes aware of the occurrence of the revoke before it becomes established. To correct a revoke, the offender withdraws the card he played in revoking and follows suit with any card. A card so withdrawn becomes a penalty card (Law 50) if it was played from a defender's unfaced hand. The card may be replaced without penalty if it was played from declarer's or dummy's hand* or if it was a defender's faced card. Each member of the nonoffending side may, without penalty, withdraw any card he may have played after the revoke but before attention was drawn to it. The partner of the offender may not withdraw his card unless it too constituted a revoke.**

---

*Subject to Law 43. A claim of revoke does not warrant inspection of quitted tricks except as permitted in Law 67.

**In such case the card withdrawn becomes a penalty card if it was played from a defender's unfaced hand.

A revoke on the twelfth trick never becomes established, but it must be corrected if discovered before the cards have been mixed together, and declarer or either defender, as the case may be, may then require the offender's partner to play to the twelfth trick either of two cards he could legally have played to that trick.

63. ESTABLISHMENT OF A REVOKE

A revoke in any of the first eleven tricks becomes established when the offender or his partner leads or plays to the following trick,* or names or otherwise designates a card to be so played, or makes a claim or concession of tricks orally or by facing his hand. The revoke may then no longer be corrected, and the trick on which the revoke occurred stands as played.

64. PROCEDURE AFTER ESTABLISHMENT OF A REVOKE

When a revoke has become established, (penalty) after play ceases, two tricks are transferred to the nonoffending side, if the side that has revoked has won two or more tricks after the revoke.** Only one trick is transferred if the side that has revoked has won only one trick after the revoke. The trick on which the revoke occurred is counted as having been won after the revoke.* There is no penalty for an established revoke:

(a) If the side that revoked did not win either the trick on which the revoke occurred or any subsequent trick.

(b) If the revoke was a subsequent revoke in the same suit by the same player.

(c) If the revoke was made in failing to play any card faced on the table or belonging to a hand faced on the table including a card from dummy's hand.

(d) If attention is first drawn to it after all players have abandoned their hands and permitted the cards to be mixed together.

65. FAILURE TO COMPLY WITH A LEAD OR PLAY PENALTY

When a player is able to lead or play from an unfaced hand a card or suit required by law or specified by an opponent in accordance with an agreed penalty, but instead plays an incorrect card:

(a) The offender must correct his error if he becomes aware of it before he or his partner plays another card. Any card played in rotation by a member of the nonoffending side may be withdrawn if it was played after the error and before its correction. An incorrect card played from a defender's unfaced hand becomes a penalty card (Law 50).

---

*Any such play, legal or illegal, establishes the revoke.

**Failure to lead or play a card or suit specified by an opponent in accordance with an agreed penalty is not a revoke but may be subject to the same penalties (see Law 65).

(b) The offender may not withdraw any incorrect card he may have played if he or his partner has led or played to the following trick; and (penalty) the offense is subject to the penalty provisions of Law 64.

There is no penalty for failure to lead or play a faced card, including a penalty card* or a card from dummy's hand, but a member of the non-offending side (except dummy) may demand rectification at any time before a member of his side has thereafter played a card.

Tricks

66. COLLECTION AND ARRANGEMENT OF TRICKS

The cards constituting each completed trick are collected by a member of the side that won the trick and are then turned face down on the table. Each trick should be identifiable as such, and all tricks taken by a side should be arranged in sequence in front of declarer or of one defender, as the case may be, in such manner that each side can determine the number of tricks it has won and the order in which they were taken.

67. INSPECTION OF TRICKS

Declarer or either defender may, until a member of his side has led or played to the following trick, inspect a trick and inquire what card each player has played to it. Thereafter, until play ceases, quitted tricks may be inspected only to account for a missing or surplus card. After play ceases, the tricks and unplayed cards may be inspected to settle a claim of a revoke, of honors, or of the number of tricks won or lost. If, after a claim has been made, a player on one side mixes the cards in such way that the facts can no longer be ascertained, the issue must be decided in favor of the other side.

68. DEFECTIVE TRICK

When a player has omitted to play to a trick, or has played too many cards to a trick, the error must be rectified if attention is drawn to the irregularity before a player on each side has played to the following trick. To rectify omission to play to a trick, the offender supplies a card he can legally play. To rectify the error of playing too many cards the offender withdraws all but one card, leaving a card he can legally play. Each card so withdrawn becomes a penalty card (Law 50) if it was played from a defender's unfaced hand. After a card has been so withdrawn each member of the nonoffending side may, without penalty, withdraw any card he played after the irregularity but before attention was drawn to it.

---

*A card played instead of the penalty card may be subject to penalty—see Law 52.

When attention is drawn to a defective trick after a player on each side has played to the following trick, the defective trick stands as played and:

(a) A player with too few cards plays the remainder of his hand with fewer cards than the other players; he does not play to the final trick (or tricks); and if he wins a trick with his last card, the lead passes in rotation.

(b) A player with too many cards forthwith faces and adds a card to the defective trick, and if possible one he could legally have played to it. A card so contributed does not change the ownership of the trick.

69. TRICK APPROPRIATED IN ERROR

A trick appropriated by the wrong side must, upon demand, be restored to the side that has in fact won the trick by contributing the winning card to it. The scoring value of the trick must be credited to that side, subject to Law 81.

Claims and Concessions

70. DECLARER'S CLAIM OR CONCESSION OF TRICKS

Declarer makes a claim whenever he announces that he will win or lose one or more of the remaining tricks, or suggests that play may be curtailed, or faces his hand. Declarer should not make a claim if there is any doubt as to the number of tricks to be won or lost.

71. PROCEDURE FOLLOWING DECLARER'S CLAIM

When declarer has made a claim, play is temporarily suspended and declarer must place and leave his hand face up on the table and forthwith make a comprehensive statement as to his proposed plan of play, including the order in which he will play his remaining cards; and

(a) Either defender may, at any time thereafter, demand that declarer clarify or amplify his statement in any particular.

(b) At any time after defender's claim, either defender may face his partner and declarer may not impose a penalty for any irregularity committed by a defender whose hand is so faced.

(c) Either defender may require that play continue as provided in Law 72.

Declarer's claim must be allowed if both defenders agree to it, or if either defender has allowed any of his remaining cards to be mixed with another player's cards.

72. CONTINUATION OF PLAY AFTER DECLARER'S CLAIM

Whenever either defender requires that play continue after declarer's claim, declarer must play on, leaving his hand face up on the table. Declarer may make no play inconsistent with any statement he may have made; and if he did not make an appropriate announcement at the time he made his claim, he may not exercise freedom of choice in making any play the success of which depends on finding either opponent with or without a particular unplayed card; and unless an opponent failed to follow to the suit of that card before the claim was made, declarer must play as directed by either defender. If declarer attempts to make a play prohibited under this law, either defender may accept the play or require declarer to withdraw the card so played and to substitute another that conforms to his obligations, provided neither defender has subsequently played. Any question not specifically dealt with should be resolved in favor of the defenders.*

73. DEFENDER'S CLAIM OR CONCESSION OF TRICKS

When a defender makes a claim or concession of tricks he may do so by showing any or all of his cards to declarer only, but this does not necessarily exempt the defender from penalty under Law 16. If in the course of making a claim or concession a defender faces his hand, names a card as being in his hand, or allows his partner to see one or more of his remaining cards, his cards do not become penalty cards but declarer may treat the remaining cards of the other defender as penalty cards.

74. CONCESSION WITHDRAWN

A concession may be withdrawn:

(a) If any player concedes a trick his side has, in fact, won; or if declarer concedes defeat of a contract he has already fulfilled; or if a defender concedes fulfillment of a contract his side has already defeated. If the score has been entered, it may be corrected, subject to Law 81.

(b) If a trick that has been conceded cannot be lost by any sequence of play of the remaining cards, however improbable, and if attention is drawn to that fact before the cards have been mixed together.

(c) If a defender concedes one or more tricks and his partner immediately objects, but Law 16 may apply.

**Example:* Declarer may be required to draw, or not to draw, an outstanding trump that he may have overlooked and that is a possible winner.

THE SCORE

75. POINTS EARNED

The result of each deal played is recorded in points, which fall into two classes:

(a) *Trick points.* Only declarer's side can earn trick points, and only by winning at least the number of odd tricks specified in the contract. Only the value of odd tricks named in the contract may be scored as trick points. (See Law 84). Trick points mark the progression of the rubber toward its completion.

(b) *Premium points.* Either side or both sides may earn premium points. Declarer's side earns premium points by winning one or more overtricks; by fulfilling a doubled or redoubled contract; by bidding and making a slam; by holding scorable honors in declarer's or dummy's hand; or by winning the final game of a rubber.* The defenders earn premium points by defeating the contract (undertrick penalty) or by holding scorable honors in either side of their hands. (See Law 84).

Each side's premium points are added to its trick points at the conclusion of the rubber.

76. PART SCORE – GAME

The basic units of trick scores are part score and game. A part score is recorded for declarer's side whenever declarer fulfills a contract for which the trick score is less than 100 points. Game is won by that side which is the first to have scored 100 or more trick points either in a single deal or by addition of two or more part scores made separately. No part score made in the course of one game is carried forward into the next game.

77. THE RUBBER

A rubber ends when a side has won two games. At the conclusion of the rubber, the winners of two games are credited in their premium score with 500 points if the other side has won one game, or with 700 points if the other side has not won a game. The trick and premium points scored by each side in the course of the rubber are then added. The side with the larger combined total wins the rubber, and the difference between the two totals represents the margin of victory computed in points.

---

*For incomplete rubber see Law 83.

78. METHOD OF SCORING

The score of each deal must be recorded and preferably a member of each side should keep score.

Scores are entered in two adjacent columns separated by a vertical line. Each scorer enters points earned by his side in the left-hand column, and points earned by his opponents in the right-hand column.

Each side has a trick score and a premium score, separated by a horizontal line intersecting the vertical line. All trick points are entered, as they are earned, in descending order below the horizontal line; all premium points in ascending order above that line.

Whenever a game is won, another horizontal line is drawn under all trick scores recorded for either side, in order to mark completion of the game. Subsequent trick scores are entered below the line so drawn. Any line prematurely drawn must be erased, and a line incorrectly omitted must be drawn upon discovery of the error.

79. RESPONSIBILITY FOR THE SCORE

When play ceases, all four players are equally responsible for ascertaining that the number of tricks won by each side is correctly determined and that all scores are promptly and correctly entered.

80. TRANSFERRED TRICKS

A transferred trick is reckoned for all scoring purposes as though it had been won in play by the side to which it has been awarded.

81. CORRECTION OF THE SCORE

Any scoring error conceded by both sides may be corrected at any time before the score of the rubber is agreed upon; except that an error made by each scorer in recording a trick score, or failing to enter one, may not be corrected after the last card of the second succeeding correct deal has been dealt, unless the majority of the players consent. In case of disagreement among two or more scores kept, the recollection of the majority of the players as to the facts governs.

82. DEALS PLAYED WITH AN INCORRECT PACK

Scores recorded for deals played with an incorrect pack are not subject to change by reason of the discovery of the imperfection after the cards have been mixed together.

83. INCOMPLETE RUBBER

When, for any reason, a rubber is not finished, the score is computed as follows:

If only one game has been completed, the winners of that game are credited with 300 points; if only one side has a part score or scores in a game not completed, that side is credited with 50 points; the trick and premium points of each side are then added, and the side with the greater number of points wins the difference between the two totals.

PROPRIETIES

1. GENERAL PRINCIPLES

Communication between partners during the auction and play periods should be effected only by means of the calls and plays themselves, not the manner in which they are made. Calls should be made in a uniform tone without special emphasis or inflection, and without undue haste or hesitation. Plays should be made without emphasis, gesture or mannerism, and so far as possible at a uniform rate.

Intentional infringement of the law is a serious breach of ethics, even if there is a prescribed penalty which one is prepared to pay. The offense may be the more serious when no penalty is prescribed.

A player should carefully avoid taking any advantage which might accrue from an impropriety committed by his side. While one should not allow partner's hesitation, remark or manner to influence one's call, lead or play, it is not improper to draw inferences from an opponent's gratuitous hesitation, remark or manner, but such inferences are drawn at one's own risk.

There is no obligation to draw attention to an inadvertent infringement of law by one's own side; however, a player should not attempt to conceal such an infringement, as by committing a second revoke, concealing a card involved in a revoke, or mixing the cards prematurely.

It is proper to warn partner against infringing a law of the game, for example, against revoking, or against calling, leading or playing out of turn.

2. VIOLATIONS OF ETHICAL CONDUCT

The following acts should be carefully avoided and are considered breaches of ethics when committed intentionally.

(a) A remark, question, gesture or mannerism which might convey information to partner or might mislead an opponent.

(b) A call made with special emphasis, inflection, haste or undue hesitation.

(c) A play made with emphasis, undue haste, or unreasonable delay, when the act might convey information to partner or might mislead an opponent.

(d) Any indication of approval or disapproval of partner's call, or of satisfaction with an opponent's call.

(e) Indication of expectation or intention of winning or losing a trick before the trick has been completed.

(f) Mixing the cards before the result of the deal has been agreed upon.

(g) A comment or act during the auction or play period, calling attention to an incident thereof, the state of the score, or the number of tricks already taken or still required.

3. OBSERVANCE OF PROPER ETIQUETTE

A player should maintain at all times a courteous attitude toward his partner and opponents. He should carefully avoid any remark or action which might cause annoyance or embarrassment to another player or interfere with the enjoyment of the game.

Every player should follow uniformly correct procedure in calling and playing, since any departure from correct standards may interfere with the orderly progress of the game.

A player should refrain from:

(a) The use of different designations for the same call.

(b) Frequent review of the auction or play due to his own inattention.

(c) Volunteering information that should be given only in response to a question.

(d) Looking intently at any other player during the auction or play periods, or at another player's hand as for the purpose of observing the place from which he draws a card.

(e) Making gratuitous comments during the play period as to the auction or the adequacy of the contract.

(f) Exchanging hands with his partner, or letting his partner see his hand, whether or not a penalty may be incurred.

(g) Detaching a card from his hand before it is his turn to lead or play.

(h) Disorderly arrangement of completed tricks, which may make it difficult to determine the sequence of plays.

(i) Making a claim or concession of tricks if there is any doubt as to the outcome of the deal.

4. USE OF CONVENTIONS

It is improper to use, in calling or playing, any convention the meaning of which may not be understood by the opponents. Conventional calls or plays should be explained to the opponents before any player has looked at his cards. Advance notice may be given of the intention to use certain conventions of which full explanation may be deferred until the occasion arises. The explanation may be given only by the player whose partner made the conventional call or play. At any time this player must reply to an inquiry by an opponent as to the significance of a call or play that may be conventional, and should supply any information that may have been withheld.

Any sponsoring organization, club or tournament committee, or group of persons playing Contract Bridge, may restrict the use of conventions in games under its jurisdiction.

5. SPECTATORS

A spectator, or a member of a table who is not playing, should refrain from gratuitous remarks or mannerisms of any kind. He should not call attention to any irregularity or mistake, or speak on any question of fact or law except by request of a member of each side.

RULES FOR CLUB PROCEDURE

The following rules, governing membership in new and existing tables, have proven satisfactory in club use over a long period of years.

A. DEFINITIONS

Member—An applicant who has acquired the right to play at a table either immediately or in his turn.

Complete Table—A table with six members.

Incomplete Table—A table with four or five members.

Cut In—Assert the right to become a member of an incomplete table, or to become a member of a complete table at such time as it may become incomplete.

B. TIME LIMIT ON RIGHT TO PLAY

An applicant may not play in a rubber unless he has become a member of a table before a card is duly drawn for the selection of players or partners.

C. NEWLY FORMED TABLES

Four to six applicants may form a table. If there are more than six applicants, the six highest-ranking ones become members. The four highest-ranking members play the first rubber. Those who have not played, ranked in their order of entry into the room, take precedence over those who have played; the latter rank equally, except that players leaving existing tables to join the new table rank lowest. Precedence between those of equal rank is determined by drawing cards, the player who draws the higher-ranking card having precedence.

D. CUTTING IN

An application establishes membership in a table either forthwith or (if the table is complete) as soon as a vacancy occurs, unless applications in excess of the number required to complete a table are made at the same time, in which case precedence between applicants is established by drawing cards, as provided in the preceding rule.

E. GOING OUT

After each rubber place must be made for any member who did not play the last rubber, by the member who has played the greatest number of consecutive rubbers at that table. Cards are drawn for precedence if necessary. A member who has left another existing table must draw cards, for his first rubber, with the member who would otherwise have played. A player who breaks up a game by leaving three players at a table may not compete against them for entry at another table until each of them has played at least one rubber.

F. MEMBERSHIP LIMITED TO ONE TABLE

No one can be a member of more than one table at the same time, unless a member consents, on request, to make a fourth at another table and announces his intention of returning to his former table as soon as his place at the new table can be filled. Failure to announce such intention results in loss of membership at his former table.

84. SCORING TABLE

TRICK SCORE

Scored below the line by declarer's side, if contract is fulfilled:

	IF TRUMPS ARE			
	♣	♢	♡	♠
For each trick over six bid and made				
Undoubled	20	20	30	30
Doubled	40	40	60	60
Redoubled	80	80	120	120

	AT A NO-TRUMP CONTRACT		
	UNDOUBLED	DOUBLED	REDOUBLED
For the first trick over six, bid and made	40	80	160
For each additional trick over six, bid and made	30	60	120

The first side to score 100 points below the line, in one or more hands, wins a GAME. When a game is won, both sides start without trick score toward the next game. First side to win two games wins the RUBBER.

PREMIUM SCORE

Scored above the line by declarer's side:

RUBBER, GAME, PART-SCORE, CONTRACT FULFILLED

For winning the RUBBER, if opponents have won no game .. 700

For winning the RUBBER, if opponents have won one game. 500

UNFINISHED RUBBER—for having won one game 300

—for having the only part-score (or scores) 50

For making any DOUBLED or REDOUBLED CONTRACT ... 50

84. SCORING TABLE (continued)

SLAMS

For making a SLAM	NOT VULNERABLE	VULNERABLE
Small Slam (12 tricks) bid and made	500	750
Grand Slam (all 13 tricks) bid and made	1000	1500

OVERTRICKS

For each OVERTRICK (tricks made in excess of contract)	NOT VULNERABLE	VULNERABLE
Undoubled	Trick value	Trick value
Doubled	100	200
Redoubled	200	400

HONORS

Scored above the line by either side:

For holding four of the five trump HONORS (A, K, Q, J, 10) in one hand 100

For holding all five trump HONORS (A, K, Q, J, 10) in one hand 150

For holding all four ACES in one hand at a no-trump contract 150

UNDERTRICK PENALTIES

Tricks by which declarer fails to fulfill the contract; scored above the line by declarer's opponents if contract is not fulfilled:

NOT VULNERABLE	UNDOUBLED	DOUBLED	REDOUBLED
For first undertrick	50	100	200
For each add'tl. undertrick	50	200	400

VULNERABLE	UNDOUBLED	DOUBLED	REDOUBLED
For first undertrick	100	200	400
For each add'tl. undertrick	100	300	600

GLOSSARY

A

ABOVE THE LINE–All scores entered above the line in scoring. These include over-tricks, doubled or redoubled over-tricks, bonuses for fulfilling contract, honors, slam bonuses, rubber bonuses and penalties received from the opponents.

A.C.B.L.–The American Contract Bridge League, under whose auspices tournament bridge is conducted in the United States.

ACE SHOWING– The act of cue-bidding each ace separately. Some players prefer to show aces rather than suits in responding to opening forcing two-bids.

ADEQUATE TRUMP SUPPORT–The minimum number of cards of partner's suit needed to raise that suit.

ADVERSARY–Either opponent.

ANALYSIS–The accurate appraisal of the trick taking possibilities of a hand, either offensively or defensively.

ARTIFICIAL BID–A bid designed to show a specific holding rather than a playable suit. Examples - a response to some slam convention; a cue-bid; a short suit bid as a means of forcing the bidding to continue.

ASKING BIDS–A slam convention devised by Ely Culbertson, where both high cards and distributional controls can be located.

ASTRO–A method of showing specific two-suited hands over an opening bid of no trump devised by Paul Allinger, Leonard Rosler and Roger Stern.

ASTRO CUE-BIDS–Extension of methods of showing specific two-suited hands over an opponent's opening suit bid, by the same authors.

ATTACKING LEAD–A lead of (or from) a high card, intended to develop a trick quickly for that side.

AUCTION–The bidding period, during which one side or both sides attempt to name the trump suit. The highest bid wins. If both sides bid the same amount, the choice is determined by the rank of the bid suits.

AVERAGE–Fifty percent of the total points possible to be won on a board, a session or an event; were 12 maximum on a board, average would be six; with 312 possible for a session, average would be 156.

B

BALANCE–To reopen the bidding in the fourth position rather than sell out cheaply to an adverse low-range contract. See protection bid.

BALANCED DISTRIBUTION–A hand in which the suits are comparatively evenly distributed, and which contains no singletons, or voids, or extremely long suits.

BATH COUP–A play, reputedly named after the Earl of Bath, who originated it in an 18th century whist game. It consists of a player holding the ace, jack and one or more cards of a suit, refusing to win the king when led by the left hand opponent. Since the lead is presumed to be from a holding headed by both the king and queen, a continuation by the left hand opponent must give the other side two tricks, since it comes into the ace-jack; or the suit must be abandoned at that point by the opponents.

BELOW THE LINE–Scores representing tricks bid and made, which count towards game, and are scored below the line.

BID–A proffered contract by any player in terms of tricks he pledges his side to win, in an attempt to name the trump.

BIDDABLE SUIT–A suit good enough to be used as a trump suit.

BIDDING–See Auction.

BLACKWOOD–A slam convention invented by Easley Blackwood of Indianapolis, Indiana, used to locate aces and kings.

BLOCK–To interpose a high card which will impede the utilization of a suit.

BOARD-A-MATCH–A form of duplicate scoring used in team of four contests, where one match point is awarded for winning the hand, a half-point for tying and a zero for a loss.

BOARD, DUPLICATE–A tray with four pockets used in duplicate and tournament bridge.

BODY–Cards that are said to possess 'body' are the high intermediate cards, as the sevens, eights and nines.

BONUS–Any premium received other than the actual trick score.

BOOK–The first six tricks taken by the declarer's side; the defenders' book is the amount of the opponents' bid subtracted from seven. Thus, if the bid were four spades, the defenders' book would be three tricks.

BUSINESS DOUBLE–A double intended to increase the penalty the opponents will pay for expected failure to fulfill their bid.

BUSINESS PASS–A pass, after partner's informatory double, to show the ability to defeat the doubled contract.

BYE–An obsolete way of saying 'pass,' or 'no bid.' The latter terms are preferable.

BYE-ROUND–A period during which a pair (or team) may have no opponents. This is sometimes known as 'drawing a bye.' It is caused by an uneven number of contestants.

C

CALL–An all-embracing term referring to any bid, double, redouble or pass.

CALL A CARD–The act of designating a card, orally, to be played.

CAMOUFLAGE BID–Bidding one suit as a psychic when holding some other suit.

CARRY-OVER–The term applied in duplicate bridge to a score or scores from previous sessions when counted in a combined score of two or more sessions of play.

CARTER CONVENTION–Devised by David Carter of Kansas City, this convention opposite an opening bid of one no trump employs a response of two clubs as showing a weak hand in a non-forcing Stayman type response whereas a response of two diamonds shows a stronger hand with eight or more points and is forcing to at least a final contract of two no trump by the partnership.

CASH–To lead a card for the purpose of taking a trick.

CLAIMING–To claim any or all of the remaining tricks to be played. This is a privilege of either defender, or declarer. Dummy may not claim tricks in advance.

CLEAR A SUIT–To force out the high cards of a suit held by the opponents in order to set up, as winners, the remaining cards of the suit held by the leader's side.

CLOSED HAND–The declarer's hand, which is not seen by the defenders, as opposed to that of dummy, which is 'open.'

CLUB CONVENTION–The use of an opening bid of one club to show a particular type of hand.

COME-ON–An encouraging card or cards played by a defender. Usually a seven spot or larger is considered encouraging, as is any high card followed by a lower card in the same suit.

CONCEDE–To give up some or all of the remaining unplayed tricks to the opponents.

CONSTRUCTIVE BID–Any bid which is encouraging and shows the possibility of making a still higher contract.

CONTRACT–The highest bid which determines the trump, and the number of tricks to be won. - Verb - to bid.

CONTROL–A high card in a suit enabling its holder to win a given round of that suit when led.

CONTROLLED PSYCHIC–A psychic bid, usually part of a bidding system, where the rebid by the psychic bidder indicates the type of hand held. The rebid is known as the 'control.'

CONVENTION–An understanding between the partnership, relating to the use of a bid or signal.

CO-OPERATIVE DOUBLE–A penalty double which must meet with the doubler's partner's approval to be left in.

COUP–A strategic play.

COURTESY BID–Responding without the required high cards to a bid by partner. This is the quickest way I know to lose money.

COVER–To play a higher card than that already played.

CROSS-RUFF–To trump back and forth between the partnership hands.

CUE BID–An artificial bid made to locate or to indicate a control.

CULBERTSON, ELY–Probably the best known name in bridge. Culbertson and his staff pioneered more innovations and improvements in contract bridge than any other group.

CUT–To separate the shuffled deck into two parts before they are re-assembled opposite to their original form and then dealt.

D

DEAL–Verb - To give out, one card at a time, to each player, the shuffled deck of cards. Noun - The hand of 52 cards, after having been distributed, 13 to each player.

DEALER–The player who dealt the cards.

DECLARATION—The final contract.

DECLARER—The player who plays the closed hand and that of the dummy. The declarer is the first player to have named the suit in which the highest bid was made, even though his partner may have made the highest bid in that suit.

DEEP FINESSE—A ducking play made without hope of winning the trick, usually against three or more higher adverse cards.

DEFENDERS—The pair that did not win the auction.

DEFENSIVE BIDDING—Bidding by the side that did not open the auction.

DEFENSIVE PLAY—A play made by a defender.

DELAYED RAISE—A raise of partner's suit not made at one's first opportunity.

DEMAND BID—See Forcing Bid.

DENIAL—A bid which denies support for partner's suit.

DESCHAPELLES COUP—Named after its inventor, the Deschapelles is a play in which a defender sacrifices a high card in order to create a winning entry in partner's hand. In the accompanying example, East has the lead, and the contract is no trump. West's hearts are winners, but his queen of spades is trapped by dummy's ace-jack. By leading the king of spades, knocking out dummy's ace, West's queen becomes an entry. This is a Deschapelles coup.

	♠ A J ◊ Q J 9	
♠ Q 7 5 ♡ K Q	N W E S	♠ K 3 2 ◊ A 2
	♠ 10 8 6 ◊ K 10	

DINK—To force the opponents to trump, shortening their trumps against their wishes.

DISCARD—Verb - To play a card (other than a trump) not in the led suit. Noun - Any card played not in the led suit.

DISTRIBUTION—The pattern in which the 52 cards are divided.

DISTRIBUTIONAL HANDS—Hands with uneven distribution, as those containing voids, singletons, long suits or two or three suiters.

DOUBLE—A call made by the side that did not make the last bid. The double increases both trick scores and penalties. Doubles are of two basic types - informatory and penalty.

DOUBLE DUMMY—To play the cards as though the location of all 52 cards were known.

DOUBLE FINESSE—To finesse against two missing cards.

DOUBLE RAISE—A raise in the same suit of one more than necessary, as from one spade to three spades.

DOUBLE SQUEEZE—A squeeze in which both defenders are forced to unguard two suits, permitting declarer to set up a low card in one of these suits as a winner.

DOUBLETON—Two cards of a suit.

DRAWING TRUMPS—The act of leading trumps to exhaust the trumps held by an opponent, or opponents.

DROP—The fall of a card under the lead of a still higher card because of the need of following suit. Thus, a player holding a singleton king would be forced to 'drop' that card were someone to play the ace.

DUCK—To deliberately lose a trick by playing a low card when holding a higher card capable of capturing the trick.

DUMMY—Declarer's partner, whose hand is placed face upwards after the opening lead.

DUMMY REVERSAL—The play of the hand by declarer in which dummy's trumps become the master trumps and are used, in the later stages of play, for drawing the opponents' trumps while in the earlier period of play, declarer's trumps are used for the purpose of trumping dummy's losing cards. Since normally declarer's losers are ruffed in dummy rather than vice-versa, hence the name of dummy-reversal.

DUPLICATE BRIDGE—A form of the game where hands are reassembled in trays after being played, and replayed by other contestants. Winners are judged on a basis of comparison.

DUPLICATION—Where both partners have the same values, or the identical distribution in both hands. A spade void in one hand facing the ace of spades in the other would be duplication.

E

ECHO—The play of a high card followed by a lower card as an encouraging signal.

ELEVEN, RULE OF—A mathematical formula permitting counting the missing high cards in the led suit when the fourth best card of a suit was originally led.

ELIMINATION PLAY—The act of stripping (playing out) two or more suits from declarer's hand and dummy's. An opponent is then thrown into the lead, forced into an unwilling lead or play.

END PLAY—Usually occuring with but a few cards remaining unplayed, end-plays involve throwing an opponent into the lead, forcing him to make some play he would otherwise not wish to make.

ENTRY—A high card or trump permitting a player (or hand) to gain the lead.

EQUALS—Cards of a sequence held by the partnership.

ESCAPE SUIT—A second suit to which the bidder plans to escape if doubled in his first suit.

ESTABLISH—To create as winners the remaining card or cards of a suit.

ESTABLISHED CARD—Any card that has become a winner.

ETHICS—The proprieties of the game such as manners, avoidance of giving information by intonation or expression, etc.

EXIT CARDS—Cards with which a player can throw the lead to an opponent.

EXPOSED CARD—A card played, accidentally or in error, by a defender so that it is subject to penalty.

F

FACED—Cards placed face upwards, as those of dummy.

FALL—The involuntary drop of a card under a higher card, as the remark, 'The ace dropped the queen.'

FALSE CARDING—Playing a card or cards in unnatural order, for the purpose of misleading the opponents.

FEATURE SHOWING—See cue-bid.

FINAL BID—The last bid of the auction. It must be followed by three passes.

FINESSE—An attempt to win a trick with a lower card than held by the opponents. For the finesse to succeed, the first opponent to play must have the higher card or cards.

FINESSING AGAINST PARTNER—The third hand defender not playing his highest card of the suit led by partner.

FISHBEIN CONVENTION—A method devised by Harry Fishbein of New York City to eliminate ambiguity in either bidding over or doubling opposing pre-emptive three bids made by the right hand opponent.

FISHBEIN CONVENTION, MODIFIED–The cheaper minor is bid over pre-emptive bids as the equivalent of an informatory double.

FIT–Supporting cards in the same suit held by partner.

FIVE CARD MAJORS–Major suits of five cards; referring to methods espoused by Roth-Stone and Kaplan-Sheinwold where opening bids of one of a major in the first and second position require at least five cards of the suit.

FLINT CONVENTION–Originated by Jeremy Flint, an English player, this convention permits the partnership to sign off in a less than game contract after an opening bid of two no trump.

FOLLOW SUIT–To play a card of the suit being led.

FORCE–To make partner bid; to shorten the opponent's trumps.

FORCED DISCARD–An unwilling discard, as in a squeeze.

FORCING PASS–A pass by one partner after an opposing bid, usually when the partnership has bid strongly. The forcing pass leaves the decision up to partner whether to bid higher or to double the opponents' bid.

FORCING RAISE–A raise which is forcing to game.

FORCING TWO BID–An opening bid of two in a suit, used to show an extremely powerful hand, and that is forcing on both partners to keep bidding until at least game has been reached.

FOSTER ECHO–The play of the second-highest, by leader's partner, against no trump when the opening lead was an honor and third hand has three cards or more. By playing lower cards, the partner can denote presence of a still higher card. Like the Rule of Eleven, it was devised by Richard F. Foster, one of the earliest American card authorities.

FOUR CLUB CONVENTION–See Gerber.

FOURTH BEST–The card fourth from the top of any four card or longer suit. Thus holding KJ86, the six would be fourth best.

FRAGMENT BID–See Ingberman Fragment Bid.

FREAK–A hand with abnormal distribution.

FREE–Any call, whether a response, rebid, overcall, raise or double, made voluntarily over an intervening bid by an opponent.

FREE DOUBLE–A double of a bid after the opponents have already reached game, with or without the aid of a part score.

The term is a misnomer, since the free double can be very costly in terms of bonuses and overtricks.

FULFILL—To complete the bid contract.

G

GAME—A score of 100 points in tricks bid and made. These points are scored 'below the line,' and need not be made at one time.

GERBER CONVENTION—A slam convention, devised by John Gerber of Houston, Texas, outstanding American player, in which the 'ask' for aces begins with a bid of four clubs rather than a bid of four no trump as in Blackwood.

GO DOWN—Fail to make the bid.

GOREN SYSTEM—The standard American bidding system, as compiled by Charles H. Goren of New York City and Miami, top American authority. It uses the standard 4-3-2-1 point count for high cards and counting distribution 3-2-1 for voids, singletons and aces.

GOULASH—A method of purposely dealing freak hands in some games of bridge. Instead of shuffling the cards as in normal play after a passed out hand, each player assorts his cards by suits, highest cards to the left and one hand is placed upon the next, beginning with the left hand opponent of the person who dealt the passed out hand. The cards are then dealt, first five at a time to each player, then five more at a time and finally, three cards to each player.

GRAND SLAM—Bidding and winning all 13 tricks.

GRAND SLAM FORCE—When a suit has been agreed on as by a direct raise, a voluntary fid of five no trump *when not preceded* by four no trump requests partner to bid seven of the agreed trump suit with two of the top three trump suit honors (ace, king or queen) or six in the agreed trump suit with one honor or no honor in the suit.

GRAND SLAM FORCE, ROMAN—A variation of the preceding where artificial responses are used to indicate the number of honors held by responder in the agreed trump suit.

GROSS SCORE—The total score of any side.

GUARD—To keep low cards as protection for high cards, so that the latter cannot be caught. The deuce of spades would be said to 'guard' the king if those were the player's only two spades.

GUARDED HONOR–See guard.

GUIDE CARD–A printed card used in duplicate bridge to give the progression of the players and hands.

H

HAND–The original 13 cards dealt a player.

HERBERT CONVENTION–A method devised by Walter Herbert, former world's champion from Austria, formerly of San Francisco and New Orleans and currently director of the Houston Opera. The response of the next ranking suit to any forcing situation is a negative response as a bid of one diamond to an opening bid of one club or, a response of one heart after partner's informatory double of one diamond. In these cases, the response *does not* show presence of the suit. It was the the fore-runner of 'ranking suit' responses to strong two-bids.

HIGH-LOW–See echo.

HOLD UP–The refusal to play a high card capable of winning a trick until a later round.

HOLDING–The hand held by a player.

HONORS–The top five cards of any suit.

HONOR TRICK-The defensive values assigned to cards, and combinations of these cards. Honor tricks are also used to evaluate opening bids and responses.

HOWELL MOVEMENT–A type of progression in duplicate, where all pairs except one move, and all pairs meet.

I

IDLE TRUMP–A trump in dummy not needed for trumping.

ILLEGAL BID–A bid that is not permitted, as a bid of eight, or a bid by a player previously barred from bidding.

INDIVIDUAL–The term most generally applied to tournaments using what is known as an 'individual movement' where players change partners and opponents after each round.

INFERENTIAL FORCE–A bid which is forcing on partner to bid because of strength already shown, and the surrounding bidding.

INFORMATORY DOUBLE–A double requesting partner to bid.

INGBERMAN FRAGMENT BID–A distribution-showing convention devised by Monroe Ingberman of Chicago.

INSUFFICIENT BID–A bid of a lesser number than required to outbid the previous call.

INTERFERENCE BID–A bid made with the intention of obstructing the opponents' bidding.

INTERIOR SEQUENCE–A sequence with a still higher card not in sequence. Example, KJ109, Q1098, etc.

INTERMEDIATES–Since the seven-spot is the middle card of each suit and aces, kings, queens and jacks the highest cards of each suit, cards between the seven and the jack, such as eights, nines and 10's are known as intermediates. They are highly desirable for bolstering the trick-taking capabilities of a suit.

INTERNATIONAL MATCH POINTS–The method used in scoring many team of four matches which is really a graded combination of match points applied to gross scoring. In other words, the greater the difference in gross score, the greater the number of international match points won or lost. This is in contrast to standard match point scoring, used in pair and individual movements, where the maximum match point score is determined by the number of times a hand is played rather by the differential in points.

Differential in Total Points	International Match Points Awarded	Differential in Total Points	International Match Points Awarded
0 to 10	0		
20 to 40	1	750 to 890	13
50 to 80	2	900 to 1090	14
90 to 120	3	1100 to 1290	15
130 to 160	4	1300 to 1490	16
170 to 210	5	1500 to 1740	17
220 to 260	6	1750 to 1990	18
270 to 310	7	2000 to 2240	19
320 to 360	8	2250 to 2490	20
370 to 420	9	2500 to 2990	21
430 to 490	10	3000 to 3490	22
500 to 590	11	3500 to 3990	23
600 to 740	12	4000 & over	24

INTERVENING BID—A bid sandwiched between two bids of the opponents.

INVERTED RAISES—The method originated by Kaplan and Sheinwold in which a single raise in a minor suit is strength-showing and a double raise weak. The term 'inverted' is derived from the fact that this is the opposite of normal procedure.

INVITATIONAL—A bid not completely forcing, but asking partner to bid with the slightest extra values.

J

JACOBY TRANSFER BIDS—A system of transfer bids devised by Oswald Jacoby of Dallas, Texas, famed American player and writer. A response other than two clubs to opener's one no trump asks the opener to bid the next higher-ranking suit.

JUMP—To bid more than the necessary minimum number.

K

KAPLAN-SHEINWOLD—A bidding system devised and made popular by Edgar Kaplan of New York and Alfred Sheinwold, now of Beverly Hills. Both are outstanding players and authors; Sheinwold a widely-read syndicated bridge columnist.

KIBITZER—A person who watches (not always silently).

KOCK-WERNER REDOUBLE—Devised by two top Swedish players, the redouble asks partner (who has been doubled for penalty) to rescue himself to any other unbid suit for which support is promised. It completely changes the meaning of the redouble from conventionally showing the ability to make the doubled contract to stating that the doubled suit is unmakeable and asking for a rescue (by himself) of the player who has been doubled. It is similar in intent to what has been known as the S.O.S. redouble except that in the latter, the doubled player redoubles for rescue; in Kock-Werner, it is his partner.

L

LAGRON ECHO–The method attributed to E. M. Lagron of Cleveland in which the size of the card led (which partner is expected to win, usually by trumping) indicates the desired suit to be returned.

LANDY CONVENTION–The method devised by Alvin Landy, executive secretary of the American Contract Bridge League to defend against weak opening no trumps.

LAVINTHAL ECHO–A signalling method originated by Hy Lavinthal of Camden, New Jersey in which the size of the card *discarded or played* is indicative of the desired suit shift. He is frequently given credit for invention of the parallel convention, together with Lagron, where the size of the card *led* indicates the suit desired to be returned.

LAWS–The laws governing contract bridge are formulated by an international body with revisions approximately each decade. There are two sets of laws – those governing rubber bridge which are included in this text and those concerning duplicate (tournament) bridge which are published by Crown Publishers, and sell for two dollars.

LAY-DOWN–A hand that requires no playing, since the tricks are immediately available.

LEAD–The first card played to a trick.

LEAD DIRECTING BID–A bid made for the purpose of telling partner what suit to lead.

LEAD DIRECTING DOUBLE–A double directing partner's lead.

LEAD OUT OF TURN–To lead when it is not one's turn.

LEAD THROUGH STRENGTH–To lead through opposing high cards.

LEAD UP TO WEAKNESS–A trite belief from whist days, "Lead through strength, and up to weakness." While generally sound, it is far from always true.

LEADER–The first person playing to a trick.

LENGTH–The number of cards in a suit.

LEVEL–The height of the bidding in referring to the number of tricks bid. Thus the three level would require a bid of three.

LIFE MASTER–The top ranking in the American Contract Bridge League, referring to players with 300 or more master points.

LIGHT BID–A bid made with minimum or sub-minimum values.

LIGHTNER CONVENTION–The lead-directing convention against slam contracts originated by Theodore Lightner of New York City.

LIMIT BID–A bid guaranteeing maximum and minimum limits.

LINE–The horizontal line used in scoring.

LITTLE SLAM–Bidding and winning 12 tricks.

M

MAJOR–The heart and spade suits are the 'majors.'

MAJOR TENACE–A tenace headed by the ace.

MAKE–An archaic term used to describe the trump suit, as a 'three spade make;' verb, to fulfill a bid.

MANDATE BIDS–See Texas Convention.

MASTER HAND–The hand containing the key cards.

MASTER POINTS–Awards given in A.C.B.L. tournaments. The more important the event, the greater the award.

MASTERS–Players with 20 or more master points.

MATCH POINT–A method of scoring duplicate. One point is awarded for every pair whose score is inferior, one-half point for every pair tied.

McCABE ADJUNCT–A bidding convention permitting a player to set the final contract after his partner has opened the bidding with a weak two-bid.

McKENNEY CONVENTION–The play of the second-highest card by the partner of the opening leader as an encouraging signal when unable to capture dummy's higher card. Thus if the opening lead was fourth-best, the five-spot, from a holding of K 10 8 5 4 and the dummy's queen was played from Q 2, third-hand defender with J 9 3 would drop the nine. This would indicate that third-hand held a still higher card than the nine. Since leader held the king and 10 and dummy the queen, there are only two possible missing higher cards, the ace and jack. Had third-hand the former card, he would have captured dummy's queen. Hence, that card is with declarer and third-hand must have the remaining higher card, the jack. The opening leader will now be aware that the suit may safely be continued since declarer does not have both the ace and jack.

MICHAELS CUE-BID–The bid of the opponent's suit at low level devised by Michael Michaels, showing a specific two-suited hand and requesting a takeout by partner.

MINOR–The club and diamond suits are the 'minor' suits.

MINOR TENACE–Any tenace headed by the king or lower card.

MISFIT–A hand in which each partner lacks supporting cards for the other's suits.

MISNOMER–A slip of the tongue in bidding, as saying 'spades' when meaning 'hearts.'

MITCHELL–A progression in duplicate where the players seated North-South remain stationary, and those sitting East-West move each round.

MIXED EVENTS–Contests where the partnerships are composed of one man and one woman.

MOREHEAD, ALBERT H.-A famous card authority, writer, player, former bridge editor of The New York Times, and author of many magazine articles and books on cards.

MOYSE, ALPHONSE JR.–Editor and publisher of the magazine *Bridge World*, and a well known writer and player.

N

NEAPOLITAN SYSTEM–An Italian bidding system based on many artificial bids and widely used in southern Italy, although not legal for American use in high tournament play.

NEGATIVE BID–A denial or weakness bid, as that of two no trump in response to an opening forcing two bid.

NEGATIVE DOUBLE–Devised by Alvin Roth and Tobias Stone, a low-range double of an opposing suit bid after partner has bid requests partner to show a second suit, if present. Conventionally, a double in this situation would be for penalty. The double is sometimes called the 'sputnik' double.

NET SCORE–The actual difference in gross scores when the smaller score is subtracted from the larger.

NEUTRAL DISCARD–Discarding a middle sized (five or six spot) for temporizing reasons.

NO BID–The equivalent of saying 'pass.'

NO TRUMP–In no trump, all suits have the same trick taking

values, Tricks are scored 40 points for the first trick, 30 for each subsequent trick.

NON-VULNERABLE–Not having won a game.

NORMAL TRUMP SUPPORT–See adequate trump support.

NOT VULNERABLE–See non-vulnerable.

O

OBLIGATORY FINESSE–A ducking play based on the hope that the opponents' high card will be singleton on the second round of the suit.

ODD TRICK–The first trick over the book of six won by declarer.

OFFENSE–The play of the cards by the side that declared the trump suit, as opposed to defense by the unsuccessful bidders (defenders).

ONE BID–A bid of one, contracting to win seven tricks.

ONE CLUB FORCING–The term applied to methods where an opening bid of one club shows a strong hand (although not necessarily clubs) and partner is compelled to respond at least once.

ONE OVER ONE–The modern bidding method in which suits are shown in an economical, ascending manner at the one level.

ONE, TWO, THREE–A recent pre-emptive development by the opening bidder with a weak hand after having received a single raise in the orininally bid suit. The free rebid to the three level is intended to make difficult or otherwise prevent a bid by the opponent as a protective measure.

OPEN HAND–The dummy's hand after being faced.

OPENING BID–The first bid, other than a pass, made at the table.

OPENING BIDDER–The first player to bid.

OPENING LEAD–The first card played to the hand, by the defender to the declarer's left.

OPPONENT–A player of the other side.

OPTIONAL DOUBLE–See co-operative double.

ORIGINAL BID–See opening bid.

OSTRICH COUP–The act of a declarer deliberately shortening his own trump suit by ruffing losers, accomplishing nothing in the process, but weakening his trump suit.

OUT–To be void of a suit.

OUT CARD–A card used to get out of the lead. See exit card.

OUT OF TURN–Bidding or playing out of rotation.

OVER–Referring to a position where a player, usually a defender, can over-trump, or, by refusal to over-trump, can promote a trump winner.

OVERBID–Bidding a greater number than warranted.

OVERCALL–A bid made by the side that did not open the bidding.

OVER-RUFF–To over-trump.

OVERTAKE–To win a trick already won by partner by playing a still higher card. Thus, if one defender leads the king, and his partner plays the ace, he is overtaking.

OVERTRICK–A trick in excess of the bid.

OVERTRUMP–See over-ruff.

P

PACK–The deck of 52 cards before being dealt.

PAIR–The two players forming the partnership.

PAR CONTEST–A match where pre-dealt hands are given contestants whose results are judged on a previously determined basis. These may be on bidding, play of the hand, defense or all three.

PART SCORE–A completed contract of less than game value.

PARTIAL–See part score.

PARTNER–The player sitting opposite another player.

PASS–Failure to bid by a player.

PASSIVE DEFENSE–Comparable to the football expression, 'kick and wait for the breaks.' In passive defense, the defender leads suits which can neither gain or cost his side a trick, waiting for the offense to expend high cards in trick development.

PASS OUT–When all four players do not bid, the hand is said to be 'passed out.'

PENALTY DOUBLE–See business double.

PENALTY PASS–See business pass.

PETER–An old whist expression meaning to echo, or high-low.

PHANTOM SAVE–A voluntary sacrifice proven unnecessary since the opponents would not have been able to win the tricks necessary to complete their contract.

PIANOLA–A hand that can play itself.

PICK UP–To catch a high card or cards by playing still higher cards. To play the ace and king of spades to drop the opponents' doubleton queen would be said 'to pick up' the queen.

PICK UP SLIP–An individual scoring card permitting only one score, used primarily in championship play.

PLAY–The period immediately following the bidding, starting with the opening lead.

PLAY OUT–To fully play out a hand as opposed to a claim or concession of remaining tricks to expedite play.

PLAYED CARD–A card that has been led or played.

PLAYING TRICKS–A trick that can be developed by the play of the cards.

POINTS–The numerical values assigned to cards in proportion to their trick taking abilities.

POSITION–A player's (or card's) location at the table in relation to other players (or cards).

POSITIVE RESPONSE–Any bid that, to a previous bid by partner, shows strength.

POST MORTEM–The analysis of the hand after being played.

PRE-EMPTIVE BID–Literally, to 'buy first.' It is a shut-out bid, usually of three or more in a suit, based on hands with long suits, and little defensive strength.

PREFERENCE–The act of showing a liking for one suit over another.

PREMIUM–The bonus paid for slams, honors, games, etc.

PREPAREDNESS–Anticipating partner's most likely response, and your own rebid to that response.

PRIVATE CONVENTION–A secret understanding between the partnership. This is strictly illegal.

PROBABLE WINNER–A trick which is expected to materialize in the play of the hand.

PROBABILITIES–The mathematical percentages of divisions.

PROGRESSION–The movement of players in tournaments.

PROGRESSIVE BRIDGE–A form of the game where, after each round, the winners move to other tables and the losers remain at the same table.

PROGRESSIVE SQUEEZE–A squeeze in which one defender is successively squeezed in three suits, being first forced to unguard one suit setting up a winning card in that suit which, when played, then squeezes him again between the remaining two suits.

PROMOTION–The act of advancing a card to higher status, usually through the capture or cover of adverse cards.

PROPRIETIES–The section of the laws dealing with manners and the niceties of the game.

PROTECTION BID–A bid made with less than normal requirements because the opponents' weak bidding, or their lack of bidding marking partner with strength which, up to now, it has been dangerous for him to show. The protective bid is made rather than sell out too cheaply to the opponents.

PROTEST–An appeal from a decision, usually in a tournament.

PROVED FINESSE–A finesse whose success has become established.

PSEUDO-SQUEEZE–An attempt by declarer to make the defenders think they are being squeezed when no squeeze exists.

PUSH–To force the opponents higher than they wish to bid.

PUT UP–To interpose, or play a high card.

PYSCHIC BID–Any bid intended to fool the opponents as bidding without the customary values or bidding a non-present suit.

PSYCHIC CONTROL–The method by which the pyschic bidder reveals to his partner that the bid was not genuine.

Q

QUALIFYING SESSIONS–The early rounds of championships to eliminate a given number of contestants.

QUICK TRICK–See honor trick.

QUITTED TRICK–A trick which has been turned.

R

RAISE–An increase in the number bid of a particular suit or no trump bid by partner.

RANK–The relation of cards to each other in terms of trick taking abilities; with suits, rank refers to their relation to each other for bidding and cutting purposes.

REBID—A second or subsequent bid by a player.

REBIDDABLE SUIT—A suit which may be safely rebid before being supported by partner.

RECTIFYING THE COUNT—The voluntary giving up of a trick early in play by declarer in order to produce a situation where he will then be able to win all of the remaining tricks save one, the condition necessary for success of almost all squeezes. Thus, if South has bid a small slam and has only 11 sure tricks, he has all of the tricks save two of the 13. By giving up one loser, he has 'rectified the count,' viz., produced an 11 of 12 situation, making a squeeze possible.

REDEAL—The act of a player dealing two or more successive times. Redeals are only permitted because of misdeals such as too few or too many cards, cards exposed during the deal, etc. See Law 10, *page 716*. When a hand is passed out, there cannot be a redeal.

REDOUBLE—In effect, a double of a penalty double, quadrupling the normal (undoubled) trick score. A redouble can only be made by the side which has been doubled.

RE-ENTRY—A card or cards permitting the return of the lead to a hand.

REFUSE—An obsolete term meaning to be unable to follow suit.

RELAY—The passing of duplicate boards back and forth between tables in duplicate.

RENEGE—See revoke.

RESCUE—To take partner out of a contract which seems bad, or hopeless, into some other contract.

RESPONDER—The player making the response.

RESPONSE—A bid made in answer to partner's bid or informatory double.

RESPONSIVE DOUBLE—Invented by Dr. H. Fielding Eliot, a second double by the partner of the original informatory doubler, after the doubled suit has received a raise intended to be pre-emptive, is also informatory. Thus, in a sequence of West, one heart; partner, North, double; East, two hearts and yourself, South, double, your double of two hearts would be informatory.

REVERSE—To bid suits in backwards order, thus showing the first suit to be longer than the second, and the hand to be very strong.

REVERSE SIGNALS–The act of playing a low card as a come-on and a high card as the play or discard of a seven or higher, as indicating a desire *not* to have the suit led or continued. This method now has little acceptance.

REVERSING DUMMY–Also known as a dummy reversal. This refers to playing the hand so that dummy's losers are trumped in declarer's hand and dummy's trumps become the master trumps, pulling those of the defenders.

REVOKE–Failue to follow suit when able to do so.

RIPSTRA CONVENTION–The method devised by J. G. Ripstra of Wichita, Kansas, for defending against weak opening no trumps.

ROMAN SYSTEM–An Italian bidding system which includes Roman Blackwood, and artificial distribution-showing bids.

ROTATION–The order in which players change partners.

ROTH-STONE SYSTEM–The bidding system devised by Alvin L. Roth and Tobias Stone primarily for tournament play. Among the ideas promulgated by them are the negative double, use of five card major suits in the first and second seat, the unusual no trump and the forcing response of one no trump facing an opening bid of one in a major.

ROUND–When each of the four players at the table have had an opportunity to bid, that constitutes a round.

RUBBER–The first two games won by a side.

RUFF–To trump.

RUFF AND SLUFF–A lead, usually by a defender, permitting declarer to trump the led suit in one hand, discard a losing card from the other hand. For this condition to be present, both declarer's hand and dummy's must be void of the led suit, and both hands should have a trump.

RUFFING TRICK–A trick won by trumping.

S

SACRIFICE–A bid made knowing that it cannot be fulfilled on the premise that the penalty to be paid will be less than the adverse score, were the opponents permitted to play the hand.

Thus a sacrifice of 300 points would be far less than permitting the opponents to bid and make a slam.

SAFETY PLAY–A play designed to avoid, or limit possible losers in playing combinations of high cards.

SAN FRANCISCO–A slam convention where aces and kings are shown in one response.

SAVE–See sacrifice.

SCORE–The points accumulated by either side.

SECOND HAND–The second player to bid, or play.

SECONDARY BID–A bid made by a player who previously passed.

SEMI-FORCING BID–A bid which, while not 100 percent forcing, requests strongly that partner bid with the slightest extra values not already disclosed.

SEQUENCE–Two or more cards of the same suit that touch each other in rank as the ace-king of spades, the queen-jack-10 of hearts, etc.

SET–Noun, a defeated contract; verb, to deafeat a contract.

SET UP–To establish, as winning tricks, cards of a suit.

SHADED BID–A bid made with less than normal requirements.

SHADED SUIT–A suit not meeting biddability requirements.

SHIFT–To change suits in leading or to go from one line of play to another.

SHORT CLUB–The term frequently applied to bidding a club suit of less than four cards as a preparedness bid or for temporizing purposes.

SHORT HAND–The hand with fewer trumps between declarer and dummy, usually the latter; a hand with an insufficient number of cards, either from a misdeal or because of having played two or more cards to an earlier trick.

SHORT SUIT LEAD–A lead made from a three card or shorter holding.

SHOW OUT–Playing a card of some other suit than that led to the current trick, thus showing no cards of the led suit.

SHUFFLE–The riffling and re-arrangement of the deck, usually by the left hand opponent of the dealer, in order to redistribute the cards in new hand patterns.

SHUT OUT BID–See pre-emptive bid.

SIDE SUIT–Any suit of four or more cards held by declarer in addition to the trump suit.

SIGNAL–The play of a card to convey a message.

SIGNOFF–A bid intended to tell partner to stop bidding.

SINGLE RAISE–A raise of one level, as from one to two.

SINGLETON–The only card of a suit.

SLAM–A bid of six or seven. See grand slam, big slam.

SLAM DOUBLES–The Lightner convention requesting an abnormal opening lead.

SLOW PASS–A pass, made after long hesitation, thus showing partner that enough high cards are present to merit thought. This practice is reprehensible.

SLUFF–To discard.

SLUFF AND RUFF–The lead of a suit in which both opponents are void. If both opponents have one or more trumps in each hand, the lead can be trumped in one hand permitting the other hand to discard a possible losing card.

SMOTHER PLAY–The lead of a suit permitting the capture of an opposing guarded trump winner. For example, East has the lead and spades are trumps.

East leads with a diamond. South trumps and West, with the guarded king, cannot win a trick.

```
          ♠A
          ♡2
          N
♠K10  W       E  ◇KQ
          S
          ♠QJ
```

The term smother is also applied to blanketing a lower missing card while finessing against a higher one as below.

South leads the queen and East's jack will be smothered.

```
          ♠A98
          N
♠K32  W       E  ♠J
          S
          ♠Q107654
```

SNEAK–A singleton.

SOLID SUIT–A suit containing sufficient high cards, or length, or both, to presumably have no intermediate losers.

S.O.S. REDOUBLE–A redouble by a player who has been doubled for penalty by the opponent. The redouble asks partner to rescue, viz., take out into the best possible suit held by partner. It denies the ability to win the required tricks. It is seldom used because of the many partnership misunderstandings arising from the convention. See Kock-Werner.

SPOTS–The number of pips on a card.

SPREAD—The act of claiming tricks, as to spread the hand.

SPUTNIK—See negative double.

SQUEEZE—The act of playing winning cards to force the other side to unguard high cards in other suits.

STAYMAN—A set of bidding conventions best known for its ability to discover major suit 'fits' between partnership hands after an opening bid of one or two no trump.

STAYMAN, SAMUEL—Co-inventor of the Stayman Convention, Sam has won many national and international championships, and is the author of "Expert Bidding."

STOPPER—A card, or combination of cards, which can be expected to win a trick when the adverse suit is led.

STRIP AND END PLAY—See elimination play.

SUICIDE SQUEEZE—The description given the leading of cards, usually winners, by one defender by which he squeezes his own partner into unguarding and discarding vital cards and tricks.

SUIT PREFERENCE SIGNAL—The lead or play of a card to signal for the lead of some particular suit.

SUPER BLACKWOOD—Advanced features of the Blackwood Convention as methods of showing voids in responding, etc.

SYMMETRY—The distributional feature appearing both ways of the table. For example, North-South having a singleton spade in one hand, together with a six card heart suit, while one of the opponents held six spades and a singleton heart.

T

TAKE OUT—To bid a new suit, or no trump, over partner's bid in another suit.

TAKE-OUT DOUBLE—See informatory double.

TEMPORIZING BID—A bid, usually on a makeshift suit, giving the bidder a second opportunity of showing additional strength, usually for a previously bid suit.

TEMPORIZING DISCARD—A discard which is neither encouraging nor discouraging, but rather stalls for time.

TENACE—An interrupted sequence. A Q, K J, Q 10 are examples.

TEXAS CONVENTION—Transfer bids employed in response to opening bids of no trump, enabling the opening no trump bidder to become the declarer with partner's major suit as trump.

THIRTEENER–The last card of a suit.

THROW-IN–A play where a player is unwillingly thrust into the lead.

TOP–The maximum score on a hand in duplicate.

TOUCHING HONORS–Honors adjacent in rank to each other.

TOUCHING SUITS–Suits adjacent in bidding rank.

TRAP BID–A bid which gets a player, or his partner into an awkward or embarassing bidding situation.

TRAPPING–Feigning weakness to coax the opponents to bid.

TRAVELLING SCORE–The score sheet accompanying a duplicate bridge board.

TRICK–Four cards, each player having contributed one card in clock-wise order.

TRIPLE RAISE–A jump of three tricks in the same suit, as from one spade to four spades.

TRIPLETON–A three card holding in a suit.

TRUMP–Noun - A card of the trump suit.

TRUMP–Verb - To play a trump card when unable to follow suit.

TRUMPING–The act of playing a trump card.

TRUMP LEAD–A lead of a trump card.

TRUMP SUIT–The suit in which the highest bid has been made.

TWO BID–An opening bid of two in a suit.

TWO SUITERS–Hands containing two suits of four or more cards each.

TWO-WAY–A bid or call which may be used in either of two ways and has two different meanings as for example, the Woodson Two-Way no trump, forcing or non-forcing Stayman, the co-operative double, etc.

U

UNBALANCED–Hands containing singletons or voids.

UNBLOCKING–Getting out of the way of partner's longer cards in the led suit. This is generally accomplished by the player with the fewer cards playing his high cards first.

UNUSUAL NO TRUMP–A Roth-Stone development. The bid of no trump either at the one or two level in situations where a player could not possibly want to play the hand in to trump or where the bidder has previously been unable to bid, hence lacks necessary high card values for the no trump bid, is the equivalent of a weak informatory double with a two-suited hand. As intended by Roth-Stone, it showed possession of the two minor suits; a variation permits its employment holding the unbid suits.

V

VANDERBILT, HAROLD–The inventor of the Vanderbilt Club Convention, now rarely used; famous yachtsman and bridge player.

VIENNA COUP–A squeeze play where declarer deliberately releases a high card, establishing a winning card for a defender, then proceeds to squeeze that defender out of that card.

VOID–To have no cards of a suit.

VON ZEDTWITZ, WALDEMAR–A former Baron, Waldy is one of the greatest figures in American contract bridge.

VULNERABLE–When a side has made a game.

W

WEAK BIDS–Bids customarily strength-showing that are made with far less strength for purposes of pre-emption as weak two-bids, weak no trumps, weak jump responses, weak jump overcalls, etc.

WINNER–A card that has been established as capable of taking a trick.

WOODSON TWO-WAY NO TRUMP–The method devised by William Woodson of Greensboro, North Carolina, in which an opening bid of one no trump can either be weak with 10 to 12 points or strong with 16 to 18 points.

X

X–Any card lower than a 10 is designated as an "x" in bridge texts.

Y

YARBOROUGH–A hand containing no card higher than a nine.

Z

ZONE–See level.

Index

INDEX

A

S

Echo 173
Lagren 174
Lavinthal 175
Negative Discards 175

EACH TRICK IN	COUNTS UNDOUBLED	DOUBLED	REDOUBLED
Clubs or Diamonds	20	40	80
Hearts or Spades	30	60	120
No Trump (first trick)	40	80	160
(subsequent tricks)	30	60	120

PREMIUM FOR OVERTRICKS
(Regardless of Suit)

	DOUBLED	REDOUBLED
When not vulnerable	100	200
When vulnerable	200	400

GAME AND RUBBER BONUSES

2 game rubber	700 points
3 game rubber	500 points
1 game unfinished rubber	300 points
Part score (unfinished rubber)	50 points

COMPLETION BONUS

For successfully completing a doubled or redoubled contract—
50 points

HONOR BONUS

Four honors in one hand (of trump suit)	100 points
Five honors in one hand (of trump suit)	150 points
Four aces in one hand in no trump only	150 points

Bonus for honors is awarded player holding them, regardless of whether that player is declarer, dummy or a defender.